LANDON OF KANSAS

Landon of Kansas

DONALD R. McCOY

UNIVERSITY OF NEBRASKA PRESS · LINCOLN

Publishers on the Plains

UNP

Copyright © 1966 by the University of Nebraska Press

All rights reserved

Library of Congress Catalog Card Number 65–16190

Manufactured in the United States of America

FOR

PATTY, BARNEY, BILLY

Contents

	FOREWORD	ix
1	BEGINNINGS	3
2	GETTING DOWN TO BUSINESS	20
3	STATE CHAIRMAN	47
4	OIL AND POLITICS MIX	67
5	FROM OIL REBEL TO GOVERNOR	91
6	THE GOVERNOR IN ACTION	118
7	AFFAIRS OF STATE	150
8	A SECOND TERM	181
9	A LONG SHOT	208
10	A CANDIDATE FOR SURE	234
11	THE EARLY CAMPAIGN	262
12	FULL-TIME CANDIDATE	291
13	SUNFLOWERS DO NOT BLOOM IN NOVEMBER	313
14	FROM UNDER THE WRECKAGE	340
15	TITULAR HEAD	353
16	A PRACTICAL LIBERAL?	381
17	DAYS OF WORLD CRISIS	407
18	POLITICS IN TIME OF PERIL—1940	423
19	THE ROAD TO WAR	454
20	POLITICAL OPPONENT IN TIME OF WAR	480
21	THE POSTWAR WORLD	513
22	TEN YEARS DOWN ON THE FARM	542

23   ELDER STATESMAN   560
     BIBLIOGRAPHICAL NOTE   583
     ACKNOWLEDGMENTS   586
     INDEX   589

A picture section follows page 310.

Foreword

Boys are natural collectors. They often load their pockets with such things as string, tin foil, rusty bolts, rocks, and dead beetles. During the late summer and early fall of 1936, the prized item was the brown tin Landon-for-President button which was set against a yellow felt background in imitation of the Kansas sunflower. Boys would beg their parents and pester party workers to get supplies of these buttons. In the author's home town, Chicago, on street corners or in vacant lots, wherever boys met, the free market trading rate was two, sometimes three Roosevelt buttons for one Landon sunflower. In October one Republican leader wrote Landon's headquarters to predict victory in Chicago for the Kansas governor. Requests there for Landon buttons, he reported, far exceeded those for Roosevelt buttons. The governor's aides could smile sadly. Buttons, however shiny, were not votes. Chicago, however much its children liked the sunflower buttons, was not Republican. Landon lost Chicago, the state of Illinois, and, in fact, forty-six of the forty-eight states.

Alf Landon is best remembered for that trouncing, but there is more to him, and to his place in American history. No man is nominated for President without a record, and no man, once he has run this race, can retire from public life. Landon, to be sure, had done the extraordinary during the early New Deal days: he was the only Republican governor to have won reelection in 1934, and he had balanced his state's budget. These feats, and a shrewd publicity campaign, led to his nomination. But most Republicans and Democrats did not know that Landon had twice bolted his party—the only politician in American history to do this and nevertheless receive a major-party presidential nomination. He had been an active opponent of the Ku Klux Klan, a rebel who had fought the major oil companies and the utility interests, a forceful advocate of conservation, and a fairly successful reform governor (indeed, one who brought a new deal to Kansas while Franklin Roosevelt was bringing the New Deal to the nation).

After his nomination, in June, 1936, Landon compiled another record. He tried to reconstruct his party, into a moderate rather than a

ix

conservative force. He hammered away at Republicans to recognize labor unions, to regulate the excesses of capitalism, to support essential welfare services, to champion free speech, and to seek world peace while maintaining adequate national defenses. All this reflected his belief that national unity and welfare could be achieved only by discussion and negotiation. His failure to make a favorable impression on the public mind was partly because of his moderation, and partly because he was occasionally immoderate. To most political observers, therefore, Landon was like the girl with a curl in the middle of her forehead: when he was good, he was very, very good, but when he was bad, he was horrid. But the Kansan, during most of his public life, was less concerned with what people thought than with saying what was on his mind. If he sometimes seemed cranky and spiteful, that was the cost of his independence. If he occasionally was platitudinous and unrealistic, that was the price he paid for his imperfect rhetoric and his zeal as a commentator on public affairs.

It is for his record of a half century in politics—not for the defeat of 1936—that Alf Landon is important. In making that record, he contributed to the changes in his nation, state, and party, he reflected the ways of a politician, and he was a fascinating amalgam of moderation and independence.

D. R. McC.

The University of Kansas
Lawrence, Kansas

Landon of Kansas

CHAPTER 1

Beginnings

Kansas has been the home of four nominees for President of the United States. The Communist party candidate, Earl Browder, the only one of the four born in the state, is seldom mentioned there. Prohibitionist John P. St. John, who ran for the office in 1884, is commonly regarded as a curiosity. Dwight D. Eisenhower, the only one to be elected, is the pride of Kansas. The state's attitude toward the fourth man, the subject of this biography, is not as easy to categorize. Kansas folk do not always know what to make of Alf Landon.

Alfred Mossman Landon's immediate family background and ancestry might have been made to order for a presidential nominee. His father was a successful businessman; his mother was a minister's daughter. On both sides of his family he came of Protestant, English-speaking stock, and his forebears were men who had fought in the wars against the British, who had pushed westward with the frontier, and who had farmed, taught school, preached the Gospel, and played the role of responsible citizens in the communities in which they had put down roots.

French, English, and German strains mingled in his father, John, a descendant of Landons who had emigrated to the Massachusetts Bay Colony in the 1640s to escape the troubles of the English civil war.

During the next 150 years, members of the family spread to Rhode Island, New Jersey, and Pennsylvania. Alfred's great-great-grandfather, Thomas, after serving in the Revolutionary War, apparently took up land in Pennsylvania, first in the Wyoming Valley, then in the Genesee Valley. Thomas Landon, Jr., who marched against the British at Detroit and Niagara in the War of 1812, moved from central Pennsylvania to Crawford County, in the northwest corner of the state, and settled in Conneautville as a farmer. One of Thomas's children, Manuel, Alfred's grandfather, lived for the rest of his life in Conneautville. A schoolteacher, and later a carpenter and joiner, Manuel, like his father, was prominent in the affairs of the small community, and he prospered sufficiently to send his only son, John, to Allegheny College. In May, 1886, at the age of thirty, John Landon married Anne Mossman.

Anne Mossman was of Scottish descent. In 1700 her ancestors had left Scotland for Ireland, whence, in 1781, they emigrated to America, settling first in Maryland, and in 1794 moving to Fayette County in southwestern Pennsylvania. Five years later Alfred's great-great-grandfather, William Herdman Mossman, led a group of pioneers to Mercer County, Pennsylvania, where he became a farmer and businessman. His son, Robert, married the daughter of the colonel of the county militia, and settled in Greenville, a few miles from the Mossman family farm. A man of substance—eventually he owned a woolen mill, a tannery, a gristmill, and a sawmill—Robert was elected sheriff by the Mercer County Whigs in 1836. One of Robert's eight children, William Herdman Mossman, named for his pioneer grandfather, departed from the family's traditional Presbyterian faith to become a Methodist minister; he served as parson in at least six Pennsylvania communities, and also was active in founding New York State's Chautauqua institution, the great adult-education and cultural movement of the nineteenth and early twentieth centuries. Anne, the eldest child of William Herdman Mossman, was thirty at the time of her marriage to John Landon.

The Landons set up housekeeping in Elba, Ohio, where John was superintendent of the Union Oil Company, one of the area's largest petroleum companies. Their son, Alfred, was born at the home of his maternal grandparents, in West Middlesex, Pennsylvania, on September 9, 1887. As soon as John had found a larger, more comfortable house, Anne and the infant returned to Ohio. A daughter, Helen, was born two years later, and her death at the age of seven was Alfred's first sorrow.[1] At this time the Landons were living in Marietta, Ohio, where they had moved in 1891. It was in Marietta—a pleasant, well-settled town, its streets lined with elms and beeches and oaks, as much like a New England town as its people could make it—that Alfred Landon spent his boyhood years and received his early education.

In the 1890s, pedagogues believed the learning process was expedited by the kind of disciplining that serves as a physical as well as a mental prod, and Alfred never forgot the disciplinary method peculiar to Frank Wheeler, principal of the Third Street School. Possessed of a long and bony middle finger, Wheeler found it useful for thumping his pupils on the back of the head to encourage more intensive application to study, and forty years later Landon retained a precise memory of the man and the method.[2]

Although Landon early acquired a genuine and enduring liking for books, particularly those dealing with history, Alfred's reading rarely fitted into his schoolwork, and he was only an average student. His scholastic record, however, was not a fair index to his attainment; he received his share of formal training in the classroom, but he got his education outside it. His extracurricular reading of history was reinforced by the tales of Civil War veterans. Religion was assiduously taught him by Grandfather Mossman, as well as by Marietta's Methodist ministers.

His chief household chores were taking care of the family horse and of his dog, and one of his hobbies was raising chickens and pigeons. Pigeon-raising was especially profitable: young pigeons, which he caught in the schoolhouse loft with the connivance of the custodian, brought 25 cents a pair when they were fully grown. By the time he was nine, Alfred was an adept bird-raiser and he attended all the local poultry shows.

The small city on the Muskingum had much to offer a boy in the 1890s. Besides the diversions common to boys everywhere—marbles, mumblety-peg, and One Old Cat—a popular sport was chasing and killing rats forced out of low-lying areas by the spring floods. There were county fairs, horse races, and occasional rides on a river packet to

[1] Laurence George, "Leaders of Men," typescript (October 3, 1936) in the Alfred M. Landon Papers, Kansas State Historical Society, Topeka (typescripts or manuscripts unless otherwise identified are those in the Landon Papers); "D.A.R. Genealogy of the Landon Family," undated typescript (ca. 1922), a copy has been filed in the library of the Kansas State Historical Society; *Titusville* (Pa.) *Herald*, August 8, 1936; "Landon-Mossman Genealogy," 1963 typescript, Library of the Kansas State Historical Society.

[2] Landon to Augusta K. Bedilion, March 27, 1936.

Hasset Island, the scene of family picnics. Another treat for Alfred was going with his father to the oil fields and being immersed in its he-man world. Summers he spent in Conneautville with the Landons or in Greenville with the Mossmans, frequently traveling from one family to the other. His favorite relative was his maternal grandfather, William Herdman Mossman, and the two would discuss religion and history and swap stories for hours on end. And there were fishing, hiking, and horseback riding with Parson Mossman, a slight but energetic man, or with Alfred's young uncle, William T. Mossman. As he grew older, Alfred rowed and swam; at fifteen, he swam the two-mile distance across Lake Conneaut.[3]

Sharing his father's interest in politics was almost as enjoyable as the sports of boyhood, and more instructive. From his earliest days, Alfred heard his father talk of politics: at home and in the oil fields, and in Pennsylvania with the Landons and Mossmans; but John Landon's interest in politics was not limited to talk. Although elected Republican county chairman in 1896, he opposed Mark Hanna and Joseph Foraker, the party's leaders in the state, and he crossed party lines; in Ohio, he sometimes supported Democrats, and, after the family moved to Kansas, he voted for Democrat William A. Harris for governor in 1906. Whenever it was convenient, Landon attended political rallies, and he sometimes took Alfred with him. In 1900 Alfred, then thirteen, accompanied his father to Parkersburg, West Virginia, to hear Theodore Roosevelt speak; in 1904 they made a trip to St. Louis to attend the international exposition and to listen to the oratory of William Jennings Bryan at the Democratic national convention. John Landon's independent Republicanism made a deep impression on his son and conditioned many of his political attitudes.

At Marietta Academy, which he entered in 1900, Alfred took to athletics, especially football. Five feet six, and weighing only 114 pounds, he made a speedy end. In his second season on the team, the end opposing him in the game with Parkersburg High School weighed 200 pounds, and Alfred suffered a dislocated shoulder. Because the repair work on his shoulder was ineptly performed, his playing days were ended, but he remained an enthusiastic sports fan.[4]

---

[3] *Ibid.*; Richard B. Fowler, *Deeds Not Deficits, The Story of Alfred M. Landon* (Kansas City: Richard B. Fowler, 1936), pp. 24 ff.; Landon to William Allen White, June 28, 1943; *Titusville Herald*, August 8, 1936; Landon to Irving Stone, July 20, 1943.

[4] Landon to William Allen White, June 28, 1943; Fowler, *Deeds Not Deficits*, pp. 29 ff.

Although Alfred's attention to his studies at the academy was adequate, his attendance at the great summer Chautauqua Lake assembly in New York State was a more impressive experience. Combining the idea of cultural progress with the methods of a religious camp meeting, the Chautauqua presented lectures, music, and readings, and offered such recreations as boating, bathing, and supervised games. Because of Grandfather Mossman's regular participation in Chautauqua affairs, a cottage was always available for John Landon's family on the assembly grounds. There, in an atmosphere of Christian fellowship, among friendly rural people, Alfred heard lectures on national issues and cultural subjects, and he joined in communal life. The conviviality and wholesomeness drew him back regularly, until 1928. Thereafter politics was to be his Chautauqua.

Over the years, John Landon had done well in Ohio, but opportunities in the state's oil industry declined as the center of petroleum production shifted to the Mid-Continent oil field of Kansas, Oklahoma, and Texas, and in 1904 he accepted the position of superintendent of field operations for the Kansas Natural Gas Company. His decision to move was the beginning of a momentous summer for his son. In June, Alfred graduated from Marietta Academy; in July, he attended the St. Louis international exposition and the Democratic national convention; in September, he traveled to the boom town of Independence, Montgomery County, Kansas, where the family would make its new home; and after a week in Independence he traveled to Lawrence to begin his studies at the University of Kansas.

Lawrence had been born in the stormy territorial days of the 1850s, but in 1904 it was a staid town whose tree-shaded streets and solidly constructed residences, set back on well-tended green lawns, reminded Alfred more of Marietta than of raw and vital Independence. The city's life centered around the university, located on Mount Oread, a rock-chalk hill that dominated the landscape. Opened in 1866, the University of Kansas at the time of Alfred's matriculation had nine instructional buildings and a student population of about 1,450.

Alfred contemplated a legal career, a plan approved by his father, and after a year in the college of liberal arts and sciences Alfred transferred to the school of law, presided over by Dean James Green—"Uncle Jimmy" Green. A dynamic and effective teacher, with an appealing personality, Dean Green believed that law required not only knowledge of precedents, principles, and procedures but also a skillful and understanding approach to interpersonal problems—the art of human relations. The application of this concept to his personal contacts with his students was an essential part of the process of converting raw material from the Kansas prairies into mainstays of the bar. Speaking of Dean Green's ability to handle young men, Landon often cited the time he and several classmates were caught chewing tobacco during the dean's class and using a ventilator as a spittoon. They braced themselves for a tongue-lashing, but the dean merely observed that gentlemen who chew tobacco do not expectorate, they swallow.

In the university, as in grammar school and at Marietta Academy, Alfred's formal academic record was not spectacular. He received A's in English and medieval history (he studied and enjoyed the latter under the not-yet-great Carl Lotus Becker) and C's in Latin, rhetoric, and English literature; he failed physics, hygiene, and physical training. In the law school, except for an A in practice court, his grades were almost evenly divided between B's and C's.[5]

He gained considerable knowledge of history and became convinced that Anglo-Saxon village moot democracy was the prime conditioning factor in the political principles, the *superior* political principles, of English and American societies. He also took to heart the lesson of Lord Acton that "power tends to corrupt." He was interested in the battles of the "boss-busters" in Kansas and of the progressives throughout the land, and thought that they upheld what he had been taught and had read. These events also seemed to point to the need for a law that would prevent the accumulation of power by an individual to the extent that it would permit corruption and inequity in economics or in politics.

Like Dean Green, Landon practiced the art of human relations, and he led a full social life on the Kansas campus. He liked football games and beer parties, Lawrence's nickel movies and soda parlors, singing and the mandolin, and—because the university was coeducational—he had many opportunities to indulge his fondness for dancing. In his freshman year Landon joined the social fraternity Phi Gamma Delta (then known as the "dancing fraternity") and soon became a leading member; in the words of the chapter's historian, he was "always the man behind the gun."

Although Landon was a very social member of a very sociable group, he was known for his seriousness. He stood for order and economy in the operation of the chapter (in 1905 he moved "that we dispense

[5] University of Kansas *Catalog*, 1905; Records of the Registrar of the University of Kansas, Academic Record of Alfred M. Landon, 1904–1908.

with the ice cream course" at dinner) and he favored the employment of a house matron and the formation of a committee to improve the fraternity's discipline and academic standing. He moved (successfully) to prohibit gambling, to force collection of overdue accounts, to establish a businesslike bookkeeping and financial system, and to prohibit visiting in private rooms after 8:30 p.m. on weekdays and piano playing after 9:00 p.m. He supported Bible lessons, and lectures and discussions by visitors and campus worthies. Despite this outwardly starchy attitude, he was popular, and was twice elected chapter president. Among other campus activities, Landon served as Phi Gamma Delta's Pan-Hellenic representative, and was chairman of the law school's "Scrim" dance and of the banquet committee in 1907.[6] Reflecting his puckish strain, he was affiliated with Theta Nu Epsilon, an interfraternity group described by William Allen White as the university's "festive and bibulous society," and more bluntly by other commentators as a "damned group of hell-raisers."

In 1907, when Landon was chairman of the committee in charge of TNE's spring initiation, one of his duties was to prevent the alumni from making off with the champagne. Having cached it in the back of a store, on the afternoon of the festivities Landon enlisted four friends to help move the champagne through an alley to the nearby initiation hall, but some chickens set up such a squawking that the "champagne squad" feared it would attract the attention of the alumni. Moving the fowl temporarily to other quarters, they encountered a policeman who mistook them for chicken thieves. Although Alfred and one of his friends got away, the others were arrested for chicken stealing. At a hearing before the university's regents, who looked into the arrests and the drinking at the initiation banquet, Landon was spokesman for TNE, and to prevent the expulsion of the three "chicken thieves" the fraternity agreed to surrender its charter. Although it continued as a sub rosa fraternal organization, Landon persuaded his Phi Gamma Delta brothers to prohibit chapter members from joining TNE, and he severed his ties with the group.

Early in his university days, Landon was nicknamed "Fox" by the Phi Gam president, and thereafter many of his friends and contemporaries never called him by any other name. The nickname stuck for a generation, apparently causing some embarrassment, for in 1929 he

[6] Donald D. Davis, "Alfred M. Landon: Kansas' Governor," *K.U. Graduate Magazine* (May, 1933), pp. 6 f.; William Allen White typescript on Landon, October 8, 1935.

wrote to the university's alumni secretary and requested that the alumni magazine stop referring to him as "Fox."[7] In 1936 Landon was apprehensive that the nickname might be used against him in the presidential campaign, and he asked if Roosevelt had a nickname that would offset it. His fears were set at rest when he learned the President's college nickname; he felt sure there would be no use of "Fox Landon" by the supporters of "Featherduster Roosevelt."

The discovery of oil and gas fields around Independence shortly after the turn of the century transformed what had been a sleepy Kansas county seat into a boom town, and by 1904, when the Landons arrived, its population had jumped from 4,000 to 12,000. Along with the gamblers, saloonkeepers, and prostitutes who appear as if by magic whenever a boom town is born, the inhabitants included such exotics as an astrologer and a visiting palmist, and there was even a uniformed concert band. Vying with neighboring Coffeyville to attract trade and newcomers, Independence promoters planted trees, paved streets and laid sidewalks, and installed an electric trolley. Not surprisingly, news about the oil industry dominated the local press, and the column "In the Kansas Oil Fields" was a page-one fixture.

Because of the large-scale oil operations, gas was abundant and cheap around Independence, and the town became field headquarters of the Kansas Natural Gas Company, which was formed early in 1904 and capitalized at $12 million. By August 2, 1904, when John Landon's appointment as field manager was announced, it had consolidated a number of small Kansas gas companies, its objective being to pipe gas to Kansas City and other Missouri towns, serving Kansas towns along the way. Landon was to have immediate charge of 130 gas wells and 28 oil wells in the Independence area and general supervision of the company's wells in all fields. The company also envisaged going to Topeka and Paola to the north and Liberty and Elk City to the east; and Landon was to be responsible for the pipe-laying operations. On August 3 he arrived in Independence to help develop the area's gas industry and build what was to become one of the nation's largest gas pipeline networks.[8]

[7] Davis, "Landon," p. 6; William Allen White, "An Old Friend Speaks," in Fowler, *Deeds Not Deficits*, p. ii; University of Kansas Chancellors' Papers, Frank Strong to Erwin H. Barbour, April 7, 1909; Landon to Fred Ellsworth, December 20, 1929.

[8] *Independence Daily Reporter*, June 2, 15, July 1, August 2, and "Special Proclamation Edition," August 16 or 17, 1904. Later in the decade John Landon quit Kansas Natural Gas because of a dissension that soon led to the company's collapse. He became a successful independent operator in the oil and gas business.

John Landon was well established in Independence by 1908, when Alfred, having graduated from the University of Kansas with the degree of Bachelor of Laws, was admitted to the Kansas bar; to the disappointment of his father and Dean Green, however, he decided against a lawyer's career. Times were still a bit hard following the panic of 1907, and the prospect of establishing a workaday law practice in a small Kansas city no longer appealed to Alfred. Uncertain of what he wanted to do, but drawn to business, he accepted a job as bookkeeper in the Independence State Bank of Commerce—later he moved down the street to work for the First National Bank—and for three years he grubbed away in the lower coils of small-town banking. Along with training in management and bookkeeping, these years gave him convictions about the importance of sound credit. Eventually he worked with oil leases, through which he gained knowledge of the area's prime industry, and he made useful personal contacts. By 1910, thanks to his steady $75.00-a-month income, he was able to invest, with modest success, in several oil-drilling projects.

In 1911 Alfred left his job with the First National Bank to become a full-time oilman. He had accumulated $2,000 from his salary and part-time oil ventures, and with this as a stake—and with credit (granted in part because of the Landon name)—he entered the unpredictable but fascinating petroleum world. Often he worked on his own, but sometimes he worked with his father or with A. H. Black, a rugged and successful veteran of the Mid-Continent exploitation, and occasionally with others who were willing to accept a share of the risk and contribute part of the capital. A few months after leaving the bank, young Landon located a good drilling site in Oklahoma, between Nowata and Bartlesville. Beating other developers to the spot, he secured a lease on 160 acres of land that was owned by an Indian, and was lucky enough to strike oil. *Lucky* is used advisedly, for this was in the days before independents made serious use of geology and seismology; "creekology"—discovery by hunch or by guess—was the method, and it worked for Landon. "In oil," as Richard B. Fowler said later, "a man had to be right or a pauper." [9]

Landon's only "office" was his father's house in Independence, but most of his operations were in Oklahoma, on the Osage Indian reservation, where the Indian Territory Illuminating Oil Company held prime

[9] Fowler, *Deeds Not Deficits*, pp. 32 f.; Landon to Irving Stone, July 20, 1943; Cal Tinney, *Is It True What They Say about Landon? A Non-Partisan Portrait* (New York: Wise-Parslow, 1936), p. 78.

rights although it subleased land to independent oilmen. Like most independents, he carried on his business mostly through personal contacts: enlisting partners, hiring contractors to do the drilling, occasionally raising extra money from creditors, and arranging for the piping of his oil to market by the big pipeline companies. In the petroleum business—as Landon recognized—judgment in deciding what to lease, speed in securing a lease once the decision was made, ability to procure good labor and equipment, and integrity in all undertakings were vitally important factors. He also realized that an independent operator, if he was to survive competition with the industry giants, had to "shop around," strike hard bargains, make things last, and spend only what was necessary to get a job properly done.

As a production boss, Landon had to know how to handle men—and the men of the oil fields were not easy to keep in line. Though he was not a big fellow—he stood five feet eight and weighed 155 pounds—Landon had to show that he was not to be intimidated; he had to learn to sober his crews up, know when to threaten and when to cajole, when to argue and when to shut up; he had to be boss, buddy, bully, and big brother. He also had to learn how to persuade farmers or ranchers to lease land and to yield right-of-way and access, along with the fine art of placating them in connection with such problems as water pollution, grassfires, damage to fences, and livestock straying when gates were left open. He had always to be alert for salt-water leakage, waste of gas and oil, and broken pipeline connections. He had to be frugal but fair: seeing that his contractors were supplied with what they needed but no more, that his hands received par wages and were paid promptly every two weeks, that his supervisors, besides being reimbursed, were encouraged with little gifts—tobacco, remembrances for their families, and authorizations to buy the "biggest turkey that you can find" on Thanksgiving or Christmas.[10]

It was a hard, demanding life, but Landon took to it. He liked the Oklahoma prairie and wearing rough work clothes—though as a college man he wore a tie, except in the summer. He enjoyed talking with fellow venturers, roustabouts, ranchers, and farmers, and sitting in on the games of pitch and poker that were the favorite pastimes of oilmen. Steady and plodding in his methods, he forged success in a risky business. Contrary to the movie stereotype—and contrary to many real-life oilmen as well—Landon was not a wheeler-dealer,

[10] Fowler, *Deeds Not Deficits*, p. 34; Tinney, *Landon*, p. 83; Landon to Irving Stone, July 20, 1943; Landon to R. T. Carey, December 21, 1917.

plunging haphazardly into one venture after another. He would not begin a new operation until he had sufficient reserve capital; and he soon gave up relying on "creekology" in favor of studying geology and consulting geologists. Moreover, like most oilmen, Landon did not confine himself to his own operations; he watched the market and traded or sold leases as conditions and his venture reserves seemed to indicate. He owned a drilling rig in the Osage country, and drilled for others on contract when it was not in use on his own leases. He even sold water that he had inadvertently struck; and in 1917 he entered into natural gas operations.

The oil leases on the Osage Indian reservation—one of the happiest hunting grounds in the Mid-Continent oil field—had been held since 1895 by the Indian Territory Illuminating Oil Company, but in 1916 the federal government decided to let the leases directly at competitive auction. Landon, who was prepared to invest $50,000 at the auction, intended to have as a partner his fellow Independencian and fraternity brother, Harry F. Sinclair, then a small oil producer, but Sinclair preferred to go into the auction as a promoter rather than as a producer. Sinclair raised several million dollars from New York bankers, and obtained—from Landon and others—the information necessary to use some of the money for intelligent leasing. This was the beginning of the Sinclair oil fortune. Landon, who stayed with his $50,000 investment and his idea of being a producer, also prospered, but on a smaller scale.[11]

Landon spent most of his time in the oil fields, but when he was in Independence his life in his father's household was congenial. Because Mrs. Landon had been reared as a minister's daughter, the church was an integral part of family life, and young Landon always felt at home with ministers and church affairs. Religion was almost as frequent a topic of conversation as politics and oil, though John and Alfred Landon were casual in their interpretations of Methodist dogmas. After his strenuous work in the oil fields, Alfred looked to his stays in Independence primarily for rest, reading, and the company of his parents; his social life was not particularly brilliant. If he was one of the town's most eligible bachelors, he was not one of the gayest. He was a Mason, and active in Chamber of Commerce and Red Cross work, and he played bridge, but he was not one for staying out late. His circle of

[11] Landon to William Allen White, January 4, 1930, in William Allen White Papers, Manuscript Division, Library of Congress, Washington, D.C.; William L. Connelly, *The Oil Business as I Saw It* (Norman: University of Oklahoma Press, 1954), pp. 60 f.

friends was small, drawn largely from the oil crowd, and although Alfred and his father had established themselves as men of integrity and ability, their politics did not make them popular members of the business community.

The traveling that was necessary in their business, the family's annual sojourns in the east, and Mrs. Landon's failing health restricted the Landon men's participation in the social and civic life of Independence. After an illness of several years, Anne Landon died at Chautauqua, New York, in the summer of 1914, her husband and son at her side. John and Alfred Landon, neither an easy man with money, memorialized her passing in a manner that would have greatly pleased her. Their contribution to the fund drive for the new First Methodist Church was the largest single donation— $5,000, which included $3,500 for a pipe organ.[12]

Politics and the press in Independence, as elsewhere in Kansas, were characterized by partisan flamboyance. The town's two daily newspapers were squarely in opposition: the *Daily Reporter* was staunchly Republican and the *Evening Star* was technically Democratic, although the latter supported the Progressive ticket in 1912 and 1914. Early in 1912 the *Daily Reporter* began directing its heaviest fire at the man it considered most dangerous to the interests of truth and Taft, former President Theodore Roosevelt, but progressive Senator Robert M. La Follette of Wisconsin—after "Tirade Teddy"—was its second target.[13] In the view of the *Reporter*, Roosevelt and La Follette were divisive influences in the national Republican party; but there were other disruptive elements among Kansas Republicans. The waning of the Populists by 1900 had been marked by the emergence of prairie progressivism as Republicans divided to fight for control of their party. In election after election the self-styled liberal Republicans, the "boss-busters," tried to depose the party's controlling members with the objectives of restricting corporate power, further democratizing the party, and securing offices for some of their group.

By 1908, making effective use of the recently passed primary election law, the boss-busters had succeeded in electing two of their nominees; Walter R. Stubbs was in the governor's chair and Joseph L. Bristow was in the United States Senate. The next four years, as these

---

[12] Fowler, *Deeds Not Deficits*, pp. 28, 35; Landon to Irving Stone, July 20, 1943; *The Phi Gamma Delta* (April, 1933), p. 534; *Independence Evening Star*, July 11, 13, October 26, 1914.

[13] *Independence Daily Reporter*, January, 1912, especially January 5–12.

reformers tried to capture every state office and congressional seat, were even more politically exciting. The contest was so hard-fought, and considered so important, that in 1910 the speaker of the House of Representatives, conservative Joseph Cannon, and Theodore Roosevelt came to Kansas. President Taft visited Kansas the following year to make three speeches in the third congressional district (which included Montgomery County, and which was represented by one of the strongest old-guard congressmen, Philip P. Campbell); and Roosevelt came again in 1912. The reform measures proposed by the boss-busters were relatively mild, and many of the progressives had interests of their own to protect, but Kansans were addicted to rip-roaring political battles, and many were drawn into the fray by the strength of rhetoric if not by the strength of the principles expounded.[14]

In 1912 Governor Stubbs led the progressive cause in Kansas, strongly supported by a squad of scrappers, among them Senator Bristow, Congressman Victor Murdock, and publishers William Allen White of Emporia and Henry J. Allen of Wichita. The fight between the conservatives and progressives was now translated into the Taft-Roosevelt fight for the presidential nomination, and feeling ran high in Montgomery County and throughout the state. In the beginning the spotlight was on Independence, for the Republican party council had named it the site of the state convention that would elect delegates-at-large to the Republican national convention in Chicago.

Montgomery County and the third congressional district were thought to be safe for the conservatives because of Congressman Campbell's strength and because of the great influence of Standard Oil's subsidiary, the Prairie Oil and Gas Company, but the progressives nevertheless won a majority of the delegates to the county Republican convention. Emerging as a leader of Montgomery County's progressive forces, John Landon was chosen as a delegate to the third district convention and was endorsed as delegate-at-large from Kansas to the Republican national convention.

At the state convention in Independence (May 7 and 8, 1912), Governor Stubbs and publishers White and Allen led the Roosevelt

[14] William F. Zornow, *Kansas, A History of the Jayhawk State* (Norman: University of Oklahoma Press, 1957), pp. 209 ff.; William Allen White, *The Autobiography of William Allen White* (New York: Macmillan, 1946), chapters 51, 55, 61–63. The most authoritative source on progressive Republicanism in Kansas is Robert S. La Forte, "The Kansas Republican Party during the Progressive Era, 1900–1917" (unpublished Ph.D. dissertation, University of Kansas, 1966).

forces to victory. White was elected national committeeman. The men named as the state's delegates to the national convention—including John Landon as one of four delegates-at-large—were pledged to Roosevelt. That same week Landon attended the third congressional district convention, at which, acting as Governor Stubbs' agent, he was instrumental in securing endorsement of William Allen White for national chairman, of Roosevelt for President, and in electing two national convention delegates who would adhere to Roosevelt.[15]

From this time on, however, the efforts of the Roosevelt men were largely frustrated. At the national convention in June, John Landon saw the nomination in danger of being stolen (as he and others viewed it) from Roosevelt. Normally a soft-spoken man, Landon publicly declared that the Republican national committee was a "bunch of horse thieves" and that the delegates—Taft men—favored by the committee in contested situations would not be seated because "we will throw them out bodily."[16] Nonetheless, much to Landon's dismay, the Taft delegates were seated and Taft was renominated for President.

Refusing to admit defeat, the Roosevelt men formed a new national party, the Progressive party, as a vehicle for Roosevelt's presidential candidacy. Wherever possible throughout the states, they tried to capture the Republican party machinery. In the mid-August primaries, Kansas Progressives (ranging from the mild Arthur Capper, who ran for governor, to the redoubtable Stubbs, who ran for senator) contested every nomination for state office and for presidential electors; they won all but one of the state Republican nominations and all of the elector posts. Although this made it appear that there was no cause for third-party action in Kansas, the Secretary of State placed Taft's name on the ballot as the pledged candidate of the Roosevelt-minded electors. These electors eventually succeeded in having their names placed on the ballot in the Independent column, but the Progressives nominated for state offices remained in the Republican column.

After the Republican national convention, John Landon was unable to play a prominent role in Progressive politics because of Mrs. Landon's illness and the press of business, but he talked to many persons about politics, gave advice on organization and tactics, and did a bit of wardheeling, and it is said he gave $1,000 to the state Progres-

[15] *Independence Daily Reporter*, April 26, 29, May 2, 1912; Zornow, *Kansas*, p. 219; *Independence Daily Reporter*, May 8, 14, 1912.
[16] *Independence Daily Reporter*, June 17, 1912.

sive effort, the largest contribution from an individual in Kansas.[17] Alfred, however, was caught up in the political excitement. Like his father, he worked for Progressive candidates over the county during the general-election campaign. He also publicized a talk by Roosevelt's friend and aide, Gifford Pinchot—at Independence in September—and he was in charge of handling Capper's campaign meeting in Montgomery County.

Although the Progressives lost the 1912 elections—national, state, and county—it was a consolation to the Landons that Theodore Roosevelt polled more votes for President in each of Independence's five wards than Woodrow Wilson or Taft.[18] Moreover, in working for the party the Landons had made many valuable political friends, including William Allen White, Victor Murdock, Arthur Capper, and Henry J. Allen. And no sooner had the vote been certified than the Kansas Progressives met at Topeka to consider future action. Two hundred Progressives, John Landon among them, organized the Kansas Progressive party at the mid-December conference; then, in late January, 1913, the Montgomery County Progressives organized by precincts, with John Landon as committeeman for Independence's fourth ward.[19]

There was little Progressive party activity during the rest of the year, but preparations for the mid-term contests began early in 1914. In Montgomery County the party's political efforts began in April with an address by Raymond Robins, the Illinois Progressive leader. A series of organizational meetings followed, culminating in a mid-June county conference at which the Progressives decided to hold their own primary. The meetings left the Progressives bursting with enthusiasm—convinced, in the words of the *Evening Star*, "that they have more than an even break ahead." [20] By June 24, Montgomery Progressives had filed for county clerk, superintendent, attorney, sheriff, clerk of the court, high school trustee, commissioner and registrar of deeds, state representative (two seats), surveyor, probate judge, and coroner.

[17] Zornow, *Kansas*, p. 220; White, *Autobiography*, p. 492; William Allen White to Harold L. Ickes, March 22, 1933, in White Papers.

[18] *Independence Daily Reporter*, September 28, November 21, 1912. Reflecting the agitated political state of mind in Kansas, the Progressive, Prohibitionist, and Socialist nominees together polled more votes than the victorious Wilson.

[19] *Independence Daily Reporter*, December 19, 1912; *Independence Evening Star*, December 19, 1912, January 28, 1913.

[20] *Independence Evening Star*, April 4, June 4, 16, 1914.

The results of the August primary were disappointing for the Progressives—in Kansas and all over the country. The new party received 6 per cent of the total Kansas vote, compared with 52 per cent for candidates running in the Republican primaries. In Montgomery County, even though their party received only 8 per cent of the votes cast,[21] the Progressives refused to be downhearted. The state party's platform, promulgated in late August, reaffirmed the national Progressive platform pledges of 1912 and added demands for national prohibition, state life insurance, antimonopoly legislation, a civil service merit system, election of federal district judges, employment of public defenders, and arbitration of labor disputes.

In September, Alfred—now simply Alf—became the Progressive chairman in Montgomery County. A hard worker for the party, he rang doorbells and made telephone calls, organized meetings, booked political speakers, arranged for the distribution of campaign posters and literature, and even formed a Bull Moose barbershop quartet. Victor Murdock and Henry J. Allen, the Progressive nominees for senator and governor, were escorted about town by Landon when they came to display their oratorical gifts to the public, and Landon arranged to have the state's Progressive national committeeman, William Allen White, in Independence for the final rally of the campaign—no small accomplishment for a twenty-seven-year-old politician.[22]

Nonetheless, Alf Landon's first political battle ended in a resounding defeat; Murdock and Allen ran far behind their opponents. In losing to former Senator Charles Curtis, Murdock got only about 23 per cent of the Montgomery County vote, the same percentage that he received in the state as a whole. Running against Arthur Capper, who had remained in the Republican party, Henry J. Allen polled only 16 per cent of the state vote and only 18 per cent in Montgomery County. In the county, the Progressives won only one office—high school trustee—and in that contest the sole opponent was a Socialist. In other county races the Progressives ran close only for one of the state representative seats.[23]

The Kansas Progressives had run their first and last campaign, and in 1916 they followed Theodore Roosevelt back into the Republican fold. But even though the Progressive party was dead and the stand-

[21] *Independence Evening Star*, June 24, 25, August 6, 1914; Zornow, *Kansas*, p. 222.

[22] *Independence Evening Star*, August 29, September 16, 25, October 2, November 2, 1914.

[23] Zornow, *Kansas*, pp. 222 f.; *Independence Evening Star*, November 9, 1914.

patters were in office, it would be a mistake to conclude, as one author has done, that the Kansas Progressive movement was finished.[24] For another generation the Kansas progressives, as a faction, would joust with the regulars for control of the Republican party, and, no less than the regulars, the factionalists would breed their successors. Alf Landon's defeat in 1914 was the beginning of his political career in Kansas, for he rose to prominence within the progressive faction to go on to political prominence in the state and throughout the nation.

[24] Zornow, *Kansas*, p. 224.

CHAPTER 2

Getting Down to Business

After striking the political "dry hole" of 1914, Alfred Landon was almost entirely inactive in politics for three years. The Kansas Progressive party, which had continued as an organization on paper, was disbanded upon the collapse of the national Progressive party in 1916, and in the summer of that year most Kansas progressives sought readmission to Republican ranks. But their record of independent action did not commend them to the state Republican party, and, because they had been partly responsible for the widespread Democratic successes in Kansas in 1912 and 1914, progressives were not allowed to carry the Republican banner for any important office in 1916.

Although Landon nominally supported the Republican ticket, he did little during the 1916 election campaign. Family life and business claimed an increasing share of his time, for he was now a married man, with new obligations and responsibilities. His bride, the former Margaret Fleming of Oil City, Pennsylvania, was the daughter of William Fleming, president of the Ohio Oil Company, the Standard Oil subsidiary for which John Landon had been field superintendent prior to moving to Kansas. The Landon and Fleming families had lived in adjoining cottages during vacations at Lake Chautauqua, and it was there that Alfred had met Margaret Fleming. He had carried on his courtship during his many trips back east, and by January, 1915, his financial position was such that he could marry her. A son, born in

1916, lived only a short time. A second child, Margaret Anne, was born in 1917.

Politics had to take a back seat while Landon devoted himself to expanding his oil enterprises, especially on the Osage reservation, but in 1918 he was able to embark on another political adventure. The political climate now looked favorable to the progressive faction. It had given generous support to the Capper administration and had worked hard to persuade its fellow Republicans that the Democratic hold on many offices could be broken only by a united party. Progressives were willing to give their loyalty to the Republican party in return for full reacceptance into the organization.

The progressives also realized that 1918 marked a time for change. Arthur Capper had served the traditional two terms as governor, and, with an incumbent Democratic senator up for election, Capper saw a chance to oppose him and advance his own career. Because this left the governorship open, the situation was an opportunity to test the quid pro quo. Many progressives joined with conservatives to support Capper for senator in the primary election, and in return they received enough support from regular Republicans to nominate Henry J. Allen for governor.[1] Landon was active on behalf of Allen, serving as a member of the state Allen-for-governor committee and as his campaign manager in the third congressional district primary.

During the early phases of the campaign, Allen's prospects looked good. After polling the Montgomery County Republican party workers in February, Landon reported that, with one exception, they were unanimously for Allen, but he cautioned the Allen Republicans to beware of overconfidence.[2] Inevitably, of course, there were problems. For one thing, many Republicans could not forgive Allen for running on the Progressive ticket in 1914. For another, the campaign had to be staged in the absence of the candidate. In February, 1918, Allen departed for war service with the Red Cross and the Y.M.C.A. in France,[3]

[1] Richard B. Fowler, *Deeds Not Deficits, The Story of Alfred M. Landon* (Kansas City: Richard B. Fowler, 1936), p. 36; William F. Zornow, *Kansas, A History of the Jayhawk State* (Norman: University of Oklahoma Press, 1957), p. 235; Homer E. Socolofsky, *Arthur Capper, Publisher, Politician, Philanthropist* (Lawrence: University of Kansas Press, 1962), pp. 89, 96, 104 f.

[2] Landon to A. H. Skidmore, January 25, February 8, 1918; Landon to C. A. Neill, February 8, 1918.

[3] Landon had considered going to France with the Red Cross, but gave it up to see Allen at least through the primary campaign.

and although this move was productive of favorable publicity and goodwill it meant that Allen's supporters had to operate without the benefit of close personal contact with their candidate in dealing with the shifting tides of state politics. The death in February of Morton Albaugh, who was the leader of the conservatives in the Allen organization, as well as its titular head, also created difficulties. It was essential, in Landon's view, that a regular Republican be designated to replace Albaugh as chairman of the Allen-for-governor committee, and Landon played a key role in persuading his fellow committee members to select former Governor Willis J. Bailey as the new chairman. This was the first occasion on which Landon revealed the talent for achieving harmony that was to serve him so well in his own gubernatorial campaigns.[4]

Spring was Landon's busiest drilling season, and while he was heading the Allen campaign in southeast Kansas he found that his politicking conflicted with his business affairs. Compounding his problems, he had run into dry holes, which prolonged the drilling time and the location of the new oil that kept him solvent. As a consequence, the organizing and fund-raising work for Allen in the district was lagging, and, in May, Harvey H. Motter, state secretary of the Allen committee, prodded Landon to step up his efforts. "From now on," Landon replied, "watch us go." But business problems continued to hamper him; moreover, the war bond and Red Cross drives were diverting the public's attention from the campaign. Landon thought a solution might be to enlist the help of sympathetic personnel on Red Cross committees, particularly in view of the prominence of Allen and Motter in Kansas Red Cross work.[5] Motter hoped that people would take greater interest in politics when the Liberty Loan and Red Cross drives were over, but he was afraid that the concern over Germany's big spring offensive and the winter wheat harvest period in June would prove distracting.

By late May, Landon's campaign activities had increased. He wrote letters urging his county leaders to perfect their organizations, and, if possible, to raise money; and he traveled around the district to talk with party workers about the forthcoming campaign. But he found the tour so engrossing that Motter soon complained of lack of information,

[4] Landon to Samuel Drybread, March 7, 1918; William Allen White to Landon, February 15, 16, 1918; Harvey H. Motter to Landon, April 2, 1918; Henry J. Allen to Landon, February 4, 1918; Fred C. Trigg to William Allen White, February 15, 1918, in William Allen White Papers, Manuscript Division, Library of Congress, Washington, D.C.; Wichita *Beacon*, February 23, 1918.

[5] Landon to J. L. Striker, May 28, 1918; Harvey H. Motter to Landon, May 24, 1918; Landon to Motter, May 26, 1918; Motter to Landon, May 31, 1918; Landon to James A. Allen, May 28, 1918.

and complained even more of lack of money. Landon visited the localities suggested by Motter to recruit supporters and to put up posters carrying photographs of the handsome candidate, but in mid-June Landon was complaining to Motter.

> Harve, this is a darn hard campaign. . . . I thought all along that people would commence to talk and take an interest in politics about this time, but from what I can hear they are not. The other fellows are not getting anywhere either. I don't [know] what we can do I must confess. The old wheelhorses, that are for Allen, say wait a little longer before starting, but we have not very much time left.[6]

The upshot was that the Allen organization worried itself into doing a superb job for its candidate, who won the primary election handily over several other contestants. Landon was elected a precinct committeeman, but he neither participated in the final weeks of the campaign nor enjoyed the victory. In June, 1918, for the third time in four years, death struck his immediate family: his wife suddenly succumbed to meningitis.

As soon as Landon recovered sufficiently from his grief, he cleared up his business affairs, arranged for the care of his baby daughter, and accepted an army commission. On October 21, 1918, he was received into the armed forces as a first lieutenant in the chemical warfare service and was sent to Camp Humphreys, Virginia, for training. On November 11, barely three weeks later, the armistice was signed. Landon was honorably discharged—"services no longer required"— and on December 9 he returned to his father's big white house at 300 West Maple Street in Independence.[7]

Back home, Landon devoted himself to his family and to business. His little daughter now held first place in his affections, and with John Landon's help he did his best to make up for the loss of her mother; they surrounded Peggy Landon with love and attention through all the stages of growing up. After the childhood years of hide-and-seek and playing horse, her father attended to her progress as a student, saw to it that her wardrobe was all it should be, looked forward to the young people's parties, and shared his interests with her. Peggy learned the landmarks around Lake Chautauqua as well as in Independence, and

[6] Harvey H. Motter to Landon, May 31, 1918; Landon to Motter, May 28, 1918; Landon to Fred Stanley, May 21, 1918; Motter to Landon, June 13, 1918; Landon to Motter, June 14, 1918.

[7] *Independence Daily Reporter*, August 13, July 8, 1918; State of Kansas, Adjutant General's Office, "Certificate of Service," issued to Landon February 3, 1936.

was initiated into the mysteries of politics and oil fields. Father and daughter shared a close comradeship through the years.

The postwar decade was a good time for the Independence family. The demand for oil as lubricants and fuel for the nation's expanding industries grew steadily. Ships also required oil products, the developing aviation industry relied on oil, and oil and gas began to challenge coal for the job of heating. Most important of all, however, was the great automotive boom of the postwar years. Automobiles, buses, and trucks were propelled by gasoline engines and lubricated by oil; and petroleum products were required to make asphalt and other commodities for the nation's burgeoning road system. Between 1919 and 1931, as a result of the universal demand, the value of oil products moved from seventh to second in rank among American products.[8]

Working the great Mid-Continent oil field, which had barely been tapped, Landon prospered in the 1920s. He continued his profitable operations on the Osage reservation and was successful in his explorations for other leases of value in Oklahoma. There was also an upsurge in Kansas during the decade, and Landon expanded his activities to southeast Kansas, initially in Greenwood County. He joined in the exploitation of the greatest oil venture in southeast Kansas, the Coleman strike, whose leasing spread over several thousand acres in Montgomery, Chautauqua, and Wilson counties. Later he roamed over the state, leasing oil lands in Barber, Butler, Cowley, Elk, McPherson, Rice, and Seward counties, and though he struck many dusters he brought in many good wells. Although he was not a millionaire, as was later rumored, his net worth in this oil-rich decade amounted to several hundred thousand dollars.[9]

Throughout the 1920s Landon engaged in a favorite American pastime: he became a joiner. He was an Elk; being a conservationist-minded fisherman and hunter, he joined the Izaak Walton League; long active in Red Cross work, he served as chairman of the Independence Red Cross drive in 1930; and he participated in the activities of the Independence and Kansas chambers of commerce. Always available to work for county, state, and regional associations of independent oilmen, he became a director of the Mid-Continent Oil and Gas

[8] Fowler, *Deeds Not Deficits*, pp. 37 f.; Record Group 48, Secretary of the Interior's Records—Solicitor, National Archives, Hale B. Soyster, "Review of the Petroleum Industry in the United States with Particular Reference to Supply and Demand and Substitutes for Motor Oil" (typescript, 1934), pp. 20 ff.

[9] *Independence Daily Reporter*, September 11, 1924; Landon to Citizens-First National Bank of Independence, December 13, 1926.

Association in 1921 and of the Independent Petroleum Association in 1930. On the strength of his brief military service he joined the American Legion and figured prominently in its affairs, holding an honorary membership in La Société des 40 Hommes et 8 Chevaux in Kansas City. He continued to take an interest in the University of Kansas, and was elected to the national committee of Phi Gamma Delta.[10] Like most other able, ambitious American businessmen of the 1920s, he served when called upon and made his service pay off, not just for the group he served but for himself as well—in terms of ever-widening local and state contacts.

In his rough leather jacket, battered hat, and bright tie, the quiet man from Independence became well known, as oilman or as politician, to hundreds of farmers, businessmen, editors, and oilmen throughout southeastern Kansas. Visiting with them, he was in a good position to combine business, politics, and pleasure; moreover, he earned a reputation for asking the right questions and for listening attentively to the answers—a habit that made him friends as he pursued his own goals. Landon early learned the importance of being a good listener.

After Henry J. Allen's election in November, 1918, Landon became a member of the new governor's "kitchen cabinet." The young oilman was often in Allen's office, and his friendship was esteemed because he could be counted on to report information accurately and to give his opinions honestly, whether or not they agreed with the governor's. Moreover, Allen was unpopular in the third congressional district and could not spare the services of his chief workhorse there.[11]

Landon's chief political concern was to keep his faction in power by ensuring that it had a broad base of support. For example, he pressed the governor's office to appoint a staunch friend of labor as labor commissioner or deputy commissioner. Another of his concerns was to maintain Republican party unity—if the necessary compromises could be worked out. Like most progressives, he had learned that stiff-necked independence did not always pay, and he solicited Senator Charles Curtis, a foe of the old progressives, to support Allen's program for a state constitutional convention.

Curtis got in contact with some of his acquaintances, and promised to do more, but he was disturbed by reports that Clyde M. Reed, the governor's secretary, was urging Allen to run for senator against Curtis

[10] Landon to E. E. Amick, October 29, 1930; Maurice L. Breidenthal to Landon, October 6, 1930; Harry W. Colmery to Harry W. Woodring, September 24, 1929.

[11] Henry J. Allen to Landon, May 7, 1919.

in 1920. When Curtis confided that he wanted to be renominated without opposition, and that he hoped the governor would not be influenced by Reed, Landon replied that he had given Allen—for use in the legislative session—the part of Curtis' letter that dealt with the constitutional convention. He added that the governor would like Curtis to continue soliciting his friends to support the convention idea. For his part, Landon gave Curtis a written undertaking that "I am doing what little I can to discourage any opposition to you in the next primary." Although the constitutional convention proposal failed in the legislature, Allen gained legislative support for amendments permitting state loans to be made to tenant farmers, expansion of the state highway system, and systematization of state taxes. Curtis encountered no serious opposition to his renomination, and did not oppose Allen's attempt to obtain the Republican presidential nomination in 1920.[12]

Like the rest of the nation, Kansas suffered from serious and long-drawn-out labor disputes in 1919. To avoid a coal shortage during the winter of 1919/20, Allen ordered state operation of the mines and forced a truce favorable to labor. As a result of this crisis, the governor sought a permanent remedy for labor problems. In January, 1920, he called a special session of the legislature to secure legislation that would protect the public interest from injury in periods of strife between labor and management. He recommended the creation of a court of industrial relations to settle labor-management disputes and (if the need arose) to operate struck businesses in five public-interest areas: food commodities processing; clothing manufacture; fuel production; transportation of food, clothing, and fuel; and public utilities and common carriers. The court was to have complete authority to deal with work limitations, stoppages, and wages and hours; and employers would be forbidden to discharge or blacklist employees for appealing to the court. The proposed court, in brief, was to have powers of compulsory arbitration. Allen wanted the court bill as much to protect labor and industry from each other as to protect the public, and although labor fought the bill energetically, it was passed by an overwhelming margin—along with antisyndicalist legislation and an act that established a bureau of employment.

[12] Landon to Clyde M. Reed, February 9, 1919; Landon to Henry J. Allen, February 21, 1919; Charles Curtis to Landon, January 25, 1919; Landon to Curtis, February 12, 1919; Zornow, *Kansas*, pp. 236 f.; A. Bower Sageser, "Political Patterns of the 1920's," in John D. Bright (ed.), *Kansas, The First Century* (New York: Lewis, 1956), II, 73.

From its beginning, the Industrial Relations Court was surrounded by controversy. It was bitterly opposed by labor and by some business-men, and in late 1922 its arbitration powers were rendered useless by a decision of the United States Supreme Court. Yet by virtue of the conditions prevailing in 1919, the industrial court had attracted national attention as soon as it had been proposed, and it remained in the limelight thanks to Governor Allen's eagerness to pose as a labor adviser to the country at large. It was further publicized in 1922 when William Allen White, in July of that year, decided to fight the Industrial Court law because he objected to the official interpretation that an expression of sympathy to strikers constituted participation in a strike. White put a poster in his office window announcing that he was 49 per cent in favor of the railroad workers, who were then on strike, and he was arrested for refusing to remove it. His arrest, and his Pulitzer prize editorial defending freedom of speech, kept the court in the news and contributed to splitting the Republican party over the issue.[13]

Landon's position in regard to the court was difficult. He was a friend of Governor Allen and of Clyde M. Reed, one of the court's first judges. As an independent oilman, on the other hand, Landon felt bound to oppose state arbitration of industrial questions because he believed that one of the disputing groups would necessarily be favored. So far as the oil industry was concerned, he thought that the favored party probably would be the big companies rather than the independ-ents or the workers. Moreover, as one who worked closely with the men in the oil fields, he knew far better than the officials in Topeka that industrial arbitration antagonized labor. He tried to discourage the enactment of the bill, and after it was passed his hope was that his political colleague in the court, Clyde Reed, would deal fairly with labor. Landon came through the episode on good terms with Allen and Reed, and without losing his friends among the oil operators and workers.[14]

Because of the national publicity he had received, Governor Allen thought he might have a chance as a dark-horse candidate in the close race for the 1920 presidential nomination. The biggest disagreement

[13] Zornow, *Kansas*, pp. 236 f.; Domenico Gagliardo, *The Kansas Industrial Court, An Experiment in Compulsory Arbitration* (Lawrence: University of Kansas Social Science Studies, 1941), pp. 19 ff., 34 f., 190 ff., 203 f., 168 f., 237, 216; Walter Johnson, *William Allen White's America* (New York: Holt, 1947), pp. 362 ff.; William Allen White, *Autobiography* (New York: Macmillan, 1946), pp. 612 ff.

[14] Landon interview, November 6, 1961.

between Landon and Allen, which concerned the selection of the third
district delegate to the Republican national convention, derived from
the governor's presidential aspirations. When Allen, either out of
courtesy or by design, asked Landon to run for delegate, Landon
refused; he doubted that a young man of his faction could be elected in
the conservative district, and he believed that Allen would gain more
politically by looking to the conservatives for a compromise candidate.
In the summer of 1919, therefore, Landon encouraged his conservative
rival in Independence, W. S. Fitzpatrick, of Prairie Oil and Gas, to
become a candidate for the delegate's post.

Fitzpatrick had supported Allen for governor in 1918, but Allen
refused to endorse him and pressed Landon either to run or to produce
another candidate acceptable to party members. Landon first recommended Wilbur Allen of Chanute, but the governor again demurred.
Landon then suggested Hugh Powell, editor of the *Coffeyville Journal*,
whom Allen accepted instantly. Fitzpatrick then decided to run for
third district delegate without the governor's endorsement, and
Landon found himself opposing the man whose candidacy he had
encouraged. He went against Independence sentiment to fight for
Powell, even though he thought well of Fitzpatrick personally and
even though Fitzpatrick was a man who could do him business
favors.

As the price of his loyalty to the governor, Landon lost several good
friends and suffered much embarrassment. Not surprisingly, he was
more than a little irked when the governor denied that he had been
involved in the third district delegate race. "After getting me into this
fight," he wrote Allen, "it now appears that you haven't the 'guts' to
'go over the top' with me....you are a hell of a captain." He later
wrote Clyde Reed that perhaps he was too hard on Allen, who after
all had been out of touch with the third district situation, but he made
it clear that he was irritated by the incident.[15]

Landon remained politically loyal to Allen because the alternative
was to abandon the party to the standpatters. He did what he could to
buttress the governor's position at the Republican national convention,
but Allen was never more than a pre-convention favorite son. Although

---

[15] W. S. Fitzpatrick to George A. Clark, December 10, 1932, enclosed in Fitzpatrick to Landon, December 12, 1932; *Independence Daily Reporter*, March 4, 9, 1920;
Landon to Henry J. Allen, March 9, 1920; Landon to Clyde M. Reed, March 14,
1920; Wesley M. Bagby, *The Road to Normalcy: The Presidential Campaign and Election
of 1920* (Baltimore: The Johns Hopkins Press, 1962), p. 48.

he was put in nomination for Vice President, and it was rumored he had the inside track because Kansas had led the shift to Warren G. Harding, Allen—according to Landon—was indifferent to the second spot on the ticket and allowed it to pass to Governor Calvin Coolidge of Massachusetts. Subsequently, Allen ran for a second term as governor, and Landon again worked for him; however, as was usually the case in Kansas, the campaign for renomination and reelection did not call for much effort.[16] In 1921, Landon supported the appointment of his controversial neighbor in the third district, Clyde Reed, to the Public Utilities Commission, which shifted him from the Industrial Relations Court. The appointment was confirmed in the state senate by a single vote.

Early in June, 1922, Landon was asked to serve as Allen's executive secretary. He was reluctant to be tied to a desk, but Allen persuaded him that he had a duty to the party and to the progressive faction, and that he should accept the position. For almost three months Landon worked in the governor's office, trying to smooth over the troubles of unhappy citizens and angry politicians, chatting with visitors, and in general working at keeping the governor and his party out of trouble. Because Allen was nearing the end of his term, the crucial decisions on his program and administration had already been made, and Landon's job was not a challenging one. The only unusual occurrence during Landon's secretaryship was a national railway strike. Allen early became involved in the strike because he insisted that the special police used to maintain order should be paid by the railroads in Kansas, not from state funds. Landon disagreed with the governor, arguing that such an arrangement would be unfair to labor because the police naturally would be loyal to those who paid them, but he was overriden.

In August Landon resigned, bored with the job and weary of the constant bickering of his two good political friends, Governor Allen and William Allen White, over the state labor law and the railroad strike.[17] Because Landon left the secretarial post as a behind-the-scenes

[16] Landon interview, November 6, 1961; Bagby, *Road to Normalcy*, p. 95. W. G. Clugston, who was almost as much a politician as a Kansas political reporter, says that Allen wanted the Vice-Presidential nomination but was maneuvered out of it by the managers of the presidential nominee, Harding; Bagby, in his book on the 1920 campaign, tends to support this view. See W. G. Clugston, *Rascals in Democracy* (New York: Smith, 1941), pp. 131 f., and Bagby, *Road to Normalcy*, p. 100.

[17] Gagliardo, *Kansas Industrial Court*, pp. 208 ff.; *Independence Daily Reporter*, June 5, 8, July 17, 1, 3, 11, 20, 24, 8, 13, August 22, 1922; White, *Autobiography*, pp. 612 f.

politician, known only to his friends in the faction and locally in Independence (where his faction was weak), his connection with the often tactless Allen administration was not damaging to his future career.

The Kansas Republicans were badly split in the 1922 primary election, partly as a result of Allen's untidy stewardship of the party. Seven candidates ran for the gubernatorial nomination, which was won by the conservative William Y. Morgan with only 29 per cent of the Republican primary vote. In the general election Morgan received little support from the progressives, many of whom were not prepared to accept a conservative candidate when they could turn to the Democratic nominee, Jonathan M. Davis, a dirt farmer whose political philosophy mingled neopopulist and progressive ideas. Davis beat Morgan by a comfortable margin, although Republicans were generally successful in other state election contests.[18]

With his friends out of office and no longer controlling the party, Landon for more than a year gave almost all his time to his business and private life. In 1924 he returned to politics, helping Clyde Reed in his fight for the Republican gubernatorial nomination. To the dismay of Reed's supporters, Walter R. Stubbs had announced his intention to run for the governorship, the fourth time he had sought state office since his last successful election in 1910. Facing primary opposition from the veteran progressive, Reed hoped that the diehards among Stubbs' friends had become disenchanted with the ever-running, never-winning ex-governor and would therefore support Reed against the conservative entry, Lieutenant Governor Ben Paulen. Landon rallied his friends in the third district, served as Reed's legman, and accompanied the candidate on several campaign tours across the state. Relying on Reed's vigorous flaying of the corporations for "looting the treasury" and on his record on the Public Utilities Commission against the railroads and utilities, the Reed forces put up a good fight, but Stubbs' opposition was too much of a burden. Although Reed went down to defeat, Paulen's margin of victory was narrow; the votes for Reed and Stubbs far exceeded those for Paulen. If nothing else, the progressives proved they could draw more votes than the conservatives, and Reed showed

[18] Marvin A. Harder, "Some Aspects of Republican and Democratic Party Factionalism in Kansas" (unpublished Ph.D. dissertation, Columbia University, 1959), p. 107; Roger W. Corley, "Jonathan M. Davis, Farmer in the State House" (unpublished M.A. thesis, Kansas State University, 1962), p. 105; John D. Bright, "The Progressive Lurch in Kansas," in Bright, *Kansas*, II, p. 34.

he could take on the Grand Old Man of Kansas progressivism and not only beat him but also come close to beating the conservative candidate as well. No one could say that Reed or the faction was dead.[19]

The political season did not end for Landon with the primary election. Usually he was willing to abide by the voters' decision in the primary, but not in 1924; more was at stake than control of office or party. The Ku Klux Klan had become an influence in Kansas, as it had in many other states, and its attempts to intimidate minority groups perturbed the tolerant, easygoing Landon and many of the state's progressives. When the Klan had begun to organize in Kansas, notably during Governor Allen's administration, it had run into strenuous opposition from Allen and his attorney general, Richard Hopkins. On the ground that it was an unregistered "foreign corporation," Hopkins had used injunctions to hamper the Klan's activities. Allen, William Allen White, and many Kansas civic and cultural leaders spoke out against the Klan, yet it continued to grow in the state, and it was rumored that Governor Davis, who was running for reelection, was sympathetic to the organization. After the 1924 primaries, efforts were made in the Republican and Democratic camps to adopt platform planks condemning the sometimes violent Klan. The Democrats adopted an anti-Klan plank but the Republicans decided to remain silent on the question, and nominee Paulen declared the Klan was not an issue in Kansas except as the Democrats injected it into the campaign to divert attention from the real issue of developing the state.

But many people were alarmed by the situation, in particular William Allen White. In White's home town of Emporia, a Klansman had been elected mayor. What was worse, in White's view, because both Davis and Paulen had been endorsed by the Klan, and even the state Socialists had taken no stand against the group, the people had no clear-cut choice between pro- and anti-Klan candidates for governor. It seemed to White that anti-Klan Kansans should have someone to vote for, and in September, at the urging of Landon and many others, the Emporia editor reluctantly decided to run for governor as an independent. Landon gave him all the support he could muster—in an unpopular campaign against not only the Klan but also against the two major parties.[20]

---

[19] *Independence Daily Reporter*, February 29, 1924; *Independence Evening Star*, March 7, 1924; Sageser, "Political Patterns," pp. 81 f.

[20] William L. White, "The Last Two Decades," in White, *Autobiography*, p. 630; Sageser, "Political Patterns," p. 79; Burton W. Marvin, "William Allen White, Senator-at-Large," in Bright, *Kansas*, II, p. 431.

Starting late, with little money at his command and only partial support from his faction, White campaigned energetically, but his use of humor in attacking the Klan disturbed Landon, who preferred a serious approach. At every opportunity White derided members of the Klan as cowards and terrorists, idiots and fools, and wearers of "nighties" and flour sacks, and he laced into Paulen and Davis for not speaking out against the organization. Landon was again on the telephone; he rousted out political workers, distributed literature, scratched for money, worked on Democrats to support White, cheered on the candidate, and arranged for him to appear at a well-publicized rally in Independence—with the result that Landon lost a few old friends, gained some new ones, and entrenched himself in White's good graces.

White made no great dent in the Montgomery County Republican vote, which was higher as a percentage of the total vote than it had been since 1918, but many Democrats fled from Davis to White, and Davis polled the smallest percentage of Montgomery County votes cast for a Democratic gubernatorial candidate since the great Populist victory of 1890. Although White received less than 25 per cent of the total vote in Kansas, and Paulen won the governorship on the issue of prosperity, the anti-Klan group was happy because the Klan was on the run. As the *Kansas City Star* put it: "White literally kidded the Ku Klux Klan out of the state. He ran third . . . but he left the state laughing and the Klan never recovered from it." The coup de grace was administered the following year when the state supreme court ruled that the Klan could not operate without a charter. Later the state charter board refused to approve the organization's application for a charter, and by 1926 the Klan was defunct.[21]

Many persons say Governor Paulen was a standpat, do-nothing governor, but he proved to be able and popular, and apparently he was not influenced by the Klan. He fought successfully for a better highway system, consolidation of government agencies, government economy and efficiency, and better tax support for the state government; and it was his administration that saw the passing of the Industrial Relations Court, which had few mourners. Paulen also

[21] Corley, "Davis," p. 82; Zornow, *Kansas*, p. 240; *Independence Daily Reporter*, August 27, September 4, October 4, 1924; Marvin, "William Allen White," pp. 431 f. There was no connection between White's candidacy and the Progressive presidential campaign of Senator Robert M. La Follette of Wisconsin. Although many Kansans undoubtedly voted for both White and La Follette, White's vote was half again as large as La Follette's.

tried to strengthen the Republican party by securing the enactment of legislation (commonly called the "Anti–Bill White Law") that prevented independent candidates from filing for office at a later date than the candidates for major party nominations. Confronted with Paulen's record of success, his Republican opponents could do little more than fume, and they supported his bid for reelection in 1926. Their support of Paulen did the progressive faction little harm, and perhaps a great deal of good, for the progressives could go into the 1928 contest declaring they had done their part in the Republican sweep in 1926.[22]

Except for keeping in touch with the leading members of his faction and broadening the range of his political contacts through his business and his membership in the American Legion, Landon's only political activity between 1924 and the 1928 campaign was in behalf of Gifford Pinchot, the governor of Pennsylvania, Landon's native state. Pinchot was again crusading against the state's machine politicians and Landon decided to put in a word for him from a distance. He wrote an editorial in praise of Pinchot, which William Allen White polished up and published in the *Emporia Gazette*. The editorial called attention to the scare thrown into the Vare and Mellon machines by Pinchot, "this strange man, who seems actually to believe in Government for the People, instead of the Vares and Mellons."[23] Presumably Landon hoped that the Pennsylvania papers would pick up and reprint the *Gazette*'s trumpet blast for Pinchot. The editorial could do little to help or hurt Landon in Kansas, but it suggests that he was not lacking in idealism.

In 1927 Alfred Landon was forty years old. As a businessman he had succeeded in an unstable industry; as a politician he had proved himself an energetic, reliable member of his faction—although he was not widely known, even in his own state, because of the nature of his work. Landon's life was pleasant and moderately exciting. He might have earned—or lost—a great deal of money in the oil business through —or despite—his adherence to sound, cautious methods. The nomination to any number of minor offices would no doubt have been his for

[22] Kansas, *Session Laws, 1925* (Topeka: State Printer, 1925), chapter 164; Kansas, *Session Laws, 1927* (Topeka: State Printer, 1927), chapter 202; Zornow, *Kansas*, pp. 241 f.; Sageser, "Political Patterns," pp. 83 f.

[23] Landon to William Allen White, October 22, 1925; White to Landon, October 30, 1925; *Emporia Gazette*, October 28, 1925.

the asking had he been the asking type. In fact, by 1927 it would have been an easy matter to propel him into the front rank of Kansas politicians. Landon was a man who could be relied upon by those within the progressive faction, and a man whom those outside it could talk to. He was liked and respected by the chiefs of his faction, Henry J. Allen, Clyde Reed, and William Allen White; indeed, if progressive Republican leaders in Kansas ever felt indebted to anyone they felt indebted to Landon. He was also respected by the Kansas leaders of the conservative Republican faction, United States Senate majority leader Charles Curtis and national committeeman David Mulvane, and by the gentle lion of compromise, Senator Arthur Capper.

Nineteen twenty-eight was a year of great promise for Kansas Republicans. Thanks to "Peace, Prosperity, Progress, Prohibition, and Paulen," they had little to fear from the Democrats within the state. And thanks to political services rendered and friendships cemented over a period of twenty years, the Kansas Republicans enjoyed considerable influence in the country at large. White was a national figure; Allen was widely known for his labor experiment, and he had ingratiated himself with Secretary of Commerce Herbert Hoover; Capper was regarded as a leader in the powerful Senate farm bloc; and Curtis' and Mulvane's decades of service to the national party, as well as their contacts within it, were beginning to bear fruit. Furthermore, the fact that the 1928 Republican national convention was to be held in Kansas City would give Kansas additional political opportunities. Later on, in 1936, the prominence of the Kansas Republicans would be important to Landon inasmuch as their continuing influence made it feasible to consider the nomination of a Kansan for President. In 1928, however, what mattered most to Landon was that the Kansas gubernatorial pendulum appeared to be swinging toward his faction, and that Clyde Reed could be the faction's standard-bearer.

After his strong showing in 1924, it was recognized that Reed might be nominated, and in the intervening years he and his allies had worked to pile up political capital. As a lawyer, Reed labored to scale down railroad freight rates for farmers and to increase safety in train operations for railroad workers. William Allen White had urged Reed to include Landon in all the faction's high councils. "He is sane and sweet and very wise," White had said; "incidentally, I love him like a son." [24] But Reed did not have to be convinced of the importance of

[24] William Allen White to Clyde Reed, November 2, 1926, in White Papers.

Landon's help in the 1928 struggle for control of the party. Having worked with Landon for many years, he believed Landon was essential in guiding his attempt for the governorship.

It was clear, however, that the venture would not be clear sailing for Reed and Landon. Progressives who habitually failed to stick with the party also habitually failed to stay hitched within the faction. Harvey H. Motter, who had been Republican state chairman during the Allen administration, decided to take the pulse of the party and of the faction; he thought that his many years of service to the faction entitled him to consideration. Joseph H. Mercer, the head of the Kansas Farmers' Union, also was testing the gubernatorial currents, thus threatening to reduce Reed's strength among farmers. Even William Allen White, after a careful survey of the field, decided to support former Congressman Charles Scott, the genial, conservative editor of the *Iola Register* and the chairman of the Kansas Good Roads Committee. Moreover, the *Kansas City Star* seemed to be flirting with the conservative forces. Worried by these developments, in June, 1927, Landon tried to stop the fragmentation of the progressive forces. In a circular letter to the state's progressive Republican leaders he opined that "we have to hang together if the old Progressive wing of the party is ever to have any more influence in Kansas." [25]

In 1927 Landon worked to secure White's support for Reed—he thought he could handle White although no one yet had been able to manage him. Responding to Landon's pleadings, White softened a bit in June, saying that his man, Scott, probably would not run. But this did not satisfy Landon, who wanted outright support for Reed. He pointed out that although Scott had supported White for governor in 1924, so had Reed and Motter. In a letter to White, Landon contended that as a national progressive Republican leader he had an obligation "to carry on the progressive fight"—to support either Reed or Motter, since to support Scott was to deny those who sought popular government. Landon also appealed to White on personal grounds, reminding him that he had followed White's lead for twenty years despite the advice of friends who had warned him this was not the thing to do if he wanted to advance in the party. But White, who thought Reed was too uncompromising, was unmoved by this outpouring. During the summer the progressive faction kept the pressure on White, and in July he seemed to weaken. He wrote Henry Allen that Scott was out of

[25] William Allen White to Charles Scott, May 10, 1927, in White Papers; Landon to White, Motter, Reed, Trigg, and Allen, June 4, 1927.

the race and that he would accept Reed for governor, though un-
enthusiastically.[26] Although Landon, Allen, and Reed may have
thought they were maneuvering White into their corner, the Sage of
Emporia was playing a skillful game of leading them on.

In the fall, the progressives' pressure on White eased as events
enabled him to counterobligate the Reed men. Two whispering
campaigns had been started against Reed: (1) The postmaster general,
it was said, was circulating damaging truths about Reed, evidently
about his earlier career with the postal railway service; (2) It was
alleged that Reed had been guilty of improper conduct with a married
woman in a Pullman car. Defending Reed, White described the latter
charge as utterly and demonstrably false; and showed that the former
charge was nothing more than a rumor about a rumor, and his challenge
to the rumormongers to reveal the basis of the story went unanswered,
thereby depriving it of its effectiveness.[27] White also urged Joseph
Mercer to stay out of the gubernatorial primary; he told the agricultural
leader that he would have to support Reed over Mercer as a vote-
getter. Again, White appeared to have put the Reed forces in his debt,
although Mercer's departure from the campaign would help Scott as
much as Reed. In November, White moved into the open: he wrote
Reed that he could not support him until Scott decided not to run. And
in December, while he was still dickering with Landon over Reed,
White wrote a confidential letter to former Senator Chester I. Long
and asked that he and his friends support Scott.[28]

In the efforts to quash the rumors, enlist White's support, and
dissuade other progressives from entering the contest, Reed drifted
from crisis to crisis, spending his own and his supporters' energy chasing
after political tumbleweeds. In October, Reed and Landon told their
friends that the whispering campaigns against Reed compelled him,
as a matter of honor, to be a candidate for the gubernatorial nomination; but no plan had been agreed on for the primary election. Late in
November, Landon pushed Reed to draw up his campaign plans:

[26] Landon to Clyde Reed, June 7, 1927; William Allen White to Landon, June 7,
1927; Landon to White, June 8, 1927; White to Landon, June 9, 1927; White to
Landon, August 10, 1927; White to Henry J. Allen, July 5, 1927, in White Papers.

[27] William Allen White to F. H. Roberts, October 4, 12, 1927; White to Clyde
Reed, October 12, November 7, 1927; Landon to White, October 21, ca. December
5, 1927, in White Papers; White to Landon, December 7, 1927.

[28] William Allen White to Joseph Mercer, November 28, 1927; White to Clyde
Reed, November 7, 1927; White to Chester I. Long, December 10, 1927, in White
Papers.

Kansas Day (January 29), on which the state's admission to the Union was celebrated, and on which Republican candidacies traditionally were announced, was only two months off, and it was obvious that the campaign preliminaries of others were well under way.[29]

Landon had been in the forefront of the Reed movement since late April, and after he returned in September from his summer vacation he accepted Reed's invitation to manage his campaign for the nomination. It was far from an ideal situation, however, largely because the candidate was a difficult man to work with. Reed was perhaps the greatest "prima donna" of all the Kansas progressive prima donnas, infatuated with himself and his issues. A poor organizer, he relied upon Landon for all the work of organization—without always giving him full support. Temperamentally, about all that Reed was capable of doing was to leave the workaday preliminaries to his campaign manager, and Landon's experience had been confined to the third district—he was a greenhorn when it came to statewide organization. Somehow or other, thanks largely to ambition and energy, the candidate and his greenhorn manager survived the crises of December and January. Through face-to-face contacts and by telephone calls and letters, Landon worked to build an enthusiastic Reed organization. In January, 1928, Allen and Landon were able to dissuade Harvey Motter from announcing for governor. In the same month Seth G. Wells, the standpat Republican state chairman and third congressional district conservative leader, decided to support Reed rather than run for governor and split the third district Republicans.[30]

On January 4, 1928, Reed set the stage for the announcement of his candidacy by charging that, because of railway rate discrimination, Kansans annually suffered a loss of between $9 million and $12 million. A week after sounding this keynote, he formally announced for governor in a statement that called for an all-out effort to improve the dire condition of farmers. Decrying, in particular, the "unfair and unjust share of the transportation burden borne by farm and ranch," he promised to continue his vigorous fight for equitable freight rates. He also pledged himself to the modernization of the state tax system in order to reduce the land-tax load, to development of an integrated state system of highways financed by an increased gasoline tax, to

[29] Landon to William Allen White, October 25, 1927, in White Papers; Landon to Clyde Reed, November 25, 1927.

[30] Landon to Sherman G. Elliott, December 6, 1927; *Kansas City Star*, January 13, 1928; *Kansas City Times*, January 14, 1928.

stronger regulation of public utilities "in the public interest," and to
an economic survey as a basis for encouraging the state's growth. In
this single statement he had declared for office, had strongly voiced the
continuing complaints of the farmers, had outlined a program the
farmers would approve—and had confirmed the enmity of the railroads, the public utilities, and the owners of business properties. The
rural press generally applauded his indictments and intentions, led by
Senator Capper's influential, farmer-oriented *Topeka Daily Capital*,
which called Reed's statement "the outline of a first-rate program for
Kansas."[31]

Kansas Day was marked by an orgy of politicking in Topeka's
hotels, speechmaking, and toasts (in ginger ale, beer, or whiskey).
Reed, Allen, Landon, and their lieutenants fought every round in the
battle for supporters and voters, offering and receiving confidences,
exchanging information, ideas, and gossip, stalking through smoke-filled
rooms, drafty corridors, and stuffy ballrooms to garner the material from
which a campaign is made. They were satisfied that they had a chance
for victory. Reed made a dramatic exit from the Kansas Day festivities,
leaving for Washington to take up his duties as counsel for the state's
farm organizations in their long struggle to convince the Interstate
Commerce Commission that railway rates should be reduced. His
departure was as well-publicized as it was well-timed.[32]

Although Landon did not publicly assume leadership of the campaign even after Reed's announcement of his candidacy, he became
increasingly busy with the details of setting up the Reed organization.
A Clyde M. Reed-for-governor executive committee was established,
and Jesse Greenleaf, Reed's former colleague on the Public Utilities
Commission, was asked to serve as chairman, fronting for Landon who
was virtually unknown with the public outside the third congressional
district. Seth Wells also was made a member of the committee, putting
to the test his profession of support for Reed.

Landon worked harder than he had ever worked before in a political
campaign. He spent hours on the telephone seeking advice and information, asking for money, arranging for publicity and meetings, suggesting
that certain persons be visited or that trips be made to this-and-that
locale to clear up problems, urging Reed's election to groups and
organizations. When Landon was not on the telephone he exhorted
his associates on the campaign committee to put forth more effort;

[31] *Topeka Capital*, January 5, 12, 13, 1928.
[32] *Topeka Capital*, January 31, 1928.

on the move by train or automobile, he met leaders in other parts of the state; he wrote letters; he briefed Reed and was briefed in return. Greenleaf found that the description of his chairmanship of the Reed committee as "nominal" was a fiction so far as work was concerned, for Landon kept him busy seeing workers and making contacts throughout the state. Greenleaf drove 15,000 miles on campaign business, made dozens of speeches, and talked with several hundred persons.[33]

Landon promoted the formation of Reed-for-governor committees in the larger towns of the state, and whenever he found time he solicited endorsements for Reed and passed them on for publication in pro-Reed newspapers. He also fed stories and editorial ideas to the papers and collected press clippings for reprinting. The farm issue was pushed hardest, but Landon saw to it that labor was canvassed, as well as minority groups, and he made sure that the latter were reminded of Reed's anti-Klan position in 1924. His immediate goal was to project Reed as a "first-class fighter," an able public servant, and a freight-rate expert—a man whose election was essential if the state was to be protected from the railroad interests. He kept pounding away at the ideas that freight rates must be reduced in the interests of farmers and businessmen, that injustices to labor (such as the check-off for company-union dues) must be eliminated, that a new industrial court that would give real justice to workingmen would be established, and that there must be strict regulation of public utilities and a house-cleaning in state government. At the same time, Landon tried to woo votes away from Scott; he reminded Scott's progressive supporters of his conservatism and of his close relationship with Senator Curtis, and he attempted to rouse the spirit of the old progressives by asserting that only Reed could implement the program they had dreamed of twenty years before.[34]

As it developed, however, the race for the Republican gubernatorial nomination was by no means a two-man affair; in addition to Reed and Scott there were four other candidates. Lieutenant Governor D. A. N. Chase, Secretary of State Frank J. Ryan, and Fred Voiland were accorded little chance of success partly because of their scattered strength and partly because they appeared to be campaigning on the Klan issue of 1924. The fourth man, John D. M. Hamilton of Topeka,

[33] Fowler, *Deeds Not Deficits*, pp. 39 f.

[34] Landon to George Webster, February 21, 1928; Landon to William Allen White, February 21, 23, 1928, in White Papers.

speaker of the Kansas house of representatives, could not be as lightly dismissed. Handsome, young (thirty-eight), and energetic, the only World War veteran in the campaign, and a leader of the legislative fight against the Klan, Hamilton showed strength. Although early reports indicated that the conservative Hamilton was attracting votes only from Scott's supporters, it 'was not long before he had to be regarded as a real threat to Reed.[35]

When on June 12 the Republican national convention met at Kansas City, Missouri, the Reed organization tried to make advantageous use of Henry J. Allen, William Allen White, and other leaders. Earlier in the year Landon had arranged with White, who was on the platform committee, that progressives would be appointed as doorkeeper and assistant sergeants-at-arms, thus ensuring attention for Reed's friends over the state when they visited the convention. Also, Reed's most prominent supporter, Henry J. Allen, was much in evidence at the Hoover-for-president Kansas City headquarters, and when Hoover won the presidential nomination the Reed-Allen men could boast of a great victory. Because of his close connection with Allen, Reed could pose as Hoover's nominee for governor of Kansas. On the other hand, Allen, as a Hoover supporter, had opposed the presidential aspirations of Senator Charles Curtis of Kansas, and this increased the enmity of the Curtis men toward Reed—an enmity that became more significant after Curtis was nominated for Vice-President.[36] Even though Reed was associated with the presidential nominee, Hoover's nomination damaged the Reed organization. In July, Allen left the state to direct publicity for Hoover's campaign; he also sold his newspaper, the *Wichita Beacon*, the only large-city newspaper in Kansas that had come out for Reed.

By July it had become obvious that Hamilton, not Scott, was the man to beat. Having outmaneuvered Scott, Hamilton carried the battle to Reed, and his adherents spread the word that Reed's men were trying to suggest to the public that veterans were unqualified for high office because of their youth and inexperience. A slate of exservicemen who were qualified for public office, with John Hamilton heading the ticket,

[35] *Chanute Tribune*, July 18, 1928; *Dodge City Daily Globe*, August 1, 1928; *Topeka State Journal*, June 28, 1928.

[36] Landon to William Allen White, February 9, 1928, in White Papers; Marian C. McKenna, *Borah* (Ann Arbor: University of Michigan Press, 1961), p. 255; *Topeka State Journal*, June 21, 1928.

was widely but anonymously circulated on postcards—a clever piece of propaganda that was probably handled by the immovable stand-patter, William Y. Morgan, through his many political contacts. In Wichita the week before the primary, Hamilton's men launched an attack designed to offset Reed's public service claims. Speaking before a Hamilton-for-governor club, lawyer John Burch accused Reed and Greenleaf of having raised Wichita's gas rates when they were public utilities commissioners. Reed's workers replied to the charge with a declaration from a former Wichita city attorney that the commission, which had raised the rates, lowered them after it had considered a petition from the city, and that later the gas company had instituted a successful suit to increase the rates.[37]

Hamilton had a good organization behind him: Senator Curtis and most of the party's conservative wing; a well-organized group of veterans; A. L. "Dutch" Shultz, whose columns of political comment appeared widely throughout the state; and the Murdock family and its powerful *Wichita Eagle*. Among these supporters, Shultz put the case against Reed most effectively. While Shultz felt that all the candidates promised too much to the voters, he asserted that Reed outdid all the others: his "assortment of promised prizes rivals a cane rack and he has more remedies for things that are wrong than a peddler at a medicine show." He also accused Reed of duplicity on various questions; for example, that Reed's legal activities in behalf of railway workers to shorten the length of trains would increase shipping prices for farmers, to whom Reed had promised lower rates. Shultz charged, moreover, that Reed not only took fees for legal services from railway workers and farmers but that he had received payment from railroads for his counsel on merger questions. Reed was also accused of having secured railroad rate reductions for Oklahoma oil interests that put their competitors in Kansas at a disadvantage. In addition, Shultz wrote that Reed's men in Klan-dominated counties were urging Reed's nomination to stop Frank Ryan, and that in anti-Klan areas they were pushing Reed as the man to stop D. A. N. Chase and Fred Voiland.[38]

Landon's organizational strategy was to sell party men on Reed and then urge them to work for their personal convictions. The Klan issue

[37] *Hutchinson News* handout, n.d., 1928; *Hutchinson News*, April 18, 1928; anonymous postcard to Charles N. McCarter, July 31, 1928; *Wichita Eagle*, July 25, 1928; *Wichita Beacon*, July 31, 1928.
[38] *Topeka State Journal*, July 12, 1928.

was dead, so far as Reed's headquarters was concerned; Reed's position, and that of his closest associates, had been so unequivocally anti-Klan that it seemed fantastic to suppose anyone would vote for Reed as a Klan candidate. The emphasis was on the economic issues with which he had begun his campaign. The appeal for the farm and labor vote continued in the form of personal statements by Reed, Wells, and Greenleaf, in pro-Reed editorials, in the active campaign participation of farm organizations and railway labor leaders, and in a big pre-primary-week advertising campaign. The stories of Reed's legal battles for lower freight rates were told and retold, and the point was made that he had continued the fight even after farm organizations no longer could pay his expenses. His exploits in seeking higher safety standards on railways were recounted again and again, and the *Railway Employees' Journal* (which compared him with Robert M. La Follette) left no doubt of its conviction that "Kansas Needs Reed." Advertisements in labor magazines and newspapers depicted Reed as the champion of collective bargaining, of government consideration of labor views, of improved labor compensation laws, and as the enemy of company unions and of the use of prison labor by private business.[39]

Other angles were not overlooked. The small towns' fear of Topeka "machine" politicians, who were supposedly in the pay of the railroads, was exploited. As the *Galena Times* put it: "We do not want to be dictated to by the Topeka crowd—Curtis and Hamilton." A particularly useful opening was unwittingly provided by Shultz, who, in his free-swinging style, had referred to Reed's supporters as "rabble." Landon instructed his workers to make the most of this epithet when they talked to workingmen, small businessmen, farmers, ministers, and small-town newspaper editors. Just before the primary, a number of newspapers carried full-page advertisements reciting Reed's virtues and pleading for the "rabble" to vote for Clyde M. Reed: "RAH FOR RABBLE! COME ON, RABBLE, LETS GO!" Other full-page ads emphasized Reed's courage, ability, and experience, all "documented" with news stories, editorials, and character references handed out by Landon's hard-working campaign team. According to the advertisements, "Every Citizen of Kansas Needs Clyde M. Reed" and "Kansas Has Already Decided on Clyde M. Reed...for Governor." The rural press supported these sentiments in editorials that discounted Voiland,

[39] *Dodge City Daily Globe*, August 2, 1928; *Galena Times*, July 24, 1928; *Railway Employees' Journal* (August, 1928), 3; unidentified labor magazine and newspaper clippings in Landon papers.

Chase, and Ryan, and that assured the reader that Scott and Hamilton would cancel each other out.[40]

The efforts of Reed, the flaming millennium-chaser, and Landon, his silent partner, were handsomely rewarded on August 7, primary election day, when Reed received approximately 100,000 votes. Hamilton ran second, with about 74,000 votes, well ahead of all of the other contestants.[41] The footrace with local destiny had resulted in a shoo-in, and—since winning the Republican nomination in Kansas in 1928 was tantamount to being governor-elect—the victors could relax for a while.

Reed's victory of course meant important changes in Landon's life. He could no longer remain a behind-the-scenes politician. Although the Republican state chairman, Seth G. Wells, had worked for Reed, the nominee decided that Landon would now have to be officially at his side. Wells, called upon to introduce his traditional third district opponent to the state rank and file, responded with generous words of praise: "[Landon] is honest, square, has vision, is shrewd, and really believes in decency in all things, even to the golden rule in politics." William Allen White also rose to the occasion in an editorial that lauded Reed's wisdom in selecting as chairman the "square kid" who "takes care to have no crooked friends, and is under obligation to no scoundrels...a prince of a guy."[42] At forty-one, Landon was hardly a "kid," but he was the youngest man ever chosen for the chairmanship of the Republican state committee.

Landon's formal election was scheduled for late August, at the meeting of the state party council; in the meantime, Reed and Landon were busy. Introducing a new feature into state politics, they traveled to Parsons, Kansas City, Beloit, and Wichita to confer with the newly nominated Republican candidates for state administrative and legislative offices about party issues and policies in the coming election. The public relations aspects of these conferences were obvious, and they enabled Reed to grasp the reins of party leadership before the usual strategy meeting of the party elders. With this end in view, Reed drafted a platform for adoption by the party council—a liberal platform,

---

[40] *Galena Times,* July 20, 1928; *Topeka State Journal,* July 11, 1928; *Topeka Capital,* August 5, 1928; *Neodesha Register,* August 2, 1928; *Ellis County News,* August 2, 1928; *Dodge City Daily Globe,* August 6, 1928; *Chanute Tribune,* July 18, 1928.

[41] Secretary of State of Kansas, *Twenty-sixth Biennial Report, 1927–1928* (Topeka: State Printer, 1928), pp. 36 ff.

[42] *Kansas City Star,* August 12, 1928; *Emporia Gazette,* August 10, 1928.

largely hammered out and sold in advance at the conferences around
the state. At the same time he cleared the way for Landon's selection as
state chairman. Because only county committee chairmen were eligible
for the post, a meeting of the Montgomery County committee was
called to take care of the eligibility requirement. Old battles and
personality clashes were forgotten, and in an atmosphere of good
feeling D. Clyde Knock relinquished the county chairmanship, not
forgetting to say some nice things about his intended successor. Attorney
Thomas Wagstaff, an old friend of Landon's, proposed him for
chairman of the county committee, and Landon was elected by
acclamation.[43]

The Kansas Republican party council, the general governing body
of the party, convened for its biennial meeting on August 28, 1928.
Despite the acrimony of the primary campaign, the gathering—as
Dutch Shultz wrote—was as harmonious "as a church meeting to feel
sorry for the Armenians." Everyone had a nominee to fight for in the
coming election—either Reed for governor or Curtis for Vice President
—and everyone had something to gain. Reed was given complete
control of the state Republican party machinery, and David Mulvane
was left in charge as the liaison with the national committee. On
August 27, at a conference of candidates for state offices and of Reed's
closest associates, the "governor-elect" outlined his strategy for the
council meeting. He announced his platform planks, and at the
meeting next day, as chairman of the platform committee, won
approval of his program.

Reed's platform pledged revision of the tax system, the reduction of
land taxes, freight-rate relief, railway safety investigations and regulation of train length, support of constitutional amendments to permit
an expanded highway construction program, and vigorous action in
reducing gas and electricity rates. A key plank looked to the adoption
of a presidential preferential primary and the popular election of
delegates to national conventions. Development of the St. Lawrence
Seaway, of the Mississippi and Missouri rivers, and a national flood-
control program also were favored. Notice was given that Kansas
Republicans expected Hoover and the Republicans in Congress to
provide economic protection for agriculture equal to that already
afforded to industry. Governmental economy and the enforcement of
prohibition were also pledged.

Soon after the council session opened, Seth G. Wells called together

[43] *Kansas City Star*, August 12, 1928; *Independence Daily Reporter*, August 17, 1928.

the state central committee. It was moved that Landon be elected state chairman, and the motion was adopted unanimously. Charles W. Steiger, Landon's attorney in El Dorado and a political conservative, was named secretary of the committee. Landon then selected another party member who had not supported Reed, state Representative Ida M. Walker, as vice chairman, representing women voters; and he appointed William M. Bradshaw assistant state chairman, marking the first time a Negro was appointed to a high Republican state committee post in Kansas. (During the election campaign three Negroes were given jobs at state committee headquarters, which also set a precedent.) Leslie Edmonds, a prominent Hamilton supporter, was named publicity director. The selection of congressional district officers and state council committeemen showed a similar movement for harmony at work in the party.[44]

The idea—a Landon touch—of creating Republican unity through representation of all party elements was a factor in Reed's election, and four years later it was to be the foundation on which Landon would build his own successful campaign for the governorship.

The year 1928 was a turning point in Landon's life, not only because of his rise to prominence in Kansas politics but also—and more important—because his efforts to achieve party harmony foreshadowed the end of his progressivism and the beginning of a pattern of thought that was to shape his future political career. His progressivism, which was an application of Theodore Roosevelt's "Square Deal" slogan, had come from a number of sources—from John Landon's examples of fairness and independence, Alfred's youthful idealism, his service and environment as a Progressive and then progressive Republican politician, and his fear of monopoly in the oil industry. As the years passed, however, Alfred Landon felt increasing dissatisfaction with the doctrinaire progressives. The Square Deal could not be attained by dividing the world into saints and sinners—those who agreed with you and those who did not. There had to be room for negotiation, for seeking broad and lasting support whenever a measure was necessary to secure social stability.

During the 1920s Landon had moved, almost unknowingly, toward a philosophy that embraced idealism and realism. That philosophy, which he later prosaically called "moderation," sought the balancing

44 *Topeka State Journal*, August 28, 1928; *Topeka Capital*, August 29, September 2, 1928; Carl Rott to C. A. Barnett, n.d. (probably March, 1936).

of group interests—not only for the general good but so that individual liberty would not be smothered and so that democratic channels for change would be kept open. Implementation of such a concept did not require consistency of thought but the willingness to fight serious threats to social balance, liberty, and democracy; the willingness to compromise on other matters; and willingness to support one's opponents if society's best interests called for it. By 1928 Landon had come—to a large extent—to believe in this broad and pragmatic philosophy, which, from 1932 on, would govern almost all that he said and did.

CHAPTER **3**

State Chairman

Party harmony was the main theme of Landon's activities as state chairman, but vigor was a close second. He traveled almost ceaselessly, visiting county chairmen, candidates, courthouse officials, American Legion and business leaders—anyone who was willing to talk politics and lend a hand. He pushed them into activity to overcome possible apathy in an election that many thought was a sure thing. He pointed out that the Democratic gubernatorial nominee, Chauncey B. Little, was an experienced and hard-hitting campaigner who in 1924 had scored an upset in winning a congressional seat, and who in 1926 had almost been reelected. He added that Alfred Smith, the Democratic presidential nominee, was a go-getter—anything could happen. Landon knew of Smith's appeal, for John Landon, though pleased with Hoover, was also fond of Smith, who, he told his friends, had been a "brilliant governor" in New York.[1]

Landon was able to move effectively among all party factions because of his manner of listening first and speaking second, his ability to recognize and praise hard workers regardless of their political quirks, and the fact that no personal opposition to him had developed among conservative Republicans. His record of insurgency was virtually unknown, and his ability to compromise differences and his skill at keeping attention focused on the future election rather than on the

[1] John M. Landon to William Gordon, June 25, 1928.

47

acrimonious past stood him well in a difficult job. If anyone disliked him it was because he insisted that a man back up his words with works.

The campaign required more than liaison work of Landon. It meant publicity, funds—never plentiful in Kansas politics—and developing an effective campaign team. It meant, most importantly, managing a candidate who was difficult to manage. Clyde M. Reed had to be kept from taking swipes at fellow Republicans and from embroiling himself in petty issues against the Democrats, which meant changing Reed's habit of carrying the fight to the opposition to allowing the opposition to attack and then parrying its blows. Landon was able to accomplish this goal with the aid of political veterans—especially Seth G. Wells and William West. One way was to relieve Reed of having to carry on the irksome task of coordinating the state campaign with the national party effort, which would have necessitated frequent contact with the Charles Curtis–David Mulvane men. Landon either did this himself or parceled it out to men like Wells and Charles Steiger. It also meant handling the vital John D. M. Hamilton forces through Leslie Edmonds, conferring with the Republican national committee chairman, Hubert Work, and his aides, and using, as the prime contact in Washington, Henry J. Allen. Allen was especially valuable, for the former governor was proving himself more flexible than ever before.[2]

Landon redoubled his efforts to gain representation of all Republican factions in the campaign posts. During the party council meeting he had declared that Reed would mobilize precinct committeemen through a series of meetings during the campaign, for mutual inspiration and information. Landon stated his belief that the committeemen "are the ones who make or break a party organization," and he issued his victory statement early in order to build up confidence. He predicted—correctly, as it turned out—that majorities of 200,000 would be given Republicans in Kansas, if they worked hard.[3]

Landon accompanied Reed as often as possible on campaign tours to avert incidents and entanglements and to activate local politicians. Reed gave strong support to local candidates, and was always surrounded by clusters of representatives of all Republican factions. Although

[2] *Independence Daily Reporter*, September 19, 1928; *Topeka Capital*, September 30, 16, 1928.

[3] *Topeka Capital*, August 29, 1928.

Reed had not fully recovered from a serious illness, his campaign was dynamic, the goal being not just to achieve election and harmony but also to drum up legislative support for his program before the 1929 legislative session. This was of great importance, for it appeared that Reed's opponents were trying to defeat him indirectly, by the election of hostile legislators.[4]

The Democratic council's platform included the traditional issues of an out-of-office party, and some issues taken from the Republican platform. The Democrats inveighed against unspecified statehouse scandals; they promised economy and efficiency, and enforcement of prohibition. They were for lower and better-distributed taxes, workmen's compensation, farm relief, and development of state resources. They went the Republicans one better on public utility regulation by calling for city home rule on such regulation.

The contest between Reed and the Democrats was vigorous. Chauncey B. Little opened his campaign early. At Columbus on August 22, Little pointed to his congressional record and his votes for legislation favoring farmers. Little picked up A. L. Shultz's charges of inconsistency against Reed and scoffed at the Republican's pledge to lower freight rates while shortening train lengths, a measure that would increase operating costs by the employment of more train crews. Little also scored Reed's record on the Public Utilities Commission, saying that Reed "did not reduce freight rates or shorten the trains"; that "in fact, the rates of nearly all companies were increased for the public to pay." He further chided Reed for being a strong advocate of Henry J. Allen's Industrial Relations Court.[5]

Reed was restrained from answering until September 4, when he made his opening speech at Emporia. Landon began the affair by pledging that the state committee and Reed were at the call of every Republican candidate for the legislature because the legislature was the key to implementing the party's platform in 1929. Reed inveighed against the anti-prohibition views of Governor Al Smith and Tammany Hall, and called for militant enforcement of the Eighteenth Amendment. He made it clear that he viewed the Democrats as being, in both senses, the "Bourbon" party. In this pro-prohibition, anti-Tammany state that prided itself on its origins as a bulwark against nineteenth-century Southern expansionism, Reed got full value out of these

[4] *Ibid.*, September 6, 23, 30, 1928.
[5] *Topeka State Journal*, August 29, 1928; *Kansas City Star*, August 22, 1928.

connections and put the Democrats on the defensive. Later in the campaign he defined prohibition as a moral issue, indeed as the biggest moral issue since slavery.

Prohibition, in turn, developed another issue: Democratic hypocrisy. On this Reed described himself as "the eagle...doing a little screaming." He said that a platform was "a covenant with the people of Kansas, and a solemn pledge" by a nominee and his party. He challenged Little to say if the supposedly prohibitionist Kansas Democrats agreed with their "wet" presidential nominee, Al Smith, or with "dry" Kansas on prohibition. One way or the other, as Reed knew, the Democrats could not give a satisfactory answer. Reed had earlier accused the Democrats of double-dealing, saying that Little and the Democratic council had violated an agreement of the two parties to support amendments to the state constitution that would authorize a state motor fuel tax and legalize federal aid for building roads.[6]

Little and the Democratic state chairman, John Wells, stuck to their charges of Reed's inconsistencies and Republican scandals. Reed adhered to his pattern of highlighting the prohibition dilemma of the Democrats and their bad faith on the amendments, and pledged a better deal for farmers, consumers, and workingmen. Landon and others successfully kept Reed from taking on unnecessary fights until the end of the campaign, when they allowed him to attack the Democratic leader in the Atchison area, Will Waggener, a Missouri-Pacific railroad attorney. While speaking in Atchison in behalf of the local Republican candidate for the state senate, Reed accused Waggener of heading the railroad lobby in Kansas.

Reed used this theme of linking Democrats with the railroads to close his campaign. On the eve of the election he charged that the railroads were allied with the public utilities and the state manufacturers' association, Associated Industries, to defeat "the people's" program by electing unfriendly legislators. Reed also condemned the railroads' request for a 40 per cent rate increase when Kansas wheat, compared with Canadian wheat, was at a 10-cent-a-bushel disadvantage on the market.

Landon also was involved in the fight against Waggener and his candidate for the state senate, Representative E. R. Sloan. The Saturday before the election Landon heard that Sloan would win. He was told by the county clerk at Holton that the only chance to beat the Democrat was to circulate handbills over the district on election morning, asking "Did you know that the Missouri-Pacific attorney,

6 *Topeka Capital*, September 5–6, 16, 25–27, 1928.

Will Waggener, brought in the notorious Wet, Senator James Reed of Missouri, to speak for Sloan?" Landon did this, and evidently succeeded in connecting Sloan with three of Clyde M. Reed's least attractive opponents—the railroads, wets, and out-of-staters—for Sloan was defeated in the election.[7]

The campaign, under Landon, had emphasized personal contact between leaders and workers within the party. Reliance had also been put on free publicity in news stories on Reed and Hoover; compared with the primary campaign, very little paid advertising was used, and as the results came in it was clear that none had been needed. Herbert Hoover and Charles Curtis carried Kansas by 320,000 votes, rolling up the greatest proportional margin of victory since Kansas' first presidential election in 1864. Reed won by 214,000 votes, with the highest popular vote that had ever been cast for a Kansas gubernatorial candidate. The state ticket swept to victory, mostly by two-to-one margins, although the eighth congressional district returned a Democratic representative. The gasoline tax and highway amendments were carried overwhelmingly. The Democratic minority was pared from 8 to 3 in the state senate, and from 33 to 24 in the state house of representatives.[8]

Normally there is time for rest after a campaign victory, but Reed was not the average governor-elect. After a respite of only two days, he began preparing his legislative program, and he issued a call for a tax conference to be attended by all legislators and other interested parties. The meeting was held November 15, with most of the state's economic groups represented, and was devoted mainly to the presentation of plans to reform the tax system—especially to relieve farmers, who were inequitably taxed. In essence, the conference committed everybody in attendance to tax reform and gave Reed many ideas to choose from. Immediately after this, the governor-elect called another conference, composed of county commissioners, but Reed, overworked, fell sick, and Landon presided. Landon emphasized that tax reform would not mean additional spoils for the counties, though he calmed the commissioners by saying there would be no important change in the apportionment of license and gasoline revenues.[9]

---

[7] *Ibid.*, November 1, 4, 1928; *Atchison Globe*, October 25, 1928; Landon interview, November 20, 1961.

[8] *Topeka Capital*, November 25, 1928; William F. Zornow, *Kansas* (Norman: University of Oklahoma Press, 1957), pp. 241, 243.

[9] A. Bower Sageser, "Political Patterns of the 1920's," in John D. Bright (ed.), *Kansas, The First Century* (New York: Lewis, 1956), II, 85 f.; *Topeka Capital*, November 9, 16, 23, 1928.

Landon's job, besides serving as "assistant governor-elect," was to fend off job-seekers, maintain liaison with legislators and other political officials, consider patronage questions, and sift the statehouse hoppers for political information and advice on the legislative program. In the midst of this, a question developed that agitated Reed and Landon, and Republican leaders generally: Senator Charles Curtis' election as Vice President meant that his seat would have to be filled by appointment. Although Curtis was unhappy that Reed might appoint his successor, he was also displeased with the lame-duck governor, Ben Paulen, who had not fully supported him for President in the 1928 Republican national convention. Pressure mounted on Reed as Curtis delayed resigning as senator, and it was said that a number of Republicans—including Hamilton, Paulen, and United States Representatives James G. Strong and Homer Hoch—were eager to receive the appointment. There was also the possibility of the appointment of Henry J. Allen. However, to relieve Reed of embarrassment with labor, which distrusted Allen, the former governor as early as August, 1928, seemed to remove himself from contention by stating that he was not a candidate to succeed Curtis.[10] Landon was uneasy with Allen's declaration and advised him against making it, for it was unnecessary.

Although Allen's statement left the impression that he was out of the running, there was a loophole in that he did not say he would refuse appointment to the Senate; and it became apparent that he was looking for a reward for his state and national campaign service. If Allen did not receive a high-level appointment from President Hoover, it was thought that he would want the senatorship. Landon warned Allen not to mislead the people: he should stick to the implication of his August statement because his appointment to the Senate would result in severe criticism—of himself, of Reed, and of Republicans generally. Landon made his position known to Reed and refused to yield to pressures to endorse Allen. Instead, Landon supported the widely respected state chief justice, William A. Johnston, for the interim appointment, and urged Reed to run for the seat in 1930.[11]

The possibility that Curtis would resign before Reed's inauguration was removed in December, when President Calvin Coolidge "commanded" him to remain as the Senate majority leader until March.

[10] *Topeka Capital*, September 9, 1928; Henry J. Allen to W. A. White, November 25, 1928, William Allen White Papers, Manuscript Division, Library of Congress, Washington, D.C.

[11] *Topeka Capital*, November 11, 1928; Landon interview, April 2, 1959.

By the end of 1928, Clifford Stratton, the political columnist of the *Topeka Capital*, counted more than a dozen possibilities for the appointment, including Landon. Landon had been mentioned for the position even during the 1928 election campaign, and had felt compelled to write a number of letters saying he was not a candidate to succeed Curtis. Denial by letter and in person was to become a familiar exercise during the next four months for Landon.[12] In January, Milton Amrine, warden-designate of the Kansas state penitentiary, said that Reed was inclined toward Landon, and that in December Landon had given the impression he wanted the appointment, but Amrine added that when he had mentioned this possibility Landon had laughed, saying "Forget it. It couldn't possibly happen." Yet Amrine, impressed with Landon, had asked William Allen White, "Reed could do worse, couldn't he?"[13] Soon after this Landon received additional and spontaneous support. The third district Grange leader, C. C. Romig, said Landon should be appointed; the legislative committee of the Brotherhood of Railway Trainmen endorsed him for the Senate; and the first congressional district Republican committee also gave Landon its endorsement.

By the middle of March, Clifford Stratton counted more than thirty candidates for the appointment, with Seth G. Wells and Landon receiving widespread support. Allen had made it clear, though, that he was in the running and that he regarded himself as the only possible choice for Reed. Although Allen had antagonized labor during his administration, and agriculture since, by belittling remarks, he knew that Reed felt indebted to him for his political start and successful career. This put Reed in a dilemma because of the esteem in which he was held by labor and farmers. White and others meanwhile tried to persuade the national administration to give Allen a high federal position in order to remove the pressure on Reed, but it became apparent that Hoover, probably because of Curtis' opposition, would not give Allen an important post—despite his strenuous efforts for Hoover's nomination and election. White finally wrote President-elect Hoover that if he saw Allen's appointment to the Senate as a way out of an embarrassing situation—for himself and for Allen—support for Allen

---

[12] *Denver Post*, August 24, 1928; *Topeka Capital*, December 20, 1928; Landon to D. G. Renfro, November 11, 1928.

[13] Milton F. Amrine to W. A. White, January 15, 1929, White Papers. Later, at a time when he was unhappy with Landon, Reed wrote that Landon had wanted the Senate appointment. Reed to W. A. White, December 16, 1931, White Papers.

must come from outside the state so that Reed could justify appointing him. Reed evidently came to the same conclusion within a couple of weeks.[14]

Curtis resigned on March 4 to assume the Vice Presidency, and the Senate seat was empty. Reed kept his own counsel; Hoover had not asked for Allen's appointment, and the governor would not name Allen to the Senate without a presidential request when so many prominent Republicans wanted the appointment. Finally, Hoover acted to break the stalemate; and word went out to Landon, Stratton, and others that Hoover would ask Governor Reed to name Allen—the President, who had been subtly pressuring Reed to appoint Allen, was forced to be more direct. Hoover's intervention was justified by the allegation that he needed Allen as his spokesman in the Senate, although it was difficult to imagine a freshman senator, an appointed one at that, as the President's spokesman in a body presided over by one of the senator's bitterest foes!

Hoover, circuitous in conveying his request, had the Secretary of War, James W. Good, ask Reed to come to Washington to discuss inland waterways, though everyone believed Reed's mission was to hash over the Senate appointment. After a ninety-minute conference with Hoover and Good, Reed announced he was appointing Allen because the President wanted it. Hoover never publicly stated that he did, though he did not contradict Reed, and thus Allen became known as the "White House Senator."[15]

Although the senatorial appointment was the prickliest problem to be encountered by Reed and Landon, the most important parts of their jobs were running the state and securing legislative cooperation. The inauguration, held on January 14, was an elaborate, well-run show and it attracted the largest crowd ever to see a governor of Kansas inaugurated. Reed's inaugural speech was eloquent but diplomatic. Speaking in Topeka's municipal auditorium, the new governor dwelt only on justice and equality, thereby preventing his critics from attacking him

[14] *Independence Daily Reporter*, February 18, 1929; *Kansas City Star*, January 30, 1929; *Topeka Capital*, March 3, 15, 1929; W. A. White to Herbert Hoover, January 29, 1929; White to Milton F. Amrine, February 21, 1929; Amrine to White, January 22, 1929; White to Henry J. Allen, January 29, 1929, White Papers; Marvin Ewy, *Charles Curtis of Kansas* (Emporia: Kansas State Teachers' College, 1961), pp. 41 f.

[15] W. A. White to Henry J. Allen, March 26, 1929, White Papers; *Topeka Capital*, March 24, 26, 30, 1929; W. G. Clugston, *Rascals in Democracy* (New York: Richard R. Smith, 1941), pp. 143 f.

before he had presented his program to the legislature. Landon presided over the affair and made, according to the *Kansas City Star*, "a snappy speech...the shortest speech on record for such an occasion." He refused to make "bombastic party pledges" for the state officials, declaring that it was the duty of every officer to be honorable in "redeeming the solemn promises made to [the public] in the party platform." [16]

Reed, with the opening of the legislature the next day, revealed his plans. He told the senators and representatives that he expected them to translate the Republican state platform into legislation. He also urged the tightening of banking standards, protection of working women and of working children between ages sixteen and eighteen, care for crippled children, and—returning to one of his primary campaign issues—creation of a state department of labor. As for what had become the most important Republican platform question—tax reform—it was the governor's responsibility to define what should be done. Convinced that new sources of revenue were necessary before the tax burden on real property could be relieved, Reed pressed the legislature for an intangibles tax law and a personal income tax. [17]

It was to be an unhappy legislative session for the new governor—marked by many petty issues, much "reconsideration" of legislation, and the obstructionist victories of 148 lobbyists (among the 165 assemblymen). The income-tax measure scuttled most effective legislation, and the chambers were swamped in the battles between intensely interested economic groups. So much of the attention of Reed's allies was focused on this question that many other important items fell by the wayside, such as the intangible-property tax and equalization arrangements, but a compromise was reached with approval of a constitutional income-tax amendment, subject to ratification by the voters in 1930.

Although Reed was dissatisfied with the action on the income tax, the legislature did not completely fail him. He was heartened by the strengthening of the state's "blue sky" laws regulating issuance of stocks and bonds. A bill was passed that provided for retroactive refunds to shippers who were overcharged by the railways. Governmental changes took place as the Public Service Commission was divided into three tightly organized agencies: the P.S.C., to regulate utilities, with less right of appeal from its decisions; the State

---

[16] *Kansas City Star*, January 14, 1929.
[17] *Topeka Capital*, January 16, 1929.

Commission on Labor and Industry, to collect labor data, enforce laws for labor's protection, and aid in the adjudication of disputes; and the State Tax Commission, to study and administer the state tax system.[18] Reed set out to make the most of the legislature's accomplishments and of his own powers. The State Tax Commission was immediately organized to make tax reform recommendations that, Reed warned, might move him to call a special session of the legislature in 1930. Reed also made plans to fight for reductions in railway and utility rates in the belief that his bellicosity would succeed where Landon's strategy of pouring oil over troubled waters had failed.[19]

Landon of course had stayed close to the governor during the legislative session and the senatorial appointment troubles, but his role naturally diminished with the coming of spring. In Kansas politics the state chairman works hardest during the election campaign and the legislative session. Landon had been cooped up in the governor's office throughout the winter, cajoling, bargaining, jollying the press, and serving as intermediary for the governor with person after person and group after group in crisis after crisis. In late March, however, politics took a back seat to administration. Landon's role until the next year was essentially to be adviser to a man who now wanted little advice, and political buffer to a man who did not always appreciate the value of "buffing." Landon had to continue to keep the groups supporting Reed happy, many of which were now displeased with his appointment of Allen or disappointed with the results of the legislative session. For Landon, this meant a variety of activities: a $50.00 contribution to the Anti-Saloon League and a letter to *Outlook* condemning critical coverage of the league; helping Negroes feel they were a part of the party by securing William M. Bradshaw's appointment as special assistant to the attorney general of Kansas, by influencing David Henderson's appointment as a special assistant United States attorney general, and by recommending two other Negroes to positions of trust; and seeing that cooperative political elements had their patronage wishes fulfilled.[20]

Landon also joined in the effort to secure the appointment of Reed's favorite, Richard J. Hopkins, as a federal district judge. Hopkins, who had the backing of the prohibitionist groups, and who Reed thought would act favorably to the public on rate cases, was anathema to the wets and the old guard. The national committeeman, David Mulvane,

[18] Sageser, "Political Patterns," 86 f.; *Topeka Capital*, March 18, 17, 1929.
[19] *Topeka Capital*, March 15, 24, 1929.
[20] *Outlook*, November 26, 1929, 5; *Topeka State Journal*, February 5, 1947.

and apparently Vice President Charles Curtis, had induced the United States Attorney General to oppose Hopkins' appointment, but Hoover was prevailed upon—by Capper, Reed, White, and Landon—to appoint Hopkins. Ironically, Senator Allen was reluctant to support his former attorney general, but as Reed and Capper would not desert Hopkins, Allen had little choice but to go along. Despite strong opposition, Hopkins was confirmed.

Landon had hoped to balance Hopkins' appointment with that of his conservative friend, Charles W. Steiger, as federal district attorney, but Allen refused to accept him because there was little party sentiment behind him. The patronage situation was aggravated when, after Hopkins' confirmation, Governor Reed commented: "For a quarter of a century, the federal judiciary of this state has been a growing stench in the nostrils of decent people." He charged that the opposition to Hopkins had been led "by the corporations of this state, joined by a coterie of lawyers who have profited from favors of the court." W. G. Clugston, of the *Kansas City Journal-Post*, stated that the old guard leaders were bitter because they had failed not only to secure high appointive office but had been branded by Reed as responsible for twenty-five years of judicial maladministration. They were reported to be seeking revenge on Reed and Allen, and perhaps Capper as well, and were even displeased with Curtis for not having resigned in time to permit the appointment of one of their own to the Senate.[21] Landon also was unhappy with the situation, not just because of its impact on the party but also because he thought Allen "double-crossed Steiger and the rest of us" in stalling on Hopkins' appointment and in opposing Steiger. In a moment of pique, Landon refused to go to Wichita to visit Allen over the Christmas holidays because of what he conceived to be the Senator's indifference to maintaining party harmony.[22]

As 1929 ended, the old guard and the progressive Republicans drifted farther apart. Reed's inability to solve the tax problem and his threat of a special legislative session were used by conservatives to attack him. The Reed forces saw this as hypocrisy in the old guard, which they blamed for blocking tax reform. Yet if the tax issue was dynamite, the

[21] Clyde M. Reed to Arthur Capper, September 19, 1929; W. A. White to Landon, October 15, 1929; Landon to White, September 23, October 11, 1929, White Papers; *Kansas City Journal-Post*, October 18, 1929; Walter Johnson, *William Allen White's America* (New York: Holt, 1947), pp. 413 f.

[22] Landon to W. A. White and Landon to Henry J. Allen, December 26, 1929, White Papers.

governor hoped to use it to blast his enemies. In mid-December, 1929, the basis was laid for renewed vigor in the tax reform fight. The State Tax Commission issued a report that recommended a luxury tax, uniform municipal records, a state system for auditing local accounts, closer supervision over municipal expenditures, and supervision of county assessors. Although this was not all that Reed wanted, it was a start, and it avoided the issues of the income and sales taxes. The report was controversial because it proposed state interference with the virtually autonomous counties and cities of Kansas, but no one could deny the value of audit or uniform recordkeeping. Later, Reed added to the commission's recommendations by urging a 2-cent cigarette tax and an extra penny per gallon levy on gasoline.

Reed had meanwhile been active on other fronts in carrying out his pledges—despite the legislature, conservative opposition, and even flagging interest among some of his supporters. Big business in the state—and elsewhere—was outraged because Reed had instituted suits against railways to secure rate reductions. Under his direction, the Public Service Commission had pressed investigation of electric power and light rates, and even insurance rates were scrutinized.[23]

The political tempo quickened as 1930 approached, but Landon could look forward to great happiness, for the new year was to make a major change in his life. In 1929 he had met Miss Theo Cobb, the daughter of a Topeka banker, a handsome, dark-haired woman of charm, quiet wit, and forthrightness. After a whirlwind courtship they were married in January, 1930, and honeymooned for two weeks in the south before Landon plunged back into the world of politics. During the difficult year of 1930—and through the troubles, opportunities, and tasks of the future—he was no longer without a partner, a most understanding one.

The new year also involved a game of political charades. Normally there was little opposition to a governor's renomination, but 1930 was an exception. Early in the year a group of more than one hundred young Republicans, American Legion members, mapped a strategy of opposition to Reed's renomination, with John D. M. Hamilton and the Kansas American Legion commander, Frank Haucke, in positions of prominence at the meeting. On Kansas Day, January 29, the uneasiness in the party became clear, as was shown in the speeches of the day. The featured speaker, Hanford MacNider, a former national

---

[23] *Topeka Capital*, December 15, 1929, January 5, 1, 1930.

American Legion commander, damned insurgency and called for unwavering adherence to the decisions made by party leaders. On the other hand, Reed, Senator Allen, and Congressman Homer Hoch demanded freedom to reconstruct the party in response to the people's wishes. The conflict erupted in candidature announcements. Even before Kansas Day, Frank "Chief" Haucke had declared his candidacy for governor, with the apparent support of the American Legion, and Congressman W. H. Sproul and businessman Ralph Snyder announced their candidacies for the senatorial nomination. Sproul, who represented the third congressional district, issued his statement through Seth G. Wells, which indicated that Wells had left the Reed camp despite his position as state oil inspector. Landon hastened to Topeka to remind job-holders and other indebted politicians that they would do well to talk up the governor.[24]

Landon, displeased with the Kansas Day developments, knew that Reed's opponents were in earnest in their battle preparations, and that Reed was unlikely to take a conciliatory course. Even if he did, that course could not extend to making concessions on the administration's program. Although Landon might disagree with Reed's tactics and his personal rigidity, he generally agreed with him on program. What worried Landon was not so much that the fight between the progressives and the old guard had been intensified during the past year but that some progressives were consorting with Mulvane's men. He knew that these activities—by men such as Victor Murdock—were motivated by a desire to achieve a quid-pro-quo arrangement, but he thought that only the conservatives could gain, for any important weakening of Reed's program would render it useless. This, as the servant of the people that he believed himself to be, he could not countenance: "I am not playing politics for the fun of it or the glory of it," he growled to William Allen White.[25]

Despite possible desertions, the administration pursued its program. In the last week in February, Reed called the long-threatened special session of the legislature to repeal the old intangibles tax law in order to prevent financial institutions from taking advantage of loopholes left by a recent state supreme court decision. Despite the obstructionism of Haucke and his supporters in the legislature, the loss of revenue and the tax inequities permitted by those loopholes were too great to bear,

[24] *Ibid.*, January 19, 5, 6, 1930; *Topeka State Journal*, January 27, 28, 1930; *Topeka Capital*, January 30, 1930.

[25] Landon to W. A. White, February 15, 1930, White Papers.

and Reed's request was granted. Under the new legislation, state and
national banks, savings, loan, and trust companies, and finance and
investment organizations were placed on the same basis for purposes
of taxation. Nothing else of note was accomplished. Reed had decided
to be content with this "must" victory and with his administrative
actions, and to await the verdict of the voters as to whether he would
be allowed further opportunities to implement his legislative program.[26]

As spring came, preparations had to be made for Reed's campaign
for renomination. William Allen White, who now supported Reed,
wrote Landon that he feared for the governor's chances, especially as
reports were circulating that David Mulvane was being considered for
appointment as Republican national committee chairman. Landon
moved to stop Mulvane's appointment by urging Senator Allen to
oppose it, which Allen agreed to do—largely because he did not want
Landon raising a ruckus over the state, thereby endangering his chances
for nomination. Allen later advised Landon that Mulvane was definitely out of the running. Originally, Mulvane and Landon had been
proposed as a counterweight team for chairman and secretary, respectively, of the national committee, with W. S. Fitzpatrick, Landon's old
Independence enemy, taking a leading role in this strategy—which
appeared to progressives as an attempt to split their faction as well as
to exalt Mulvane. Later there was talk of appointing only Landon, as
Republican national committee secretary. Although Landon was
intrigued by the possibility, he decided it would endanger Reed and
might be considered treason by his faction. The question of Mulvane's
appointment as Republican national chairman arose again, and
Landon asked White to write a stiff letter to Senator Allen telling him
to block Mulvane's appointment.[27]

In mid-April Landon began to lay definite plans for Reed's primary
election campaign, a campaign greatly burdened with drawbacks.
Once again a rumor had to be combated, this time that Reed's health
was failing. While Reed had intermittently suffered from bad health,
it had not stopped him from being an energetic governor, but during
the spring of 1930 he needed rest to recover from a long spell of flu.

26 *Topeka Capital*, February 23, March 2, 1930; Zornow, *Kansas*, p. 244.

27 Richard B. Fowler, *Deeds Not Deficits, The Story of Alfred M. Landon* (Kansas City,
1936), p. 43; William T. Mossman to James F. Burke, February 14, 1930; W. A.
White to Landon, April 3, 1930, and Landon to White, April 8, May 17, 1930, White
Papers.

This meant that Reed was unable to campaign until late June, though Haucke had been campaigning since winter.[28]

Reed presented difficulties as a candidate because of his uncompromising, fiery personality, his health, his occasional appointment of Democrats to state office when Republicans were available, and his difficulties in carrying out his program. Other charges against him were his liberality toward labor and his criticism of the Federal Farm Board activities, and he was accused of "persecuting" public utilities and railroads, failing to enforce prohibition properly, not keeping his promises, and insobriety.

But the governor was not Landon's only campaign problem; he also had to campaign for Senator Allen because Allen was Reed's appointee. The senator was accused not only of failing to keep his word but of double-crossing progressive and old guard Republicans, developing a "statesman" complex—thereby becoming arrogant—and championing the unsuccessful nomination of John J. Parker of North Carolina to the federal Supreme Court. The last accusation hurt particularly, and Landon knew it would add no votes for Allen because of the strenuous opposition to Parker, who then had the reputation of being antilabor and anti-Negro; and it might also detract from Reed's labor following.[29]

Reed's position, however, was not without its strong points, as contrasted with the 1928 primary. His chief campaign aides, Landon and William G. West, the governor's secretary, were experienced, and Reed had a better feel of the state as a result of the 1928 campaign and his term as governor. He had the patronage rolls with him, and his issues were clear, so that he did not have to cast in a dozen directions in search of campaign material. The *Kansas City Star* and the *Emporia Gazette* were firmly in his camp; moreover, early campaign contacts convinced Landon that Reed was riding a favorable trend.

But Reed's opposition also was in better condition. The conservative forces, instead of being scattered among a number of gubernatorial primary candidates, were concentrated behind Frank Haucke. Those forces had no doubt that Reed was the enemy, one well worth disposing of. Haucke had many political attributes: he was thirty-six, a World War veteran, the Kansas American Legion commander, and personable and hard-working. Although he had served only one term as a

[28] *Topeka Capital*, June 22, 1930.
[29] C. Q. Chandler to Landon, May 12, 1930; Landon to Henry J. Allen, June 13, 1930.

state representative, as a farmer he could be expected to emphasize agricultural problems.[30] It was obvious that he could give real opposition to Reed.

Reed opened his campaign on June 25, 1930, with a scorching speech reminiscent of Walter R. Stubbs. He accused his political enemies of having launched the worst campaign of abuse, misrepresentation, and vilification in thirty years, and of trying to defeat him so that they might turn the state government over to the big utility corporations. That the people might know them, Reed named the men responsible for this: David Mulvane, John Hamilton, Will J. French, William Y. Morgan, former United States District Attorney Al F. Williams, John W. Breyfogle (Haucke's campaign manager), and Harry Sharp of Associated Industries.[31] This speech reflected his chief campaign issues: the bosses against the people and the monied against Reed.

Landon backed up Reed, but he pointed out that the governor's forces would never descend to unfair campaign tactics. Landon gave Haucke's workers the names of all the precinct committeemen they asked for, a courtesy not always followed by state chairmen. On issues, Landon charged that the nomination of Haucke would mean only that the Republicans were repudiating themselves. He characterized Haucke's campaign as "simply a smoke screen to organize the legislature to prevent any change of the present inequitable tax situation." The state chairman also went to work on his friends in the oil industry about Haucke's suggestion that tax relief could be achieved merely by reducing the real estate tax. Landon asked them how the state would compensate for this loss of revenue, the implication being that increased taxes would be levied on the oil industry.[32]

While the tax battle went on, Reed began his bid for farm and labor support. Writing to his commissioner of labor, the governor outlined his labor program: repeal of antistrike laws, minimum competition between free and convict labor, an eight-hour day on public work, better regulation of health and hazardous work conditions, and increased protection for women and children in industry. The agitation before the Interstate Commerce Commission resulted in a campaign bonus for Reed, or so it appeared, when in late July the commission

---

[30] Henry J. Allen to Landon, June 9, 1930; Landon to Allen, June 6, 1930; Zornow, *Kansas*, pp. 244 f.; *Topeka Capital*, July 26, 1930.

[31] *Topeka Capital*, June 26, 1930.

[32] Landon to Roy Bailey, May 22, 1930; Landon to Albert Weaver, May 24, 1930; Landon circular letter, n.d. (ca. June, 1930).

lowered freight rates for wheat shipments from Kansas, though corn rates were permitted to go up. The week before the primary election, moreover, the State Tax Commission made a nominal reduction in the mill levy, from 1.45 to 1.43 mills. Reed still had the backing of labor unions and farm organizations. For example, Clyde W. Coffman, the legislative representative of the major Kansas farm organizations, went on the radio as a spokesman for Reed. He enumerated Reed's accomplishments: a reduction of $3.25 million in state taxes over the previous administration; from April, 1929, to April, 1930, 1,606 miles of highways completed—half as much as in the preceding 12 years; $3.6 million in insurance reimbursements and $600,000 in insurance rate reductions for policyholders; greater enforcement of prohibition; an increased school fund; and lower freight and utility rates.[33]

The Haucke campaign soon shifted beyond personalities and pledges to do what Reed had not done as John Hamilton enumerated the many sins—in his view—of Reed's administration. Hamilton accused Reed of using state agencies and departments for political purposes, the standard campaign charge in Kansas politics; of favoritism in letting state contracts; of a political levy on state employees; of offering to trade state improvements for votes; of smearing persons and personalities; and of glossing over the fact that while the ICC decision would help wheat farmers it would cost the state $2 million in increased freight rates on other crops. In short, Hamilton charged, Reed's accomplishments were mere "political gestures." Landon countered: "Let's have more political gestures."[34]

By July the weather was unusually hot—this was the first summer of the six-and-a-half-year drought—and so was the campaign. Landon and Reed felt that things were not going right, and Reed, who was still recuperating, could not travel as often as was necessary. The initial impact of the depression was being felt in Kansas and the governor was blamed for the disturbing economic phenomena (the depression was not yet seen as national in scope). Another situation plaguing the campaign was that Allen was not helping Reed, not even in the senator's home town, Wichita. Wichita was the base of a very strong anti-Reed movement, but Allen, wanting to play it safe at home, did not visit the city.

[33] Clyde M. Reed to C. J. Beckman, June 3, 1930; *Topeka Capital,* July 27, 29, 30, August 1, 1930.
[34] *Topeka State Journal,* July 31, August 1, 1930; *Topeka Capital,* August 4, 1930.

Landon was blunt with Allen about Wichita. "Clyde is being crucified there between the attitude of your friends and the fellows that are your enemies. Your enemies are more loyal to their hates than your friends are to you." Landon, especially distressed by information that the Allen workers in Wichita had been instructed to say they did not care about Clyde Reed, told the senator that he realized this was a legitimate attempt to separate the Allen and Reed campaigns, yet Allen's appearance in Wichita and throughout the state could help the whole ticket without mixing the two campaigns. "The fight on Reed is very bitter," Landon wrote. "I rather misjudged it at the start. . . . The great difficulty has been to get our friends to realize that he has a hard fight." [35]

Although Landon was soon able to convince some of Reed's friends of the seriousness of the situation, he had to continue pressing Allen. He told the senator: "With the price of cattle and the price of wheat and other farm products where it is, we are facing a most difficult campaign, not only for the renomination of Reed, but also for the election of the entire ticket this fall." As for personalities, it appeared that people were not so much for Haucke as against Reed because of his tactlessness. Because of this, Landon wrote: "We have . . . been fighting with our backs to the wall and anything might happen."

An encouraging development was that the Kansas visit of Secretary of Agriculture Arthur M. Hyde and the Federal Farm Board chairman, Alexander Legge, had pointed up the righteousness of Reed's opposition to Federal Farm Board policy, even if it had hurt the national administration. Legge had told the farmers that if they did not like what the board had been doing "it did not make any difference to him, and they could go to hell." Hyde boasted of the amount of money—deemed insufficient in Kansas—given to the farm board, and indicated that he was not concerned with maintaining the farm population on the farms. Landon thought that though this might help Reed in the primary election, it was also a good issue for the Democrats that fall because Hyde and Legge's trip had dealt the administration "a terrific blow in Kansas and the whole Middle West." Landon advised Allen against standing behind the administration on the Federal Farm Board's policies, especially its proposal to reduce the wheat acreage.[36]

Allen replied that he had instructed his Wichita manager to de-emphasize the separation of the Allen and Reed campaigns there, and

[35] Zornow, *Kansas*, pp. 244 ff.; Landon to Henry J. Allen, July 12, 1930.
[36] Landon to Henry J. Allen, July 15, 21, 1930.

he passed on the cheery news that Reed seemed to be gaining in Wichita. The senator said it was impossible for him to leave Washington before the London naval disarmament treaty was disposed of by the senate, for he was counted upon to maintain the quorum—he hoped the treaty would be acted on before the end of July. To help Kansas and the campaign, Allen and Capper had brought what they considered to be successful pressure on Hyde and Hoover to get the Federal Farm Board to resume wheat purchases. Allen also sent a check for $3,000 for the campaign.[37]

Allen's optimism was supported by word from party workers over the state, which indicated that Reed would do better than in 1928. These reassurances led Landon to write Allen on July 21 that perhaps the "intense hate at Reed" was too much, and, because of the heartening reports, Landon thought "that we have the swing definitely coming our way at last and that Reed will go over. It sure has been a terrific campaign and one that I will be glad to have over. The Haucke fellows have the most elaborate and well-organized campaign, I think Kansas has ever seen."[38]

Allen did not return to Kansas before the primary, though on August 1, during the last week of the campaign, he made a press statement in support of Reed. By then Landon found that the old guard campaign was aimed not just against Reed and Allen but also against himself. His political foes were out to remove him as a precinct committeeman in Montgomery County, which would automatically eliminate him as county chairman and as state chairman even if Reed won renomination. The Prairie Oil and Gas Company spearheaded this drive, and Landon, unable to return home, had to look to others to organize his campaign for reelection as precinct committeeman in Montgomery County. As the going became increasingly difficult for both Landon and Reed, reports showed that the corporation campaign was hard at work. It was said that W. S. Fitzpatrick had called a meeting of the Independence employees of Prairie Oil and Gas and "laid before them that the best interests of Prairie demanded that they vote for Haucke and against Reed." The Reed forces contended that this message went to all Prairie and Standard Oil employees in Kansas. Fitzpatrick denied the story, though he admitted that while he had told the employees to vote as they pleased he had also told them that he was voting for Haucke in the interests of the company. The final

[37] Henry J. Allen to Landon, July 16, 18, 1930.
[38] Landon to Henry J. Allen, July 21, 1930.

week saw a flurry of speeches, charges, and countercharges. Landon placed advertising announcing Reed's record and the need for permitting him to complete his program. He lined up press release statements of support for Reed from Allen, White, and others in an attempt to offset Haucke's Legion appeal.[39]

After a hard-fought campaign came election day's bitter results. While Allen, running against three opponents, was renominated, Reed was decisively beaten. In Montgomery County, Reed was routed two to one, and Landon—and even his local allies—lost their places as precinct committeemen. Landon's only solace was that the reports from his workers had been correct: Reed received more votes than he had in 1928—but Haucke received even more than that. Landon made a perfunctory loser's statement, saying he was "willing to help all I can to elect the entire Republican ticket." On August 26 the Republican state central committee elected John D. M. Hamilton as state chairman. Landon, after a little speech wishing Hamilton might receive as much loyalty and support as Landon himself had received in 1928, retired from the scene.[40]

Although the 1930 general election in Kansas was exciting, Landon was not part of it. He was given nominal membership in his party's state finance committee; and Hamilton once invited him to come to state headquarters, but Landon was busy with an oil well and felt he had to decline. Like most progressive Republicans, Landon sat out the general-election campaign, which was undoubtedly a factor in Frank Haucke's narrow defeat by Democrat Harry Woodring.

Landon had risen to prominence rapidly in 1928 and had fallen from it just as quickly in 1930. To most observers, he was politically dead. It was logical to assume that the services of a politician who could not win renomination for his governor would not be in great demand.

[39] Landon to P. G. Bredehoft, July 18, 1930; *Topeka Capital*, August 1–5, 1930.

[40] *Independence Daily Reporter*, August 6, 1930; *Topeka Capital*, August 6, 7, 27, 1930; *Topeka State Journal*, August 26, 1930.

CHAPTER 4

Oil and Politics Mix

Landon was dismissed from politics just in time to watch an accelerating slump in oil prices; indeed, the price of petroleum had been declining since 1926, when a barrel of crude oil commanded as much as $2.31. A series of discoveries of oil fields and the onset of the depression had forced prices as low as a dollar a barrel by the summer of 1930. In October, less than a month after Landon lost the state chairmanship, the greatest production area in the industry's history, east Texas, was discovered; and prices dipped again, more disastrously than ever. The inability or unwillingness of the east Texas producers to control their output led to increased production—as everything else in the national economy was going down. In panic, operators in other areas removed self-imposed limits on their production, thereby unpropping the price structure of the petroleum market. In late 1930, Mid-Continent crude oil prices were down to 18 cents a barrel and east Texas prices were down to 10 cents a barrel—evidence that one state—California, Oklahoma, or Texas—could supply the nation's demand for oil. The oil industry seemed to be drowning in its surplus.[1]

Landon was in no immediate danger of going bankrupt, but he was

[1] Record Group 48, Secretary's Records—Solicitor, National Archives, Hale B. Soyster, "Review of the Petroleum Industry in the United States with Particular Reference to Supply and Demand and Substitutes for Motor Fuel" (mimeograph, 1934); Federal Oil Conservation Board, *Report V of the Federal Oil Conservation Board to*

67

disturbed by the unbalanced state of the industry. He and other small oil producers saw in the galloping increase of supply over demand the possibility of monopolization of the industry by a few large companies that could emerge solvent from the fierce struggles for markets that low prices had brought. It had become apparent as early as June, 1929, that the dominant trade association of the industry, the American Petroleum Institute, which was controlled by the major companies, would not take effective steps to balance production and demand; and the small producers were moved to act for themselves. On June 11, 1929, they organized the Independent Petroleum Association of America, under the leadership of Wirt Franklin of Oklahoma, to fight for limitations on domestic production and for restrictions on petroleum imports. They had some success in securing voluntary limits on production, but they were repulsed by Congress in 1930 in their attempts to secure a dollar-a-barrel tariff on oil imports.[2]

In December, 1930, while the I.P.A. was regrouping its forces to approach Congress again on the tariff, a new crisis developed, one that particularly threatened Oklahoma and Kansas, the third and fourth largest oil-producing states. Landon, as a newly elected director of I.P.A., found himself in the center of the fight to resolve the situation. The crisis proclaimed itself with the announcement of Prairie Oil and Gas Company, the sole pipeline connection for thousands of oil producers, that it would stop purchasing and piping crude oil on January 1, 1931. Its withdrawal would affect some 33,000 wells, thousands of operators, lessors, and fieldworkers, and would involve the daily production of 54,000 barrels in Kansas and Oklahoma. Prairie justified its action on the ground that it had in storage 60 million barrels of oil at a time when demand was slow. It might have added that its chief customers, particularly Standard Oil, had found cheaper and better-quality petroleum sources elsewhere, and were in business to earn

the President of the United States (Washington, D.C.: Government Printing Office, 1932), p. 2. See also Edgar E. Robinson and Paul C. Edwards, *The Memoirs of Ray Lyman Wilbur, 1875–1949* (Stanford: Stanford University Press, 1960), p. 559; J. Stanley Clark, *The Oil Century* (Norman: University of Oklahoma Press, 1958), pp. 134, 177 ff.; Carl Coke Rister, *Oil! Titan of the Southwest* (Norman: University of Oklahoma Press, 1949), p. 309.

[2] Independent Petroleum Association, *The Independent Petroleum Association of America Represents the Domestic Petroleum Industry* (Tulsa, 1935), p. 1; *Congressional Record* (Washington, D.C., Government Printing Office), 71st Cong., 2d sess., LXXII, 5578–5604.

money, not to gratify their long-existing sources of supply. The major companies seemed to have concluded that the independents were doomed and should be forced out of business, especially the many "costly" small wells, such as those serviced by Prairie.[3]

Landon had no direct economic stake in the small "stripper" wells, which produced less than 10 barrels of oil a day—his interests were in larger production units on major-company pipeline connections and in his investments in Sinclair and Standard—but he saw Prairie's action as a threat to all independents. Oversupply, the reason for cutting off the strippers today, could be used against big independents tomorrow. Landon, moreover, was outraged that abandonment of most stripper wells by their only market connection meant the complete loss of their production forever because of water seepage into unused wells and their oil beds—a violation, as he saw it, of the basic precepts of conservation.[4]

Landon, after Prairie's announcement, telephoned and wrote his influential friends to explain the situation. Hundreds of millions of barrels of oil would be lost because of Prairie's withdrawal—reason enough, he thought, to expect Standard Oil and other major firms to help the strippers. But Landon also contended "there is the moral responsibility of a business concern to its life-long customers, whose business was solicited." He noted that Prairie did not intend to shut down its wells, which drained oil "from adjacent farms of the independent operator who was their customer."[5] Help was needed. Spurred by Landon, by other oil independents, and by public officials like Governor Clyde M. Reed, the newspapers of Kansas bristled with stories and editorials on the evils that the closing down of the stripper wells would cause. Similar efforts occurred in Oklahoma.[6]

There was a meeting of independent oil producers in Tulsa on December 11, and Landon was on hand with a pocketful of resolutions

[3] *Topeka Capital,* December 6, 1930; *Independence Reporter,* December 5, 1930; Jack Harris to Fred Palmer, February 15, 1936, Harold McGugin to Arthur Capper, December 19, 1930, Alfred M. Landon Papers; Harold McGugin to W. A. White, December 23, 1930, White Papers; Clark, *Oil Century,* p. 230; Paul H. Giddens, *Standard Oil Company* (Indiana), *Oil Pioneer of the Middle West* (New York: Appleton-Century-Crofts, 1955), pp. 444 f., 458.

[4] Jack Harris to Fred Palmer, February 15, 1936, Landon to Dan T. Pierce, July 28, 1931.

[5] Landon to W. A. White, December 8, 1930, White Papers.

[6] *Topeka Capital,* December 22, 23, 1930; Harold McGugin to W. A. White, December 23, 1930, White Papers.

for derogation and action; but the producers were so frightened and confused that the meeting was fruitless. Other action had to be taken. Alarmed by the situation, Thomas C. Johnson, the Kansas state umpire on oil disputes, named a committee of three to consider means of providing markets for the "distress" oil. Landon was named chairman, with Arthur Denman of Sedan and Carl Weiner of Chanute serving as the other members. The committee called independent oil operators to meet at Chanute on December 19 to consider the problem caused by Prairie's withdrawal. The call was accompanied by Landon's statement that innumerable shallow wells would be permanently ruined by salt-water seepage if they were shut down for any length of time. It was time for action: markets, or at least some form of storage, must be found.[7]

Landon forcefully presided over the Chanute meeting, and a sheaf of resolutions was passed. The threatened loss of at least 200 million barrels of oil to the national economy was stressed, as was the loss of employment to thousands of fieldworkers and the financial ruin of hundreds of small producers. The independents demanded a state plan to prorate purchases of oil among the various oil producers, a national tariff on oil, and price relief action by President Herbert Hoover and by industry leaders. They also advocated meetings between representatives of the major petroleum companies and state and national officials. On behalf of the owners of 12,000 Kansas wells, they asked for aid "to prevent the greatest economic waste civilization has ever witnessed in times of peace." Warning that the small producers had been "sentenced to be shot at sunrise on January first," Landon sent the Chanute resolutions and related letters and telegrams to congressmen, Kansas and Oklahoma state officials, fellow independents, executives of major oil companies, the John D. Rockefellers, and federal officials—"to everybody but Santa Claus."[8]

The answers to Landon's letters and telegrams, indicated sympathy for the strippers' plight, or blamed ten years of industrywide waste and folly, or vaguely stated that one's company would help relieve the situation if the others would agree to a specific plan, or stated that one's company could not help because it had no pipelines in the area. Landon

[7] Jack Harris to Fred Palmer, February 15, 1936; *Wichita Beacon*, December 12, 1930; *Chanute Tribune*, December 17, 20, 1930; *Topeka Capital*, December 18, 1930.

[8] *Chanute Tribune*, December 19, 1930; *Topeka Capital*, December 20, 1930; Landon to John D. Rockefeller, Sr., December 19, 1930; Landon to U.S. Guyer, December 20, 1930.

was not satisfied with these condolences, explanations, and vague offers of help; only action would suffice. He telegraphed industry leaders that the problem was "not the problem of small independent producers but of leaders of industry who will be held responsible by public opinion for social and economic waste." He also hinted at the possibility of a boycott of their companies' retail products, saying that "the ordinary comity of business relationships causes you to have a direct interest in state in which you have thousands of filling stations."

Landon expanded his thinking in a reply to the president of the American Petroleum Institute, Edward B. Reeser, of the Barnsdall Oil Company. He asserted that overproduction and depression, wherever they occurred, were caused by transgression of sound economic laws, by the greed of all business participants. It was the responsibility of those who caused the crisis to resolve it. The public would not permit those who brought on depressions to avoid prompt and effective counteraction. Capitalism must act to justify its existence. In the oil industry, Landon emphasized, a complete program was required, not just the continuation of stripper production; proration of purchasing and conservation had to be applied to all producers.[9]

By December 23 it appeared that federal intervention had secured a solution of the problem. Secretary of the Interior Ray Lyman Wilbur was notified by the major oil companies that they would resolve the problem: they were sending representatives to Independence, Kansas, for consultation, and they announced that Prairie would cooperate in any forthcoming plan. Wilbur cautioned, though, that it would take time to establish a satisfactory plan. Landon expressed pleasure at the announcement but stated that he assumed the current arrangements with Prairie would continue until the plan of the major companies went into operation. Governor Reed hoped the large companies would do something, but cautioned that the incident was not yet closed. Democratic Governor-elect Harry Woodring expressed his intention of creating a state natural resources commission to deal with oil problems in the future; Kansas, he warned, would "not sit idly by."

E. B. Reeser scheduled a meeting of major purchasers for Tulsa on December 26. When questioned about this development, Landon said he did not expect to be invited to Reeser's "closed-door" meeting, but

9 Harry Doherty to Landon, December 21, 1930; R. C. Holmes to Landon, December 22, 1930; *Topeka Capital*, December 23, 1930; Landon to W. R. Boyd, December 22, 1930; Landon to E. G. Seubert, December 24, 1930; Landon to R. C. Holmes, December 23, 1930; Landon to E. B. Reeser, December 23, 1930.

he gave some advice. The participants should recognize, he said, that it would be foolhardy if, in protecting natural resources, the value of the stripper wells, was discounted, for with pressure recovery methods these wells could produce as much in the future as they had in the past. In any event, the major purchasers must keep in mind that the burden of relief fell on them.[10]

The Tulsa meeting was attended by representatives from Standard of Indiana, Standolind Pipeline, Prairie, Texas, Carter, Oklahoma Pipeline, Gypsy, Gulf Pipeline, Empire, Dutch Shell Pipeline, Dixie, and Barnsdall companies. Because a plan of action could not be devised during the first conference, the representatives adjourned until the next day. Reeser emphasized that any action taken by the major companies would be a public service because of the availability of flush-pool crude oil at cheaper handling costs. He repeated what was by now the shibboleth of the major companies on the crisis: "The condition of said small wells is not the fault of any purchasing company but merely evidence of the workings of an inexorable economic law." He cautioned that a boycott of the retail products of the purchasing companies would be ill-advised, for it would retard settlement.[11]

The secret meeting reassembled on December 27 and yielded only an announcement by Reeser that, although the group had agreed something would be done, "Nothing has been settled as yet and it is dangerous to be too optimistic." The specific allotment of distress crude oil among the purchasing companies was said to be the obstacle. December 28, 29, and 30 went by without a solution. Although Landon had suggested that Standard of Indiana, which had been the largest purchaser of stripper oil, was most responsible for the crisis, he now diplomatically decried any attempt "to charge a few major concerns with the responsibility of relieving the distressed oil producers. The problem belonged to all the major companies and all of them must share in its solution. This is practical, for if the burden is spread equally no one company will have to buy too much and the future stripper production will be preserved." Although Landon was quoted on December 29 as being optimistic, he was fully aware that time was running out.[12]

Finally, on December 31, the major companies announced a plan of

[10] *Kansas City Star*, December 23, 24, 1930; *Topeka Capital*, December 24, 26, 1930.

[11] *Independence Reporter*, December 27, 1930; *Topeka Capital*, December 27, 1930.

[12] *Topeka Capital*, December 28, 29, 31, 1930; *Independence Reporter*, December 29, 1930.

relief for the strippers: the major companies would take half of the distress crude oil if Prairie would take the other half. W. S. Fitzpatrick was unable to give an immediate answer, and could not arrange for a decision by Prairie until January 2, 1931. This meant, of course, that the pipeline to the stripper wells would be cut off as scheduled—the oil industry had not taken care of its own. It was not a happy New Year's Day in the oil fields. At seven in the morning, Prairie Oil and Gas Company cut its stripper pipeline connections after thirty years of service in the Mid-Continent field. Then, on January 2, Fitzpatrick told Landon that Prairie could not buy half of the distress oil. The news spread rapidly, and that night the boycott of retail products that Landon had hinted at and that Reeser had feared began to creep up on the majors. It was unorganized and spontaneous; and it proved painful, especially to Standard Oil of Indiana.[13]

Landon was to abet the boycott with more formal action; in fact, everything was to be tried. As Landon said, "We've got to pull their hair, poke them in the eyes, and kick them in the belly." He issued a statement that, unless buying commenced soon, the Kansas oil industry might be wiped out. After his conferences with the state's affected producers, it was reported that the longest they could hold out was two weeks because salt water, rising slowly but constantly, would ruin the stripper oil pools. The strippers had to keep pumping and to have storage space to meet the problem, for once the water got a good start in the wells, it would push back into the oil sands and reduce the pressure so that nothing could bring out the oil later.

E. B. Lawson, who headed the stripper fight in Oklahoma, and Landon were in constant touch with their states' officials and congressional delegations. They traveled throughout the distressed area and telephoned all over the country, begging or demanding assistance. Reaction in Washington was quick, as Senator Arthur Capper and others further pressed the federal government for help. Capper reported that President Hoover and Secretary of the Interior Wilbur were making every effort to persuade the major companies to enter into an effective agreement to protect the stripper wells. Wilbur stated that two-thirds of the distress oil, largely outside of Kansas, had been taken care of because of switchovers to other nearby pipeline connections. The trouble was that most of the Kansas and Oklahoma Prairie customers had no competing pipelines in the vicinity to take care of

[13] *Independence Reporter*, December 31, 1930; *Topeka Capital*, January 2, 3, 1931; Jack Harris to Fred Palmer, February 15, 1936; Giddens, *Standard Oil*, p. 458.

them. It was reported that 14,500 wells in Kansas—with daily production of 9,985 barrels, 621 operators, and 1,396 leases—were directly affected by Prairie's withdrawal; twenty-two Kansas counties were involved. In Oklahoma 19,125 wells—producing 44,307 barrels per day, with 449 operators and 3,318 leases—were involved. All of these leases, as well as the producers and their workers, and the income they spent, were now out of economic circulation.[14]

In early January, Landon went to Topeka to work on a solution with Governor Reed. Governors Reed of Kansas and W. J. Holloway of Oklahoma called for a January 15 conference in Washington of representatives of the oil states, and the call had the full approval of Governors-elect Woodring and Murray. The governors of Texas, Louisiana, Arkansas, Colorado, Wyoming, New Mexico, Montana, and California were invited to send representatives. Favorable responses were received immediately from Texas, Wyoming, and Montana, and the cabinet-level Federal Oil Conservation Board announced its willingness to assist the conferees.

Governor Reed, after directing Kansas Attorney General Roland Boynton to give oil matters precedence, issued a statement declaring that because the stripper wells had given Prairie Oil and Gas its start, Prairie bore partial responsibility for solving the stripper problem. He described the company's proposal to resume handling stripper oil at a service charge of 30 cents a barrel as financially absurd—the oil itself was selling for only slightly more. Reed also telephoned A. W. Peake, vice president of Standard of Indiana, to discuss the problem and to demand a solution, and Peake assured the governor that the problem would be solved. Meanwhile, E. G. Seubert, Standard of Indiana president, told Landon his company had proposed that the major purchasers absorb Prairie's load so that Prairie, in turn, could take the stripper production without a loss. Seubert said that the major companies were ready to proceed on this basis but that Prairie had not yet consented. Fitzpatrick replied (in the press) that conditions prevented Prairie from cooperating, insisting that his company was not responsible for the stripper crisis because its market had dwindled disastrously. He pointed out that Standard of Indiana's purchases from Prairie had recently been reduced from almost 80,000 barrels a day to 12,000, and would, he had been advised, soon be cut to nothing.[15]

[14] Jack Harris to Fred Palmer, February 15, 1936; *Wichita Beacon*, January 4, 1931; *Topeka Capital*, January 4, 1931.

[15] *Wichita Beacon*, January 5, 6, 1931; *Topeka Capital*, January 5–7, 1931; *Independence Reporter*, January 6, 1931.

Pressures on the major companies continued to come from congressional elements and the executive branch. Senator Arthur Capper was in constant touch and frequent conference with Hoover, Wilbur, and Secretary of Commerce Robert P. Lamont. During the first week in January, Landon sent a telegram to Capper explaining the situation at considerable length, and Capper showed the wire to President Hoover, who commended Landon's presentation. Landon's message emphasized that the independents were not trying to blame anyone, they were trying to get a solution; and the major oil companies—despite their claims—had not done all they could. He chided the major pipeline companies: If Prairie's service charges were too high, so were those of the other pipeline companies, for the charges were all the same; the Interstate Commerce Commission should reduce these charges, and promptly. Landon asserted that the major purchasers of crude oil should forget about Prairie and buy through their own Oklahoma facilities. As for the companies' offer of December 31 : " It looks to us that a relief offer was made that the other companies knew would be rejected when it was made." If Prairie had no market, it was unfair for the major companies to force it to purchase the distress oil; but, said Landon, the independents did not really know the facts of the secret negotiations between the major companies. "We are only urging that something be done to save us and a great section of two states from the utter ruin that is now confronting us while the oil industry is quarreling about who is to blame for it." [16]

The representatives of the major companies then met in New York, and again were unable to accomplish anything. The matter was referred back to the purchasing committee set up earlier by their representatives in Tulsa. Standard of Indiana offered to buy 3,000 barrels of distress oil daily through Prairie, but Fitzpatrick refused to accept this offer unless other major companies arranged to take the balance—whereupon Standard announced it was already taking 12,000 barrels of distress crude oil through Standolind lines. The major companies were confident of a settlement, but a headline in the *Topeka Capital* read " BIG SHOTS DO NOTHING." [17]

Other pressures developed during the first two weeks of January, 1931. As voluntary proration broke down among oilmen throughout Kansas, new complaints reached Secretary Wilbur from those affected by the wild competition of producers to secure purchasers. Businessmen

[16] *Topeka Capital*, January 8, 1931.
[17] *Wichita Beacon*, January 9, 1931; *Topeka Capital*, January 10, 1931.

in Wichita screamed, in a full-page advertisement: "TALK OIL TARIFF!
...Now is the Time to Act! Let No Effort Be Left Undone for the
Protection of the Oil Industry on Which our Prosperity Depends!"
In Oklahoma, the house of representatives asked for an embargo and
tariff on oil imports.[18] These actions prefaced a vigorous, almost
desperate renewal of efforts to secure congressional action to rectify
the situation in the oil industry.

Earlier—in December, 1930—preparations were made by oilmen to
renew their demand for a tariff on oil imports. On December 6, in
Dallas, the Mid-Continent Oil and Gas Association called for a protective tariff on oil as well as equitable state proration systems, and
within a week a group of 300 Kansas Independent Petroleum Association members, meeting in Wichita, seconded these demands. The I.P.A.
had been working on the matter of an oil tariff since the defeat of a
similar measure in Congress the preceding March. Imports of foreign
oil in 1929 had totaled 108,710,000 barrels, an average of 298,000
barrels daily. This was, of course, more than the estimated total output
of the nation's stripper wells, and more than one-ninth of the 1927–33
average annual domestic production of 900 million barrels.[19]

Early in January, 1931, Secretary Wilbur stated his opposition to a
protective tariff on oil. He gave two reasons: (1) petroleum exports
exceeded imports by 50 per cent; (2) imports allowed the country to
conserve its oil resources. The second reason, although perhaps theoretically valid, was scoffed at when great waste characterized American
petroleum operations. Wilbur's first reason, although based on sound
international economics, made no sense to producers, lessors, and
workers whose income had been cut off. They forcefully presented their
viewpoints to the government, and, by the end of January, Wilbur and
the administration leaders flagged in their opposition to the movement
for a protective tariff on oil.[20]

The oil-states conference convened on January 15, soon after Congress reassembled, and the representatives of the thirteen states at the
conference limited themselves to urging congressional action and White
House pressure on industry leaders to solve the problems of the
independents. The conference then divided into lobbying units to effect

[18] *Wichita Beacon*, January 11–13, 1931.

[19] *Wichita Beacon*, December 10, 14, 1930; Clark, *Oil Century*, pp. 231 ff.; *I.P.A.
Represents*, pp. 2, 8; Soyster, "Petroleum Industry," p. 13.

[20] *Topeka Capital*, January 7, 1931; *Kansas City Star*, January 30, 1931; *New York
Times*, January 31, 1931.

their tactical goals. Senator-elect Thomas Gore of Oklahoma would lead the lobbying activities in Congress and Senator Capper and Representative Homer Hoch would prepare resolutions for investigations of the oil industry, resolutions designed to find a basis for antitrust action. Wirt Franklin, the I.P.A. leader, again led the independent oil forces in Washington, naming a committee of three, which included Landon, to press for congressional action. A spirit of urgency pervaded the independents' actions, as 13,000 stripper wells were still without markets, but, fortunately for the owners, damage to the unconnected wells was negligible because most of them were pumping oil into makeshift storage facilities or waste dumps.

Although Landon had been cool toward a tariff on oil imports, he now supported such a measure, though neither he nor Franklin regarded a tariff as a panacea—or were optimistic about congressional action. It was obvious that most progressive Republicans and Democrats in the Senate would not accept a tariff increase. In the House, moreover, the chairman of the powerful Rules Committee, Bertrand H. Snell of New York, had said the oil tariff would not be considered because it would reopen the whole tariff question. Landon knew that the depression and the controversy over the Hawley-Smoot Tariff Act of 1930 had heightened sensitivity to the tariff question, but he thought this was no excuse for permitting ruin in the oil fields and the development of a monopoly of oil properties through forced sales by independents to the major companies. Landon made a compromise proposal, which he hoped would succeed in Congress: imports should be limited, on a pro rata basis, to 25 per cent of 1928 crude oil imports—to 19 million barrels.[21]

On January 17 the Hoch investigation resolution was introduced; also submitted was a bill—by Representative Milton C. Garber of Oklahoma—providing for a dollar-a-barrel crude oil tariff, a 50 per cent ad valorem tariff on petroleum products, and presidential authority to stop imports. In the Senate, Gerald Nye of North Dakota demanded an investigation of the oil industry. Five days later, Capper introduced a bill, based on Landon's proposal, to restrict crude imports to one-fifth of the 1928 level, or 16 million barrels, the limitation to be effective for three years. The Capper bill also provided for an embargo on imports of refined petroleum products. Toward the end of January Representative Hoch, after a conference with Landon, introduced an amendment

[21] Landon to A. D. Allison, December 31, 1930, February 11, 1931; *Topeka Capital*, January 16, 17, 1931; *New York Times*, January 16, 1931.

to the Interstate Commerce Act that would limit pipeline companies to transporting crude oil. Landon had told Hoch that the pipelines would have to be divorced from production, purchasing, and refining operations if the oil monopoly was to be broken. "The country just can't stand [the] results much longer."[22]

Landon was increasingly impatient for action on the immediate issue of marketing the production of the stripper wells. Although the congressional hoppers were filling and the national administration was still conferring with the big companies, the stripper problem had not been met. Landon repeatedly trod a circuit of government offices, talking to members of Congress and conferring with administration leaders. In late January he concentrated on Robert P. Lamont, hoping that the Secretary of Commerce, who impressed him as being genuinely sympathetic toward the strippers, could secure a negotiated settlement.[23]

Despite intensive efforts, Lamont achieved nothing in his negotiations with the representatives of the big oil companies, and Landon was despondent. Of one of Lamont's conferences, Landon said, two and a half billion dollars of wealth "sat down" to talk for three hours.

> And that two and one-half billions refused to turn a finger to help save the distress in their own industry. It looks to me as if too much power in the oil industry, as in the public utility fields, has been centered in too few people. I don't know just what can be done about this in Kansas, but I am beginning to believe it will have to be along the lines of breaking down monopolistic control.

Landon saw the need for legislation to remove interstate oil pipeline and refining companies from the filling station business, to prohibit natural gas companies from owning and operating local distributing companies, and to take gas and electric power companies out of the business of selling appliances.

> The time has come about for return of the Roosevelt policies in dealing with huge combinations and mergers that tend to produce monopolies, and I think we might as well take that attitude in Kansas and in the nation.[24]

The pressures on government and industry were sustained by home sources to help Landon and the other independents in their fight.

[22] *Topeka Capital*, January 18, 23, 25, 29, 1931.

[23] *Topeka Capital*, January 21, 22, 1931; Landon to W. A. White, January 16, February 2, January 22, 1931, White Papers.

[24] *Topeka Capital*, January 28, 1931.

Outrage over the oil situation continued to be a familiar editorial theme in Kansas newspapers. Senator Capper's newspaper warned that to "destroy [the stripper wells] is to confess that the oil industry as now conducted is reckless of waste and loss of incalculable national wealth in natural resources." On January 30, Governor Woodring wrote President Hoover and E. G. Seubert of Standard of Indiana that he was appalled to think that the destruction of thousands of wells would be allowed. He held the big producers responsible, requested immediate action by the federal government, and urged the sponsorship by Standard Oil of a new conference of purchasers. The governor declared his support of the tariff bill and warned of state action to deal with the stripper problem; in fact, he threatened Standard with state action—perhaps a state inquiry into the business arrangements between the ostensibly divorced Standard Oil companies of Kansas and Indiana. Woodring also warned Fitzpatrick that if Prairie went into the retail oil trade, as was rumored, its products would not be well received in Kansas; and Standard and Prairie were given until February 10 to act. The governor's statements followed reports that Kansas producers were burning crude oil for lack of market and storage facilities.[25]

Despite discouragements, Secretary Lamont's conferences continued; Woodring entered into negotiations with Standard of Indiana; and Landon conferred with officials of the major oil companies in New York. Soon their efforts began to bear fruit. Lamont told Landon, on February 7, that Standard Oil of New Jersey, Standard of Indiana, Gulf, and Texaco had offered to take almost all of the available stripper oil in Kansas and Oklahoma; if Gulf and Texaco would accept another 1,000 barrels daily, a permanent solution could be implemented. Then, on February 8, Governor Woodring announced that he and a representative of Standard Oil of Indiana had reached an acceptable agreement whereby Standard would purchase 6,000 barrels daily of unconnected Kansas crude oil, for a period of 60 days, up to a total of 300,000 barrels. The governor viewed this truce as providing the time necessary to find a permanent settlement.

Landon was a bit discouraged, for he believed Lamont was on the verge of arranging a continuing agreement when Woodring had accepted a temporary one. Yet Woodring's truce—and a similar agreement concluded in Oklahoma—meant that negotiations could be

conducted under more relaxed conditions. On behalf of the oil independents, Landon thanked Lamont, Woodring, and Capper for their
efforts.[26] Woodring, in March and April, with Landon serving as his
adviser, negotiated a continuing agreement with the major companies
to buy Kansas' stripper well output.[27] Thus with bludgeoning publicity,
blunt talk, persistent lobbying, state and national governmental
pressures, and informal boycotts, the stripper markets were retrieved.

After the temporary settlement of the stripper problem, Landon
returned to Kansas. His work as an oil crusader was far from over,
however, for the stripper question had spurred interest in other matters.
Upon Landon's return, in the middle of February, 1931, he assumed
the task of securing state oil conservation and production control
legislation, with the support of many Democratic and Republican
legislators—as well as that of Governor Woodring. Landon was chiefly
interested in two proposals that were before the Kansas legislature.
One proposal would place intrastate pipelines under the jurisdiction of
the Public Service Commission and would prohibit preference in
pipeline connections and purchasing. The other was a conservancy
measure that would adjust—on a pro rata basis—production to
demand, thus stopping waste.

A political problem in pipeline control came from the fact that some
major producers supported it; and Landon worked hard to persuade
party progressives and oil independents that they should not oppose
pipeline control on the basis of guilt by association. The chief problem
with oil conservancy was usually the reverse: major oil companies
bitterly opposed it. These difficulties were somewhat mitigated by
consolidating the pipeline control and conservancy proposals into one
bill, later known as the Geddes-Carpenter Bill, and Landon worked
constantly with legislators to enlist their support for the bill. He testified
before the oil and gas committees of the Kansas senate and house of
representatives. He saw to it that delegations of independent oilmen
lobbied for the bill, and that those who could not be in Topeka wrote,
wired, and telephoned their support of the legislation. Landon

[26] *Topeka Capital*, February 3, 4, 6, 1931; Landon to W. A. White, February 10,
1931, White Papers; *Topeka Capital*, February 9, 15, March 28, 1931; *Wichita Eagle*,
February 10, 1931; Giddens, *Standard Oil*, p. 460.

[27] Landon to Stephen Frazier, February 23, 1931; *Topeka State Journal*, March 6,
1931; Landon to Harry Woodring, March 24, 1931; Harry Woodring to Landon,
April 2, 1931; *Topeka Capital*, April 11, 12, 1931.

had earlier been successful in manipulating the election of a friendly progressive Republican as speaker of the Kansas house of representatives.[28]

Some success was achieved when, on March 3, the bill was approved in the Kansas house of representatives; the battle then shifted to the state senate, and the opposition became more vocal. Pat Malloy, the general counsel of the Sinclair Gas and Oil Company, stated that proration of production would not work, and he cited the reductions in crude petroleum prices where such measures had been instituted. Landon in reply, using Standolind's recent 40-cent-a-barrel price cut, asserted that if Kansas did not enact proration Oklahoma would repeal its wobbly proration law to try to beat such price cuts by increased production, and increased Oklahoma production would demolish what remained of the crude-oil price structure. Under considerable pressure from "big business" lobbyists, however, the senate oil and gas committee killed the Geddes-Carpenter Bill on March 7. Telegrams of protest immediately flooded the committee's mailbox, and oil independents in Topeka buttonholed senators to urge reconsideration of the committee's action. These tactics succeeded, and the bill was revived and reported out of committee. It was passed in the senate on March 13, 22 to 17, and Governor Woodring promptly signed it. Woodring, Landon, and the independents had achieved state-enforced control of Kansas oil production. Kansas was the first state to adopt an effective conservancy-proration law, a measure that over the years greatly contributed to supporting crude oil prices and that also served as an example for other states.[29]

The new conservancy-proration law gave the Public Service Commission full power to make rules for managing production and preventing waste in petroleum operations. The key criterion was that the production of individual wells be limited to the amount that could be marketed; oil would not be pumped indiscriminately and thereby create a price-depressing surplus, much of which would be lost forever. Under this law, corporations and their officials were liable to fine and/or imprisonment for violating the commission's rulings. Wells that produced less than 15 barrels a day were exempt, thus protecting the strippers from being restricted by other than natural limitations on

[28] Landon to Randolph Carpenter, February 18, 1931, Landon to S. C. Bloss, February 18, 1931; *Topeka Capital*, February 26, March 3, 1931.

[29] *Topeka Capital*, March 3, 5, 8, 9, 14, 1931; Kansas, *Session Laws, 1931* (Topeka: State Printer, 1931), chapter 226; Rister, *Oil!*, p. 369; Clark, *Oil Century*, pp. 237 ff.

their production. The independents were further protected because it was made virtually impossible for a big producer to pump a common source of oil dry by multiple drilling.[30]

The passage of the conservancy-proration law afforded great personal satisfaction to Landon. He had fought successfully not only for state production control but also for petroleum conservation; nevertheless, more had to be done. Having concluded the battles for relief of the stripper well owners and for the conservancy-proration law, Landon sought national and regional action to help the oil industry regain its health and to make the industry competitive for the independent operator.

In Congress, as has been seen, Landon helped spur men like Senator Capper and Congressman Hoch to action. He fed them ideas and material, and they relied upon him to gather the evidence to support their legislative maneuvers. Early in the 1931 session of the Kansas legislature, Landon and his political friends secured a resolution for an oil tariff, which Capper could use in the fight in Congress. Landon also helped round up not only oil independents from Kansas and Oklahoma but also representatives of banks and labor unions as witnesses for the Capper tariff and embargo bill before the Senate Commerce Committee. In his testimony before the committee, Landon followed the theme that not just the industry's current financial losses—in excess of $100 million a year—should be considered but also (contradictorily, because he favored restricting production) the loss of the development of untapped lands. Senator Capper, whose testimony followed, asserted that the oil import volume fixed the crude oil prices in the United States; Capper saw a direct relation between imports and the fall of crude prices from $2.04 per barrel in 1926, to $1.29 in 1930, and to 87 cents in early 1931. He saw supporting evidence in the retail gasoline prices, which averaged 18.09 cents per gallon in 1926 and 18.49 cents in 1930 and 1931. He concluded that the only reason for the fall in home crude oil prices, while retail gasoline prices increased, was the flooding of the market with imported oil.[31]

After Capper's testimony, the major operators spoke against his bill—their view being that its provisions would deprive the people of cheap

---

[30] Kansas, *Session Laws, 1931*, chapter 226.

[31] *Topeka Capital*, January 22, 28, 1931; *Kansas City Star*, January 29, 1931; *Wichita Eagle*, January 28, 1931; *Topeka Capital*, January 31, 30, 1931; *Congressional Record*, 71st Cong., 3d sess., LXXIV, 4122–4123.

gasoline and oil products. R. G. Stewart, president of Standard of Indiana's importing subsidiary, the Pan-American Petroleum and Transportation Company, stated that the four largest oil companies had agreed to import only enough to supply the market. (Showing an awareness of antitrust legislation, he later contradicted himself by saying that no agreement had been made.) Aiming a blow at those who called for more regulation of the industry, Stewart suggested that the antitrust laws be repealed so that the oil companies could get together to solve the industry's problems; and he condemned regulations and tariffs as contrary to all laws of economics. Despite his testimony, the Senate Commerce Committee decided on February 5, 1931, less than a month before the end of the Seventy-first Congress, to report the Capper bill. By this time, W. H. Sproul of Kansas had offered two oil tariff bills in the House and Garber of Oklahoma had offered a companion House measure to the Capper bill.[32]

The Capper bill was given preferred consideration by the Senate Steering Committee, but success eluded the bill's advocates as the major oil companies launched their main attack. Using a naval construction bill as a lever, the majors' Senate allies toppled the Capper oil embargo bill from its preferred position. Kansas Senators Allen and Capper tried to counter by securing President Hoover's support for the Capper bill, but Hoover's reaction was mixed, indicating sympathy for the bill but opposition to its embargo provision.

Landon, assisted by Marvin Lee of Wichita, recruited a trainload of oilmen and farm leaders to travel to Washington to press Congress, and a campaign of wires from businessmen was also unleashed. The independent oil lobby, which had been perambulating over the capital for almost a month, began to sprint. In the House, after representatives from twenty-five oil states asked the speaker, Nicholas Longworth, where he stood on the tariff, Longworth replied that he favored its passage—and told his junior colleagues that they could tell that to their friends in the Senate.[33] Despite Longworth's statement, and the oil independents' agitations, the Ways and Means Committee voted, on February 23, to reject all embargo and tariff bills. Speaker Longworth told the Ways and Means chairman, William C. Hawley, that his committee should reconsider its decision because something had to be done. Other House Republican leaders had by this time come to

---

32 *Topeka Capital*, February 3, 6, 8, 1931.
33 *New York Times*, February 8, 1931; *Topeka Capital*, February 10–12, 1931; *Wichita Eagle*, February 10, 11, 1931.

support reconsideration, including the majority leader, John Q. Tilson, and Bertrand Snell, chairman of the Rules Committee. From Topeka, Landon demanded that oil-state Republicans support for speaker of the next House of Representatives, which would be narrowly divided between Republicans and Democrats, someone who would agree to prompt hearings on the oil tariff. Counterpressures were again brought to bear in the House. Several New England representatives told Longworth to forget the oil tariff if he wanted their support for reelection as speaker, and Longworth sought to appease everybody—or at least absolve himself of responsibility—by appointing a special committee to deal with the oil tariff. The hopes of the oil independents slumped, for, of the five committee members, three were known to oppose an oil tariff.[34]

The Kansas delegation was enraged. Following Landon's suggestion, six of the seven Kansas Republican representatives refused to attend the House Republican caucus. Meanwhile in the Senate, Capper was unable to secure a vote on his bill, and despite a last-minute filibuster in the Seventy-first Congress by Senator Thomas the Nye resolution for investigation of the oil industry was lost. While the oil independents failed completely in the Senate, a minor concession was granted by the House in the establishment of a committee to investigate the need for tariff protection for oil and agriculture. The Hoch pipeline divorcement bill also failed.[35] The oil independents had received little help from Congress, but they had learned a lot about politics. They thought they would be better prepared to renew their fight at the opening of the Seventy-second Congress in December, 1931.

Action was developing in other areas. The states encompassing the Mid-Continent field were seeking a cooperative way to meliorate the oil situation. The governors of these states and representatives of the independent oilmen had been in increasingly closer contact since December, 1930, and as Congress faltered they decided to consult formally on the crisis. A meeting was scheduled for March 1, 1931, in Fort Worth, Texas. Governors William H. Murray of Oklahoma and Ross S. Sterling of Texas were there, as well as a representative of the governor of New Mexico and Landon as Governor Woodring's representative. Although the only actions taken by the representatives of the

[34] *Topeka Capital*, February 15, 24–26, 1931; *New York Times*, February 24, 1931.

[35] *Wichita Eagle*, November 29, 1931; *Topeka Capital*, February 27, March 1, 1931; *Congressional Record*, 71st Cong., 3d sess., LXXIV, 6706, 7297 ff., 6767 ff.

four states were to schedule a second meeting and to send a strong message to President Hoover asking him to urge the major companies to limit imports, some favorable results followed the conference. Within the week, the Federal Oil Conservation Board announced that all of the major oil importers (except one) had voluntarily agreed to cut imports. Shell, Gulf, and Standard of New Jersey soon limited their imports, and, by the end of March, Standard of Indiana, the hold-out importer, reported that it too would restrict its imports. The result was a substantial reduction of imports, from 105,619,000 barrels in 1930 to 86,087,000 in 1931.[36]

The second Mid-Continent states governors' meeting was held March 9, but Landon did not attend because of the critical position of the proration bill in the Kansas senate. The idea of an interstate compact between the states to limit oil shipments from the area was favorably received. Again, regional conversation coincided with federal activities as the Federal Oil Conservation Board tried to negotiate industrywide production restrictions to balance supply and demand; the federal government also encouraged an interstate compact to deal with the oil crisis.

A third regional meeting, on April 8, attended by representatives of ten oil states and presided over by Governor Murray's cousin, Colonel Cicero Murray, made further efforts to secure an interstate compact. Landon, now freed from his other interests in the oil fight, showed great concern over the nature of the proposed compact, which would establish an interstate oil commerce commission to act as an umpire in allocating a production quota to each state. He wrote to many Kansas oilmen for their reactions to this proposal. Landon, who opposed its provisions, wanted such a commission to act only in an advisory capacity, as an information exchange, and to aid in coordinating state stabilization programs. The states would then be expected to implement stabilization programs through their own proration apparatus. This was best in terms of effective stabilization action, he thought, for an umpire committee would be severely limited in its enforcement power and might be easily influenced by the national power of the major companies. Landon voiced these ideas in the following governors' conferences, and, because they were widely shared by oilmen in the Mid-Continent area, Landon's views influenced the character of the informal regional

36 *New York Times*, March 2, 6, 1931; *Topeka Capital*, March 1, 2, 6, 12, 1931; Federal Oil Conservation Board, *Report V*, p. 8; *Wichita Beacon*, March 31, 1931; *I.P.A. Represents*, p. 9.

compact that was established in April by Kansas, Oklahoma, and Texas. This agreement set up the Oil States Advisory Committee, which functioned, somewhat weakly, as an information exchange and a stabilization coordinator. Yet it was the forerunner of the 1935 Interstate Oil Compact, which has functioned with considerable effectiveness as an information exchange, an advisory body, and a conservation coordinator.[37]

The oil independents and their allies, exhausted from a winter of fighting, relaxed their efforts during the spring of 1931. This was true of Landon, too, for about all he did was encourage his friends in Congress to be prepared for the December session. The respite was short-lived. While demand for oil continued to decline as the depression grew worse, production and importation had not dropped enough to balance the curtailed demand, much less reduce the tremendous stocks of petroleum in storage. The result was a further snipping away at the depressed price levels. By early June the market appeared to crack: Mid-Continent prices dropped to between 25 cents and 37 cents a barrel.

The independents did nothing for almost a month, hoping that the price would soon "naturally" go up or that the major petroleum companies would further curtail their production and imports; but they were wrong on both counts. By July the price level had dropped to a top figure of 22 cents—from $1.57 the year before. Meetings were held in Oklahoma and Kansas to take action. The Oklahoma oil independents met on July 10, in Oklahoma City, to arrange a complete shutdown of production; a meeting of Kansas independents was scheduled for Wichita on July 11. The Oklahoma shut-down came, and Wirt Franklin wired Landon that the independents must stand together in the two states. Landon had worked for a large turnout at the Wichita meeting but was pessimistic that anything would be accomplished. Some 300 Kansas independents came, representing 60 per cent of the state's production. Landon's pessimism was not completely warranted,

---

[37] *Topeka Capital*, March 9, 10, 22, April 11, 12, 1931; Federal Oil Conservation Board, *Report V*, pp. 3 f.; *New York Times*, April 10, 11, 14, 1931; Landon to Walter Fees, April 4, 1931; Landon to Robert H. Bradford, April 4, 1931. See also Robinson and Edwards, *Ray Lyman Wilbur*, p. 424; Innis D. Harris, "Legal History of Conservation of Oil and Gas in Kansas" in Section of Mineral Law of the American Bar Association, *Legal History of Conservation of Oil and Gas. A Symposium* (Chicago, 1939), p. 48; Clark, *Oil Century*, pp. 192 f.

for they showed that they had emerged from their three-month hibernation. They voted unanimously to join the Oklahomans in closing their wells to retaliate for the price slashes.[38] Yet the shut-down was incomplete, for all of the independents were not represented at the Wichita meeting, and many of those in attendance later weakened in their resolve.

Prices improved a bit during the next month and Landon continued to urge better organization to enforce the shut-down—and whatever else might be decided by the oilmen. He gave a fighting speech—the first lengthy speech of his life—before a large meeting of independent oil producers at Tulsa on July 27. There he likened their fight to that of the "rag-tag, bob-tailed" men of the American Revolution, and equated their plight with that of the small merchants and farmers in 1931. He pinned the blame on monopoly.

> Every thinker knows that the greatest issue in the world today is the communistic system versus the capitalistic or individualistic system. But when the capitalistic system ceases to be an individualistic system by reason of this tendency to monopolize all branches of industry and finance, what then? When you eliminate the small business man, whether he be in the oil or merchandising business, or in the farming business, or in the banking business, you have removed the solid foundation that this government and business system rests upon. . . . It would be foolish to refuse to face the fact that it is this kind of a situation that makes rebels.

Something drastic must happen to save the system, Landon asserted. Small businessmen, farmers, and oilmen must organize with the motto "Don't tread on me" in order to survive. Oilmen must buy only from top payers and must boycott others. A situation that maintained retail gasoline and motor oil prices while crude oil prices fell must be subjected to public scrutiny and to harsh revision.[39]

That these thoughts were not just for publicity's sake was indicated in a letter Landon sent to an acquaintance, a Sinclair Oil Corporation official, who disagreed with his ideas. Landon even expanded on the dangers: "If we keep on going the way we are headed, I do not think there is much question but what there will be a revolution in this country." According to Landon, many conservative oil producers, who believed there was no place for them in a monopolistic society, could well provide leadership to the radicals of the country—instead of

[38] *Wichita Beacon*, June 7, 1931; *Topeka Capital*, June 7, July 12, 1931; Wirt Franklin to Landon, July 10, 1931; Landon to Walter Fees, July 10, 1931.

[39] Landon speech, Tulsa, Oklahoma, July 27, 1931.

being, as in the past, a stabilizing force. The big corporations had better realize that they could lose the support of the middle class. If radicalism broke loose, Landon knew that men of modest fortune, like himself, would be lost, but he also believed they might be lost if monopoly succeeded.[40]

The voluntary shut-downs had an effect by the end of July, when the top crude oil price was 42 cents a barrel. Later, state public service agencies in Oklahoma and Texas issued shut-down orders to oil producers that contributed to boosting the price to 70 cents by the third week of August. These were followed by an order of the Kansas Public Service Commission for a 90 per cent shut-down of the Ritz and Canton pools, where 20 per cent of the state's oil was produced. The strict production control implemented in the three states helped boost the price of crude to 85 cents a barrel by December, 1931.[41]

Meanwhile the oil tariff issue was again becoming active. A mail and visitation campaign was being conducted by the major companies to undercut support for the tariff. The election of the speaker of the federal House of Representatives was again part of the issue, for early in the fall it still appeared that the Republicans would control the House. As every Republican vote would be needed to organize the House under Republican control, Landon hoped to trade the vote of the Kansas congressional delegation for favorable consideration of the oil tariff. "The people of Kansas should insist that their delegation vote for a Speaker of the House who would favor the oil tariff." Landon suggested Congressman Homer Hoch for the speakership.[42]

By November it was clear that the Democrats had picked up enough strength in special elections to organize the House of Representatives. That fact cheered the oil independents because Representative John Nance Garner of Texas, an ardent advocate of the oil tariff, was the leading Democratic choice for speaker. It also appeared that a chairman of the Ways and Means Committee would be selected who would be favorable to the tariff. Landon was optimistic: "It wouldn't surprise me if the oil tariff measure would come up the very opening day of Congress. The shoe is on the other foot. . . . There's one thing we oilmen are not going to do this year, and that's wait until it's too late to make our noise."

[40] Landon to Dan T. Pierce, July 28, 1931.

[41] *Topeka Capital*, August 23, 30, October 11, 1931; Federal Oil Conservation Board, *Report V*, p. 3; *Kansas City Star*, December 10, 1931.

[42] *Wichita Beacon*, September 8, 1931.

Early in December, Wirt Franklin called Landon to Washington to assist in formulating oil legislation, and Landon had previously volunteered to spend two weeks in the capital for the Independent Petroleum Association. The tariff campaign was to be based on a demand for a dollar-a-barrel duty on crude oil and a 50 per cent ad valorem duty on refined products. The independents' main argument in support of the tariff was that recovery of the oil industry—which had now slipped to third place in national importance—was possible, and that its recovery would help revive agriculture and transportation.[43]

As Landon became increasingly involved in state politics, in preparation for the 1932 elections, he became less of a force in the oil battle; but he kept in contact with—and on occasion joined—the front-rank fighters. Landon's optimism about the Democratic House proved excessive. The tariff proposal, taken up rather early in the session, appeared to have been killed on January 9, 1932, though it was revived two weeks later. Landon continued to dramatize the subject in Kansas —and elsewhere—by condemning monopoly and its "pirate" pricing practices, and by demanding tariff and antitrust action. In April, Landon lobbied in Washington for the oil tariff, now euphemistically called an excise tax. He later engaged in raising money to finance the independent oil lobby in Washington, and he participated in the attempts to secure state and national Republican platform pledges for the relief of oil independents.[44]

Some of the pressure on Congress was reduced as crude oil prices rose—up to a maximum of a dollar per barrel. In late March, 1932, however, the House adopted a compromise measure—an excise tax of one cent a gallon on imported crude oil. The Senate, with many of the oil tariff foes from the Seventy-first Congress still on hand, presented another problem. Yet, after a great deal of fencing in the Finance Committee, a measure was reported to impose a $\frac{1}{2}$-cent-per-gallon or a 21-cents-a-barrel excise tax on crude oil, in addition to $2\frac{1}{2}$ cents a gallon on gasoline and 4 cents a gallon on other imported petroleum products. Assiduous efforts by the bill's opponents to stalemate its final consideration failed, and the Senate approved the measure the day after Memorial Day. It went to a conference committee, where House conferees accepted the Senate version, and victory was at last

[43] *Wichita Eagle*, November 29, 1931; *Independence Reporter*, December 1, 6, 1931; *Kansas City Star*, December 10, 1931.

[44] *Topeka Capital*, January 10, 26, February 7, May 1, April 16, 1932; John M. Franklin to Landon, March 2, 1932; Landon to John M. Franklin, March 6, 1932.

achieved.[45] Although Landon and the I.P.A. were not completely satisfied by the new tax rates, the excise virtually eliminated imports of motor fuel and it considerably reduced imports of crude oil and other oil products—65 per cent between the first and second halves of 1932.[46]

Although the developments of 1930, 1931, and 1932 did not save the petroleum industry from near-calamity in 1933 and 1934, they established the bases for lasting public oil policies. Some protection for independent oil operators has constantly been a theme of legislation, and tariff protection for oil has been an integral part of federal policy. Moreover, since 1932 all of the important petroleum states have enacted fairly effective laws for allotting production quotas among oilmen and for curbing the waste of crude oil.

As for Landon, the fight for stabilization of the oil industry was the key to his political future. Without the oil crusade, he probably would not have sought the governorship in 1932, and in 1936 he would not have had "an experience that comes to few," the Republican presidential nomination. Oil made possible not only his business fortune, but also his political fame.

[45] *Congressional Record*, 72d Cong., 1st sess., LXXV, 7329; *Topeka Capital*, April 10, 16, 1932; *Kansas City Star*, April 25, 1932; *Topeka Capital*, April 29, May 10, 19, 25, 1932; *New York Times*, May 21, 1932; *Congressional Record*, LXXV, 9808, 11666, 12038, 12069 ff.; Rister, *Oil!*, p. 373.

[46] Landon to John M. Franklin, October 26, 1932; *I.P.A. Represents*, pp. 2, 9; Landon to W. A. White, May 24, 1932.

CHAPTER 5

From Oil Rebel to Governor

Kansas politics had changed considerably after Clyde M. Reed's defeat in August, 1930. Frank Haucke's nomination for governor had been generally considered by Republicans as tantamount to his election, but they soon came to realize that his success was not guaranteed. The state Democratic party, which after the 1928 elections had been called "a thing of the past," had been reinvigorated under the leadership of national committeeman Jouett Shouse. In 1930 the Democrats, by then keenly aware of the American Legion's political importance, nominated the energetic Harry Woodring, a former state Legion commander, for Governor.[1]

More sensational was the entry of a write-in candidate, Dr. John R. Brinkley of Milford. In the 1920s the degree-mill graduate had attracted a national clientele and a fortune with his goat-gland transplantations and compounds, which were advertised as methods of restoring virility. His powerful radio transmitter, KFKB, increased his advertising power, and it later provided radio diagnoses of ills that his listeners described to him in their letters. As his radio activities increased, alarm spread among physicians and competing radio stations. Attempts were made to restrict his efforts, and Brinkley had to contend with the hostility of the American Medical Association, the Federal Radio Commission,

[1] William F. Zornow, *Kansas* (Norman: University of Oklahoma Press, 1957), pp. 243 f.

the Kansas Medical Society, and the *Kansas City Star*. During the summer of 1930 the state Medical Registration and Examination Board revoked his license to practice, and the Federal Radio Commission refused to renew KFKB's broadcasting license.

In September, crying "persecution," Brinkley declared himself an independent candidate for governor, but as he had made his decision too late to put his name on the ballot, his declaration was scoffed at. As the campaign developed, however, Democratic and Republican party workers sent increasingly alarming reports about voters' determination to write Brinkley's name on their ballots. Both parties were in a panic by election day, when it became clear that the colorful Brinkley, with his promises to accomplish everything for everybody, had found a following. Accounts of vote frauds were wholesale.[2] When the votes were tabulated, Woodring had 217,171, Haucke had 216,920, and Brinkley had 183,278.

It was widely conceded that Haucke could have won over Woodring had he requested a recount, but the Republicans decided to accede Woodring's election rather than take a chance that uncounted or miscounted Brinkley votes might give victory to the goat-gland doctor (not being on the ballot, he could not request a recount) or that a recount might confirm the rumors of voting fraud by the major parties. The election of a Democratic governor and the cries of "cheated" by Brinkley's supporters almost obscured the fact that Henry J. Allen had been defeated by Democrat George McGill for a two-year Senate term and that Clyde Reed's income-tax amendment had failed.[3]

Because of Woodring's election, the possibility that Brinkley would again run for governor in 1932, and the growing severity of the depression, Kansas politics was more profoundly unsettled than it had been since the Populist successes of the 1890s. It was in this situation that Alf Landon was to develop as a candidate for governor. Landon's battle to solve the problems of the oil independents led to a remarkable development of his political capital, transforming a leader of a repudiated Republican faction into the chief hope of his party in Kansas. During the winter of 1930/31, and throughout the following year, there

[2] Gerald Carson, *The Roguish World of Doctor Brinkley* (New York: Holt, Rinehart & Winston, 1960), *passim*.

[3] *Ibid.*, pp. 165 f.; A. Bower Sageser, "Political Patterns of the 1920's," in John D. Bright (ed.), *Kansas, The First Century* (New York: Lewis, 1956), II, 87; Zornow, *Kansas*, pp. 245 ff.

was scarcely a day in which Landon's name did not appear in one or more of the state's newspapers.

During the stripper well fight, Landon thought of politics only as a way to save the stripper well operators; there was no time for considering personal ambitions. When in February, 1931, a friend suggested that Landon look toward the gubernatorial candidacy the following year, he bluntly wrote: "As far as the governorship is concerned, I don't give a damn." [4] Several things contributed to his reaction besides being under pressure around the clock. He had been disillusioned with the political process because of the government's lassitude in helping the small oilmen, and he felt that the worsening economic outlook made the political situation in Kansas unpromising for a Republican. Furthermore, as he wrote in March, 1931, "Woodring has given pretty general satisfaction and I am afraid will be a hard man to beat, especially with the party torn to pieces the way it is." Landon thought consequently that the Republican nomination for governor was not worth much; even if it was, "there seems to be no particular outstanding candidate for governor." [5]

Although Landon was perhaps unaware of it, he had developed into a good potential candidate. He was an experienced politician and had extensive contacts—as a politician, a joiner, and a businessman. He had fought, with drama and some success, for the "little fellow" and for Kansas, and had received widespread credit for it, and it was not surprising that he came to mind when the question of the governorship arose. The idea started trickling into newspapers as early as April, 1931, and, by the middle of May, one of the state's leading political columnists, Clifford Stratton, listed Landon first among the "frequently mentioned" Republican gubernatorial possibilities. In July, the young leaders of the progressive Republican faction met secretly in Emporia to consider ways of restoring party harmony, and Landon as a harmony candidate was a chief topic of discussion. A few days later the *Independence Daily Reporter*, which was not always friendly to Landon, profiled him in its "Pillars of Industry" column—with a good summary of his career and connections, and a line-sketch likeness. The spontaneity of support and his successes in the oil fights soon led him to decide to make himself available for governor. By September it was clear that the Independence oilman was running for office when he spoke out on

[4] Landon to A. D. Allison, February 11, 1931, Alfred M. Landon Papers.
[5] Landon to Lewis J. Pettijohn, March 26, 1931.

the problems of the wheat farmer—a certain sign in Kansas of impending candidacy.[6]

Landon sensed that Kansas Republicans, despite their many quarrels, would realize that only party unity could bring them success in 1932. He handled himself accordingly. His position as a potential harmony nominee was enhanced by the fact that he had often bargained dispassionately with Republican conservatives and yet maintained his standing as a progressive Republican. Moreover, Landon's approach to the nomination seemed to be partisanly responsible rather than self-serving: he was willing rather than eager to run for governor. To his old oil partner, A. H. Black, he wrote:

> My feet have not been itching to get into the kind of a campaign that next year promises to be. I have not run after [the nomination] and on the other hand I have not run away from it. As I have told some of my friends who have been concerned about my political future, that is the most intangible thing in the world. I have had a lot of fun in politics by not giving a darn about that and politics becomes a burden when you commence to worry about your political future.

As for 1932's unhappy omens for a Republican candidate, Landon felt "there are lots worse things than taking a licking and one of them is to run away from a fight because it is hard."[7]

Preparing for his political venture, Landon enlisted as chief of staff the *Kansas City Star*'s Lacy Haynes, who was William Allen White's brother-in-law. At Haynes's urging, Landon faithfully attended alumni, chamber of commerce, American Legion, and oil association meetings, where he had many opportunities to discuss politics. He even became a speechmaker, appearing at the Kansas Oil Conference at El Dorado, the Kansas City Armistice Day ceremonies, and the Kansas City Women's Chamber of Commerce. Landon, in his political visits, kept conservatives and progressives, moderates and reactionaries, and cranks and elder statesmen fairly well separated. Meeting them alone, he could survive their sizings-up by letting them talk and by drifting with their conversation. In the middle of December, however, he went out on the prairie, to Hays, for a harmony meeting of forty Republican leaders from northwest Kansas. A real test had come:

[6] *Winfield Daily Courier*, April 10, 1931; *Topeka Capital*, May 17, 1931; *Kansas City Journal-Post*, July 16, 1931; *Independence Daily Reporter*, July 21, 1931; *Kansas City Times*, September 8, 1931.

[7] Landon to A. H. Black, October 22, 1931.

could he hold a middle course when he was the center of attention, surrounded by representatives of every faction and personality type in the party? Lacy Haynes told him to talk harmony and harmony and more harmony—on campaigning, on accepting the primary election results, on devising a platform, on supporting the ticket in the general election, and on implementing a program. The point was that only with harmony could the Republican party win Kansas in 1932.

When Landon arrived in Hays, on December 15, accusations were made as to responsibility for party chaos, and Landon, who was often chided for being a Reed man, replied that this had nothing to do with harmony. Encouraged by progressives and irritated by conservatives, he came close to suggesting that the conservatives had sold out the party. Lacy Haynes, in Topeka, had tried to forestall this development by sending a telegram, which Landon received soon after his arrival in Hays, telling him to ignore the panning that had been prepared for him, and Landon did so, using his well-developed sense of humor. The chiding was as irksome the following day, but Landon's harmony-and-humor approach appeased everyone. The Republican leaders of northwest Kansas unanimously endorsed Alf Landon for governor.[8]

By January of 1932, Landon's intentions were known; as the *Hiawatha World* said, with exaggeration, "He is as crazy to be Governor as a mule is to eat hay." On January 20, with the release of a printed brochure, Landon announced his candidacy for the Republican gubernatorial nomination. In an appeal for unity for meeting Kansas' economic challenges, he declared: "We Kansans, regardless of party, want to do two things: one, to make this state materially progress—second, to cut taxes." To achieve material progress, Landon pledged he would work for the development of manufacturing industries in the state and for recovery in Kansas' two largest businesses, agriculture and oil. Tax relief, he contended, required economy in public expenditures and an equitable distribution of the tax burden—taxes must be shifted to accumulated wealth by imposing taxes on income and investments. The announcement brochure also included editorial quotations from seven newspapers that depicted Landon as "a fearless, intelligent, constructive leader," "clean, capable and competent," "harmonious," and "a businessman of much ability, a student of affairs with ability to express his views." The brochure might have added that he "must be

[8] Lacy Haynes to Landon, December 15, 1931; *Hays Daily News*, December 16, 1931.

honest," because, as one Kansan put it, "he shore ain't a speaker."[9]

The announcement of Landon's candidacy was immediately followed by an editorial barrage in his favor, but it also led to a counterattack by conservative newspapers. The *Eskridge Independent* combined two common lines of complaint when it stated:

> Alf's candidacy, we truly believe, has no potent influence behind it except that of the [Kansas City] *Star* and William Allen White's *Emporia Gazette*. Haucke Republicans detest Landon because they feel he deserted his party after the primary of two years ago when his boss, Clyde Reed, was honestly licked at the polls.

The *Independent* also lauded Haucke's withdrawal from the primary election to permit a capable Republican desirous of party harmony to run. Broadly hinting that Landon should withdraw, the newspaper asserted that Haucke

> could poll just as many votes as he did against Clyde Reed and he could beat Millionaire Landon, too, don't ever forget that, but what good would that do toward harmony in the ranks of the party?[10]

A few days after Landon's announcement, the conservative wing's harmony candidate, Lacey Simpson of McPherson, entered the race for the nomination. Simpson, who had supported Reed in 1930, was a dirt farmer. He had been a member of the state senate for four years, had spent two terms in the state house of representatives, and had served on the Kansas Board of Administration from 1925 to 1931;[11] he was to wage an energetic campaign against the Independence oilman. Landon's and Simpson's campaigns started with their announcements and were carried on over the state—for six months—in one of the dullest, but most strenuous, primary contests ever seen in Kansas.

Simpson was obviously the candidate of Frank Haucke and national committeeman David Mulvane, who were trying to control the party. When Haucke withdrew from the race he had called upon Landon to withdraw and to show his sincere interest in party harmony by supporting Simpson. Landon refused to withdraw; he emphasized that factionalism must be set aside and that the campaign must be fought on issues, not personalities, because the people would decide the election on

---

[9] *Hiawatha World*, January 18, 1932; *Topeka Capital*, January 21, 1932; *Landon Announces for Governorship* (leaflet), January 20, 1931; Richard B. Fowler, *Deeds Not Deficits, The Story of Alfred M. Landon* (Kansas City, 1936), p. 51.

[10] *Eskridge Independent*, February 4, 1932.

[11] *Topeka State Journal*, January 25, 1932.

issues.[12] A basic part of Landon's approach during his primary campaign was that the people would decide, the issues were most important —he would not indulge in party-wrecking references to personalities.

Against this attitude, Simpson was unable to overcome identification with his faction. He found no issues to distinguish himself from the front-running Landon; both favored agricultural and business recovery, lower taxes, an oil tariff, and efficiency in government. During the campaign Simpson preached harmony yet blasted Landon and his wealth and connections—especially "the funny man of Kansas politics," William Allen White, and Clyde Reed and the *Kansas City Star*.[13] His attack was buttressed by the strictures of political columnist A. L. "Dutch" Shultz against "Fox" Landon, which characterized the contest as "a farmer boy against a rich oil man." Landon, Shultz wrote, was "campaigning on the theory that the hand is quicker than the eye. . . . Quite craftily he counsels in private with his old friends and walks in the open with old enemies of his party group."[14] Late in the contest, Simpson implied that Landon was a party-wrecker, citing Landon's support of White's independent candidacy for governor in 1924. In a bid for the poor man's vote, Simpson also charged that Landon's campaign was backed by big business, newspaper publishers, and other dominant interests—while claiming that he had none of this support.[15]

Simpson's assessment was partly true, for Landon's harmony campaign had undercut much of Simpson's prospective support. The staunch conservative leader, William Y. Morgan, just before his death in 1932, had written one of his chief political allies that he wanted his friends to go along with Landon for governor. Leslie Edmonds of Wichita, an American Legion leader and one of Hamilton's chief backers in 1928, came out strongly for Landon because of his ability and the bifactional support he had garnered. Former Governor Ben Paulen, who was running for the Republican senatorial nomination, supported no one, but he wrote his friends that he favored Landon. In fact, as the primary approached its end a large number of conservatives either backed Landon or became politically silent.[16]

[12] *Ibid.*, January 26, 27, 1932.
[13] *Topeka Capital*, May 1, 8, July 25, 1932; *Norton Telegram*, May 10, 1932.
[14] *Norton Courier*, May 19, 1932; *Topeka State Journal*, June 2, 1932.
[15] *Topeka Capital*, July 28, 1932.
[16] *Kansas City Times*, February 20, 1932; *Topeka Capital*, July 30, 1932; Ben S. Paulen to Sherman G. Elliott, April 13, 1932.

Landon had gathered a strong organization in the primary contest. The *Kansas City Star* had swung behind him, and the newspaper's Kansas correspondent, Lacy Haynes, had become Landon's principal adviser. William Allen White had also backed Landon, and continued to do so strongly during the campaign: "I am following the banner of flaming youth." Landon's campaign manager was a practicing farmer, Frank Carlson of Concordia, who early displayed his adeptness at political diplomacy. Reed's former secretary, William G. West, and former attorney general, William Smith, also played leading roles as advisers and contact men. William M. Bradshaw was in charge of contacting Negro workers and voters. A Landon-for-governor committee was carefully selected for representativeness—with members from the Republican factions, from every section of the state, from every significant economic interest, and with a Methodist, a Presbyterian, a Lutheran, and a Baptist minister (representing the state's chief denominations).[17]

The harmony approach of the pre-announcement campaign was followed throughout the primary campaign. The old Progressive party leader, Victor Murdock, had told Landon:

> Now, Alf when you are making a speech and take a crack at your opponent, the crowd will yell. You take another crack at him and they will yell again. That eggs you on to go further than you intended and the crowd keeps yelling. When you get through you say to yourself, "I got away good." But the next morning there is an unfavorable reaction.[18]

Landon knew that his only chance to rally Republicans behind his campaign was to avoid unfavorable reactions, and he did this by taking the Democrats to task and by transcending factional issues.

In his first major campaign speech, given at Emporia in January, he concentrated his fire on the Democratic state chairman, Guy Helvering, and even this was put humorously: "I think it is sad for Mr. Helvering to have to work so hard running the highway commission and the Democratic party both. I am going to try to relieve him of some of that work." As for the Republicans, Landon said "that if we stop cussing the present and past and start planning for the future, we will have plenty to do." These ideas, along with remarks on the need for farm

---

[17] W. A. White to Landon, April 18, 1932, letterhead (1932) of Landon-for-governor committee.

[18] Landon to Lewis H. Brown, January 26, 1945.

recovery, an oil tariff, industrial development, impartial law enforcement, government efficiency, and income-tax reform, were the backbone of his campaign. His insistence that Kansans must talk principles not panaceas, and must "concentrate on building up the state instead of tearing it down," won him much support.[19]

All this was accompanied by hard work. Landon was constantly campaigning, hitting first one congressional district, then another, until all eight had been visited; then starting all over again. He visited newspaper offices, hotel lobbies, chambers of commerce, precinct committeemen, and officeholders; he walked up and down main streets, talking with everyone he met. He urged petition signatures by his workers as a way of gaining additional contact with the voters. He was always willing to listen to people with grievances—factionalists, Democrats, Brinkleyites, or whatever. He always emphasized that the Republican party could win, if unified, and he declared that the party must win if Kansas was to secure recovery, honesty, and constructive statesmanship. He conceded to Republican conservatives what was theirs, supported the endorsement of Herbert Hoover and Charles Curtis at the state convention, and avoided conflict with Simpson, state chairman Hamilton, and national committeeman Mulvane. All this, in turn, was played up by Landon's editorial supporters or by observers. Here is a man, the *Garden City Telegram* wrote, who talked

> man to man, plain, simple, Kansas language; . . . no flag waving, ranting or striving for oratorical effect, no parading the shortcomings of others . . . Alf Landon is just a plain, everyday citizen with a lot of ability, a lot of stick-to-itiveness and a vast capacity for making and holding friends by his earnestness and sincerity.[20]

Although Landon's campaign progressed smoothly, the state increasingly suffered from the effects of depression and drought. Crop production and value, retail and wholesale receipts, and industrial and mineral output and sales slumped toward disaster, as unemployment steadily climbed. By spring, Landon was sure he would win the primary election, and his efforts took on the character of a campaign

[19] *Topeka Capital*, January 27, May 1, 20, 1932; *Manhattan Mercury*, June 14, 1932.
[20] *Garden City Telegram*, quoted in *Topeka Capital*, May 8, 1932. For similar estimates of Landon's campaign impressions by conflicting political newspapers, see *Topeka State Journal*, May 18, 1932, and *Topeka Capital*, May 9, 1932.

for the general election—an election in which his success was much in doubt. His chief oil field aide, H. R. Allen, wrote Landon of his fears:

> I believe that 2/3 of the Republicans are going Democratic. I have had a number of them give me a cussing, when I tried to talk to them. The farmers are *Hot*, they are selling brood sows for $2.00 and $3.00 per head. I think you better get some "dope" to fight the Farm Board—and the Packing House—with, to get the farm vote, for they are Red.[21]

This and similar reports led Landon to give greater emphasis to the farm problem. Before he left for Washington (in April) to fight for the oil excise tax, he issued a strong and quixotic statement on the farm situation. He said that a second purpose of his trip was to bring forcibly to the attention of farm leaders and government officials the "alarming short crop in the winter wheat belt" and the "ruinously low prices of farm products." The year's crop would not satisfy American wheat needs, and, with Russian yields down, the European market for wheat should revive. Because of this, he would demand that the prices of wheat and other cereals "be promptly advanced."[22]

In May, Landon undertook to publicize the state's farm problem in analytical terms. Speaking of Kansas' agricultural nature, he said:

> With more acres under the plow than any other state in the Union except Texas, it is evident that the prosperity of her people depends upon the economic condition of agriculture. [Yet] farm prices have fallen to a lower level than at any time in this century [and] far below production costs. . . . Our farm mortgage debt has been increased threefold above what it was in 1910 and our taxes have been boosted 250 per cent higher than before the war.

Probably drawing on the ideas of his acquaintances in the Farmers' Union, he demanded a readjustment of these economic factors so that the "costs of production plus a reasonable profit may be realized." This could be achieved, for with an increasing population and with "millions of hungry and starving in this country and abroad, there is a place for our Kansas wheat and hogs." He also called for a better system of distributing products, expansion of currency, more liberal bank loans, and, of course, reduction of the taxes paid by farmers. These improvements could be achieved, now that the nation's "best business

21 H. R. Allen to Landon, April 22, 1932.
22 Landon press release, n.d. (ca. April, 1932).

minds...are awakening" and "a greater cooperative spirit prevails among all our classes than has ever before been evidenced." [23]

Starting at the end of May, 1932, thousands of letters signed by Landon were sent out over the state to buttress his press releases and speeches. These letters solicited support, and enclosed in them the recipients found a copy of the candidate's announcement program. The letter said:

> You will note my position on agriculture; enforcement of ALL laws, including the Eighteenth Amendment; consolidation of needless boards in state affairs. My stand for tax reduction and rigid economy in government is sound business doctrine. [24]

By the latter part of June, Landon's itinerary had led him to 90 of the state's 105 counties, and his petition method of filing his candidacy had gained him more than 70,000 signatures. [25]

Despite the strenuous campaigns waged by Landon and Simpson, no unusual interest had been aroused in the contest. Landon's oratory and confidence put the voters to sleep, and Simpson could not wake them up. Landon intentionally followed this course, knowing that "waking up" the voters meant alienating votes that would be desperately needed for the general election. A strident appeal by Landon might antagonize too many party workers; also, it might give Woodring and John Brinkley—who had again declared himself the independent candidate for governor—something substantial to attack. Furthermore, it might put Landon in the position of repudiating the national administration, thereby alienating those Republicans closely tied to Vice President Curtis or President Hoover.

Landon decided to complete his primary campaign in a mildly dramatic way, however, in order to arouse Republicans enough to go to the polls. In late July he condemned the Democratic political levy of 5 per cent on the salaries of state employees; this was a traditional opposition tactic in Kansas, and one used earlier by and—as state chairman—against Landon. He pledged, if elected, not to make the levy. He also proposed a plan to relieve unemployment. This could be done, under the supervision of the United States Department of Labor, by reducing the average number of hours worked a week to a level that

[23] Landon press release, enclosed in Frank Carlson to Landon, May 16, 1932; *Great Bend Tribune*, May 31, 1932.

[24] Landon to T. A. Reeves, May 31, 1932.

[25] *Norton Courier*, June 23, 1932.

would make employment available to the jobless. A Simpson spokesman derided Landon's proposal as "all wet."[26]

Landon by July 26, visiting as many as ten towns a day, had covered all of the counties in the state, and just before the August primary he experienced two vote-boosters. A daughter, Nancy Jo, was born, and on the way home for her birth he had stopped to carry furniture out of a burning farmhouse and had injured two fingers. His happiness and hurt were probably supplemented by the votes that the publicity of these events drew. Little use, however, had been made of newspaper advertising before the election; reliance was mainly on Landon's campaigning and the confident statements by Frank Carlson—to the effect that Landon would win the nomination because of his constructive issues, wide business experience, great civic interest, knowledge of state problems, appeal as a harmonizer, and ability to transcend personalities.[27]

Landon won an overwhelming victory. He polled 160,345 votes—to 59,326 for Simpson, and 28,456 for a late entry, Joseph H. Brady, of Kansas City. Landon carried ninety-four counties.[28]

Landon had the gubernatorial nomination, but no one was certain it was worth having. He was facing Harry Woodring, an affable governor with a good record, who was abetted by a hard-working state chairman, Guy Helvering; and the situation had been complicated by Brinkley's entry into the contest. Since June, 1931, it had been apparent that the medical maverick was running for office, and Brinkley formally announced his intention to run as the independent candidate for governor early in June, 1932.

The race for governor, therefore, was as it had been in the fall of 1930, with Landon substituting for Haucke—but the Republican position appeared to be worse than in 1930. Woodring had won overwhelming endorsement in the Democratic primary election, and because he was now the incumbent the power of state offices could be used in his support. Moreover, the strong national Democratic campaign, led by Franklin D. Roosevelt against the "Hoover Republican Depression," was certain to buoy the efforts of the Kansas Democrats. Brinkley in 1930 had been a hastily entered write-in candidate, and his campaigning time had been limited, as was his political support. Now

26 *Topeka Capital*, July 19, 25, 1932.
27 *Ibid.*, July 27, 30, August 2, 1932.
28 *Ibid.*, August 27, 1932.

he had been campaigning for over a year and had the backing of several political veterans, including former Governor Jonathan Davis; he had also developed an organization—with Burt Comer running for attorney general, Ella J. Burton for superintendent of public instruction, and G. A. Brown for United States senator. Brinkley also now had his name printed on the ballot. The Woodring and Brinkley forces looked so formidable that Landon later said he did not expect to be elected.[29]

Although things looked unfavorable for Landon and the Kansas Republicans, the 1932 campaign had several aspects that were lacking in 1930. The Republicans knew something of their opponents: Brinkley could not take them by surprise, nor would they discount him; and Woodring had a record to shoot at, and therefore might be put on the defensive. While Woodring could receive assistance from his national ticket, many Republicans thought—inadvisedly, as it turned out— that Vice President Curtis would carry Kansas for himself and President Hoover, and therefore help elect the state ticket. Also, the Kansas Republican leaders were fairly well unified, thanks to Landon and their own recognition that only party harmony could help them in their critical situation.

The general-election contest started well before the primary campaign was over. Landon's primary activities were of a piece with his general campaign, and Woodring had been preparing for the race since spring.

Brinkley's general campaign started with the announcement of his candidacy and the promulgation of his platform in June. While he did not actually stump the state until the traditional time, his radio station—now moved to Mexico, with call letters XER, and possessing unlimited power—was used to good effect in 1931 and 1932. Many newspaper speculations about his plans had given him valuable publicity. Brinkley's platform promised something big for everybody: pensions for the aged, a lake in each of Kansas' 105 counties, free state medical care for those otherwise unable to afford it, a state hospital for Negroes, free school books, reforestation, three-dollar automobile license tags, conservation, and industrial development. He pledged opposition to a state income tax, and, as a threat to his "hypocritical" persecutors, he promised annual examination of

[29] *Ibid.*, June 21, 1931; *Topeka State Journal*, June 5, 1932; Francis W. Schruben, "Kansas During the Great Depression, 1930–1936" (Ph.D. dissertation, University of California, Los Angeles, 1961), p. 210; *Topeka Capital*, October 8, 1932; Landon to Roy W. Howard, June 13, 1938.

physicians' qualifications. To be on the safe side, he also promised economy in government and elimination of unnecessary public offices.[30]

Soon after the announcement of Brinkley's candidacy, the goat-gland doctor was transported throughout Kansas in his airplane or in his $20,000, silver-mounted, sixteen-cylinder limousine. Kansans heard his voice, purring sweet somethings and sermonizing on his martyrdom, in person or on radio, in almost every town of the state. Floods of Brinkley stickers, tire covers, and banners were distributed, and a campaign song, "He's the Man," was heard night and day on Kansas radio stations. All this, as A. L. Shultz wrote, was "just as pleasing to orthodox party folks as the knowledge that the elevator is going to break a cable when the car is about six floors from the basement."[31]

The Democratic and Republican parties stuck to traditional political forms. The Democrats, at the end of August, met in a formal election-year council to grow nostalgic about the virtues of farmers, praise the record, cheer the candidates, and adopt a platform. The Democrats' cheers were hearty, for they were in office and they expected to be reelected for the first time in Kansas history. They lauded Woodring's "dynamic," "efficient," and "economical" (expenditures had been reduced by $3 million) government. Part of the platform followed Brinkley's in calling for cheaper textbooks, industrial development, better public welfare, reduced automobile-tag rates, consolidation of state departments, equality for Negroes in state benefits and rights— and, of course, economical government. Other planks were more technical but no less appealing: curbing public utilities, strengthening workmen's compensation, just taxation of banks, lower property tax, stronger budgetary controls, school-budget equalization, regulation of motor carriers, unemployment relief, help for the state's oil industry, further curbs on stock speculation, reorganization of county governments, and adherence to state prohibition.[32]

The Republicans also met for their party council at the end of August, and also cheered their candidates, extolled agricultural virtues, adopted a platform, and praised the "record"—the record they offered to set during 1933 and 1934. Landon's choice for state central committee chairman, Frank Carlson, was ratified; and, at Landon's

[30] *Topeka Capital*, June 5, 1932.

[31] Carson, *Brinkley*, pp. 168 ff.; Fowler, *Deeds Not Deficits*, p. 47; *Topeka Capital*, August 7, 1932; *Topeka State Journal*, June 2, 1932.

[32] *Topeka State Journal*, August 30, 31, 1932.

suggestion, Arthur Ericsson, who was Lacey Simpson's campaign manager, was named secretary of the committee. Carrying the idea of harmony further, Landon had Simpson named chairman of the party council's rules committee, but Landon headed the resolutions committee so that he could guide formulation of the platform.

The Republican platform was partly constructed to head off some of Brinkley's proposals. The Republicans undercut him considerably on the automobile-license rate issue, using Landon's suggestion for a graduated tag fee that began at 60 cents; any deficit this caused was to be offset by tightening the application of the state gasoline tax. The Republicans called for reduction of textbook prices to minimum cost, industrial development, equality for Negroes in sharing public benefits and rights, and development of natural resources, and of course insisted on economy and efficient organization in government. Aiming at Guy Helvering, they also proposed an investigation of the Highway Department and they pledged operation of that department on a businesslike and politics-free basis. They demanded better regulation of common carriers, of public utilities, and of sales of stocks and bonds. They promised to work toward restoration of farm income and to maintain reasonable foreclosure redemption periods. They favored collective bargaining by labor's freely chosen representatives, state law prohibiting injunctions in labor disputes, payment of prevailing wages on public work, betterment of the state workmen's compensation system, and state aid to communities so that "no Kansas citizen willing to work shall see his family go hungry." They inveighed against chain stores and chain banks. The Republican national ticket and the national platform—especially the planks promising tariff protection for foodstuffs and oil—were endorsed.[33]

Landon was well-received as the party's leader at the beginning of the council meeting, but he handled himself so well in compromising conflicting interests and personalities that he emerged as even a stronger leader. The party entered the campaign with its top-level organization harmonious and intact. As in 1928, each of the important Republican leaders had something to fight for, whether for Landon, Curtis, senatorial nominee Paulen, or part of the platform. Landon's chief aides—William Smith, Lacy Haynes, Frank Carlson, and William G. West—prepared for a general-campaign battle of the same strenuous nature given during the primary campaign, and others fell in line to support the campaign.

[33] *Ibid.*

Lacey Simpson worked to repair any breaches made in party ranks during the primary. The retired state chairman, John D. M. Hamilton, gave six weeks of service to the party. W. S. Fitzpatrick, Arthur Capper, and Frank Haucke worked hard. Although Paulen initially remained aloof, he cooperated fully toward the end. Henry J. Allen, again publicity director for the Republican national committee, Vice President Curtis, and national committeeman Mulvane gave full support to the state campaign. In short, it seemed as though the days when progressives had viewed standpatters as Uriah Heeps and the standpatters saw progressives as Wackford Squeerses had never existed. The party was on the spot, and all the factional leaders knew it; if the party lost in 1932, no one would get anything. Only Clyde M. Reed, who was irked because Landon had not frequently consulted him, was missing from the concert of Republican leadership.[34]

Landon opened his campaign before the party councils met. Speaking at the Johnson County fair, he asserted optimistically—if not inspiringly—that the Republican party could be depended upon to bring the country out of depression, as it had done in the past. He pledged to do his part as governor by extending the state's full cooperation in the task of national economic reconstruction. In late August the Republican nominee also made clear his position on two constitutional questions, which revolved around the two state constitutional amendments up for consideration at the polls: one to limit the levy that a local government could impose upon property owners, the other to authorize legislation of a graduated income tax. Brinkley opposed both amendments, and Woodring favored them. Landon, who declared his staunch support of the graduated income-tax amendment, also favored the purpose of the property-tax-limitation amendment, but he said that freezing a limitation into the constitution was inadvisable because the legislature should keep the power to set levy restrictions and to alter them as conditions warranted.[35]

The formal opening of Landon's campaign was in Abilene on September 16, at a dinner attended by 400 Republicans. Landon addressed himself to three issues, which for him were recurring campaign issues: taxes, "scandalous" government, and prohibition.

[34] *Topeka Capital*, September 11, 1932; Landon to John Blood, December 6, 1932; Clyde M. Reed to W. A. White, January 16, 1932, William Allen White Papers, Manuscript Division, Library of Congress, Washington, D.C.

[35] *Topeka Capital*, August 27, 28, 1932.

(Brinkley was brushed aside as "responsible to no organization.") He asserted that the most important question before the state was reduction of the taxes so burdensome to business and agriculture, and that this must be achieved by retrenchment and a graduated income tax. Guy Helvering was charged with "the most BRAZEN demonstration of political duress ever practiced in Kansas" because of his assessment of state employees for political purposes. Because the Democratic state chairman was also the director of the Highway Department, its administration had been "one of graft, waste, and incompetence." Landon reiterated that Republicans were on record favoring an investigation of the department, and he pledged that he would not appoint the Republican state chairman as head of the department. On top of this came the irresistible question that had worked so well in 1928: Are the Kansas Democrats really for prohibition? Landon suggested that the answer was "wet in Albany and dry in Kansas." [36]

From Abilene, Landon commenced to campaign through western Kansas, repeatedly emphasizing tax reduction and economy, Highway Department "politics," and the prohibition issue. From time to time he added calls for tariff protection for agriculture and oil. By September 19, Woodring—showing that Landon's attack on the Highway Department was effective—said that the "contributions" gleaned through the department reflected forty years of political practice, and he suggested that it was a better way to finance a campaign than by accepting corporation backing. Brinkley exploited the issue the following day when his state organizer ran a full-page advertisement in a number of newspapers that played upon the inefficacy and corruption of "the old parties that the people are sick and tired of." The ads reprinted—as a clean contrast—Brinkley's platform. Kansans were advised that they could count on Brinkley: he would not be a party to a sell-out. [37]

The campaign was now well under way, with all three gubernatorial candidates on the road. Landon was visiting five towns a day, more than either the governor or the doctor. All three were reported drawing good crowds, the largest in years. At least one observer, *Topeka Daily Capital* columnist Clifford Stratton, drew fun out of the campaign, pointing out that Brinkley was ahead of Landon in one respect: Landon had promised to reduce expenditures $5 million by lowering

[36] Landon speech, Abilene, September 16, 1932; *Topeka Capital*, September 17, 1932.
[37] *Topeka Capital*, September 20, 21, 1932.

automobile license fees, but Brinkley "is going to have free textbooks, free clinics, lakes in every county—and reduce taxes anyway." [38] The campaign roared ahead as the little doctor with the bristling goatee sped over the state, as Woodring's happy oval-shaped face appeared on main streets and at crossroads, as Landon's earnest eyes peered through his rimless glasses beneath a battered fedora at a new crowd every hour.

This was a campaign of distinct personalities. The diamond-studded Brinkley hurriedly arrived in his airplane or limousine, accompanied by an entertainment troupe and a minister of the gospel to introduce him, and told of the defalcation of the two old parties, of his persecution for pursuing medical "truth," of his vision of a Kansas wonderland under his administration—then hastily departed with scarcely a goodby. Woodring arrived in a town in the governor's automobile; he sauntered down the main street, patting people on the back, and in a bluff manner exchanging words—expounding on his administration, his "second" term, and his opponents in the manner of a football coach who has just tied for the conference championship. Landon arrived almost inconspicuously, in a 1928 car; he accosted friends and strangers, heard them out, told them an appropriate campaign idea, perhaps bummed a cigarette; he stood awkwardly at a meeting, perhaps telling a story—or forgetting to tell it—delivering his talk about tax relief and efficient government in a blunt, sometimes stumbling manner.

Brinkley's campaign, of course, scared party regulars; Republican and Democratic workers were upset by his influence. Landon said, aiming more at Brinkley than Woodring, that the important thing in the election was not who would win but "who is going to manage the business affairs of the state of Kansas the next two years." [39] By late September, Brinkley was drawing the largest crowds, but Landon was visiting as many as ten towns a day—more than Brinkley and Woodring together. Landon felt prompted to call publicly for Republican unity, something he had not considered necessary to do since the primary. He warned that the Republicans in Kansas had never been defeated when united, and he said there was no party discontent in 1932. He acted like a shepherd, whistling for lost sheep, as reports came in of precinct workers and committeemen going over to Brinkley. As the scare developed, so did some joint campaigning. Wirt Franklin, the Republican nominee for the United States Senate from Oklahoma, appeared with Landon at a rally in the oil town of El Dorado; and

[38] *Ibid.*, September 25, 1932.
[39] *Ibid.*, September 26, 27, 1932.

Ben Paulen and Landon also stumped together to display Republican harmony.[40]

Landon's basic issues did not change, except as they were punctuated with additional, almost meaningless, pleas: "Keep the priceless home-rule heritage in taxes" and "Kansas jobs for Kansas men."[41] Carlson, the state chairman, spoke out too, charging that Woodring was a wet, and responsible for wasting 60 per cent of the revenue of the Highway Department. Carlson also asserted that Brinkley had no program, and Brinkley retorted by condemning the assessment of state employees for political purposes—saying that Landon, under Reed, had been just as guilty of the practice as was Helvering under Woodring. Carlson's aggressiveness was probably in response to newspaper reports that placed Landon third in voter popularity, and, although Landon and his aides were worried by these reports, they decided not to do anything that would detract from the picture Landon had constructed of himself as a calm, sound politician. Their strategy relied on the probability that Woodring and Brinkley would tar each other and that the jabs Landon could make at them toward the campaign's end would turn the tide.

During most of October, Governor Woodring concentrated on showing how his administration had kept Kansas up with other states—it had surfaced more roads the preceding year than any other state—and still had reduced expenditures.[42] On October 20, Woodring came up with the big charge of the contest, accusing Brinkley of receiving funds from Henry Doherty of Cities Service and being a tool of the natural gas operator in his efforts to prevent the state from reducing gas rates for Kansas consumers. He offered photostatic evidence in support of his charge, and Brinkley retorted "That's about as wild a jackass story as I ever heard of." This storm raged between the two men the rest of the campaign, with Brinkley calling the governor the instrument of Missouri interests, especially the *Kansas City Star*. This charge was "proved" for the goat-gland doctor when the *Star* came out in support of Woodring, but Brinkley also alleged that this was the newspaper's way of helping Landon. To Brinkley's way of thinking, the *Star*'s support of Woodring should cost the governor more votes than it could attract to him.[43]

---

[40] *Ibid.*, October 2–5, 1932.
[41] *Ibid.*, September 30, October 4, 1932.
[42] *Ibid.*, October 7, 9, 12, 15, 1932; *Lyons Daily News*, October 9, 1932.
[43] *Topeka State Journal*, October 21, 1932; *Topeka Capital*, October 21, 30, 1932.

Landon had to rely largely on his own appeal. The visit to Topeka, in September, of the Democratic presidential nominee, Franklin D. Roosevelt, had made a good impression, and had probably helped Woodring. Landon believed that Hoover could not help him because of the predominant Kansas sentiment against the President. Nevertheless, Landon regularly indicated his support of Hoover as a gesture of party harmony. The Kansas Republicans even invited Hoover to speak in the state as a courtesy owed the head of their national party. Landon took care, however, to urge Henry J. Allen to keep Hoover from antagonizing the desperate farmers by saying that he could not do anything for them. In his own campaign, Landon stuck to simple ideas: "If you don't need it, don't buy it; if you can't afford it, don't buy it; if you do buy it, get your money's worth." [44]

During the last three weeks of the campaign the Republican organization intensified its efforts. The state committee's speaker bureau, headed by Ben Franklin of Topeka, did a superb job of getting the oratory flowing, with Capper, Haucke, and Simpson—as well as Landon's closest political associates—stumping the state on Landon's behalf. The state Republican headquarters on October 22 predicted that Landon would win, hoping to encourage a Republican victory psychology over the state. Landon threw in some extra promises. On October 21 he said that lower gas and utility rates would be achieved through a Republican administration, a slap at Woodring's claims and at the alleged Doherty-Brinkley connection. This was followed by Jesse Greenleaf's assertion that, as chairman of the Public Service Commission, he had found that Woodring bungled rate-reduction matters—in contrast with Landon, who had always worked smoothly with the commission during both the Reed and Woodring administrations. [45]

Landon used some sarcasm on his opponents during the last week in October, calling Brinkley the "great promiser" and Woodring "the greatest little claimer Kansas has had in a long time." [46] Landon, observing the widespread use of radio and billboard advertising by Brinkley, took further advantage of Woodring's charge that Doherty was giving substantial financial support to the goat-gland doctor. Estimating that the Brinkley campaign was costing between $100,000

[44] *Topeka Capital*, September 18, October 7, 14–16, 1932; Landon to Henry J. Allen, October 9, 1932.

[45] *Topeka Capital*, October 12, 23, 24, 1932.

[46] *Ibid.*, October 26, 29, 27, 1932.

and $200,000, he asked "Where's the money coming from?" Republican Roland Boynton, running for reelection as attorney general, repeatedly asked a similar question, of the source of the unusually large amount of money spent by the Democrats.[47]

In the last week of the campaign the Republicans used sound trucks, considerable newspaper advertising, and, in the larger cities, parades with elephants to trumpet the party's virtues. The message in one of the full-page Republican advertisements was typical of their appeal in the newspapers: "LANDON or BRINKLEY. Cast your vote in the biggest pile. The Republican party is the dominant party in Kansas this year—a United party." This was supported by the argument that the Democrats could not win when the Republicans were united, and that, in any event, no Democratic governor had ever been reelected in Kansas. The choice was clearly between the able Landon or the inexperienced Brinkley: "The way to beat Brinkley is vote for Landon."[48]

Landon complemented this publicity campaign with increasingly aggressive statements the week before election. Woodring's tax reductions were ridiculed as amounting to a mere 1 cent per $1,000 of valuation. Landon deplored the feud between Brinkley and Woodring, as offering no relief to the people who wanted the issues discussed. Landon blasted Woodring's economy claims, asserting that the number of state employees had increased since 1930. The governor replied by accusing Landon of issuing "half-truths and distortions" on tax data. On election eve, November 7, Woodring urged the voters to check their tax reductions before voting.[49]

The gubernatorial campaign had been an exciting one, and, with all three of the candidates accounted a chance of winning, the excitement continued to election day. Frank Carlson predicted a Hoover-Curtis victory and a plurality for Landon of 6,500. The campaigning continued even on election day. Party workers were out in force, trying to talk to voters before they entered the polls. Radio advertising continued. Telephone circuits were loaded with calls from party workers, receiving

[47] *Ibid.*, October 30, 1932. The Democrats spent heavily in 1932: $81,357.57; Brinkley reported expenditures of $55,928, and the Republicans reported $19,823. *Wichita Beacon*, December 11, 1932; "Democratic State Central Committee Receipts and Expenditures—General Election of 1932," certified undated typescript.

[48] *Topeka Capital*, October 30, 1932.

[49] *Ibid.*, November 2, 5, 7, 1932.

orders and asking their friends to vote for their candidates, and urging others to do likewise.

The fear of Brinkley was in Republican and Democratic hearts. William Allen White reported this, as did innumerable county leaders over the state. Willard Mayberry's report was typical of those from western Kansas: Brinkley-fever struck even veteran committeemen, who switched to the goat-gland doctor; farmers, who a month before the election ridiculed Brinkley as a quack, had gone over to him.[50] Rumors were flying that Brinkley was being counted out by voting registrars; that Democrats were spreading the idea that Landon was supporting Woodring in order to defeat Brinkley; that Woodring's strength was being undermined by anti-Woodring Democrats supporting Brinkley; that Republicans and Democrats locally were trading off candidates in order to achieve a united front against Brinkley. Sharp tactics were undoubtedly used by some Democratic, Republican, and independent leaders in their efforts to get votes, and Brinkley votes may have been "miscounted" or thrown out, but the fact that no one asked for a recount showed that this was not widespread or that all three headquarters—Brinkley was now eligible to request a recount—feared what it might show.

On November 8 the votes trickled in, giving no one a clear edge, though by afternoon it seemed that Brinkley had fallen too far behind to catch up. By 8:45 p.m., John Hamilton correctly concluded that Landon would win. Landon polled 278,581 votes—to 272,944 for Woodring and 244,607 for Brinkley—which bore out predictions of how close the gubernatorial race would be. Landon could also take satisfaction in knowing that the people had followed his lead on the income tax and the levy limitations amendments, approving the former and rejecting the latter by substantial margins.

A good case can be made that Landon won the governorship in 1932 because most of the votes that Brinkley received in that depression year would otherwise have been cast for Woodring, but this case is not conclusive. Although Kansas voted for Roosevelt and Democratic Senator George McGill, Republicans won all the other statewide offices—and the question remains whether Woodring would have been elected in 1930 if it had not been for Brinkley's campaign that year. Of the percentage of the total vote received, Woodring's decreased between 1930 and 1932 from 35 per cent to 34.1 per cent, the Republican nominee's decreased from 34.9 per cent to 34.8 per cent, and

---

[50] *Ibid.*, November 6, 8, 1932; W. A. White to Henry J. Allen, November 9, 1932, White Papers; Willard Mayberry to Landon, November 16, 1932.

Brinkley's increased from 29.5 per cent to 30.5 per cent; the "other" vote stayed constant at 0.6 per cent. This proves only that Landon's forces were a bit more effective than Woodring's in staving off Brinkley's inroads, but, whether Landon won because of a fluke or because he was more successful in conserving his strength than Woodring, the paramount fact is that Landon won. He was the only Republican governor elected west of the Hudson River; he was one of four Republican governors elected in the land; and he was one of the seven Republican governors to be in office in 1933.[51]

"I lie awake nights," Governor-elect Landon wrote, "thinking about the pleas that I hear every day from men who, a few years ago, would never think of wanting a public job, and are now willing to take anything." A newly elected governor is always pressed with demands for jobs, but at the height of the great depression the pressure was almost unbearable, and Landon was swamped with job requests. Five weeks after his election he had received 8,000 letters asking for jobs. Patronage requests flooded in even from political leaders who previously had been little concerned with patronage—at least seventy came from William Allen White.[52] Landon was busy from morning to night talking to job applicants, with "ten, twelve, fourteen waiting all the time." Men approached him "with tears running down their cheeks begging for something to save their homes."[53] Landon was in a heartsickening position. Not only was there to be only a small turnover in state jobs, but it was clear that the legislature would abolish and consolidate several public offices. Landon's position was complicated by the fact that, with only a small Republican majority in the legislature, he felt required to make maximum use of patronage to get his program enacted. All this meant that the jobless would have to wait until the legislature acted, and even then the prospect was that only "a sprinkling" of them would find state jobs.[54] Public and private relief agencies would have to take care of most of the unemployed.

There were, however, four positions that Landon found it necessary

---

[51] John D. M. Hamilton to Landon, November 8, 1932; Zornow, *Kansas*, p. 250; *Topeka Capital*, November 27, 1932; *Kansas City Star*, November 27, 1932.

[52] Landon to Athol E. Dunham, December 10, 1932; *Arkansas City Traveler*, December 13, 1932.

[53] Landon to James B. Kelsey, December 8, 1932; Landon to J. H. Jenson, November 26, 1932.

[54] Landon to George M. Lindsay, December 30, 1932; Landon to James B. Kelsey, December 8, 1932.

to fill soon after his election. The most pressing choice was that of his secretary, and here he looked to William G. West, who was a splendid selection. West had served Landon well in the primary campaign and as publicity chief of the state committee during the general-election contest; he had also served in many state positions, had been Governor Reed's secretary, and over the years he had been able to maintain his popularity and a reputation for integrity with members of the legislature. Landon also planned to press the regulation of utilities, and he therefore acted quickly to fortify the Public Service Commission. Jesse Greenleaf's term as chairman was running out, but Landon designated his friend to a regular membership on the commission to take advantage of his decade of experience on that body. As the new chairman of the commission, Landon chose the recently defeated congressman, Homer Hoch, a well-known public figure with a liberal agrarian viewpoint and considerable experience in regulatory matters. Hoch's designation did not make the conservatives happy, but Landon's next choice did. The day after the election David Mulvane died, leaving vacant the Republican national committeeman's post that he had filled for almost a quarter of a century. John D. M. Hamilton, the dynamic young spirit of the state's conservatives, was elected to the position with Landon's sponsorship. The selection did much to perpetuate harmony within the party, though Landon had no difficulty making his decision because the overwhelming majority of county leaders and state committeemen had urged Hamilton's appointment.[55]

Although patronage was a problem of unusual proportions, program was also of intense concern. Because of the state's economic problems, much interest was expressed in the development of a more positive state government, but conservatives feared they might lose something as a result of increased state action and became unusually vigorous in their representations against increased state powers. Landon was caught in between; he had to act vigorously to relieve burdens and to solve problems, but he was pledged to economy and tax reduction, was confronted by a legislature of Democrats and Republicans similarly pledged, and was constitutionally obliged to balance the budget. He had to satisfy his progressive friends, yet keep his conservative allies for legislative success. A new time had come to Kansas, and everybody knew it. The man most responsible for defining and administering the

[55] Benjamin F. Endres to Landon, November 28, 1932; Landon to Leslie Edmonds, December 6, 1932; *Topeka State Journal*, December 20, 1932.

new day was Alf Landon, and everybody knew that, too. He was on the spot.

During the election struggle, and afterward, the Kansas political atmosphere crackled with talk of economy. Strong talk for budget reductions—as much as 25 per cent—was heard among Democrats and Republicans. Landon, uncertain of measures that would bring recovery, knew "of one sure thing to help business and agriculture, and that is to reduce the cost of government." [56] He would not permit the customary purchase of a new car for the governor or new dishes for the governor's mansion. The inauguration ceremonies would be simple— no parade, no invitations, no tickets, and music by volunteers if possible. Money must not be wasted on such things, while men, women, and children were going hungry.[57] Landon told a dinner of Arkansas City civic organizations on December 12:

> I see no reason why the government should not retrench the same as the rest of us are compelled to retrench. . . . There is only one way for the government to give prosperity to its citizens. That is to reduce the cost of government to business and to agriculture.

Two days later he told the state convention of the Grange that he intended "to attack the cost of government from every angle, whether it be on road construction, in township government, county, city or state." In short, as Landon directed the labor commissioner: "Save money without impairing the service." [58]

Of course, Landon was under strong pressure not to touch various boards or departments, not to reduce certain expenditures, not to redistribute taxes "unfairly." He found it ironic that the tax-conscious elements that should be supporting his economy-efficiency drive "are organized in favor of appropriations for this or that project in which they are interested." [59] He was particularly irked by pressures from the state chamber of commerce not to cut down on road building. In a widely publicized letter to Roy Bailey, a chamber of commerce leader

---

[56] Landon to C. H. Friedberg, December 10, 1932.

[57] Landon to R. H. Smith, December 7, 1932; *Wichita Beacon,* December 11, 1932; *Sylvia Sun,* December 15, 1932.

[58] *Arkansas City Traveler,* December 13, 1932; *Coffeyville Journal,* December 15, 1932; Landon to C. J. Beckman, December 10, 1932.

[59] *Arkansas City Traveler,* December 13, 1932.

and the publisher of the *Salina Journal*, Landon admonished the state chamber to be realistic.

> I think we are in the midst of a revolution, the far reaching effects of which we have not yet felt and cannot yet see the end. Every program that is being offered as at least a partial panacea for our ills is fundamentally based on prosperity by government aid. Maybe that is the spark that is necessary to turn the engine over; the dose of digitalis that is necessary in the emergency. But in my judgment the only safe and sure footing is that we must save our way out.

Landon contended that money that goes from an individual's hands to dealers in materials and to artisans was not a waste, but that money given to government—as World War I proved—could be wasteful. Landon declared that he too wanted good roads, because the more cars that were driven the better was his business, but one must, as Edmund Burke had pointed out, be able to change one's wishes and plans to accommodate circumstances. Because the circumstances of depression dictated economy, the "guiding and governing policy of my administration is going to be—How much does it cost?—Not whether we need it. I would not favor that as a permanent policy for government, but I think it is what we need under these circumstances." [60]

That circumstances were dire was easily seen in Topeka when Landon arrived there, on January 8, 1933, for his inauguration: Topeka, then a city of 70,000, had 4,000 men out of work. The city's construction relief program was unable to employ single men, and a married man who got a job with the program received about $10.00 every three weeks if he had children, or $5.00 every three weeks if he did not. Newspaper advertisements told of the state of business in the capital: "Sales!!," "You Don't Need Cash," "No interest," "Sacrifice Prices," "Big Reduction," " $1.00 Down Secures a Radio," "FREE! 2 Roll-A-Tubs—100 Bars Soap/Copper Boiler/With Every Prima Washer Sold Monday." Oldsmobile advertised: "Prices Reduced $130 to $145"; quality men's shoes were priced at $3.85, blankets at 50 cents, and from as far away as Davenport, Iowa, came an advertisement of hotel rooms at $1.50 up.

Landon, who stayed at the Kansan Hotel, was forced to dodge mobs of job hunters. On January 9 the morning *Topeka Capital*'s front page carried a two-column photograph of Landon, "Our New Governor." It was his day—but it was surrounded by reminders of misery and

[60] Landon to Roy Bailey, December 14, 1932.

unrest. "Student Hangs Self," "300,000,000 for Relief," "Grain Dealers Offer Own Farm Relief Plan," "Would Aid Small Banks," "30 Hurt in Irish Riot," "17 Die in Riots" (Spain), "Three Die in Riot" (India). The day Landon was inaugurated, Calvin Coolidge was buried. Something was ending, but no one knew what was beginning. [61]

[61] *Topeka Capital*, January 8, 9, 1933.

CHAPTER 6

The Governor in Action

January 9, 1933, was a fine day in Topeka—fair, mild, and sunny. As the governor-elect's automobile arrived at the city auditorium, one small artillery piece—a symbol of economy—fired a seventeen-gun salute. The auditorium, filled with people, was aglow with the bright lights of movie and still photographers as the venerable chief justice of the Kansas supreme court, William A. Johnston, administered the oath of office to Landon. The new governor then turned to the audience to speak.

"Time and again during seventy-two years of statehood Kansas and her citizens faced severe difficulties and conquered them," but common sense, perseverance, courage, and cooperation had extricated the state from its previous troubles, and those values could serve the people well again. During the boom years, he declared, the country had led itself astray, thinking that its extravagant ways had developed new economic laws. Now, "the pathway from the swamp of despair must be built with planks of economy devoted to the principle that we must not spend that which we do not have."

At this point the auditorium lights went out, and a wave of chuckles rolled through the crowd, launched by thoughts of the connection between the governor's comment and this unintentional conservation of electricity. In the dim light coming in through the auditorium's few windows, the governor was seen to smile and wave his hands in gratitude for this underscoring of his point. Continuing his address, he said that people must realize that they cannot get something for nothing, that they must rely upon themselves for the energy to solve their problems. If the people can return to basic values, and if they can accept the necessary burdens, they can generate the public will requisite for the state government to help put society back on the road to prosperity.[1]

The inaugural address, Landon's first task as governor, marked the beginning of three uninterrupted months of work, day and night; his second major task was to hammer out a program with the legislature. Of course, Landon had been preparing for the legislative session for weeks before his inauguration, consulting widely on program and staying in close touch with house and senate leaders.

Originally he had intended to remain aloof from the organization of the legislature, thinking that the legislature and the administration would work better if he affronted no one by his interference, but he was finally persuaded by friendly legislators that he would have to be actively concerned with the appointments to the key legislative committees if he wanted his proposals to be favorably considered. Landon also became convinced that intensive efforts had to be made to head off division among Republican legislators on the speaker of the house, for a split could result in the election of a Democratic speaker. William G. West was the chief worker in guiding the organization of the Republican legislators along lines as favorable as possible to Landon. With small Republican majorities in the house and senate—5 and 6, respectively—it was essential that the administration handle the legislators diplomatically but firmly if Landon's legislative proposals were to have any chance of enactment.[2]

The legislature was organized soon after Landon's inauguration. Dallas Knapp of Coffeyville, an old acquaintance of Landon, was elected president pro tem of the senate; in the house, William H. Vernon was unanimously elected speaker. Cooperation was reported to be the spirit among Democratic and Republican legislators, and members of both parties had called on the new governor to pledge their support for governmental economy and tax-reduction measures. The

[1] *Topeka Capital*, January 10, 1933; *Inaugural Address of Alf M. Landon, Governor, January 9, 1933* (Topeka: State Printer, 1933).

[2] Landon to P. G. Abell, December 8, 1932; John W. Blood to Landon, November 17, 1932, Alfred M. Landon Papers, Kansas State Historical Society, Topeka.

farm organizations favored an income-tax law and a reduction in the automobile license fee, and it was observed that greater pressure than usual was being exerted on the legislature for action on these measures. Circumstances seemed propitious, on January 11, as Landon arrived at the chamber of the house of representatives to deliver his general message to the senators and representatives.[3]

At 11 a.m. the governor was escorted to the rostrum; he laid out the final draft of his message, paused for photographs and to acknowledge friendly greetings, and then began to speak in his uneven but firm manner. He stressed the gravity of the responsibilities of the government and the legislature in times of "unrest and almost rebellious spirit." "The credit of our state, counties, cities, and other municipal subdivisions is at stake. A successful solution of our problems means the saving of our homes, property and government; our failure means their loss."

He then presented his recommendations, which emphasized ways to achieve economy and a reduction of taxes. He demanded "a general paring down of salaries and the elimination of all unnecessary public employees," and, particularly, an investigation of the Highway Department—the state's largest spending unit. As for taxes, "reorganization of an antiquated tax system must be made certain" so that taxes could come down; and he called for an income tax, not as "*just another tax*" but so that "the tax on property [could] be proportionately reduced." License fees on motor vehicles, except trucks and buses, should be reduced by the establishment of "a system of fees graduated upward from a minimum of sixty cents." Provision should be made for the full collection of all taxes, especially gasoline taxes, due the state. Landon's tax program, in effect, demanded placing the cost of government most heavily on those who could best afford to pay for it and tightening the loopholes used by those who least needed tax relief.

As for local governments, he proposed that, except for poor relief, "obligations contracted in any one year should not be in excess of the actual revenue for that year" unless approved by the voters. A uniform system of auditing and accounting and the standardization and greater itemization of local budgets were requested. Landon also asked that steps be taken to prevent "juggling of funds" by any taxing unit, that tax levies be cut, and that the payment of fees to public officials over and above their salaries be eliminated. For further relief to property

[3] *Topeka State Journal*, January 10, 1933; *Topeka Capital*, January 9–11, 1933.

owners, especially farmers, he advised against shortening the time allowance—eighteen months—given mortgagors for the redemption of foreclosed property. He suggested that penalties and interest rates on delinquent real estate taxes be lowered, and that the state assist the localities in meeting the unemployment and relief problem. The governor also called for further protection of Kansas insurance policy-holders and authorization that would permit lending institutions to become members of the Federal Home Loan Bank. He urged considera-tion of strengthening the regulation of public utilities and truck and bus businesses, ratification of the Twentieth Amendment of the federal Constitution, and amendment of the state constitution to provide for a short ballot for state and county officers. He concluded by again enjoining the legislature to consider economy its first duty: "The total tax bill should be measured by our ability to pay. The answer to our legislative program must be: reduced taxes—positively reduced—and they must be reduced this year." [4]

Landon implied, in his inaugural and legislative addresses, that he did not know where the nation was going, but he made it clear that the country must have faith that it was going to extricate itself from its problems on the basis of respect for work and law. He considered himself pledged to economize and to provide relief and reform, but he felt that the people and their government would have to search further. As he told the state Board of Agriculture: "We Kansans may feel like the little boy who was met trudging down the road carrying a cat rifle on his shoulder. 'What are you hunting, Buddy?' he was asked. 'Dunno, I ain't seen it yet.' Now we are like that...we are hunting." [5] This attitude was to characterize Landon during his first year and a half in office. He was hunting; and this could be seen as he pumped his legislature with fresh new proposals, and even called special sessions—indeed, more special sessions than any other Kansas governor. His hunting was amply justified as he saw the character of the governor's office change radically, in a matter of months, in response to the people's demands to meet the crisis of depression.

In the beginning his search was for efficiency in government in a state where that idea had been more of a campaign slogan than an administrative practice. One of the efficiency proposals pushed hardest

[4] *Topeka Capital*, January 12, 1933; *Kansas City Star*, January 11, 1933; *Message of Alf M. Landon, Governor of Kansas, to the Legislature of 1933* (Topeka: State Printer, 1933).

[5] Landon speech, Topeka, January 11, 1933.

by Landon was the collection of gasoline taxes. Despite the opposition of the farm organizations, Landon and his aides gave high priority to tightening the collection of these taxes, and as a result the legislature promptly started working on the matter—along with the popular automobile-tag fee reduction. More pressure was put on the legislature on January 17, when the governor delivered a special message to clarify the relationship between gasoline-tax collection and tag-fee reduction, pointing out that the gasoline tax and the vehicular registration fees were the chief support of the state Highway Department.

Although the primary purpose of registration was identification, Kansas, like other states, had also been using it as a source of revenue, charging a minimum fee of $8.00. Landon called for graduated registration fees, from a minimum of 60 cents to a maximum of $25.35. His plan would achieve identification of vehicles, produce some revenue for highway maintenance and construction, and yet reduce fees on some 267,000 cars to less than $3.00—while putting larger fees on trucks. To offset the loss of revenue in tag-fee reduction, Landon proposed rigid collection of the taxes on the gross-ton miles traveled by trucks and buses, and, more importantly, of the tax on motor fuel (evasion of which was scandalous). He contended that implementation of these three measures would result in a fairer distribution of the tax burden, according to use and ability to pay, at the same time liquidating the Highway Department's indebtedness and providing enough funds for a basic program of highway maintenance and construction.[6]

By the time the session—a scheduled fifty-day session—was only nine days old, it seemed as though the body was buckling down to work. Although only four actions had been taken, these included two of the governor's recommendations: the granting of authority for lending companies to take advantage of the Federal Home Loan Act and approval of the Twentieth Amendment. Moreover, the deliberative work of the legislative committees appeared to be ahead of schedule. The legislators were obviously in an economy mood; they even sliced their postage and telephone funds. A spirit of nonpartisanship also appeared to reign as Democrats repeatedly joined Republicans in pushing the economy-efficiency proposals. Even some of the pressure

[6] *Topeka Capital*, January 14, 16, 1933; *Special Message of Alf M. Landon, Governor of Kansas, to the Legislature of 1933, January 17, 1933* (Topeka: State Printer, 1933).

groups cooperated, with the Kansas State Teachers' Association drafting model legislation to trim the authorized maximum school levies by 25 per cent.[7]

On January 26, Governor Landon delivered a second special message to the legislature, asking for legislation "to do away with waste, extravagance, duplication and unnecessary service"; he especially urged the reorganization of many departments of state government. A new department was requested that would combine the duties of the state oil inspector, the state fire marshal, the state hotel commissioner, and the cigarette-tax collectors in order to stop the practice of two or three inspectors visiting the same places of business when one could do the job. This new department should have the vehicular licensing responsibility of the state vehicle commissioner, and the inspection function should be transferred to the Highway Department. It was also recommended that the regulation of trucks and buses should be shifted from the Public Service Commission to the Highway Department. These and other consolidations, the governor explained, should mean that fewer employees would be needed. Landon then suggested the creation of a state corporation commission to regulate and enforce the laws pertaining to the issuance and sale of stocks and securities; these powers were to be transferred from the two agencies that were then competitively handling such matters.

This lengthy message also contained the germ of Landon's pioneering legislative council proposal: his request for a permanent five-man legislative committee to investigate tax matters, advise the governor on them between legislative sessions, and recommend pertinent measures to the legislature. (The objective was to free the state government from reliance on the services of the tax experts of the Santa Fe Railway and the Kansas Chamber of Commerce.) Landon demanded establishment of a report system so that the financial condition of any state department might be known exactly at any time. He also invited the legislature to search out any expenditures and fees, regardless of how minor, that might be reduced; for example, he suggested that car allowances for state employees could be reduced to 5 cents a mile and grain inspection fees from $1.00 per carload to 75 cents. He again called upon the legislature to look to the reduction and equalization of the salaries of all state employees, elected or otherwise. "Let us cut out the red tape,

[7] *Topeka Capital*, January 21, 22, 26, 1933.

disregard all pork-barrel propositions, provide what help is actually needed at reasonable salaries only, and see that the state receives honest values for every dollar spent. Let economy be the watchword."[8]

Toward the end of January it was obvious that the legislative process was becoming clogged. To spur the legislature, Landon called in legislators—individually and in small groups—to urge action. He also brought out the big club he had kept behind the door: the warning, on the eve of the Kansas Day Republican meetings, that no appointments would be made until the legislature acted on his economy program. Landon's threat—as well as a Democratic proposal of a flat $1.00 fee—probably hurried action on the reduction of automobile tag fees, even though it had encountered increasingly stiff opposition from those who saw it as leading to the ruination of the highways. This opposition became so strong that he decided to compromise, as he probably knew from the beginning he must; nevertheless, he was able to achieve legislation—acceptable to Republicans and Democrats—that reduced fees on motor cars and that increased them on trucks and buses. The compromise law provided for a $4.00 fee on cars of up to 2,000 pounds, with 25 cents extra required for every additional 100 pounds. Heavy vehicles were to be taxed on a graduated basis, from $5.00 for the first 1,000 pounds to $100 for up to 8,000 pounds. This reduction, while well over the 60-cent minimum fee originally proposed, was substantially under the existing $8.00 rate.[9]

Yet the passage of the tag measure did not move the legislature to further actions. The house and senate Republicans disagreed on how to investigate the Highway Department; and Senator C. C. Bradney killed the house plan in the senate State Affairs Committee, and Representative Henry Buzick killed the senate's resolution in the house Ways and Means Committee. And other important proposals still lingered in committee rooms. Bills for further mortgage relief were snagged, and Landon had to sponsor conferences with the representatives of farmers, banks, and loan companies to secure more lenient arrangements for mortgagors. Although the legislature was reported to be planning sizable cuts in appropriations, fees, and salaries, Landon and the public waited—and waited some more—for formal action. The state appeared to be restive. The *Pleasanton Herald* complained:

[8] *Special Message of Alf M. Landon, Governor of Kansas, to the Legislature of 1933, January 26, 1933* (Topeka: State Printer, 1933).

[9] *Topeka Capital*, January 29, February 2, 3, 7, 1933.

No Governor ever worked harder to secure into law the promises of his party and fulfill his pledges made to the people during the campaign, yet with the end of this legislature but a short time off but few of these promises have been fulfilled. . . . It's time this legislature gets down to brass tacks. . . . If this legislature fleets its time away and fails to make good the promises made during the campaign pull of 1932 the party will be a "blowed up sucker" in Kansas in 1934.[10]

Although Landon still followed his tactic of urging the legislators to act rather than trying to bully them into it, and although the no-appointments club was still held over their heads, and although Landon intervened forcefully to resurrect the Highway Department investigation resolution, legislative progress eluded the governor during most of February. Lobbyists worked against administration measures and for their own unsanctioned proposals, just as many legislators insisted on pushing their pet bills—the concept of the pork barrel had not disappeared from the legislative deliberations. Action was so slow that the Democrats considered asking the governor if he would permit them to handle economy measures, but Landon was convinced that public pressure and his persuasion would ultimately lead to action. He felt he had no choice, because undue pressure from him might disintegrate the small Republican majorities in the house and senate. He even defended the legislature, saying the delay was not disturbing, for careful consideration of the mass of proposed legislation was essential.[11]

Finally, at the end of February, the two houses began to disgorge a number of measures. A joint resolution for investigation of the Highway Department was approved; the house passed a bill providing for a new inspections and registration department, consolidating the duties of oil inspector, hotel commissioner, fire marshal, and cigarette inspectors—reducing the number of inspectors from seventy-eight to twenty-one. The house also approved a stricter system for collecting gasoline taxes.[12]

It was at this time that a banking crisis developed in Kansas, largely because of withdrawals of funds from the relatively solvent Kansas banks by banks elsewhere. Moreover, bank troubles in Missouri and Oklahoma suggested that unnecessary runs might be made on Kansas banks, with disastrous results. Bank Commissioner H. W. Koeneke advised the governor that, to avoid a state-bank holiday, a law should

[10] *Ibid.*, February 15, 19, 23, 1933; Landon to Grover C. Talbot, February 21, 1933; *Pleasanton Herald*, February 24, 1933.

[11] *Topeka Capital*, February 23, 26, 27, 1933.

[12] *Ibid.*, March 1, 1933.

be enacted limiting the amount of withdrawals. Landon agreed on the
need for such legislation but he insisted on discussing it with the
directors of the state banking association, and a meeting was held on
March 3. Landon read the proposal to the directors, which called for
a 5 per cent limit on withdrawals of funds. Then he called for each
director to express himself on the proposal, and found that one after
another the directors opposed it. Then, in the middle of the polling,
a couple of the men were called from the room—word had come that
there were runs on the First National and the Commerce Trust banks
in Kansas City, Missouri—and now the banking association directors
shifted in favor of the proposal. Landon rushed to the speaker's office
in the house of representatives and called together the legislative leaders
of both parties to urge them to take immediate action. A banking bill
was introduced at two o'clock that afternoon and was enacted into law
within two hours—a pace unprecedented in the legislature's history.
The legislation established a "bank dictatorship" for Kansas. The
Bank Commissioner, subject to the governor's approval, was given the
power to make rules for the governing of banks, savings companies, and
trust companies for two years. Koeneke and Landon immediately set a
5 per cent withdrawal limit, and they advised banks and savings and
trust companies by telegraph that the limit would be effective the next
day, March 4. The firms were also instructed to set up new account
ledgers—overnight.

The state's financial institutions accepted the restriction, and worked
through the night preparing to put it into effect; but in Washington
others were also working overnight. On March 4, Landon was asked
by the Comptroller of Currency to temporarily close all banks in
Kansas, an action already taken in many other states, and Landon
called the banking association directors for another meeting to consider
the request. Meanwhile, in telephone talks with federal officials, he
learned accidentally that a presidential proclamation closing all banks
in the United States was being drafted. He passed this information on
to the directors, and the meeting was adjourned. Reporters asked the
governor what he intended to do. "We are not going to do anything,"
he replied, "and it does not make any difference because a Presidential
proclamation is coming this afternoon." Thus news of the national bank
holiday first reached the country's press.

Kansas complied with the national bank holiday—although the
Kansas banks then operating were believed to be able to handle their

problems under state laws [13]—the state went ahead to consider the problems posed by the bank holiday. A special economic advisory committee of bankers had been set up, on March 4, to consider ways of helping business continue to meet private needs if withdrawal restrictions cramped commerce. With the issuance of the presidential proclamation, the committee intensified its efforts, because no one knew how long the bank holiday would last. The committee laid plans to issue scrip as a substitute for currency, and by March 7 almost every county in Kansas was reported ready to handle state scrip if this was necessary for meeting commercial exchange needs. During the banking crisis, Landon and his insurance commissioner, Charles F. Hobbs, secured from the legislature complete regulatory power over the state's insurance companies. The immediate object of this "insurance dictatorship" was to make rules to save life insurance policies from lapsing for nonpayment during the bank holiday. Hobbs also placed a moratorium on payments over $100 by insurance companies in order to cut down on bank withdrawals and to maintain the companies' stability.[14]

On March 11 it was announced from Washington that banks would be permitted to open, on a restricted basis, on Monday, March 13. Kansas was ready, and its banks began opening on that day. The confidence of Kansas officials in the state's banks was generally upheld, as 582 of the 624 banks open on March 3 immediately resumed business.[15] With the ending of the national bank holiday, the worst seemed to be over.

The battle on tax measures continued during the banking crisis as the corporation lobbies increased their fight against Landon's income-tax proposal. Unable to stop its consideration, however, the lobbyists tried to persuade the legislators to adjourn because they had been at work longer than usual. Landon thwarted this by telling the legislators he expected them to stay in session to deal with the rapidly worsening economic crisis and to cooperate, if called upon to do so, with the new national administration. The lobbyists then counterattacked, stampeding the senate into destroying the house-approved income-tax bill, but the senators soon regained their poise and indicated that they would strive for a satisfactory compromise with the house. The next move of

[13] Ruth Friedrich, "The Threadbare Thirties," in John D. Bright (ed.), *Kansas, The First Century* (New York: Lewis, 1956), II, pp. 95 f.; *Topeka Capital*, March 4, 6, 1933.

[14] *Topeka Capital*, March 5–8, 12, 1933.

[15] *Ibid.*, March 12, 16, 1933.

the lobbyists was to propose a sales-tax bill, in exchange for a drastic weakening of the house income-tax bill. When the lobbyists found that the sales tax was being taken seriously, they were dismayed, for they no more wanted that than the income tax.[16] By the middle of March, new pressures were felt on tax questions as public and small-business resentment over the proposed sales tax arose.

As mass protest meetings were held, newspaper support of the accomplished items of the agenda came in. The *Kansas City Times* congratulated the governor and the legislators, regardless of party, for "pulling together to lift the tax load from Kansas property." The *Wichita Beacon* congratulated the legislature on replacing the Public Service Commission with the new, more powerful Corporation Commission. The praise was written partly in the belief that a satisfactory compromise would be found between house and senate conferees on an income tax, but by March 17 the two houses were at a standoff. When the senate adjourned to March 20, Landon intervened, stressing the importance of prompt reconsideration of the tax, and new conferees were appointed to take up the struggle and hammer out a mutually satisfactory bill.[17]

Two other actions were taken to ease the legislative stalemate. Landon announced a number of appointments, some to start a trickle of patronage and others to create favorable public reaction for the administration. The expected appointments of Homer Hoch and Jesse Greenleaf as chairman and member, respectively, of the new Corporation Commission came, satisfying progressive and moderate Republicans. The appointment of former Lieutenant Governor D. A. N. Chase as state budget director was a boon to conservatives. In the legislature, the obstinacy of western Kansas senators was softened as reapportionment shifted two senate seats from eastern Kansas to the western part of the state. Finally, in the early hours of March 22, a graduated income tax was passed. It provided for a 2 per cent tax on net corporation income, and a graduated tax—from 1 to 4 per cent— on net incomes over $2,000 of individuals. Landon's pressure to enact the tax had been continuous but unobtrusive, and, when word came that passage of the tax was imminent, he went to the legislative halls to congratulate the members of the house and senate.[18]

[16] *Ibid.*, March 2, 9, 10, 1933.

[17] *Kansas City Times*, March 15, 1933; *Wichita Beacon*, March 19, 1933; *Topeka Capital*, March 15, 18–20, 1933.

[18] *Kansas City Times*, March 18, 1933; *Wichita Beacon*, March 19, 1933; *Topeka Capital*, March 21, 22, 1933.

The income tax was the last important item considered by the legislature, which adjourned its unusually long session two days later, on March 24. Landon was pleased with the legislature's record; they had been contentious but they had risen to the governor's challenge. Direct appropriations were cut by almost a quarter, and it was estimated that tax burdens would be reduced between $10 million and $20 million for the biennium. State and local payrolls had been slashed by 10 to 40 per cent, and a measure of salary equalization had been achieved. The income-tax and the tax-levy limitations laws had been passed. Legislation had been approved to simplify tax collections and local government business procedures. Restrictions were placed on the weights, lengths, and widths of buses and trucks. The Inspections Department and the Corporation Commission had been established. License-tag fees were reduced, and the cash-basis law—restricting expenditure to income—had been approved. The eighteen-month mortgage-redemption provision had been retained, and the governor was given power to extend it by six months. Deficiency judgments on real estate foreclosures were abolished. Land sold for taxes was made redeemable by former owners for a period of four years after the tax sale, and tax penalties and interest on real estate sold to pay 1932 taxes were abolished.

The Twentieth Amendment had been ratified. The legislature had moved to halt gasoline-tax evasion and to lower exemptions from the tax. Grain inspection fees were reduced by 25 per cent, and the reimbursable car allowance for state officials was limited to 5 cents a mile. Cities and counties were authorized to borrow to aid home-owners. The Legislative Council was established to study the state's needs. The poll tax was abolished, and oil and gas proration laws were strengthened. The only major administration measure lost was uniform accounting and auditing for localities.[19]

Landon could be pleased, for never before had a Kansas governor had such a high proportion of his proposals adopted by the legislature. He was to find, however, that legislation was but a small part of government in 1933.

Franklin D. Roosevelt has been called a "confidence man," in both senses of the phrase, but this description was also true of Alf Landon, and in fact of almost every public official early in 1933. The country was then, by any measure, at rock bottom, confused as to where it was

[19] *Topeka Capital*, March 22, 23, 1933; *Topeka State Journal*, March 21–23, 1933.

going; and there was a desperate need for courage and a lifting of spirits. Politicians, who were no less confused than the people, tried to lend confidence and borrow courage by well-intended actions and reassuring rhetoric. They also relied on each other to a surprising extent. Most of the old partisan jealousies and factional rivalries were put aside during the great emergency of 1933.

Landon in his first few months as governor spent much time exhorting people to confidence, to confidence that with hard work and co-operation the nation could extricate itself from the dire circumstances of depression. He also became a beater of drums for the incoming national administration. "We are at war," he told Missouri Young Republicans in a Lincoln Day speech that urged cooperation with the new government. He looked to Franklin D. Roosevelt to prove himself the spiritual kinsman of Teddy Roosevelt, and he approved giving the new President the "big stick" for use in budgetary and reorganization matters. After the bank holiday was promulgated from Washington, Landon praised the move, saying that Kansas would "gladly cooperate in every way with the President's plans." [20] Landon soon volunteered for more than verbal cooperation with the New Deal.

One of the earliest and most baffling problems facing the new national administration was the oil situation. Although the petroleum excise tax of 1932 and the states' regulatory laws had contributed to removing some of the industry's problems, they could not lift petroleum out of depression. "Hot oil"—oil produced in violation of state laws—flooded the market from Texas, and of course the general depression further contributed to low oil prices. Oil-producing states were foundering in treating the situation. Little could be done in outlying oil-producing areas, like the Rocky Mountains, unless the gigantic Mid-Continent field was properly regulated, and the Mid-Continent area could not be properly regulated as long as any of its major producing states had inadequate legislation or enforcement.[21] Like many governors, Landon called for—and gained—a strengthening of his state's oil regulations. He urged major producers not to store oil unnecessarily, thereby making future price drops inevitable. But one governor, or even a number of governors, acting on only part of the situation, could not bolster the whole industry; and Landon knew that the situation required the

[20] *Topeka Capital*, February 12, March 7, 1933.
[21] Leslie A. Miller to Landon, January 27, 1933; Landon to Miller, February 10, 1933.

cooperation of all.[22] In an attempt to impress upon the new administration the chaotic situation in the American oil industry, the Independent Petroleum Association (and others) sponsored a conference of oil-state governors or their representatives in Washington on March 6. This conference, though limited in scope, roused some congressional and administration interest in the industry's plight. It led to planning for a second, more widely publicized meeting, to be held late in March under the sponsorship of the President and the Secretary of the Interior, Harold L. Ickes.

Landon, unable to attend the first oil conference because of the prolonged session of the legislature, was strongly urged to attend the second conference by Wirt Franklin, the leader of the Independent Petroleum Association, and others.[23] While Landon had an abundance of work in Kansas, he decided to go to Washington because he had more intimate knowledge of the oil industry than any other governor in the land. He left for Washington on March 25, the day after the legislature's adjournment, and he had arranged, while in the capital, to confer with the Kansas congressional delegation, to discuss with the Secretary of Agriculture arrangements to meet the state's need for seed loans, and to ask Reconstruction Finance Corporation officials why they accepted commercial real estate mortgages but not other types of mortgages as collateral for loans. But, as he said on leaving Topeka and after arriving in Washington, the main purpose of his trip was "to acknowledge in a tangible way the appreciation of the people of my state of the courage with which President Roosevelt has attacked the depression." Landon's participation in the oil conference was "one way in which a member of that species thought by many to be extinct—a Republican Governor in a Mid-Western state—can aid in the fight, and I now enlist for the duration of the war."[24]

The Department of the Interior officials were evidently pleased that Landon could come. Secretary Ickes' chief aide at the conference, E. S. Rochester, had earlier and happily reported that "Kansas has

[22] Landon to W. G. Skelly, February 24, 1933; Landon to Arthur A. Seeligson, February 28, 1933.

[23] Wirt Franklin to Landon, March 16, 1933; George T. McDermott to Landon, March 16, 1933.

[24] *Topeka Capital*, March 26, 1933. See also Arthur M. Schlesinger, Jr., *The Coming of the New Deal* (Boston: Houghton Mifflin, 1958), p. 3, and *New York Times*, March 27, 1933.

regulation pretty well in hand." [25] Rochester and Ickes, however, were not pleased with the early sessions of the oil conference. Ickes had hoped that the oilmen could devise a working plan for their industry, but it immediately became evident that they could not fruitfully work together without his intervention. Ickes called a meeting of the official representatives of the sixteen oil states for 2 p.m. on March 27. In a sixth-floor office of the Department of the Interior, Ickes met with them and suggested that they appoint a committee of five, hopefully as a stabilizing force, to meet with two other committees of five, one representing the independents and the other representing the major oil companies. He then went to the oil-industry representatives to ask them to appoint their two committees, so that the three committees could sit down together to work out a program. [26] The committees were appointed, and were amalgamated into a committee-of-fifteen, with the objective of working out a cooperative federal-state-private program to cope with oil problems and to restrict production with minimum federal control.

Landon, the only governor at the conference, was named chairman of the Committee of Fifteen, and in this role he addressed the conference. He began by pledging once again his "enlistment for the duration of the war," and then went on to give the oilmen a genteel piece of his mind. In the oil meetings he had attended, "much was said and little done," although it was clear the problems of the industry, especially that of the surplus of crude oil, must be vigorously attacked. While all the oil states now had laws for conservation and proration of petroleum purchases from producers, they were not being satisfactorily enforced, nor were the penalties for violations stiff enough. There must be active cooperation between oilmen and the states in enforcing the laws, and "imprisonment must await the violator." As for fixing fair quotas for oil production and purchasing, Landon conceded that producers and the states were not always in a position to set them.

He suggested that the "total current consumption of the United States can be arrived at by agreement or fixed by federal authority." When the consumption figure is set, "give the states and the industry a reasonable time—a few months is enough—to demonstrate their

[25] E. S. Rochester to Harold L. Ickes, March 15, 1933, Harold L. Ickes Papers, Manuscript Division, Library of Congress, Washington, D.C.

[26] E. S. Rochester to Harold L. Ickes, March 27, 1933, Ickes Papers; Harold L. Ickes, *The Secret Diary of Harold L. Ickes: The First Thousand Days* (New York: Simon & Schuster, 1953–54), pp. 9 f.

ability fairly to allocate this demand among the states and the industry;
to produce the oil with a minimum waste of gas; to keep unneeded oil
in its natural reservoir—the ground. If they fail, if bickering and
jealousy stand in the way of conservation of a national resource, or if
the irresponsible ten per cent cannot be policed by state authority, then
recourse must be had to more drastic measures. For even the iron hand
of a national dictator is preferable to paralytic stroke." He also asked
for relaxation of the Sherman Antitrust Act to ease the fierce competition
in the marketing of petroleum products, and he called for help from
the federal government in stopping the frequent evasion by oil
companies of state gasoline taxes.[27]

Landon then went to work with the Committee of Fifteen to devise
a plan that incorporated his suggestions, holding the committee on the
job for three days and two nights in order to reach agreement on a
workable plan. Because the committee members had been spurred to
action by Ickes' warning that the federal government might have to
regulate the oil industry directly if the oilmen could not get together
to save themselves, and because Landon's speech had forcefully buttressed the Secretary's statement, the bespectacled governor was able
to ride herd on the untamed stallions of the industry.

Policy agreement was unanimously arrived at by the Committee of
Fifteen on March 29. The committee recommended that President
Roosevelt call upon the governors of California, Kansas, Oklahoma,
Texas, and New Mexico to close all highly productive, or flush, pools—
except the few that would be damaged by water encroachment—until
April 15. He should ask the principal producing states to enact adequate
oil and gas conservancy laws, and he should recommend to Congress
legislation prohibiting interstate and foreign transportation of oil and
oil products produced in violation of the laws of the state where they
were produced. The President should strictly enforce federal gasoline
and pipeline tax collections, and should direct the Bureau of Internal
Revenue to send information to the states about those who paid these
taxes so that the states could collect their full taxes.

The President was also asked to assign a personal representative to
work with the states in bringing about industrial and governmental
cooperation in all of these matters and in a fair allocation of production
quotas during the economic emergency. The committee also requested

[27] *Topeka Capital*, March 28, 1933; Landon speech, Washington, D.C., March 27,
1933.

an increase of the oil tariff, elimination of federal taxes on oil products
and pipelines, delayed drilling on public lands, continuation of the
Federal Oil Conservation Board, and a comprehensive federal study
of the oil and gas industry in order to further conservation practices.
The committee called upon the states to arrive at equitable allocations
of production among oil pools and among producing states. Oilmen
were asked to support and cooperate with government agencies in these
activities, to refrain from violating oil legislation or from handling
products produced in violation of the laws, and to limit drilling,
imports, and storage withdrawals of oil. It was hoped that these
activities could achieve a margin of profit for all branches of the oil
industry and that waste would be reduced.[28]

The report was remarkable in view of the heel-dragging that had
occurred in the industry since prices began dropping in 1926, and it
was the first instance of agreement on major oil policies among representatives of the independent and major producers and the states. But
the report was not fully acceptable to the federal government, which
was suspicious of anything smacking of oil; nor was the report acceptable to all segments of the industry. This was foreshadowed by an
incident during the second day of the conference, when Ickes was
accosted by an angry group of independents, mainly from southern
California. Headed by John B. Elliott, the group made it clear it did
not want curtailment of production, it wanted instead antitrust action.
Elliott especially attacked the Independent Petroleum Association,
charging it was really under the thumb of the major companies.[29]

Despite intense opposition from the few independents who believed
they could afford to compete in a market floundering in surpluses,
Landon and his allies, with Ickes' encouragement, acted to secure
favorable response to the proposals of the Committee of Fifteen. The
representatives of the sixteen oil-state governors were assembled to
review the committee's report, and they unanimously resolved to
approve it. Also, they recommended that the governors appoint
representatives to facilitate cooperation between the federal and the
state governments on oil conservation matters. They urged that the
governors of the oil-producing states—particularly California, Kansas,
Louisiana, Oklahoma, and Texas—meet personally to coordinate the
actions of their states on oil problems. Representatives of the twenty
oil and gas associations who were present voted unanimously for the

[28] Committee of Fifteen to Harold L. Ickes, March 29, 1933, Ickes Papers.
[29] Ickes, *First Thousand Days*, pp. 10 f.

proposals for federal action, and overwhelmingly for the proposals for action by the states and the industry.[30]

But the government still was not ready to accept the committee's recommendations. John B. Elliott had hastily organized a dissenting group, the Independent Petroleum Association Opposed to Monopoly, and the Elliott group—joined by the I.P.A. of California and the I.P.A. of Texas—said that petroleum was sounder than most American industries and that overproduction was not a problem. The chief problems, Elliott and his associates declared, were monopoly and overcharges on pipeline rates; and conservation and control of production were asserted to reside within the exclusive domain of the individual states.[31]

The Committee of Fifteen proposals were laid before President Roosevelt and the cabinet by Secretary Ickes, and discussed at length. The President, who had been influenced by some of the arguments of Elliott's group, indicated that he could not agree with all of the committee's recommendations. In a restrained letter (drafted by Ickes) to the oil-state governors, Roosevelt said that some of the actions recommended by the committee were beyond his authority. He wrote that he could not go far in calling upon the governors to act, especially in closing flush pools and in requesting state conservancy legislation. He did, however, suggest that appropriate action should be taken by the states, and, most significantly, he declared for a legislative ban on "hot oil," for strict federal tax enforcement, and for giving federal tax data to the states. Trying to appease the Elliott group, he also called for legislation to divorce oil pipelines from other oil enterprises.[32]

Although the oil conference had been hectic and demanding, Landon returned to Kansas thinking that the basis had been laid for action that would bring prompt relief to the industry.[33] He was wrong. The drive for federal legislation and state actions proceeded slowly, and oil prices remained low.

[30] Record Group 48, Federal Oil Conservation Board Correspondence, Resolution of the Conference of Governors of the Oil Producing States, March 27–29, 1933, National Archives, Washington, D.C.; Committee of Fifteen to Harold L. Ickes, March 29, 1933, Ickes Papers.

[31] I.P.A. Opposed to Monopoly and others to Harold L. Ickes, March 29, 1933; Ickes, *First Thousand Days*, pp. 11 f.

[32] Ickes, *First Thousand Days*, pp. 14, 16; Franklin D. Roosevelt to Landon, April 1, 1933; *Topeka Capital*, April 4, 1933; Record Group 48, Federal Oil Conservation Board Correspondence, Interior Department Press Release, April 3, 1933, National Archives.

[33] Landon to Clyde I. Layton, April 3, 1933.

By early April the crusty governor of Oklahoma, William H. "Alfalfa Bill" Murray, had joined Landon as one of the most forceful leaders of the oil movement,[34] and Landon suggested that Murray call a conference of governors to discuss oil problems. Murray agreed, and asked the governors of California, Colorado, Kansas, Texas, and New Mexico to meet with him in Amarillo, although the meeting had to be postponed because of conflicts in schedules.[35] Landon, after hearing of the postponement of the Amarillo conference, asked Murray to confer with Texas Governor Miriam "Ma" Ferguson on ways of meeting overproduction in Texas. Landon had acted to strengthen the Kansas Corporation Commission in enforcing his state's oil legislation, and, thanks to Murray, the Oklahoma City flush pool was now under control; but east Texas, where prices were as low as 8 cents a barrel, was still running wild. Landon was convinced that the government of Texas could do much more to stop illegal production, thereby easing the price crisis in the entire oil industry. The Kansas and Oklahoma forces also tried, along with I.P.A., to shake up the national government through Congress. Senator Arthur Capper of Kansas and Representative E. W. Marland of Oklahoma were preparing legislation to name a federal production arbiter, to ban "hot oil," to legalize the sharing of federal internal revenue data with the states, and to separate pipeline companies from oil-production companies.[36]

Murray, unable to make progress with Governor Ferguson, called another oil conference of governors, which also was unable to meet. Landon, conferring with oil producers of Kansas, Oklahoma, and Texas, urged their support for increased regulation. By May the situation was worse than ever; marketed production was higher than in any month since the peak production of 1929, violation of the ratable taking laws—designed to restrict production—was common, and prices continued low.[37] Landon and Murray, who conferred in Oklahoma City on May 3 with oilmen from their states, tried to win increased support for the national administration's new plan for industrial regulatory codes. Each governor appointed a committee to go to Washington to press for federal legislation that would balance supply and demand, that would provide for a fair apportionment of

[34] Ickes, *First Thousand Days, passim*; W. H. Murray to Landon, April 4, 1933; Murray to Franklin D. Roosevelt, April 4, 1933.

[35] *Topeka Capital*, April 5, 7, 1933; Landon to Carl Weiner, April 9, 1933.

[36] *I.P.A. Represents*, p. 3; *Topeka Capital*, April 9, 1933.

[37] *Topeka Capital*, April 23, 1933; *I.P.A. Represents*, p. 3; Ickes, *First Thousand Days, passim*.

production quotas, and that would limit imports. A few days after the Oklahoma City meeting, the Kansas Oil Advisory Committee, which met in Wichita, unanimously recommended that Landon urge all Kansas producers to shut their wells (wherever technically possible), that he request the state Corporation Commission to restrain increases in production, and that he take steps to prevent refiners from purchasing oil at low prices in order to store it for sale at higher prices. Landon immediately discussed these recommendations with the Corporation Commission, which on May 8 approved a voluntary shut-down of oil wells and began restriction of pipeline purchases of oil to the supply believed needed to meet consumer demands.[38]

President Roosevelt had not yet sent an oil bill to Congress, something he had promised to do. Crude oil was selling at between 10 and 25 cents a barrel in the Mid-Continent field, and the national government's delay, as Landon saw it, was unnecessarily prolonging the distress in the industry. On May 11, Landon telephoned the President to plead for help for the industry; he was assured that it was on the way. The next day he wired governors Murray and Ferguson for help, especially for the independents. Murray answered that he would await the action of Congress, inferring that Oklahoma and Kansas could not control the situation without the help of Texas.[39] Landon again telegraphed Murray and Ferguson, on May 15, asking that their states act to limit purchases, as Kansas had done, in order to stop the large companies from storing oil purchased at rock-bottom prices. He urged that the three states cooperatively measure their storage capacity to find out how much cheap oil had been stored. "The public is entitled to know what companies are preparing to repeat the indefensible practices carried on in the past in filling storage at destructive prices and reaping unholy profits [later] at the expense of struggling producers and the public."[40]

Murray then took the matter up with the Oklahoma Corporation Commission, and Ferguson stated that Landon's position was "well-founded." Governor Ferguson referred Landon's telegram to the appropriate state agency, the not-very-vigorous Texas State Railroad Commission, for consideration—a meaningless answer for Landon, who wrote Murray that he was "afraid this is the end of the matter as far as Texas is concerned." Nevertheless, Landon declared that Kansas

[38] *Wichita Beacon*, May 3–10, 1933; T. C. Johnson to Landon, May 6, 1933.
[39] Landon to Arthur Capper, May 16, 1933; Ickes, *First Thousand Days, passim.*
[40] Landon to W. H. Murray, May 15, 1933; Landon to Miriam A. Ferguson, May 15, 1933.

and Oklahoma should do what they could to prevent the storing of oil by the major purchasing companies, but Murray replied that he could not help. Political pressures, the unfavorable mood of the Oklahoma legislature, and the temper of the oilmen made action impossible.[41]

Landon had already become convinced that Murray's hands were tied, and he looked again to Washington for a solution; he also asked his Kansas cohorts to sustain their pressure on the national capital and to stir up mass meetings of oil people in Kansas and other states. Within the week, the situation brightened. The plans to restrict purchases of oil for storage had been successfully implemented in Kansas, and it appeared that Oklahoma, despite Governor Murray's pessimism, had also found ways to curtail unnecessary storing of oil. The national administration's oil control bill was introduced in Congress, under Ickes' sponsorship, by Senator Capper and Representative Marland. The bill would give the Secretary of the Interior broad powers, for two years, to regulate production and to limit imports.[42]

All this, however, was only a small counteroffensive—no real battles had been won; and President Roosevelt did not fully back the bill;[43] but there was a new possibility that might save the industry. On June 16 the President signed the National Industrial Recovery Act, one aim of which was to encourage American business to stop cut-throat competition. The Independent Petroleum Association and the American Petroleum Institute immediately called for a conference of representatives of domestic petroleum associations to meet in Chicago to draft, under the act, a code of fair practices for the industry. At the same time Landon called upon American Petroleum Institute members to take action voluntarily, or, through an NIRA code, to attack the industry's problems—and especially to prevent the negotiation of long-term contracts to buy oil at the prevailing low prices. The A.P.I. leadership was agreeable to Landon's requests.[44]

The provisions of the NIRA brought enough confidence, and fear, to force prices up to a top of 52 cents a barrel by the time the code conference met; indeed, the producers went so far as to ask the President to fix petroleum prices. Things soon began to happen. On July 11,

[41] W. H. Murray to Landon, May 15, 1933; Miriam Ferguson to Landon, May 16, 1933; Landon to Murray, May 16, 1933; Murray to Landon, May 17, 1933.

[42] Landon to T. C. Johnson, May 16, 1933; Landon to C. L. McMahon, May 24, 1933; Landon to A. D. Allison, May 25, 1933; *Topeka Capital*, May 20, 1933.

[43] Landon to Harold McGugin, May 31, 1933; Ickes, *First Thousand Days, passim*.

[44] *I.P.A. Represents*, pp. 3 f.; Landon to Axtell J. Byles, June 16, 1933; Byles to Landon, June 17, 1933.

President Roosevelt issued—under NIRA authority—an order forbidding interstate transportation of illegally produced oil, and, on July 15, Secretary Ickes issued regulations and organized a special bureau to enforce this order. Meanwhile, a code that had been written by the oil associations was being studied and revised by government officials, who were being pressed by the oil states and the industry to see that every grievance, real or fancied, would be taken care of.[45] Landon contributed to the pressure with repeated demands that independent producers be protected from price discrimination and manipulation by the major oil companies.[46]

On August 19, 1933, the Petroleum Code was signed by the President; it provided for increased wages, fewer hours of work, and holding production in line with demand; and it gave the President discretionary power to fix maximum and minimum crude oil prices. Although the code was far from satisfactory for many oil independents because it increased their labor costs and did not provide for strict control of the major oil companies, they were pleased to find themselves heavily represented on the Planning and Coordination Committee and its subcommittees, which had been established to make modifications in the code.[47] Secretary Ickes, who had been appointed administrator of the Petroleum Code, moved rapidly—first in setting up the Planning and Coordination Committee in late August, and then, in early September, in setting state oil-production quotas and import restrictions. The Planning and Coordination Committee also moved rapidly; by the second week in September it had drawn up modifications of the code that eased its effect on stripper wells, that permitted more flexible administration of the code, and that made a more "scientific" basis for price fixing. These modifications were approved by the President on September 13, 1933.[48]

[45] *Topeka Capital*, June 17, 18, 1933; "Rules and regulations . . . prescribed in conformity with the requirements of the Act of Congress of June 16, 1933" (mimeograph), signed by Harold L. Ickes, July 15, 1933, enclosed in R. B. Brown to Wirt Franklin, July 17, 1933; *Topeka Capital*, July 16, 1933; Ickes, *First Thousand Days*, *passim*.

[46] Landon to Hugh S. Johnson, August 2, 1933; Gifford Pinchot, Landon, *et al.* to Franklin D. Roosevelt, August 12, 1933, Franklin D. Roosevelt Library, Hyde Park, N.Y. (hereafter called FDRL); Pinchot to Landon, August 21, 1933.

[47] *Topeka Capital*, August 20, 1933; R. B. Brown to Wirt Franklin, September 1, 1933.

[48] *Topeka Capital*, September 3, 1933; Clark, *Oil Century*, p. 239; Franklin D. Roosevelt, *Modifications of Code of Fair Competition for the Petroleum Industry* (Washington, D.C.: Planning and Coordination Committee, 1933).

Landon, generally satisfied with the government's action, telegraphed his congratulations to Ickes on allocating to the various states "practically the fullest possible amount of the present consuming demand." He was particularly pleased with Ickes' order that daily production, rather than storage withdrawals and imports, was to be used to satisfy demand. Landon knew the code would not solve the oil industry's problems, but he recognized that it would afford appreciable relief in a short period of time.[49] Along with the other oil-state governors, he was content to wait to see if this relief would be enduring, and if the code, in the course of time, would meliorate other pressing problems of the industry.

Although the petroleum crisis was closest to Landon's experience and emotion, it was not the most vexatious problem he faced; his saddest problem was finding relief for the unemployed. Landon, knowing the state's limited resources—though he constantly encouraged state and local agencies and private groups to greater efforts to meet relief needs—looked to the federal government for the greatest amount of assistance. During the Washington oil conference (in March), he had urged congressmen and administrative officials to act promptly on the relief question, and in a meeting with President Roosevelt he had spent most of his time pleading for an expansion of the scope of the reforestation bill—which promised some job relief for the unemployed— then before Congress. This legislation, like most conservation bills, did not touch on the most important conservation problems—water conservation and flood control—of drought-stricken states like Kansas, which were without a large federal public domain. Landon urged the President to consider broadening the legislation, or its administration, so that state lands could be improved and water conservation projects could qualify for federal aid.[50] Landon's position was not unique, though he was a strenuous advocate of this view. Pressure for a broader interpretation of conservation and of acceptable project sites came from the many states with great water problems and no great tracts of federally owned public lands. This movement contributed significantly to expanding the scope of federal conservation efforts.

The forestation legislation, amended to provide for state lands, was

[49] Landon to Harold L. Ickes, September 5, 1933.
[50] *Topeka Capital*, March 29, 1933.

passed a few days after Landon's visit with the President. The governor immediately dispatched two state officials to Washington to lay plans before the Secretary of Agriculture for four state lakes and six flood control projects to put some of the unemployed to work, but the representatives returned dejectedly a few days later with the information that there was nothing in the President's conservation plans for Kansas. Landon was not discouraged. He, like other midwestern governors, persisted in his efforts to get federal funds for relief-conservation projects [51]—which were ultimately successful.

Unemployment relief was also the most pressing problem facing Landon. He had received more than 15,000 applications for the 200 state jobs that were available for his appointment after the legislature's adjournment. Day after day his reception room was crowded with applicants—and their county chairmen and state legislators. It was disheartening to listen to their tales, but it was sadder to contemplate that these men represented only a small part of the unemployed of Kansas—and an infinitesimal part of the nation's jobless. After three weeks of interviewing, all the state jobs available to the governor's office had gone to the most experienced applicants. Landon, when in Topeka, had daily talked with 200 and 300 applicants; although he could seldom give them jobs, he had tried to give them hope.[52]

Worn out by three months of day-and-night work and worry, Landon began a brief fishing excursion on April 12, having left orders for his subordinates to think of every way possible to alleviate the state's unemployment problems. The state itself could do little to help, but it could explore every possibility for self-help and for federal and private assistance. Landon, upon his return, telegraphed the President and petitioned that the National Guard training program not be reduced because it was an important means of support of the states, national defense, and unemployment relief. The governor also applied to the Reconstruction Finance Corporation for supplemental funds for meeting the estimated relief needs of fifty-five counties; and the application was approved, subject to monthly review.

By April 19 the state Labor Department had completed an unemployment survey that showed that 75,000 Kansas families required

[51] *Ibid.*, April 2, 1933; *Topeka State Journal*, April 10, 1933; Edgar B. Nixon (ed. and comp.), *Franklin D. Roosevelt and Conservation, 1911–1945* (Hyde Park, N.Y.: Franklin D. Roosevelt Library, 1957), I, pp. 161 f.

[52] *Topeka Capital*, April 6, 12, 1933.

assistance. The assistance programs developed during the Woodring and Landon administrations included the use of county, municipal, and state poor-funds; federal money; private help (more than $3 million was raised in the past six months); and utilization of vacant land for gardening programs that involved over 15,000 needy families.[53] But this, clearly, was not sufficient, and in a state suffering from low farm and oil prices, and from drought and debt, relief had to be sought elsewhere. The federal government was the main target and work relief was the main proposal.

The first federal work-relief program in Kansas operated under provisions of the Reforestation Act. In late April it was announced that recruits for the program, the Civilian Conservation Corps, would be accepted for six months' service, with a maximum of 3,750 to be drawn from Kansas—which could mean an income of $90,000 a month to the state in relief to dependents. In May, the state again tried to secure favorable consideration from the federal government for its lake and flood control projects. When Landon had talked with the President, in March, Roosevelt had suggested that a project involving the timber lands in southeastern Kansas might be acceptable; and by May the state had drawn up proposals for five CCC projects, which were promptly approved. It was announced that some 1,000 CCC men would be assigned to work on the projects.[54]

The $3-billion public works bill before Congress also stirred hope in Kansas. When it appeared, in May, that this bill would pass, Landon appointed a Works Projects Development Committee to develop plans to make the best use of the expected federal money. The state administration was alarmed when, in mid-May, Harry Woodring, now the assistant secretary of war, tried to pull a *démarche*: Woodring made banner headlines in the state's newspapers with his announcement of plans to construct a huge dam across the Kaw River at Kiro. This dam was to be part of a Mississippi Valley flood control project, then under discussion in Washington, and would be financed from funds appropriated under the anticipated public works act. It would cost $45 million and would create a lake 40 miles long, inundating several sizable towns and some of the most valuable land and transportation

[53] Landon to Franklin D. Roosevelt, April 18, 1933; Fred C. Croxton to Landon, April 19, 1933, Kansas State Archives, Governors' Papers, Kansas State Historical Society, Topeka (hereafter called KSA); *Topeka Capital*, April 20, June 4, 1933.

[54] *Topeka Capital*, April 26, May 26, June 7, 1933; Landon to Robert Fechner, May 20, 1933, KSA.

routes in the state. "Indignation meetings" were held, angry delegations poured into Topeka, and telegrams of protest were sent to Washington. Democratic Senator George McGill protested to President Roosevelt, asserting that the property, even in its depressed state, was worth at least as much as Woodring's improvement would be.[55] Although Woodring did not abandon the Kiro dam proposal, the opposition made it virtually impossible for him to squeeze any political profit from it—and, in effect, the protest movement preserved Kansas' share of federal public-works funds for projects developed by the state's Republican administration.

Although these were tense days, they were not without humor. After two months of strenuous work trying to arrange for federal aid, and nervously waiting to hear of presidential and agency decisions, a letter from the White House arrived in Topeka. Fumbling hands slit it open, and it was read that the President took great pleasure in informing Governor Landon that a matter about which Roosevelt "felt very strongly" had been settled: thenceforth governors would receive, instead of seventeen-gun salutes, nineteen-gun salutes—the same as was "accorded to the members of the federal cabinet."[56]

Only in May, with the establishment of the Federal Emergency Relief Administration—with a $3-billion budget—was a real beginning made in coping with the relief problem; but the states and the federal government then discovered they were inadequately prepared for the effective allocation and spending of FERA money. In June, George S. Knapp, the secretary of Landon's Plans and Projects Committee, complained that opportunities to get federal aid were being lost because of the inadequate amount of time and money invested by local and state agencies in planning relief projects. Despite this, the committee had cleared project-proposal requests for $17 million in federal funds for developing state lakes, for building highways, and for making local improvements. By late June, 1933, only $400 million of the appropriation had been allotted over the nation, of which Kansas was to receive over $10 million for highway construction.[57]

Landon had become interested in the plight of young people entering the depressed job market, and in July he telegraphed Harry Hopkins, the Federal Emergency Relief administrator, asking that serious consideration be given to providing "for relief on the basis of

[55] *Topeka State Journal*, May 16, 20, 22, 1933; *Topeka Capital*, May 24, 1933.
[56] Franklin D. Roosevelt to Landon, May 5, 1933, KSA.
[57] *Topeka Capital*, June 13, 21, 24, July 1, 1933.

not only the physical needs of families but also of the educational requirements of the next generation." Relief should also be offered to the many graduates of high schools and colleges who were unable to find jobs. Hopkins replied that FERA and the Federal Board of Vocational Education were developing plans to help these young people. Unsatisfied with the slow progress made in giving aid to those who wanted to go to college, Landon, late in August, asked his fellow Kansan, Carroll B. Merriam of the Reconstruction Finance Corporation, to work for the establishment of a self-liquidating federal loan fund to assist capable but indigent students. "We can't afford to lose this resource." [58]

By summer, FERA and public-works money began to have a salutary effect on Kansas and the nation. The slack in unemployment relief was beginning to be reeled in. Other early New Deal measures had caused a welcome upswing in business activity, and, when the NRA codes began going into effect in August, the situation further improved. All this was reflected in correspondence from the governor's office, which changed by late July from pleas of urgency to notes of disgruntlement with the red tape and the large overhead cost of federal work relief. [59]

Although the unemployment relief question became less pressing by summer, a second vexing problem, agricultural relief, became critical, for 1933 was the fourth consecutive year of drought for Kansas and the other plains states. Whatever crops and grasses had grown since winter began to wither with the heat of late spring and summer. Feed for cattle was desperately short in much of Kansas, Oklahoma, Colorado, New Mexico, and Texas, and the cash necessary for exporting cattle to pasture elsewhere was unavailable in the dust bowl area. In Kansas, farmers and livestock men met at every crossroads community and adopted resolutions; they wired Washington and Topeka, and the few who could afford it visited these cities in search of help.

When it became evident, by the middle of June, that there would not be enough rain to relieve the situation, the state acted to cope with this problem. Landon requested Senator Capper to canvass Washington for federal assistance. Red Cross aid was sought. All of the

[58] Landon to Harry Hopkins, July 16, 1933, and Hopkins to Landon, July 17, 1933, KSA; Landon to Carroll B. Merriam, August 30, 1933.

[59] *E.g.*, Landon to Alexander Howatt, July 31, 1933, and Landon to Harry Hopkins, July 31, 1933, KSA.

railroads serving Kansas—the Santa Fe, the Rock Island, the Missouri-Pacific, the Frisco, and the Union Pacific—were asked to cut their shipping rates during the emergency. The Farm Credit Administration offered livestock feed-loans on a collateral basis. The Red Cross indicated that it would give what help it could, and the FERA pledged its aid. The railroads offered help, though they did not specify what form it would take.[60]

Plans were also being made in Washington to begin payments for restriction of farm production under the terms of the Agricultural Adjustment Act. Secretary of Agriculture Henry A. Wallace, Landon, and Congressman Clifford Hope (one of the Republican supporters of the act), toured parts of Kansas, toward the end of June, to explain the legislation. Wallace announced that Kansas wheat farmers would receive $30 million in 1933 because of their lowered crop yields; and $20 million of this would be paid by September. The farmers were urged to restrict their wheat acreage in order to cut down the surplus that was depressing the market,[61] a plea that was considered almost hilarious in Kansas because the drought had done more to reduce wheat yields than would the AAA. In fact, much of the idle acreage for which farmers would be paid was wheat land that had been abandoned to drought. Nevertheless, the program gave needed cash relief to tens of thousands of Kansas farmers. Acceptance of acreage control was peaceful because of these payments and because few farmers could harvest enough wheat to profit from dollar-a-bushel prices in Chicago. During drought times agrarian myths of abundance were easily replaced by Washington's plans for balancing supply and demand.

Although the state had moved rapidly to procure pledges of help, they remained largely unfulfilled as July dragged by. The plains had become scorched and the land increasingly barren, and little relief had been received. Official representatives of Kansas, Colorado, Oklahoma, and Texas—who met to discuss and publicize the situation—declared that FERA efforts were lagging in anticipation of AAA farm payments in order to avoid overlapping between the two agencies. The result was distress, for business was also withering in the drought areas; credit

[60] Arthur Capper to Landon, June 17, 1933; F. A. Winfrey to Landon, June 17, 1933; Harry Hopkins to Landon, June 23, 1933; L. W. Baldwin to Landon, June 19, 1933; R. G. Merrick to Landon, June 28, 1933; J. E. Gorman to Landon, June 19, 1933, all KSA.

[61] *Topeka Capital*, June 29, 30, 1933.

and assets were virtually nonexistent; even food was short. Appeals to private sources of assistance were made more dramatic. Landon, who had been negotiating with the railroads for substantial shipping-rate reductions since mid-June, called a conference of Kansas farm and relief officials and railroad representatives for August 9. The state officials impressed upon the railroad men that the farmers of western Kansas were losing everything they owned for lack of relief, and that many of them were blaming the railroads. The railroad representatives, in turn, were successful in recommending that their companies substantially reduce rates on shipments of feed into and cattle out of thirty-nine drought-stricken Kansas counties. Free return of herd foundation cattle was also recommended, and the effective dates of these reductions were set for the period of greatest traffic.[62]

By the middle of August the farm crisis—like the unemployment problem—had eased, as private and federal assistance became effective. It was not forgotten, however, that winter would bring bitter problems, and planning was in order to tide the state over during the winter ahead. There were signs that there was insufficient meat for families on relief, but one of the food surpluses in the nation at the time was pork, and Kansas officials thought that this could be used to strengthen relief programs. Landon suggested to Harry Hopkins that surplus salt pork should be distributed free of charge to the states, according to the number of families on relief in each state. The Kansas Emergency Relief Commission had volunteered to handle distribution in Kansas, and E. L. Kirkpatrick of the AAA soon notified the governor that arrangements were being made to distribute surplus pork among the states according to "plans suggested by your wire." Landon told John G. Stutz, director of the K.E.R.C., to make plans to parcel out the pork when it became available. Stutz said that 1,408,000 pounds of pork was expected for distribution among the state's 50,000 relief families between October 11 and January 1, and that a large range of recipes would also be distributed.[63]

Meanwhile, public-works money was being allocated to the states under the careful supervision of Harold L. Ickes, and Ickes called upon the state governors for haste in letting the federal highway contracts

---

[62] *Ibid.*, July 17, 1933; Landon to S. T. Bledsoe, August 4, 1933, and memorandum of conference with railroad officials, August 9, 1933, enclosed in D. E. Ackers to Landon, August 15, 1933, KSA; *Topeka Capital*, August 10, 1933.

[63] Landon to Harry Hopkins, September 5, 1933; E. L. Kirkpatrick to Landon, September 8, 1933; John G. Stutz to Landon, October 7, 1933; all KSA.

that were to be financed under his Public Works Administration program. Landon replied that all contracts for Kansas would be let by January 1, and he took the occasion to request an additional $5 million from Ickes for the elimination of railway grade crossings. Ickes answered that $2.1 million, to help relieve unemployment in the drought area, was available for extra highway projects in twelve western and central Kansas counties, and that other projects for Kansas were under consideration.[64] A half million dollars also came from the Civil Works Administration, which had been established in early November to help the states take care of the problem of winter relief.[65]

In October the farm situation flared up again because prices for agricultural products had not kept up with general commodity prices. In fact, the farm purchasing-power ratio had declined from 72 in July to 61 in late October. While Kansas farmers were generally calm, elsewhere clashes between agrarians and law officers occurred, and preparations were made for a large-scale farm strike. Kansas was asked to join with other states in attempting to remove the causes of discontent. Governor William Langer of North Dakota called on the governors of the wheat-growing states to place an embargo on spring wheat shipments in order to force market prices up. Landon was out of town, but his secretary answered that there was little wheat then to be harvested in Kansas because very little spring-sown wheat was raised in the state. Landon, upon his return to Topeka, said the states could not handle the price situation, and he called for action by the federal government—particularly for long-term, low-interest loans to farmers to enable them to survive the effects of the low market prices.[66]

Landon forcefully followed this up in correspondence with federal officials, whom he had been pressing for more liberal agricultural loan arrangements since March. He wrote Henry Morgenthau, Jr., the governor of the Farm Credit Administration, that the "agricultural situation in Kansas and other farm-belt states is lamentable...prompt and vigorous action is necessary to save scores of farmers from eviction from farms and homes." In 94 Kansas counties, he pointed out, 1,518 farm foreclosure actions were pending. Hundreds of other farms had

64 *Topeka Capital*, October 11, 14, 1933; press release, October 19, 1933, KSA.

65 Robert G. Sherwood, *Roosevelt and Hopkins* (New York: Harper, 1948), pp. 51 ff.; Harry Hopkins to Landon, November 11, D. E. Ackers to Hopkins, November 10, 1933, and Hopkins to Landon, November 13, 1933, KSA.

66 *Topeka Capital*, October 26, 20, 21, 1933; William Langer to Landon, October 17, 1933, and Willard Mayberry to Langer, October 18, 1933, KSA.

already been sold at sheriffs' sales, and others would have gone had it not been for the Kansas mortgage-redemption law. He demanded action by the FCA to facilitate long-term, low-interest loans, and he pledged the state's help in administering them.[67]

New state action was also undertaken as Governor Clyde L. Herring of Iowa called a conference of the governors of ten midwestern states to meet in Des Moines on October 30 to consider the farm situation. A presidential representative would be present. Landon, who believed the conference could be very helpful, especially in speeding federal action in the crisis, suggested that Governor Herring invite Morgenthau and Secretary Wallace to the conference. Landon could not attend because of the opening of a special session of the legislature, but he sent Joseph M. Mercer, the Kansas livestock commissioner, as his representative. Landon also telegraphed the President, on October 26, to convey his ideas about what should be done for the farmer. "Put farm commodity prices up to where they belong thus restoring... purchasing power and [the farmer] will be able thereafter to care for himself and most other businesses will improve accordingly."

Landon also called for a stabilized dollar and for diplomatic recognition of Russia. In fact, he suggested extending a billion-dollar loan to Russia, to be spent in the United States for cattle, fats, cotton, and other surplus farm and manufactured goods. He again urged that federal credit machinery be expanded to reach farmers who, without choice, were being victimized by high private interest rates and by the exorbitant costs of shipping animals and maintaining foundation herds. This wire was released by Landon to the public through the International News Service office in Des Moines.[68]

The fall farm crisis stimulated further activity by the federal government. AAA corn-loan payments began to be disbursed in the middle west, and Morgenthau scheduled a regional meeting, for October 31, to facilitate the extension of federal farm credit. These measures were not enough, though, for in early November the farm strike began in sections of the middle west. Kansas remained quiet, and Landon stuck to his demand for a larger federal loan program while other governors called for drastic programs that involved price-fixing and regimented production and sales. At the same time, the federal loan program was

[67] Landon to Henry Morgenthau, Jr., October 25, 1933, KSA.

[68] Clyde L. Herring to Landon, October 25, 1933; Landon to Herring, October 25, 1933; Landon to Franklin D. Roosevelt, October 26, 1933; Landon to T. A. Pledge, October 26, 30, 1933, all KSA.

reaching larger numbers of farmers as collateral requirements were loosened, and the FCA began to ask the states to help screen loan applications. Kansas, at Landon's urging, had already established a State Debt Conciliation Committee for adjusting debts and payments between creditors and debtors. Using this committee, Landon was in a good position to set up a series of state and local screening committees to assist farmers in adjusting their debts and getting refinancing from the FCA.[69]

But Landon was not enamored of the federal programs. At Secretary of Agriculture Wallace's request, he sent an assessment of the AAA corn program to Washington on December 22. Efforts must be made, he contended, to raise livestock and crop prices. The tax on processors of commodities had not helped to do this, and the pegged corn prices had prevented a decent functioning of the market. The only solution was to find markets. A day earlier he had written the new governor of the Farm Credit Administration, William I. Myers, that FCA operations were weak. The agency's reliance on Federal Land Bank officials meant that banking rather than relief criteria would continue to be used in making loans. The credit program was also being bottlenecked by FCA's inability to process the unexpectedly large number of credit applications that had been received. Greater cooperation between Land Bank officials and the county debt-conciliation committees was needed, as well as a better understanding by federal officials of the farmers' problems. Landon urged Myers to provide for higher appraisals of the value of farm property and to facilitate the scaling down of farmers' debts to the government, as well as to private creditors.[70]

It was clear to Landon that the prosperity of Kansas rested on the economic recovery of its farmers. It was equally clear that farmers could not achieve recovery until they were secure in their property.

[69] Henry Morgenthau, Jr., to Landon, October 25, 1933, and Landon to Sam Edwards, October 26, 1933, KSA; *Topeka Capital*, October 26, November 5, 6, 27, 1933.

[70] Landon to Henry A. Wallace, December 22, 1933, and Landon to William I. Myers, December 21, 1933, KSA; *Topeka Capital*, December 25, 1933.

CHAPTER 7

Affairs of State

The year 1933 did not see the solution of depression and drought problems in Kansas, but it had seen many attempts at solution. Landon had played the roles of supplicant, federal agent, and sovereign participant in trying to secure relief and recovery. He—and his fellow governors—would continue to play these roles, almost without realizing that the function of a governor in the United States had changed radically. For Kansas, the governor's federal relations during the early New Deal days were to be more important in tackling the state's problems than his state powers. But the state functions, which existed separately and parallel to his federal functions, were nonetheless demanding.

After the adjournment of the state legislature in March, 1933, Governor Landon was confronted with a variety of state tasks. The roster of state appointive offices had to be filled, which was difficult in those depression days—not so much in acquiring talent as in deciding which capable men to select. Harry Darby, a dynamic young businessman and past president of the state chamber of commerce, was appointed—with sweeping powers of reorganization—director of the state's largest department, the Highway Department. John G. Stutz, director of the state relief organization under Governor Woodring, was continued in that office under Landon. Seth G. Wells was made director of the new Department of Inspections, and Ellis D. Bever was drawn from federal service to organize and head the Kansas Income Tax Division. Former Lieutenant Governor D. A. N. Chase became state budget director, and Topeka businessman Ben Franklin became state business manager. After William G. West resigned as Landon's secretary, in July, to become clerk of the federal district court, Willard Mayberry assumed the secretaryship. These and other Landon appointees were to give Kansas excellent service during his administration. They constituted a team upon which Landon could rely.

Appointed personnel was no great problem to the governor, but money was; the inescapable tax decreases left the state in the dilemma of maintaining, and even adding to, state services with less revenue on hand. Landon's answer was that nonessentials should be cut out; this was the course he had promised and the course he would follow, except when federal assistance was available. Landon led the way to economy by slashing his own salary and his official household expenses. Soon after taking office, he ordered the state departments not to add employees or fill vacancies unless this was absolutely justified, and he persuaded agency heads to cut their expenditures by 25 per cent. Landon cut his salary from $5,000 a year to $3,750, and it remained at that figure throughout his four years in office.[1]

The new, consolidated Department of Inspections and Registration led to sizable personnel slashes, and 300 employees were let out of other offices in Topeka. Twenty-three jobs in the penitentiary at Lansing were eliminated, and a cafeteria program was inaugurated there that was supposed to save the state some $10,000 a year. Highway Department wages were lowered 5 per cent, and consolidations were made with the aim of saving $3 million annually. The administration's tax-enforcement policy, however, created jobs in order to collect more revenue. Roving patrols and thirty-nine ports of entry, requiring the services of over a hundred gasoline inspectors, were established to catch gasoline bootleggers and to enforce the truck-mileage tax. These ports (a Kansas contribution to state government in America) and the patrols increased the tax yield far more than enough to pay for themselves. As a result of the economy drive, eleven of the fourteen institutions under the Board of Administration showed a substantial drop in per capita cost by the end of April. Efforts also were made to de-emphasize politics in the public service, and a number of Democrats were kept on in state jobs. Landon ordered that Highway Department

[1] Report of the Division of Auditing and Accounting to Walter A. Huxman, February 2, 1937; *Topeka Capital*, March 26, January 25, 29, 1933.

supervisors have sole power in hiring and firing; they were not to hire through Republican county committees, even for temporary help. The primary object was to get qualified, satisfactory help.[2]

Ironically, the federal government added another ingredient to the fiscal dilemma the state was struggling to resolve. In trying to revive the national economy, New Deal measures caused some inflation, which in turn increased operating costs for state institutions. The enactment of the National Industrial Recovery Act placed pressure on state agencies to reduce hours of work and yet maintain wages. Responding to this, the Highway Department, for example, shifted to a 40-hour week without cutting wages, which required 200 additional employees. Rumors circulated that the state legislature would have to be called upon to pass supplemental appropriations, but by pushing economy, efficiency, and the collection of taxes—and a good deal of balancing and juggling—the administration was able to announce at the end of October that there was no need to request extra funds for regular state institutions.[3]

All, however, was not strictly business for Landon. There were fund-raising drives to help disabled veterans; an honorary degree—an LL.D. from Washburn College—and a Pottawatomie "chieftainship" to be received, both with appropriate ceremonies; speeches and appearances to be made before Republican clubs, chambers of commerce, agricultural groups, bankers, the American Legion, the Y.M.C.A., the Knights of Columbus, and the Women's Christian Temperance Union. Landon most enjoyed his visits to Kansas National Guard encampments or to the new Civilian Conservation Corps camps, to chat with the boys, share their corned beef and cabbage with them, and catch fly balls or even demonstrate his ability at pitch.[4]

Tending to fiscal and ceremonial matters was routine for Landon in 1933. He also had to contend with those incidents that make public life alarming but exciting: the escape from the penitentiary of eleven convicts who took as hostages the warden and two guards; tornadoes,

[2] *Topeka Capital*, April 16, 11, 26, 30, May 7, 1933; Memorandum Concerning the Work of the State Corporation Commission, December 17, 1935, and Landon to Harry Darby, June 3, 1933, Kansas State Archives, Governors' Papers, Kansas State Historical Society, Topeka (hereafter called KSA).

[3] *Topeka Capital*, July 23, August 8, October 30, 1933.

[4] *Ibid.*, June 2, 17, 16, August 1, 1933; Landon speech file, 1933, Alfred M. Landon Papers, Kansas State Historical Society, Topeka.

including one at Liberal that left 700 persons in need of aid; the fight against the attempts of out-of-state insurance companies to absorb and remove Kansas companies; the commissioning of ten uniformed motor-vehicle inspectors (the origin of the Kansas Highway Patrol) to enforce vehicle laws on the road; and the battle against the rise of high-powered crime, especially bank robbery, by using units of the Kansas National Guard to set up roadblocks—a Landon innovation.[5]

Yet all this was minor compared to the crisis that descended on the state on August 7, the first disclosure of the greatest scandal in Kansas history, the Finney scandal. A federal bank examiner advised United States District Attorney Sardius M. Brewster that he had discovered evidence of serious irregularities in the Kansas state treasury. Brewster, after he had verified the story, notified Landon, who immediately asked the state adjutant general at Fort Riley to send a guard to take control of the treasurer's office. The adjutant general replied that he could not release men immediately, but he gave the governor the names of two national guardsmen in Topeka who could be ordered to duty. Landon rousted out a lieutenant and a sergeant from their civilian jobs in Topeka, and without taking time even to change to military clothes they rushed to the capitol to regulate the use of the treasurer's records. This was the beginning of day-and-night martial law for the office, with all its funds and books impounded. It soon appeared that at least $150,000 of state school-fund bonds had been duplicated and were being held as collateral by Kansas City and Chicago bond houses against the account of Ronald Finney, the son of one of the state's leading businessmen, Warren W. Finney of Emporia. Landon immediately requested the Shawnee County Attorney, Lester Goodell, to arrest and start prosecution against Ronald Finney. The governor then directed the state treasurer, Tom Boyd, to check the school fund. When Boyd replied that the governor's "request" would be presented to the School Fund commissioners for action, Landon countered: "That won't be necessary; I am issuing the order now, and if you cannot see your way clear to grant it I shall put the school fund under martial law." Boyd complied; and Landon promised the public that he would get to the bottom of the situation.[6]

[5] *Topeka Capital*, May 31, June 4, 18, July 18, 24, 23, August 5, 1933; *Hays City News*, August 10, 1933.

[6] Landon to Lester Goodell, August 7, 1933, KSA; Kansas Senate, *Trial of Will J. French, Auditor of the State of Kansas* (Topeka: State Printer, 1934), pp. 54 f.; *Topeka Capital*, August 8, 1933.

The warrant for young Finney's arrest charged him with selling
school fund bonds to the National Bank of Topeka and with resale to
his father. Finney surrendered at 1 p.m. on August 8, in Topeka—at
which time it appeared that some $500,000 in duplicate bonds had
been made. Of that amount, $329,000 had been deposited with
Boyd's office as security for state funds in three banks, the Fidelity
State and Savings Bank of Emporia, the Eureka Bank, and the Farmers'
State Bank of Neosho Falls. The Emporia and Neosho Falls banks were
operated by Warren W. Finney, and the Eureka bank was operated by
Ronald Finney's uncle, Howard Tucker. Bank Commissioner H. W.
Koeneke immediately closed the three banks, pending investigation.

Boyd first told the press that the bonds were not out of his office,
though Ronald Finney may have had access to the treasury vault.
Later, the treasurer said he had let Finney take $150,000 of bonds out
of the vault, "on loan," for personal use; he did not know if they had
ever been returned. "I loved and trusted him like a brother. And he
lied to me." This caused Landon to declare that "Mr. Boyd's statement,
if true, indicates that Mr. Boyd was either a party to permitting
$150,000 of state bonds to be taken by Ronald Finney to Chicago for a
purely personal transaction, or was a party to sending $150,000 of
forged bonds to Chicago in the same transaction." The governor
ordered the state accountant to start an exhaustive examination of the
treasurer's office.[7]

The state was becoming alarmed: many persons could have been in
on the scandal—including such elected officials as Treasurer Boyd, who
was the custodian for the bonds, Auditor of State Will J. French, who
had to sign all school bonds, the Attorney General Roland Boynton,
who was the legal watchdog of the School Fund Board. Landon ordered
an investigation of every office and every person who could con-
ceivably have been involved. Because Attorney General Boynton was
a member of the School Fund Board, he was relieved of responsibility
for the investigation, and the Shawnee County attorney, Lester Goodell,
was asked to take charge. Legislators were also requested to study the
case. The *Manhattan Tribune* indicated the apprehensions of the state—
"This gigantic bond forgery and swindle is reaching greater proportions
with every issue of the Topeka newspapers"—and it commended
Landon for his quick action in the affair.

[7] *Topeka Capital*, August 8, 9, 1933; Landon press release, August 9, 1933, KSA.

The Governor at this time no doubt has not the slightest idea how far this investigation will reach or how many of his official family will be implicated. The chances are that this scandal is going to take in some of the prominent politicians of the capital city and also the state house. In the reports that emanate from the state house it indicates that several state officers are as shaky as a boy with the St. Vitus dance.[8]

Clifford Stratton, in the *Topeka Capital*, gave some indications of Ronald Finney's operations. Taking advantage of depression prices, Finney had purchased ranches, farms, and businesses all over Kansas. From a plush business suite in the Hotel Jayhawk, he had kept his financial operations going, using fraudulent government bonds to keep solvent. This, Stratton asserted, required friends in the offices of the treasurer, the auditor, and the attorney general. Such friends the thirty-four-year-old Ronald Finney could easily have had, for he was the well-known son of a well-known father, and a long-time acquaintance of Attorney General Boynton (a cousin of William Allen White). Warren Finney was one of Emporia's leading citizens, a former member of the state legislature, and a neighbor and friend of the Whites. The elder Finney had been a liberal contributor to both parties and to individual Democratic and Republican candidates for state office. He had been accounted a friend of most high officeholders, and his friends were his son's friends. Who could escape suspicion? Not even Harry Woodring, or Alf Landon, both of whom knew the Finneys.

While speculation was mounting, Landon continued to act; he had instituted a search of Ronald Finney's office in Emporia and had placed the state accountant, A. R. Jones, in charge of the treasurer's office during the audit. To expedite matters, Budget Director D. A. N. Chase was assigned to help in the audit; Ronald Finney's confidential secretary, Leland Caldwell, had been arrested; impeachments were planned. On August 11, Landon directed Superintendent of Public Instruction W. T. Markham, Attorney General Boynton, and Auditor French to deliver all their office correspondence and to give access to all their records to the state's investigators.[9] This action was probably based on Leland Caldwell's admission of having taken bond copy to a

[8] *Topeka Capital*, August 9, 1933; *Manhattan Tribune*, August 10, 1933.

[9] *Topeka Capital*, August 10, 1933; Kansas Senate, *Trial of Roland Boynton, Attorney-general of the State of Kansas* (Topeka: State Printer, 1934), p. 97; Landon to Roland Boynton, Landon to Will J. French, Landon to W. T. Markham, all August 11, 1933, KSA.

Kansas City, Kansas, printshop on the pretext of reprinting them to correct errors in the original printing. He said that Finney had received the bond copy from friends in the capitol, that Auditor French's receipt books would verify this; and that municipal bonds also had been duplicated. The total duplications, Caldwell said, ran to almost $800,000.

Landon appointed a former state senator, Fred Harris of Ottawa, as his special counsel in the investigation. A. R. Jones asked all banks that held state bonds to check their holdings. Some relief was afforded by the knowledge that surety bonds in the treasury would help pay for losses, but there were more reports on the extent of Ronald Finney's operations.[10] They had begun in April, 1931, when he started buying, at a discount, 5 per cent bonds from hard-pressed—and ill-informed—school boards for sale to the state School Fund Board at face value and at only 4.5 per cent interest. By 1932 he had branched out. Finney arranged, without giving adequate security, the deposit of $136,000 in state funds in his father's Emporia bank; he persuaded the state treasurer to give him drafts for more than $1.4 million, payable on demand by county treasurers; he forged municipal bonds and placed them in the state treasury as security for state deposits in banks he claimed to represent; he procured canceled school-debt warrants from state offices, valued at $102,000, for his own use as legitimate exchange. There was also information that he had carried on similar operations in Colorado and Wyoming.[11]

By August 12, $926,000 of duplicate Kansas bonds had been traced. It was also discovered that four employees of the treasurer and the auditor had been guests at Ronald Finney's ranch in Colorado, and these employees were interrogated by state and federal officers. By August 14 enough evidence had come to light against Treasurer Boyd that Landon could ask Lester Goodell to institute prosecution against him for converting $150,000 of state bonds to personal use, and he asked Boyd to resign immediately. On August 26 the federal government also took action: Boyd, Caldwell, and Ronald Finney, who was out of the Shawnee County jail on bond, were arrested on federal warrants, charged with misusing the United States mail. Two days later Warren W. Finney, who had been uncovered as a large-scale embezzler through the investigation of his son, was arrested by the

[10] *Topeka Capital*, August 11, 1933.
[11] *Boynton Trial*, pp. 66 ff.; *French Trial*, pp. viii f., xiii, 27 f., 48 f., 280; *Topeka Capital*, August 11, 12, 1933.

Lyon County attorney, Clarence V. Beck. The state's Legislative Council, at Landon's suggestion, discussed whether impeachment action should be taken against French and Boynton.[12]

Landon meanwhile was speaking over the state about the scandal, trying to maintain confidence in the state government by pledging that the guilty would not escape. The Democrats entered the picture when Thurman Hill, Landon's former Independence neighbor and an obvious aspirant for the governorship, demanded that the statehouse be cleaned out. Harry Woodring, who found time in early September to visit Kansas, pledged Landon his full support in the investigation. He warned, though, that "neither I nor the people of Kansas, in my judgment, will accept oft-reiterated statements that he is going to the bottom of the mess, without fear or favor, in lieu of actually doing so." Reaction to the assistant secretary of war's statement was strong. The *Arkansas City Traveler* found it lacking in "good taste" and "a direct imputation of insincerity." The independent *Hutchinson News* chided Woodring, pointing out "that the evidence shows the irregularities were going on for a year and a half before Landon took office, and his predecessor never even heard about them." There were, however, those who agreed with the former governor, and the *Pittsburg Advertiser* praised Woodring's comment: "The whole rotten business is the Republicans' baby. . . . Repudiation of the present regime is the only action Kansas can take if it would again set itself right in the eyes of the nation."[13]

While the presses were whirring, the investigation made progress. It was revealed that Boynton had received over $1,000 in campaign contributions from Ronald Finney, and the attorney general had, at Finney's suggestion, invested $400 with Finney and received a profit of $1,700 over a period of four months. It further developed that the seal of state Auditor French had been used on all of the fraudulent bonds, which indicated that someone in his office had given Finney access to the seal.[14] By the middle of September a backwash of the case hit Landon, who at the outset of the investigation had suspended the retirement of bonds and the payment of interest on municipal bonds,

[12] *Topeka Capital*, August 13–15, 20, 27, 29, 30, 1933; Landon to Lester Goodell, Landon to T. B. Boyd, both August 14, 1933, KSA; Landon statement to the Legislative Council, August 15, 1933.

[13] *Topeka Capital*, September 2, 7, August 30, 1933; *Arkansas City Traveler*, September 11, 1933; *Hutchinson News*, September 9, 1933; *Pittsburg Advertiser*, September 14, 1933.

[14] *Arkansas City Traveler*, September 16, 1933; *Boynton Trial*, pp. xii, xxii, 798 f.

as well as closed the treasury. This inconvenienced the state's bankers, who pressed increasingly for the reopening of the treasurer's office, but Landon stood by his order that the office would not function until everything could be accounted for. The standoff between the governor and the bankers was instrumental in forcing Boyd's resignation, effective October 1; he declared that his resignation offered "no imputation of guilt" but was tendered to permit the opening of the office under the guidance of a person acceptable to Landon.

In the meantime, launching a counterattack, Boyd studied the 1932 election campaign records to find out who had contributed to Landon's campaign. On September 20 it was revealed that Warren Finney had given $500 to the Landon campaign. Finney had also worked after the election to erase the campaign deficit.[15] But circumstances arose that permitted Landon to counter public reaction to this information; the following day he announced that a plot to kidnap his daughter, Peggy, had been discovered. For three weeks, while the plot was being broken, the governor's mansion and the Landon family had been protected by public and private guards.

Landon was not yet off the spot. By the end of the month newspapers were carrying stories about a check for $10,046.67 from Ronald Finney made out to Mrs. Landon in March, 1933. This proved to be the return of the capital, with interest, that Mrs. Landon had invested in the Hill Packing Company, a legitimate Finney business interest, on the recommendation of the National Bank of Topeka. The check had been issued on the company's account as a cashier's check through the Finney bank in Emporia. Although there were those who wanted to see it as a bribe, the logic broke down, for the check had been issued and delivered before Landon had initiated the Finney investigation. The transaction was thoroughly investigated by state and federal investigators, as well as by counsel for Will French, who found no evidence to substantiate any charge of wrongdoing.[16]

While Boyd's resignation had solved one problem for Landon, it created the problem of finding a new treasurer, one of stature and ability who could command public trust. The governor offered the post

[15] *Topeka Capital*, September 16, 27, 20, 21, 1933; Warren W. Finney to Landon, December 3, 1932; Landon to Finney, December 8, 1932.

[16] *Topeka State Journal*, September 21, 1933; cashier's check from Ronald Finney to Theo Cobb Landon, March 24, 1933; *Topeka Capital*, August 2, 1934; *French Trial*, *passim*; Landon to Henry F. Draper, August 17, 1934, and Landon to James M. Rhodes, June 19, 1934, KSA.

to Dr. Ernest Pihlblad—the highly respected president of Bethany College, a man of substantial attainments as an educator, pastor, and former public servant—but Dr. Pihlblad declined the appointment because of the needs of the college. Landon was then struck with an audacious idea: one of the most distinguished Kansans of the time was then leaving a holdover position in the federal government. Landon wired William M. Jardine—former president of Kansas State College, former Secretary of Agriculture, and retiring ambassador to Egypt— asking that he take the treasury post. Jardine, happily for Landon, accepted—with the reservation that he would not be a candidate for election as treasurer in 1934. Dr. Jardine, after rushing from New York to Kansas to be sworn in, performed an excellent job in rectifying the affairs of the treasury. The office was opened by late October, and interest payments and the retirement of public securities were resumed. Jardine also began to remedy the impact of years of amateur management of the office by setting up records and management systems for its running. Viewing the administrative mess he had found, Jardine concluded that Kansas was "lucky to have any money left." [17]

Meanwhile, additional action had been taken against others connected with the scandal. Before an investigating committee of the state house of representatives, the governor's special counsel, Fred Harris, questioned the conduct of Attorney General Boynton and Auditor French with regard to Ronald Finney's operations. Harris charged that Boynton had ignored questions (raised before November, 1932) about Finney's conduct—and that French's office had permitted unauthorized use of the auditor's seal, had allowed eight vital transcripts to be "lost," and had perhaps destroyed letters of inquiry about fraudulent warrants. On November 2 the committee recommended the impeachments of Boynton and French, and later in the month the two officials were impeached by the house, virtually without opposition. [18] In October, the trial of Warren Finney had commenced in Emporia, and Hugo T. Wedell was appointed an assistant attorney general by Landon to help in the prosecution. On November 9 the elder Finney was found guilty on twelve counts of embezzlement and was sentenced to a minimum of thirty-six years in prison.

In December, Wedell joined Goodell, the Shawnee County attorney, in prosecuting Ronald Finney. The younger Finney later pleaded

[17] *Topeka Capital*, September 29, 30, October 2, 27, 28, 1933, January 28, 1934.

[18] *Topeka State Journal*, October 2, 1933; *Boynton Trial*, pp. v ff.; *French Trial*, pp. v ff.

guilty, hoping to make a deal with the state on his sentence. A deal was made, but it fell through, and Finney received a minimum prison sentence of thirty-one years. During World War II, Ronald Finney's sentence was reduced by Governor Andrew Schoeppel, and he was later released after having served eleven years in the state penitentiary.[19]

On January 8, 1934, Attorney General Boynton's impeachment trial before the state senate—the sixth in Kansas history—began. Boynton's famous cousin, William Allen White, had been working in his behalf, writing that the attorney general was no more guilty of misdeeds than was Landon, and that Landon was guilty of nothing. The fact that trial counsel found no evidence of illegal action by Boynton and that Boynton cooperated fully in the investigation of the scandal led to his acquittal after fourteen days of hearing. Neither the votes for or against him were on partisan lines. On January 27, two days after the conclusion of Boynton's trial, Tom Boyd was convicted in a criminal court for illegally removing state bonds from the treasury; he was sentenced to four to ten years in the penitentiary, of which he served six. Auditor French's impeachment trial began on January 25. Based on its experience during Boynton's trial, the senate saw fit to dismiss three of the four charges against French on February 2, and four days later it acquitted him on the remaining charge.

The votes again were not on partisan lines and it appeared that all were satisfied with the results, especially with the detailed accounting to the public of the various ramifications of the Finney scandal.[20] Boynton's credulity and naïveté were astounding but not incriminating. Likewise, French's lack of control over his office was blameworthy but not implicating. Although the two officials were acquitted, their public

---

[19] *Emporia Gazette*, October 25, November 10, December 2, 1933; *Topeka Capital*, December 2, 24, 31, 1933, January 3, 4, 1934; *Lawrence Journal-World*, October 12, 1961. It was later rumored that Landon sought heavy sentences for the Finneys— their maximum sentences ran to 600 years—to push himself for reelection and as a presidential candidate. Although it was clear that the governor was interested in reelection—few governors are not—he was also under heavy pressure from Republicans and Democrats to crack down on the Finneys. Moreover, he was outraged at the scandal and felt obliged to clear himself and his party in the matter. As for the Presidency, it was absurd to think of him as a candidate for nomination in 1933.

[20] W. A. White to Rodney Edward, November 9, 1933, William Allen White Papers, Manuscript Division, Library of Congress, Washington, D.C.; *Boynton Trial*, *passim* and pp. 908 f.; *Topeka State Journal*, January 28, February 17, 1934; *Topeka Capital-Journal*, December 17, 1961; *French Trial*, pp. 359 ff., 496. The emotional involvement of the White family with the principals in the Finney scandal is revealed in William L. White's novel, *What People Said* (New York: Viking, 1938).

careers were ruined. Boynton heeded the advice of his friends and never again ran for office; French ran for reelection in 1934, but was soundly defeated by a Democrat.

On February 15, Leland Caldwell was convicted of forgery on forty counts and received a minimum sentence of forty years in the state penitentiary. Warren W. Finney fought to overturn his own conviction as long as possible, but when, by June, 1935, all legal resorts had been exhausted, he committed suicide rather than surrender to the marshal who was to have taken him to prison.

The total loss to the state was $708,166, but the state was able to recover most of this loss by action against the Finney banks and by returns from surety bonds held by the treasury. Over $500,000 was claimed to have been lost by individuals, businesses, and local governments who had placed their trust in the Finneys.[21]

The high drama and the low implications of the Finney scandal constituted only an unpleasant diversion from Landon's chief concerns and duties. Indeed the demands of the time made it impossible for the governor and a regular session of the legislature to meet the problems confronting the state. Less than six weeks had elapsed after the adjournment of the legislature—in March, 1933—when demands for a special session were heard. They first came from those who wanted Kansas quickly recorded on the Twenty-first Amendment, which provided for the repeal of prohibition. Landon indicated that he would not call a special session for this purpose unless a majority of the legislators wanted it—and would vote to pay their own expenses.[22]

In June, a new issue arose to revive talk of a special session. The Glass-Steagall bank bill, which was then before Congress, was seen by Landon, Senator Arthur Capper, and Bank Commissioner H. W. Koeneke as potentially injurious to Kansas banking. Its provisions for insured deposits and minimum capitalization could ruin the state's many small banks, which were essential to banking and credit operations in the sparsely settled rural areas of Kansas. The passage of the Glass-Steagall measure, which would take effect January 1, 1934, spurred the state government to study the act's ramifications for Kansas banking. It appeared certain that a special session of the legislature

[21] *Topeka Capital*, February 16, March 4, 17, 1934, June 7, 1935; Summary of Spurious Bond Transactions, July 19, 1932, to August 8, 1933, dated August 27, 1934, KSA.

[22] *Topeka State Journal*, May 6, 1933.

would have to be called to establish a state system for those banks—about 200 in number—that would be unable to meet the minimum federal capitalization requirement of $25,000.[23]

Additional pressure for a special session came on July 13, when the Kansas supreme court held that the state laws prohibiting intoxicants had not established air-tight rules for defining beer as an intoxicating beverage. This decision left it to local courts to determine whether beer was intoxicating. The police, prosecutors, and judges were thrown into confusion by the ruling, and the result was the open selling of 3.2 per cent beer in the state's larger cities. The *Atchison Globe* cried that "the Kansas legislature must do something," but it quoted with approval a *Pittsburg Sun* editorial stating that Governor Landon was correct in not allowing himself to be stampeded into calling for an immediate special session: Landon should continue with his plan "to have the legislation that is necessary on the Roosevelt relief program and the beer legislation attended to at one session."[24] Kansas' sentiments were still "dry," but her principles were those of economy.

Toward the end of July, the NRA administrator, Hugh Johnson, requested that the states take action within sixty days to provide for complete cooperation with the national recovery program, and Governor Landon announced that he would call a special session for September to comply with Johnson's request. The bond scandal, and, later in August, the announcement that new federal relief requirements would be issued sometime in September made it necessary for Landon to defer setting a date for the special session. In the meantime he gave the Legislative Council plenty of grist to use in planning the session, including suggestions that it consider a short ballot, a referendum on the repeal of prohibition, the definition of intoxicants, ratification of the federal child-labor amendment, and the raising of $4.5 million for work relief.[25]

Landon, in early September, sent a statement to the convention of the American Bankers Association in Chicago. He told the bankers of

[23] *Ibid.*, June 14, 27, July 7, 1933; Landon press release, n.d. (probably June 26, 1933). Although the federal deposit-insurance plan was designed to protect small banks, even President Roosevelt and Senator Glass were skeptical that it would work. William E. Leuchtenburg, *Franklin D. Roosevelt and the New Deal, 1932–1940* (New York: Harper & Row, 1963), p. 60.

[24] *Topeka Capital*, July 14, 15, 21, 1933; *Atchison Globe*, July 19, 1933.

[25] *Topeka State Journal*, July 28, 1933; Landon to Frank Sponable, August 24, 1933, KSA; Landon statement to the Legislative Council, n.d. (probably August 15, 1933); *Kansas City Journal-Post*, August 16, 1933.

his lack of confidence in the Glass-Steagall Act's deposit-insurance
concept because it had been tried in eight states, including Kansas,
and had failed in all of them because of excessive costs of operation.
He also told of his fear that the act might be the first step in the
development of a nationally unified and politically controlled banking
system. If the bankers were to avoid this, they had to establish a banking system, probably a nonpolitical state or national system, "that
makes the earnings and savings of the people safe." Such a system would
have to be free from domination by a financial clique. As an example
of what was needed, Landon outlined his proposal for a new Kansas
state banking system, a system that would be controlled by a board,
with a majority of bankers as members, all appointed by the governor
from a list submitted by the board. The board would designate permissible out-of-state correspondents and bonds acceptable for purchase
by banks, supervise bank personnel and policies, determine capitalization, conduct the auditing and evaluation of assets, and remove
negligent bank officers or directors. He hoped this proposal would

> jar the bankers of my state enough that they will at least make some
> intelligent suggestion about legislation. For make no mistake, the public is
> not going to be satisfied with conditions as they are and have been. The
> banker who is satisfied with the system as is will find that if he does not help
> make a constructive and sound program, one will be written for him.[26]

In response to Landon's address, Kansas bankers organized the
Allied Independent Banks of Kansas and voted to back his efforts to
remove politics from banking. Landon was pleased with this and with
other gestures of support by the state's bankers. Yet six weeks later, on
October 14, when Landon formally revealed his bank plan, he found
that the bankers' lobby—perhaps piqued by the closing of the state
treasury during the Finney scandal—did not intend to support him.
The Kansas Banking Association stated that the records of every bank
board would have to be secret, even from the governor; that branch
banks would have to be forbidden; and that the board would have to
be supported by state funds.[27]

Yet Landon had not only the bankers to cope with but also that
bane of Kansas politicians, the liquor question. Considerable public
sentiment existed, if not for repeal, at least for a chance to vote on the
question. The governor personally did not care a great deal one way

[26] Landon statement, Chicago, September 2, 1933.
[27] *Topeka Capital*, September 3, October 15, 19, 1933.

or the other; although he was not a teetotaler (though he scrupulously obeyed the law as governor when in Kansas), he knew the evils of overindulgence and he was not opposed to state prohibition. More important, though, was that the people be permitted to vote on repeal if they wished to, and he went before the Women's Christian Temperance Union convention at Newton in late September to make his position clear. He praised the women for their courage and conviction. He did not mind being labeled a W.C.T.U. friend, but he reminded them that repeal of national prohibition was an accomplished fact. While he inveighed against the "saloon interests," he pointed out that there were "honest wets" who wanted repeal with guards against the excessive use of intoxicants. He implored the ladies to work for their convictions by appealing to the voters rather than by legislative maneuvering. "Majority has a right to rule if we are to maintain a representative government. So, therefore, I will not oppose the submission of the state prohibition amendment to the people of Kansas in the firm belief that it will be reaffirmed and not repealed." Even if he had equivocated, he had made his point clear: majority rule was more important than the prohibition of "demon liquor." [28]

Although the banking and the beer and liquor questions were important, Landon emphasized to legislators, in briefing them on the special session, that the greatest problem was how to provide unemployment relief. It was also the greatest problem he faced in finding legislative support. In fact, he encountered so much resistance on the relief issue that he postponed the session to October 30 so that he might seek support for an adequate relief program from the county commissioners and the Legislative Council, which were meeting in Topeka the last week of October. Although both groups failed to support him,[29] he nevertheless determined to push the relief question before the legislature.

October 30 came, and the legislature spent the day organizing itself for action. The next day, like an unwelcome Halloween spirit, Landon entered the house chamber to deliver his message to the assembled legislators. Economy was still the watchword, he said, but there were problems that required immediate action, and his first concern was unemployment relief. The $7 million needed for relief through June 30, 1934, could be raised from federal and state sources if county

---

[28] Landon speech, Newton, September 28, 1933.

[29] Landon to R. C. Russell, September 27, 1933, KSA; *Topeka Capital*, October 8, 25–27, 1933; Landon press release, October 19, 1933.

commissioners were required to budget sufficient funds to fulfill federal requirements. He asked that counties be allowed to issue bonds to meet emergency relief demands, and that they be authorized to issue $2.2 million in bonds—the latter to be amortized from the state highway funds allotted to the counties. Money raised in this way, along with the matching federal relief funds, would be used to build streets and roads, and thereby road construction would not suffer; no new tax burden would be created, and federal relief money would not be lost to those in need. "The state," he declared, "has a responsibility to discharge to those unfortunately situated through no fault of their own. Women and children must not suffer."

The governor then called for establishment of his bank board plan, which had been recommended by the Legislative Council. As for the bond scandal, he charged that it spotlighted the need for greater centralization of authority in the state government. It was impossible to fix responsibility for the operation of the administrative branch when six popularly elected constitutional state officials operated independently. He suggested election of only the governor, lieutenant governor, and auditor, so that a cabinet system of state administration could be developed. Landon also called for clarification of the statutes dealing with the alcoholic content of malt beverages, and he asked that Kansas join the fifteen states that had ratified the federal child-labor amendment—now more important than ever, because capable adult workers lacked employment. He also suggested that the legislature make any revisions in state laws that were needed to coordinate them with federal recovery legislation.[30]

The legislature, reluctant to deal with the issues raised in his message, moved slowly. The house ratified the federal child-labor amendment, but the senate voted it down. The legislators, however, renewed the life of the Legislative Council to "let it try to make good."

The governor bided his time, hoping that the legislature would eventually take affirmative action. He had little choice because dictation on his part would probably have been resented, and he had no clubs or lures to back up dictation.[31] After three weeks, Landon tried to pump life into the legislature by raising another issue: utility regulation. Kansas for years had wrestled with the problems of determining utility rates.

[30] *Message of Governor Alf M. Landon to the Special Session of the Legislature, 1933* (Topeka: State Printer, 1933).
[31] *Topeka Capital*, November 9, 12, 1933.

The rate question became aggravated when, during the depression, utility company costs and consumer income dropped without corresponding rate reductions. Laws providing for federal regulation of rates, requested by Senator Capper and others, had not been enacted, and the state's efforts were therefore spurred. Governor Woodring had received an appropriation of $100,000 to enable the Public Service Commission to investigate Cities Service gas rates and to cover the court costs in pursuing a revision of rates. A three-judge federal court had restrained the commission from reducing natural gas rates, but the decision had been appealed to the United States Supreme Court, which had indicated that it would overrule the lower court. State funds for the litigation, however, had been exhausted by the fall of 1933.

Landon went before the legislature on November 21 to review this information. He said that the state had spent so much money it would be foolhardy to drop the proceedings. Moreover, much of the power of the Corporation Commission—the P.S.C.'s successor—would be rendered useless if the state could not meet the legal challenges of public utilities and common carriers. As the legislature had not seen fit to assess carriers and utilities to support the rate determination work of the commission, it must appropriate funds to carry on the commission's work. He requested $50,000 for this purpose.[32]

Although this message served to put the legislature on the spot on an issue of great public interest, it did not soften its attitude toward Landon's program for the special session. The senate, two days later, responding to pressure from the state's bankers, ripped the governor's bank board bill to shreds, but Landon's patient and nonpartisan approach worked fairly well on other proposals. The legislature gave substantial aid to the financing of relief and public construction programs. The counties were authorized to use more than $1 million of their state highway funds for work programs, and were empowered to float $2 million in bonds for poor relief; and municipalities were permitted to issue bonds to help finance Public Works Administration projects. All political subdivisions were allowed to issue bonds to pay for materials required to meet Civil Works Administration needs, and the Highway Department was permitted to contract for a maximum $14-million federal loan.

The legislators also authorized the construction of buildings for the

[32] *Ibid.*, November 22, 1933; Landon message "To the Senate and House of Representatives, November 21, 1933" (mimeograph).

Deaf School at Olathe and the 4-H Fair at Hutchinson, to be financed by federal loans and state appropriations. Although Landon's state bank board had been killed, permission was given to establish a separate state system of nonguaranteed banks, and the federal deposit-insurance plan for larger banks was accepted. The short-ballot proposal was unsuccessful. A referendum on state prohibition was approved, but the legislators failed to define intoxicants; and money was appropriated to help the Corporation Commission pursue reductions in utility rates.

By and large, the legislation would permit the state and its people to take advantage of New Deal programs. The governor was unstinting in his praise of the legislature; he knew that the special session, when compared to legislative sessions in past years, was a success.[33] But the legislature's biennial chores were not done. By January, 1934, a new crisis developed that required legislative action.

Farm debt was still so heavy that it appeared a disastrous wave of foreclosure actions would take place after the expiration of the state's moratorium law on March 4. Landon called a conference of farmers and representatives of insurance and mortgage companies to discuss the problem and to gather support for further mortgage-moratorium legislation. He also polled the members of the house and senate on calling another special session, writing them that the emergency on foreclosures still existed—and that it was aggravated by the unlikelihood that Kansas' statutes, even if reenacted, would be upheld by the United States Supreme Court. The legislature should consider passage of an act patterned after the Minnesota mortgage-moratorium law, which had been found constitutional. Landon pointed out that the provisions of the Minnesota measure would not only meet the distress of threatened homesteads but would also eliminate abuses of Kansas' statute. The Minnesota law provided for court determination of each application for moratorium on its merits, and for extension over a period of time only if a reasonable sum could be paid the mortgagee for application against taxes, insurance, interest, and perhaps principal. In effect, this assisted the responsible mortgagor, and gave minimal protection to the mortgagee. Landon also asked that the legislators not introduce their own pet proposals if the session was called.[34]

The great majority of legislators replied that they favored the special session, and Landon called it for March 1, hoping that the short time

---

[33] *Topeka Capital*, November 24, 30, 1933.

[34] *Ibid.*, January 14, February 6, 1934; Landon to Members of the Kansas Legislature, February 9, 1934.

before the expiration of the moratorium law would force the legislature to waste no time in acting. He also sought to stimulate support for effective legislation in pre-session statements, pointing out that the rise in land values the previous year had seen "sharpies" increase pressures to foreclose. Between 7,000 and 10,000 families were in danger of losing their homes unless something was done immediately.[35]

The governor went before the legislature on March 1 and asked for the enactment of a moratorium law, effective for one year, modeled after the Minnesota statute. In view of the large number of foreclosure actions waiting upon the expiration of the current law, he urged that the new statute be passed before March 4: "This is an emergency matter and will require the careful and painstaking efforts of all." The house passed the recommended legislation that day, 80 to 4. On March 2 the senate passed it with minor changes, 35 to 5, and Landon signed it. The two houses also stayed in session long enough to take action to comply with Public Works Administration requirements for the granting of $22 million in federal loans.[36]

Although 1934 saw only one legislative crisis, emergency continued to be the normal state of affairs for Landon; however, the worst problems in finances were soon solved. In 1933 state officials had to juggle funds in order to balance the budget, and as late as January, 1934, many observers thought that the legislature might have to relieve the situation by the imposition of a sales tax. Only half of the taxes due in December, 1933, were in; and the governor could only urge further economy. Tax collections soon rose to normal, though, and by February little need was seen for a sales tax.

The Landon administration, faced with serious financial problems since its inauguration, had urged and had received a subsistence budget, believing that its economies would permit it to live on its skimpy means. Unhappily, the administration saw the cost of commodities rise with the national inflation of the first year of the New Deal. The state's tax collections faltered in several instances, its new income tax yielded only half of what had been expected, new burdens were thrown upon it, and its institutional population took an upward swing; but in 1934 tax collections rose to normal. Thanks to improvements in

[35] "Mortgage Session Letter" file, February, 1934; Landon to John Frost, February 24, 1934; *Topeka Capital*, February 27, March 1, 1934.

[36] *Message of Governor Alf M. Landon to the Special Session of the Kansas Legislature, March 1, 1934* (Topeka: State Printer, 1934); *Topeka Capital*, March 2, 3, 1934.

the state's economy and to stringent enforcement of the collection of gasoline and cigarette taxes, revenues increased substantially.[37]

By summer the administration was pleased with its economy program. The laws limiting local spending and budgeting practices had not only made for greater public honesty but had saved the taxpayers considerable amounts of money. Although local officials deserved a great deal of credit for operating successfully within the new laws and for effecting economies of their own, the state could share the credit with them because of its reduction of assessed property taxes in 1933—by more than 10 per cent, almost $7.5 million—as compared with 1932. As for the money spent from appropriations, another real saving was made: the expenditures of the state offices—except those of the Highway Department—were about $2.5 million under the appropriated amounts.[38]

One may wonder, of course, about the effect of all this. Several hundred public servants were discharged, swelling the army of the jobless; the salaries of those who remained were reduced and workloads often were increased. Supplies were perhaps short. Maybe it was true, as one rumor went, that toilet paper and hand towels were often absent from rest rooms in public buildings, but employee efficiency went up; pay cuts, which ranged from 5 to 25 per cent, generally were not out of line with the drops in commodity prices since 1929; and greater efficiency was achieved in the use of supplies. In short, public needs were being handled just as well as before because they were being handled more efficiently.

As had been predicted, the United States Supreme Court, in January, 1934, held that it would not permit a gas company—Cities Service in this case—to secure a federal court injunction against a Kansas Corporation Commission rate-change order, which meant that the struggle against the utilities could be started again—with a better chance of success. Commissioner Homer Hoch ordered new hearings; and the Supreme Court decision and the determination of Landon and Hoch to continue the fight soon brought results. Electric power

[37] "Charitable, Penal and Patriotic Institutions, Operating Expenses," April 9, 1934, KSA; *Topeka Capital*, January 14, February 6, 27, April 15, July 17, March 22, 1934.

[38] "Governor Landon's Administration—Good Government at Lower Costs, January, 1933, to May 1, 1934" (mimeograph), p. 3; Memorandum from Carl A. Rott, n.d. (probably August, 1934), KSA.

companies decided to reduce their rates; then, in April, Hoch announced that Cities Service had "voluntarily" reduced its rates in sixteen of the state's largest cities.[39] Landon sought to force the telephone and natural gas pipeline companies to comply by suggesting that the state was considering setting up publicly operated pipeline and telephone systems; and the companies, deciding not to call his bluff, made satisfactory rate adjustments. But the administration was not content with these successes: railroads were thwarted by the Corporation Commission in 1933 and 1935 when they attempted to secure freight-rate increases, and in 1936 the Cities Service gas case was finally settled, with rates being reduced by about 20 per cent.[40]

Petroleum had not been a major problem for Landon since the NRA Oil Code went into effect in July, 1933. In September, 1934, however, the United States district court in Oklahoma City invalidated part of the code. Prices soon edged lower, and there were indications that some of the oil companies were planning to take advantage of the situation by collapsing the market's price structure. Landon wired Roosevelt and asked that steps be immediately taken to protect the industry from such a debacle. Although market prices temporarily dipped in the Mid-Continent field, vigorous enforcement of the remaining provisions of the Oil Code, and actions and threats by the states, helped to force prices up.[41]

Landon used a daring threat to help stop the lowering of crude oil prices. The major oil companies had invested heavily in tanks to store the oil they had purchased at low prices. Landon knew that if the major companies lost these facilities, they would lose their investments in them and in the cheap oil they contained. In October he told James Veasey, the general counsel of Carter Oil Company, and John Wilson, a Standard of Indiana official, that if prices were cut further "the Kansas Corporation Commission will prohibit the storage of oil in tank farms on the grounds of physical waste, leakage, evaporation and so forth." Veasey replied that this would stop the price cuts.

[39] Landon to William E. Hannan, December 26, 1934, KSA; *Topeka Capital*, January 9, April 25, 1934.

[40] Arthur M. Schlesinger, Jr., *The Politics of Upheaval* (Boston: Houghton Mifflin, 1960), p. 624; *Topeka Capital*, June 14, April 24, 1936; Memorandum Concerning the Work of the State Corporation Commission, December 17, 1935, KSA.

[41] *Topeka Capital*, September 23, October 24, 1934; Landon to Franklin D. Roosevelt, October 23, 1934; Harold L. Ickes, *The Secret Diary of Harold L. Ickes: The First Thousand Days* (New York: Simon & Schuster, 1953–54), pp. 217 f.

Landon, who had called Governor Murray of Oklahoma and persuaded him to make the same threat to the major companies, then called Edward B. Reeser, the president of the Mid-Continent Refineries Association, to tell him to pass on another warning. If price cuts came, the first company to cut would run into an all-out retail boycott in Kansas, like the one that had hit Standard Oil of Indiana in 1931. "You can't call ten or twelve fellows sons of bitches; there can only be one"—and that one would catch it. Landon also warned that if all the major companies cut prices at the same time, his attorney general would investigate the situation. The threats worked, and crude oil prices held in Kansas.[42]

Landon was not as successful in handling the penal system. Another group escape from the penitentiary at Lansing took place on January 19, 1934; in a comedy of confusion, seven convicts made their way to freedom. Several guards froze at the sight of danger and others shot scores of bullets at the escapees without hitting one of them—or, fortunately, any of the other guards. The official investigation of the break held that the warden, the officers, and the guards were negligent in maintaining security, had little or no training in their jobs or in handling firearms, and had no clear operating procedure or lines of responsibility and discipline. The newspapers of the state, even the mild *Topeka Capital*, called for a reorganization, and Landon was criticized for his appointment of Lacey Simpson as warden—who was not performing his principal duties at Lansing. Simpson, it was conceded, was a good businessman, but business was not a warden's first concern.

Action was soon taken to correct the situation. Many prison personnel were demoted or discharged, and plans were effected to increase security. In the matter of reorganization, Landon and the Board of Administration called upon one of the nation's best authorities, Sanford Bates, to make recommendations. Following Bates' advice, the board established civil service regulations to govern the guards, set up a training system and forbade the guards to fraternize with the inmates, and appointed E. M. Stubblefield—of the state prison at Joliet, Illinois—as deputy warden to establish discipline at the penitentiary. Simpson remained as warden, but he was responsible mainly for business affairs. As for the escapees, some surrendered voluntarily (one

42 Landon to Russell B. Brown, September 9, 1949.

complained that it was tougher "outside" than in prison), and the others were not captured until late July—when Kansas highway patrol officers conducted raids in Missouri and Oklahoma to arrest them.[43]

During 1934, relief matters continued to be of almost overwhelming importance to Landon. Kansas had handled work relief efficiently, under the supervision of the bipartisan Kansas Emergency Relief Committee, and the state was to receive the maximum amount of federal money available under the Civil Works Administration program. During November, 1933, Kansas had made the transition from the Federal Emergency Relief Administration to the CWA smoothly, with 32,000 persons on the payroll by the end of the first week of the new program. Missouri reported only 4,310 and Colorado only 91 on the rolls that same week. Kansas was also proud of its record in using money from the Public Works Administration's highway fund: it was the first state to contract for all work possible, with 99 per cent of its contracts let by January 1, 1934. By April 14, Kansas had an additional 6,762 men at work on the roads, ranking only behind Texas in the number of men employed. Landon credited the bipartisan nature of the Highway Commission for this achievement.[44]

Despite the rosy official record, crisis seemed always to threaten. CWA funds were available only to February 15, and governors pressed the President to extend the program. In response to a telegram from Governor Miriam Ferguson of Texas, Landon wrote Roosevelt in January, urging the continuance of the CWA as "one of the soundest, most constructive policies of your administration." Landon also praised the CCC; and he asked Roosevelt to consider recommending a program to assist needy college students, pointing out that many college students —50 per cent in Kansas' denominational colleges—were wholly or partially self-supporting. "These students do not desire a subsidy, but an opportunity to work for a few hours a day in order to continue their education."[45] President Roosevelt replied that the CWA would be continued a while longer and would aid needy students (they did not receive substantial assistance until the coming of the National Youth Administration in 1935); and he hoped that, upon the CWA's termina-

---

[43] State Board of Administration and Parole Attorney to Landon, January 25, 1934, KSA; *Topeka Capital*, January 30, 1934; Ben Franklin to Landon, February 16, 1934, KSA; *Topeka Capital*, February 15, August 1, 1934.

[44] "Governor Landon's Administration," pp. 4 ff.

[45] Miriam A. Ferguson to Landon, January 15, 1934, KSA; Landon to Franklin D. Roosevelt, January 16, 1934.

tion, the Public Works Administration and an upturn in private employment would absorb the jobless.[46]

The President was wrong in his thinking about unemployment: with the gradual demobilization of the CWA beginning in the latter part of February, a crisis arose in Kansas. Some 17,000 persons were thrown off the payrolls during the last half of the month, and the state worked to place them in public works and on local relief. By April, the local agencies were unable to accommodate all of the unemployed, and on April 2 there was a march of the unemployed on the state capitol. This orderly demonstration was met by Landon, who talked to the group and to individuals in it. The governor tried to use the occasion to bring pressure on local communities to relieve the plight of the unemployed. Pointing out that local communities had not exhausted their permissible borrowing opportunities, Landon urged the localities to take maximum advantage of federal loans. The situation seemed even darker a few days later, when John Stutz of the K.E.R.C. reported that 4,000 state relief recipients would be dropped from the list early in the summer because of lack of funds. By the end of the week, Landon and Stutz were touring the state, checking the unemployment situation, especially in the drought-stricken communities of southwest Kansas.[47]

From Wichita, later in April, there was a report that supporters of Thurman Hill's candidacy for governor were spreading rumors that large amounts of relief money were being withheld by the state. Mass demonstrations were held to demand release of this money. A Sedgwick County commissioner, George E. Rogers, declared this was a maneuver by Hill to gain political advantage at the expense of the unemployed. In actuality, relief funds had been held up for Wichita because the city had not fully complied with state laws and FERA regulations, or given adequate police protection to relief administrators; as soon as these things were done, relief funds would be restored.[48]

Demonstrations were held not only in Wichita but also in Pittsburg and Coffeyville, where relief funds failed to meet the needs. The worst incident came on May 10, when riots broke out in Wichita, causing the destruction of property and injury to policemen. Mayor Schuyler Crawford and City Manager Bert Wells requested that Landon send troops to preserve order, and the police informed Adjutant General

[46] Franklin D. Roosevelt to Landon, February 10, 1934.

[47] *Topeka Capital*, February 27, April 3, 5, 8, 1934.

[48] George E. Rogers to Landon, April 24, 27, 1934, John Stutz to Rogers, n.d. (probably late April, 1934), KSA.

M. R. McLean that the situation was out of control. Landon sent the troops, as he was required by law to do; seventy arrests were made and thirty persons were jailed after the mob, estimated at a thousand, had been checked. John Stutz went to Wichita to investigate, and Harry Hopkins warned that all federal relief would be cut off if the troops were not withdrawn by May 12. McLean worked successfully to get Mayor Crawford to release the troops, and Stutz got the city to comply with relief regulations.[49]

Landon increased his efforts to secure additional federal assistance. On May 12 he announced that Kansas would seek $22 million in federal loans and grants for highway relief, which was twice Kansas' share of these funds. "We will take all the money we can get in order to furnish employment to as many men as possible next fall and winter." He was dismayed to discover that President Roosevelt had requested only a quarter as much federal money for highway relief work in the following fiscal year as had been appropriated in 1933. Great pressure was exerted on Washington, by Republicans and Democrats, to see that adequate relief funds were made available, and, although the entreaties of the states led to Congress' appropriating far more than the President had requested, the amount was still less than had been granted the previous year. Kansas was allotted, as its share of the highway work-relief fund, only some $5 million.[50]

Despite this setback, Kansas had been relatively successful in procuring federal relief assistance—but its record of providing relief from state funds was poor; it relied primarily upon its traditional system of local responsibility. The state contributed very little to relief, ranking thirty-ninth among the states in per capita relief grants from May 23, 1933, to July 31, 1934—with $4.60.[51]

Under Landon, however, Kansas aimed at securing job relief, agricultural relief, and conservation—all in one program. Looking toward the 1935 session of the legislature, and probably to the up-coming campaign for reelection, Landon in January, 1934, recommended that plans be drawn up for a comprehensive water-storage program.[52] This was vital for the state's economy: when water was short, Kansas suffered; when water was plentiful, the state prospered—

[49] Memorandum from General McLean, May 11, 1934, and Landon to John W. Bricker, May 15, 1935, KSA.

[50] George McGill to Landon, June 6, 1934, and Landon to McGill, June 7, 1934, KSA; *Topeka Capital*, May 13, 16, 19, August 20, 1934.

[51] "The [relief] disbursements by states," n.d. (1934), KSA.

[52] Landon to the State Planning Board, January 22, 1934, KSA.

but when water was plentiful Kansas also was ravaged by floods. The problem was to stop the floods and to capture rainwater before it reached the rivers. This was a challenge, Landon reasoned, that would command attention not only in the state but that would attract the fancy of the money-givers in Washington.

Landon, of course, was not alone in his concern for water; the National Resources Board in Washington was interested, and Landon and his planners were in touch with the board. Water legislation was also of interest to Congress, which had already established the Tennessee Valley Authority. Landon wrote Roosevelt in June, 1934, to acquaint him with Kansas' water problems and to urge a "complete [Kansas] program of water conservation and flood control," as part of a regional watershed and a national plan of water conservation that would be developed by the states and the federal government. Landon requested immediate action by the President or Congress.[53]

This proposal, although largely Landon's way of trying to pry more relief money from the federal government, was also recommended in the hope that the government—at the urging of a President who welcomed pressure for conservation measures—might decide to deal in a dramatic way with the critical problems of water conservation that faced the plains states. Roosevelt's response was prompt: "This whole matter is having the most careful consideration, and I am sending your letter on to those who are studying it for me." Soon, an FERA representative, J. F. Stone, was sent from Washington.

To take advantage of Stone's presence, Landon held a conference on water problems at which a detailed water conservation plan for Kansas was presented. Proposals included the development of farm ponds to nourish gardens and trees in arid areas; 50,000 large farm ponds—of 5 to 30 acres—created by dams to store water for stock, to raise the groundwater levels, and to contribute to flood control; 200 lakes—of 100 to 400 acres—for storage, stream-flow regulation, fish culture, and recreation; 20 lakes, on the state's larger streams, to hold from 100,000 to 1 million acre-feet of water for storage and flood-control purposes; and 100 storage and flood-control dams on smaller streams. The total costs to the government for these projects, except for the garden ponds, would be about $70 million for labor and $87 million for other expenses. Kansas felt it was organized to implement such a program expeditiously if the funds could be raised.[54]

[53] Landon to Franklin D. Roosevelt, June 2, 1934.
[54] Franklin D. Roosevelt to Landon, June 6, 1934; Memorandum of June 16, 1934, on water storage conference, KSA.

After hearing of the plan from Stone and Senator Capper, and commenting "but that is a lot of money," Harry Hopkins acted quickly. On June 27 it was announced that Kansas would receive about $500,000 a month in relief money for the construction of lakes and ponds.[55] The more expensive aspects of the Kansas plan had been shelved, but at least a substantial water conservation program could be started. Through Landon's bold move, Kansas received not only badly needed relief money but the promise of real melioration of its perennial water problems.

Because the water conservation program was the link between unemployment relief and the state's most pressing problem, farm relief, much of the money spent on the program found its way into the farmers' hands; and the new ponds and lakes helped to keep much of the sparse rainfall from fleeing the plains. Other federal programs also helped. By January, 1934, Kansas had received $8 million under the wheat- and hog-loan programs, and $630,000 in drought relief. Moreover, other relief money—amounting to some $19.5 million—had contributed to offset the continued low prices for farm products. The Kansas Farm Debt Adjustment Committee also achieved great success in paring the farm debts of distressed farmers.[56]

But the drought continued. Winter wheat suffered almost as badly as in 1933. Landon, in late May, sought permission from Secretary of Agriculture Henry Wallace for farmers to grow what crops they could on their best acreage and yet qualify for federal crop-reduction loans. Senator Capper, at Landon's request, took the matter up in Washington; he reported that Wallace was out of the capital but that he had conferred with Agricultural Adjustment Administrator Chester Davis, who was agreeable to the idea. On May 31, Capper telegraphed that Davis had authorized drought-area farmers to raise and cut for hay any forage crop, except corn and grain sorghums, on contracted acreage; Davis also removed crop restrictions on non-contract acres. This probably prevented the state's worst year of hay production from becoming catastrophic.[57]

[55] *Topeka Capital*, June 27, 28, 1934.

[56] *Topeka Capital*, January 21, April 22, 1934.

[57] Landon to Henry A. Wallace, May 25, 1934, and Arthur Capper to Landon, May 26, 31, 1934, KSA; Kansas State Board of Agriculture, *Kansas Agriculture—Centennial Report* (Topeka: State Printer, 1961–62), pp. 525 ff.

The impact of the drought was nonetheless frightening. Corn yielded 13 million bushels, compared with an annual average of 124 million during the 1920s; oats yielded 20 million bushels, compared with 30 million; winter wheat yielded 84 million bushels, compared with 131 million. Grain sorghums were down to 500,000 bushels, compared with 12 million; barley 1 million, compared with 8 million; hays were less than 2 million tons, compared with more than 5 million tons.[58] Livestock prices were down drastically because farmers and ranchers were forced to sell their animals for lack of feed. In Smith Center, pigs were going at 1 cent a pound and calves as low as $1.00 a head.

The plight of people in the drought area that summer was revealed in a letter from a bank official in Plains, Kansas. Pasture was so short that most of the cattle had to be shipped out, and feed was so expensive that families would soon find it impossible to keep even one cow apiece for their own butter and milk. After three local crop failures, clothing was becoming a problem. It was difficult to see how people would find enough to live on during the winter. People were willing to work, but relief jobs paid only $2.40 a week for single men and $4.80 for married men, and there were not enough of those jobs to go around.[59]

In early June, Landon stepped up his drought-relief activities, working in close cooperation with Dean Harry Umberger of Kansas State College, who had just been named Federal Drought Relief Administrator for Kansas. With Joseph H. Mercer, secretary of the Kansas Livestock Association, Landon once again pressed successfully for lower freight rates in the drought areas, and he recommended that the federal government work for a 50 per cent reduction in freight rates for all cattle and feed shipments. Oilmen were asked to help in the crisis by making their pumps and spare pipe available for the movement of water to the farms, and $950,000 was secured from FERA for drought relief. Landon also asked Secretary Wallace and the War Department that pasturage at Fort Riley be opened to grazing for 10,000 breeding cattle. The answer, dictated by military officers, was "No."[60]

The federal cattle-buying program was put into high gear through

[58] Board of Agriculture, *Centennial Report*, pp. 516 ff.
[59] F. E. Lull to Landon, KSA; William P. Elliott to Arthur Capper, August 23, 1934, Arthur Capper Papers, Kansas State Historical Society, Topeka.
[60] *Topeka Capital*, June 9, 10, 1934; Harry Hopkins to Landon, June 28, 1934; Landon to Henry A. Wallace, July 21, 1934, KSA; *Topeka Capital*, August 3, 1934.

Umberger's and Landon's efforts. The tedious problem of determining
the priority by which cattle would escape the parched pastures was
encountered daily in July and August, but it was handled successfully.
More than a million head of Kansas cattle, the second-largest number
from any state, were sold under the program by farmers who were not
only desperately in need of cash but were constantly threatened with
completely losing their livestock investments because of the flesh-
shrinking drought.[61]

Exhortation was needed as well as relief. On July 24, Landon took
to the radio to urge Kansans to save straw for use as feed during the
winter. He later pointed out that the practice of burning off straw could
be suicidal for livestock raisers: "There is not enough feed in Kansas,
no matter how much money we might get hold of to buy it." He also
advised farmers of the available government loan funds, and how to
apply for them.[62] During the final week of his primary election
campaign, he collected information on the drought and continued to
work on the problem—actions that were certainly politically effective.

On August 4, the day before the election, he again made a broadcast
on the situation. Every effort was being made to fight the effects of the
drought, Landon said. Railway rates had been reduced, and oil-
company equipment was being used to transport water. The Kansas
Emergency Relief Committee had put teams of geologists in the field
to locate emergency well sites, and the county poor commissioners were
supporting the digging and drilling of water wells. The Federal
Emergency Relief Administration was giving farmers relief funds and
distributing feed for livestock and poultry, and other federal aid was
being given in the form of production-credit loans, emergency crop
loans, feed and forage loans, and work relief. Farmers were told to
contact their county farm agents and poor commissioners to obtain
help. The governor advised that all forage, including straw, hay, and
cornstalks, should be conserved. Urging people not to panic, he
asserted that courage, patience, cooperation, and resourcefulness would
pull the state through the drought; and he concluded his talk with a
pledge of continuing economy and sound business operations in
government.[63]

[61] "Agricultural Relief" file, 1934, H. Umberger to Joyce F. Blackman, August 18,
1934, Chester C. Davis to Landon, October 4, 1934, Victor Christgau to Landon,
October 10, 1934, all KSA; Schruben, "Kansas During the Great Depression," p. 245.
[62] *Topeka Capital*, July 25, 31, 1934.
[63] *Ibid.*, August 5, 1934; *Kansas Relief News-Bulletin*, July 23, 1934, p. 1.

Landon, having discovered that some millers were profiteering on cottonseed cake and other feeds that were in short supply, sent a strong protest to the Consumers' Council in Washington. In early August he asked Secretary Wallace to form a corporation to finance the purchase and sale of feed to hard-pressed livestock owners at fair prices, warning that if the federal government did not do so, Kansas would. Landon, Umberger, Mercer, and J. F. Farrell (of the Santa Fe Railroad) had already devised a plan for a $50,000 state corporation, with a borrowing reserve of $500,000, that would be underwritten by the state's bankers and the Reconstruction Finance Corporation. Toward the end of August, Landon again pressed Wallace on the question, asserting that cattlemen needed feed at lower prices or higher sale prices for their livestock. It was announced, within a week, that the federal government would in effect implement Landon's loan plan by giving additional feed loans on easier terms than before. It was hoped that this extra financing would enable livestock owners to be more selective in buying feeds, thereby forcing profiteers to reduce their prices.[64]

Meanwhile, the struggle for emergency railway freight rates had continued. Landon and Kansas farm leaders constantly pressed railroad officials not only to extend the lower rates but to grant further rate reductions. In August, water for human consumption was so short in drought areas that the governor appealed—successfully—for the establishment of emergency freight rates on the transportation of drinking water, but by the end of the month word came that the railroads would charge their regular rates after September 4. The battle was taken up again, as Landon entreated for extension of emergency rates. He declared that the railroads' interests were at stake because, without their help, there might be no cattle left in the state, and the railroads would have lost their greatest market in Kansas. Landon pressed the fight, and by the end of September he succeeded in securing restoration of most of the emergency freight rates. This permitted him to observe that the cooperation of the railroads and oil companies showed that much could be done with private resources in meeting emergency situations; one need not, and should not, rely solely on federal aid.[65]

In 1934, the fifth year of the seven-year drought, agricultural distress

[64] Landon Memorandum, August 11, 1934, Landon, Mercer, Umberger to Chester C. Davis, October 15, 1934, Landon to Henry A. Wallace, August 28, 1934, all KSA; *Topeka Capital*, August 6, 15, September 5, 1934.

[65] E. B. Boyd to Landon, August 9, 1934, and Landon to J. M. Kurn, August 31, 1934, KSA; *Topeka Capital*, August 30, 31, September 26, 1934.

lessened considerably, thanks largely to federal assistance and energetic state efforts in procuring and distributing it. Landon was critical of the national government's crop-control plan because Kansas' problem was one of harvesting enough to survive, and because he believed there were markets—at home and abroad—that had not been developed. He would later oppose, as unnecessary intervention, further federal efforts to inflate prices; but in the hard years of 1933 and 1934 he generally had kind words for Washington's subsidy, loan, and buying programs.[66] His reasoning was simple: Emergency measures were justifiable until the time came when the emergency they were designed to meet had vanished. Landon was to convince himself, partly out of conviction and partly out of political expediency, that 1936 was that time.

[66] *E.g.*, Landon to the editor of *MacFadden's Weekly*, November 13, 1934.

CHAPTER 8

A Second Term

Landon had been an exceptionally good governor during his first term. He had lowered the tax burden, reorganized the state government, fought successfully for farm and unemployment relief, started a water conservation program, reformed the finances of local governments, forced utility rates down, overcome the Finney scandal, met oil crises, and—because many of these could not have been done without federal assistance—proved to be a top-notch cooperator with the New Deal. Because of his record, he looked forward to a second term.

In March, Landon's forces began warming up for the 1934 campaign. Willard Mayberry, the governor's secretary, and Fred Seaton, president of the Kansas Young Republicans, spent two weeks organizing Young Republican clubs in western Kansas. By late March, Landon revealed the basis of his campaign: he was going to campaign on a record of accomplishment, a record that downplayed partisanship.

At the top of the list of achievements was his administration's cooperation with the federal government.[1] Landon elaborated upon this in a speech at Fort Scott, in which he told the Young Republican district convention: "It should be a source of great satisfaction and pride to the citizens of Kansas that our legislature did not indulge in blind and bitter partisan squabbles but worked for the best interests of the state." Tying Democrats in with his administration's actions, he

[1] *Topeka Capital*, March 11, 25, 1934.

called "attention to the fact that while the Democratic minority in the Kansas legislature was cooperating with the Republican state administration, so was the Republican majority cooperating with the recovery program of the national administration although not agreeing with it in its entirety."[2] Landon's administration had boasted that Kansas was listed by the national recovery administrator, Hugh Johnson, as a leading cooperator with the objectives of the NRA. Landon also procured—and publicized—a statement from Harry Hopkins' midwest field representative that the planning and execution of relief programs in Kansas was outstanding and that the work of the Kansas Emergency Relief Committee director, John G. Stutz, was "unexcelled in any state."[3] The path of cooperation between Democrats and Republicans was still open, remarkably so, in 1934.

On May 29, Governor Landon formally announced his decision to run for reelection. He pledged "a continuation of rigid economy and sound business principles applied to state government," and the pursuit of improved agricultural, industrial, and business conditions; adequate relief; and the preservation of the country's institutions. Within a few days another announcement was made: John R. Brinkley declared he would run for the Republican gubernatorial nomination.

Soon after the 1932 election Brinkley had stated that he did not expect to run again for office, but "if I should run it is quite probable that it will be on a party ticket."[4] Brinkley, who had established his clinical and business headquarters in Del Rio, Texas, returned to Kansas to establish his Republican affiliation and to keep the primary election from being "a droll affair."[5] More likely, he was looking for additional publicity, and thought that the Finney scandal offered possibilities for political exploitation. Actually, the Republican primary election was unexciting; Brinkley did little campaigning until about a week before the election, and Landon did even less. A flurry of excitement was caused in July with the announcement that a movement was under way to challenge Brinkley's right to run, on the grounds that he

[2] Landon speech, Fort Scott, April 17, 1934, Alfred M. Landon Papers, Kansas State Historical Society, Topeka.

[3] "Governor Landon's Administration—Good Government at Lower Costs, January, 1933, to May 1, 1934" (mimeograph), p. 7; T. J. Edmonds to Landon, April 9, 1934, Kansas State Archives, Governors' Papers, Kansas State Historical Society, Topeka.

[4] *Topeka Capital*, May 30, 1934; *Topeka State Journal*, June 1, 1934; *Pittsburg Headlight*, November 14, 1932.

[5] *Topeka Capital*, June 21, 1934.

was not a citizen of Kansas. The recently elected Republican state chairman, Will T. Beck, stated that this was an unwise move, and Landon also discouraged it.[6]

Brinkley opened his campaign by radio at the end of July, attacking the state's "puny" lake program and Landon's chumminess with the Finneys. He charged that the governor had accepted $10,000 from Ronald Finney, branding the explanation that it was a repayment to Mrs. Landon as an alibi; and he declared that Landon, if reelected, would pardon Ronald Finney. Brinkley's bond-scandal charges brought immediate replies. Cliff Stratton, of the *Topeka Capital*—whom many credited with whipping up the widespread sentiment for stiff penalities for those connected with the scandal—wrote that Brinkley's "Statements Don't Jibe with Facts." He pointed out that the former federal district attorney, Sardius M. Brewster, whom Brinkley had lauded, had thoroughly checked Mrs. Landon's investment transaction and had proved that the money had been invested by her in the Hill Packing Company on the advice of the National Bank of Topeka.[7] And Brewster himself said that state and federal investigations showed that Brinkley's charges were without foundation. Brinkley immediately switched his attack, warning Republicans that a primary vote for Landon was a vote for a Democratic governor in November. The voters then went to the polls, and Landon defeated Brinkley 233,956 to 58,938 in the heaviest primary election vote that had ever been recorded in Kansas.[8]

Jubilant and united, the Republicans met for their party council on August 28. State Senator Kirke Dale gave the main address, citing the party's record and lauding Landon. The platform also recited the party's achievements, revealing the impact of federal activity on state administration. The document, devised under Landon's direction, demanded of the federal government "a parity price for agricultural products" to assure the farmer his "cost of production, plus a reasonable profit." It demanded that the National Industrial Recovery Act be amended to prevent monopoly and to provide additional protection to small businesses, farmers, and workingmen. The party pledged its cooperation in developing "plans for a sound system of unemployment insurance and of old age pensions," and called for a state anti-injunction law for labor disputes; it promised to continue the fight to

6 *Ibid.*, July 15, August 7, 1934.
7 *Ibid.*, August 1, 2, 1934.
8 *Ibid.*, August 3, 4, 21, 1934.

reduce utility rates, to champion "the cause of the colored citizens of the state," to push industrial development, to be nonpartisan and equitable in administering relief, and to perform with economy and efficiency. The Democrats, who had nominated the young mayor of Topeka, Omar Ketchum, also met in the state capital on August 28 for their party council. Displaying enthusiasm if not ingenuity, the Democrats tied their fortunes to the New Deal, pledging their complete support of the New Deal and its extension to Kansas' state government —along with economy and "house-cleaning." [9]

Landon did not worry greatly about reelection. He had easily won renomination; he had suffered little from the political criticism of the Democrats—indeed he had benefited from their official coöperation. Moreover, the Democrats were far from united in their areas of strength, as intraparty struggles in Wyandotte and Sedgwick counties showed; and several Democrats had indicated that they would support Landon. The prohibition referendum would probably help him, for he had successfully straddled the fence, calling for the referendum yet indicating that the state prohibition amendment should not be repealed (in October he contributed $100 to the campaign against repeal). This had been his position from the first, and it had been incorporated in the party's platform plank. The printing presses produced tens of thousands of copies of the party platform and Landon-for-governor cards, which emphasized relief and recovery, cooperation, economy, tax relief, and the lakes program.[10]

As in 1932, Landon formally opened his campaign in a speech at Abilene. He reviewed his administration's accomplishments and emphasized the importance of a nonpartisan approach to government. He suggested, however, that the prime question before the voters was which of the two parties had contributed most in the economic emergency, and he asserted that in Kansas the Republican party had provided "progressive and constructive measures which have made the state outstanding among the states of the Union." He also reiterated his support of adequate powers for President Roosevelt and he gave a word of support to local Republican candidates, who were "big enough to

[9] *Address of Senator Kirke Dale at Republican Party Council* (Topeka: Republican State Central Committee, 1934); *Topeka Capital*, August 29, 1934.

[10] Landon to Henry F. Draper, August 17, 1934; John R. Golden to Landon, October 11, 1934; card entitled "Alf M. Landon for Governor," n.d. (probably September, 1934).

cooperate with the opposing party." Landon's entire campaign was patterned on the approach used in this opening speech in Abilene.[11]

He conducted an active campaign, "visiting and swapping experiences with Kansas folks," and politicking for himself and the Republican ticket. He methodically visited a congressional district every week, which underscored his reliability, but Ketchum jumped from one part of the state to the other, back and forth. According to Ketchum and his aides, the prime issue was that Kansas would get more help from the national government if a Democratic state administration was elected, and Ketchum confidently indicated that he could do things better because he would cooperate better with Washington.[12] Meanwhile, the anti-repeal group had swung into action, and nationally prominent religious figures—like Daniel A. Poling and Homer Rodeheaver—tramped over the state stirring up "dry" sentiment. This agitation hurt the Democrats; although they had not taken a stand on the question of state prohibition, it was assumed that they favored repeal. By mid-October many thought that Landon was a shoo-in. Clarence Cook, in the *New York Times*, stated: "The New Deal in Kansas so far has been a grand slam for the Republicans, with the Democrats doing a fine job at playing dummy." Cook held that Landon had sewed up federal and state patronage to such an extent that the Democrats could not claim credit for a thing.[13]

As the campaign went on, Landon grew stronger, which was partly attributable to Ketchum's difficulty in raising new issues and partly to Landon's ability to attract organizational backing. Landon not only received the expected support of Joseph H. Mercer, the head of the Kansas Livestock Association, but also that of Carl C. Cogswell, the master of the state Grange. Moreover, the Kansas State Federation of Labor commented favorably on many of the governor's policies, especially those concerning relief. Landon had made a point of consulting several labor leaders on policy, and he was on record as favoring an expertly determined reduction of working hours, an enforceable prevailing-wage law, unemployment insurance, and old-age pensions.[14]

By late October the Republicans, again countering charges of involvement in the bond scandal, pictured Landon as the model of a forceful, dutiful governor, creating an image that probably more than

---

[11] Landon speech, Abilene, September 5, 1934.

[12] *Fort Scott Tribune*, September 5, 1934; *Topeka Capital*, October 14, 7, 1934.

[13] *Topeka Capital*, October 14, 1934; *New York Times*, October 21, 1934.

[14] *Topeka Capital*, August 7, November 1, October 21, 1934.

offset the Democrats' charges. Their defense of the administration also permitted them to raise embarrassing questions about the Democrats in an issue that arose with some force—partly because some Democrats could not resist using the Finney issue and partly because Brinkley had also raised it in an attempt to swing his following to Ketchum. Fred Harris, Landon's chief investigator of the bond scandal, went on the radio to assert that most of the forged bonds found their way into the state Treasury during the Woodring administration. Cleverly, Harris declared that Woodring did not know that the forgeries were there, though if he had he would have acted as vigorously as Landon. A Republican press release asked, "Which kind of a Governor do you want?" and pointed up that though the Finneys and Boyd were friends of Landon, Landon had not hesitated to investigate and prosecute. As for Ketchum, it was alleged that officials of Topeka who were admittedly guilty of illegal activities had not been prosecuted, or even removed from office. Ketchum was also said to be inexperienced, opposed to municipal ownership of utilities, and less than fully cooperative in the administration of relief.[15]

Ketchum abandoned his confident approach in late October. On October 26 he charged Landon with political hypocrisy, saying that the governor, although professing cooperation with the New Deal, was advocating the election of congressional candidates who had obstructed —or would obstruct—the Roosevelt administration. Three days later Ketchum flew to Washington to discuss Kansas politics with President Roosevelt, which finally got him space on the front pages of the state's Republican press. He reported that the White House did not concede Kansas to the Republicans, but it was observed that the President did not endorse Ketchum—and probably had not invited him to Washington. At this point Harry Woodring took the front pages away from Ketchum: the Assistant Secretary of War declared that if the Kansas Republicans did not stop connecting his administration with the forged bonds, he would demand that the United States Attorney General start a new investigation—and he said that very few bonds had been forged during his administration. Sardius Brewster and Fred Harris immediately contradicted this. It has been said that Woodring was warned that if he did not refrain from speaking on this issue the Republicans would stop saying that he would have dealt as vigorously

[15] *Topeka State Journal*, November 1, 1934; *Topeka Capital*, October 25, 1934; Republican State Headquarters, press release, n.d. (probably October, 1934).

with the scandal, if he had known about it, as had Landon. Whatever his reason, Woodring dropped the issue.[16]

Landon continued to cite his record, unruffled by the bond-scandal sideshow. Thrift, efficiency, cooperation with the federal agencies, and promises of support for unemployment insurance and old-age pensions —these were the issues with which to win the election. Ketchum summed up his campaign on November 5: Kansas needed an administration that would effectively cooperate with President Roosevelt; and Landon's record was weak because he sheltered political obstructionists and rode the prohibition referendum as a hobbyhorse. Ketchum said he advocated a state old-age pension, equalization of the state's school opportunities, and providing schoolbooks at cost.[17]

Landon went into the election confidently, and was relected by a substantial margin: 422,030 votes to 359,877.[18] Although Ketchum had contributed to his own defeat with a weak, me-too campaign, Landon won by adroit use of his record, the issues, and federal aid. He was the only Republican governor who was reelected in the Democratic landslide year of 1934.

Landon's second inauguration took place on January 14, 1935, a clear, cold winter day; in a sense, however, his new term had begun five days earlier, when he had presented his legislative requests to the Kansas senate and house of representatives. Landon prefaced his legislative message, on January 9, with an appeal that the legislators consider the slender financial resources of the state's citizens in making appropriations. The impact of drought made economy and low taxes essential, but it was equally important that unemployment and other depression-born emergencies be dealt with effectively. Landon then itemized his legislative requests. He called for a revision of the valuation of property for assessment so that properties that had escaped taxation would fairly share the tax burden and so that over-assessed properties would be relieved. He also asked for a reduction of the exemption rate on the inheritance tax, and he again requested the imposition of a uniform system of accounting and auditing on county governments. Insisting that the requirements of federal relief agencies for full

[16] *Topeka Capital*, October 27, 30, 31, November 1, 1934.

[17] Landon speech, Topeka, November 3, 1934; *Topeka Capital*, November 3, 6, 1934.

[18] Landon to R. E. Wilson, November 6, 1934; William F. Zornow, *Kansas* (Norman: University of Oklahoma Press, 1957), p. 253.

assistance be met by making the necessary changes in the state laws, Landon suggested that the legislature be prepared to comply with whatever federal old-age pension and unemployment insurance plan might eventuate. He also called for an appropriation to make the state Planning Board—then supported by a foundation grant—a permanent agency, for reenactment of an enforceable prevailing-wage law, for passage of legislation to restrict the use of injunctions against labor, and he again requested ratification of the federal child-labor amendment. He asked for legislative consideration of a state amendment that would permit the short ballot in voting for state officers. He concluded by complimenting the legislators on their prompt and beneficial decisions in 1933, and he expressed confidence that the work of this legislature would be equally prompt and beneficial.[19]

Landon's position vis-à-vis the legislature in 1935 was different from what it had been two years before. The Republicans now had working majorities in the senate—twenty-six Republicans to fourteen Democrats—and in the house—seventy-five to fifty.[20] This situation, however, did not guarantee that the governor's program would be enacted, because dissenting Republicans could not be blamed for its failure—nor could the Democrats, now decidedly in the minority, be blamed for defeating the "people's program." Moreover, the sharp edge of crisis, so keenly felt in 1933, was lacking in 1935, even though depression conditions remained.

Yet, although Landon had little patronage to dispense in 1935, he could use his experience in office and his knowledge of the senate and house leaders in dealing with the legislature—as well as his larger margin of victory. He could, if he pleased, be harsh with those who opposed his program—one or two votes would probably not make a difference—but he again chose the easy-mannered way. He made his goals clear, in conferences and chats with the legislators; he tried to persuade, not to bully. He counted—not with great success—on the large Republican majorities and on the relative goodwill of the Democratic legislators for gaining his objectives, yet, though he lost on many of the important legislative issues, he maintained political equanimity in the state. He also gained considerable freedom from the sharper forms of criticism that had obstructed the legislative programs and administrations of previous governors. In short he probably gained

[19] *Message of Governor Alf M. Landon to the Kansas Legislature of 1935* (Topeka: State Printer, 1935).

[20] *Legislative Directory, January, 1935* (Topeka: State Printer, 1935).

more from the legislators—and his party—than if he had used stronger tactics.

In preparing for the legislative session, Landon had consulted farm, labor, and business leaders. His program, as a result, was generally acceptable throughout the state; it included something for everybody, but it did not go to extremes. Of course, Landon was pressed by the federal government to seek the passage of state laws that would fit into federal relief and conservation programs, and he reacted positively in his legislative messages, but this legislation moved slowly in the house and senate—so slowly that on February 16 Landon used one of his few weapons: the threat of a special session if the complementary relief legislation was not passed. The legislature was also slow in passing appropriations to match federal grants, jeopardizing the $2.3 million in aid due from the federal government in March. Finally, after constant wheedling by the governor, the legislature appropriated the $775,000 needed to complement federal grants for the following two years—a relatively small sum that federal agencies had agreed to only after a superb job of negotiation by John G. Stutz of the Kansas Emergency Relief Committee ($4 million had originally been required). Still, the legislature had not enacted enough complementary legislation, and Landon indicated—after adjournment—that a special session would have to be called.[21] Fortunately for the legislators, changes in federal requirements and slowness in implementing certain federal programs postponed the necessity of a special session until the summer of 1936.

Landon's chief interest during the session was passage of the bill for uniform accounting and auditing in the counties. He believed

> the first principle of good business, and I might say good morals is accurate accounting methods so that we do not deceive ourselves. . . . An officer who is shown by the results of an audit to have administered his office well and honestly merits the confidence of the public. To those public officials who might be inclined to a loose use of public funds, an audit is an effective deterrent.

That this was important was revealed by the fact that in most Kansas counties there were no formal audits. Landon tied this reform to his

---

[21] *Topeka Capital*, December 16, 22, 1934; Franklin D. Roosevelt to Landon, December 22, 1934, January 2, 1935; Alf M. Landon, "To Legislature, Special Message," Session 1935 (mimeograph), KSA; *Topeka Capital*, February 16, 28, March 1, 17, 1935.

request for uniformity of assessment. The enactment of both these measures, he declared, would save the taxpayers large sums of money and would serve the cause of justice and honesty in procuring and using revenue.[22]

Although Landon secured a uniform accounting and auditing act, he did not get much else. The inheritance-tax adjustment failed, as did uniform assessment; and the bill to make Kansas' Planning Board a permanent state agency was also defeated. On the other issues the legislature involved itself in its own arguments, instead of following the governor's lead. An unsuccessful drive to outlaw 3.2 beer, furor over a capital-punishment law, and a fight against compulsory R.O.T.C. at Kansas State College diverted attention from Landon's main proposals.[23]

The legislature adjourned early in the morning of March 10. "Harmony" and "trust" had been sustained, but only a part of the governor's program had been enacted. The Legislative Council, which Kansas was pioneering in the nation, was perpetuated. Uniform accounting, auditing, and records were required of local governments —Landon's chief victory. A law was passed, which Landon favored, that required public utilities to pay for litigation arising from Corporation Commission actions on their rates and practices, and, at the governor's request, the Mortgage Moratorium Redemption Act was extended to January 15, 1937. Economy was fairly well upheld: the legislature appropriated $15,891,086 for the biennium, compared to the $15,142,070 requested by the governor. The legislature also approved, with Landon's support, the appointment of a special committee, headed by Dr. William M. Blount, a Negro member of the state house of representatives, to investigate and publicize discrimination in state institutions.[24]

Administration during Landon's second term was virtually a continuation of the practices of his first term. Although the state business manager, Ben Franklin, with Landon's approval, urged expansion of institutional facilities, increases in civil service salaries, and the

[22] Landon speech, Goodland, January 31, 1935.

[23] *Topeka Capital*, February 12, 28, 2, 4, 7, March 10, 1935; Landon to Franklin D. Roosevelt, February 19, 1935.

[24] *Topeka Capital*, March 1, 10, 1935; D. A. N. Chase to the Governor, State Legislators and Taxpayers of Kansas, March 21, 1935 (mimeograph), KSA; *Kansas City* (Mo.) *Call*, March 22, 1935.

establishment of a contingency fund, the legislature did not respond favorably. Franklin, one of Landon's chief aides in the management of state affairs, was responsible to the Board of Administration, but he frequently found that the board was unsympathetic to his recommendations and he therefore relied upon the governor for action. Finding himself unable to achieve his objectives with the board or the legislature, Franklin tried to keep state agencies within their budgets— by cutting purchase requests, personnel, and even salaries if necessary —but the state's problems worsened as commodity prices climbed upward. Confronted by an inflationary trend, Landon and Franklin increased their efforts to get the most for the state's dollars, and Franklin was constantly engaged in studying the patterns of institutional purchasing. Specifications were carefully set so as to obtain the best items, at the lowest bid, in terms of the cost and quality of the commodities needed; moreover, contracts were often renegotiated at lower costs.[25]

Some improvements that were needed for maintaining services—but at lower costs—were not implemented in time. The penitentiary, which had been a sore spot throughout Landon's first term, was still a problem, and a deficiency appropriation for the prison—one of only two requested for the hundred activities of the state—was passed by the 1935 legislature (as was money for its physical improvement). The funds, however, were applied too late to forestall another major crisis at Lansing—in June, 1935. While the state was building new kitchen and dining facilities, a recreation hall, and a trustees' dormitory, 347 prisoners mutinied in the prison coal mine, held nine guards hostage, and refused to leave the mine (they were eventually "smoked out"). Their main grievance was reported to be the state's parole policy, which, although it had been liberalized in terms of the number of paroles granted, had been placed on a psychological basis—which made it impossible for convicts to calculate when they might be released. Overcrowding was probably another grievance, for almost 2,000 men prisoners were housed in quarters originally built for 1,200. Landon stated that either a more liberal parole policy was needed or a bigger, more modern prison; and he favored the latter, for he was convinced that a stringent policy was needed with dangerous criminals. He hoped

[25] Ben Franklin to Landon, November 15, 1934, December 6, 1934; Ben Franklin to H. S. Buzick, April 1, 1935; Ben Franklin to Landon, November 22, 1935, November 16, 1935; all KSA.

that completion of the building program would relieve the cause of complaints.[26]

The state achieved its goal of providing essential services economically during Landon's administration. It had little choice but to do so. Not only was the administration required by the constitution to balance the budget, but the people and the legislators were tax-conscious at a time when every dollar counted. Basic services were maintained and the tax load was lightened, according to the mandate from the people. The per-person cost of state government dropped from $15.68 in 1932 to an average of $12.93 in 1933, 1934, and 1935; the cost of local government was reduced from $51.67 in 1932 to an average of $40.00 in 1933, 1934, and 1935. The state had also been able to increase the unencumbered balance on hand to something like its normal level. When Landon took office the balance stood at $513,200, but by June, 1936, it was $1,572,481.

The Highway Department's deficit of $3 million was not only wiped out by 1936, but a surplus of $750,000 was on hand; and the only authorized state indebtedness, the soldiers' bonus bonds, was reduced from $21 million in 1932 to $18.25 million by July 1, 1936. Local bonded indebtedness dropped from $139,651,328 in 1932 to $122,889,370 by July 1, 1935, a reduction—almost 12 per cent—that had been facilitated by the operation of the cash-basis and budget laws. Several hundred municipalities had extricated themselves from debt, and almost all had reduced their debt. As a result of state and local tax-reduction measures, taxes on farm lands dipped from 58 cents an acre in 1929 to 36 cents in 1934 (the average reduction nationally was 58 cents an acre to 39 cents).[27] It was on these bases that it was claimed that Landon was a tax-reducing, budget-balancing governor, a unique phenomenon during depression times.

Another untoward episode during the second Landon administration—besides the prison mutiny—was a violent labor dispute in south-

[26] D. A. N. Chase to the Governor, State Legislators and Taxpayers of Kansas, March 21, 1935 (mimeograph), KSA; *Topeka State Journal*, June 18, 19, 1935; Landon speech, Topeka, June 20, 1935.

[27] Research Department, Kansas Legislative Council, *Cost of Government in Kansas* (Topeka: State Printer, 1935); Governor's Office press release, "Depression in Kansas Budget Is Halted," n.d. (probably June, 1936); *Topeka Capital*, June 20, 1936, February 17, October 13, 1935; *Thirtieth Biennial Report of the Treasurer of State, Kansas* (Topeka: State Printer, 1936), 44; State Accountant's press release, "Facts and Figures about Kansas, August 24, 1936."

eastern Kansas. The conditions of the zinc and lead miners in the area (and in neighboring Oklahoma and Missouri) had been characterized by low pay and crowded and inferior housing. In the spring of 1935, the union that had organized the workers there—the International Union of Mine and Smelter Workers—requested negotiation of these issues with the Tri-State Zinc and Lead Ore Producers Association. When the request was rejected, a strike call was issued, and on May 8 the operators closed the mines. The operators organized a company union and planned to open a mine (on June 7) with company-union men. The undersheriff and the county attorney of Cherokee County asked the state for assistance in policing the opening of the mine, saying that some 150 pickets, who had allegedly threatened violence, refused to disperse.

As was required by state law, Landon ordered units of the Kansas National Guard to police the Cherokee County lead and zinc mining area. Under Colonel Charles H. Browne, two cavalry troops, an under-strength infantry company, and a medical detachment—a total of 15 officers and 228 men—were dispatched. Harry Burr, a former United Mine Workers official, was also sent to the area, as Labor Commissioner George Blakely's observer. Burr reported there was little justification for the request to send troops because no incidents had occurred. Landon did not withdraw the troops, however, because of fear of clashes between the rival unions—as had occurred earlier in Oklahoma. The National Guard officers held a series of conciliatory conferences in the area to reduce tension, and in Topeka the governor conferred with mine owners and miners in an attempt to achieve a strike settlement.[28]

Violence—a shooting incident and the dynamiting of two high-tension electric towers—broke out on June 8. Landon ordered the troops to maintain order, to disarm all armed civilians (including the mine guards, if they stepped off the mine properties), and to require the company guards to surrender their deputy constable commissions. The Guardsmen were also told "not to interfere with labor meetings and other activities of the strikers, so long as they were peaceably conducted. . . . Picketing, and . . . meetings and pickets were [to be] protected from possible violence of any kind." Street assemblages, however, were prohibited, as were publications that reflected

---

[28] George Blakely to Landon, June 6, 1936, Dick Helman and C. E. Shouse to Landon, June 7, 1935, June 10, 1935, Harry Burr to George Blakely, June 8, 1935, all KSA; *Topeka Capital*, June 8, 1935.

disparagingly upon the work or action of federal or state authorities.[29] Colonel Browne assigned an intelligence officer to check on the re- actions of the union men, and the officer reported that people were pleased with the impartial behavior of the troops. A picket spokesman reported that the Guard had protected the union hall from a scab raid; another union man was reported as having said the Guard was "hard as hell but fair to both sides."[30]

Because the virtual imposition of martial law had ended the violence, the troops were gradually reduced, and were completely withdrawn by June 27; but other action had been taken to maintain order. Deputy sheriffs, previously paid by the mine owners, were ordered by the governor to be paid by the county, and when the sheriff refused to obey, Landon kept pressing him until the sheriff resigned. A new sheriff, Earl Neeley, though initially resisted by the Democratic county commissioners, with Landon's forceful backing was able to add sixteen deputies to his staff. Despite all precautions, the danger of clashes be- tween union and company men had not passed, and violence broke out again on June 28 as seventy-five to one hundred armed strikers be- sieged the fortified Eagle-Picher lead smelter at Galena. At least five persons were injured, and twenty-eight special guards were pinned down inside the smelter by the strikers' fire.

Sheriff Neeley's deputies were unable to control the situation, and assistance was again requested from the state. Landon responded by declaring martial law and ordering the National Guard to disperse the armed strikers. He also issued a statement blaming the operators for this outbreak, saying they had tried to open the mine without settle- ment or notice and had thereby inflamed union sentiment.[31]

The Galena incident was a gesture of futility; the strike, in effect, had already been broken because 90 per cent of the mines were operating, with company-union men, by the end of June. Martial law continued in the area until July 21. Although Landon regretted that such action had to be taken, and although state officials were not un- sympathetic to the grievances of the strikers, they saw their duty only

[29] *Topeka Capital*, June 9, 1935; Landon to Norman Thomas, July 29, 1936; "Proclamation, General Orders No. 1, Headquarters, Cherokee County Military District," n.d. (probably June 8, 1935), KSA.

[30] Ellis B. Christensen to Charles H. Browne, June 12, 1935, KSA.

[31] George Blakely to Landon, June 6, 1936, and memoranda from Adjutant General's Department, June 20, 1935, July 1, 1935, KSA; *Topeka Capital*, June 29, 1935.

as impressing "the citizens of the mining district with a wholesale regard for law and order"—and they tried to protect the strikers as well as other citizens from violence. Mass picketing was not allowed, but peaceful, small-scale picketing was permitted, as were labor meetings.[32]

Conferences with owners and labor representatives came to naught— why should they? the owners had won—and labor opposition flagged. The efforts of the Kansas State Federation of Labor to arrange a meeting between Governors Landon, Marland of Oklahoma, and Park of Missouri for tri-state action to settle the strike were unsuccessful. Because 85 per cent of the men employed when the strike began were back at work, such a conference did not seem worthwhile to the three governors, and by October it was reported that more miners were employed in the mines than before the strike was called.[33] Thus the episode ended unhappily for organized labor; law and order had been obtained, and fairly, but this did not help compose the labor dispute.

Meanwhile, the struggle for relief continued. The administration of unemployment relief was generally delegated to the Kansas Emergency Relief Committee, and federal relief formulas had been so well established that the governor played only a perfunctory role in unemployment relief by the winter of 1934–35. By spring, the federal Works Progress Administration had been established. It was organized on the basis that its high-level administrators were to be confirmed by the United States Senate, which in effect placed the WPA—and therefore a large part of federal relief work—in the category of national administration patronage. The WPA, by June, assumed responsibility for most of the work supervised by the Kansas Emergency Relief Committee, and a Democrat, Evan Griffith of Manhattan, was appointed from Washington a state WPA director. Although Landon could do little about the situation, he expressed his disappointment, for the K.E.R.C. had been maintained intact from the Woodring administration, and was, as he saw it, free from political manipulation. Landon regretted that a partisan politician had been named to direct the WPA in Kansas, but he hoped that Griffith would administer relief and work funds impartially.

[32] *Topeka Capital*, July 1, 10, 1935; George Blakely to Landon, June 6, 1936, and Landon to L. B. Boicourt, July 11, 1935, KSA; Landon to Norman Thomas, July 29, 1936.

[33] Thomas Crowe to Landon, July 24, 1935; Landon to Crowe, July 27, 1935; A. Scott Thompson to Landon, October 23, 1935; all KSA.

The K.E.R.C. had accomplished a great deal with federal funds. It had spent $40 million, and had coped with an increase in families on relief—from 30,000 in April, 1934, to 88,747 in February, 1935. It had purchased 521,000 cattle, canned 13 million cans of meat, and processed 25,000 hides and 430,000 sheep pelts. Its federally-supported work relief construction projects had changed the face of Kansas between October, 1932, and October, 1935. Over 15,500 miles of roads and streets had been improved, and 1,515 bridges and large culverts had been built. Seventy-four courthouses had been improved, 7 schools built and 971 improved, 326 other public buildings built or improved, and innumerable sewers and water mains installed. K.E.R.C. had also developed recreation facilities, including 25 new and 221 improved parks, and 55 new and 206 improved playgrounds; in water conservation work, 2,391 ponds and 26 lakes had been constructed. Twenty-four airports had been built or improved, and 11 mattress factories, 4 garment, 9 furniture, and 8 canning factories were built and operated.[34]

The operations of the K.E.R.C.—as a cooperative federal-state agency—had reflected Landon's conviction that relief could be administered in a relatively nonpartisan way, and in 1936 it provided him with one of his chief issues. The agency's operations—financed largely with federal funds—also reflected his belief that state and local governments could not shoulder the greater part of the relief burden— that the federal government had to do the job. This view, however, which might have seemed justifiable in fiscally conservative Kansas in a time of both depression and drought, left Landon vulnerable during the 1936 presidential campaign to the charge that he had shifted the relief burden to Washington in order to balance his state's budget.

Of course, the work of the K.E.R.C. was only one part of the relief picture. Relief came directly, or indirectly, from various sources: the Farm Credit Administration, the Federal Land Bank, the Civilian Conservation Corps, the Bureau of Public Roads, the Public Works Administration, the Home Owners Loan Corporation, the Emergency Crop Loan Corporation, the Rural Resettlement Administration, the Shelterbelt project, the Reconstruction Finance Corporation, and the Forest Service—among others. Landon's main relief concern during his second term, however, was agriculture: the drought persisted, and in fact worsened. Grain was so scarce in late 1934 that

[34] *Topeka Capital,* June 2, 17, August 8, 1935; John G. Stutz to Landon, February 6, 1936, KSA; Arthur M. Schlesinger, Jr., *The Politics of Upheaval* (Boston: Houghton Mifflin, 1960), p. 355.

Landon gave serious consideration to arranging for wholesale shipment of Kansas livestock to out-of-state feeding places. While emergency rates for shipping cattle were continued by the railways, Landon was unsuccessful in his efforts to secure lower rates for cottonseed cake and other feed concentrates.[35]

It was hoped that the winter of 1935 would see the return of sufficient rainfall, but a dry winter followed the dry fall. The amount of wind erosion and the size of the drought area were said by Landon to be unprecedented. All parts of the state were visited by dust storms; electric lights often had to be left burning all day; trains crept along; and automobile traffic, on occasion, was completely stopped—only grasshoppers seemed to thrive on the dust and wind. On March 20, Landon wired President Roosevelt, pointing out that the best crop prospects—meager though they were—were dying and that the land itself was being damaged; moreover, the health of people and livestock was threatened by dust inhalation. He urged that the facilities of the United States government be put to work immediately to relieve the drought states. "This catastrophe is of such size and importance that it is more than the problem of a single state."[36]

Landon also asked Senator Capper to confer with Relief Administrator Hopkins and Secretary of Agriculture Wallace, from whom promises of help were secured. It was pointed out to those officials that some of the drought-area soil was so pulverized that it would be unaffected by any rain that might come. Listing of the soil—plowing deep furrows every ten yards or so against the prevailing winds in order to catch drifting dust—was essential; and Landon's aides, after making a survey of tractors in the area, found that there were enough to do the work. The problem was to secure a sufficient supply of oil and gasoline. Landon urged the governors of Nebraska, Colorado, Oklahoma, Wyoming, Texas, and New Mexico to join with him to get federal assistance for listing in the entire drought area.[37]

Landon went to Washington on March 23 to plead for prompt federal help, and he and Capper made the rounds of the relief agencies. Colonel Lawrence Westbrook, of the Federal Emergency Relief

[35] Landon to H. Umberger, November 13, 1934, and I. C. Peterson to A. H. Bennett, December 28, 1934, KSA.

[36] Landon to Roosevelt, March 20, 1935, Franklin D. Roosevelt Library, Hyde Park, N.Y.

[37] *Topeka Capital*, March 22, 23, 1935; Landon to the governors of Colorado, Wyoming, Oklahoma, New Mexico, Nebraska, and Texas, March 22, 1935, KSA.

Administration, promised $250,000 for strip-listing in western Kansas, and Landon immediately applied for the money, which was granted. Hoping this would buy enough tractor fuel for strip-listing a million acres, Landon immediately directed county commissioners and county farm agents in the drought area to mobilize tractors and volunteer labor for the battle to save the soil; and arrangements were made with the Soil Erosion Service to supervise the project.[38]

Hoping for additional federal assistance, Kansas drew up plans for listing more than a million acres. The initial planning conference on the matter on March 10 (with experts from the Kansas State Agricultural College serving as the chief technical advisers) had estimated that two and a half million acres needed listing, but by mid-April the figure was increased to 6 million acres. Landon was discouraged; it seemed the problem was growing out of control, and the withering heat of summer had not yet arrived. He wrote Capper on April 15: "There was another bad storm yesterday. I don't know the answer."[39] In the meantime, Landon and other Kansas leaders had urged citizens to send letters and telegrams to Congress and Secretary Wallace demanding help and action—a campaign that had been stimulated by the slowness of the federal government's response to Landon's March 20 appeal to the President. Roosevelt, it seems, had promptly asked the F.E.R.A. and the Department of Agriculture to look into the situation, but Washington got snarled in its own complexities. On April 10, Hopkins wrote Roosevelt expressing his regret for the delay, blaming it on an inexcusable, but unspecified, mix-up.[40]

The Assistant Secretary of Agriculture, M. L. Wilson, was dispatched to Kansas to study the situation, and a meeting of spokesmen from the affected areas was arranged with Landon and Wilson in Garden City. The governor hoped this meeting would provide some answers—that it could at least determine whether the listing approach was outmoded. Landon and Wilson left Topeka by car, on April 15, to inspect the dust-choked areas of the state, and by the time they arrived in Colby, in western Kansas, they were impressed with the necessity for vigorous and prompt action. It was apparent that more acres needed listing than had been originally estimated, and that the 10-cent-per-acre allotment for listing was insufficient. In preparation

[38] *Topeka Capital*, March 24, 26, 1935.

[39] *Ibid.*, April 4, 1935; Landon to Arthur Capper, April 15, 1935, KSA.

[40] Harry Hopkins to Roosevelt, April 10, 1935, FDRL.

for the Garden City meeting with the spokesmen from five states (on April 16), twenty-five truckloads of dust had been raked off the Finney County courthouse lawn—a 300-foot-square block—to save the grass, or what was left of it. The plight of the dust bowl was further dramatized by the midnight darkness that prevailed in the town from 2:00 p.m. on, and the dust conditions were so bad that Landon and Wilson were forced to cancel a night trip to Liberal.

Some encouragement came from the Garden City meeting, for it was reported that less than 400,000 Kansas acres had been permanently damaged and that only some 3 million acres needed listing. The representatives of the five states—Colorado, Kansas, New Mexico, Oklahoma, and Texas—recommended an increase of the listing acreage allotment, that federal listing grants be made to the other four states, and that Kansas' grant be increased. The representatives also called for integrating soil-conservation work with the agricultural adjustment programs and experimental stations in each state, for more research on resodding and land care, for a federal land-buying program, and for more strenuous efforts to conserve water. It was estimated that dust and drought threatened the lives and livelihoods of 180,000 people in Kansas, 100,000 in Texas, 76,500 in Colorado, 60,000 in New Mexico, and 27,000 in Oklahoma.[41]

The initial stages of the listing program started the week before Wilson's visit, and by the end of the first week of May additional assistance arrived in the form of fodder from the Agricultural Adjustment Administration. The time had also arrived to request more funds for listing, and Dean Umberger of Kansas State College asked Landon to apply for an extra $2 million for this purpose. The dean reported that 513,928 acres in 37 counties had already been listed; but 80 per cent of the original grant of $250,000 had been spent by April 27, and the remainder was being held in reserve as the counties waited for moisture—any moisture—that would help listing in areas of the greatest soil pulverization. Support in the dust bowl's plight came from conservationists—most dramatically from Rexford Tugwell, who declared that the midwest would be a depopulated desert in 300 years without proper conservation measures.[42]

Landon, meanwhile, had pointed out another aspect of the problem. In a statement to the National Rivers and Harbors Congress in early

[41] Landon to Capper, April 15, 1935, KSA; *Topeka Capital*, April 16–18, 1935.
[42] *Topeka Capital*, May 8, 9, 16, 1935.

May, he declared: "The prolonged drought and its tragic effects upon the people have served to dramatize the water problems of the Great Plains." The insufficiency of rain had resulted in a tremendous reduction of agricultural productivity and in a serious loss of topsoil from the 98th meridian to the foothills of the Rocky Mountains, and from the border of Canada into Texas and New Mexico. An irony of the situation was that but a few years previously this area had been ravaged by floods, caused by unusually heavy rains. Landon said steps must be taken to solve a water situation that was unable to supply people's basic needs, and that at other times caused rampaging floods. Although the causes of flood and drought could not be removed, people could be protected from their destructive effects by the conservation and storage of water, and Landon then outlined the start Kansas had made—with federal and state funds—in establishing a system of ponds, lakes, dams, and reservoirs for water storage. He suggested that Congress be petitioned "to give more consideration to the conservation and storage of water on the headwater streams in connection with a broad Mississippi Valley water program." [43]

As if to underscore his message about the double jeopardy of the water problem, rains in northeast Kansas in early June quickly ran off down the muddy river beds, causing damage at a number of points along the Kaw River. In one part of Kansas, water could destroy, yet it could not be used to relieve the disaster of drought in another part of the state. [44]

With the coming of summer's heat, the farm situation grew worse. Drought led to further unemployment, for there were few crops to harvest. The FERA had made few provisions to care for farm workers, and in August Landon appealed to Hopkins for immediate relief. Of course, farm owners were also affected, and at least 13,000 of them were short on seed for the following year. In September, Landon asked President Roosevelt for funds for seed-wheat purchases, pointing out that the lending regulations of the Resettlement, Farm Credit, and Works Progress administrations had to be modified so that the most desperate farmers could apply for loans not only to buy seed and livestock feed but also to maintain their families. He urged that the modifications be made within thirty days, but in less than two weeks Washington had acted to meet the crisis—though, as a result of federal

[43] Statement by Governor Alf M. Landon to National Rivers and Harbors Congress, May 2–3, 1935.
[44] *Topeka State Journal*, June 4, 5, 1935.

red tape, needy farmers did not begin to receive the loans until November.[45]

Landon's efforts during the 1935 farm crisis brought compliments from Victor Christgau, the assistant to Chester Davis, the Agricultural Adjustment administrator. Christgau said that because of the excellent state work in culling herds and conserving feed, and Landon's successful efforts in securing continuation of reduced freight rates, Kansas would be in relatively good shape during the winter of 1935–36; and the federal government should be able to meet quickly any unexpected farm problems that arose in Kansas. Christgau, however, did not mention that Landon had been remarkably successful in another way: Kansas by the end of 1935 had received $87.5 million in AAA benefits, ranking behind only Texas and Iowa in the amount received.[46]

Landon put his private business almost completely aside when he became governor; time did not permit him to explore or drill for oil or gas, and even his oil properties received only superficial attention. As governor, he was scrupulous in matters that affected the state's oil and gas properties. Only one lease—a renewal of a previous oil lease, in which Landon had no interest—was granted on state property while he was in office, and it provided the state with a better return than the original lease.[47] Yet, as the governor of an oil state, Landon could not escape oil matters, nor could he forget his earlier associations and opinions. Although he tried to be impartial with small and large producers, in disagreements between them he was likely to favor the small, independent producers. He had obviously believed that the interests of Kansas and its people lay with the small and independent producers, like himself, who maintained the state's income and prevented complete control of the industry by the large companies. He was, however, eager to achieve compromises between the large and small oil interests so that they might cooperate in reviving the industry.

Although the National Recovery Administration's Petroleum Code had helped reduce oil production to a more reasonable level and raise the price of crude oil, the situation was tenuous. The flush-pool

[45] Landon to Harry Hopkins, August 21, 1935, KSA; Landon to Roosevelt, September 16, 1935, FDRL; Cal A. Ward to Clifford R. Hope, September 30, 1935, November 13, 1935, Clifford R. Hope Papers, Kansas State Historical Society, Topeka.

[46] *Pittsburg Headlight*, September 28, 1935; Schruben, "Kansas During the Great Depression," 324.

[47] Mark Bridges to Willard Mayberry, September 3, 1935, KSA.

producers were angry because they thought the strippers were allowed to produce too much—and the strippers were angry because they thought the flush-pool operators were allowed to produce too much. The problem was simply that overproduction still dogged the petroleum market, and that the large companies were still trying—or at least operating as though they were trying—to force the small and independent producers out of the industry.[48]

The Petroleum Code, which had been given a trial period of several months by Kansas producers, had not solved all their problems, and the producers pressed Landon to seek further federal action. On December 18, 1933, Landon wrote Secretary of the Interior Ickes to express his constituents' concern about indications that up to 60,000 barrels of illegal oil were daily being sold from east Texas and that oil was being withdrawn from storage by the major companies in excess of the amount permitted under the code. Legal production, therefore, was not as high as it could be, and market prices were being depressed by the flow of "hot oil." Landon called upon the federal government to use all its powers to stop the illegal production and sale of oil and to enforce the regulation that the applications for storage withdrawals be passed upon by Ickes and the Code Planning and Coordination Committee—there would then be "an absolute and accurate balance between supply and consumptive demand." Ickes replied that the reports of illegal oil production were perhaps exaggerated, but he wanted Landon to know he was vigorously pushing enforcement of the code, though he was hampered by the need for judicial clarification of his powers.[49]

Although the financial position of oilmen improved during 1933 and 1934, independent producers made little more than the cost of production, and even the large companies were not receiving their customary profits. Therefore, early in 1934, efforts were renewed to limit further petroleum imports, to establish a legal balance between supply and demand, and to enforce this balance by fixing quotas for the movement of oil in commerce. These provisions were embodied in bills introduced in Congress in April by Representative Wesley Disney and Senator Elmer Thomas of Oklahoma. Landon, although not enthused by the

[48] Paul H. Giddens, *Standard Oil Company (Indiana), Oil Pioneer of the Middle West* (New York: Appleton-Century-Crofts, 1955), pp. 517, 524 f.; J. Stanley Clark, *The Oil Century* (Norman: University of Oklahoma Press, 1958), p. 195; Landon to Carl Weiner, December 16, 1933.

[49] Landon to Harold L. Ickes, December 18, 1933; Ickes to Landon, December 28, 1933.

proposed legislation, offered his support because "we are lost if we don't get some federal head to the industry." Although the bills had administration support, they encountered opposition from the major oil companies and the extreme independents, and died in committee. All that was salvaged was the establishment of a subcommittee (headed by Representative William P. Cole, Jr., of Maryland) to collect data on the oil industry.[50]

In November, 1934, Cole's committee investigations began in Oklahoma. Landon's connection with the committee was minimal because he believed that the facts would be collected whether he contributed or not, but he wired Cole that additional federal regulation of the industry was necessary for economic recovery.[51] Meanwhile, other steps had been taken to try to deal with oil problems. On October 11, 1934, the Code Planning and Coordination Committee resolved in favor of an interstate compact on oil within a system of federally set production quotas for each state. Landon and the Independent Petroleum Association were not happy with this movement because they preferred federal legislation that would effect a balancing of supply and demand, and that would coordinate the states' production proration and conservation measures. Nevertheless, Landon and the I.P.A. supported the development of an interstate compact in the event the Disney and Thomas regulatory bills could not be revived and passed in Congress.

The issue of further federal regulation versus an interstate compact soon came to a head. One of the leading proponents of a compact, Governor-elect E. W. Marland of Oklahoma, sponsored a governors' conference on December 3 at his home in Ponca City. The I.P.A. representatives went to the meeting to urge further federal regulation, and representatives of the American Petroleum Institute, which was dominated by the major oil companies, were on hand to champion an interstate compact. A conciliatory attitude prevailed at the meeting, as Landon—backed by the I.P.A.—and Marland agreed in theory to the desirability of a compact and of additional federal action.[52]

Landon was unable to attend a second governors' conference, in Ponca City on January 3, 1935, and he sent Thomas C. Johnson and

---

[50] Independent Petroleum Association, *The Independent Petroleum Association Represents the Domestic Petroleum Industry* (Tulsa, 1935), p. 4; Clark, *Oil Century*, pp. 195 f.; Landon to Arthur Capper, May 19, 1934.

[51] Landon to William P. Cole, Jr., November 13, 1934.

[52] Wirt Franklin to Harold L. Ickes, December 5, 1934; Clark, *Oil Century*, pp. 196 f.

Ernest B. Shawver of Wichita as his representatives. Support for an interstate compact with federal supervision had increased, and Kansas endorsed it as an acceptable compromise. Governor Marland had persuaded Congressman Cole of the virtues of such an arrangement, and, on January 2, Cole proposed the compact in the House of Representatives. The Marland-Cole plan called for a fact-finding agency of federal and state representatives that would study supply and demand, and allot quotas, and it would empower the President to restrict imports; interstate movements of oil, in excess of allocations, would be prohibited. At the governors' conference, only the representatives of Texas opposed the plan.[53]

The entire question was clouded when, on January 7, the United States Supreme Court struck down the Petroleum Code, which had been established under the National Industrial Recovery Act. The oil industry was now defenseless against a flooding of the market. Landon immediately tried to see Secretary Ickes to urge that action be taken to remedy the invalidation of the code. Murray and Marland, the retiring and the succeeding Oklahoma governors, also sought immediate action; along with Landon, they contended that the Mid-Continent price levels were about to crack. The market soon began to be flooded, especially with oil from east Texas. The Connally bill, formulated as a stop-gap measure, declared that oil and oil products produced or taken from storage in excess of the amounts permitted by state laws were contraband in interstate commerce. The bill was rushed through Congress under pressure from the national administration and the oil-state governors, including Landon, and it became law on February 22.[54]

In the middle of February, another conference of governors was held on the question of an interstate oil compact, and Texas won Marland over to a plan that did not provide for federal regulation. The result was that the conference drew up a compact that would require the signatory states cooperatively "to conserve oil and gas by the prevention of physical waste thereof from any cause." Conservation was the

[53] Minutes of the Second Conference of the Governors of the Oil-producing States, Ponca City, Oklahoma, January 3, 1935, KSA; Thomas C. Johnson to Landon, January 9, 1935; Henry T. Hunt, "An Appraisal of the Oil-Gas Compact" (Washington, D.C., 1937) (mimeograph), pp. 16 ff.

[54] *Panama Refining Co.* v. *Ryan,* 293 U.S. 388; Hunt, "Oil-Gas Compact," pp. 7 f.; Landon to Wirt Franklin, January 8, 1935; Landon to Franklin D. Roosevelt, February 1, 1935; *I.P.A. Represents,* p. 4.

tool, but proration of production without federal interference was the obvious objective of the compact. Colorado, New Mexico, Oklahoma, and Texas signed the compact immediately, and the representatives from Arkansas, California, Illinois, Kansas, and Michigan agreed to recommend its approval to their governors and legislatures. As Texas won the major concession at the conference, Governor Marland placed the burden for the compact's success on Texas, saying that it depended completely on that state's good faith; and to many people this meant the failure of the compact. Landon and the I.P.A. leaders shared this view, and they continued the fight to secure enactment of the revived Thomas bill to regulate supply and demand.[55]

By April, Colorado, Kansas, New Mexico, Oklahoma, and Texas had ratified the compact, and the American Petroleum Institute and the Independent Petroleum Association had endorsed it (the I.P.A. had also urged passage of the Thomas bill, upon which the A.P.I. remained silent). Governor Marland, on April 22, transmitted the interstate compact to President Roosevelt, asking him to submit it to Congress with his recommendation for ratification. On May 17, President Roosevelt, aware of the weaknesses of the compact, wrote Governor Marland that he hoped to be able to ask Congress to ratify the compact, but he warned that he must also concurrently recommend appropriate oil legislation for conservation, methods of extraction, and market regulation. This, of course, represented a shift in the President's position—from support for a new Petroleum Code to support for something like the Thomas bill; but Roosevelt was unable to influence Marland.[56]

A few weeks later Landon tried to win Marland, the Oklahoma governor, to the cause of federal legislation. "Opinion in the oil industry has at all times been united on the proposition that limitation of production to consumptive demand is necessary and desirable." Such control was not only in the interest of oil producers but also of the landowners, mostly farmers, who received royalties from oil production. The oil states and their populations looked to a prosperous petroleum industry to help the economy—as did the states that manufactured and provided the supplies used in the industry, the consumer who wanted

[55] *Topeka Capital*, February 17, 1935; Hunt, "Oil-Gas Compact," pp. 22 ff.; Clark, *Oil Century*, pp. 197 ff., 255 ff.; Landon to Elbert Thomas, April 15, 1935.

[56] *Dallas Morning News*, May 12, 1935; E. W. Marland to the President, April 22, 1935; Franklin D. Roosevelt to Marland, May 17, 1935.

stabilized business conditions and recovery, and finally the entire nation, which viewed oil as a vital resource that must be conserved. Because of this, there must be federal regulation.

Landon called upon Marland, because of his leadership on the inter-state compact, to sponsor a conference of oil-state officials to consider ways and means for the states to limit production to consumptive demand if Congress failed to act. Again, Marland reacted by urging congressional ratification of the compact. He then wrote Landon of the necessity of the compact: if it was not passed, no effective state action was likely until the next regular round of legislative sessions, in 1937.[57] Marland had concluded that the Thomas bill, rather than being a complement to the compact, was a diversion that would jeopardize ratification of the compact, and Marland was right in being anxious for the compact. The Thomas bill was blocked because of the opposi-tion of the major companies and the Texas producers, and Congress might adjourn without ratifying the interstate compact. Marland implored Landon to wire Representative Cole and the Kansas con-gressional delegation to urge ratification of the compact.

Although Landon urged Senator Capper to push for ratification of the compact—the oil market was "getting in worse shape every day"—he did not abandon hope for complementary federal legislation. He wired Secretary Ickes several times, backing him in the fight for federal oil regulation. He also wrote Representative Cole, declaring that Congress must limit oil imports, approve the compact, make the Connally Act permanent, and authorize the Bureau of Mines to as-certain the amount of consumptive demand in order to assist the states in fixing effective production quotas.[58] Cole responded to the sugges-tions of Landon (and others) by introducing a bill that provided for congressional consent to the interstate compact and for the establish-ment of a Petroleum Administrative Board that would collect data, investigate, and periodically determine "reasonable market demand" (the amount that dealers expect they can sell rather than the amount for which there actually is a market) so that each state could be assigned

---

[57] Landon to E. W. Marland, June 4, 1935; Marland to Roosevelt, June 6, 1935; Marland to Landon, June 6, 1935.

[58] E. W. Marland to Landon, July 16, 1935; Landon to Arthur Capper, July 18, 1935; Landon to Marland, July 27, 1935; Landon to William P. Cole, Jr., July 18, 1935. See Harold L. Ickes, *The Secret Diary of Harold L. Ickes: The First Thousand Days* (New York: Simon & Schuster, 1953–54), pp. 374, 383, 413 ff., for information on some of the activities in Washington on federal oil legislation in 1935.

production quotas. Also, the bill would have limited imports, made the Connally Act permanent, and provided for federal assistance in making voluntary industrial agreements for fair production, refining, market, and wage-and-hour practices.[59]

Landon, as well as Secretary Ickes, was unhappy with the Cole bill because of the "reasonable market demand" criterion and because it would withdraw oil regulation from the Interior Department. Because it did not get support from Ickes, Landon, and most of the petroleum independents, the Cole bill was lost. The interstate compact, which was all that remained, had the support of almost everyone concerned with the oil industry. It was ratified by Congress on August 27, 1935. The compact, as Governor Marland readily admitted, fell short of what many—including himself—wanted, but he thought it was "a tremendous step in the right direction."

While Landon and the I.P.A. had lost the fight for increased federal regulation, they set about to make the most of the compact. Since 1930 their constant pressure had helped shape the industry, so that there would be a niche in it for the small producer, and minimum waste in the exploitation of oil and gas. They had contributed to more effective state regulation, to making restrictions on oil imports a permanent feature of national policy, to developing the stop-gap NRA Petroleum Code, to the passage and later extension of the Connally Act to prevent the running of hot oil, and even to the formulation of the interstate compact. Landon and the independents now joined to make the compact a relatively effective instrument of stabilization and conservation. This leaky canoe was not the vessel they preferred to navigate in on a sea of oil, but—with an astonishing amount of help from other segments of the industry—it was kept afloat.[60]

[59] *United States House of Representatives Bill 9053, 74th Cong., 1st Sess., August 6, 1935* (reprint) (Washington, D.C.: Government Printing Office, 1935).

[60] Landon to Arthur Capper, August 10, 1935; Ickes, *First Thousand Days*, pp. 414 ff.; E. W. Marland, "The Interstate Oil Compact," press release of a paper given at 16th Annual Meeting, American Petroleum Institute, Los Angeles, November 13, 1935; Clark, *Oil Century*, pp. 198 ff.; Giddens, *Standard Oil*, p. 542.

CHAPTER 9

A Long Shot

Early in the winter of 1933–34 there had been considerable discussion in Republican circles about 1936 presidential possibilities. Although the Republicans had been badly beaten in the 1932 elections, many of them, such as Chicago publisher Frank Knox, believed there would be a turn against the New Deal at the polls in 1934 (there had to be, they reasoned, for it was traditional that the party that lost the Presidency gained congressional seats in the following mid-term elections). Although far behind the Democrats in the number of Senate and House seats they held, the Republicans were not so weak that they could not—with the seats they should pick up in 1934—powerfully contest Roosevelt's bid for reelection. Many Republicans were convinced, however, that Hoover's renomination would preclude the possibility of electing a President in 1936; therefore, alternative nominees had to be discussed early, and almost every Republican congressman and governor who had won in 1932 was discussed in the spring of 1932.

Ben Hibbs, an editor of *Country Gentleman*, wrote Landon of this talk, and said that Landon was being considered, but the governor laughed it off, saying the Republican party was not "so hard up as to name a man from Kansas." "Not that Kansas couldn't furnish a good President," he added, "but the leaders of both parties just don't think of us that way."[1] Then came the debacle of 1934. The tradition had been broken: the Republicans lost seats in the mid-term elections in both the House and the Senate, and the great majority of contested governorships to boot. Perhaps the party *would* be sufficiently "hard up" to consider a man from Kansas, a man who was one of a kind—the only Republican governor reelected in 1934. This unique feat made Landon one of his party's most prominent personalities, which meant that he would be subject to much discussion as a possible presidential nominee by newsmen and Republican politicians.[2]

Because of the occasional comments about Landon as a presidential possibility, William T. Mossman, his uncle and a public-relations man in Pittsburgh, urged him to work for the nomination, and offered him his services and contacts in Pennsylvania. Landon's reply was shrewdly realistic.

I have had a good time in politics by not worrying about my political future. I have seen too many fellows who were made unhappy by seeking a job higher up as soon as they were elected to one. It also handicaps their efficiency in the work they have on hand, because they shape every decision with a view to its effect on the next campaign. I didn't expect to be elected Governor when I ran; I didn't expect to be re-elected, and I don't have any political bees in my bonnet. However, the situation is in such shape that it is hard to tell what will develop in the next fourteen months. But I would be glad to have you drop a friendly word to your friends and keep me posted as to the developments in the East on this situation.

Also, he prepared his uncle for dealing with charges that Landon was a New Dealer.

[1] Frank Knox to Landon, February 26, 1934, Kansas State Archives, Governors' Papers, Kansas State Historical Society, Topeka; Chester C. Bolton to Ogden Mills, March 30, 1934, Ogden Mills Papers, Manuscript Division, Library of Congress, Washington, D.C.; Landon to Ben Hibbs, June 9, 1934, Alfred M. Landon Papers, Kansas State Historical Society, Topeka.

[2] George Rothwell Brown, "Washington Sideshow," *Pittsburgh Post-Gazette*, November 12, 1934; Ben Hibbs, "Governor Landon Answers," *Country Gentleman*, January, 1935. Senator James Couzens of Michigan, writing to Senate minority leader Charles L. McNary in November, 1934, listed Landon as one of the four men likely to receive the Republican presidential nomination in 1936. Couzens to McNary, November 19, 1934, Charles L. McNary Papers, Manuscript Division, Library of Congress, Washington, D.C.

I cooperated to the fullest with the New Deal legislation, as far as our state was concerned, without endorsing any of it. I simply took the position that we should give every opportunity for the experiment to work.[3]

Landon's letter to his uncle pointed up several interesting aspects of his attitude toward the Presidency. He was nonchalant about the nomination, but he did not overlook the possibility of nomination or ignore the fact that the publicity of a presidential build-up could be helpful in his political future—and helpful to Kansas and Kansas Republicanism. Moreover, there was the problem and the promise of his record. It was a problem because it could hurt him with the conservative elements, which were essential in any campaign for the Presidency, yet to win conservative support by denying the liberal aspects of his record would court the disfavor of liberals and moderates, whose support also was needed: to make a broad appeal, he would have to carry water on both shoulders.

Carrying water on both shoulders did not bother Landon because he had been doing it—in the best sense of the phrase—for years in Kansas. He believed that the states, as he had often said, must try to solve their problems by themselves, but if they could not do the job the federal government must step in, acting cooperatively with the states if possible, or by itself if cooperation was not possible. His opinions about the New Deal were honest but mixed: the cattle-buying, wheat allotment, and corn-loan programs had been good, at least in Kansas, but he feared that crop-control measures would ultimately fail because of the problems of enforcement and competitive foreign production; and he thought the federal oil program was working satisfactorily, but only because of the oil industry's willingness to cooperate in it.

His splitting-the-difference showed in other ways. While he boasted about the accomplishments of his administration, he also gave credit to the opposition party, the legislature, and the local governments for their roles in the achievements. As for that occasional pastime of American state legislatures, Red-hunting, he let "the boys" talk about it but he personally would not hunt Reds. He criticized socialism, but he had introduced Socialist leader Norman Thomas at a speaking engagement in Topeka with Voltaire's reputed phrase: "I disapprove of what you say, but I will defend to the death your right to say it." He opposed the repeal of prohibition in Kansas, but he encouraged the submission of the question to the people in referendum. Even in

[3] Landon to W. T. Mossman, November 24, 1934.

fiscal matters Landon walked a middle path: he was in earnest about efficient and economical operations, and about balancing the budget and reducing taxes, but he believed that government had an obligation to help people when they could not help themselves; if this involved the expenditure of more money, it would have to be done, even if taxes were maintained or the federal treasury was tapped.

In short, Landon's record and viewpoint hampered, and enhanced, his national candidature: he could be seen as a hypocrite from the right or from the left, yet he gave promise of meeting problems in a way that conserved human and financial resources—and that also kept tempers low. His position did not lack reason or a rationale but drama and dash. The twentieth-century world—though not the Republican party —has rarely been attracted to a man who believed that government should act only when action is clearly essential.

In December, 1934, and into 1935, events were quietly developing that would make Alf Landon a national figure. Landon-for-President clubs were being organized, and Landon was being solicited by newspaper and magazine editors for his views on national and world problems. National committeeman John D. M. Hamilton arranged for people from Colorado, Illinois, Iowa, Missouri, Nebraska, and Oklahoma to meet the Kansas governor. Kansas Day approached, and Hamilton worked to get leaders from other states to attend the festivities (ironically, Frank Knox, the most active candidate for the 1936 presidential nomination, was the chief speaker). Hamilton invited fifty national committeemen and other Republican leaders, as well as three members of Hoover's former cabinet: William Jardine, Arthur Hyde, and Patrick Hurley. But more important than Hamilton in the early stages of the Landon build-up was Richard Lloyd Jones, of the *Tulsa Tribune*, who after the 1934 election had begun stumping the midwest and the border states in behalf of his "Kansas Lincoln," playing effectively upon the wish of many Republicans for an emancipator who would free them from the federal government.[4]

Landon was becoming popular. His mail began to bulge and journalistic and political visits became more frequent; and Landon began to make some of his decisions, political if not governmental, "with a view to [their] effect on the next campaign." A strategy was developing. Landon, by concentrating upon Kansas affairs, would do his job as

[4] *Topeka Capital*, December 2, 1934, January 30, 1935; John D. M. Hamilton to Landon, December 27, 1934.

governor, would avoid sticking his neck out, would not appear ambitious, would not get pushed into unwanted positions by slicker politicians elsewhere, and would not get caught in the cross-fire between
Republican liberals and conservatives. In February, although he
received invitations to address party meetings in six states, he declined
them because he did not "want to take too big a lead off of first base."
Yet he listened more and more to the political winds that murmured
his name. He wrote William Mossman:

> If you can have some of your newspaper friends keep dropping in a good
> line once in a while,—if you can get some second- or third-choice delegates
> from some of your Pennsylvania friends; if you can take the time to read
> that great document, my inaugural address, and circulate it where you
> think it will do the most good . . . then we would be in a position to govern
> ourselves by the situation as it may exist a year from now.

Even so, Landon made it clear to his uncle that he was doing no more
than playing the game. "I haven't much idea that the nomination
would come as far west as Kansas." [5]

So things went for a while. Nobody in Kansas, including Landon,
took the possibility of his nomination seriously—and anyway, the
governor was busy. The legislature had to be dealt with, as did administrative problems and federal relations. In spring, 1935, the dust
situation worsened, and Landon had little time for contemplating a
national candidacy. Nevertheless, late in March, during a visit to
Washington to secure aid for the dust bowl and to lend his support to
the Thomas oil bill, Landon did not avoid politics. Two *Kansas City
Star* correspondents, Theodore Alford and Duke Shoop, invited a score
of capital correspondents (headed by Mark Sullivan) to a luncheon to
size up Landon—a move that gave the reporters a good deal of
background material for use during the summer's political prophesying.
On his return west, the governor called on Frank Knox, who was not
impressed by the reports that Landon was seeking a place on the
national ticket—or, as Knox put it, "a ticket composed of Knox and
Landon." ("The Governor quite evidently has his lightning rod up
but I think his real target is Arthur Capper's seat in the Senate when
the latter retires.") Yet an observer who was closer to Landon, Clifford
Stratton of the *Topeka Capital*, did not think that the relation between
national politics and Landon could be overlooked in view of Landon's
unique position as the only reelected Republican governor. [6]

[5] Landon to W. T. Mossman, February 19, 1935.

[6] *Topeka Capital*, March 27, 31, 1935; Frank Knox to Annie Knox, March 30, 1935,
Frank Knox Papers, Manuscript Division, Library of Congress, Washington, D.C.

Meanwhile, John Hamilton had been busy trying to maneuver Kansas Republicans, and himself, into a prominent position for the 1936 campaign. Hamilton, much like Landon, had since 1932 tried to become acceptable to all groups within the state Republican party. As national committeeman for Kansas, he was in a position to boom Landon for the presidential nomination and to use that campaign to find a role of greater responsibility for himself in the national party. In March, Hamilton discussed the organization of middle west Republicans with Republican leaders from the region. His scheme grew out of the Kansas Day meeting, where he had talked with visitors from other states about developing a "virile Republican organization on principles" and preparing "to fight" for these principles.[7] A planning session for a general meeting of midwestern Republicans was held in Kansas City on April 1; although Landon was interested in Hamilton's project, he later said that April Fool's Day was an appropriate day for planning the foolishness that was to come out of the conference. The planning session was significant, however, because it showed that the region's Republican leaders clearly opposed eastern control of the party. The Kansas state chairman, Will Beck, endorsed this opposition, and the hopes for midwestern domination of the party, asserting: "As Eastern Republicans have been somewhat phlegmatic or static about it, I believe the Midwestern Republicans might as well take the lead." Landon was, however, irked that some reporters interpreted the project as a revolt—instigated by Landon—against Hoover and the Republican national committee, when Landon's main interest was to stir up party sentiment for Republican programs and action.[8]

William Allen White, Henry J. Allen, and John Hamilton went to Washington later in April to discuss with Republican national committee members and congressional leaders the rebuilding of the party on the basis of the projected midwest meeting. It had also been announced that the Republicans of New England would hold a regional conference on April 30 to stimulate a Republican resurgence, and this regionalist fervor had its influence on the national committee. During the committee sessions much was said about a reborn Republican party, based on Constitutional and fundamental American principles, that would strive to sweep the nation in 1936. The national chairman, Henry P. Fletcher, endorsed the proposed conferences, saying that regional meetings were to be viewed as "a grass roots

[7] *Topeka Capital*, March 17, 1935.
[8] *Ibid.*, April 2, 1935; Landon to Richard Lloyd Jones, April 2, March 21, 1935.

revival" of the party. Although it was made clear that the party was not yet ready for a 1936 candidate, Landon was mentioned as a possibility.[9]

Landon stayed out of all this, saying he was too busy to heed talk of the Presidency. The midwestern "grass roots" committee decided that its regional conference would meet in June in Springfield, Illinois, rather than in Kansas City, in order to take advantage of the city's association with the Great Emancipator—and also not to embarrass Governor Landon. Landon was not being coy about the grass roots developments or about the premature boom in Washington, he was embarrassed. On April 24 he wrote his uncle that he was not sanguine about the conference: "They can take it to any seaport, and I am not sure but what the farther the better." [10] While Alf Landon was skeptical about April's developments, Frank Knox was encouraged; the latter saw a growing disposition among Republican leaders for a presidential candidate from outside the congressional ranks, "for a candidate who can oppose the whole New Deal program without apology or embarrassment." Knox also thought the conviction was widely held that the candidate should be from the midwest, which "narrows the choice to Landon and myself." Knox apparently was betting that he would be the candidate, for he came from the most important midwestern state, an unsure one, while Landon came from a sparsely populated and supposedly sure state.[11]

Although Landon was not campaigning, and although it was not yet certain whether his fellow Kansans were pushing him or bucking for themselves, he was broadening his contacts, especially with newspapermen. A sturdy correspondence grew with Mark Sullivan, as Landon and Sullivan agreed that people of property (of "at least one mule," as Landon put it) should set aside traditional politics (as had been done in England) to fight inflation—which perhaps meant a coalition of Republicans and southern Democrats. The President's Republican cousin, Nicholas Roosevelt of the *New York Herald Tribune*, visited Landon during the spring to gather material for a magazine article. Landon felt that many of Roosevelt's ideas were "bully," but he feared that a major story at that time might "work me into the national picture maybe a little prematurely." [12] To W. M. Kiplinger,

[9] *Topeka Capital*, April 18, 20, 21, 1935.

[10] *Ibid.*, April 23, 27–29, 1935; Landon to W. T. Mossman, April 24, 1935.

[11] Frank Knox to Annie Knox, May 5, 1935, Knox Papers.

[12] Landon to Mark Sullivan, April 9, 1935; Landon to Nicholas Roosevelt, May 20, 1935. Roosevelt wrote the article anyway, "Pay-as-You-Go Landon," *This Week*, *New York Herald Tribune*, June 16, 1935.

another publicist of note who was interested in the Kansas governor, Landon told his concern over changes in the American spirit.

> We shall muddle through in the end, but the cost worries me; not in the balance sheet of an unbalanced budget, but in the terms of society. There is a rising trend of intolerance which may prevent a fair and just solution of our problems.[13]

In the meantime, to further disconnect the Springfield conference from a Landon boom, Iowa national committeeman Harrison E. Spangler, a Hoover man, was authorized to issue the call for the conference. Kansas, which showed great enthusiasm for the meeting, planned to send at least 350 delegates—and it was reported that at least three persons wanted to attend for each place available. But one Kansas Republican, Landon, did not want to go; and he said he would be unable to attend the conference because of conflicting engagements. He was dissociating himself from the conference because he was displeased that John Hamilton (and others) intended to use it to slash at the New Deal and to purge the Republican party of members of questionable loyalty. Landon's sentiments were expressed by William Allen White, who wrote Hamilton:

> Roosevelt . . . is getting nowhere. And unless the Republicans can come in and offer some constructive suggestion that will recast our distributive system and make the American market replace our lost foreign market, it is going to be done under some kind of dirty, tyrannical Bolshevism or Fascism which will deny the liberties guaranteed by the Bill of Rights, kick a hole in the Constitution big enough to drive the despotism in, and it will take bloodshed to chase it out.
>
> And before this terrible threat to our institutions you talk about party purge and "fair weather Republicans." O my God John! You can't win the next election on that basis.[14]

In May, Hamilton was appointed counsel of the Republican national committee, as an executive officer to the national chairman, Fletcher. His new position was described in some Republican circles as enlisting the "shock troops that will lead the victory march in 1936."[15] Hamilton was too encouraged by this to pay much attention to White.

Landon remained aloof from the coming Springfield conference, but

[13] Landon to W. M. Kiplinger, May 14, 1935.
[14] *Topeka Capital,* May 10, 15, 1935; W. A. White to John D. M. Hamilton, May 11, 1935, William Allen White Papers, Manuscript Division, Library of Congress, Washington, D.C.
[15] *Topeka Capital,* May 29, 1935.

developments late in May were to obscure the differences between Republicans on the conference. President Roosevelt's reaction to the invalidation of the National Industrial Recovery Act by the Supreme Court was seen by many as auspicious for a Republican victory in 1936. Landon shared this view. He wrote Hamilton that "the President 'cracked up'" in his famous May 31 "horse and buggy" press conference, during which he severely criticized the court. Landon saw an unfavorable reaction to the President's implication that economic problems could be handled only by the national government. Republicans could benefit by pursuing a

> line of criticism . . . that it is a terrible thing for the President to gamble with the social and economic welfare of a hundred and thirty million people because he is peeved at the Supreme Court's decision and trying to create a psychology of fear in order to bolster up an unsound plan.[16]

With the court issue as background, Hamilton felt more encouraged in using the Springfield meeting as a forum for criticism rather than for constructive planning, and in terms of participation he was correct. The accredited delegates to the conference numbered 5,698—including 778 Kansans—from ten midwestern states; some 7,000 "observers" were also milling around the Illinois capital. William Allen White and Landon avoided the conference, though Herbert Hoover did a "lot of touring" in the area. Although Carl C. Cogswell, the chairman of the Kansas delegation, warned against finding fault with the Agricultural Adjustment Act, most of the conference speakers proceeded on a fighting, negative note. Illinois' former governor, Frank O. Lowden, took President Roosevelt's swipe at the Supreme Court as the point of departure for his speech, and he called upon Republicans to take the lead in the "preservation of the basic principles of the Constitution." Other speeches also hinged on defending the Constitution against the New Deal; and it was predicted that this was an issue that would draw Americans of all kinds—including innumerable Democrats—to Republican banners.

The platform of the conference was more comprehensive and less negative than the speechmaking. Although the conference statement made it clear that the group opposed centralization of power, monopolies, simultaneous reclamation and retirement of land, economic instability, and arbitrary and bureaucratic government, it recommended several positive measures. Among these were economy, relief

[16] Landon to John D. M. Hamilton, June 4, 1935.

for the needy, a balanced budget, a sound currency (based on gold), antitrust action, a breaking down of world trade barriers (such as quotas and exchange restrictions), protection of homeownership, "work for workers," and a better deal for agriculture (including a higher tariff, better market research, and government farm loans at low interest).

Democrats, of course, were not impressed with the Springfield meeting. National chairman James Farley said no one was concerned with what happened there, and James Roosevelt was quoted as saying that the Republican party was "dead and the grass roots convention looking for the body." Most Republicans, however, were pleased with the venture.[17] Landon even wrote Hamilton that the reaction to his management at Springfield was good. "I was glad to see you emphasize the waste angle; that is the thing to keep pounding away on."[18]

The success of the conference convinced many Republicans that they might have a chance in 1936. This conviction was bolstered by the fact that Roosevelt was losing ground in the polls, probably because of his attack on the Supreme Court and his legislative difficulties during the late spring. Landon wrote to Nicholas Roosevelt in June, 1935:

> Politically, Mr. Roosevelt has slipped more in the last month than in any previous time. If he did not have the $5 billion [of relief money] his election would be very much in doubt, and the waste with which that is going to be spent may at last shock the country. He has discarded the one element in this program which was sound, that is, of making permanent improvements.[19]

By August, Landon had become more certain that it was possible to defeat the President. He had been influenced by William Allen White to believe that Republican chances would become better as economic conditions improved, yet he cautioned William Mossman that, although people were turning against Roosevelt, "they are also just as much opposed to the old-guard leadership of the Republican party."[20]

[17] William T. Hutchinson, *Lowden of Illinois: The Life of Frank O. Lowden* (Chicago: University of Chicago Press, 1957), II, 679 ff.; *New York Times*, June 11, 1935; *Topeka Capital*, June 9, 10, 12, 1935.

[18] Landon to John D. M. Hamilton, June 12, 1935.

[19] "Senator Capper discusses 'Where Are We At? Where Do We Go From Here?' over CBS," June 30, 1935, Arthur Capper Papers, Kansas State Historical Society, Topeka; Landon to Nicholas Roosevelt, June 18, 1935.

[20] Landon to Richard Lloyd Jones, August 8, 1935; William Allen White to Landon, July 19, 1935; Landon to W. T. Mossman, August 10, 1935.

During the summer of 1935 there was again much speculation about possible Republican candidates for 1936. Senators William E. Borah of Idaho and Arthur H. Vandenberg of Michigan were mentioned, as was Senator Lester Dickinson of Iowa. Frank Knox continued to tour the country, though denying he was a candidate for the nomination. Knox suspected that Herbert Hoover was trying to make a comeback; John Hamilton was writing to Landon as though the Kansas governor were in the running; and Landon, like a candidate, was acting cautiously. Hamilton reported that party leaders generally did not think Hoover was a candidate, which made talk about the nomination freer.

Hamilton was in touch with Edward Colladay, the District of Columbia national committeeman, who in turn was in close touch with a great variety of leaders. According to Colladay, Bascom Slemp, who had been President Coolidge's secretary, thought that the Republican nominee must come from "the west," and that Vandenberg was best. Knox appeared to be impressing no one of importance, though Lawrence Richey, Hoover's aide, was for Knox—which indicated the former President's support of the Illinois publisher. Colladay was for Landon. A former Senate leader, James Watson of Indiana, probably was for Dickinson, but he felt that Landon had a good record; Watson warned, however, that the Republican party could not accept a man who had backed the New Deal. This led Hamilton to suggest that Landon begin criticizing Roosevelt and the New Deal; the Kansas national committeeman, who was working hard to secure sentiment for Landon, added: "Boy if your record is half as good as I tell it, the Lord himself wouldn't have a chance to equal it." [21]

Opinions soon came in that greatly encouraged the Landon men. The leader of Pennsylvania's conservatives, Joseph R. Grundy, wrote William Mossman that, though he knew little of Landon, the Kansan appeared to be the best hope of the party. Landon later wrote that Stanley High, the liberal publicist, had told Roy Roberts "I was the best bet of all"; and Landon suggested to Mossman that some of his newspaper friends might editorialize on High's comment that "Landon may not be a candidate, but his record is." [22]

Most encouraging was the widespread press comment that Landon received after his national broadcast for the National Economy

[21] Frank Knox to Annie Knox, July 22, 1935, Knox Papers; John D. M. Hamilton to Landon, July 1, 1935.

[22] Joseph R. Grundy to W. T. Mossman, August 30, 1935; Landon to W. T. Mossman, September 10, 1935.

League (on July 2). He had told the story of Kansas' balanced budget in a matter-of-fact, nonpartisan way. He gave credit for the accomplishment to the "Kansas people," and he warned: "We must so guard the use of public funds that government does not become such a burden as to destroy that which it is designed to protect." Newspapers widely applauded Landon's speech, as was illustrated by the editorial headlines: "HE PRACTICES AS WELL AS PREACHES THRIFT" (New York); "COMMON SENSE LANDON" (Missouri); "LUCKY KANSAS" (Nebraska); "KANSAS SETS THE EXAMPLE" (Boston); "THIS IS THE KIND OF A GOVERNOR WE NEED" (Wisconsin); "LOOK AT KANSAS" (Providence); "KANSAS GOVERNOR LOOMS AS PRESIDENTIAL TIMBER" (Pittsburgh); "EYES SHIFT TOWARD LANDON" (Denver); and "LANDON SHOWS HOW" (Newark). The most pointed comment came from the *Ohio State Journal*:

> Franklin D. Roosevelt, candidate for President, promised to reduce government costs, cut taxation and balance the budget. Alfred M. Landon, candidate for Governor of Kansas, promised the same things. President Roosevelt has not done them, but Governor Landon has.[23]

Dozens of favorable editorials were reproduced in Topeka and sent out around the land, wherever they might stimulate more editorials; and additional comments developed to push Landon further into the national picture. Congressman Frank Carlson, in an Associated Press story, stated that Landon was a national figure because of his budget-balancing feat. Columnist John T. Lambert hailed Landon as "the likely Republican Presidential nominee to oppose Mr. Roosevelt."[24] Damon Runyon, as a Hearst writer who had recently interviewed Landon, described him as "a leading potential candidate for the Presidency of the United States, so far as the Eastern press is able to determine. . . . [He] is receiving more headline attention in New York, Boston, Philadelphia, Baltimore, Pittsburgh and Washington than any and all other Midwestern possibilities combined." The *Boston Transcript* began a series of articles on leading candidates for the Republican nomination with a story on Landon, "A Calvin Coolidge from the West!"[25]

[23] Landon speech, Kansas City, Mo., July 2, 1935; *New York Herald Tribune*, July 8, 1935; *Kansas City Times*, July 2, 1935; *Lincoln Evening Journal*, July 8, 1935; *Boston Herald*, July 10, 1935; *Janesville Gazette*, July 10, 1935; *Providence Journal*, July 14, 1935; *Pittsburgh Post-Gazette*, July 29, 1935; *Denver Post*, August 6, 1935; *Newark Sunday Call*, August 18, 1935; *Ohio State Journal* (Columbus), July 10, 1935.

[24] *Topeka Capital*, July 26, 1935; *Washington Herald*, July 28, 1935.

[25] *Wichita Beacon*, August 2, 1935; *Boston Transcript*, August 10, 1935.

In Kansas, the *Wichita Beacon* exulted: "The rural and the metropolitan press, from New York, Boston and Washington, to Los Angeles, San Diego, Seattle and Portland, are ringing with the praises of the Governor of Kansas." The *Topeka State Journal* could hardly contain itself:

> Long since we noted the admiring gaze—which we thought at first must be directed at someone else—we also have heard the flattering remarks previously saved for more favored members of the family of states—such as California. . . . Cinderella at the ball, being petted openly if not scandalously by the prince, was no more self-conscious than Kansas, too long the ill-favored stepchild. . . . But, Oh boy, are we enjoying it![26]

The press commentary continued, fed by the Kansas Press Association, by Kansas state officials, and by the governor's staff. Favorable opinion about Landon developed even among calloused politicians. Hamilton, toward the end of July, reported that Landon's name was well known even in New England, where the Kansas national committeeman had recently talked with Republican leaders. Hamilton later reported that former Senator James Watson was impressed with the general talk about Landon in Ohio, Michigan, Indiana, and Illinois. In September, the former executive director of the Republican national committee, Robert H. Lucas, polled 3,200 party leaders on their preference for Republican presidential nominees. Borah led, with 367 votes; Knox received 260; Landon 176; Lowden 126; Vandenberg 122; and Hoover 75.[27] The race was wide open, and Landon was in a good starting position. Borah, who was seventy, was considered by Landon's supporters as too old and too controversial for the nomination; Lowden also was too old; Knox had no record of public office, was too eager, and was opposed by the leading Republican newspaper of his state, the *Chicago Tribune*. Hoover was regarded as unacceptable to most Republicans; and Vandenberg, it was hoped, would be considered by most as a fence-straddler.

Landon's campaign strategy developed slowly. He had little money, and few political contacts outside Kansas, so he could not stump the country; and he was aware that by venturing outside the state he could be caught in the cross-fire of the party's factions. Furthermore, he was

[26] *Wichita Beacon*, August 12, 1935; *Topeka State Journal*, August 6, 1935.

[27] John D. M. Hamilton, July 30, October 29, 1935; *Topeka Capital*, September 6, 1935.

occupied with state affairs, especially drought matters, which he felt he should attend to personally. But he found that, with his strong press contacts, his campaign could be carried on over the press wires, and that people would come to see him. Landon's early campaign, therefore, was conducted without a campaign manager. The governor let his friends and associates carry the burden, and such men as Roy Roberts and Lacy Haynes of the *Kansas City Star*, John Hamilton, William Mossman, Richard Lloyd Jones, and William Allen White did a remarkably good job. By staying in Topeka, with the things he knew best, the candidate conserved his strength.

Landon hoped to win the nomination without an all-out convention fight: he doubted he could compete in a serious struggle for delegates because of his lack of funds and political contacts and his deficiencies as an orator. In June he wrote to Nicholas Roosevelt that Republican chances for winning the 1936 election depended not only on *who* was nominated but on *how* he was nominated. "If the tactics are followed which I anticipate, . . . of having a host of favorite-son candidates, especially in the primary states, with the nomination coming from a convention dominated by the old influences, it will, to a considerable extent, handicap the nominee." He also wrote Richard Lloyd Jones, on June 19, that the candidate could not be hand-picked if the party hoped to win in 1936: the nominee must wrest it from the convention.[28]

In less than two weeks, however, Landon had shifted his position. He wrote Nicholas Roosevelt:

> If a group of influential leaders who will have considerable to say in the convention could this fall settle on someone, and that man could go out and campaign in a number of states and come to the convention in his own right with a big block of delegates, and then to get the nomination, the candidate would be in a much better position before the country. Furthermore it is evident that the nominee of the convention, whoever he is, will not be so well known to the country. A pre-convention campaign in [key] states will help lay the foundation for a better campaign in November.

Roosevelt replied that, after a personal canvass on Landon's idea, he did not believe a nominee could be agreed upon; the eastern conservatives would not surrender.[28a] Landon, however, had meanwhile

---

[28] Landon to Nicholas Roosevelt, June 18, 1935; Landon to Richard Lloyd Jones, June 19, 1935.

[28a] Landon to Nicholas Roosevelt, July 2, 1935; Roosevelt to Landon, July 29, 1935.

despaired of achieving early agreement on a nominee, having already noted a strong trend toward favorite-son candidates.

But Landon still thought his position was good. He was convinced that the Republican nominee would not come from congressional ranks because of the controversial votes which Republicans in the House and Senate had cast. Certainly, no nominee for President could "hope to carry the west" if he had voted against the AAA.[29] Only a moderate, he believed, stood a chance with the public. If those who "want to hang, quarter, and shoot at sunrise" controlled the 1936 Republican convention, "it will drive a lot of the moderates into the Roosevelt camp at election time." Moreover, if the "bitter-enders" won the election, the political pendulum might swing left of Roosevelt by 1940. Only a moderate would make a good President in 1937, Landon believed, because only a moderate could clear up the administrative disorder in Washington and yet salvage the best of the New Deal experiments.

> I want to see a man who will go in with a fair and open frame of mind and attempt to adjust and manage them, plus a genuine budget balancing, tax reduction program. [Whoever] succeeds Mr. Roosevelt when, as, and if, is in a good bit the same position as the captain of a tugboat which is hitched on to a liner that is on the rocks. If he tightens up his cable too quickly it will part, and the liner with its load of passengers will then be completely wrecked. His job is to ease the liner off the rocks, and he can't do that by any sudden strain on his cable.[30]

Landon thought of himself as this kind of moderate, and he ran his pre-convention campaign accordingly.

Mossman, in late July, advised Landon: "1. Stay away from Hoover, 2. Ignore Roosevelt—say nothing about his administration, 3. Stick tight to your present job." Landon followed these principles, and he refused to criticize other Republicans and to run after newspapermen. He believed, as Clifford Stratton put it, that his "chances of being a candidate in 1936 will be so much better if he is not a candidate in 1935."[31] Landon waited to see how things would develop; he stayed in Topeka, talking with his many visitors and trying to impress them with his depth and personality. One of these visitors, columnist Paul Mallon, wrote:

[29] Landon to W. T. Mossman, July 25, 1935.
[30] Landon to Richard Lloyd Jones, July 29, 1935.
[31] W. T. Mossman to Landon, July 25, 1935; *Topeka Capital*, August 18, 1935.

They call Landon a "Kansas Coolidge," but he is like Coolidge in only one respect. He is the kind of fellow who always would be the last to buy a round of drinks. . . . He is warmer, more friendly, less reticent in conversation, much more emotional, more human. Also he has a good face for political posters. In fact he is the kind of personality which many a political publicity man would pray for in a campaign against a spending opposition.

This does not mean that Landon is provincially minded. Out here on the prairies, he gets yesterday's Eastern newspapers by airplane each day, follows the European financial situation closely. He has definite ideas about what will happen in France, Italy, Ethiopia.[32]

In the fall, a Landon-for-President committee was formed and a headquarters was opened. On September 23, Oscar Stauffer, the publisher of the *Arkansas City Traveler*, had called Fred Brinkerhoff of the *Pittsburg Headlight* and had said it was time for Landon's friends to organize behind him. Then, on October 5, Stauffer and Brinkerhoff had dinner with Landon, Lacy Haynes, and Roy Roberts to discuss the matter, and a few days later two rooms in the Muehlebach Hotel in Kansas City were set aside as headquarters for the Landon committee. The Landon-for-President headquarters would have drawn laughs from most big-time politicians. No free drinks or cigars were offered to visitors, and there were no pamphlets for distribution. There were only Oscar Stauffer, who talked with visitors, and a girl who typed letters to those who had written in, telling them the governor appreciated their interest but had not yet decided to campaign for the nomination.

By November, Landon was discussing—for publication—the national situation. To the suggestion that Republicans should wait until 1940 for an all-out campaign, Landon replied: "It seems to me that, if we are going to stop the New Deal, it's 1936 or never. . . . By 1940 the national government will have assumed so much authority [and] become so powerful that it will be useless to fight it. This country is not far from fascism." While the Kansas governor was sympathetic with many New Deal objectives, he declared himself "thoroughly out of sympathy with its technique, its over-spending, its wastefulness, its unbalanced budget and its usurpation of the rights of states." As for what Landon would do if he were in the White House, W. E. Christenson of the *Omaha World-Herald* wrote:

He doesn't pretend to know all the answers. But this much of his "platform" I gleaned from informal conversations: He would continue federal relief, in some form, so long as unemployment remains acute. He would give every

[32] *Washington Star*, September 26, 1935.

encouragement to business to resume its normal gait, and so take up the slack in employment. His first objective would be to balance the budget. Farm aid, in some workable and effective form, would be continued. He would tolerate no "coercive legislation." His aim would be to decentralize the government and place local authority unequivocally in the hands of local governments.

Those planks are certainly not specific. Landon realizes that. He does not claim to be a Messiah, or to have offhand remedy for all the ills he sees in the Roosevelt administration. He also recognizes that his best chance of becoming President lies in the possibility that the people are becoming weary of Messiahship and are ready for some plain, Kansas horse sense.[33]

Partly out of conviction and partly because of ambition, Landon by November encouraged attacks on Roosevelt. He wrote Mark Sullivan:

Mr. Roosevelt's record of broken promises should be stressed. I really think it is a very regrettable thing that the statements of the President of the United States on a public policy are not believed. . . . it never was so necessary to defeat a President of the United States for a second term if we are to preserve our parliamentary government.

Later, in a letter to Congressman Clifford Hope, he suggested a well-publicized investigation of the staffs of the federal spending agencies and their salaries.[34]

Landon carefully avoided involvement with Republican factions or other candidates for the nomination. He avoided contact with Herbert Hoover, rejected an overture from the Borah camp to consider joining forces,[35] and tried to fend off eastern capitalists who were trying to capture him—while securing their support with no strings attached. Reports of eastern business interest in his candidacy had reached him through Hamilton and through some of the newsmen who were visiting Topeka. The most substantial report, in late September, was William Mossman's:

The business interests of the country are going into politics direct, and for the sole purpose of ousting Roosevelt from the White House. They will utilize political channels, of course, but will oblige political leaders to work *under*

[33] *Topeka State Journal*, October 9, 1935; *Omaha World-Herald*, November 17, 1935.
[34] Landon to Mark Sullivan, November 4, 1935; Landon to Clifford R. Hope, December 20, 1935, Clifford R. Hope Papers, Kansas State Historical Society, Topeka.
[35] W. A. White to Herbert Hoover, July 24, 1935, White Papers; Landon to Richard Lloyd Jones, July 29, 1935; Ray McKaig to Landon, December 14, 1935; Landon to McKaig, December 19, 1935.

them, taking orders, giving their practical political counsel, of course, but actually doing what business wants done. For the first time in our history business is faced with the necessity of doing its own political work and is determined to do it and make a good job of it too, no matter what the expense or how great the effort required.

Mossman mentioned two Pittsburgh industrialists, steel magnate Ernest T. Weir and Koppers Coke Company president H. B. Rust, who were connected with this movement (which was apparently the conservative American Liberty League). Weir thought that the Republican nominee must come from the west, not Wall Street, and "must be a progressive but above all a businessman"; he seemed to think that Landon was the logical candidate. Rust agreed with Weir. "In his [Rust's] opinion," Mossman wrote, "a man who can rule a province as you have done demonstrates his qualifications for the rulership of a nation." The likelihood of a Democratic Congress even if a Republican were elected President did not discourage Rust, who thought it would be too argumentative to pass legislation on its own. Rust and Weir urged Landon to come east, without fanfare, to meet with groups of businessmen.[36] Mossman suggested that his nephew vacation at Atlantic City in order to meet his prospective industrial backers, cautioning Landon not to do anything that would disturb their confidence in him. He urged Landon not to make any public appearances in the east, and, if possible, to cancel a speech before the Ohio State Chamber of Commerce that was scheduled for November 6. Landon replied that the Ohio talk had to be given, that the Pittsburgh leaders could meet him on that occasion, and that he thought he should not take an Atlantic City "vacation."[37] Actually, Landon did not intend to be caught caucusing with industrialists, or give them the impression that he would be "their" candidate; yet it would be foolish to discourage them. He would avoid them, and let them court him in Topeka.

In October, in a scribbled note, Mossman told Landon that Dr. Edward Weidlein of the Mellon Institute had been instructed to communicate the following information through Mossman. Ogden Mills had given a dinner for Hoover in New York, attended by a dozen men who were "absolutely the tops in industry and national politics" (including Weir and the Republican national chairman), who had

[36] W. T. Mossman to Landon, September 25, 1935.

[37] W. T. Mossman to Landon, October 1, 1935; Landon to Mossman, October 3, 1935.

bluntly told Hoover that he must not be the Republican nominee—
and that he would not have the support of business if he were nominated. Hoover was said to reply that he was not a candidate for the
nomination. The group then indicated that Knox and Borah were
unacceptable, but it expressed great interest in Landon. "It was assured that there will be no Harding finish to the next Republican
convention. By the time the convention assembles the candidate will
be picked and the delegates assured to put him over with a swoop—and
at present the man looks like Landon." Mossman also told Landon
that money for the campaign was ready; the first million dollars had
already been spent for lining up the small political fry and "plenty
more [is] forthcoming."[38]

Indications of business interest in Landon mounted steadily during
the last half of 1935, as did journalistic interest. During the late
summer, moreover, some of Landon's political friends made statements
in his behalf: in August, Representative William Lambertson announced his support of Landon for President, as did Senator Arthur
Capper and former Vice-President Charles Curtis shortly afterward.
Letters from those who were close to Landon were widely circulated.
Roy Roberts lauded the governor as "probably the best we have ever
had"; the *Kansas City Star* publisher said that the Republicans, in order
to defeat Roosevelt, must work together and must carry the west—and
that "if anyone can do it, Landon can."[39] From Harvey H. Fremming,
president of the International Association of Oil Field, Gas Well, and
Refinery Workers, came great praise for Landon's record in the
stabilization of the oil industry. William Allen White described
Landon to the public as a "diligent, prudent, conscientious young
Republican who . . . will go straight and not devious into his work."
He added that "if the Republican party does not name some such
honest, clear-headed, high-visioned, liberal Republican on a broad-
gauged liberal platform, the country will suffer for the selfishness of
the Republican leaders."[40]

Landon, in the meantime, had made several public statements. In
July, at Eugene Meyer's solicitation, he had condemned the "in-
tolerant and drastic treatment of minorities in Germany," charging

[38] W. T. Mossman to Landon, n.d. (probably mid-October, 1935).

[39] *Chicago Tribune*, September 5, 1935; Roy Roberts' circular letter, n.d. (probably
September, 1935).

[40] *Topeka Capital*, September 3, 1935; *Kansas City Star*, October 16, 1935.

that the German leaders "have forgotten all teachings of justice and love." In September, he praised the Salvation Army (at a tent meeting in Topeka) for promoting "Christian helpfulness and Godliness and in helping all of us to live more like a good Samaritan." At the state fair, at Hutchinson, he warned that "wasteful public spending" would undermine the national credit, which could lead to an instability that could destroy the Constitution. He described, as a threat to liberty, the increased centralization of power in private and governmental hands, and he praised the "small home, small business and small American farm." It was also in September that Landon left the state, for the first time since March, to make a highly publicized visit to the national American Legion convention, which was meeting in St. Louis. In October, he sent a message to the Western States Republican Convention—through his Young Republican adviser, Fred Seaton—warning of national destruction unless waste and extravagance in government were stopped. In November, in a talk to the Lutheran Brotherhood in Kansas City, he expressed pride in "the part Scandinavian peoples and Lutheran churches played in our state's development." He declared, in December, before Young Republicans in Topeka, that the 1936 election would show whether the American people "are determined to maintain parliamentary government or if they wish to accept more centralization of power." [41]

But Landon's most important speech was saved for his appearance before the Ohio State Chamber of Commerce, on November 6 (the day after Republicans had elected the mayor of Philadelphia, recaptured the New York state legislature, and made gains in New Jersey). Designed to maintain suspense about his candidacy and yet to attract a following, the speech stuck to what Landon knew best, Kansas and fiscal soundness, but it was interspersed with some admonitions to the businessmen.

> If the situation in Kansas seems unusual it is only because the type of government which the citizen has a right to expect has become the unusual in a day of theory and experimentation. What we have done in Kansas is what a sensible family does in the face of reduced income. We have cut out

[41] Landon to Eugene Meyer, July 23, 1935; Landon speeches: Topeka, September 8, 1935, and Hutchinson, September 17, 1935; *St. Louis Post-Dispatch*, September 26, 1935; *Topeka Capital*, October 7, 1935; Landon speeches: Kansas City, Mo., November 8, 1935, and Topeka, December 7, 1935.

the frills. We have maintained essential services, but at minimum cost. We have insisted that every dollar buys more, not less, of government. We have tried to run all departments of government on business principles and by business methods.

The surest way either an individual or a state learns is by experience. We all admit that our modern industrial state is complicated, and far from the simple structure of our founding fathers. But does the fact that we have changed and grown, make it wise to abandon, out of hand, the course which the wisdom of our forefathers charted for us. . . .

If the wind rips the roof off a house out in our country, we don't tear down the walls, also, and abandon the whole structure. We put on a new and better roof—strengthening those parts which we have discovered to be weak. Similarly, we must not abandon what remains of our American institutions or jeopardize the remainder of our freedom simply because an economic storm has devastated our nation and shaken confidence. Rather let us replace what is destroyed, rebuild what is torn away, and in so doing strengthen our structure in every way that experience can suggest.

Landon also declared that the farmer was not seeking special privilege but equality, and that unemployment relief was neither a vested right or a charity but a common obligation, caused "by our inability to cope successfully with situations as fast as they have arisen." He called for genuine cooperation between national and state governments and business and financial leaders in dealing with the nation's problems, preferably on a pay-as-you-go basis.[42]

Landon's Ohio speech set off a new wave of press adulation. Dale Cox, in the *Cleveland Plain Dealer*, wrote: "We are convinced that as Lincoln left a profound impression in the East in 1860, Landon left behind a similar impression in the East in 1935." The *Washington Post* observed: "The homely nature of [his] principles plus the moderate tone of the entire address clearly indicate that Gov. Landon is much more than a politician seeking office." The *Ohio State Journal* commented that Landon "merely reiterated what is the common American belief and attitude. . . . If it happened that Roosevelt and his New Deal were in the line of the Landon fire, it was too bad for the President and his theories." The formal Democratic reply, from Attorney General Homer Commings and national chairman James Farley, was that the New Deal's spending was more than made up by the economic recovery.[43]

[42] Landon speech, Cleveland, November 6, 1935.
[43] *Cleveland Plain Dealer*, November 8, 1935; *Washington Post*, November 7, 1935; *Ohio State Journal* (Columbus), November 8, 1935; *Topeka Capital*, November 10, 1935.

That Landon was now a national figure was testified to by the attacks of the Democrats. According to Harry Hopkins, "Kansas has never put up a thin dime for relief," and the state's budget, he said, was balanced by "taking it out of the hides of the people."[44] Charles Michelson, the publicity chief of the Democratic national committee, fired "wet" ammunition at the supposedly "dry" Landon. Secretary of Labor Frances Perkins was scornful: "And who is Landon?"[45] Not all Democrats attacked him, however. As early as July, 1935, Landon had been helped by the desertion of four young Kansas Democratic leaders, who had switched to the Republican party. In December, a former Democratic governor, George Hodges, pointed out in his newspaper that although Kansas had contributed little to relief, Landon had always been fair in explaining the balancing of the state budget, and that, in the event of his nomination and election as President, Landon would have "the well wishes of comparatively the whole state. He is careful and he is sane, and as this paper has stated on several occasions, he knows his limitations." Although Landon received some Democratic support, he also drew criticism from the right. Dan Casement, the president of an ultraconservative agrarian organization, the Farmers' Independence Council, pointing out that Landon advocated direct subsidies to farmers, concluded: that "any true American should follow Landon in this crisis is unthinkable."[46]

Landon paid little attention to the attacks on him because he was too busy developing his candidacy. He exchanged views with historian John Truslow Adams, who saw a trend toward dictatorship. He asked a free-lance journalist, Duncan Aikman, a political independent, for his views on the social and economic conditions facing the nation. He talked with Francis Townsend for two hours, commending the doctor's sincerity but flatly refusing to go along with Townsend's radical old-age security plan. Landon lined up William Allen White to help him with platform ideas, Clifford Stratton to serve as a general critic, and Lacy Haynes as general factotum. He drew on such visitors as Eugene Meyer of the *Washington Post* and economist Ben Anderson of New York's Chase National Bank for ideas, and, through men like Anderson, he

[44] *Kansas City Star*, November 3, 1935.

[45] *Dispelling the Fog*, November 10, 1935; *Lincoln* (Nebraska) *State Journal*, November 20, 1935.

[46] *Topeka Capital*, July 20, 1935, February 4, 1936; *Johnson County Democrat*, December 19, 1935.

was put in contact with others—such as the 1924 Democratic presidential nominee, John W. Davis. He wrote a former Kansan, the Scripps-Howard news analyst, Raymond Clapper: "I would like your help, [but] not for my own sake. . . . I think four more years of the same policies that we have had will wreck our parliamentary government, and four years of the old policies will do the job also." He confided to Clapper that "as the possibility of defeating Roosevelt increases, the probability of my nomination increases." [47]

From newspapermen and politicians the governor picked up stories and material about waste and inefficiency in government, an issue he was to make much of during his campaign. In September, Representative Hamilton Fish of New York—a "Red-baiter," as the *Topeka Capital* called him—was feted at Emporia by the Kansas Republican leaders, but Landon said that Kansas had an open mind. Fish, who soon came out for Borah, became one of the Idaho senator's leaders in New York, and Landon's camp counterattacked, inviting Melvin C. Eaton, New York's state Republican chairman, to Topeka for dinner. Eaton declined, saying "that's a long way to go for dinner," and the bid for New York's support thereafter swung toward the New York Young Republicans and the conservative national committeeman, Charles D. Hilles. It was hoped that the Young Republicans would support Landon because of the liberal aspects of his record, and that Hilles would support him out of fear of Senator Borah. [48]

William Randolph Hearst (a conservative and highly nationalistic Democrat) and his vast newspaper and magazine empire was a force that Landon had to reckon with. In July, 1935, Richard E. Berlin, the head of Hearst's magazine chain, told Landon he was assigning Damon Runyon and Adela Rogers St. Johns to write articles about the Landons, for *Cosmopolitan* and *Good Housekeeping* respectively. Two weeks later, John Hamilton wrote Landon that he had met Homer Guck, Hearst's newspaper chief-of-staff, who said he wanted to see the governor. Landon was soon aware that he was being checked out by the Hearst people. "The County Chairman of Linn county . . . in visiting with me one day said, 'Two Hearst men were in my county a

[47] Landon to John Truslow Adams, December 3, 1935; Adams to Landon, December 10, 1935; Landon to Duncan Aikman, August 15, 1935; *Topeka Capital*, October 15, 1935; Ben M. Anderson, Jr., to Landon, February 15, 1936; Landon to Raymond Clapper, November 2, 1935.

[48] *Topeka Capital*, September 14, 15, December 27, 1935; W. T. Mossman to Landon, December 31, 1935; Landon to Mossman, January 2, 1936.

few weeks ago asking a lot of questions about you.'" Landon's thought was that they might be investigating the market potential for a new newspaper in Kansas City, but the chairman said "'No, they seem to be representing more the Hearst magazines, soliciting subscriptions, but they spent more time in asking questions about you.'" In the next few weeks similar reports came in from over the state. John Lambert, of the Hearst papers, who came to Topeka in September, checked through local newspaper files and visited with the governor. Landon asked him: "Did you discover any ring bones on the pony that might show up in dry weather?" and Lambert replied: "I wish your opposition to the World Court and League of Nations was more definite."[49]

In late September the news broke that Hearst was supporting Landon, and many were dismayed. Bill Mossman wrote: "Adopted by Hearst! Well, that's that!" William Allen White was disturbed, but he justified the endorsement: "Doubtless any statesman many times has to ally himself with worse men than Hearst. Probably in my own career I have worked with deeper-dyed villains. But a man should be allowed his fancies in villains, this being the glorious free country that it is."[50] Sentiment in statehouse circles was mixed, but Landon's attitude was clear: It was better that Hearst be for him than against— as long as he exacted no promises and did not interfere. Columnists Clifford Stratton and Paul Mallon probably sized up the endorsement correctly. Stratton said that Hearst believed Landon could be elected President, and that, above all, he did not want to see Roosevelt or Hoover elected—though he preferred Roosevelt to Hoover. Mallon thought Hearst believed that no Democrat could take the nomination away from Roosevelt but that Landon could take it from Hoover.[51]

The build-up of Landon in Hearst's newspapers and magazines started in October, 1935, and continued throughout the campaign. Stories and photographs of the Landons were regular features in the Hearst publications in order to make the family "the best-loved family in America." Paeans of praise were sung about the Kansas governor, and the following—from Arthur Brisbane's column, "Today"—is a typical sample of that prose:

[49] Richard E. Berlin to Landon, July 29, 1935; John D. M. Hamilton to Landon, August 13, 1935; Landon to Westbrook Pegler, December 6, 1954.
[50] W. T. Mossman to Landon, December 30, 1935; W. A. White to W. O. Hart, May 12, 1936, White Papers.
[51] *Topeka Capital*, October 1, 1935.

Governor Landon, an American of average height and far above average ability, a thorough man. He knows American conditions and problems, knows the farmer and his trouble, and knows business, for his intelligence made him a successful, prosperous business man before he became Governor.

He has broad shoulders, made to carry a load, and walks with as firm a stride as any West Pointer. His eyes are brown, his expression cheerful; his nerves are not frazzled.

He prefers listening to talking, and he really LISTENS; does not simply wait for his turn to talk again. He has a strong chin, which means determination, and a forehead to balance it!

All of this interests you, because Governor Landon will probably be nominated for President by the Republicans.

Paul Block says, "He is a great man"; Mr. Hearst says, "He is an able, direct man." There is no doubt that he is a powerful, determined, thoughtful man, and one who may be President needs all of that.[52]

Landon had not met Hearst before Hearst's decision to support him, nor had they negotiated with each other. Unlike Hoover in 1928 and Roosevelt in 1932 (both of whom Hearst had backed), Landon had not solicited the publisher's support, and it was not until December, 1935, that the two men met. On December 10 three private railway cars pulled into Topeka, with Hearst, Paul Block of the Block newspaper chain, and Eleanor Patterson, the publisher of the *Washington Herald*; and Landon met them in the governor's mansion for lunch. Views were exchanged at the luncheon session, during which general agreement was reached on the necessity for prudent fiscal government and the need for defeating Roosevelt. The publishers departed from Topeka, satisfied with Landon's character, but little had been said about policies and no promises had been made. The Hearst people brought in businessmen and others for Landon to meet, pushed Landon in their publications, and fed him information. They also gave him much conflicting advice, which left him free to choose his own ideas.[53]

Contrary to the charge often made in 1936 that Landon was Hearst's puppet, the governor had formed most of his campaign ideas before he met the publisher. Landon, though a strong advocate of state action, was convinced that the states' rights doctrine could not be an excuse for state inaction. When the social security bill was before the Senate, Senator Harry Byrd of Virginia tried to enlist Landon's support in opposing it, because the states could not afford to match its federal

[52] *Columbus Dispatch*, December 11, 1935.

[53] *Topeka Capital*, December 11, 1935; Landon to Westbrook Pegler, December 6, 1954.

grants, but Landon wired back saying the states must match federal social security funds, although allowance should be made for a state's needs and capacity. Landon wrote Senator Capper in support of this position on the matter of relief and unemployment insurance. "As long as a national government is able to withdraw relief arbitrarily and without notice from any state, it can dictate to that state," but the matching of federal money with state funds would help prevent this.[54]

Landon's thoughts on currency were also solidified before the fall of 1935. He wrote his uncle (in August) that there was only one basic issue: the stabilization of currency. He had read Kemmerer of Princeton and other economists for years, and had been impressed by the impact of inflation on Germany in the 1920s and its contribution to Germany's turbulent politics. He felt that "we are following the German pattern of inflation."[55] Landon moderated his views for the press, but his message was clear. He wrote Mark Sullivan: "I don't know whether extravagant expenditures will lead us into Socialism . . . but . . . a continually unbalanced budget leading to a debasing of our currency will throw a greater strain on our form of government than has confronted it since the Civil War." It might even lead to revolution, as in France almost 150 years before.

Landon also told Sullivan, the elder statesman of journalism:

> I do not believe that the solution of our social and economic difficulties lies in a program based on an economy of scarcity. As I have said, the difficulty with a planned agriculture is that you can't plan the weather.
>
> Unquestionably the price of agricultural products has been out of line with the price of industrial products to an unhealthy degree since the war. World events seem to be forcing us on to more of a nationalistic basis than our own domestic policies such as the tariff. If we are to maintain what is known as the American standard of living on a level above the rest of the world, then agriculture must be prosperous in order to furnish a market for our industrial products, but I believe the answer can be found in an economy of plenty.[56]

These were Landon's ideas before he met Hearst, and they were to remain his ideas throughout the campaign for the Presidency.

[54] H. F. Byrd to Landon, February 4, 1935; Landon to Byrd, February 7, 1935; Landon to Arthur Capper, February 21, 1935; all KSA.
[55] Landon to W. T. Mossman, August 23, 1935.
[56] Landon to Mark Sullivan, October 17, 1935.

CHAPTER 10

A Candidate for Sure

John Landon once wrote of his son: "He is about the busiest man you ever heard of—telephone is ringing day and night and men from every state in the union [are] coming here to see him." The old gentleman marveled that "one man came in an airship from Los Angeles for no other purpose than just to talk with him. One day the Santa Fe brought in three private cars, all coming to see the Governor." This increasing activity reflected Alf Landon's development as a national figure and his gradual entry in the 1936 presidential sweepstakes. As a result of his reelection in 1934, he was a prominent Republican; by the spring of 1935, he was an influential Republican; by summer, he was seriously mentioned as a possibility for the nomination; by fall, he had received considerable support and was discussed in the press more often than any of the other possible Republican nominees. In December, *Time* commented:

Still withholding formal acknowledgment of his candidacy, Governor Landon continued last week to play his role of conscientious public servant modestly awaiting a call to higher service. But . . . [the] picture services were ready to bet 1,000 to 1 on the Governor's yearnings when they were furnished with a series of photographs depicting Alf M. Landon at six months in long skirts; Alf M. Landon going on 3 years in sailor straw and enormous kilts; Alf M. Landon at 4 in an embroidered collar; Alf M.

234

Landon at 7 in breeches and sweater with his lop-eared dog; Alf M. Landon at 10 in long coat and pancake hat.[1]

Time was right. Landon was campaigning for the Republican nomination for President, and his campaign was going well, but he had opposition. Only in retrospect might the 1936 Republican presidential nomination appear to have been unwanted or worthless: the Kansas governor had active opposition from Frank Knox and William E. Borah, and shadowy opposition from Herbert Hoover, Arthur H. Vandenberg, and half a dozen "favorite sons." Knox's opposition generally took the form of stop-Landon efforts, but everyone except Knox himself knew that he was almost out of the running. Because of this blindspot, however, Knox could be encouraged to slash away at Borah and Landon, both of whom were considered too liberal by many conservative Republicans. Hoover, for example, urged the *Chicago Daily News* publisher on, discussing the steps he should take against Landon. Knox, who failed to see not only his own political weaknesses but also Landon's strength, thought in late April that the "Landon cause seems to be slipping." Although it was apparent that Hoover was leading a stop-Landon movement, a Hearst writer, James T. Williams, Jr., exulted that Hoover's opposition could almost ensure Landon's election as President, as Harry Hopkins' attack in fall, 1935, had almost clinched the Kansan's nomination.[2]

Landon's biggest problem was Senator Borah, who criticized the Kansas governor in many damaging ways. Arthur Capper, William Allen White, and Roy Roberts tried to use their influence with Borah to keep friendly relations between the two camps, and Landon stayed out of primaries to avoid antagonizing the old progressive warrior (Capper even got Borah to say that he regarded Landon as a friend). Although Borah intended to stay in the race, Capper believed he looked to Landon as his second choice, but, unfortunately for Landon, Borah was not known to keep his commitments—or, as the Idahoan saw it, to wear fetters. The Borah situation was dangerous because many westerners would go with Borah if it seemed he had a chance for the nomination.[3]

[1] John M. Landon to J. H. Grundish, January 22, 1936, Alfred M. Landon Papers, Kansas State Historical Society, Topeka; *Time*, December 23, 1935, p. 11.

[2] Marian McKenna, *Borah* (Ann Arbor: University of Michigan Press, 1961), pp. 322 ff.; Frank Knox to Annie Knox, April 8, 12, 27, 1936, Frank Knox Papers, Manuscript Division, Library of Congress, Washington, D.C.; James T. Williams, Jr., to Landon, April 7, 1936.

[3] McKenna, *Borah*, p. 331; Arthur Capper to Landon, January 4, 1936.

The fight between Landon and Borah broke out in March, 1936, and both men emerged the worse for it. Borah's correspondence files show that his most fervent supporters viewed Landon as an old guard candidate, one whom Borah should fight, and Borah could not very well disappoint his followers, men with whom he had had dealings for years. Unfortunately for Landon and himself, the old senator allowed himself to be taken in by Landon's bitterest enemies in the oil industry. These men made strong charges against the governor, and Borah adopted many of them without investigation. The leader in the attack against Landon was John B. Elliott, the maverick of the 1933 Washington oil conference, who implied that Landon was a tool of Standard Oil. Landon was condemned because he was well-to-do and because he refused to write Elliott (with whom he had learned to be cautious) his views on monopolization.[4] Other men made similar accusations, and the immediate result was that Borah charged Standard Oil with trying to influence the selection of Oklahoma's delegates to the Republican national convention. Borah also called for a Senate investigation of the matter. Because Oklahoma was to send a Landon delegation, the senator concluded that Standard Oil was backing Landon.

All this brought angry responses from Landon's friends. Louis Levand, the publisher of the *Wichita Beacon*, said it was mud-slinging, and Borah dodged, writing Levand that Standard, not Landon, was the sinister influence. Richard Lloyd Jones publicly challenged Borah to prove his statement, and wrote to Hoover that Borah had lied.[5] The episode, however, brought more "evidence" that seemed to support Borah's suspicions—flimsy indications that Landon was linked with Standard Oil, the American Liberty League, the Republican old guard, the Chamber of Commerce, and the Finney scandal; that he was a "bolter" and an Anti-Saloon Leaguer, and a millionaire who favored big business and Wall Street. The old progressive, Chester Rowell, now a Hoover admirer, told Borah that the clinching damnation was Hearst's support of Landon.[6]

Landon worried about his opposition for the nomination, but he was confident enough that he did not think it necessary to enter the

[4] Harry Sommers to William E. Borah, April 23, 1936, and John B. Elliott to Borah, March 9, 10, 1936, William E. Borah Papers, Manuscript Division, Library of Congress, Washington, D.C.

[5] *Columbus Dispatch*, March 15, 1936; Louis Levand to William E. Borah, March 14, 1936, and Borah to Levand, March 16, 1936, Borah Papers; Richard Lloyd Jones to Herbert Hoover, April 23, 1936.

[6] File 401, Chester Rowell to William E. Borah, April 11, 1936, Borah Papers.

primary elections in any of the thirteen states that determined convention delegates in this way. Moreover, an active primary campaign would have conflicted with the image of sitting back and receiving the nomination as the harmony candidate. Furthermore, primaries cost money, and, as William Allen White wrote Landon: "You have no money. You cannot get much honest money"[7] (but his name was entered in some of the primaries, against his wishes, by overly enthusiastic supporters). Later in the spring Landon wrote that he did not have to go into the primaries because his boom was based not on the bosses but on the sentiments of rural counties. In New York, Missouri, and Oklahoma, he said, the bosses preferred uninstructed delegates, but sentiment in the counties forced them to go along with the Landon boom. Landon also refused to make any deals in exchange for backing, though some of his zealous supporters hinted at deals in his name. Landon told all those close to him that he would not make any promises to win support, nor be bound by promises made in his name. "I am not going to be under any embarrassing obligations either for financial or personal support."[8]

The Landon forces strongly asserted themselves in early 1936. Fifty Kansans attended Republican Lincoln Day dinners throughout the country to push Landon. In March, John D. M. Hamilton opened the national headquarters of the Landon-for-President movement in the Carlton Hotel in Washington. Although they were not authorized, Landon-for-President clubs sprang up throughout the land. Other Landon supporters were hitting the campaign trail. Representative Clifford Hope, who was politicking among Republicans in Washington and among farm groups, went to New York on a scouting mission. Kansas editors plugged for Landon at the convention of the American Society of Newspaper Editors, and it was reported that most ed tors and Washington correspondents were for Landon. William Allen White was second only to Hamilton in trooping about in support of Landon. Before the New York Young Republican Club, in an effort to stop comparisons of Landon and Coolidge, White said the Kansan was

[7] W. A. White to Landon, February 15, 1936. By May, 1936, the Landon-for-President Committee had spent no more than $100,000, a small sum for a successful candidacy for the Republican presidential nomination. William Allen White, *What It's All About* (New York: Macmillan, 1936), pp. 18 f.; Cal Tinney, *Is It True What They Say about Landon? A Non-Partisan Portrait* (New York: Wise-Parslow, 1936), p. 158.

[8] Landon to Raymond Clapper, March 1, 1936; Landon to James McMullin, May 11, 1936; Landon to W. A. Sheaffer, March 14, 1936.

"about as much like Coolidge as the Wild Man of Borneo is like Billy Sunday."[9]

On March 26, John Hamilton presented Landon to the nation over the Blue Network of the National Broadcasting Company, after reviewing Landon's personal background and official record, and emphasizing his attributes of economy and efficiency. The governor, Hamilton said, promised stability rather than Utopia.

> If the country wishes to regain its self-confidence, if it wishes to get back to something real, if it wants action that is calm and considerate, and speech that is quiet and to the point, if it is tired of the show and wants something that is substance and not shadow, it will, I believe, look with increasing eagerness to Governor Landon as the leader best-qualified to bring back reality into national affairs and to make liberalism something besides a cloak for usurpation of power by little men and something that will benefit the ordinary man and woman. . . . And anyone who counts on his being "handled" or discounts him because he can be "handled" by any little group of smart men, whether politicians or financiers, does not know Governor Landon. He is as sympathetic with the problems of business men as he is with the problems of the farmer, the industrial worker, or the family on relief, but he will not plead the cause of any one group against the good of the whole.[10]

This was the beginning of Landon's formal bid for the nomination. Until that week his movement did not have letterhead stationery, and Landon never had a coordinated, professionally organized preconvention movement. Although the build-up was formidable, it was carried on largely by his supporters rather than his entourage. Even so, the build-up, he complained, was "hard on Mrs. Landon and the kids. I worry sometimes as to the psychological effect hereafter of the atmosphere in which they are being raised. . . . Nothing we do is normal, no matter if we are doing the same things today that we did last year and in the same way, somebody gives it an abnormal slant."[11]

The campaign, of course, intruded on the life of the family. Innumerable photographs were taken of the Landons; rotogravure sections of newspapers around the country week after week carried

[9] *Topeka Capital*, February 12, March 11, April 17, 25, 1936; Clifford R. Hope to Landon, February 10, 1936, Clifford R. Hope Papers, Kansas State Historical Society, Topeka.

[10] John D. M. Hamilton, *Presenting Governor Landon* (Ottawa, Kan.; Landon-for-President Committee, 1936).

[11] Landon to W. M. Kiplinger, March 27, 1936.

pictures of the governor walking, talking, reading, working, speaking, relaxing; the children, Peggy, Nancy Jo, and Jack, were snapped playing, running, and walking, and with and without their parents. It seemed that wherever the Landons turned they confronted newspaper photographers, but this was a key part of the build-up: it would be impossible to make the Landons America's Best-loved Family without a constant splurge of pictures and newspaper coverage. The Kansas Daily Newspaper Association distributed thousands of "Facts about Landon" sheets, with stories and pictures about Landon, his record, his family, his business, his epigrams, and comments about him from friends, associates, and newspapermen. By April, the Landon-for-President committee provided similar material in its weekly four-page *Landon Marches On* bulletin; and photographs filled the pages of *Landon Marches On*, with titles such as "Nancy Jo and Her Easter Bunny," "A Portrait Study of Mrs. Landon," "EARNEST ALFRED M. LANDON," and "Governor Landon spends an evening with his family in the upstairs library of the Executive Mansion."[12] If the Landons were not becoming America's Best-loved Family they were certainly becoming America's Most-photographed Family.

Adding to the material on Landon was Richard B. Fowler's fairly reliable though pro-Landon biography of the governor, *Deeds Not Deficits, The Story of Alfred M. Landon*. This small book, with an introduction by William Allen White, appeared at the end of March and had gone through its "fifth large printing" by May 10. In February an old acquaintance, William Hard, listened for hours as Landon talked on the need for a sound, sensible approach to national politics. This exposition was readied for the July issue of *Redbook*: "The Spirit of Republicanism, by Alf M. Landon as told to William Hard." During the fall and winter, Colonel Frederick Palmer roamed about Topeka and Kansas City to get material for *This Man Landon*, a long but sketchy biography of Landon.

Although biographical material was circulated lavishly, very little of it presented the whole Landon; the basic theme was that Landon was a fiscal wizard. Like most Hearst papers, the *San Francisco Examiner* proclaimed, over a full-page color photograph of the governor: "Governor Alf M. Landon—Balancer of Budgets." The organ of the National Economy League, *The Watch Dog*, headlined: ALF M. LANDON, THE BUDGET–BALANCING GOVERNOR OF KANSAS. The letterhead of the

---

[12] *E.g., Landon Marches On*, April 21, 1936.

Landon-for-President clubs of California proclaimed: "He reduces taxes."[13]

Information was prepared and sent out to meet some of the expected criticism of Landon. Barney L. Allis, president of Kansas City's Muehlebach Hotel, answered the question of the president of the American Hotel Association about Landon's views on prohibition: In Kansas, he upheld the law; outside prohibitionist territory, he enjoyed an occasional drink, and did not object if others did likewise.[14] As for Hopkins' charge that he achieved balanced budgets by depriving Kansans of necessary services, data were provided by state officers and Landon supporters that showed the state's budget was balanced despite—not because of—federal assistance, which so often required state contributions.[15] Although the pro-Landon accounts failed to convince the governor's critics, few observers noted that he had *combined* federal aid and a tight fiscal policy to give Kansas what most other states had in relief and state services, and yet, *unlike* the other states, had balanced the budget and reduced taxes. Most often, Landon's supporters ignored federal aid and his denigrators played up the state's parsimony.

The administration of the Kansas school system had been attacked on the ground that it had been weakened to balance the state budget, and again there was a counter-flood of defensive material. William M. Jardine, the president of the University of Wichita, called this criticism "ridiculous" and "impossible" because, as the schools were the responsibility of local government, there was no way the state could tap school funds. Moreover, the cash-basis law, which required that expenditures not exceed cash on hand, assured the payment of teachers' salaries—and emergency aid had been granted to school districts in distress. Then, in a bid for Negro support, the Associated Negro Press was told that Landon was opposed to the lily-white Republicanism of the south, that he condemned lynching (Kansas' stringent anti-lynching law was highly touted), and that he favored nondiscriminatory civil service examinations.[16]

Landon also stepped up his personal efforts to win the nomination.

[13] *San Francisco Examiner*, February 2, 1936; *The Watch Dog*, February, 1936.

[14] Barney L. Allis to Thomas D. Green, February 28, 1936.

[15] An example of official literature is the state accountant's press release, "Facts and Figures about Kansas," May 28, 1936.

[16] Governor's office press release, "Educators Find Gov. Landon Friend of Schools," n.d. (probably April, 1936); Carl A. Rott to C. A. Barnett, March 4, April 3, 1936.

On January 8 he told a meeting of the Kansas Board of Agriculture that he had given the Agricultural Adjustment Administration full co-operation because it was the only agency that could meet the farm crisis, and that the disruption of its activities by the Supreme Court was only temporary; he foresaw stabilization of the farm situation on a new basis. A new farm program, he contended, must find permanent markets rather than provide temporary relief, and also must work to-ward soil and water conservation.[17] He used the Kansas Day meeting at Topeka to declare: "Change does not necessarily mean progress. A social philosophy is not always bad because it is old, nor good because it is merely new." He warned that the Constitution cannot be flouted "by executive evasion, loose legislation or insidious propaganda" if the people are to be protected against oppression. He deplored an un-balanced federal budget, waste in relief expenditures, and patronage spoilsmen, and again he spoke out for soil conservation and flood control. At the end of February, at the Nebraska Founders' Day dinner in Lincoln, he repeated these sentiments—along with his usual homilies on the pioneer spirit—and ended with a quotation from Theodore Roosevelt: "The old pioneer days are gone, but the need for the pioneer virtues remains." The Lincoln and Topeka speeches were reprinted (as well as the November, 1935, Ohio State Chamber of Commerce speech) in a widely circulated pamphlet that capsulized the bases of Landon's nomination campaign: economy, efficiency, abundance, recovery, equal opportunity, adherence to the Constitu-tion, federalism, integrity, conservation of resources, opposition to a concentration of power in private or in public hands, and the civil-service merit system.[18]

Landon did not speak publicly again until May, when he made five speeches, three of them only a few days before the Republican national convention. His first engagement was a nationwide radio interview by H. V. Kaltenborn, on May 7, in which he presented himself as a public servant who "can be a liberal without squandering [the public's] money." He also used this opportunity to declare his approval of social security, and to say that relief must be given where it was needed—but with the warning that "*There is no future on the relief roll.*" On May 18 he traveled to the small high school at Attica, Kansas, to address the twenty-nine boys and girls who were graduating that day (an act

[17] Landon speech, Topeka, January 8, 1936.
[18] *Three Speeches by Governor Alfred M. Landon of Kansas* (Topeka; Landon-for-President Committee, 1936).

hailed by Richard Lloyd Jones' *Tulsa Tribune* as dramatizing "the bigness of the man "). Landon asked the students to resist the temptations offered by those "who would solve your difficulties by changing everything" or by those who would "be shocked at the thought of changing anything." [19] Two weeks later, addressing the American Medical Association convention at Kansas City, he lauded the physicians' adherence to individualism; and at the University of Kansas commencement, on June 8, he affirmed his belief that "America has not come to the end of the road of individual opportunity." At the Baker University commencement, Landon voiced similar ideas:

> I don't think you should rely upon society or government for your "piece of pie," any more than you should rely upon it coming to you automatically in the sky, bye and bye. If you want a piece of pie, you've got to go out and get it yourself. You have a right to insist that government keep the door of opportunity open for you so you can do that.[20]

During the late winter of 1935 and early spring of 1936, Landon was perpetually busy. In addition to making speeches, consulting with advisers, and planning platform proposals, the governor had visitors, as Malcolm Bingay put it, "from all parts of America" who regarded him as a strange "zoological specimen." Day after day Landon sat at his office desk—an American flag and maroon velvet drapes as a backdrop, and near a bust of humorist Will Rogers—listening to the leaders and the humble of his party, and talking to them in turn. Landon impressed his visitors as an extremely likable person, "a cross between a popular 'grad' and the most astute politician of the old school," an informant reported to Senator Borah.

> In meeting him face to face, one is immediately disarmed by his friendly smile and warmth of his welcome. . . . His ease of manner makes the interviewer feel immediately at home in his presence; propping his feet on the top of his desk, . . . producing a package of cigarettes and asking you to join him in a real homey way, he starts you off with a cordial, "Well what can I do for you?"[21]

[19] *Landon Philosophy, A Trio of Public Utterances* (Ottawa, Kan.; Landon-for-President Committee, 1936); *Tulsa Tribune*, May 18, 1936.
[20] Landon speech, Kansas City, June 3, 1936; *Landon Philosophy*; Landon speech, Baldwin City (Baker University), June 5, 1936.
[21] Malcolm Bingay to Landon, May 25, 1936; Unsigned and undated (1936) typescript in Presidency/Landon file, Borah Papers. The report in the Borah files is borne out in Raymond Gram Swing's excellent article, "Alf Landon Is Not Calvin Coolidge," *The Nation*, January 8, 1936.

All visitors were seen, if not by Landon, by one of his aides; but all of the political, industrial, and farm leaders, the few labor leaders who dared call, and the publishers, editors, and correspondents of big newspapers and magazines could always see the governor (and anyone else in the machinery of the state) if they wanted. By a refinement of the open-door policy of earlier, less pressing days, others could see him if they were in groups—and occasionally even if they were not. They would certainly see Fred Seaton, or A. R. Jones, or lesser officials who had been pressed into service to praise Kansas and Landon. All visitors were welcome: if they could not help Landon they could spend money in Topeka, which hugely enjoyed the great "barbecue" at the capital. The city took on the aspects of a tourist center with one big attraction, Landon—about whom every merchant and clerk on Kansas Avenue, and every bellhop and waitress had opinions and stories.

The famous correspondents, editors, and publishers visited, wrote, and telephoned Landon; and scarcely a day passed that a nationally prominent political, industrial, or religious figure did not drop in.[22] These people advised Landon not to attack Roosevelt directly—or to attack him directly; to speak out on foreign affairs—or not to speak out; to take a liberal position—or not to touch anything the New Deal favored; to improve his speaking ability—or not to improve it. But Landon made his strategy clear. He would not be pushed into an illiberal position, as Hoover had been. He would not make an aggressive campaign for the nomination—except for a few appearances in neighboring states, he would not leave Kansas. The nomination must come free of entanglements.

The Landon movement, spearheaded by the press and increasingly supported by rank-and-file Republican sentiment, moved along with remarkably few setbacks. Although some declarations of support from convention delegates had come as early as 1935, the important signs of Landon's developing strength came in 1936. Landon's forces won a round in their fight for New York when the state's Association of Young Republican Clubs declared Landon the number-one candidate in the west. Although the association denied that this was an endorsement, it concluded that as there was no eastern candidate "we must look to the West."[23]

Kansas Day, January 29, was a boon to the movement; it was the seventy-fifth celebration of Kansas' statehood and the state made

[22] Governor's office datebook, 1936.
[23] *Topeka Capital*, January 12, 1936.

the most of it. The largest crowd ever recorded assembled in Topeka for the event, including dozens of newspapermen and some 500 visitors from other states. The usual candidacy announcements were canceled to give Landon center stage, and the governor was billed as the chief speaker, an honor traditionally given to an out-of-state politician. Landon (who appeared in a dress suit) spoke over a national radio hook-up and flayed the "spendthrift" administration in Washington. The consensus was that the speech was very effective and that Landon had greatly enhanced his position.[24]

In the actual pledging of delegates, which began toward the end of February, Landon's strategy was to avoid doing anything that might be divisive of Republican strength. The Iowa state Republican convention met, and great enthusiasm for Landon was reported, despite the fact that the party leaders were offering Senator Lester Dickinson as a favorite son. Clyde Miller, Landon's observer at the convention, had to work hard to dissuade delegates from voting for Landon, which would have split the state convention and incurred the wrath of the Iowa leadership. A similar situation occurred in Ohio, where the state leaders, although favoring Landon, wanted an uninstructed delegation. Borah had entered the Ohio primary, opposed by Robert A. Taft, who had entered in order to gain control of the delegation for the state leadership; Landon fought to stay off the ballot, so as not to offend Borah or the Ohio organization. Landon also avoided running against Borah in Nebraska.[25] At the end of February the California Republican Assembly overwhelmingly approved sending an uninstructed delegation to the national convention. The Landon forces were displeased by this, interpreting it not as a harmony move (the description of the state chairman, Earl Warren) but as a stop-Landon maneuver. Landon, however, intended to stay out of California to avoid antagonizing Hoover and the state organization. Encouraging news came early in March: the New Mexico state convention had endorsed Landon, and an Ohio poll showed Landon was the favorite in the Buckeye state. In Oklahoma, despite Borah's blast about a Standard Oil–bought convention, Landon won all twenty-one delegates.[26]

On March 10 the California situation began to unravel when Governor Frank F. Merriam announced he was for Landon, and a

[24] *Topeka State Journal,* January 29, 1936; *Topeka Capital,* January 30, 1936.
[25] *Topeka Capital,* February 28, 29, March 6, 1936.
[26] *Ibid.,* March 1, 3, 12, 17, 1936.

Landon slate was entered a week later (without Landon's permission) in the contest for delegates. Ohio began to warm up: Borah challenged the voters of Ohio to permit "no hotel-room decisions," but, to convince the voters of his party loyalty, he said he would support the successful nominee. In New Jersey, Governor Harold G. Hoffman announced for Landon; and a little later Governor C. Douglass Buck of Delaware predicted Landon's nomination.[27]

By March 28 it appeared that Landon's stay-at-home, harmony strategy was paying off: he could boast fifty-one delegates to Knox's eleven, and none of the other Republican aspirants had delegates as yet. Three days later Kentucky gave Landon eighteen votes, and the following day Landon was entered (against his wishes) in the New Jersey primary—against Borah. By April 4 the delegate total was Landon 74 and Knox 24; there were rumors that Vandenberg and Hoover were engaged in a stop-Landon movement, and Borah had changed his mind about bolting, saying there was "no chain about my neck."[28]

By spring, Landon had a commanding lead in the Gallup Poll— 43 per cent of the Republicans had favored him in February, and on the March 15 poll he scored 56 per cent (Borah, the runner-up, had only 20 per cent). Landon led in forty-three states and Borah in four. Landon's greatest strength was with farmers and he was weakest with relief recipients. Roosevelt, however, led the entire Republican group in strength: 54 per cent to 46 per cent. The March poll also showed that Republican women, farmers, people on relief, and youth wanted a liberal program. It was clear that Landon had to devise a program that could balance the budget and yet not disturb relief and farm benefits.[29]

The job of securing delegates went on. On April 11 the Virginia convention endorsed Landon, and his total climbed to 107 delegates (502 were needed to nominate). The same day Borah won most of the Wisconsin delegates, but a few days later he was defeated in Illinois by Knox. Knox, by April 19, claimed 130 delegates, apparently having forged ahead of Landon, but Borah was surprised that he got only 41,000 votes in the Nebraska preferential primary while Landon received 10,000 write-ins.[30] One week later, Nebraska national committeeman C. A.

[27] *Ibid.*, March 11, 18, 20, 22, 31, 1936.
[28] *Ibid.*, March 29, April 1, 2, 5, 6, 1936.
[29] *New York Herald Tribune*, April 5, 1936.
[30] *Topeka Capital*, April 12, 16, 19, 1936.

McCloud declared that twelve of Nebraska's uninstructed fourteen delegates favored Landon; and it was reported that most of Colorado's delegates also favored Landon. The delegate estimates stood at 130 for Knox, 123 for Landon, and 47 for Borah. Then, in the Massachusetts primary, Landon won five to one over all the write-in votes cast for Borah, Hoover, Knox, and Vandenberg, though President Roosevelt won far more votes than all of the Republicans together.[31]

The Gallup Poll taken in April showed that Landon held his strength among the Republicans, again receiving 56 per cent, while Borah dropped to 19 per cent. In three crucial states, whose primaries were still to be held, Landon polled 55 per cent in New Jersey, and 59 per cent in Ohio (though he was not on the ballot), but in one month he had dropped from 64 per cent to 46 per cent in California. The Kansan's ardent California supporters were hurting him there.[32]

The California situation was becoming sticky as the Hoover and nonpreferential forces campaigned against Hearst, and incidentally against Landon. Because the California Republican Assembly had charged that Landon was splitting the party, William Allen White tried to mend fences with the outraged Hoover, telling the former President that Landon had opposed the entry of his slate. Hoover was temporarily assuaged, but he made it clear he would consider a victory by the Hearst forces (who were backing the Landon slate) a personal insult; and he implied that if this happened he would probably withdraw from all political activity. Three days later Hoover wrote White that Landon should do something to show his independence of Hearst, but he doubted that the governor had the courage to do so. In any event, if Landon's California backers did not stop attacking Hoover, he could no longer restrain his supporters from opening up on Landon. Soon after, the Landon-for-President club of Los Angeles advised all Landon supporters to vote for the uninstructed slate.[33] Landon was involved in reconciling the factions, with White trying to calm Hoover and Henry J. Allen trying to soothe the Hearst group. The uninstructed forces, however, demanded that the Landon group in California withdraw, which so angered the group that it pursued its

31 *Ibid.*, April 25, 26, 30, 1936; *Washington Post*, May 3, 1936.

32 *Washington Post*, May 3, 1936.

33 *Topeka Capital*, April 8, 19, 1936; Herbert Hoover to W. A. White, April 14, April 17, 1936, William Allen White Papers, Manuscript Division, Library of Congress, Washington, D.C.

activities. Hearst, on the other hand, did not threaten Landon, and gave no reason for offense.[34]

The California primary had unpleasant results for Landon. Stuck with a slate he did not want, he was defeated by some 90,000 votes. Even more disheartening, more than 600,000 votes were cast in the Republican primary, but almost 1 million votes were cast in the Democratic primary. The only consolation at the time was that Landon had beaten Borah in the South Dakota primary. Although White also was unhappy with the California fiasco, he discounted its effect on the overall campaign; he was more worried about the uninstructed, boss-controlled delegates of the eastern states.[35]

Meanwhile Borah had been defeated in Ohio, and the New Jersey campaign had ended happily for Landon. Because of a struggle between Governor Hoffman and ex-Representative Franklin W. Fort for control of the party machinery, Landon had been in danger of being tied in with the Hoffman faction, which had supported him. Moreover, most of the New Jersey leaders wanted an unpledged delegation, and Borah had campaigned in the state. Yet Landon's reform backers skillfully played on their debtors, their good name, and the ideas of national party harmony and backing the winning man. With little money and no visible organization, they pulled Landon through to a four-to-one victory over Borah, allowing the Kansan to claim more than 300 delegates to Knox's 230.[36] In the same week that Landon won his stunning New Jersey victory, he received inadvertent help from James Farley. On May 20 the Democratic national committee chairman, in belittling tones, predicted that the Republican nominee would be "the governor of a typical prairie state." The reaction to this snobbishness was ferocious among western Republicans, and redounded to Landon's advantage.[37]

Throughout late winter and early spring the Landon forces were generally confident of his nomination, and they proceeded on this

[34] Henry J. Allen to W. A. White, May 6, 1936, White Papers.

[35] *Los Angeles Times*, May 7, 1936; W. A. White to Henry J. Allen, May 8, 1936, White Papers.

[36] Arthur T. Vanderbilt, "The Landon Campaign in New Jersey," n.d. (probably late May, 1936) (typescript); *Topeka Capital*, May 18, 21, 25, 1936.

[37] *Topeka Capital*, May 21, 1936; *Washington Post*, May 22, 1936; *New York Times*, June 14, 1936.

assumption in preparing for the tussle over the platform. On certain issues, Landon had strong ideas. He believed a great deal more could be—and should have been—accomplished in public works through the expenditures of relief money. Moreover, very little money had been used for gathering "the necessary facts and statistics that would enable an intelligent study of our unemployment problem," and Landon feared that "the minute we stop spending this federal money we shall have a slump in the consuming industries in this country." Landon, who several years before had been a member of the Civil Service League, renewed his interest in the merit system: "With the tremendous expansion of bureaucracy, which I think we all realize is more or less permanent, it seems to me a real Civil Service becomes imperative." So strongly did he feel about this that he declared the merit principle should apply not only to routine jobs but also to high governmental positions, as in Great Britain.[38]

Although Landon was being touted all over the land as a man who knew the farmers' problems, he had been wary of speaking on these problems (except as they pertained to flood control, water conservation, and abundance); therefore, in January, the governor and his supporters went to work drawing up an agricultural plank. Representative Clifford Hope, Landon's chief coordinator on the plank, searched widely for ideas and knowledgeable people. Landon also consulted E. H. Taylor of *Country Gentleman*, J. M. Collins of the *Kansas City Star*, and Robert Laubengayer of the *Salina Journal*. They looked for ways to manipulate the tariff to the American farmer's advantage and for ways to provide for commodity loans, crop insurance, and soil conservation —as instruments for stopping land depletion and through which relief payments could be made. By the time Hope had completed the trial draft of the plank, it had been seen by a platoon of farm experts, researchers, and politicians. When he sent it to Henry J. Allen for polishing, in late May, Landon noted:

> I believe you should give especial emphasis to the provision for encouraging the family type of farm. By limiting the payment of benefits to the normal production of the family type of farm several things may be accomplished. One is the avoidance of such large individual benefits as occurred under the AAA; another is a reduction in the cost of the program; a third is some degree of control over surpluses, as the large-scale farm enterprises contribute

[38] Landon to William Hard, March 27, 1936; Landon to Ellery Sedgwick, March 13, 1936.

more to creating surpluses than the family type of farm; finally is . . . the preservation of individual opportunity.[39]

On other issues and planks, Landon received suggestions from all elements of the party. He corresponded on budget and finance problems with Professor Channing J. Bullock of Harvard, asking his consideration of a congressional resolution that would provide (on the British pattern) that appropriations must be accompanied by a supporting tax measure. Landon also gave a great deal of consideration to social security, working with his general platform coordinator, Charles P. Taft, and with Raymond Gram Swing, who in turn worked with Dr. Frederic Dewhurst (of The Brookings Institution), Gifford and Cornelia Pinchot, and William Hard. Landon, who did not like the compulsory insurance established in the Social Security Act, favored old-age pensions, but he felt that the nation was stuck with compulsory insurance. He made a special point of saying that whatever system was used for pensions and assistance, a test of an applicant's means should not be used to determine his eligibility. He felt that government pensions and assistance came from taxes, and that taxpayers should not be embarrassed in taking advantage of federal payments.

On foreign affairs, Landon depended chiefly upon former Under Secretary of State J. Reuben Clark. Clark drafted planks on tariff reciprocity, most-favored-nation agreements, and the Monroe Doctrine. He believed in a literal interpretation of the Monroe Doctrine, which would let the Latin-American nations feel real pressures from Europe—which would relieve the United States from Latin-American and European criticism, and might even result in Latin America drawing closer to the United States. Clark saw tariff reciprocity as an instrument for removing unnecessary and artificial trade barriers, but felt that reciprocity should not extend to most-favored-nation privileges, for this would make both concepts meaningless.[40]

William Allen White, selected by Landon as his chief emissary on platform questions, spent a good deal of time in the east that spring

[39] Clifford R. Hope to Landon, January 10, 1936; J. M. Collins to Hope, January 9, 1936; Hope to Collins, January 13, 1936; all Hope Papers; Landon to Henry J. Allen, May 25, 1936.

[40] Landon to Channing J. Bullock, February 25, 1936; White, *What It's All About*, pp. 28 f.; Landon to Raymond Gram Swing, February 26, May 15, 1936; J. Reuben Clark to Landon, April 20, 1936.

ferreting out platform ideas and reactions. He gathered that the New
England Republicans would not only support Landon for the nomination but would let his forces write the platform. He warned Landon
that the liberal attitude was the only successful approach, and that
even Vandenberg would accept a liberal platform. White reported
that the Republican national chairman, Henry P. Fletcher, thought "it
would be a fine thing for Borah to go in and strut his stuff and carry
the convention as far to the 'left' as he can. The further he carries it the
better for you." This would not only liberalize the platform, it might
keep the Idahoan from bolting.[41]

While the Landon platform proposals were being completed, public
attention in late May turned to the forthcoming Republican national
convention in Cleveland. Kansas, with only 18 of the 1,003 delegates,
was in the odd position of sporting the leading candidate for the
presidential nomination, thanks to strong press and delegate support
drawn from all over the east, midwest, and west. Yet Landon's leading
position did not ensure him the nomination: forces were afoot to stop
him. Hoover, who was unhappy with Landon, had not been invited to
the convention, but Frank Knox remedied this. Believing the former
President was "doing everything he can to bring about my nomination," Knox got Fletcher to invite Hoover. John Hamilton, not to seem
ungracious, soon requested that Hoover be asked to address the
delegates, and Fletcher, a few days later, formally asked Hoover to
speak. This crowded Hoover into the limelight and unsettled the
convention picture.[42]

On June 3, state chairman Beck reiterated that no deals would be
made and that no pledges would be given on Landon's behalf. At
the same time, Robert A. Taft of Ohio withdrew as a candidate, telling
his delegates to vote as they pleased; and it was presumed that most of
them would vote for Landon. J. Henry Roraback, the Connecticut
national committeeman, was quoted as saying, "It's all over." On the
counterattack, Borah's manager, Carl Bachmann, said that all the
candidates for the nomination should address the convention (a wag
suggested that all the candidates might just as well model bathing
suits). The next day, June 4, after Bachmann called Landon an
"avowed friend of the New Deal," Borah's supporters also charged

[41] W. A. White to Leonard Ayres, May 11, 1936; White to B. M. Anderson, May
14, 1936, White Papers; White to Landon, April 21, 1936.

[42] Frank Knox to Annie Knox, May 21, 1936, Knox Papers; *Topeka Capital*, May 30,
June 3, 1936.

that national-committee funds had been used against the senator in the Ohio primary. Moreover, national committeeman Charles D. Hilles and state chairman Melvin Eaton, both of New York, refused to endorse Landon because they were working to keep the state's delegates uncommitted in order to make a trade, which supposedly involved the nomination of Representative James Wadsworth for Vice President. Edwin F. Jaeckle, the Erie County chairman, declared that half of the New York delegates wanted Landon, and should not be hog-tied.[43]

Meanwhile, the Kansans had congregated in Cleveland's Hollenden Hotel, and on June 5 they began holding Landon-for-President open houses. (A hundred Kansas women, by shifts, welcomed guests and served soft drinks and cookies—also distributing Landon buttons and publicity—amid huge photographs of Landon, including one that showed him expertly guiding his horse, "Old Si," over a hurdle.) When word came that Pennsylvania would support Landon, Hamilton predicted 400 delegates for the Kansan on the first ballot (but Knox and Borah denied that the nomination was clinched, and the stop-Landon efforts were intensified). Kansas, boasting an "all-star" delegation, had Capper, Allen, and White as three of its delegates-at-large, and Hamilton was a district delegate. The delegation was balanced in terms of the political factions in Kansas; and Frank Haucke was on hand to tell why (despite charges that Landon had betrayed him in 1930) Landon was a great man, Joseph H. Mercer to tell why stockmen idolized Landon, Harry Colmery to tell why Legionnaires admired Landon, Walter Fees to tell why oilmen lauded Landon, and Thomas Wagstaff to tell why the home folk in Montgomery County loved Landon.[44]

Landon, who had decided to stay away from the convention, advised the delegation and his supporters to go easy on Borah, and not to be disturbed by what the senator or his managers said. To J. Reuben Clark, who complimented Landon on this strategy because it

[43] *Topeka Capital*, June 4, 5, 1936. The disagreement among New Yorkers on Landon reflected the bitter struggle between Hilles and Jaeckle for Republican leadership in the state; Wadsworth, the pawn in the situation, was not opposed to Landon. Charles D. Hilles to James W. Wadsworth, Jr., May 27, 1936, Wadsworth to H. A. Hopkins, March 2, 1936, James W. Wadsworth Papers, Manuscript Division, Library of Congress, Washington, D.C.; Alden Hatch, *The Wadsworths of the Genesee* (New York: Coward-McCann, 1959), p. 244.

[44] *Topeka Capital*, June 6, 11, 1936; *Cleveland Plain Dealer*, June 8, 1936.

might keep Borah from bolting, Landon replied that it was not entirely a matter of strategy: "I have the highest regard for Senator Borah . . . he is entitled to all credit and consideration. He has been a great statesman and a great patriot for twenty-five years." Landon, moreover, wrote to his Oklahoma boomer, Richard Lloyd Jones, about an editorial Jones had written charging that Borah had joined with the old guard to defeat Landon. He asked that Jones also go easy: "I am not sure your comments on Borah will be justified. After all, we must remember he has been a grand fighter for many years in behalf of the things you and I believe in, and is entitled to all the honors of a veteran warrior for righteous justice."[45]

In the meantime, rumors and reports continued to flood the convention city. It was said that George H. Moses, Charles Hilles, and David Reed—the old guard leaders of New Hampshire, New York, and Pennsylvania—were fighting against the control of the convention by the young, including Landon. White broadcast sophisticated homilies on the virtues of the Kansas governor on the N.B.C. network. On June 6, Hamilton contended that Landon's nomination was certain; there would be no smoke-filled-room selection this time. Many stop-Landon circulars were distributed, one of which charged that Landon had bolted the party in 1912, 1924, and 1930, and that White had said Landon "followed me in and out of the Republican party four times"; the same circular also condemned the "Landon-controlled press." Another circular said the Landon leaders "have a SECRET BAR" and that "they have offered our boys . . . almost anything they want to SELL OUT TO THEM," but—referring to the Kansas state flower—it warned "Sun Flowers do not Bloom in November."[46]

On Sunday, June 7, there were reports that Senator Vandenberg was trying to spur a stop-Landon movement and that he had visited the headquarters of the other candidates. George H. Moses, a Knox leader, took to the radio to demand that the convention not be a "rubber stamp." Senator Dickinson, when warned by the Iowa delegation against becoming active in a stop-Landon movement, said that he was not trying to stop anyone. There were discussions of former Governor Frank O. Lowden of Illinois as a dark-horse candidate. (Secretary of the Interior Harold Ickes contributed a barb, saying the Republican nominee would be the man "whose record is most color-

[45] J. Reuben Clark to Landon, June 4, 1936; Landon to Clark, June 10, 1936; Landon to Richard Lloyd Jones, June 8, 1936.

[46] *Topeka Capital*, June 7, 1936; pamphlet enclosed in George Dixon to Landon, June 7, 1936.

less, whose views on the burning issues of the day are the least known, and whose convictions are the most accommodating.") On June 8, Frank S. Gannett, a Borah leader, visited Vandenberg, and later, soon after his arrival in Cleveland, Borah talked with the Michigan senator for an hour. That evening, Knox-man George Moses met with Vandenberg until after midnight. Borah had meanwhile attacked Landon, saying he had turned the money plank over to the financial interests. This sent White scurrying to try to soothe the senator and arrange for a mutually satisfactory monetary plank.[47]

The platform was now being given a good deal of attention. Although Charles P. Taft had served as Landon's general coordinator in framing his platform, William Allen White was placed on the resolutions committee to unite as many of the Landon proposals as possible into the final document. The Landon platform draft was meant to appeal to as many interests of the party as possible, while being more liberal than the 1932 document, but this did not prevent battles from arising in the deliberations of the resolutions committee. Fights developed over tariff questions, and over the gold standard as opposed to managed money that was based on stable commodity prices, with Landon taking the position that the gold standard should be readopted upon the return of prosperity. There was disagreement even with the suggestion, supported by Landon's forces, that the platform be short and snappy. There were sharp skirmishes on June 7 because of White's advocacy of a Constitutional amendment that would authorize the states to regulate working wages and hours; Vandenberg and Dickinson questioned the need for "tampering" with the Constitution.[48]

Borah again entered the platform fight, on June 9, differing with Landon's foreign policy plank because it did not definitely oppose American membership in the League of Nations and the World Court and because it failed to support strict neutrality and embargo legislation: Landon's plank vaguely called for international cooperation to preserve peace and it merely "opposed" entangling alliances. Borah also indicated that he was against altering the Constitution, but Representative Fish later stated that Landon's Constitutional amendment was satisfactory to the senator. A happy development came when Herman Langworthy of Missouri, a Landon supporter, was chosen to chair the resolutions committee; and former Treasury Secretary Ogden Mills and Henry J. Allen maneuvered behind the scenes with Langworthy (and White) in trying to work the Landon planks into the

---

[47] *Washington Post*, June 8, 1936; *Topeka Capital*, June 9, 1936.
[48] *Topeka Capital*, June 7, 1936; *Washington Post*, June 8, 1936.

platform.[49] As the committee went to work, however, it became apparent that the Landon forces did not control it—that they had, in fact, permitted it to be loaded with such anti-Landon men as ex-Senator Hiram Bingham of Connecticut, ex-Governor James R. Goodrich of Indiana, ex-Senator George H. Moses of New Hampshire, ex-Senator Walter Edge of New Jersey, and ex-Senator David Reed of Pennsylvania: all were out of office, all were quite conservative, and all were expert at committee work and in-fighting. The anti-Landon group was an informal subcommittee that manipulated the large majority of "newcomers" on the committee. Overnight, on June 9/10, they were able to scuttle the Landon proposals and to substitute ideas of their own.

Only William Allen White had the force and the experience for launching a successful counterattack, but, by the afternoon of June 10, the Landon forces had somewhat recovered from their shock. Landon, who had been in almost constant touch with his leaders by long-distance telephone, directed the comeback; he told Hamilton, Taft, White, Allen, Hope, and others to make a determined fight to replace his planks, and, if they failed to do this, to carry the fight to the floor. They had the votes, the necessary indignation, and the governor's confidence, and were able to achieve considerable success. The upshot was that Landon was portrayed as a tiger, and the ideas of the old guard were largely repudiated. White, however, having fought hard for days, gave out before all of Landon's planks were restored, and as a result, vital elements of Landon's civil service, labor, and monetary planks were missing. Borah took advantage of the struggle in the resolutions committee to secure concessions from the Landon men, notably a strong antimonopoly statement and a statement of opposition to American membership in the League of Nations and the World Court. (Landon did not greatly care about either issue, though he favored the first and disliked the second.) Borah also took advantage of the situation to eliminate a statement advocating return to the gold standard. By the time the resolutions committee completed its work, the platform was considerably shorter than the platform of 1932: 2,600 words, compared to 12,000 words.[50]

The fight was not yet over; there was still the nomination, of course, and Landon had not capitulated on all of the platform changes. The

[49] *New York Times*, June 10, 1936.

[50] White, *What It's All About*, pp. 29 ff.; McKenna, *Borah*, pp. 334 f.; *Cleveland Plain Dealer*, June 11, 1936; *Topeka Capital*, June 12, 1936; *Wall Street Journal*, June 12, 1936; *Chicago Herald and Examiner*, June 12, 1936.

formal sessions began at 11:41 a.m., Tuesday, June 9, with the distinguished-looking national chairman, Henry Fletcher, presiding. More than 2,000 delegates and alternates were on the floor, and about 10,000 guests were seated in the huge civic auditorium. The usual rituals ensued: the invocation, singing, the mayor's welcome, more singing, a roll call, election of the convention's temporary chairman and other officers, and various reports and announcements. The convention then adjourned until the evening, when it reconvened to hear the temporary chairman (and dark-horse vice-presidential candidate), Senator Frederick Steiwer of Oregon, deliver a long, lusty, anti-New Deal, anti-Roosevelt keynote address. The Landon delegates were jittery, partly because of the news leaks of their platform reverses and partly because of rumors that Landon sentiment was subsiding among the California, Washington, and Pennsylvania delegations. Moreover, all of the chief elements for a stop-Landon movement were on hand; Knox and Hoover had arrived in Cleveland.[51]

The nervousness lessened somewhat on the second day of the convention—thanks to the efforts of White, Roy Roberts, and floor manager Joseph W. Martin—as the Landon forces regrouped on the platform and nomination fights. And there were rumors (later confirmed) that Borah had refused to take part in a stop-Landon coalition. That night, however, Herbert Hoover came before the convention, which brought the delegates to their feet in a spontaneous tribute and welcome. His address sustained the ebullience his appearance had evoked, as he called for a "crusade for liberty" to preserve America and the reestablishment of "Peace, Plenty and Security,"[52] and the ex-President left the rostrum amid thunderous cries of "We want Hoover!" (It was said that, behind the staging, he had begun to return to the rostrum when an aide tugged at his elbow and reminded him of his intention to leave the auditorium as soon as possible.) Hoover conferred that night with Vandenberg and Knox in an effort to form an anti-Landon coalition, but because Borah held out, and because Hoover refused to announce that he would not accept the nomination, the plan fell through.[53] The next morning, it was generally

[51] *New York Times*, June 10, 1936; *Official Report of the Proceedings of the Twenty-first Republican National Convention* (New York: Tenny Press, 1936), pp. 7 ff.

[52] *New York Times*, June 11, 1936.

[53] Chester Rowell to Myrtle (?), June 11, 1936, quoted in George H. Mayer to Donald R. McCoy, December 14, 1960; Oswald Garrison Villard to Franklin D. Roosevelt, June 16, 1936, Franklin D. Roosevelt Library, Hyde Park, N.Y.; *New York Times*, October 13, 1936.

conceded that Landon would be nominated on the first ballot. The hassle over the platform continued during the day, with the old guard refusing to yield further ground, but Landon decided not to wage a floor fight. He had thought of a more dramatic and less dangerous way of defeating the conservatives.

Before the opening of the morning session on June 11, word was out that the other candidates had withdrawn. Borah was the first to announce his withdrawal. Then Knox, Vandenberg, Dickinson, and several favorite sons eliminated themselves. The permanent convention chairman, Bertrand H. Snell, after opening the session at 11:40 a.m., indicated that the report of the resolutions committee would not be ready until two that afternoon, and only routine business was transacted until the noon adjournment. At 2:30 p.m. the convention reassembled, expecting to hear the reading of the platform, and was informed that the platform would not be ready until evening. (The Landon men were still doing battle, although with little success on civil service, labor, and money questions.) The delegates assembled again at 8:02 p.m., but it was another twenty-five minutes before the resolutions committee began its report, which took thirty-five minutes to read—and which was adopted unanimously by the impatient delegates. The platform motion also stated: "The acceptance of the nomination tendered by this convention carries with it, as a matter of private honor and public faith, an undertaking by each candidate to be true to the principles and program herein set forth." [54]

After the agreement on the platform by the resolutions committee, Landon, who had been in constant touch with his aides, telegraphed a message for John D. M. Hamilton to read to the delegates. Hamilton, who was to nominate Landon, was introduced to the convention at 9:07 p.m., and received a five-minute demonstration. Hamilton then read Landon's telegram, in which the governor stated that the delegates should have his interpretations of certain platform planks before they considered his nomination.

Referring to the plank that supported the adoption of state laws and interstate compacts for regulating the conditions under which women and children work, Landon said: "If nominated and elected, I shall favor a Constitutional amendment permitting the states to adopt such legislation as may be necessary to adequately protect women and

[54] *Twenty-first Republican National Convention Proceedings*, pp. 127 ff.; *New York Times*, *Topeka Capital, Chicago Herald and Examiner*, and *Cleveland Plain Dealer*, all June 12, 1936.

children in the matter of maximum hours, minimum wages, and work-ing conditions." Because the convention advocated "a sound currency to be preserved at all hazards," Landon said he interpreted sound money as "a currency expressed in terms of gold and convertible into gold"; but asserted that such a currency should not "be made effective until and unless it can be done without penalizing our domestic economy and without injury to our producers of agricultural products and other raw materials." As for the party's adherence to the civil-service merit system, and its improvement and extension, Landon said the merit system should include "every position in the administrative service below the rank of assistant secretaries of major departments and agencies, and . . . the entire post office department." [55]

After mild applause, Hamilton turned to the text of his speech. He nominated a man of experience, efficiency, honesty, and courage; the man who had clear conceptions of the problems of labor, of the needs of the distressed, of farmers, and of businessmen; and the man who was fully aware that "the disbursement of public funds is a public trust and not a political revelry." At this point—having delivered little more than the customary preamble—Hamilton surprised the convention by departing from tradition, by declaring the name of his candidate. Before he could proceed, it seemed that the entire audience of 16,000 had sprung to its feet at the mention of Landon's name, caught up as enthusiastic participants in the great American ceremony of a conven-tion demonstration. The aisles were jammed. "Oh, Susanna!"— Landon's campaign song—boomed forth; banners, sunflowers, and state standards were waved about; cowbells clanged; pictures of Landon, mounted on long poles, appeared; a frenzied joyous intoxica-tion filled the cavernous hall. Hamilton pleaded in vain: "Can I go on? Can I go on?" After half an hour, he was permitted to finish his speech, which he ended by again naming "the one man who can rally to a glorious cause the rank and file of all America . . . Alfred Mossman Landon." And again the demonstrations broke loose.

Gaspar Bacon of Massachusetts was the first of the eight persons who made the routine seconding speeches; then Hamilton, in a surprise move, presented Vandenberg, Knox, Dickinson, Governor Nice of Maryland, and Robert A. Taft as further seconds of Landon's nomination. The delegates then began to vote. Alabama, thirteen votes for Landon, Arizona, nine votes for Landon, Arkansas, eleven votes for

[55] *Twenty-first Republican National Convention Proceedings*, pp. 148 ff.; Landon to John D. M. Hamilton, June 11, 1936.

Landon, and on it went—until, near the end of the roll call, and after Landon's nomination was clinched, one West Virginia vote, Carl Bachmann's, went to Borah—and eighteen Wisconsin votes as well. When the total vote was announced—984 for Landon, 19 for Borah— Wisconsin asked that the vote be made unanimous, Bachmann agreed, and it was so declared. Then the third Landon demonstration of the evening took place, as balloons and Landon feathers showered down from the ceiling.[56]

During the remainder of the night, and into the morning, the search for a vice-presidential nominee went on, as Hamilton and other Landon leaders called on state leaders to sound them out before the convention reconvened. Vandenberg seemed to be the most popular selection, but substantial support also was indicated for Colonel Knox. Strangely, the all-night interviewing and dickering belied the amount of consideration that Landon and his advisers had given the vice-presidential nomination; the problem was that they had not agreed. As early as November, 1935, Landon had thought of a coalition ticket, speaking most often of Lewis Douglas, Franklin Roosevelt's former Director of the Budget, for the Vice Presidency. There had also been talk of Virginia's Senator Harry Byrd, former Massachusetts Governor Joseph Ely, and former War Secretary Newton Baker (who was as amused as he was uninterested)—all Democrats who might be good possibilities.

Although publisher Paul Block encouraged the idea of a coalition ticket, and Richard Lloyd Jones suggested Governor Herbert Lehman of New York, those closest to Landon opposed the idea.[57] William Mossman wrote his nephew on May 1 : "Keep off the coalition fallacy," explaining that it could also be used by the Democrats—with even greater effect. And William Allen White declared that western Republicans could not countenance a coalition ticket, because—unlike the so-called Jeffersonian Democrats—they disagreed with Roosevelt's methods, not his aims. To quash the coalition idea before it became

[56] *New York Times, Chicago Herald and Examiner, Topeka Capital, Cleveland Plain Dealer,* all June 12, 1936; *Twenty-first Republican National Convention Proceedings,* pp. 152 ff.

[57] Nicholas Roosevelt to Landon, November 29, 1935; Landon to Roosevelt, December 5, 1936; Newton D. Baker to Ralph Hayes, June 2, 1936, Newton D. Baker Papers, Manuscript Division, Library of Congress, Washington, D.C.; *Cleveland Plain Dealer,* June 8, 1936; Paul Block to Landon, April 23, 1936; Richard Lloyd Jones to Landon, June 3, 4, 1936.

noised about the convention, White said publicly (on June 3) that a coalition ticket would be a catastrophe.[58] Landon's position by then was to let things develop naturally. Although he still favored a coalition ticket with Lewis Douglas, Hamilton had convinced the governor there was insufficient support for the notion. Moreover, plenty of Republicans seemed to want the second-place nomination, including Wadsworth, Vandenberg, Nice, Knox, and Styles Bridges (mention of Bridges inspired the Democrats' quip that the Republican slogan could be "Landon Bridges falling down)." [59]

By the time the convention had convened in Cleveland, the Landon forces were so occupied with platform and delegate matters that they had little time to think about a vice-presidential nominee. Then, when the convention recessed after Landon's nomination, "Off the Rocks with Landon and Knox" and "Landon and Vandenberg" movements got under way. A Knox spokesman indicated the publisher was receptive to the idea of the runner-up spot, but Knox said: "I will cross that bridge when I come to it." Actually, Landon's managers at the convention preferred Senator Vandenberg, whom they liked personally. Not only would his nomination keep the congressional Republicans happy, the Landon men saw Vandenberg as an easterner and as a moderate who could work well with Landon; moreover, he had won reelection in an industrial state in the dismal election year of 1934.

Landon agreed to accept Vandenberg in order to avoid prolonging the convention, and, by dawn of June 12, the objections of some state leaders to Vandenberg had been smoothed over. Landon's representatives were ready to ask the senator to accept the nomination. Roy Roberts, who was sent to Vandenberg's suite to tell him of Landon's decision, pounded on the door but received no answer. By early morning, however, Vandenberg had indicated that he would not accept the nomination, and Hamilton, Roberts, and the others had to huddle again.

Frank Knox was the choice this time; his representatives assured the Landon men that he would accept, although he had already left town and could not be reached. Knox, a favorite of the party's conservatives, was not an unhappy choice for Landon, who had convinced himself that the publisher, despite his conservative pronouncements, had not

---

[58] W. T. Mossman to Landon, May 1, 1936; W. A. White to Landon, May 2, 1936, White Papers; *Topeka Capital*, June 4, 1936.

[59] *Topeka Capital*, June 9–11, 1936; *Cleveland Plain Dealer*, June 8, 1936.

laid aside all of his Bull Moose sentiments.[60] The convention re-assembled on Friday morning, June 12, and Hamilton told the delegates that Landon wanted them to choose the vice-presidential nominee. Styles Bridges nominated Knox; and Senator Edge of New Jersey, Maryland's Governor Nice, and Arthur W. Little of New York also were nominated. Edge and Nice withdrew, asking that Knox be given the nomination. Then Little withdrew, and Knox was unanimously nominated for Vice President.[61]

In the 1936 Republican national convention the party's old guard professionals did not throw the nomination to Landon as a sop to the west or because they did not care who got it. Weakened and dis-credited by their political losses since 1928, and lacking a candidate upon whom they could agree, they were unable to turn back the assaults of the younger Republicans who were eager to assume direc-tion of the party. The veteran columnist, Irvin S. Cobb, characterized the result as "a quiet interment for the old guard. With no flowers and derned few mourners." The *Washington Post* thought the convention marked a change, "the interim period between the displacement of traditional leadership and the establishment of a new command." It explained the platform compromises as a necessary evil of the interim period and as a bid for a united Republican front.[62]

The *Post*'s evaluation of the convention was accurate. A group of relatively inexperienced western Republicans, who were adept only in securing national newspaper support, had nominated its man for President, fought at least a draw with the old guard on the platform, and had thereby won control of the national committee headquarters. But a similar development had also occurred among the delegates on

[60] Landon interview, February 16, 1963; Arthur H. Vandenberg, Jr. (ed.), *The Private Papers of Senator Vandenberg* (Boston: Houghton Mifflin, 1952), p. xi. This account of how Knox received the vice-presidential nomination appears to be verifiable only in its general outline. None of my sources—most of whom did not wish their versions to be attributed to them—agrees on the timing involved, or the degree of Vandenberg's reluctance, or Knox's willingness to be nominated. Several conflicting accounts of the matter are given in Clapper's diaries and entries for July 29, August 3, September 13, 1936, Raymond Clapper Papers, Manuscript Division, Library of Congress, Washing-ton, D.C., in Arthur M. Schlesinger, Jr., *The Politics of Upheaval* (Boston: Houghton Mifflin, 1960), p. 546, and in a letter from Paul Leach (Knox's Washington corre-spondent) to Landon, August 25, 1962.

[61] *Twenty-first Republican National Convention Proceedings*, pp. 182 ff.

[62] *Los Angeles Times*, June 25, 1936; *Washington Post*, June 13, 1936.

the convention floor: most of them were younger than the delegates to past conventions, and inexperienced in politics. And this change had been reflected in the dropping of many old hands from the national committee: Walter Brown of Ohio, Mark Requa of California, Frank Smith of Illinois, David Reed of Pennsylvania, George Wingfield of Nevada, and Earl Kinsley of Vermont. In fact, a third of the committee members were replaced; and John Hamilton replaced Henry Fletcher as national chairman.[63] Roosevelt had removed most of these men from public office, and the forces behind Landon were now removing them from party office.

The 1936 delegates were not of the private club and Wall Street, but of the small-town country club and Main Street. They had struck against the old guard with telling effect, and a new deal had been dealt for the Grand Old Party. The delegates wanted down-to-earth ideals, and they got them—along with a folksy nominee and a relatively liberal platform. Now it was up to the nominee. What was he going to do? How was he going to do it? Who was going to help him? An honor that comes to few had come to Landon; but it was accompanied by a gruelling experience and an agonizing responsibility.

[63] *Topeka Capital*, June 12, 1936; *New York Times*, June 14, 1936; List of Republican national committee members, October 1, 1935 (mimeograph); *Twenty-first Republican National Convention Proceedings*, pp. 129 ff.

CHAPTER 11

The Early Campaign

The 1936 campaign was one of the strangest in the history of American politics, and some observers at the time compared it to the campaigns that preceded the Civil War. In the 1930s, as in the 1850s, the political parties were in flux. The composition of the Democratic party had not changed for several generations, but, in the 1930s, Negroes flocked to its banners and organized labor virtually declared the party its own. This formerly conservative party, now under the leadership of the aristocratic Franklin D. Roosevelt, became the haven of liberals and progressives of all kinds, and Republicans, agrarians, and even socialists entered its ranks to an extent that was alarming to the party's regulars. The Republican party also was reconstituted, not only by the loss of many of its Negro, labor, and urban constituents but also by the addition of some conservative Democrats. Ironically, in 1936 the Republican ticket was headed by two old Bull Moosers, and its national committee was loaded with Main Street rather than Wall Street figures.

Third parties were still in abundance, colorful if weak. The Socialists and Communists fielded noisy campaign teams and joined in the race for power with the new Coughlin-Smith-and-Townsend Union party. Strong independent state parties arose to harass the major parties in Wisconsin, Minnesota, and New York; and many Democrats abandoned their nominees to assist third-party and independent candidates.

Republican leaders also were less able to count on support from nominal Republicans. Consequently, the two major parties reached out for support wherever they could find it. Before their 1935 national convention, some Republicans had talked of a coalition ticket, and during the campaign Landon promised he would appoint a coalition cabinet. President Roosevelt, however, by including Henry A. Wallace and Harold L. Ickes in his cabinet, had already formed a coalition, and, through the use of such organizations as the Progressive National Committee and the Good Neighbor League, he extended his support even farther beyond the traditional boundaries of his party. Democratic Senator Rush Holt of West Virginia was hobnobbing with Governor Landon and Republican-Fusion Mayor Fiorello La Guardia of New York City supported President Roosevelt. The Republican mayor of Philadelphia declared his neutrality of the Republican ticket, and the Democratic mayor of Pittsburgh battled the New Deal.

These alignments reflected some of the changes in American society that the depression had brought about. Where the changes would lead, no one could see, but everyone predicted dire results if their favorite candidates were not elected; the situation was viewed as serious as that which had led to the Civil War. To many Republicans a Roosevelt victory in 1936 meant the end of Constitutional government, and to others it meant the beginning of communism or socialism. To many Democrats a Republican victory meant a return to a 1932 economy, or the beginning of fascism. Many Socialists, Unionists, and state third-party men thought action had to be taken in 1936, or "there may be no election of 1940!" To Communists, less worried about elections, the problem was that the entire world might be fascist by 1940. Although these fears were overstated, they reflected an uneasiness about the country's future that was comparable to the disturbed feelings of the 1850s. All perceived that the nation was in a period of flux, and they fought—each by his own lights—to salvage what they wanted from the past and to fashion a better future. A new society—better or worse—was in the making, which meant that some would lose and some would gain in the scramble.

It was in this context that Landon had to organize a campaign. Although many progressive Republicans, such as Senators George W. Norris and Gerald P. Nye, were disappointed by the convention results, Landon's agents reported that the party had been buoyed up

by the convention and by Landon's nomination. Representative Frank
Carlson said that Republicans were greatly pleased with the party
harmony that had been engendered by the convention; Senator Arthur
Capper said the reaction was highly favorable and that he had not
heard an unfriendly comment on Landon's nomination; and Representative Clifford Hope said the convention had left good feelings and
enthusiasm among Republicans.[1] James P. Warburg, a "refugee"
from the Democratic party and a seeker of reduced trade barriers, said
Landon's nomination was the wisest choice, and that he was thrilled
by Landon's telegram to the convention. Gifford Pinchot believed the
Kansan could win "if I help him." Ogden Mills was well satisfied with
the convention's results and was "more and more confident . . . that
the Republican party will be reinvigorated by the kind of leadership
which Landon and those around him can give us." Mills thought the
Republicans had a better-than-even chance of beating Roosevelt.[2]

Other Republicans found additional reasons for optimism. The
Literary Digest poll indicated that the majority of the people were
opposed to the New Deal. The National Association of Manufacturers,
the national Chamber of Commerce, and that supposedly influential
association of the wealthy, the American Liberty League, stood
opposed to the administration. According to a Du Pont Company
statistician, the President's family life was considered offensive by large
numbers of Americans, as was the sharpness and "amorality" of his
advisers; the New Deal was based on class distinctions and was highly
politically motivated; the New Deal advocated centralization, ruinous
taxation, and reckless spending; the cost of living had increased under
the New Deal without corresponding wage increases, and the unemployed had not received jobs despite Roosevelt's promises. Moreover, the statistician said, women did not like the abandonment of
prohibition without safeguards for the young, and the majority of
adults were beginning to tire of Roosevelt's affected voice and manners.[3]

Having convinced themselves they could win, the Republicans went

[1] *Topeka Capital*, June 13, 1936; Frank Carlson to Landon, June 16, 1936; Arthur
Capper, June 13, 1936; Clifford Hope to Landon, June 15, 1936; Alfred M. Landon
Papers, Kansas State Historical Society, Topeka.

[2] James P. Warburg to George T. McDermott, June 15, 1936; M. Nelson McGeary,
Gifford Pinchot, Forester, Politician (Princeton: Princeton University Press, 1960), p. 415;
Ogden Mills to Gordon O'Neill, June 18, 1936, Ogden Mills Papers, Manuscript
Division, Library of Congress, Washington, D.C.

[3] Edmond E. Lincoln, "Some Reasons Why the Present Administration Can and
Will Be Defeated" (Wilmington, Del., 1936) (mimeograph).

to work on the electorate. Landon, however, did not share the optimism of the hard-core, coupon-clipping Republicans; he saw many reasons why the Republicans could lose. Economic conditions were improving, and Roosevelt was getting the credit for it; Republicans were often ignorant of the thinking of the man in the street; and the Republican party—compared to the well-organized Democratic party—was a weak organization. He would not concede Roosevelt the election, however; as the opposition leader, he had an obligation to fulfill, and he would fight to the finish regardless of the odds.

After Knox's nomination, Landon began preparing for the campaign. He immediately called a meeting of Knox, Hamilton, and key figures of the Republican national committee, and scheduled appointments with Republican leaders from all over the country. This had its awkward and amusing aspects because many of the leaders knew each other only slightly, or not at all. Landon and Knox, for example, knew little about one another, as was evidenced by their affectation of such Teddy Rooseveltian terms as "delightful," "bully," "standing at Armageddon," etc.—but how else were old Bull Moosers expected to talk or to write to each other?[4] The meetings began in Topeka, on June 16, and it was soon agreed that the Republicans would wage an all-out campaign. Landon, Knox, and Hamilton would make national speaking tours; radio would be used as often as possible; there would be a big publicity budget, and frequent press conferences. (Landon sought to meet with newsmen almost daily, and Knox and Hamilton used every opportunity for press conferences.)[5]

Landon was convinced that Constitutional government was imperiled in America by the threat of a debased currency and by the fiscal and quasi-legislative powers that Congress had given to the executive branch. He contended that the government's many broken promises, and the President's cavalier attitude, could impose unbearable strains on democratic government—and on the most hardy attributes of American society. The country needed "clear-cut, definite, and vigorous administrative leadership" if it was to eliminate waste in government, inspire business confidence, and permit Americans to use tax savings for personal spending. All this should be done; but relief must be given where needed, business must be protected from government interference, labor from business, and agriculture from itself; and the budget must be balanced and taxes reduced as soon as

[4] Landon to Frank Knox, June 12, 1936; Knox to Landon, June 12, 1936.
[5] *Topeka Capital*, June 17, 28, 1936.

possible. Landon saw the Roosevelt government's policies as leading to an economy of scarcity, whereas America's hope was in raising its standard of living to the level allowed by its potential productivity.[6] The Republican campaign would try to build on these ideas—according to one observer, the "year-around, full dinner pail, with liberty and justice for all."

But organization, not issues, was the weightiest problem for the Republicans. Landon saw the convention as the basis for an effective Republican organization: it had displayed remarkable unity in nominating Landon and Knox on the first ballots and in accepting a platform with a liberal tinge. By telegraphing the convention his interpretation of the platform, Landon had shown an element of leadership that had bolstered the morale of many Republicans. Also, the national committee had received new blood, and its head-quarters—reorganized under John Hamilton's direction—tried to revitalize the party's withered state and county organizations.

In addition to defining issues and reorganizing the party, Landon tried, as it would be popular to say a generation later, to project an image. He believed he had been nominated because of the party's grass roots' reaction to his display of simple attributes, which the rank-and-file understood and liked to think it possessed—and Landon hoped these virtues would appeal to the country. This image, of being unglamorous but sound, homely, and forthright, was to be projected as the antithesis of President Roosevelt's image. In a Topeka speech, early in the campaign, Knox lauded Landon's

> sturdy spirit of independence, the practical good sense, that quiet dis-crimination. . . . He represents in his personality those qualities and characteristics . . . that settled our colonies, that won independence, that sent the prairie schooners across the Mississippi to bring families to a virgin soil. It is the spirit that drove the buffalo away to break the stubborn sod for future American homes.

The government, Knox declared, would be safe in Landon's hands.[7]

Meanwhile a staff—a young one—was being recruited. Less than two weeks after the convention, Charles P. Taft, Ralph Robey, Frederick D. Enfield, and Earl Taylor (all but Taft were former Democrats) had been enlisted to dig up material for Landon, advise him, and help write speeches. Kirby Hawkes, Arthur Calvert Smith,

[6] Landon to George Rothwell Brown, June 18, 1936.
[7] Landon to Henry J. Allen, June 20, 1936; Knox speech, Topeka, July 15, 1936.

and Sherwin Badger joined the staff later, and many others were pressed into part-time service as the campaign progressed. These included Charles F. Roos, of the Cowles Economic Research Commission; Frederic Dewhurst of the Twentieth Century Fund; William Hard; Ogden Mills; Ben M. Anderson, of the Chase National Bank; Jay N. Darling, the cartoonist and former New Deal conservation official; Gifford and Cornelia Pinchot; Amos Pinchot; Leonard P. Ayres, of the Cleveland Trust Company; William B. Bell, of American Cyanamide; Representative John M. Hollister, of Taft, Stettinius and Hollister of Cincinnati; former Under Secretary of State J. Reuben Clark; James P. Warburg; Eugene and Agnes Meyer, of the *Washington Post*; Lewis Douglas; and Robert P. Bass, the Progressive governor of New Hampshire in the Bull Moose days. Seldom has a stew had so many rich cooks.

Of course, Roy Roberts, William Allen White, and other Kansas newspapermen continued to work in Landon's campaign. Oscar Stauffer became Landon's personal campaign manager; Lacy Haynes was the chief liaison man between Landon, national committee headquarters, and Colonel Knox; and Landon's secretary, Willard Mayberry, and his assistant secretary, Carl Rott, served as spokesmen, aides, and troubleshooters. Fred Seaton continued to work with the Young Republicans; and E. Ross Bartley, formerly Vice President Dawes' press secretary, became Landon's press relations chief. Clifford Hope, the governor's farm adviser, also headed the Republican national committee's agricultural advisory staff. Roger W. Straus was Landon's liaison man with Jewish organizations.

Although Hamilton and Knox opened their speaking campaigns on June 26, Landon decided he would wait until July 23, when he would formally accept the presidential nomination in Topeka. He wanted more time to prepare for the campaign; he wanted a vacation; and he had to meet a special session of the legislature in early July.[8] Landon and his aides laid the groundwork for his acceptance speech, which was planned to highlight the issues he intended to stress during the campaign; the rest of his time was spent on state business, conferring with visitors, and discussing campaign plans. On June 24 the governor began a twelve-day vacation at the Irene McGraw ranch in Colorado, accompanied by reporters and photographers.

[8] *Washington Post*, June 27, 1936; Landon to Charles Spencer, June 20, 1936.

Day after day, pictures of the vacationing governor were dispatched throughout the country. There were newspaper pictures of Landon in leather jacket and boots—fishing, riding, cooking over an outdoor stove, relaxing with his family, eating luncheon or dinner outdoors, throwing snowballs, scrambling up hills, contemplating nature, and sitting around a campfire. There were interviews, "profiles," human-interest stories, and background articles. On June 30, Robey, Taft, Taylor, and Enfield arrived to confer with Landon on his speeches and campaign itinerary. William B. Bell, head of the party's finance committee, Senator Frederick Steiwer, and other party notables also conferred with the candidate.[9]

When Landon returned to Topeka he was nevertheless refreshed, and he plunged into the work connected with the July 7 special session, which he had called for the authorization of constitutional amendments that would enable Kansans to obtain social security benefits from the federal government. On July 8 he issued a press release, hoping to prod the legislators to action. Because the depression had brought economic disaster to many people, and especially to the aged, Landon said, the state must "protect us from a repetition of the troubles of the past years or minimize their effects." He asked the legislature to initiate the amendments that would enable Kansas "to join in securing all proper assistance to our people." The legislature acted promptly, with only one dissenting vote, to submit the amendments to the vote of the people.[10]

Buoyed by the bipartisan victory, which indicated that he had been reasonable on social security, Landon also was pleased by other indications of support. He wrote Ogden Mills: "The tide is running very strong in our direction." He felt his ticket would carry Iowa, Nebraska, Colorado, Missouri, South Dakota, Oklahoma, Wisconsin, and Kansas, and that he had a good chance of winning in Minnesota, Wyoming, and Montana. He did not presume to foretell the impact of the Union party's presidential candidate, North Dakota Congressman William Lemke, but he doubted that the new movement had popular strength behind it.[11]

A split in the Democratic party, which had been rumored since the

[9] *Washington Post*, June 27, 1936; *Chicago Daily News*, July 1, 1936; *Denver Post*, July 1, 4, 1936; *Los Angeles Examiner*, June 30, 1936.

[10] *Message to the Legislature of Kansas, Special Session, July 7, 1936, By Alf M. Landon, Governor* (Topeka: State Printer, 1936); Landon press release, July 8, 1936; *Topeka Capital*, July 10, 1936.

[11] Landon to Ogden Mills, July 6, 1936; *Topeka Capital*, June 22, 1936.

formation of the American Liberty League (in the summer of 1934) particularly cheered Landon. One of the leaders of the league, Henry Breckinridge, President Wilson's Assistant Secretary of War, had been in touch with Republican national committee chairman Henry Fletcher as early as December, 1935, about Democratic aid to the Republican cause and a sharing of "responsibility and power in case the 'aid and cooperation' are given and success is won." [12] Breckinridge also encouraged other disaffected Democrats to oppose Roosevelt in the state primaries—as he himself had done (but with little effect) in New Jersey, Ohio, Pennsylvania, and Maryland. Alfred Smith, the Democratic presidential nominee in 1928, and Bainbridge Colby, Wilson's Secretary of State from 1920–21, were to become increasingly critical of Roosevelt during 1936, as were former Governors Joseph Ely of Massachusetts and Albert Ritchie of Maryland, and former Senator James Reed of Missouri. Breckinridge summarized the complaints of the dissident Democrats as "the subversion of the Constitution, the scrapping of the platform of '32 and the repudiation of all Democratic principles." [13] He might have added that Roosevelt had ignored the advice of these proud men.

Breckinridge, who visited Landon in Topeka after the Colorado vacation, said the Landon-Knox ticket would end "the present and future menace to the American system of constitutional freedom." A bit later, former Governor Ely conferred with Republican national chairman John Hamilton, who told Landon that Ely was delighted with the meeting and would follow Landon's instructions. [14] Hamilton later conferred with Alfred Smith, with inconclusive results. Ely, Breckinridge, and other Democrats were in frequent touch with Landon during the campaign, but William Allen White, who was hostile toward this coalition movement, flayed the "cross-overs" and "turncoats." The Democratic "auxiliaries" protested to Landon about White, and about Charles Taft's acid comments on Smith's newly

[12] Henry Breckinridge to Henry P. Fletcher, December 18, 1935, Henry Breckinridge Papers, Manuscript Division, Library of Congress, Washington, D.C.

[13] Henry Breckinridge to D. List Warner, January 3, 1936, Breckinridge Papers. Excellent accounts of the background of disgruntlement among Democrats are given in George Wolfskill, *The Revolt of the Conservatives* (Boston: Houghton Mifflin, 1962), especially ch. 7, and in Arthur Schlesinger, Jr., *The Politics of Upheaval* (Boston: Houghton Mifflin, 1960), ch. 28.

[14] Nathan Miller to Landon, June 4, 1936; Landon to Miller, June 11, 1936; Statement by Colonel Henry Breckinridge, Topeka, July 7, 1936; W. E. Mullins to Landon, July 17, 1936.

found "political principles," and Breckinridge thought "practical political sense, if nothing else, suggests the wisdom of Republicans restraining their utterance, at least until after election." White also drew criticism for other statements about the exclusiveness of some "hyphenated" Americans, especially Scandinavian Americans, for which statements Landon was partly blamed. Landon tried to soothe all these injured feelings, though he wrote White: "Say what you durn please."[15] Landon knew he could not gag White, and he believed that the dissident Democrats could support only him.

Early in August the anti-Roosevelt Democrats, calling themselves the National Jeffersonian Democrats, met in Detroit to decide what action they should take against the President. Forty prominent men, from twenty-two states, attended the meeting; and although Ely, Breckinridge, Colby, and former Congressman Joseph W. Bailey of Texas said they would support Landon, the group as such produced only a scathing criticism of the New Deal.[16]

Many prominent anti-New Deal Democrats supported Landon in 1936, but there was constant friction because of their sensitivity to Republican partisanship. After Sterling Edmunds, the secretary of the Jeffersonian Democrats supporting Landon, complained to Hamilton of Landon's partisanship, and Hamilton had suggested that Landon tone down his partisan references, Landon reacted testily.

> I have never referred to the present administration as the Democratic party. I have never made any partisan appeal to the Republicans and I have only referred to the Republican party when it was necessary to state our position on the issues as expressed in the platform. I don't see how this can be avoided. . . . I am fully conscious of the wisdom of his advice [but] I am the candidate of the Republican party and I must mention it occasionally.[17]

In October, other prominent Democrats, especially from Wall Street circles, embraced the Landon banner, issuing "A Declaration of Independence by Democrats." The newcomers included Eugene W. Stetson, Robert L. Garner, and Albert Rathbone, and their statement,

[15] Henry Breckinridge to Landon, July 27, 1936, Breckinridge Papers; G. F. Hedstrand to Landon, August 3, 1936; W. A. White to Landon, August 8, 1936; Landon to White, August 10, 1936.

[16] *Detroit Evening Times*, August 7, 1936; *Detroit Free Press*, August 8, 1936; *Chicago Tribune*, August 9, 1936; Henry Breckinridge to Landon, August 10, 1936, Breckinridge Papers.

[17] John D. M. Hamilton to Landon, September 28, 1936; Landon to Hamilton, September 30, 1936.

which was widely circulated in support of Landon (by the Landon Volunteers and the American Liberty League), was later endorsed by Alfred Smith and by John W. Davis, the Democrats' nominees for President in 1928 and 1924.[18] Jeffersonian Democratic organizations were formed in several states—with the assistance of Colby, Breckinridge, Reed, Ely, Smith, and Richard Cleveland (President Cleveland's son)—under the Landon banner.

After the special legislative session in Kansas, plans were completed for the acceptance ceremonies in Topeka; July 23 was to be, as the *Wichita Beacon* put it, "Kansas' Most Glorious Day!" No single event in the state's history had received as much comment in Kansas' newspapers. For several days before—and after—it was the chief news item. Even the newspaper advertisements were keyed to Landon themes. ("A Balanced Budget! that's what LANDON did for Kansas and a Balanced Budget Is What The Economy of ELECTROLUX Is Daily Doing for Their Users." An optometrist advertised: "The Eyes of the Nation Are Upon Topeka Today. . . . It Pays to See Accurately."[19]) The capital had never before had such attention. And why not? Landon was the first Kansan to receive a major-party presidential nomination.

Cecil B. De Mille, the maker of movie "spectaculars," was one of those who worked out the pageantry, the highlight of which was a two-hour parade of elephants, choirs, floats, soldiers, cheering groups, bands, drum corps, prairie schooners, stage coaches, and cowboys and Indians. This—and more—was watched by tens of thousands of people, in sweltering, 100-degree heat. A 40- by 60-foot picture of a smiling Landon, draped down the side of a downtown office building, looked on as participants and spectators—to band accompaniments, and the tune of "Oh, Susanna!"—sang:

"Landon, oh Landon/will lead to Victory—
With the dear old Constitution,/and it's good enough for me."

In the evening, it was said, 100,000 people—the greatest crowd in Topeka's history—assembled on the statehouse grounds for the notification and acceptance ceremony. A massive concentration of kleig lights played upon the wooden stands and platforms that had been set up—and decorated with red, white, and blue bunting—in

[18] Kenneth C. Hogate to Landon, October 13, 1936; Wolfskill, *Revolt of the Conservatives*, p. 216.

[19] *Wichita Beacon*, July 23, 1936; *Topeka Capital*, July 23, 1936.

front of the steps leading to the south entrance of the capitol. The minority leader of the United States House of Representatives, Bertrand H. Snell, formally notified Landon that he had been nominated for President, and charged him with the "high responsibility of representing and defending the cause of freedom, of opportunity, of a better life for 125 million men and women and children."[20] Then Landon took the speaker's stand, to the most enthusiastic ovation he had ever heard; there were cheers, yells, and the bands struck up. Landon lifted his hand and asked for silence (the millions of radio listeners must not be kept waiting); then he accepted the nomination and offered a prayer for divine guidance.

Landon vowed, if he was elected, to keep inviolate the President's oath to "preserve, protect, and defend the Constitution of the United States." Identifying the chief campaign issue, as he saw it, Landon said: "If we are to go forward permanently, it must be with a united nation—not with a people torn by appeals to prejudice and divided by class feeling. The time has come to pull together." He lashed out at the New Deal, on substantive issues, for failing to achieve recovery and provide full employment, which required the restoration of confidence that would allow free enterprise to stimulate consumer demand for products. This could be done by a government that would free American enterprise from "incessant governmental intimidation and hostility, . . . excessive expenditures and crippling taxation," and "an arbitrary and uncertain monetary policy"; and Landon promised an efficient government, composed of the best-qualified men, with a President who stood behind them but held them responsible for their jobs.

Landon would reorganize the government in order "to eliminate duplication, to insure better administration, and to save the taxpayers' money," but he promised that relief would be given to those who needed it: "We will not take our economies out of the allotments to the unemployed." The policy that took "the American farmer out of foreign markets and put the foreign farmer into the American market" must be reversed, though cash benefits to the farmer would be continued until this reversal could be made. The soil must also be protected, through a national land-use program; and the right of labor to organize would be fully protected, with the government serving as a mediator in disputes between business and labor. Landon would

[20] *Kansas City Star*, July 26, 1936; *Topeka Capital*, July 23, 24, 1936; *Topeka State Journal*, July 24, 1936; Snell speech, Topeka, July 23, 1936.

spur his party to further efforts "in creating international understanding, in removing the causes of war, and in reducing and limiting arms." The Constitution would be followed, not evaded; although changes were not out of order, they "must come by and through the people and not by usurpation." The Republicans, he said, proposed to

> maintain the Constitutional balance of power between the states and the federal government. We propose to use the full power of the federal government to break up private monopolies and to eliminate private monopolistic practices. In other words, the Republican Party proposes to restore and to maintain a free competitive system—a system under which, and only under which, can there be independence, equality of opportunity, and work for all.

With this program, Landon believed, the people could develop

> a country which produces more and more until there is plenty for all, with a fair chance for all to earn their share . . . a land in which equal opportunity shall prevail and special privilege shall have no place . . . an America that shall bring to bear the whole of her great spiritual force in a common effort to drive the curse of war from the earth; an America that, for the sake of all mankind as well as ourselves, shall never lose the faith that human freedom is a practical ideal.[21]

His address, delivered in flat but forceful accents, drew seventy-one rounds of cheers and applause. Landon's presidential election campaign had begun.

The Hearst press gave a thunderous ovation to Landon's acceptance speech, which it asserted "will be a text for patriots, as long as America remains free." Labor, on the other hand, led the attack on the speech. George L. Berry, president of the Printing Pressmen's Union, charged that Landon's labor ideas favored employers. Berry also leveled many specific charges against the Kansas governor: that he had acted as a strike-breaker in the 1935 miners' strike, had not fought for a state minimum-wage law for women and children, had not fully enforced Kansas' law for an eight-hour day and prevailing wages on public works, had permitted work-weeks of forty-eight and fifty-four hours in various occupational categories, had not established a state civil service system, had permitted prison and non-union labor on public projects, had opposed the National Recovery Administration (except for

[21] *Address of Governor Alf M. Landon, July 23, 1936* (Topeka: Republican National Committee, 1936).

oil), and had favored Governor Allen's "fascist-like" Industrial Relations Court.[22] Berry was somewhat correct—except on the last two items—but similar charges could have been made against most state governors during the same period, and usually with greater truthfulness.

On August 3, Secretary Harold Ickes answered Landon for the New Deal, insisting that the governor was supported by "the men who ruthlessly wield the money power of America." Ickes said the Republicans had a platform that "faces both ways upon which stands a candidate whom the West is asked to support because he is a 'progressive,' while, at the same time, he is entirely satisfactory to Wall Street and the predatory interests because he is 'practical.'" Ickes also recalled Landon's 1933 "enlistment" under Roosevelt "for the duration of the war" against the depression. "It would appear that Candidate Landon has gone A.W.O.L. from the war."[23]

Immediately after Landon's acceptance speech, the Socialist nominee, Norman Thomas, asked Landon for clarification of some of his labor ideas, and Landon answered in an unprecedented (and widely publicized) exchange of letters between presidential nominees during a campaign. Thomas asked what Landon meant in saying employees should be "free from interference from any source" in organizing unions: did it mean that organizing had to be spontaneous, or could union organizers be introduced? Landon replied, saying the courtesy and candor of Thomas' letter merited an answer:

> The workers have the right to meet among themselves or with others of their own choice to promote organization, with complete freedom from interference from anyone whatsoever. The workers should be fully protected in this right by the public authorities. This necessarily includes the right of a labor union to promote by lawful and proper means the organization of an unorganized industry, which includes the right to send in an organizer.

Landon cited the Cherokee County mine and smelter strike of 1935 in explaining the protection that must be afforded.

> The troops . . . were directed not to interfere with labor meetings and other activities of the strikers, so long as they were peaceably conducted. This included picketing, and both meetings and pickets were protected from possible violence of any kind.

[22] *Los Angeles Examiner*, July 26, 1936; *Kansas City Star*, July 25, 1936.
[23] *New York Times*, August 4, 1936.

Thomas, in his reply, thanked Landon for his letter, and said he hoped the governor's principles could be applied to the organization of the steelworkers and sharecroppers during the campaign. Thomas thought, however, that Landon's actions in Cherokee County had contributed to the reopening of the mines under the company's armed guards, and that his provision for two pickets at each mine had been insufficient for effective picketing. Thomas—who asserted that the provisions for the workers' health and safety, as well as their wages and living conditions, had been outrageously inadequate—concluded that the general condition of this tri-state industry was a good argument for federal control.[24]

The Landon-Thomas exchange revealed the serious difference of opinion between Landon and the chief defenders of organized labor upon the essential safeguards for workingmen. Although the charge that health and safety were not protected in Cherokee County was exaggerated, it could not be denied that wages and living conditions were substandard, but, according to Landon, the latter were matters in which the state could not interfere. Moreover, the improvement of all these conditions depended upon a general economic upswing and the effective organization of labor. Landon spoke with candor because he believed he could not attract most of the nation's labor leaders (they were already in Roosevelt's camp) but he could appeal to that "large group of people who have no connection with labor, that more or less judge a man's views on social and economic questions by the position he takes on organized labor." Landon also felt that his statement on labor, compared with the statements of the President, revealed that "I have gone further than he in a friendly recognition of the right of labor to organize."[25]

Landon was still governor of Kansas, and in the summer of 1936 the state was again ravaged by drought. As bad in many areas as it had ever been, the drought was worse than ever in other areas because the summer was the hottest the state had experienced in half a century. Landon, between his acceptance of the nomination and the start of his campaign tours, was preoccupied with the drought problem; again, he requested federal aid, as he helped mobilize private and state resources. Then, in late July, he resumed the battle for continued—and

[24] Norman Thomas to Landon, July 24, 1936; Landon to Thomas, July 29, 1936; Thomas to Landon, August 1, 1936.
[25] Landon to A. M. Curtis, August 7, 1936.

expanded—railway rate reductions, but he met great resistance from
the railways, which, financially weak themselves, contended that
many feed and cattle dealers and water handlers had taken advantage
of past rate reductions to pad their incomes. The tired and work-
burdened presidential nominee pressed the railroads for the reductions
well into August, and delayed a second vacation trip to Colorado until
the railroads finally agreed to slash cattle, feed, and water freight
rates.[26] President Roosevelt, under pressure for drought relief, in
early August indicated great concern over the drought and proposed
a meeting with the governors of the affected states. Landon replied
immediately: "I will go any place at any time if it is for the good of
Kansas." He also urged the President to take steps to see that cattle
did not die for want of feed and to prevent profiteering in food commodities and livestock feeds.[27]

Before his departure to Colorado (on August 11), as governor and
presidential nominee, Landon conferred with such visiting dignitaries
as Senators Dickinson (Iowa), Steiwer (Oregon), and Townsend
(Delaware), Louis Taber of the Grange, and Governors Fitzgerald of
Michigan and Welford of North Dakota. (Dr. Francis E. Townsend,
the self-styled champion of the country's aged, was in Topeka, too,
but did not call on Landon, saying he would rather vote for "a
Chinaman from Hawaii than either Landon or Roosevelt.") Landon
also found time to review the artillery forces at Fort Riley and to travel
to Emporia to see William Allen White and to Independence to visit
the home folks. Newsmen—at least a dozen—were always on hand, and
Landon everywhere had to contend with the curious. There were
interviews, and shaking hands and talking with the powerful and the
humble, and being photographed with the aspiring. Then, shortly
before he left for Colorado, the governor came down with an attack of
summer flu and pleurisy, the first of the minor ailments that were to
harass him during the campaign. This was followed by threats to
kidnap one of his children, and guards were placed around them in
Colorado, where they had preceded him.

Landon had now reached the point where he was doing less listening

26 Ogden S. Jones, "Drought Report," August 28, 1936 (mimeograph), Kansas State
Archives, Governors' Papers, Kansas State Historical Society, Topeka. *Topeka Capital*,
August 1, 7, 1936.

27 *Topeka Capital*, August 10, 8, 1936; Drought files, O.F. 987, Box 3 (1936),
Franklin D. Roosevelt Library, Hyde Park, N.Y.; Victor Anderson (one of Landon's
bodyguards), "Observations of the Campaign," p. 6 (undated carbon-copy typescript); Landon to Franklin D. Roosevelt, August 14, 1936.

and more speaking, occasionally with a sharp tongue. He needed a rest. This time at the McGraw Ranch he really took it easy. Little news was issued, except that the governor was "resting at the ranch." The reporters and photographers were at their wits' ends for lack of material, but the candidate was getting a real rest.[28]

The preliminaries for the campaign were vexatious. Roosevelt's aides were worried because of Landon's strong showing in winning the nomination, and many in Landon's camp wondered if the Republican national committee was not behind schedule in its organization work. Then, by the middle of August, the Republican national committee headquarters was apparently ready for the campaign, having organized its various divisions and blocs: the south, women, agriculture, industry, labor, naturalized citizens, Negroes, taxpayers, Young Republicans, veterans, and speaker bureau. *On The March with Landon and Knox* was put together to give information to campaign workers; and provisions were made to issue pamphlets in foreign languages for the foreign-born, to begin William Hard's powerful series of broadcasts building up Landon and criticizing Roosevelt, and to outfit thirty sound trucks for carrying the Republican message. A personal campaign headquarters for Landon was established in Topeka, and by the middle of August it had nineteen people on the pay roll. Fifty-five different form letters had been prepared for answering the governor's campaign mail.[29]

All this activity, however—if the critics were to be believed—was insufficient. Moreover, the summer heat was scorching on the Great Plains, which, in the days when air-conditioning was rare, hindered the staff members from doing their best. The heat, at least in part, accounted for Landon's two vacations to Colorado—and for a third one that was scheduled but later called off. July and August, 1936, were the hottest on record, and even September had five days of more than 100 degrees. Topeka that summer had fifty-nine days of readings of 100 degrees or over, and thirty-one days in which the thermometer hovered between 90 and 100.[30]

[28] *Topeka Capital*, August 4, 1936; Anderson, "Observations," p. 3.

[29] James MacGregor Burns, *Roosevelt: The Lion and the Fox* (New York: Harcourt, Brace, 1956) pp. 270 f.; Carl A. Rott to Mildred Creighton, August 6, 1936; Republican national committee's "Alphabetical Directory by Departments, August 17, 1936" (typescript); M. W. Tuthill to Landon, August 15, 1936; *On The March with Landon and Knox*, September 5, 1936; *Los Angeles Times*, August 17, 1936; Carl A. Rott to Clyde Miller, August 31, 1936.

[30] *Kansas City Star*, June 25, 1961; *Topeka Capital*, July 25, 1963.

More problems arose in July. The Kansas school system was being attacked as substandard, an issue that Landon and his aides, despite numerous testimonials and denials, were unable to quash. Anti-Semitism was also a persistent charge against the governor, probably because he had discharged the head of a state hospital who was a Jew, though he had been replaced by another Jewish doctor. Governor Hoffman had invited Landon to speak at Sea Girt but did not receive a reply, which intensified intraparty wrangles in New Jersey. Because Landon was being pictured as a reactionary, Raymond Gram Swing urged him to counteract this by being gracious to conservatives but keeping his distance from them.[31]

In August, Agnes Meyer, the head of the Landon radio clubs, warned the Kansan the public-opinion polls would show him slipping because of the widespread impression that he was in the grip of the old guard, an impression that was bolstered by the operations of the party's eastern headquarters in New York City, and that, despite the efforts of its manager, Joseph W. Martin, Jr., showed no signs of an infusion of moderation. Landon, alarmed by the New York situation, assigned Lacy Haynes to help Martin, but the effort was unsuccessful. Landon was also dismayed because he had no one who knew, to his satisfaction, what was going on in Washington and who could help him get material to meet the sudden thrusts of such antagonists as Harold Ickes. By early August, Landon was a harassed man; he wrote Mossman:

> It is just impossible for me to handle any details of the campaign. In addition to my regular work and the conferences, I am probably shaking hands with over a hundred people a day.[32]

Although the governor was vexed, he refused to resort to what he regarded as trickery. In August, W. F. Bigelow, the editor of Hearst's *Good Housekeeping*, demanded that Landon call for a Constitutional amendment that—except in case of attack on the United States—would subject a congressional declaration of war to ratification in a national referendum. Bigelow said this would attract the women's

[31] Fred Brinkerhoff to Landon, July 25, 1936; A. H. Kirchhofer to Roy Roberts, October 20, 1936; "Digest of Mail Received at Jayhawk Hotel Headquarters, Aug. 31 to Sept. 5" (typescript from Rolla Clymer); John D. M. Hamilton to Landon, August 1, 1936; Landon to Hamilton, August 11, 1936; Raymond Gram Swing to Landon, July 27, 1936.

[32] Agnes Meyer to Landon, August 2, 1936; Lacy Haynes to Landon, August 30, 1936; James L. Wright to Landon, August 3, 1936; Landon to Wright, August 10, 1936; Landon to W. T. Mossman, August 3, 1936.

vote, but Landon did not reply to the editor nor did he call for a "war referendum." In a letter he wrote but did not send, Landon said: "I am just as much opposed to war as anyone else, but I do not think you are going to prevent war by a Constitutional amendment such as you are advocating." Just as he would not use a simple answer for such a complicated question, Landon also refused to reply to those who suggested "whispering campaigns" or the exploitation of religious issues.[33]

One problem partially resolved itself when, in early August, William Randolph Hearst sailed for Europe, not to return until the day before the election. Although his departure eliminated some of the political sting of the campaign, Hearst had already created serious trouble with his insistence that because the Communists had called the Landon-Knox ticket their chief enemy, "loyal" Americans must support the ticket. As for Roosevelt, Hearst had said: "Naturally the Communists flock to him. 'Every bird knows its own nest.'"[34] The implication— that many of the President's supporters were disloyal—was used by the Hearst newspapers repeatedly during the campaign, as well as by some of the Republican and Jeffersonian Democratic spokesmen. In September, the Republican national committee even issued a statement that said "the men who advocated revolution, who calmly discussed the amount of blood that ought to be shed, are still in Roosevelt's confidence and controlling his actions." The President— and most Americans—could not take these and similar charges lightly. Roosevelt responded by repudiating the support of those "taking orders from alien sources," but later in September he counter-smeared Hearst and the other Red-baiters by aligning them with the unpatriotic, indecent, and dishonorable elements of the country.[35]

Herbert Hoover was another problem. Landon had long been unhappy about the former President, an attitude that stemmed from Landon's disappointment with Hoover's role in the stripper well crisis of 1930–31, and that grew over the years because of—in Landon's judgment—Hoover's ineptitude in meeting the effects of the depression

---

[33] W. F. Bigelow to Landon, August 14, 1936; Landon to Bigelow, August 17, 1936 (not sent); Landon to John D. M. Hamilton, September 30, 1936.

[34] W. A. Swanberg, *Citizen Hearst* (New York: Scribners, 1961), pp. 477 ff.; *Los Angeles Examiner*, June 30, 1936. Hearst's bitterness was perhaps aggravated by the fact that he was on the verge of bankruptcy.

[35] *Topeka Capital*, September 22, 1936; *New York Times*, September 26, 1936; *Time*, September 28, 1936, pp. 12 f.; *Kansas City Star*, September 18, 1936.

and in leading the Republican party. It was further bolstered by Hoover's apparent back-door attempt to gain the 1936 Republican nomination. As far as Landon was concerned, Hoover could sun himself in California during the campaign; if he came to Landon, the governor would be polite, but no more. Landon was counseled, however, to show some recognition of Hoover's prominence in the party, and, with this in mind, Landon wrote Hoover to thank him for his statement that employment opportunities would be improved if the Republican party were returned to power. The governor also wrote: "I would appreciate your views as the campaign progresses."[36] This was as far as Landon intended to go in asking Hoover for help.

Hoover, a proud man, refused to answer when his friends asked him what his role would be in the campaign. This reticence disturbed national chairman John Hamilton, who hoped that Landon would assign a task to Hoover; but Landon believed that the former President would try to dominate the campaign, which he thought would lose innumerable votes for the Landon-Knox ticket. Hamilton called upon Hoover in Palo Alto in the latter part of August, and Hoover, placing himself at the party's disposal, asked what he could do to help during the campaign. Hoover insisted, however, that he must first be invited to participate (as was customary) by the party's presidential nominee; and he indicated that he would make no more than three speeches. On August 21, Hamilton wrote to Landon and urged him to set aside his personal views and ask Hoover to serve the party during the campaign; even Hearst's chief adviser (Francis Neylan), Hamilton said, believed that Hoover must participate because he was the obvious person to answer the Democratic criticisms of his administration. It was also feared that Hoover's supporters would be alienated and that California would be lost if the former President did not take part in the campaign—and that the Democrats would use the rift between Landon and Hoover to advantage.[37]

The matter was not decided until September 2—in a telephone conversation between Landon and Hoover. Hoover said that Landon (or one of Landon's aides) had called him for help; Landon said that Hoover (or one of Hoover's assistants) had placed the call. The possibilities of who called whom are endless, but the important fact is

[36] Landon to W. T. Mossman, April 22, 1936; Landon to Herbert Hoover, August 7, 1936.

[37] John D. M. Hamilton to Landon, August 21, 1936.

that, finding himself on the telephone with the expectant Hoover on the other end of the line, Landon could do no less than to ask Hoover to help in the campaign and to invite him to visit Topeka. Hoover, despite the unusual circumstances of the telephone call, interpreted Landon's words as an urgent call for his assistance and for a conference in Topeka.[38] The former President had been "unleashed."

Landon encountered another personality problem in John D. M. Hamilton, the Republican national chairman, who in his travel over the country and in his many speeches made it appear that he might be the real nominee. Moreover, Landon often disapproved of Hamilton's aggressive statements. Although he was happy with the national chairman's work in reviving the moribund organs of the party, Landon thought that Hamilton was ignoring the party's liberals (Hamilton later wrote that, unlike Landon, he and Knox were trying to build a conservative party). In August, complaining that a conservative businessman was being sent out as the advance man to make arrangements for his campaign tour, Landon told Hamilton:

> This again is an illustration of getting too many businessmen, employers of labor, in our campaign organization. I am hearing again and again that the old guard is functioning too prominently in the picture, that the great effect of the new leadership in the party, as demonstrated at the Cleveland convention is being lost.[39]

Landon often prodded his national chairman to use Progressives, like Gifford Pinchot and Robert Bass, in the campaign, and he reminded Hamilton of the contributions that could be made by liberals, and by moderates (such as Richard Lloyd Jones, whom Hamilton did not like).

Although Hamilton resisted Landon's suggestions, he did not always stress the party's conservative aspects; indeed, he was anxious to develop an appeal to labor, based on Landon's record and on his endorsements by national and local labor officials, but the Republican chairman was usually frustrated in this by the scarcity of endorsements

[38] Herbert Hoover to Landon, September 2, 1936; *Topeka Capital*, September 5, 6, 1936.

[39] John D. M. Hamilton to Donald R. McCoy, February 6, 1959; Landon to Hamilton, two letters, both dated August 7, 1936. Hamilton's conservatism rankled Landon, who later thought that Oscar Stauffer, his personal campaign manager, might have been a better Republican national chairman in 1936: *e.g.*, Landon interview, November 28, 1958.

and by the comparative unattractiveness of Landon's labor record. Landon, also unhappy with this situation, once put it to Hamilton: "Why don't you ever bring workingmen to see me? All I ever see are stuffed-shirt businessmen and bankers."[40]

The important reason for the differences between Landon and Hamilton, however, was the poor coordination of their campaign efforts. For that matter, the efforts of Hamilton and his eastern representative, Joseph W. Martin, Jr.—and even those of Hamilton and the Chicago national committee headquarters—were not properly coordinated. All went out to work their hardest, but they often worked at cross-purposes.[41]

Landon had decided to make at least four major campaign tours: one from the middle west to the east, one through the farm belt, a third tour through the east, and a tour of the Rocky Mountain area. Still suffering from pleurisy, Landon terminated his Colorado vacation on August 20 to begin the first tour. Accompanied by his Kansas aides and a group of Colorado politicians, he journeyed by train to the Nebraska border, where the Coloradans were replaced by Nebraska's Republican worthies. Large and receptive crowds— 7,000 at North Platte and 8,000 at Grand Island—greeted Landon at his stops in the small towns of the dust-dry area. Intermittent light rain fell as the train moved eastward. At Grand Island, Landon closed his remarks with "I hope you get rain," the rain began to fall, and the crowd cheered; it seemed a good omen. The train arrived in Omaha late at night, off schedule, but a crowd of 20,000 was on hand. On August 21 the Landon Special entered Iowa, again accompanied by rain (and area politicians), and Landon was introduced by congressional candidate Fred Gilchrist as "the man who brought rain to Iowa." Landon dispensed corny humor to his Iowa audiences: "If you think your crops are bad, you ought to see ours."[42] During the day the train rolled through Iowa, stopping at Council Grove, Carroll,

[40] Landon to John D. M. Hamilton, August 17, 1936; Hamilton to Carl Rott, September 1, 1936; Landon interview, November 28, 1958.

[41] Raymond Clapper's Diaries, August 27, 28, 1936, Raymond Clapper Papers, Manuscript Division, Library of Congress, Washington, D.C.; Landon to Walter F. Jones, November 26, 1945.

[42] Anderson, "Observations," pp. 10 f.; *Topeka Capital*, August 18, 20, 22, 1936; E. Ross Bartley to Mrs. Alfred Landon, August 21, 1936; E. Ross Bartley to Mildred Creighton, August 24, 1936.

Boone, Ames, Marshalltown, Iowa City, Cedar Rapids, and Clinton, and then into Illinois for stops at Sterling, Dixon, Rochelle, and De Kalb. During the night and morning of August 21 and 22, the train passed through Indiana and Ohio, arriving at 2:30 in the afternoon in West Middlesex, Pennsylvania.

It was estimated that between 75,000 and 110,000 people were on hand, in the vicinity of Landon's birthplace, to hear the first major speech of his campaign tours. His voice and delivery were smooth, and he talked to the crowd in his plain-folks manner. The address had been prepared by various Republican elements and polished by his speech-writing team, a procedure that—with only one or two exceptions—Landon avoided in the future by giving his writers ideas for speeches and then working over their drafts. The West Middlesex address was neither male nor female nor Landon. It included many words and phrases that Landon did not normally use: "attributes," "supplant," "mutual obligations," "more leisure for spiritual and cultural things," and—worst of all—"Wherever I have gone in this country, I have found Americans."

Despite its language and "style," the speech emphasized ideas that Landon would often repeat during the campaign. He warned that "in many parts of the world, democracy is in retreat and dictatorships are advancing" and that the American way of life was in danger because "we may not prize it as we should." He exalted free enterprise in a terminology, though not the theory, that John F. Kennedy would use a generation later.

> A new frontier had been discovered—the frontier of invention and new wants. Under our American way of life, men with courage and imagination were free to occupy this new frontier and develop it. They built a greater America. Our people were able to buy the new luxuries, comforts, and conveniences, because they had new purchasing power,—new purchasing power that came not in checks from the Treasury, but from the production of goods.

Government's role in the United States was to be ever "on the alert to repress violence and fraud, to terminate special privilege and unfair practices, to protect the everyday American in carrying on projects that are beyond the scope of private enterprise"; but Landon opposed "the transfer to Washington of any power which can be more safely and efficiently administered by state and local governments."

The candidate touched upon economic matters:

> The remedy for unemployment is not a permanent dole. . . . How can it be
> said that we have over-production, when so many Americans are badly fed,
> badly clothed and badly housed? How can it be said we have over-pro-
> duction when large groups of our fellow citizens are neglected, underpaid,
> or unemployed?

Landon contended that the great choice before the country was
"between the 'pig in the poke' policies of the present administration
and those American institutions under which we have enjoyed more
liberty and attained a higher standard of living than any other people
in the world."[43]

Although the words were not Landon's, the speech nevertheless set a
pattern of plainness of expression and simplicity of ideas that Landon
retained throughout the campaign. To his opponents, of course, the
speech was dull, simple-minded, chamber-of-commerce nonsense.

While he was in Pennsylvania, Landon gave reporters a field day:
the candidate returned to his birthplace, visited old family friends, and
attended church at his grandfather's old pastorate in West Middlesex.
But the nominee was also occupied with serious political chestnuts as
he tried to patch up the quarrels between the state Republican
organization and Senator James Davis on the one hand, and Gifford
Pinchot on the other. (Davis was the darling of whatever labor supporters the party had in Pennsylvania and Pinchot was the darling of
its intellectuals and old Bull Moose supporters.) The organization
wanted to exclude Pinchot from the homecoming ceremonies, but
Landon insisted that the former governor, an old acquaintance, ride
with him in his private railway car and in his automobile, and that he
be introduced at a banquet in New Castle on August 22. Landon
also lectured the Pennsylvania leaders on the necessity of using and
honoring Pinchot during the campaign, and they did, grudgingly,
but only for a short while.[44]

On August 24, Landon traveled through familiar places on his way
to make the second major address of the eastern tour, at Chautauqua,
New York—a speech that elicited considerable controversy among his
conservative supporters. Speaking to some 10,000 people on education

[43] Landon to Raymond Clapper, November 10, 1936 (not sent); Ralph Robey to
D. R. McCoy, March 4, 1959; Anderson, "Observations," p. 11; *Salina Journal*,
October 16, 1964; Landon address, West Middlesex, Pa., August 22, 1936.

[44] Landon interview, October 24, 1961. Pinchot campaigned for Landon largely in
midwestern and western states; McGeary, *Pinchot*, p. 416.

—in an attempt to offset criticism of Kansas' schools and to exalt a school system free from political influence—Landon declared that because the schools had been kept relatively free from political intervention and bureaucratic control, they could

> usually be counted upon to encourage change when change means progress. ... In these days of widespread propaganda, it is imperative that our teachers be kept free and that our educational institutions, our newspapers and the radio, be kept independent, either from control of autocratic government or from the influence of any selfish interest.

Taking a swipe at one of William Randolph Hearst's favorite demands, which was supported by the American Legion, he said: "In Kansas we insist that no teacher should be required to take any oath not required of all other citizens."

Landon then touched on academic freedom, a subject hitherto unmentioned in presidential campaigns. Perhaps thinking of the tribulations of his friend and college classmate, John Ise, a controversial liberal professor of economics at the University of Kansas, Landon said that although a teacher must not become a propagandist for his pet theories in the classroom, out of class "a teacher has a right to the same freedom of speech in expressing his political, social, or religious convictions as any other citizen. And I believe that a teacher has the same right to work for the accomplishment of his political and social ideals as any other citizen." Moreover, a teacher is obliged to follow the truth wherever it leads.

> The right of free inquiry is one of the essentials of free government. It is the very bedrock of democracy. We must realize that academic freedom, political freedom, religious freedom and freedom of opportunity, are all bound together. Infringement upon one will soon lead to infringement upon the others.

Although the speech was well received at Chautauqua, the Hearst press squealed, calling Landon's opposition to the teachers' oath "a regrettable departure from the high plane of true Americanism to which he has consistently adhered." Others also protested to Landon about the speech, but his reaction was: "The evidence of the need of this speech is the fact that I have received a large number of letters from Legionnaires all over the country protesting against it." [45]

[45] Landon address, Chautauqua, N.Y., August 24, 1936; *Los Angeles Examiner*, September 1, 1936; Landon to W. W. Waymack, September 2, 1936.

Landon arrived in Buffalo, the metropolis of western New York, on the morning of August 25, and he received his fanciest welcome to date, with a large parade and all the trimmings. As the governor approached his hotel, huge pictures of himself and Knox were moved by wires across the street, high above the crowd. Landon spent the rest of the day conferring with Republican and disaffected Democratic leaders,[46] and the next day, after seeing more callers and attending several local functions, he delivered a speech in Offerman Stadium. The stadium, which seated 30,000, was not filled, but some 22,000 people turned out to hear the governor lambast the administration for living "beyond its income" and warn that "someone, sometime, will have to pay the bill." The remedy to the squandering of resources and public credit was contained in four principles:

> 1. The government must guard and preserve its source of income. 2. The government must make sure that it gets a dollar's worth for every dollar it spends. 3. The government must not get in the habit of spending more than it receives. 4. Finally, the government must prepare for the rainy day.

Landon then scored the Roosevelt administration for raising much of its income from hidden taxes, which fell most heavily on those with small incomes. The housewife would not be misled much longer "with the pretense that only the rich will pay. . . . Those of our citizens with small incomes have had to pay an increased proportion of the cost of the Federal government."[47]

Landon left Buffalo immediately after the speech and arrived in Joliet, Illinois, early on August 27 for the first of a day of trainside talks in Illinois and Missouri. Then back to Topeka. The first tour had tired Landon, but he was happy with the receptions he had received. John Hamilton was elated: "Everywhere, Governor Landon's sincerity and frank and candid manner carried a most impressive appeal. . . . Reactions leave no doubt as to the leadership which will be chosen in November."[48]

The day after Landon had begun his first speaking tour, President Roosevelt made arrangements to meet in Des Moines with the drought-state governors on September 1; but the death, within the week, of Secretary of War Dern necessitated postponement of the conference

---

[46] Anderson, "Observations," p. 13.

[47] *Topeka Capital*, August 27, 1936; Landon address, Buffalo, N.Y., August 26, 1936.

[48] *Topeka Capital*, August 31, 1936.

to September 3.[49] The drought caused special difficulties for Roosevelt and Landon because they had to work together in meeting the situation and yet try to "top" each other politically. Because Landon was the Republican presidential nominee and the governor most active in fighting the drought, the President could not attack him in the time-honored way; Roosevelt had to act decisively while seeming not to respond directly to Landon's demands. How to act and yet not seem to be rewarding his adversary was Roosevelt's problem. Once he had solved this problem, it was up to Landon to see that the solution was not a campaign disadvantage and that Kansas was not deprived of its fair share of drought relief. Nevertheless, the possibility that large-scale federal aid for Kansas might swing the state to Roosevelt was a risk Landon gladly took; there was, after all, a chance that the governor might receive credit for it. And even if Roosevelt got all the credit, Landon believed it was better for the state to get assistance than for him to get votes.

President Roosevelt solved his dilemma by arranging the non-partisan, fact-finding conference of drought-state governors—in this way taking the initiative away from Landon, who would have to attend as just another governor responding to the call of his nation's chief executive. Yet the conference would have advantages for Landon: the confrontation with Roosevelt would yield him as much publicity as it would the President, and would spotlight the drought problem as nothing else could. Moreover, because President Roosevelt would have to deal with the drought as a regional problem, Kansas was assured of receiving a fair share of relief. As it turned out, Kansas received more than its proportionate share of assistance inasmuch as its relief allocations were increased—possibly to bolster the Democrats' Kansas campaign.[50]

[49] Franklin D. Roosevelt to Landon, August 21, 1936, and M. H. McIntyre to Landon, August 27, 1936, FDRL.

[50] Although the author found no evidence that would prove that relief money was largely allocated on the basis of political criteria, a case can be made in support of that contention. State figures, according to Landon, showed that the number of Works Progress Administration relief recipients in Kansas increased from 46,966 on June 27, 1936, to a peak of 69,163 the week before election: Landon to Arthur Krock, June 25, 1938. The Secretary of the Treasury, Henry Morgenthau, Jr., said that there were heavy pressures to increase federal spending in order to win the election, and it is true that WPA spent beyond its assets during the campaign and was forced to cut its program back sharply after the election: John Morton Blum (ed.), *From the Morgenthau Diaries* (Boston: Houghton Mifflin, 1959), pp. 244, 268, 272 f., 276.

During the week after his return from the east, Landon received callers, worked on his campaign speeches, and prepared for the Des Moines conference. The morning of September 3 he traveled to Des Moines by automobile—across the parched country-side—and was met by a motorcade that passed through welcoming crowds on the way to the Iowa capitol. Immediately after luncheon, in Governor Clyde Herring's outer office, the meetings with President Roosevelt started. Governors and United States senators from Missouri, Nebraska, and Oklahoma—as well as from Kansas and Iowa—were present. Because each delegation was called in the order of its state's admission to the Union to confer with the President, the Kansans went in third.

Landon and his advisers, after presenting the President with information about the drought in Kansas, proposed several measures for immediate relief: water supply and storage projects, the improvement of farm-to-market roads, control of wind erosion, federal purchase of livestock, surveys of the availability of feed, loans to needy farmers, and reduced freight rates on shipments of cattle and feeds. Their long-range measures included the retirement of depleted lands, grass restoration, land conservation education, surveys of underground water resources, and the conservation of water resources (as outlined in the comprehensive pond, lake, and reservoir program proposed by Kansas in June, 1934).

F. S. Bartlett to H. L. Hopkins, November 18, 1936, WPA file 100, National Archives, Washington, D.C. WPA expenditures in Kansas soared during the fiscal year 1936–37 to $27,888,660, compared to $15,820,351 the preceding year, WPA, "Relief Financing for States and Territories 1933–1940" (WP 1.2 R 3), Kansas, Part I, pp. 2 f. (typescript), National Archives. The WPA also authorized adding 5,000 people to the rolls in southeast Kansas, which was neither a drought area nor in as bad a situation as in previous years. Aubrey Williams to Congressman E. W. Patterson, August 10, 1936, WPA file 610, Kansas, National Archives. A remarkably high number of authorizations to use funds from prior allocations—forty-four in October, for example—were received during the campaign by the Kansas Works Progress administrator, Evan Griffith: Corrington Gill to Evan Griffith, October correspondence, WPA file 610, Kansas, National Archives. In view of the drought crisis, this does not prove that winning the election was the prime motivation. Harry Hopkins, though not averse to helping the Democratic party, as a matter of principle worked to step up his agency's efforts (whenever possible) in the belief that additional funds would be found to make up his deficits. Moreover, President Roosevelt, although he allowed Hopkins some additional funds during the fall of 1936, sharply refused to grant most of the extra money he requested for WPA: Searle F. Charles, *Minister of Relief, Harry Hopkins and the Depression* (Syracuse, N.Y.: Syracuse University Press, 1963), p. 167. Blum (ed.), *Morgenthau Diaries*, p. 243. Roosevelt to Hopkins, October 12, 1936, WPA file 100, National Archives.

Roosevelt, who had come to the conference after a "non-political" tour of the drought areas, met Landon at Governor Herring's luncheon before the meetings; they shook hands, ate lunch together, and chatted for almost forty minutes; then, after the conference, Landon and his advisers went to the Hotel Fort Des Moines for a short rest before dinner—a dinner, on the presidential train, to which Roosevelt had invited the governors and their staffs. It was a pleasant affair, and at its end Landon and Roosevelt again shook hands. At these meetings— the first in modern times between contending presidential nominees— Roosevelt and Landon were genial but restrained; each guarded himself against embarrassment, and both were unembarrassed, for the drought was of great personal interest to them. Senator Capper said: "Harmony dripped so steadily from every rafter that I fully expected one of the candidates to withdraw." [51] The only victors were the newsmen, who filed reams of colorful commentary, and the victims of drought, who received more attention in one day than they had normally received in a year. Only one exchange between the two nominees touched on the election. "Governor," Roosevelt remarked, "if you get my job at the White House you had better get a small boat to take weekend fishing trips upon the Potomac. Large ones hold too many people, and it is a pretty hard job without these trips." "Thanks, Mr. President," Landon replied, "I will remember that."

Landon's party stopped for the night at St. Joseph, Missouri. On the road again the next morning, it stopped to discuss the situation around Wathena and Troy, in Kansas; then Landon traveled to Atchison to visit Ed Howe, the "Sage of Potato Hill." The famous author told the candidate that his advisers were overworking him, and that he should drop them and go his own way. After a tour of the state orphanage, the party left for Topeka, where it was welcomed by a shower of rain.

On September 5, Landon posed for newsreel photographers, and sat for an oil painting, and the same day it was announced—to the horror of many Republicans—that the governor had decided not to make a western speaking tour. The next day Landon spoke to a conference of Young Republican leaders in Topeka, met with his advisers in Kansas City, and took a night train to Wichita to address the state American Legion convention. On the morning of September 7, in the Allis Hotel, he

[51] Landon to Franklin D. Roosevelt, September 2, 1936 (mimeograph); *Topeka Capital*, September 2, 3, 4, 1936; Burns, *Roosevelt*, p. 277; Schlesinger, *Politics of Upheaval*, pp. 609–610. For a dissenting view, see Rexford G. Tugwell, *The Democratic Roosevelt* (Garden City, N.Y.: Doubleday, 1957), p. 425.

exchanged greetings with past department commanders of the Legion, then went to the Forum to deliver a little-publicized speech on tolerance to 3,000 World War I veterans.[52]

"It ought not to be necessary to stress tolerance in America. . . . But of late there has been disquieting evidence of attempts to stir up racial antagonisms"—probably, Landon thought, because of the persecutions then breaking out in parts of Europe, the strain of depression, and "pure orneriness." Because the legionnaires represented all of America's various racial strains, and because the Legion was influential, the members and the group had a "responsibility to oppose every move to . . . break up the country into hostile groups. Also, we must insist upon the preservation and protection of American freedom, and above all the freedom of expression." After calling for unity in meeting the nation's problems, Landon discussed labor unions, and deplored the split between craft and industrial unions. "Here again, unity is requisite for progress and achievement. . . . All labor will be in a stronger position if it eliminates the cut-throat competition of cheap labor in the sweatshops. Low living standards for some of our people in this competitive age are a continuing threat to the standards of workers in other sections more fortunately situated." Emphasizing the duty of keeping the peace, Landon then condemned war's futility, its waste, and "its meaningless cruelty"—but, in the event of war—he demanded that profiteering be eliminated and that all the nation's "manpower, industry and resources" be put "on an equal footing."[53]

With this noble speech the preparatory phase of Landon's campaign for President ended. Three days later he would board a train for what would seem to be an unending series of speeches across the land.

[52] Anderson, "Observations," pp. 16 ff.; *Topeka Capital*, September 7, 1936.
[53] Landon speech, Wichita, September 7, 1936.

CHAPTER 12

Full-Time Candidate

Until the early part of September, Landon had been beset by illness and fatigue; he had lacked luster and decisiveness—had been, in effect, a part-time candidate. The Gallup polls, however, had recorded little change in the relative attractiveness of Roosevelt and Landon: in June, the sample showed 55.8 per cent in favor of the President, 52.5 per cent in August, and 52.6 per cent in September. During the late summer of 1936 the *Literary Digest* poll, which had been highly accurate in past elections, showed that Landon had a two-to-one lead, but private polls—made for the Republicans by the Nielsen Corporation— showed that Landon was running well behind Roosevelt.[1] Criticism of the campaign effort streamed in. Frank Altschul wrote that, despite Landon's appealing personality, forcefulness, and honesty, he was not "coming across" on the radio; he suggested better editing of Landon's radio speeches and the avoidance of certain sounds in his delivery. Landon answered: "What is one man's dish is another man's poison" —convinced that Roosevelt could be beaten only by an opponent with an antithetical personality. William Allen White wrote, "Boy, how I do want to help you," and he feared that "the stuff that is coming out of headquarters is picturing you as too dark and dour a

[1] *Topeka State Journal*, September 14, 1936; Hill Blackett to Landon, August 27, 1936, Alfred M. Landon Papers, Kansas State Historical Society, Topeka.

conservative."[2] It was widely rumored that Landon advocated an average of only $1.08 a week for a family for relief; another rumor said that he was an anti-Semite, and still another that he favored Jews over Germans. Landon also was said to be linked with the utility interests, and antilabor, and in favor of ending relief immediately, and of restoring prohibition. The campaign, moreover, was plagued by factional feuds in New Jersey, Pennsylvania, Missouri, California, and New York, making it difficult for Landon to decide whom he should see and where he should stay when he visited these states. Further, there were reports that the Republican national committee was pinched for money; and there were complaints that the committee's headquarters was not responding to requests for campaign literature.[3]

Many Democratic leaders were afflicted by similar worries for Roosevelt because of the lack of visible campaign activity, but, although the President was biding his time in taking to the stump, much effort was being devoted to the campaign. Roosevelt had suggested, as early as February, that the Department of Agriculture and Harry Hopkins "prepare a little history of Governor Landon's requests and demands on Washington and a history of what the Federal agencies did for Kansas." The Democratic national chairman, James Farley, was busy organizing his party's campaign workers; at Louis Howe's suggestion, many different nonpartisan organizations were being established to support Roosevelt; and it must have been apparent to most appointed federal officials that they were expected to do what they could to help the party in order to save their jobs. All kinds of people were sending "dirt" on Landon to the President and to his political aides. Frank Hodges, a Reconstruction Finance Corporation official in Kansas City, wrote Farley that someone should see a former Kansas state treasurer who would supply inside information about the Finney scandal. Oswald Garrison Villard, the veteran reformer—among others—sent the President a catalog of curious charges, *Meet Mr. Landon*, written by John Wells. Copies of Burt Comer's equally uncomplimentary book, *The Tale of a Fox*, also found their way to Roosevelt (Comer was

[2] Frank Altschul to Landon, August 27, 1936; Landon to Altschul, September 2, 1936; W. A. White to Landon, August 31, 1936.

[3] "Digest of Mail Received at Jayhawk Hotel Headquarters," August 31 to September 5, September 7 to 16, September 17 to 26, September 26 to October 3 (typescripts from Rolla Clymer); John D. M. Hamilton to Landon, September 12, October 2, 1936.

a close friend of Dr. Brinkley).[4] Roosevelt, to his credit, decided not to use or circulate such material.

The Democrats again made strenuous efforts to capture Republican supporters, as in 1932, when Henry Wallace, Harold Ickes, and Senators George Norris and Robert La Follette, Jr., had declared for Roosevelt. In 1936, La Follette became chairman of the Progressive National Committee for Roosevelt, Norris became honorary chairman, and Mayor Fiorello La Guardia of New York took an active part in its organization. The P.N.C. attacked Landon as the candidate of "the oligarchy of special privilege," declaring: A VOTE AGAINST ROOSE-VELT IS A VOTE FOR LANDON—AND THE DANGER OF: WAR, HOOVER STARVATION, REPUBLICAN REACTION, SUPPRESSION OF CIVIL LIBERTIES. Dr. Stanley High, a Republican, and the former editor of the *Christian Herald*, was enlisted to help write Roosevelt's speeches and to head his organ for peace and piety, the Good Neighbor League. Although High's organization emphasized the positive aspects of Roosevelt's record, it also hit at the President's opposition, calling them "party hacks and disappointed politicians."[5]

Roosevelt's press support, although small, was vitriolic in supporting him. The *Los Angeles Daily News* mounted a wide range of attacks upon Landon and "his Liberty League pals," and upon the "sacrifice" of Kansas' tuberculous and mental institutions, schools, and highways for the sake of achieving a balanced budget. The Democratic national committee bludgeoned Landon in its releases:

> Kansas has suffered for four years now from "soak the poor" taxation. . . .
> Gov. Landon's administration closed the last fiscal year with a surplus of over $1 million. This was done by contributing nothing for social security and only a trifling amount for the administrative expenses of relief.

According to the Democratic national committee, Landon's forces, in order to pay for distressed schools and social security, would impose

[4] Franklin D. Roosevelt to Rudolph Forster, February 26, 1936; Frank Hodges to James A. Farley, July 28, 1936; Oswald Garrison Villard to Roosevelt, September 25, 1936, all Franklin D. Roosevelt Library, Hyde Park, N.Y.; James MacGregor Burns, *Roosevelt: The Lion and the Fox* (New York: Harcourt, Brace, 1956), p. 275; Donald R. McCoy, "The Good Neighbor League and the Presidential Campaign of 1936," *Western Political Quarterly*, XIII (December, 1960), 1011.

[5] McCoy, "The Good Neighbor League," pp. 1012, 1018; Donald R. McCoy, "The Progressive National Committee of 1936," *Western Political Quarterly*, IX (June, 1956), 456 ff., 465 ff.

higher taxes and a sales tax on Kansas' "little folks," including teachers
(who allegedly earned as little as $25.00 a month). The light touch
also was used against Landon, as in Senator Burton Wheeler's talk to
the Montana Democratic convention:

> I have made diligent study of the speeches delivered by Governor Landon
> since the nominating convention. His thoughts were expressed after much
> deliberation following a sojourn of some weeks at a secluded mountain
> resort in Colorado. I was hopeful they would throw much light upon the
> problems that confront the people. After careful study, I conclude that
> Governor Landon is in favor of good health, sunshine, a temperate climate
> and a long and happy life. I do not wish to misquote him. I believe he is in
> favor of sunshine, but only when accompanied by adequate precipitation, a
> temperate climate, but one sufficiently bracing, a long and happy life, but
> not too long nor too happy.[6]

The attacks against Landon by liberals and radicals were particularly
harsh; they repeatedly charged that he was insincere, a prohibitionist,
a tool of Wall Street, the darling of the munitions-makers and the
American Liberty League, an instrument of Hearst, and an encourager
of the Union party's leaders: William Lemke, Charles Coughlin, and
Gerald L. K. Smith. Despite his record, it was hinted that Landon was
the political heir of the Teapot Dome oil intriguers. His Kansas record,
though outstanding among farm states, suffered by comparison with
the endeavors and accomplishments of wealthier and more populous
industrial states. Landon's balancing of his state budget was sneered
at by those who contended that it resulted from federal financial support of the state, that it was a very small budget, and that a deficit was
prohibited by the state constitution.[7] The fact that all of the other

[6] *Los Angeles Illustrated Daily News*, August 28, September 1, 1936; *New York Daily News*, October 7, 1936; *Great Falls* (Mont.) *Tribune*, September 13, 1936.

[7] Representative of such criticism are Harold L. Ickes to A. R. E. Pinchot, October 19, 1936 (mimeograph), Harold L. Ickes Papers, Manuscript Division, Library of Congress, Washington, D.C.; Earl Browder, *Democracy or Fascism: Report to the Ninth Annual Convention of the Communist Party* (New York: International Publishers, 1936), *passim*; Norman Thomas, *After the New Deal, What?* (New York: Macmillan, 1936), p. 3; Progressive National Committee Supporting Franklin D. Roosevelt for President, *Declaration of Principles* (New York, 1936). For other materials, see the miscellany of criticism in the weekly press releases written by Charles Michelson and published by the Democratic national committee serially as *Dispelling the Fog*; National Restaurant Institute, *Landon—The Dry Challenge* (New York, 1936); "Presidency/Landon" file, William E. Borah Papers, Manuscript Division, Library of Congress, Washington, D.C.; George H. Mayer, *The Political Career of Floyd B. Olson* (Minneapolis: University of Minnesota Press, 1951), p. 297; and Wilbur L. Cross, *Connecticut Yankee: An Autobiography* (New Haven: Yale University Press, 1943), pp. 344 f.

states had received federal aid and had nevertheless run up deficits, and that a constitutional requirement is not self-fulfilling, were not successfully explained by the Republicans during the campaign.

Of course, the Republicans printed vast amounts of campaign literature to try to counteract all this and to create a counteroffensive. About 400 million copies of some 200 different pamphlets and leaflets were distributed. These contained speeches by Landon and Knox, reviews of Landon's record, the party platform, and jibes at the Roosevelt administration. One of the most popular pamphlets was "Landon Epigrams," which included such sayings as "American initiative is not a commodity to be delivered in pound packages through a governmental bureau" and "A people begin to decay when they do not resist burdensome taxation." "Relief for Votes," which showed James Farley on the telephone, was subtitled: "Will the American people accept the imputation that their votes can be bought with relief money? That you can't beat $5 billion?" "Death Flies the Mail" said that Roosevelt and Farley had canceled contracts for commercial airmail delivery and had instead used army planes, with the result that "Twelve Army air pilots [were] sent to their death." It was reported in "The New Deal Confesses" that the United States lagged behind other countries in economic recovery, and that the "American Market Supports Foreigners—The Home Market for Agriculture Has Been Given to Foreigners By the NEW DEAL." "And lay up corn under the hand of Pharaoh . . . Genesis: Chapter 41" attacked the New Deal's agricultural scarcity program, and "Canada Invites You" pointed up the huge increase in imports of Canadian hogs, fresh pork, and cheese in 1935 and 1936. "What will Daddy bring for dinner?" pictured two children peering sadly from a rain-streaked window, obviously looking for their father and the bundle of food he would bring home—a bundle smaller in 1936 than in 1933 because "it takes exactly $1.44 to buy what they could have bought for $1.00 in 1933." "The Bad News" proclaimed that there were "58 Taxes on a Loaf of Bread," that "the Big Boys say DEBT is for the little fellows own good," that "THE PUBLIC DEBT IS $34 BILLION," that "If We Don't Stop the New Deal the Nation Will Be Bankrupt," and that "YOU PAY OVER THREE MONTHS OF YOUR WAGES EACH YEAR FOR THE COST OF GOVERNMENT." The most controversial piece of Republican literature was a handbill, "Notice of Pay Deduction"; it was given out late in the campaign at factory gates and it said that on January 1, 1937, because of the Social Security

Act, "your employer will be compelled by law to deduct a certain amount from your pay check every week."

The national committee headquarters also distributed 18 million Landon and Knox portrait posters, 42 million campaign buttons, 15 million automobile stickers, and over 4 million pieces of rotogravure publicity. Millions of gummed labels were given out to remind voters that "Every Minute the New Deal Spends $16,894.59," and to ask them to "VOTE FOR LANDON AND LAND A JOB—REGULAR JOBS AT REGULAR PAY." Press releases flooded out of national committee headquarters into the offices of press representatives all over the country; and William Hard went on the air three times a week during the campaign to explain Landon's record, the Republican platform, and the deficiencies of the Roosevelt administration. His broadcasts carried such titles as "Calls Mr. Landon Complete Liberal," "Shows Roosevelt Had Hearst's Support," "Roosevelt Not on Road to Peace but War," "Roosevelt and Collectivism! Landon and Sanity!" "Roosevelt Prevents New Jobs," "New Deal Supports 'Economic Royalists' of Cotton," "Party Funds Forced from WPA Workers," and "Nails Campaign Lie! Proves Landon *NOT* Against Jews." The American Liberty League, that curious combination of angry and rich Democrats and Republicans, also did its share; it poured money and venom into the campaign and tried to create the impression that the things Roosevelt stood for "constitute a great stride towards actual communism." Jim Farley was right when, in September, he had said that this would become a "dirty campaign."[8]

Landon's campaign reached its turning point in early September. Spurred by criticism of his early campaign, influenced by the rising voices of hate around him, and having acquired some momentum and zest for the battle, he set out to put more punch in his efforts. The result was a potpourri—based, in part, on Charles Taft's idea that the Republican nominee had to make a broad appeal in the hope that some of the wild horses in Roosevelt's coalition would break away, in part on Hamilton's view that "people vote their dislikes," and in part on Landon's conviction that he had a duty to soften conservative resistance

[8] Miscellaneous printed campaign materials, Landon Papers; Ralph D. Casey, "Republican Propaganda in the 1936 Campaign," *Public Opinion Quarterly*, I (April, 1937), 34, 43; George Wolfskill, *The Revolt of the Conservatives* (Boston: Houghton Mifflin, 1962), pp. 208, 223; *Kansas City Star*, September 20, 1936.

to necessary reforms.[9] The rest of Landon's campaign was therefore increasingly combative in tone and vote-catching in nature, an amalgam of alarms and promises seasoned with liberalism.

This became clear immediately after his September 7 address to the Kansas American Legion, when he arranged a well-publicized meeting with Jesse Owens, the Negro Olympic star, who declared that he would stump for Landon. Also, through the colored voters' section of the Republican national committee, the governor appealed to Negro citizens for their votes, the first presidential nominee to do so. (Later in the month President Roosevelt also sent a message directly to colored voters.) On September 8, Landon announced that he would go to Maine to speak—just before that state's election. Despite the arguments of other advisers, Ogden Mills successfully urged him to do this to help save Senator Wallace White, whose reelection seemed jeopardized by unfavorable reactions to Frank Knox's condemnation of the AAA. Moreover, a victory in Maine's early national election and, after a Landon visit, would give some credence to the national committee's contention that "The Country Seems to Be Switching to Landon."[10]

On the evening of September 10 Landon boarded the train for Maine on his second campaign tour. He stopped in Chicago the next day for a hastily drawn together conference with midwestern party leaders and national committee officials. That afternoon, in Indiana, in Gary, Valparaiso, Plymouth, Warsaw, and Fort Wayne, Landon made folksy water-stop appeals.

> I am delighted to see so many of you here this afternoon. I know you have come down to look me over. Well, that goes both ways. I am glad to look you over, too. It is not convenient for you to come out to visit me on my front porch in Topeka, so I am glad to visit with you, as it were, from my back porch here. . . . This is going to be a back-porch and a front-porch campaign, as well as a fighting campaign—a fighting campaign on the part of Republicans and Independents and Democrats for good government.
>
> We want a government that is concerned about the economic rights and

[9] Charles P. Taft, *You and I—and Roosevelt* (New York: Farrar & Rinehart, 1936), pp. 12 f.; Harold F. Gosnell, *Champion Campaigner: Franklin D. Roosevelt* (New York: Macmillan, 1952), p. 156; Raymond Clapper's Diaries, September 13, 1936, Raymond Clapper Papers, Manuscript Division, Library of Congress, Washington, D.C.

[10] Victor Anderson, "Observations of the Campaign" (undated carbon-copy typescript), p. 18; *Los Angeles Eagle Home News*, September 11, 1936; *Kansas City Star*, September 10, 1936; Landon interview, March 18, 1963.

the opportunities of the average man. We want a government that is also concerned about the pocketbooks of everybody. Whether you know it or not, we are all paying taxes every day in our lives.

I don't blame this present administration for trying to hide behind a non-political campaign plea. I would too if I had to defend such a record as they have made in Washington in the last three years.[11]

Landon had never before participated in a national campaign, or even in a big campaign, for Kansas politicking was not like that of the cross-country tour or the big city. He was also unused to the big stadium and auditorium crowds; 5,000 people made a huge crowd in Kansas. He had to learn a great deal very quickly, but by the time of the Maine tour he had begun to hit his stride. He had perfected his water-stop technique, and had learned something of handling large crowds at major stops and speaking engagements. And he and his staff had also learned something about showmanship: before his train arrived in a town, advancemen alerted the local papers and party leaders; people were turned out and a band was present. Landon would be on the rear platform of the train as it stopped, a technique that lacked suspense but was in keeping with his straightforward approach. He would appeal to local interests and would praise local worthies; then, for a few minutes after his speech, he would wave to the crowd, give them lots of his infectious smile, and shake hands all around. After the train pulled out, he would return to his private car and talk with small groups of local dignitaries for ten or fifteen minutes each. Then, passing through a car jammed with the second-rank politicos of the area, he would walk down the aisle, shaking hands and making cheerful small talk.

Erwin Canham, of the *Christian Science Monitor*, put it well: "Here is a ruddy-faced man, with twinkling eyes and a grin as broad as his drawl, and a square jaw and square glasses, who likes people and enjoys greeting them if there aren't too many." With individuals and small groups, Landon created the impression of "a sincere, warm, friendly person," but he was unable to convey this impression to the millions who were to know him only from his radio speeches or from newspaper reports.[12] A man can be honest, friendly, well-intentioned, and even competent, and still not win a presidential election.

Landon's speeches started again September 12 at Stamford, Con-

[11] *Kansas City Times*, September 11, 1936; Landon speeches, September 11, 1936.
[12] *Topeka State Journal*, September 26, 1936; *Geneva* (N.Y.) *Times*, November 3, 1936.

necticut: "No nation can prosper while one-fifth of those who earn their own living are denied real work and left dependent upon the work of others for their support." Bridgeport: "There is no future for any American on the relief rolls." New Haven: "We must continue to provide relief for all those that need relief; but we owe it to ourselves . . . to purge relief of all partisanship, waste and incompetence." Worcester, Massachusetts: The characteristics of New England and Kansas are "old-fashioned honesty, courage, common sense, self-reliance, self-respect, and respect for the rights of others." Lowell: "It is beneath the dignity of a great nation to dole out bread for votes." Lawrence: "Jobs will be made secure when free American enterprise is restored."[13] The day was balmy and the crowds were big, though quiet.

Landon was welcomed in Portland, Maine, by the state's leading Republican politicians and by the Democratic governor, Louis J. Brann, who was running for the Senate. Because his train was late, Landon drove directly to the stadium where his speech was to be given, but he was disappointed to find that less than 15,000 people were present—fewer than in some of the train-side crowds during the day.[14] Then Landon lashed at the government as he had not done before; his target was the National Recovery Administration, which he called "the beginning in America of the [worldwide] movement which has been substituting arbitrary personal authority for constitutional self-government." The NRA was dead but its spirit lived on in the New Deal.

> It lives on in the efforts of this administration to get around the decisions of the Supreme Court. . . . But above all it lives on in the spirit of the President, who has confessed to no error—who has let it be clearly known that he considered it would be a catastrophe if the American farmer should "once more become a lord on his own farm."
>
> If this does not mean that the present administration wants to establish government domination of industry and agriculture, what does it mean?
>
> If the President has changed his mind and recognizes his errors, let him say so. Let him say so in plain language. Until we have such an admission of error, the choice before us is clear.
>
> On one side is the system of free competitive enterprise, which, while not perfect, at least does not dole out opportunity according to a governmental yardstick—a system under which this country is still a freer, a happier place to live in than any other country in the world. . . .

[13] Landon speeches, September 12, 1936.

[14] Anderson, "Observations," p. 20; *Topeka Capital*, September 12, 1936; *Portland* (Me.) *Telegram*, September 13, 1936.

On the other side is a system under which the minutest doings of every citizen are scrutinized and regulated; under which the privacy of our homes is invaded. Our fields lie idle by government edict—and across the length and breadth of America a million signs spring up "By Order of the Government, Keep Off." There is no half-way house between these two systems.[15]

Maine's Republican leaders were happy with Landon's performance, but Landon was not impressed with the response. Senator Frederick Hale told him, as they drove from the stadium, that it was one of the warmest political meetings ever held in the state. Landon replied: "Senator, it may have been warm for Maine, but it was damn cold for Kansas."[16] Landon spent the night at Hale's house, and on September 13 he drove around upper New England and visited political figures. On September 14 he boarded his train at Nashua, New Hampshire, and during the day made a number of short train-side speeches. At Springfield, Massachusetts, he referred to the Connecticut River Valley floods the previous spring to emphasize the need for "a sound soil conservation, erosion control, and water resources program," and he blasted the administration for not having developed a national land-use program. In the industrial cities of central New York he flayed the New Deal because 11 million were still unemployed. He promised he would establish a back-to-work government and would "keep politics out of relief while the job was being done."[17] The crowd that heard him in Albany was said to rival in size the crowds that listened to Al Smith at the height of his political career. Some 10,000 people were on hand in Rochester when Landon pulled in after midnight. He arrived in Chicago the next morning, and after conferring for several hours with John D. M. Hamilton and other national committee headquarters officers, he left for a series of train-side speeches in Illinois, Iowa, and Missouri.

At Coal City, Illinois, after hearing of his victory in Maine's early election, Landon gave the news to his audience, adding:

[15] Landon speech, Portland, Me., September 12, 1936. Although Landon's increased pugnacity, as seen in this speech, undoubtedly came in part from the alarmists around him, it should not be overlooked that Landon for some time had brooded on the rise of authoritarianism in Europe. This had led him to conclude, as he told Raymond Clapper in August, that it was "vital to resist any tampering with [public opinion] in this country." Raymond Clapper Diaries, n.d. (probably August 25, 1936), Clapper Papers.

[16] Arthur M. Schlesinger, Jr., *The Politics of Upheaval* (Boston: Houghton Mifflin, 1960), p. 611.

[17] Landon speeches, Springfield, Mass., and Albany, Schenectady, Utica, Syracuse, and Rochester, N.Y., September 14, 1936.

You all know that old saying, "As Maine goes, so goes the nation." . . . The victory parade has been started that will span the nation. It goes far beyond mere partisanship. Republicans, Democrats and Independents alike are taking part. . . . The American people are aroused at the waste and extravagance of their national government. . . . The spirit evidenced yesterday in Maine has stirred the entire country. And the voice of the nation will speak in November in no uncertain terms.

Despite the exhilarating news of the Maine victory, Landon soon ran into a crushing instance of labor's indifference to him. At Shopton, Iowa, the site of the great Santa Fe Railroad shops, he left his train to shake hands with a group of employees who were sitting on a porch railing. He had to go to them, and almost had to drag them to their feet to shake hands, in order to be photographed.[18]

There were, nevertheless, several reasons why Republicans could be happy in September. The crowds that greeted Landon on the Maine trip had been large; and Frank Knox, a bit earlier, had also reported large crowds. The Landon–Knox victory in Maine was heartening because the vote for Roosevelt had been less than in 1932 while Landon had surpassed Hoover's 1932 popular vote. Further, Landon's visit to Maine was credited as the decisive factor in the victory of all of the Republican candidates for state and federal offices (but many Landon supporters conveniently overlooked the disproportionate attention given the state by Jeffersonian Democrats and other Republicans, and the tens of thousands of dollars poured in by the American Liberty League). Of the national opinion polls, only the Gallup Poll showed Roosevelt winning; the rural press poll of 3,000 publications and the *Literary Digest* had Landon well ahead of the President. In the primary elections in Michigan and New Hampshire, Republicans drew more votes than Democrats, and in Massachusetts about as many as the Democrats. Moreover, the *Baltimore Sun* and the *St. Louis Post-Dispatch*, both normally Democratic, came out in support of Landon.[19] Many Republicans thought the Kansan had a good chance.

Landon was in Topeka for almost a week, working on speeches and campaign plans, before he began his third tour. He made only one

[18] *Kansas City Star*, September 15, 1936; *New York Times*, September 15, 1936; Landon speech, Coal City, Ill., September 15, 1936; Anderson, "Observations," p. 22.

[19] Frank Knox to Landon, September 5, 1936; Edgar E. Robinson, *They Voted For Roosevelt* (Stanford: Stanford University Press, 1947), p. 42; *Kansas City Star*, September 16, 1936; Wolfskill, *Revolt of the Conservatives*, p. 220; *New York Times*, September 15, 1936; *St. Louis Post Dispatch*, September 26, 1936.

lengthy speech during that week—on September 18, to a national youth conference—in which he defined what he thought was the chief difference between the New Deal and the Republicans.

> The present administration apparently believes that there is no future for this country. It has accepted the idea that we have reached our peak—that ahead of us is a large standing army of unemployed; that, in consequence, the government must play a greater and greater part in managing the details of our daily lives instead of confining itself to the expanding field of regulation in the public interest.
>
> The Republican party, on the other hand, utterly rejects this philosophy. It believes that America is still on the upgrade, that we can eliminate unemployment, that the government should tighten the rules governing business, but should not attempt to manage business.

In short, under the latter policy, "the government tells us what we can*not* do. Under the other, the government tells us what we *must* do."[20]

The governor's third campaign tour was a week-long visit through the farm belt states of Missouri, Iowa, Minnesota, Wisconsin, and Illinois; and he had made intensive preparations for discussing agricultural matters. He left Topeka on the morning of September 22 and made eight stops for brief speeches and handshaking in northern Missouri and southern Iowa, which was virtually virgin territory for a presidential nominee. At 4:15 p.m. the train arrived in Des Moines, where that evening Landon went to the state fairgrounds to tell some 20,000 people of his farm security program.

After homely remarks about the great values of farm life, he pledged to work to make the farmer "a good provider and a good customer," which was to be achieved by an increasing demand for farm products— stimulated by returning the unemployed to work, by government development of new crops and new crop uses, by a program of subsidies on exportable surpluses, and by conservation measures for operators of family-size farms. Also, his program would lower retail prices in order to benefit the consumer. Landon promised prompt drought relief, seed loans, consideration of a federal crop-insurance program, equalization of rural and urban educational opportunities, a comprehensive conservation program, and the fulfillment of outstanding New Deal obligations to individual farmers "with no waste

[20] *Governor Landon Speaks to Youth* (El Dorado, Kan.: Republican National Committee, 1936).

and no politics." Landon also touched on a problem, farm tenantry, that the New Deal had found difficult to handle because of the pressures of southern landowners. Pointing out that 42 per cent of the nation's farms were operated by tenants, he declared: "It is our pledge to extend, within the limits of sound finance, adequate credit at reasonable rates, to capable tenants and experienced farmers, for the purchase or refinancing of farm homes."[21]

The local response to Landon's speech was such that many in the governor's party regarded Iowa as in the bag. Landon remained in Des Moines the following day, conferring with representatives of farm and political organizations, including J. P. Wallace, an uncle of Secretary of Agriculture Henry A. Wallace, and George Peek, the former Agricultural Adjustment administrator. Landon also spoke at a luncheon, at the Kirkwood Hotel, in which he praised Iowa's contributions to agriculture—and even conceded that Iowan Henry A. Wallace "has done some good things."[22]

On September 24 the governor was on the road again; he stopped at a number of places in northern Iowa and southern Minnesota to lament the drought, foreign agricultural competition, and waste and politics in relief.[23] Privately, he must also have bemoaned the fact that President Roosevelt had beat him to the punch in promising—the day before Landon's Des Moines speech—crop-insurance, land-use, and farm-tenant aid programs, thereby forcing Landon to reveal some of the key parts of his address in advance press releases.

The man who had almost everything was stealing the few positive issues still available to the Republicans. Roosevelt had also held a series of conferences with the representatives of leading utilities, banks, and insurance companies to allay their suspicions, wiggle the carrot in front of their noses, charm their teeth away, and coax admissions that—contrary to Frank Knox's rash charges—their sectors of the economy were not only in good condition but were getting better.[24] This not only damaged Knox's and Landon's appeal to the voters, it led to unpleasantness between the two Republican nominees. When, before the President's meetings with financial leaders, Knox had charged

[21] Anderson, "Observations," p. 24; Landon speech, Des Moines, September 22, 1936.

[22] Anderson, "Observations," pp. 24 f.; Landon speech, Des Moines, September 23, 1936.

[23] Landon speeches, Nevada, Ia., and Albert Lea, Minn., September 24, 1936.

[24] *New York Times*, September 26, 1936; *Time*, September 28, 1936, p. 11.

that the New Deal had put insurance companies in danger of bankruptcy, Landon telephoned immediately to restrain him. Knox thereupon called in three newsmen to have a drink with him, and, striking a Teddy Roosevelt pose, said "Boys, I've got another McKinley on my hands." [25]

The crowds Landon met on his way to Minneapolis were warm in their greetings, and more politicians and farm leaders piled on and off the campaign train—including Dan Wallace, another uncle of the Secretary of Agriculture. In the Minnesota metropolis, the governor went to the auditorium, where an overflow crowd had come to hear him speak about international trade. Landon charged that although the Administration's reciprocal trade program had been called a boon to the farmer, it had, in its two years of operation, "delayed recovery for our farmers." The program had "sold the American farmer down the river" because all the countries involved had not made concessions. New Deal reciprocity had further worked to America's disadvantage because it had failed to deal with such trade-constricting factors as foreign embargoes, exchange restrictions, trade quotas, and the drive toward national economic self-sufficiency. Landon also criticized the government for not requiring sanitary standards on agricultural imports equal to those demanded of America's farmers, for "star chamber" hearings on new trade agreements, and for negotiating agreements that increased imports of commodities that were in surplus at home—such as cheese from Canada. Landon said the Republicans would revise the tariff in order to restrict imports of competitive foreign products, especially dairy and livestock commodities. They would also encourage real reciprocal trade on noncompetitive products, thereby helping the farmer recapture his markets abroad. [26]

The Des Moines and Minneapolis speeches were the most controversial of Landon's campaign. His farm program, as outlined in the Iowa capital, promised far more than the AAA, and left the impression that it would cost far more. Despite Landon's belief that his farm program, by restoring agricultural markets and income, would reduce rather than swell public spending, those seeking governmental economy never accepted his analysis. His Minneapolis speech on trade agreements—which compromised his low-tariff views—was even more

[25] Lyle C. Wilson to Landon, June 28, 1947.

[26] Anderson, "Observations," p. 25; Landon speech, Minneapolis, September 24, 1936.

controversial. Not only did it antagonize rather than draw together many of his supporters who favored reciprocity *or* high tariffs, it caused Secretary of State Cordell Hull to enter the campaign to denounce Landon's "wild misrepresentations." It is fair to say that although these two speeches may have brought him votes from farmers, as the Kansan wanted, they cost him dearly in the east and in the large cities. They further hurt him because he never explained, to the satisfaction of the voters, how the government could give more aid to farmers and still reduce expenditures, and how trade barriers could be lowered while giving farmers additional tariff protection.[27]

After his Minneapolis speech, Landon chatted with local Republican hopefuls and hasbeens, and the next morning the Sunflower Special moved eastward for a two-day tour of Wisconsin. Again, as in Iowa and Minnesota, Landon was well received, but he made only six platform appearances on September 25, taking time out for some relaxation (a high school football game at Oshkosh) and some good eating (Minnesota lake trout for breakfast and Lake Superior whitefish for lunch, on orders from a nominee who had been robbed of a day of fishing to put in some extra campaigning). More politicians got on and off the train, and one, the treasurer of the state central committee, arrived with 500 sunflowers, which he had grown, to decorate the train. Landon spent the night in Oshkosh, and plugged the local industry before his departure the next morning: "Overalls is right. I don't think there are very many Kansans that have not worn 'Oshkosh, By Gosh!' products." After Oshkosh, the nominee made stops at almost every place that boasted a high school band, again lashing out at waste and partisanship in relief administration, calling for the preservation of liberties, and blasting the "rising tide of intolerance, of racial prejudice, creeping on this country."[28]

Landon's train arrived in Milwaukee on September 26, and the candidate gave one of his most vigorously delivered speeches of the campaign. He spoke on economic security, and sharply criticized the Social Security Act. Under the act's old age insurance provisions, he said, none of the country's old people would receive a penny until 1942, yet 26 million workers and their employers would begin paying

---

[27] Schlesinger, *Politics of Upheaval*, pp. 611 ff.; *New York Times*, October 4, 7, 1936; *Washington Post*, October 2, 1936; Cross, *Connecticut Yankee*, p. 345.

[28] *Kansas City Star*, September 26, 1936; Anderson, "Observations," p. 26; Landon speeches, September 26, 1936.

taxes in 1937 to finance these pensions. Unfortunately, only about half of America's working force would be eligible for benefits— niggardly at best—which would be based on the expectation that the insured parties would earn $125 every month for full coverage. These taxes were a "cruel hoax" because the contributions of employees and employers would gradually increase over the years, for each group from 1 to 3 per cent of wages, and one could be sure that employees would wind up paying the entire tax because "if the employer is to stay in business he must shift the tax to someone else." Landon also accurately predicted that the cash paid into the social security fund would be used to cover the government's deficits of the moment. He did not, however, dispute the objectives of the act: "We can afford old-age pensions . . . in a highly industrialized country they are necessary. I believe in them as a matter of social justice." He proposed legislation that would give "every American citizen over sixty-five the supplementary payment necessary to give a minimum of income sufficient to protect him or her from want." Such a program "will be much less expensive than the plan of the present administration, because we will not create a needless reserve fund." Landon's pensions would be administered by the states, the funds coming from a direct, widely distributed federal tax earmarked for this purpose. As for unemployment insurance, Landon said this was an appropriate area for experimentation by the states.[29]

The morning after the Milwaukee speech, Landon traveled to Sinnissippi, Illinois, to spend the day with Frank Lowden, the elder statesman of midwestern Republicanism, who told him: "I liked the farm speeches very much." The campaign train was on the move again the next morning, and Landon barnstormed through Illinois, Iowa, and Missouri on his way back to Topeka. Gifts of apples came aboard the train, and were placed with the dairy products given the governor in Minnesota and Wisconsin. In Iowa, crowds gathered to wave and yell, even at cities and villages where no stops were made.

This tour was Landon's most exhilarating of the campaign. The crowds were large, attentive, and eager, and the Kansan had made a good impression. But the publisher of the *Des Moines Register* asked nineteen newspapermen who had accompanied Landon whom they favored for President and who they thought would win. Although

[29] Anderson, "Observations," p. 27; Landon speech, Milwaukee, September 26, 1936.

twelve were for Landon, four for Roosevelt, and three for others, only six thought Landon would win.[30]

Landon spent the rest of September and the first week of October catching up on state business and planning further campaign strategy, and he issued a series of statements, the earliest of which dealt with patronage. On September 18, John Hamilton said that Landon, if elected, would not appoint him—as Roosevelt had appointed his national committee chairman—to head that great patronage dispensary, the Post Office Department. The following day Landon commented that Hamilton's statement was "further evidence of the intention of the Republican party to carry out its pledge for a merit system and civil service requirements in the public service." He added that "No one could be a member of my cabinet and a member of the national committee at the same time," and said he intended "to select the most competent executives I can find, or draft, to head the departments and to put them on an efficient basis." When asked whether it would make any difference if the men considered were Republicans, Democrats, or Progressives, he replied: "No, it would not." Interpreting this as a promise of a coalition cabinet, the *San Francisco Chronicle* exaggeratedly hailed it as "a revolution in American politics," and the *Toledo Blade* predicted it would "appeal to all fair-thinking Americans." [31]

Landon's most serious political troubles began about this time: Franklin D. Roosevelt had finally taken to the stump. At Syracuse, New York, on September 29, the President gave a biting speech before the Democratic state convention, in which he was particularly concerned with Red-baiting: "Desperate in mood, angry at failure, cunning in purpose, individuals and groups are seeking to make Communism an issue in an election where Communism is not a controversy between the two major parties." While the two parties thought alike about communism, the Democrats had done something to eliminate the social unrest on which communism feeds. The Republican leadership, the President said, "is not against the way we have

---

[30] Anderson, "Observations," pp. 27 f.; *Topeka Capital*, September 28, 1936; William A. Wyman to Landon, October 12, 1936.

[31] *Topeka Capital*, September 29, 30, 1936; *San Francisco Chronicle*, September 30, 1936; *Toledo Blade*, October 7, 1936; see also John D. M. Hamilton, "What Landon Will Do with the Spoils System," *Review of Reviews*, XCIV (October, 1936).

done the job. The Republican leadership is against the job being done." The Republicans could make promises but they could not accomplish them, because the "same lack of purpose for fulfillment" lies behind their 1936 promises as behind the promises of earlier years. Roosevelt obviously aimed at Landon when he said: "You cannot be an old-guard Republican in the east, and a New Deal Republican in the west. You cannot promise to repeal taxes before one audience and promise to spend more of the taxpayers' money before another audience. . . . You simply cannot make good on both promises at the same time." The President's aim was accurate, for it led to speculation in the press, even among Landon's supporters (like Walter Lippmann), that Landon's campaign strategy had become one of making vote-catching promises that would involve raids on the Treasury.[32]

Further trouble was encountered on September 30, when Landon was accused of leaking criticisms of the Social Security Act from a confidential report made by a staff member of the highly respected Twentieth Century Fund; the fund, and the Edward A. Filene Foundation, which financed the study, made the charge. Landon replied that he neither had been given the report by a fund staff member nor had received it in confidence.[33] On October 1 a third blow fell as the nation's leading newspaper, the *New York Times*, rejected the narrow nationalism it saw in the Republican cause and called for Roosevelt's reelection as a hedge against radicalism.[34]

Republicans could hope, however, that all this would be offset by the announcement of the 1928 Democratic presidential nominee, Alfred E. Smith, for Landon on October 1. Speaking at Carnegie Hall in New York, Smith revealed his bitterness against Roosevelt when he said that the administration had "betrayed the party." Smith also declared:

> I am an American before I am a Democrat, before I am a Republican, or before I am anything. I have never in my long public career ducked, dodged, or pussyfooted. I have never found fault with anything unless I was prepared to suggest a remedy. . . . I firmly believe that the remedy for all the ills that we are suffering from today is the election of Alfred M. Landon.[35]

[32] *Topeka Capital*, September 30, 1936; *Topeka State Journal*, October 3, 1936; *Canton* (O.) *Repository*, October 8, 1936.

[33] *Topeka Capital*, October 2, 1936.

[34] *New York Times*, October 1, 1936.

[35] *Topeka Capital*, October 2, 1936.

October 1 was not only the day when the *New York Times* declared against Landon and Smith declared for him, it was also the day when Herbert Hoover came to Topeka on his way east. The former President arrived in the afternoon at the Union Pacific depot, looking poised and almost cheerful. He made no predictions on the outcome of the election, but he observed that there seemed to be a "forward movement for Governor Landon." He then motored to the executive mansion to confer with Landon. That night Landon, Hoover, and Senator Capper were the guests of honor at a chicken dinner given by the newsmen covering Landon's campaign. After the dinner the group listened to the broadcast of President Roosevelt's address at Pittsburgh, while waiting for Smith's address from New York. Hoover and Landon listened with sour looks on their faces, Hoover because of Roosevelt and Landon perhaps because of Hoover. As Roosevelt—in a forceful repudiation of Hoover's ideas—repledged the use of the power of government for achieving recovery rather than retrenchment, the enthusiastic reaction of his audience, as heard over the radio, caused the dinner group at Topeka to become embarrassed for Hoover, and restless. Landon took him away before Roosevelt's speech was completed, saying: "We had better rush if we're going to catch the train." Hoover, along with Landon, heard Smith's speech while he waited in the depot for his train.[36] Whether political boon or boomerang, Hoover's visit was a bother for Landon.

Meanwhile there were other problems. Organized labor was still implacable in its opposition to Landon. Labor delegations avoided Topeka, just as union men resisted shaking hands with the governor. During the first half of September the Republican national committee reported that large industrial plants refused to cooperate in distributing Republican campaign materials among workers. The plea of one of the division's officials was desperate—"We must have those votes." An alternative suggestion was to give paying work to unemployed Republican men by placing them at the entrances of all large factories to hand out campaign literature. Yet this plan was impracticable, except where local donors were willing to finance it, because the national committee again reported that it was short of money.[37]

The desertion of some leading Republicans to Roosevelt and the

[36] *Ibid.*; Landon interview, January 9, 1962. For another version, see Schlesinger, *Politics of Upheaval*, p. 622.

[37] H. S. Buck note to Landon written on copy of H. S. Buck to Sterling Morton, September 21, 1936; John D. M. Hamilton to Landon, October 2, 1936.

refusal of others to support the Landon–Knox ticket also vexed the party throughout the campaign. Senator George W. Norris of Nebraska had become an independent and was supporting Roosevelt again. Senators James Couzens of Michigan and Peter Norbeck of South Dakota, while remaining in the party, also supported Roosevelt. Others, like Senators William E. Borah, Hiram W. Johnson, Gerald P. Nye, and even Senate minority leader Charles L. McNary took no part in the campaign. Of course, Representative William Lemke was heading the Union party's ticket, and Representative Usher Burdick, also of North Dakota, was serving as one of his campaign managers. By October a number of former Roosevelt supporters, like James P. Warburg, who had switched to Landon, were backing off from the governor.[38] In Kansas, it had even been feared that Landon's old mentor, Clyde M. Reed, would declare for Roosevelt, but this was neutralized. Efforts were made to line up Nye, Norris, Borah, Couzens, and Democrat Newton D. Baker for Landon—by William Allen White and others—but all that was achieved was that Norris canceled his plans to speak in Kansas and Borah asked the Idaho Republican headquarters to circulate Landon's Minneapolis speech.[39] Landon had been deprived of the support he most wanted, that of the party's liberal wing.

The troubles that afflicted Landon's campaign also seemed to be reflected in the public opinion polls. Hill Blackett, of the national committee headquarters, wrote Landon, in mid-September, that he was running far behind on the special polls of druggists and factories. Even Landon's lead in the *Literary Digest* poll was dwindling, from about two to one in early September to less than three to two on October 1. The Gallup Poll for early October showed another increase for the President, from 52.6 per cent in September to 53.2 per cent—his highest rating since June. The polls showed Michigan, Ohio, Colorado, Wisconsin, Minnesota, Indiana, Iowa, West Virginia, New York, Nebraska, New Jersey, Illinois, Pennsylvania, and Rhode Island as the marginal political states[40]—to most of which Landon was

[38] Schlesinger, *Politics of Upheaval*, pp. 596, 634; Harry Barnard, *Independent Man, The Life of Senator James Couzens* (New York: Scribners, 1958), p. 309.

[39] W. A. White to Lacy Haynes, October 17, 1936, Lacy Haynes Papers, Kansas State Historical Society, Topeka; Marian McKenna, *Borah* (Ann Arbor: University of Michigan Press, 1961), pp. 338 ff.; White to Landon, September 18, November 14, 1936; J. Reuben Clark to Landon, September 28, 1936.

[40] Hill Blackett to Landon, September 18, 1936; *Topeka Capital*, September 12, 1936; *Kansas City Times*, October 2, 1936; *Topeka State Journal*, October 5, 1936.

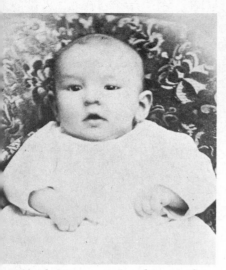

Alfred Mossman Landon at six months

Landon and his uncle, William Mossman

Landon and his sister, Helen

Landon at age ten

First Lieutenant Landon, 1918

Landon, aged nineteen, as a student in the University of Kansas

The Landon home, Independence, Kansas

enator Charles Curtis, Governor Ben S. Paulen, and Senator Arthur Capper

William Allen White in Emporia

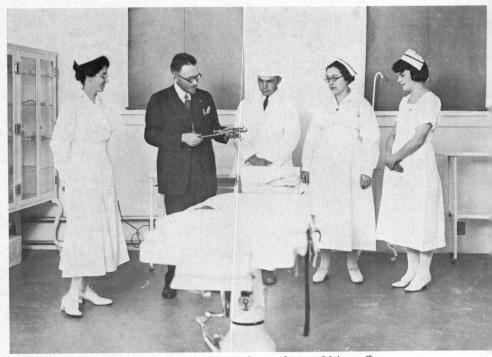

John R. Brinkley and members of his staff

Governor Henry J. Allen

Governor Harry Woodring

A Solid Front.

Cartoon of Landon's campaign
for Governor, 1932

Landon as the newly-elected
Governor

Governor Landon Addresses the Legislature

Landon and his daughter Peggy Ann

Governor and Mrs. Landon and their two children, John and Nancy Jo

Landon as a horseman

LANDON'S STUMPING ENGAGEMENT.

OHIO PRIMARY STUMPS

LANDON

PROBLEMS OF KANSAS GOVERNORSHIP

Cartoon of Landon's stay-at-home campaign for the Republican Presidential nomination

National Chairman John D. M. Hamilton

Colonel Frank Knox

Courtesy New York Post

Courtesy Cincinnati Times-Star

Echoes Out of the Past

"They Said the Same Thing About Lincoln"

Courtesy Republican National Committee

Courtesy Detroit News

1936 campaign cartoons

Landon and Knox

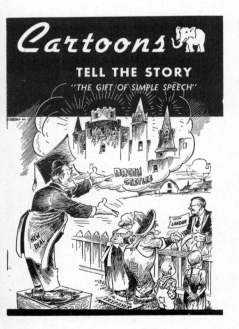

Republican National Committee campaign leaflets, 1936

Popular campaign photograph of Landon in the 1936 campaign

Landon speaking from observation platform of the Sunflower Special at Canton Ohio

The Landon family votes

Cartoon of Landon's visit with President Roosevelt after the 1936 election

Landon, Capper, and Hamilton discussing party affairs, 1937

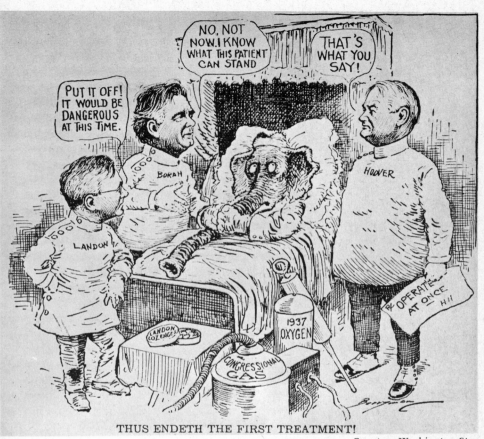

Cartoon of the fight for control of the Republican party

Landon in the oil fields

When He Thought He Had Something

Courtesy Pittsburgh Press

Cartoon reflecting frequent Republican dismay when Landon supported Roosevelt's foreign policy, 1937–39

Landon campaigning in Iowa for the Willkie-McNary ticket, 1940

Cartoon on fight among Republican leaders regarding foreign policy, 1941

Herbert Hoover and Landon, 1943 .

Landon after a courtesy call at the White House, 1942

Landon during the mid-1950's

Courtesy News Associates, Inc.

Landon calling for a lowering of world trade barriers before the National Press Club, Washington, December, 1961

In the 1950's and 1960's Landon could usually be found at lunch time talking politics in Topeka's Chocolate Shop

Landon, at 78, in his office

to devote considerable attention in October. There was a tide, but it was retreating from the Kansan, which partly explains the rising pugnacity of his campaign speeches.

During his stay in Topeka, in late September and early October, Landon tried to attend to a facet of the campaign that hurt him deeply, the ugly rumors that he was anti-Semitic and anti-Negro. These rumors had led him to raise the issue of tolerance increasingly in September. Soon after his return to Topeka, he disclaimed the support of "any elements who are endeavoring to bring racial prejudices and religious bigotries into American life." Just before Hoover's visit (on October 1), he held another press conference to elaborate on that statement. "I think there can be a suspicion that the Democratic party is not above reproach for attempting to misrepresent my position. The attempts to stir up racial prejudice and one thing or another are evident in many ways."[41] If the President was injured by charges of Red influence, Landon was equally hurt by charges of prejudice.

In the next few days Landon took steps to get backing from Jewish and Negro spokesmen on this matter. Landon's disclaimer of support from the elements of prejudice and bigotry drew commendatory messages from a large number of Kansas City Jewish leaders, as well as from prominent Jews in New York, Boston, and Pittsburgh. Mrs. Oscar D. Straus, the widow of the first Jewish cabinet member, announced her support of Landon for President.[42] Even more attention was given to Negroes, as Landon fought to recapture their support, but the Good Neighbor League's Negro division was exercising great influence in favor of Roosevelt, and much of the Negro press showed unhappiness with Republicanism. Many Negroes viewed Roosevelt's relief programs as economic salvation and looked to the federal government to afford increased protection of minority rights. The *Afro-American* of Baltimore interpreted Landon's program as a states' rights platform, the support of which would be "plain suicide."[43]

Most of the Republican counterattack came in October. Hoover was its first big gun, calling attention, while he was in Topeka on October 1, to the "unnatural alliance" on racial questions between the Democratic south and the big cities. Robert R. Church of Memphis, a

[41] *Topeka Capital*, October 2, 1936; *New York American*, October 2, 1936.

[42] *Kansas City Times*, October 5, 1936; *Washington Herald*, October 5, 1936; *New York American*, October 6, 1936.

[43] McCoy, "Good Neighbor League," pp. 10–14; *Baltimore Afro-American*, September 26, 1936.

prominent colored leader, and Colonel Arthur W. Little, who had commanded the colored 15th New York infantry regiment during World War I, conferred with Landon on October 5. They discussed the problems of lynching and economic discrimination, and afterward Church issued a statement in Landon's name: "I am unalterably opposed to lawlessness in all forms, and of course, this includes lynching which is a blot on our American civilization. We must devise some legal means which will be effective in ending this great menace to our institutions." (During the campaign, Roosevelt did not try to match Landon on the lynching issue.) Landon also assured Negroes not only of equal treatment in the civil service and in relief matters but that he would strive to see that the Negro was "reemployed and integrated into the great productive life of our country." He added: "The attempt of the New Deal to use relief rolls as modern reservation[s] on which the great colored race is to be confined forever as a ward of the federal government . . . is not only disastrous to a great people but of alarming consequence to our entire economic and social life."[44]

This was immediately hailed by the Republican national committee as "a new 'emancipation proclamation' for the victims of UNDISGUISED MOB LAW and of ILL-DISGUISED NEW DEAL DISCRIMINATION." These statements were soon followed by P. G. Porter, the Negro principal of Atchison's Lincoln high school, who vigorously defended Landon's record on race relations. Porter pointed out that Landon was the first Kansas governor to appoint a Negro as a state committee vice-chairman, that under his administration more Negroes were employed in a greater number of state offices, and that he had energetically supported William Allen White's fight against the Ku Klux Klan in 1924.[45]

All this drew some favorable Negro response. The Los Angeles *Eagle Home News* asserted that another change was necessary, and urged its readers to vote for Landon. Roscoe Simmons, in the *Chicago Defender*, declared: "Your Party never had a better candidate than Landon," and he compared Roosevelt's evasiveness on lynching with Landon's outspokenness on Negro problems. Yet Negroes generally voted with the idea in mind, as the *Baltimore Afro-American* put it, that "ABRAHAM LINCOLN IS NOT A CANDIDATE IN THE PRESENT CAMPAIGN."[46] The Emancipator's place was to be taken by Roosevelt, not Landon.

[44] *Topeka Capital*, October 2, 1936; press release of Robert R. Church, Topeka, October 5, 1936.

[45] *New York Daily News*, October 7, 1936; *Chicago Defender*, October 17, 1936.

[46] *Los Angeles Eagle Home News*, October 12, 1936; *Chicago Defender*, October 17, 1936; *Baltimore Afro-American*, October 17, 1936.

CHAPTER 13

Sunflowers Do Not
Bloom in November

Landon spent almost all of the last four weeks of the 1936 campaign on the road. He again toured the middle west, and later he traveled from coast to coast in his search for votes. He prefaced his swing through the middle west by sharply criticizing the New Deal for having closed WPA records to public inspection, for saying that the veterans' bonus payments—most of which had been bonded—were no longer a public debt, and for claiming sole credit for the upturn in farm prices. Landon was also in a promising mood, giving his support to the long-obstructed St. Lawrence seaway project.[1] It was obvious from the tone of these statements that he was worried. His only "victory" at this time came through Francis Townsend, the medicine man of the old-age-pension radicals, when he urged Californians who were unable to vote for Lemke, to support Landon.[2]

On the evening of October 8 the Sunflower Special left Topeka, traveling eastward. At Freeport, Illinois, the next morning, Landon revealed a new fire, saying there would be no slackening of the fight until the last ballot had been cast.

[1] *New York American*, October 7, 1936; *New York Times*, October 8, 1936.
[2] *Topeka Capital*, October 8, 1936. Townsend later asked people everywhere to vote for Landon—wherever Lemke was not on the ballot. *Ibid.*, October 12, 1936.

313

That fight is going to be won. . . . The New Deal can be beaten. . . . the New Deal is going to be beaten for the simple reason that you and I now realize the job can be done. It has left us enough shreds of democratic self-government for the will of the American people to be expressed at the polls next month. On their ballots they are going to demand in no uncertain way that their country be given back to them."[3]

Landon's train arrived at Chicago at 11 a.m., but heavy rain had ruined the planned welcome at the station, though several thousand persons were on hand to welcome him. Along Michigan Boulevard, from the Illinois Central station to the Congress Hotel, several thousands more braved the pounding rain to see the parade that had been organized for the occasion. Landon rode in an open car and was thoroughly drenched by the time he arrived at the hotel. He then held conferences with the local Republican leaders, and that night went to the Chicago Stadium to give one of his most effectively delivered speeches of the campaign. He was introduced by Michael J. Kennedy, the business agent for the Electrical Workers' Union of Chicago (at last, a labor leader who would publicly admit to being for Landon). Landon began by saying: "First, let me make my position absolutely clear. If I am elected, the budget is going to be balanced," and he was interrupted by an explosion of cheers and whistles. Buoyed by this, he continued:

> It is going to be balanced, not by depriving our needy of relief, not by refusing necessary aid to our farmers, not by swamping the country with taxes. The budget is going to be balanced by cutting out waste and extravagance; by putting an end to the use of public funds for political purposes; by restoring hard-working, painstaking, commonsense administration.

With reductions in public expenses, he added, "I am convinced there will be such a rebirth of confidence that we will have a real recovery."

He then chided "Candidate Roosevelt" for violating his 1932 campaign pledges to run an economy government and to permit no tax increases. Instead of redeeming those pledges, he had pushed fourteen measures increasing the tax burden through Congress, and unbalanced budgets had "become annual fixtures." This reversal had stemmed from John Maynard Keynes' "amazing" theory that if the government spent

[3] Landon speech, Freeport, Ill., October 9, 1936, Alfred M. Landon Papers, Kansas State Historical Society, Topeka.

$400 million a month, it would prime the pump and all would be well. Of course, as a foreigner, he found ardent followers in this administration, although he had none in his own government. His formula was eagerly adopted, with one important change. The administration concluded that if $400 million a month for useful projects would be good medicine, $600 million a month thrown around at random would be even better.

The consequence of this was that every family's future income had been mortgaged because the growing national debt must be paid, "not out of some impersonal fund known as 'national income,' but 'in the sweat of every man that labors.' "

Landon, in conclusion, warned:

> We must put the spenders out. For remember: Those who preach spending, practice spending and brag about spending, cannot stop spending. That is the lesson of history. That is the record of this administration. They are proud of spending. They talk of it as though preserving the financial integrity of the United States were only a game.
>
> The American people know that it is more than a game—that our very existence depends upon keeping our financial house in order. But if the administration wants a baseball analogy—if they want the score—it is easy to give. It is written clear across this country:
>> Twenty-five billion dollars spent.
>> Thirteen billion dollars added to the public debt.
>> Eleven million unemployed left on base.

The uproar that followed the speech was deafening. Miniature American flags were waved about by almost all of the 25,000 shrieking, whooping, cheering people in the stadium (probably, one jokester said, they were all the Republicans from Chicago and its suburbs, with some thrown in from downstate Illinois as well). The newspapers were tougher than the crowd in their evaluations; their reactions were summed up by the *Baltimore Sun*, which said that although the speech was "easily the best he has made since his nomination," the Kansan would have to "find more searching remedies than mere efficiency to reduce Federal expenditures to the point to which they ought to be reduced." [4]

The campaign train pulled out of Chicago at 11 p.m. and arrived at

---

[4] Victor Anderson, "Observations of the Campaign" (undated carbon-copy typescript), pp. 30 f.; *Kansas City Star*, October 9, 1936; Landon speech, Chicago, October 9, 1936; *Kansas City Times*, October 10, 1936; *New York Times*, October 10, 1936; *Baltimore Sun*, October 10, 1936.

Cincinnati the next morning. On entering the station, Landon congratulated Cincinnati on its charter form of government and on having such citizens as Charles P. Taft. This reference was calculated to back Taft and the local reform movement, despite the fact that the charter government and the son of the former President were controversial among Republicans as well as Democrats in Cincinnati. Although Landon had been warned to "go slow" on the matter by Taft and Taft's opponents, he decided to speak his mind. It caused consternation, but, as some local politicians observed, Cincinnati's Republicans "had nowhere to go except to Landon." The governor then went downtown to breakfast with the city's Republican workers. In his breakfast talk he again praised Cincinnati's nonpartisan form of government, recalled his childhood in Ohio, and urged the party workers to get out the vote in this "battle of the century" that "will determine what sort of a nation we are to hand down to our children."[5] Afterward he reboarded his train to travel to Columbus to attend the Ohio State–Pittsburgh football game, making half a dozen train-side talks on the way.

The Sunflower Special arrived in Columbus at 1:40 p.m., and the governor went to the stadium to watch the game; at half-time he was introduced and said a few words to the 71,000 football fans. After the game he went to the O.S.U. chapter house of his fraternity, Phi Gamma Delta, where he joshed the upperclassmen because the chapter did not have a better scholastic record. Pausing before photographs of fellow Phi Gams Calvin Coolidge and Newton D. Baker, he remarked about Wilson's War Secretary, who had not yet committed himself in the election, "He's a fine fellow."[6] That evening the Kansan went to the Deshler-Wallick Hotel to a Republican dinner, where he spoke on conservation. Talking as one well acquainted with the results of drought, flood, and erosion, there was conviction in his demand for carrying on the work started by Theodore Roosevelt by strengthening public efforts to conserve natural resources. (Franklin D. Roosevelt, meanwhile, was in Omaha, rapping Landon's farm program as a wasteful subsidy that would wreck agriculture by piling up surpluses— as Hoover's Federal Farm Board had done.)[7]

[5] Landon speech, Cincinnati breakfast meeting, October 10, 1936; *Kansas City Star*, October 11, 1936.

[6] Anderson, "Observations," p. 31; *Topeka Capital*, October 11, 1936; *Kansas City Star*, October 11, 1936.

[7] Landon speech, Columbus, October 10, 1936; *New York Times*, October 11, 1936.

Sunday, October 11, was a day of rest, and Landon attended Columbus' King Avenue Methodist Church, which had been William McKinley's church when he was Ohio's governor. Landon used most of his Sundays as vacations, an escape from the din and clamor of the campaign, to find time for a bit of meditation and soul-searching. He was up early the next day to journey to Cleveland, making stops at Mount Vernon, Millersburg, Orrville, and Akron, where Landon proclaimed: "I stand for . . . real jobs at real wages." (Roosevelt, who was barnstorming Kansas, said at Dodge City: "I want to remind you here in Western Kansas that I am making the same kind of talk I make back East.")[8] The Sunflower Special arrived in Cleveland shortly after 1 p.m., and the campaign party paraded over a two-mile route to the hotel. That afternoon Landon visited the Cleveland Exposition and spent the rest of the afternoon in political conferences, after which an official of the Brotherhood of Locomotive Engineers announced his belief that if Landon were elected "Labor will be given every consideration." Now Landon had two labor votes outside Kansas. The Kansan went to Cleveland's public auditorium that night, where he spoke under a twenty-foot-wide sunflower adorned with pictures of Landon, Knox, and John W. Bricker, Ohio's Republican nominee for governor, before an overflow crowd of some 15,000 people. The crowd cheered, and sang "The Sidewalks of New York" and "Oh, Susanna!" Landon's text was relief and work. He chastised the New Deal for its "tragic neglect" in spending $7.5 billion for relief, but finding "neither time nor money to inform itself of the extent and nature of the relief problem." America, he said, had been and would be liberal in providing for those deprived of a livelihood through no fault of their own, but that was not enough; the country had to get "real jobs at real pay" for the unemployed. The diversion of relief money "to the building up of a shameless political machine" had to be stopped. More importantly, the nation had to overrule "those members of this administration who say this nation has passed its last frontier of opportunity—those prophets of despair who claim that never again will there be work in this country for everybody." Landon demanded that politics, red tape, and secrecy be abolished so that economic recovery could be achieved and necessary relief could be administered, competently and humanely, through state programs assisted by federal grants-in-aid. He also proposed to give

[8] Anderson, "Observations," p. 32; Landon speech, Akron, October 12, 1936; *Washington Post*, October 12, 1936; *Kansas City Times*, October 13, 1936.

special encouragement, through a program of job retraining, to citizens who were trying to become self-supporting.[9]

Landon was tired when he left the hall; it had been a strenuous day. He gave Ohio's political and industrial leaders farewell handshakes and words of cheer, and then went to bed, but he was up early the next morning to complete his Ohio tour and to enter Michigan. At Toledo he left the train for the Valentine Theater, where he took a swing at Labor's Non-Partisan League, which, under the leadership of John L. Lewis and George Berry, was working effectively for Roosevelt among workingmen. Landon exalted the advice of Samuel Gompers, the founder of the American Federation of Labor, who had "repeatedly declared that once organized labor engaged in party politics, and once it permitted itself to be affiliated with the government, it would lose its independence and its power to promote the interests of the working people effectively." The Kansan warned: "Labor today has its false friends. In other nations they have already betrayed the men and women who work" and had made them "serfs of the state." He exhorted labor to beware the temptations offered it by government because these offers, if accepted, "mean ultimate dictation by politics." His only promise was that he would oppose "any infringement on the rights of labor to organize and any curtailment of the right of freedom of assembly. It is the government's duty to protect labor and the people in these rights." Landon's appearance brought little applause in this strong labor city.[10]

As the governor entered Michigan he was joined by groups of Michigan politicians and industrialists, including Senator Arthur Vandenberg, Governor Frank Fitzgerald, and officials of General Motors and Chrysler corporations. His train arrived in Detroit shortly after noon, where it was greeted by a thousand well-wishers. The campaign motorcade, accompanied by a band and several drum and bugle corps, wound through three miles of city streets as undemonstrative crowds looked on. At the Book Cadillac Hotel, where Landon was to stay, the cheerless atmosphere was broken by the shouts and shrieks of 1,500 rabid partisans. After visiting a luncheon of 750 Republican women to say hello, Landon left the hotel for Henry Ford's Dearborn home. The auto magnate, who had been in the business of endorsing Republican presidential nominees since 1924, gave Landon his

[9] Anderson, "Observations," pp. 32 f.; *Kansas City Times*, October 13, 1936; Landon speech, Cleveland, October 12, 1936.

[10] *New York Times*, October 14, 1936; Landon speech, Toledo, October 13, 1936.

blessing and lauded him as a man who was "well-informed," experienced, honest, and had "thought things through."[11] That evening the governor went to chill, wind-swept Navin Field, where he declared that unnecessary increments of executive power under the New Deal were the "first steps" toward destruction of the "American form of government." Landon promised, if elected, to ask for repeal of all laws "giving autocratic powers to the chief executive." If increased federal authority was needed to protect the people from the abuses of power concentrated in other hands, he would seek amendments to the Constitution to confer it.

It was in Detroit that Landon added a new ingredient to his campaign formula, asking Roosevelt to say "whether he intends to change the form of our government—whether labor, agriculture, and business are to be directed and managed by government." This question, which the Kansan was to ask again—and most forcefully in his Madison Square Garden address—was a campaign tactic that he and Knox had agreed upon. It was based on their opinion that the President would probably evade the question, and would therefore be unable, if reelected, to claim a popular mandate for any radical shift in his policies.[12]

Landon was on the train again the next day, campaigning further in Michigan. "Some of us are getting weary of the ridicule of American institutions by men on the public payroll," he told a crowd at Flint. At Lansing, he said that America's sugar beet farmers should have the opportunity to fill the nation's sugar bowl. At Battle Creek, a banner at the station proclaimed "The World's Health City Welcomes the Nation's Next President—Alfred M. Landon." "Bouquets" of celery were sent aboard the train at Kalamazoo, and Landon spent the night at Grand Rapids. It was at Grand Rapids that Landon told a crowd of almost 30,000 people:

> Let me say here what I said East and West. If I am elected chief executive, the budget is going to be balanced, but it is not going to be balanced by depriving our needy unemployed of the relief that is their right until they can recover real jobs at real wages. It is not going to be balanced by denying the aid to the American farmer which he ought to have.[13]

[11] Anderson, "Observations," p. 33; *New York Times*, October 14, 1936; *Topeka State Journal*, October 13, 14, 1936.

[12] Landon speech, Detroit, October 13, 1936; Landon to Verne Marshall, January 20, 1938.

[13] Landon speeches, Flint, Lansing, and Grand Rapids, October 14, 1936; Anderson, "Observations," p. 34; *Topeka State Journal*, October 14, 1936.

The next day, October 15, the governor carried the battle from Michigan through Indiana and into Illinois. He showed more fight than during the past two days, when he had been bothered by a cold and depressed by the usually undemonstrative crowds. Then too, he was weary of the urging of big businessmen that he fight Red influences, an urging to which he refused to respond—he would not cry "Red" at Roosevelt. The crowds at the stations, and even along the way, were sizable. At his many stops on this last day of the tour he reiterated the ideas that the indebtedness of the government was the indebtedness of every citizen and that America's form of government had been changing without the consent of the people. "What recovery we have had has come since the Supreme Court gave the country a REAL breathing spell from the President's MUST legislation."[14]

The reaction of the press to Landon's October tour was generally the same as it had been to his earlier campaign ventures. His analysis of the government's defects was good, it was said, but he overdid the vote-catching, and his outline of remedial action was disappointing. The *Baltimore Sun* pointedly suggested that the governor's speeches showed that Republicans were "willing to exceed Mr. Roosevelt in public expenditures as a means of stopping Mr. Roosevelt's lavish expenditures." Partly because Landon was not saying what many newspapers thought he should, and partly because he now had to compete not only with Roosevelt but also with Hamilton, Hoover, Knox, and Al Smith for news space, Landon's coverage by the nation's press was dwindling. The Hearst newspapers tried to take up the slack with such statements as "Gov. Landon's Dare that the Raw Deal End Its Dictatorial Powers . . . the Raw Deal DARE NOT answer that challenge. It realizes that to do so would be an ADMISSION OF GUILT THAT WOULD AWAKEN THE AMERICAN PEOPLE."

The Democrats, who through the summer and even into September had been apprehensive, had become optimistic. The presidential press secretary, Stephen T. Early, wrote that reaction to the President was "entirely favorable. . . . Every sign points to rapidly diminishing influence of Republicans [and] hate-Roosevelt democrats." Early was jubilant because a confidential poll of the political writers in Washington showed a consensus that Roosevelt was assured of 400 electoral votes. Reports were also coming to the President's headquarters that greatly discounted the published estimates of Landon's crowds and

[14] Landon interview, January 9, 1962; Landon speeches, October 15, 1936.

their reactions to his speeches. The mid-October *Literary Digest* poll showed Landon slipping, and the *Farm Journal* poll showed that he did not have enough rural votes to offset Roosevelt's urban majorities.[15]

In order to keep his western supporters happy—and perhaps searching for a political miracle—Landon decided to take a swing through the southwest and to California, though no undecided states were shown there in the Gallup Poll. Frank Knox, who was in Topeka on October 17 for a brief conference with Landon, tried to cheer Republicans by stating that the Kansan's trip to the Pacific coast would tip the scales of victory. The evening of the following day, Landon left Topeka for the west: the campaign wind-up was on, and he would be on the road for two weeks. The Sunflower Special raced across the Kansas prairies and wound into the highlands of Colorado and New Mexico, stopping occasionally for train-side speeches by the nominee. At Albuquerque, Landon warned vaguely of an "attack on our freedom . . . from within." He also showed his sensitivity to criticisms of his tariff statements when he pledged to continue reciprocal tariff-making, except on competitive farm products. The governor then tried to answer his critics by summarizing the chief features of his program, as though repetition would drive into their heads what he was aiming at.[16]

The tragedy for Landon was that his scheme for recovery—which was theoretically as defensible as any other—was not obvious to his enemies, to the uncommitted, or even to many of his supporters. It would not have won him the Presidency had he made it clear, but it could have given him additional prestige as titular leader of his party after the election. To Landon, however, it was all very simple— probably as simple as it had seemed to Roosevelt in 1932. Elect a fair-minded, skillful manager as President: let him recruit a group of like-minded subordinate administrators. As a team, they could work to cut expenditures by eliminating waste and extravagance; this way the budget could be balanced and perhaps taxes could be cut (especially for the "little fellow")—though not at the expense of needed relief and farm subsidies. The administrators would also work to find markets for the nation's produce at home and (through "real reciprocity") abroad. Dabbling in fuzzy-minded experiments would be

[15] *Baltimore Sun*, October 16, 1936; *New York Evening Journal*, October 16, 1936; Stephen Early to Marvin McIntyre, October 13, 1936, Franklin D. Roosevelt Library, Hyde Park, N.Y.; *Topeka Capital*, October 16, 1936; "*Farm Journal* Presidential Straw Ballot to October 10" [1936].

[16] *Topeka Capital*, October 18, 1936; *Christian Science Monitor*, October 20, 1936; Landon speech, Albuquerque, October 19, 1936.

replaced by a drive to guard labor in its rights to organize and to protect business from harassment by petty bureaucrats.

All this would lead, Landon thought, to an upswing in business confidence and activity, which in turn would result in an expansion of jobs. With an increase in employment, the demand for manufactured and farm products would rise, thereby swelling employment opportunities, business and farm profits, and government tax yields. Soon, recovery would be achieved, the federal budget and debt made manageable, and some "extras"—such as a larger-scale national conservation program—could be afforded. This is what Landon meant to say but never did; he believed his pattern of thought was obvious to everybody.

From Albuquerque the Governor's train streaked across New Mexico and Arizona to Barstow, California, where Landon for the first time spoke on the Civilian Conservation Corps. He pointed out his past support of the CCC and he pledged, if elected, to continue the program and make it more effective.[17] Landon arrived early the afternoon of October 20 in Pasadena, where he was greeted by 5,000 frenzied partisans. He then motored with Governor Merriam to Los Angeles, along an eighteen-mile route, and at times it was almost impossible to drive through the crowd that turned out in downtown Los Angeles. Confetti and tape added to the commotion, as did the occasional jeering, which the Kansan encountered for the first time during the campaign.

During this busy day, Landon and Harold Ickes engaged in a cross-country political exchange. The Secretary of the Interior charged Landon with being the "changeling candidate," shifting from liberalism to conservatism. He said that Landon had been a "state socialist" until 1935, advocating state-owned telephone and natural gas distributing systems. Landon replied that this charge was typical of the "confusion and contradictory policies that have characterized this administration from the beginning." Until now, he said, he had been attacked as a puppet of big business; now he was a Socialist and an enemy of big business. He explained his position: "I have always been in favor of public ownership as a gun behind the door in the adjustment of proper and fair utility rates." Ickes responded: "I wonder how many other concealed weapons he carries about. The utility interests had better frisk him before they go any further."[18]

[17] *Christian Science Monitor*, October 20, 1936; *Kansas City Star*, October 20, 1936.

[18] *Topeka Capital*, October 21, 1936; Arthur M. Schlesinger, Jr., *The Politics of Upheaval* (Boston: Houghton Mifflin, 1960), pp. 623 f.

Landon was scheduled to speak at the Los Angeles coliseum that night—at "the largest gathering at a political meeting west of the Mississippi River." To the disappointment of local Republican leaders, the 105,000-seat stadium was only two-thirds filled (but news photographs were edited to make it appear that a full house was on hand). Entertainment by show-business celebrities warmed up the crowd, after which national committeeman Earl Warren introduced Governor Landon. "We glory in this opportunity to welcome to California this Governor of a typical prairie state. . . . Let me present to you the next President of the United States." Then, with a sweeping arm motion, Warren directed the crowd's attention to the coliseum's tunnel entrance, through which Landon's car came, into the spotlights, the nominee standing, with tousled hair, waving his hat. The crowd stood and cheered as Landon proceeded to the rostrum (there were also some boos),[19] and Landon spoke out slowly and deliberately, trying to pound his points home by thumping his hand on the lectern. The Roosevelt administration, he said, was undermining the rights guaranteed to citizens by the Constitution.

> This administration came into power at a time of great national crisis. Unusual powers were granted to the chief executive. But when the crisis was over, the administration refused to give up its extraordinary powers. Instead, it asked for more. It seemed obsessed with the idea that it had a mandate to direct and control American business, American agriculture and American life.
>
> Recall a few of the things they tried to do. They tried to tell our farmers how much they could plant and how much they could not plant. They tried to tell our businessmen how much they could produce and under what conditions they could run their business. They tried to tell labor who could and who could not represent them in negotiations with their employers.
>
> Was this an undermining of our liberties? I think so. And the proof of it is, so many of our fellow citizens rebelled at these tactics that the administration was forced to abandon the subterfuge of voluntary cooperation. It cracked the whip on those individuals who refused to be led like sheep. It resented any criticism which recalled what American initiative and free enterprise had done for the country. And when the Supreme Court declared its methods unconstitutional, the administration actually attempted to bring the Supreme Court into disrepute. . . .
>
> Even the President joined in this undermining attack on men who were only doing their duty—men sworn to uphold the Constitution of the United

[19] *Los Angeles Times*, October 21, 1936; Zach Lamar Cobb to Marvin McIntyre, October 21, 1936, FDRL.

States. The President predicted disaster if his plans were held unconstitutional. They were held unconstitutional. Now he claims credit for the improvement that followed. He says, "We planned it that way."

Landon elaborated, charging the administration had used scorn, threats to cancel government contracts, and arbitrary interpretations of administrative rules to keep business in line. The spending power of the President had been employed to keep congressmen and local officials in line, and "to prevent freedom of choice at the polls." Congress' investigatory powers had been used not just "to get the crooks" but also "to get the critics." Landon urged the people to rally around the Bill of Rights so that it could serve its purpose of ensuring "that tyranny could never exist." "If we would maintain our nation, we must brook no tampering with our freedom."[20]

Landon immediately left Los Angeles to return east, but on October 21, at Yuma and at Phoenix, he made brief addresses. "I am not questioning the humanitarian intentions of the present administration. But . . . there can be no question as to the road down which we are being led. Regimentation of the individual and curbing of his liberties underlie every one of the New Deal's plans." Landon charged Roosevelt with concealing facts and challenged him "to be candid with the American people."[21] On the morning of October 23, at El Reno, Oklahoma, ex-Governor William Murray boarded the train to accompany the Republican nominee to Oklahoma City, where Landon's party paraded to the local coliseum and a capacity crowd. The colorful "Alfalfa Bill" introduced Landon and recounted the Kansan's many associations, over the years, with Oklahoma. Landon, in turn, lauded Murray for coming out on his side in the campaign.

> You know what it means when a former Democratic Governor with a life-long record of party regularity introduces the Republican nominee for the Presidency. It means severing political friendships of long standing. It means opening himself to political penalties in the years to come. It means endangering the whole political future of many of his loyal supporters of the past. . . . Only a threat to our form of government itself could cause a man like Governor Murray to take this step.[22]

[20] Landon speech, Los Angeles, October 20, 1936; Anderson, "Observations," pp. 36 f.

[21] Landon speech, Phoenix, October 21, 1936; *Pueblo Chieftain,* October 23, 1936.

[22] Anderson, "Observations," p. 38; Landon speech, Oklahoma City, October 23, 1936.

Landon left Oklahoma City at two in the afternoon and arrived in Indianapolis the next morning, October 24; he attended a luncheon for Republican workers, and afterward headed an elaborate two-and-a-half-hour parade that was witnessed by crowds estimated at between 100,000 and 150,000. That night, 20,000 people heard his speech, and thousands of others had to be turned away. (One of Landon's aides wrote: "There is one thing quite noticeable of all our crowds. They have that clean upstanding appearance.") The theme of the governor's Indianapolis address was foreign relations, and his pledge was to "encourage with all my power the cause of peace."

The first thing to be done was to restore world confidence in America's good faith, which, Landon said, had been shattered by the President's disruption of the London Economic Conference of 1933. Landon would restore world confidence, if he was elected, by having the United States participate "in international conferences on matters affecting the common welfare where it is distinctly understood no political commitments are involved." He also said the nation should work for the reduction of armaments, and should "assist in lowering world-wide trade barriers." These efforts, along with attempts to develop international law so that disputes could be settled by mediation or arbitration, might forestall another general war. As for an American anti-war policy, Landon said neutrality was the best path to follow. Then, obviously referring to the Neutrality Act of 1935, he warned:

> Specific pledges not to go to war under any condition, risk encouraging belligerents to attempt aggression which would, in fact, precipitate us into war. In view of our enormous potential strength, demonstrated in 1917 and 1918, I believe hereafter nations will be reluctant to violate any neutral rights upon which we insist.

He called for legislation that would take "the profits out of war" as an act that would discourage private interests from seeking war; and should war come anyway, such legislation would also require sacrifices from capital as well as from the doughboys.[23]

The day after his Indianapolis speech—a Sunday—Landon prepared himself for the rigors of the last full week of the campaign, a week in which many of his supporters expected him to perform miracles. For weeks he had been beset by advisers, official and otherwise, who

[23] Anderson, "Observations," p. 38; Landon speech, Indianapolis, October 24, 1936.

alternately told him how wonderful things looked or how badly he was doing. "The Man on the Street," an anonymous letter-writer (one unusually well-informed on Republican affairs) who was taken seriously by some national committee staff members, wrote that every time Landon "SPEAKS IT JUST CONVINCES A CERTAIN CLASS OF PEOPLE THAT WHAT THE DEM COMMITTEE HAS BEEN PUTTING OUT ABOUT HIM BEING VAGUE AND HAZY AND HESITANT AND WISHY–WASHY IS TRUE. . . . FOR GAWD'S SAKE GET DOWN TO BRASS TACKS." Later, "The Man" wrote Hamilton: "I'm afraid you're going to be the worst-fooled party manager in political history when you meet the dawn November 4. . . . Never in my life . . . have I seen among Republican workers such *wishful thinking*, such rationalizing, such self-hypnotism."[24]

Former Governor Nathan Miller of New York urged Landon to emphasize Constitutional questions and the radical, communist nature of the New Deal. J. Reuben Clark and William Castle kept hitting the Kansan, effectively, with foreign policy ideas, especially that of international arbitration. Others, like Roy Roberts, asked the governor to point up the difference between the President's humanitarian statements and the intimidation of those on relief by Democratic party workers. Cornelia Bryce Pinchot urged Landon to hit out at influence-peddling and to crack down on the myth that he was opposed to relief. Her brother-in-law, Amos, pressed the nominee to emphasize the necessity of reviving production. Walter Lippmann criticized Landon for speaking on a half-dozen subjects of no great importance instead of hammering home the issue of concentration of power that he had raised in his Portland and Detroit addresses. Landon replied that although this concentration of power was the main issue, it had been "knocked out of the lot in the 1934 campaign"; he contended that his cause would be hopeless without a constructive program on such important questions as farm supports, social security, and tariff reciprocity.[25]

In the middle of October, Agnes Meyer told Landon that he was doing a great job; she had never felt more sure of an election's result, and she asked him to keep stressing the issue of waste and extravagance.

[24] "The Man on the Street" to John D. M. Hamilton, September 12, 18, 1936.
[25] Nathan L. Miller to Landon, September 16, 29, 30, 1936; J. Reuben Clark to Landon, September 28, October 14, 1936; Roy Roberts to Landon, October 14, 1936; Cornelia Bryce Pinchot to Landon, October 12, 1936; Amos R. E. Pinchot to Landon, October 16, 1936; Walter Lippmann to Malcolm Bingay, October 14, 1936, enclosed in Bingay to Landon, October 16, 1936; Landon to Bingay, October 24, 1936.

William Allen White wrote: "I most earnestly hope you will find some place to put in that shot for peace. There are more unattached votes hovering between Roosevelt with his big navy expenditures and Norman Thomas with his pacific ideas who would go to you if you make this straightaway declaration, more, I say, than any other block now drifting around." George A. Hormel, the Iowa meat packer, wired that the campaigners should stop talking about Roosevelt's spending and the Constitution and should let Landon make a concentrated appeal to the unemployed workers, telling them that his highest priority job would be putting them back to work. Russell M. McFarland, of the national committee's publicity department, urged the governor to don working garb and pose for photographs with workingmen to offset the propaganda that he was a tool of big business.[26]

October also confronted Landon with the problem of being overshadowed in tone and coverage by those less moderate than he: Hamilton, Hoover, Knox, and the American Liberty League predicted immediate calamity for the nation should the Democrats win. Their alarm revealed their disagreement with Landon having accepted any New Deal goals, a strategy of compromise that had been adopted in the Republican national convention and that had been followed by Landon.[27] Pressures from the right wing contributed to Landon's flirtations with political immoderation, and made the Republican campaign more frantic and confusing than it otherwise would have been. Landon's strength in the public-opinion polls also kept dropping, which caused additional Republican hurry and scurry. Special polls, compiled October 26 by the Nielsen organization, showed Roosevelt ahead among drug retailers by 48 per cent to 32 per cent, among grocers and other retailers by 51 per cent to 24 per cent, and among individual voters by 50 per cent to 33 per cent.[28]

Although the Nielsen polls showed that the contest was not close, the contest was "hot," and was becoming hotter all the time; indeed,

[26] Agnes Meyer to Landon, October 16, 1936; W. A. White to Landon, October 22, 1936; George A. Hormel to Landon, October 24, 1936; Russell M. McFarland to Mrs. Landon, October 27, 1936.

[27] Rexford G. Tugwell, *The Democratic Roosevelt* (Garden City, N.Y.: Doubleday, 1957), p. 430; Basil Rauch, *The History of the New Deal, 1933–1938* (New York: Creative Age Press, 1944), pp. 238, 260 f.; John D. M. Hamilton to D. R. McCoy, February 6, 1959; Ralph Robey to D. R. McCoy, March 4, 1959.

[28] Hill Blackett to Landon, October 30, 1936.

some found the campaign so hot and so ugly that they avoided participation in it. Newton D. Baker echoed the sentiments of some Democrats: "I find it extremely difficult to be a Democrat and impossible to be a Republican." Most people, however, were caught up in the contest and saw it as crucial in determining the nation's destiny. Bainbridge Colby called the "New Deal leadership false to the Democratic party and traitorous to the country." Felix Frankfurter declared that the fate of the Western world was at stake; that Roosevelt's election would bolster the democratic forces in the world while Landon's would encourage the antidemocratic elements.

Because of this feeling, that the nation and the world were at a turning point, many who held Landon in high esteem turned to Roosevelt for leadership. Coca Cola Company vice-president Ralph Hayes wrote that although Landon's character was admirable, he was managed by a group of men who did not deserve to be put into office. Duncan Aikman, a *New York Times* reporter who became acquainted with Landon in 1935 and 1936, wished the Kansan luck but said he could not believe that the men around Landon knew as much about where the world was going as did—despite their many imbecilities—the Roosevelt people. Raymond Clapper, one of Landon's closest newspaper friends, said that it had been impossible for him to follow Landon because of the policies of Hamilton and other Republican conservatives.[29] The election results would soon confirm that fears of the men around Landon were shared by most other Americans.

Landon left Indianapolis on the afternoon of Sunday, October 25, to continue his eastward tour. He arrived late the next morning in Baltimore, where he left the train to deliver a fighting speech—and one of his best-composed speeches—to more than 5,000 people in the station yard. The New Deal leaders, Landon said,

> ask for another four years of power because back in 1933 for a few weeks they remembered their platform pledges. They hope the country will forget how those pledges were then thrown out the window. . . . They hope the country will forget that . . . they fostered monopoly and suspended the antitrust

[29] Newton D. Baker to P. H. Callahan, September 3, 1936, Newton D. Baker Papers, Manuscript Division, Library of Congress, Washington, D.C.; *Topeka Capital*, October 20, 1936; Felix Frankfurter to Harold L. Ickes, October 28, 1936, Harold L. Ickes Papers, Manuscript Division, Library of Congress, Washington, D.C.; Ralph Hayes to John H. Clarke, November 3, 1936, Baker Papers; Douglas Aikman to Landon, November 1, 1936; Raymond Clapper to Landon, November 4, 1936.

laws. . . . They hope the country will forget what millstones they hung about the little fellow's neck in the NRA, the invisible taxes, and in the latest [undistributed profits] tax act. . . . They hope the country will forget that their continued squandering threatens to destroy the value of all savings. . . . They hope the country will forget that nine out of the eleven major statutes enacted by their administration have been held unconstitutional by the Supreme Court . . . they hope the country will forget that it went into a slump after the New Deal measures became operative, and became really better only when the Supreme Court of the United States knocked off some of its shackles by holding the NRA unconstitutional . . . they hope the country will forget that eleven million persons are still unemployed and twenty million are still on the relief rolls.

Yet, the Kansan said, these and other issues, which would be major ones "in any ordinary campaign," were subordinate to the disagreement on philosophy of government.

On the one side, on the side of the New Deal, we find a strange new group. They believe in an all-powerful chief executive. . . . They believe in the destruction of states rights and of home rule. They believe in the concentration of political and economic authority in the White House. . . . On the other side, supporting your cause, stand those who believe in the American form of government. . . . They recognize that this strange New Deal has betrayed the principles of the . . . American form of government.

This issue was matched by another of prime importance.

There can be an honest difference of opinion as to whether the proposals of the administration for one-man government hold the solution of our social and economic problems, *but* there can be no difference of opinion on this: The President's theory of government should be presented frankly to the people at the polls. He has no right to ask for votes without telling the people his intentions. Frankness in government is just as vital as truth in securities.[30]

From Baltimore, Landon went to Philadelphia, where huge crowds slowed his travel through the city. The governor's party visited Independence Hall before proceeding to its headquarters at the Bellview Stratford Hotel, and that night some 25,000 people watched and heard Landon as he again said the chief issue was whether "we want a free and popular government or a government which concentrates increasing power in the chief executive." He ripped into the administration for drafting revenue bills that constitutionally should have been initiated in the House of Representatives, and for driving these bills

---

[30] Landon speech, Baltimore, October 26, 1936.

"through Congress without adequate debate." Even worse, Congress had acceded to the President's demand that it "transfer to him its control over the spending of public funds." This power had enabled the President to bypass state governments, and, Landon said, referring to a current scandal in Pennsylvania, this power had been used by Works Progress Administration agents to coerce voters, to tell the unemployed "that if they do not support the President they will be thrown off the relief rolls." Landon then shifted to the broader effects that he was convinced would result if the United States continued its "spendthrift course" to insolvency.

> The lesson of national bankruptcy is clear for all to read. We have seen what happens in nation after nation of the modern world. We have seen democracies fall and dictatorships rise. We have seen societies planned and liberties destroyed. And we have seen hard-won constitutions first ridiculed and then, section by section, discarded and thrown away.
>
> Human liberty, like a tree, grows slowly. For more than seven hundred years the race has struggled for the liberties embodied in our Constitution. But an axe can fell the sturdiest tree in a few short hours. Our liberties can be lost almost as quickly. This administration wields the same axe which has destroyed the liberties of much of the old world—an unbalanced budget, inflation of the currency, delegation of power to the chief executive, destruction of local self-government.
>
> Let us then, here in Philadelphia, where the charter of our liberty was born, make this high resolve. Let us take an oath that the bell which rang here one hundred and sixty years ago shall not have rung in vain.[31]

Landon was in Pittsburgh the next day, where he worked on final arrangements for the campaign and met with friends and politicians. That night he went to Duquesne Gardens to speak on civil service reform and to pay tribute to Teddy Roosevelt on his birthday, recalling "that Theodore Roosevelt began his national career in Washington as a member of the Civil Service Commission and he put this commission on the map." The governor then contrasted Franklin D. Roosevelt's statements in favor of a stronger and broader civil service with the New Deal's record. In 1933, he said, 100,000 federal jobs had been available for patronage distribution; by 1936 the number had reached 325,000—with the result that the proportion of executive employees under civil service had dropped from 80 per cent to 60 per cent during these years. Landon said that he would get rid of the bloated patronage machine that had been created by the New Deal.

[31] Anderson, "Observations," p. 39; Landon speech, Philadelphia, October 26, 1936.

He offered to assume the "grinding undramatic responsibility" of paring it and reorganizing it into an efficient, money-saving apparatus. In the executive branch, the merit system would be applied to every position below the rank of Assistant Secretary, and the system of promotion on merit would be broadened "so that employees may look forward to continuous advancement." He assured classified civil servants that they had nothing to fear from this reorganization. He promised them: "I shall ask that the Civil Service Commission provide open hearings—a court of appeals—for employees against whom charges have been made that may lead to the loss of their jobs. When such charges are made the accuser should face the accused." [32]

The next morning, October 28, Landon arrived in Newark, New Jersey, to speak at the Mosque Theater, where he gave his major speech on labor. He tried to identify himself with labor and distinguish himself from the aristocratic Roosevelt (a tactic he might have used with greater effect earlier in the campaign) by pointing out that he had worked with his hands and earned wages. He credited labor with bringing about a general recognition of the principle that "national prosperity depends upon labor's receiving an increasing share of the value of everything we produce." He pledged himself, "when I am President," to protect labor's rights to organize, to picket peacefully, and to "bargain collectively through representatives of its own choosing without interference by employers."

Landon then warned of those who tried to deliver bloc votes. "Such a person is sowing the seeds of destruction for all of us. He threatens to destroy the one classless nation in the world." And Landon once again warned that the forthcoming social security payroll deductions would fall "almost entirely on workers," and that about half of the nation's workers were excluded from the old-age and survivors' insurance program. He repeated the Republican platform pledges to assist the needy, blind, and crippled, to promote child welfare and state unemployment-insurance programs, and to improve public health services. "To these—our old people and our workers struggling for better conditions I will not promise the moon. I promise only what I know can be performed: economy, a living pension and such security as can be provided by a generous people." [33]

After the speech Landon joined former Senators Joseph Frelinghuysen and Walter Edge, and one other man, for lunch. Frelinghuysen

[32] Landon speech, Pittsburgh, October 27, 1936.
[33] Landon speech, Newark, October 28, 1936.

and Edge told Landon that he would not carry New Jersey, and they asked him if he had a chance of carrying the country; and Landon replied: "No chance." Then they looked to the fourth man—whom Landon thought to be an associate of the New Jersey leaders, and whom the former senators took to be a Landon aide—for an opinion, and the man identified himself as a reporter for a Newark newspaper. Frelinghuysen and Edge upbraided him for sneaking into the luncheon under false pretenses. Landon, however, admired the reporter's audacity and initiative, and he told him he could do what he wanted with the story but that if it was printed the election might as well be called off. The story was never published.[34]

On the afternoon of October 28, Landon entered New York City. The crowd on hand to greet him was so large that he found it almost impossible to make his way into his headquarters at the Murray Hill Hotel, the gay spot of the "horse and buggy" era. President Roosevelt had been in New York City that morning, and a Republican newsman who had covered both campaign processions reported that the Landon crowd was less enthusiastic than Roosevelt's. The President was buoyant and obviously enjoying himself, while Landon, though he felt fine, looked preoccupied. One of Landon's bodyguards saw New York City's greeting as a sign that the tide was turning for the Kansan; but, the guard wondered, would it turn rapidly enough—would people rise to the theme of "Save America," written on the governor's campaign banners?

That night Landon met with Al Smith for some pleasant conversation, and the next morning he drove to Sagamore Hill to pay homage at the grave of Theodore Roosevelt and to visit his widow. The Kansan then went to Brooklyn for lunch with the borough's Republican leaders. At 5 p.m., from his hotel suite, he gave a radio talk that was directed to naturalized citizens, asking them to resist efforts by bigots of any party to divide the people "on racial and religious grounds." Taking aim at those who tried to link him with the racists among the Jeffersonian Democrats and with the anti-Semitism of Father Coughlin, he said bluntly:

> I want no support from any elements that are trying to inject racial prejudices and religious bigotries in this campaign. I have never countenanced them in my own state. I fought the forces of bigotry in Kansas,

[34] Landon interview, January 9, 1962.

[and] helped to destroy them. I intend to fight them in the United States whenever and wherever they may appear.

He then pledged that "if ever in this country there is an attempt to persecute any minority on grounds of race, religion or class, I will take my stand by the side of the minority."[35]

The most tumultuous rally of the Landon campaign was staged the evening of October 29. Three hours before the governor's arrival, Madison Square Garden was packed with people—over 20,000 of them—and in the surrounding streets some 50,000 people stood hoping to catch a glimpse of the nominee. American flags and artificial sunflowers were everywhere, and for an hour before the program started group singing and jazz music were alternated to entertain the crowd. The oratory began with introductions of celebrities and with short speeches by Theodore Roosevelt, Jr., Alice Roosevelt Longworth, John Hamilton, Al Smith, and—the party's New York gubernatorial candidate—William F. Bleakley. When Landon appeared he was greeted by a fifteen-minute demonstration of cheers and frenzied group singings of "Oh, Susanna!" Finally, Landon was able to speak from the rostrum, which was flanked by giant sunflower replicas against the background of a huge "YOU CAN BELIEVE LANDON" banner.

"We are drawing to the end of a great campaign," Landon said—"a campaign that transcends all party lines. Tonight I am here, not alone as the representative of a great party; I am here as the representative of a great cause." He then proceeded to summarize the principles of his political creed.

I believe in our Constitutional form of government—a government established by the people, responsible to the people, and alterable only in accordance with the will of the people. I believe in our indivisible union of indestructible states. I believe in the American system of free enterprise, regulated by law. I believe in the liberty of the individual as guaranteed by the Constitution. I believe in the rights of minorities as protected by the Constitution. I believe in the liberties secured by the Bill of Rights and in their maintenance as the best protection against bigotry and all intolerance,

---

[35] *Kansas City Times*, October 30, 1936; Anderson, "Observations," p. 40; Landon speech, Naturalized Citizens League, New York, October 29, 1936. Landon, who had heard from publisher Paul Block that Roosevelt might try to pack the Supreme Court, raised that issue in this speech in the belief that the President would evade it and therefore be deprived of a mandate in altering the Court's composition. Landon interview, January 9, 1962.

whether of race, color or creed. I believe in an independent Supreme Court and judiciary, secure from executive or legislative invasion.

Landon went on to review the New Deal's record, as he saw it, and to state his own positions on the chief issues before the nation. He began with agriculture, saying that the administration had not only failed to correct agriculture's ills but had added to them. The Republicans proposed "to stop muddling and meddling and to begin mending." Then the governor posed the first of his series of questions meant to point up Roosevelt's evasiveness on campaign issues. He asked what the President intended "to do for agriculture?" "The answer is," Landon said, "no one can be sure." As for industry, Landon charged that the administration had favored monopoly, and, with the NRA, had attempted "to supplant American initiative with Washington dictation." The Republicans, on the other hand, would strengthen initiative and trade. Landon again asked what the President intended to do. "The answer is: no one can be sure."

Turning to unemployment, Landon scored the President's "boasts of recovery" when, in 1936, as in 1932, eleven million people remained unemployed. What was needed, Landon asserted, was confidence, and he would restore confidence by being "open and aboveboard on the policies of my administration," by making "use of the best talent available, irrespective of party," by throwing "out all plans based on scarcity," by putting "a steady hand at the wheel." "And how does the President propose to restore confidence? . . . The answer is: no one can be sure."

As for relief, the administration had used "public money for political purposes," a policy the Republicans would end, because "the votes of the American people are not for sale." But what would the President do about relief problems? "The answer is: no one can be sure."

The administration, with its Social Security Act, had given the nation an unworkable hodgepodge, which only partially covered the people and which would lead to unfair taxation and fiscal waste. What would the President do about this? At this point the crowd, which had been unusually responsive, began to chant the refrain with Landon: "The answer is: no one can be sure." Landon condemned the administration for the policy of "spending for spending's sake" and promised that he would "put an end to extravagance and waste . . . [and] balance the budget." "And what is the President going to do? . . . The answer is: no one can be sure."

Then came the great question of the campaign, as the Republican nominee saw it, "the question of whether our American form of government is to be preserved." He charged the President with responsibility for the implementation of nine unconstitutional laws, for urging Congress to pass laws when he doubted their Constitutionality, for publicly belittling the Supreme Court, for publicly suggesting that the Constitution was outworn, and for retaining in high office men who were boldly contemptuous of the American form of government. "Every one of these actions—and the list is by no means complete—strikes at the heart of the American form of government. . . . What are the intentions of the President with respect to the Constitution? Does he believe changes are required? If so, will an amendment be submitted to the people, or will he attempt to get around the Constitution by tampering with the Supreme Court? The answer is: no one can be sure."

Landon then issued a challenge to the President.

> Forty-eight hours from tonight, standing where I am standing, there will be a President of the United States. He will be seeking reelection. A little more than forty-eight hours after he has spoken, the American people will be streaming to the polls. . . . I leave a challenge with the President. I say to him: Mr. President, I am willing to trust the people. I am willing to stand up and say openly that I am against economic planning by the government. I am against the principles of the Agricultural Adjustment Act. I am against the concentration of power in the hands of the chief executive. Tell us where you stand, Mr. President. Tell us not in generalities, but clearly so that no one can mistake your meaning. And tell us why you have evaded the issue until the eve of the election.

The crowd stood and cheered enthusiastically, for this, the liveliest of Landon's speeches. Landon responded by grinning and waving energetically. As he left, the audience remained standing and sang "America." This was the emotional highpoint of Landon's campaign. It even affected most of his aides, who now believed he had a chance to win.[36]

The next day the Sunflower Special made its way through the mountains of Pennsylvania and West Virginia, and Landon made platform talks at White Sulphur Springs and Huntington. He departed from the train at Charleston to speak at Middleburg Auditorium, where he reminded the audience that the "Constitution is the charter of our liberties," praised the "old-fashioned principle of making both ends

[36] Landon speech, Madison Square Garden, New York, October 29, 1936; *Kansas City Times*, October 30, 1936; *New York Times*, October 30, 1936.

meet," and pledged to do everything possible to keep America out of future wars.[37]

His train sped across southern Ohio, Indiana, and Illinois during the night, and arrived in St. Louis the next morning. It was the last full day of campaigning before the election. Mrs. Landon and Peggy were waiting at the terminal for the governor, and that day Mrs. Landon participated in campaigning for the first time during the contest. Early in the evening Landon headed a parade through the city, shortly before he gave his last major speech of the campaign— in which he joined his fellow Republican campaigners in the concerted drive to scare workingmen to vote for "salvation." Landon repeated his warning that workers would bear a large part of social security taxes, but he added that keeping track of those covered under the program would open the field to "federal snooping," perhaps even fingerprinting, photographing, and the wearing of identification tags. But the burden of his remarks was more soundly conceived. He blasted the Roosevelt administration for thinking "the way to real and lasting prosperity is by the spending of borrowed money. It is financial madness to delude ourselves into thinking that the more we borrow, the easier it will be to get out of debt." Landon also showed that he, like Roosevelt, could use political parables.

> Two weeks ago, in Chicago, [the President] said that when he came into office he found the train of this country's business and industry in the ditch. He said he pulled it out of the ditch. He said he put it on the rails and ran it into the shop. He said he repaired it. He said that now, as a result of his efforts, the train is running again.
>
> I should like to make a few comments on this parable of the derailed train. The President assumes that his administration deserves all the credit. Surely, the courage, industry, and sacrifices of our people had something to do with getting the train out of the ditch.
>
> Further, the President fails to state that after the train got into the shop it stayed there for nearly two years. It stayed there nearly two years because the repair work was intrusted to thumble-fingers who were long on theory, but short on practical experience. And it wasn't this administration which finally got the train out of the shop. It was the Supreme Court, when it decided the NRA was unconstitutional.
>
> Then there is the repair bill, which is not taken into account. This bill is a large part of the $25 billion spent by this administration of which $13 billion has not been paid.

[37] Landon speech, Charleston, W. Va., October 30, 1936.

Finally the train was in the shop so long that it is far behind its schedule. It is so far behind that eleven million unemployed men and women are still standing along the tracks, waiting to be carried to their destination—the destination of full-time work and full-time pay.

Landon pledged that he would restore prosperity and good government to the nation. He ended by declaring (much as Roosevelt had in 1932 and 1933): "Let us look forward to an America with faith revived; faith in our government; faith in those qualities of heart and soul and mind that have given us so proud a history; and above all, faith in the eternal God thru whose mighty power our fathers won their liberties of old." [38]

Landon's train left St. Louis at midnight, and for the only time during the campaign he thought he might win the election. The response to his speeches in Pennsylvania, New York, West Virginia, and Missouri had been enthusiastic; and most of the local politicians had given him reports that indicated he might carry those pivotal states. The temper of his aides also was optimistic. Yet, as he awoke the next morning, he knew that his moment of hope had been a delusion, that Roosevelt would be reelected.[39] The Sunflower Special arrived in Topeka in time for the Landons to attend church, and perhaps for the governor to pray that his instincts were wrong.

Others tussled with the same question as the last day of the political battle approached. James Rudolph Garfield, son of the martyred President, and in his own right a progressive member of Theodore Roosevelt's cabinet, wrote in his diary (on October 31) that the result was "absolutely uncertain but I feel Landon will win as he ought to win." James A. Reed wrote Bainbridge Colby that the anti-Roosevelt forces deserved the verdict at the polls whether they got it or not. The *Literary Digest* poll showed that Landon had essentially maintained his

[38] Anderson, "Observations," p. 41; Schlesinger, *Politics of Upheaval*, pp. 635 ff.; Landon speech, St. Louis, October 31, 1936.

[39] Landon interview, January 9, 1962; Landon to Oscar Stauffer, November 23, 1936. It should be noted that Raymond Clapper on October 27 thought that Landon believed he would win, though on November 19 Clapper reported that James Wright, who covered Landon for the Scripps-Howard newspapers throughout the campaign, said the governor did not think he would be elected (Diaries, October 27, November 19, 1936, Raymond Clapper Papers, Manuscript Division, Library of Congress, Washington, D.C.). Although there is no direct evidence that Landon, during the campaign, was convinced he was going to be defeated, the private and public polls especially followed by his campaign headquarters in Topeka clearly showed that Roosevelt would be reelected.

position over Roosevelt during the last two weeks of October, 54.43 per cent against 40.98 per cent for the President. As Landon was campaigning in St. Louis, John Hamilton predicted that Landon would sweep the country.[40]

On November 2, the day before the election, the governor occupied himself with visitors and Kansas state business. That evening, on the radio, he told the voters he was confident that they would "go to the polls tomorrow united in one aim—to vote as Americans for the future of America." He called upon them to emulate the virtues of the pioneers, "their simplicity, their steadfastness and their abiding faith." He asked the people "to look beyond the present and see the world in which their children would prosper and be free."[41] This talk represented what Landon had hoped his campaign would be—a middle-of-the-road approach that was as constructive as it was critical, that called to mind the glories of the past without defending its failures, that looked to a future quite different from the present, that would appeal to the great majority of Republicans, to dissident Democrats, and to independent voters. His campaign was meant to be, like Landon himself, the direct antithesis of the President.

At midnight, Governor and Mrs. Landon boarded a train for Independence, where they were to vote; they cast their ballots in the morning, visited around the town, and then had lunch before returning to Topeka. The Landons went to the governor's mansion immediately upon their arrival in the capital and stayed there for election evening. For the first time in months, the family secluded itself for dinner. At 8:30 p.m. the mansion was opened to notables and reporters. Doughnuts, sandwiches, and coffee were served; and the reception room was decorated with a huge "Landon Victory Cake" and an even larger, five-foot-wide "sunflower," made of yellow and brown chrysanthemums. The governor played the role of genial host, and chatted amiably with his visitors.

At one point, while the early tidings of Roosevelt's triumph were being reported over the radio, a photographer asked Landon to pose

[40] James Rudolph Garfield Diary, October 31, 1936, James Rudolph Garfield Papers, Manuscript Division, Library of Congress, Washington, D.C.; James A. Reed to Bainbridge Colby, November 3, 1936, Bainbridge Colby Papers, Manuscript Division, Library of Congress, Washington, D.C.; *Topeka Capital*, October 30, 31, 1936. The huge error—20 per cent of the popular vote—made by the *Literary Digest* was explained by its reliance on telephone directories in drawing its polling samples—at a time when many people could not afford to have a telephone.

[41] Landon speech, Topeka, November 2, 1936.

beside the victory cake. The incongruity of the situation appealed to the governor, who turned to Mrs. Landon and said in rustic accents: "Come on, Mother, and get your picture took. It will be the last chance." Before midnight it was obvious that the Sunflower Special had been derailed, and the Landons retired from the party. Before going to bed Landon wired President Roosevelt: "THE NATION HAS SPOKEN. EVERY AMERICAN WILL ACCEPT THE VERDICT AND WORK FOR THE COMMON CAUSE OF THE GOOD OF OUR COUNTRY. THAT IS THE SPIRIT OF DEMOCRACY. YOU HAVE MY SINCERE CONGRATULATIONS." [42]

[42] Anderson, "Observations," p. 43; *Topeka Capital*, November 4, 1936; *Kansas City Times*, November 4, 1936; *Kansas City Star*, October 24, 1943; Landon to Franklin D. Roosevelt, November 4, 1936.

CHAPTER 14

From Under the Wreckage

"An overwhelming disaster," wrote James Rudolph Garfield of the election results.[1] Roosevelt received 27,478,945 votes and Landon 16,674,665. As James Farley had predicted, Landon received the electoral votes—a total of 8—only of Maine and Vermont; 523 electoral votes went to the President. The Republicans now had only skeletal representation in Congress—eighty-nine seats in the House and sixteen in the Senate. Moreover, Landon not only lost in Kansas but William G. West, his hand-picked successor as governor, was also defeated. Perhaps there was some consolation in the fact that Landon received 915,000 more votes than Hoover had in 1932, and carried 87 more counties. The governor had attracted a larger proportion of the votes than Hoover in Iowa, Missouri, South Dakota, Nebraska, Kansas, Maryland, Georgia, Arkansas, Louisiana, Oklahoma, Texas, and New Mexico. Landon did even better than Wendell Willkie would do, in 1940, in Vermont, Maine, New Hampshire, Georgia, and North Carolina. The Kansan's gains over Hoover in the midwestern states probably were attributable to his strong emphasis on agricultural issues and his midwestern background, though he did not come within 4 per cent of capturing a majority of the popular vote in any of those states. His gains in the southern and border states also were probably

[1] James Rudolph Garfield diary, November 4, 1936, James Rudolph Garfield Papers, Manuscript Division, Library of Congress, Washington, D.C.

based on his farm issues, especially that of lending money to tenant farmers to buy their own farms, and on his attractiveness to conservative Democrats. Yet the closest Landon came to capturing one of those states was in Missouri, where he polled 38 per cent of the popular vote. The fact, dismaying to Republicans, was that Landon had captured 45 per cent or more of the popular vote in only four states; and only in ten states had he polled between 40 per cent and 45 per cent of the total vote. The Lemke vote had not helped him, for it was immaterial in Maine and Vermont, where Landon received over 55 per cent of the vote; it perhaps hurt him only in New Hampshire, where the number of votes cast for Lemke slightly exceeded Roosevelt's margin of victory. The plain fact was that Roosevelt had won a smashing victory.[2]

Landon received considerable praise from the press after his defeat. The *Cincinnati Times-Star* said: "It Was a Gallant Campaign." The *Washington Post* wrote: "Thanks to Mr. Landon's persistent and intelligent discussion of the fundamentals of good government, the country is much more keenly aware of the dangers of drifting into dictatorship." It added: "The liberal direction which Mr. Landon has given to Republicanism augurs well for a further regeneration [of the party]." Calling him a "gentleman and a sportsman," the *Boston Post* commented: "Governor Landon faced an impossible task. He and his Western advisers made many blunders. But would the party leaders in the East, who sought to run his campaign, have done any better? They probably would have done worse."

The *Boston Post* was right when it added that Landon had been beaten from the start. Whether he was right or wrong in goals and strategy was immaterial to the election, and Landon himself expected to lose, for the country's economic improvement in 1936 made it unlikely that the voters would demand a change. Landon, however, thought that the Republican party suffered from too much "stuffed-shirt and blind leadership," and that a candidate could not hope to correct this in the midst of a campaign. Landon also knew that "the

---

[2] *Topeka Capital*, November 5, 1936; Edgar E. Robinson, *They Voted for Roosevelt* (Stanford: Stanford University Press, 1947), pp. 41 f. Landon and Knox's percentage —36.5—of the popular vote was the second-lowest received by a major party's national nominees in the twentieth century when there was not a substantial third-party ticket in the field. The lowest, ironically, was in the 1920 election, when James Cox and Franklin D. Roosevelt received only 34.1 per cent of the ballots.

Republican party has a lot to live down," and that "much of the ground I covered in the closing weeks of the campaign was discredited because of the Liberty League, Economy League, etc. One trouble was that I had no one [except Charles P. Taft] to pick up the progressive and moderate side of my speeches." [3]

Landon could have added that three and a half years of demoralization and disintegration had atrophied the functional organs of the Republican party. During the 1936 campaign it was difficult to rebuild the national committee organization, and it had been impossible to make effective political groups of many state and local units. Serious party rifts were apparent during the campaign in—at least—California, Missouri, Ohio, New York, New Jersey, and Pennsylvania. Although the national committee experienced a remarkable revival in 1936, it still had several pitiful weaknesses. For example, there were twenty-four workers in its industrial division but only three people on its labor staff. The responsibilities of the committee's various divisions were not clearly defined, and committee publicity failed to support the party's national standard-bearers adequately. The Republican effort was further fragmented because not one but several campaigns were conducted. Herbert Hoover, Bainbridge Colby, Al Smith, and John D. M. Hamilton ran personalized speaking campaigns, largely because Landon could not dismiss or effectively discipline an ex-President or the leaders of dissident Democratic forces or, in the middle of the campaign, even a national committee chairman (whom he considered otherwise efficient). As for Frank Knox's campaign independence, it appears that Governor Landon overestimated the vice-presidential nominee's ability to correlate his efforts with Landon's. Even worse their campaigns were so quixotically conservative, and employed so much name-calling, that they offset much of Landon's moderation. This was even truer of the wild efforts of the Hearst newspapers and the American Liberty League, which Landon later called the "kiss of death." [4]

Problems of communication between campaign headquarters at

[3] *Cincinnati Star-Times*, November 6, 1936; *Washington Post*, November 4, 1936; *Boston Post*, November 7, 1936; Landon to Raymond Clapper, November 16, 1936, Alfred M. Landon Papers, Kansas State Historical Society, Topeka.

[4] George Wolfskill, *The Revolt of the Conservatives* (Boston: Houghton Mifflin, 1962), p. 215. Although Landon during the campaign saw a number of Liberty League members in their roles as Republican or dissident Democratic leaders, he had no formal contact with the League. Ralph Robey to D. R. McCoy, March 4, 1959.

Topeka, Chicago, New York, and Washington—and en route with the various campaigners—complicated the achievement of a relatively concerted political effort. It was also significant that a number of Republicans, lulled by the *Literary Digest* polls, contributed little to the campaign; and the extraordinary enthusiasm of many leading Republicans early in the campaign changed into pessimism. Some of these men lost their confidence in Landon because they believed he had accepted too many New Deal objectives, although if they had known more about him before the campaign, they would have been less surprised.[5] Other Republicans, dismayed by the party's general conservatism, had already left or would, during the campaign, leave the party, like the La Follette brothers and Senator George Norris. Some, like Senator James Couzens, remained in the party but supported President Roosevelt; others, like Senators William E. Borah and Hiram W. Johnson, publicly backed none of the candidates for President.[6]

There was also the intentional strategy of keeping Landon's speaking delivery amateurish, to make Roosevelt appear flippant by contrast. This not only failed, it stole from Landon's speeches much of their effectiveness and made him appear personally mediocre. In many of his speeches he appeared exactly as he felt, "like the country boy going to take a job in Toronto for the first time." It was ironic that a man who had used his personality to great advantage in winning the nomination could rarely project it to large groups.[7] Governor Landon's efforts were also hurt because he spoke in an idiom that was not pleasing to labor or to city dwellers: they could not eat the pioneer virtues to which he so often alluded, nor could they swallow the Republican party or digest the eulogies of economy and efficiency.

Certainly, Landon suffered from apparent inconsistencies in his speeches. He was unable to explain satisfactorily how he could lower

[5] Ralph Robey to D. R. McCoy, March 4, 1959; John D. M. Hamilton to D. R. McCoy, February 6, 1959; William T. Hutchinson, *Lowden of Illinois: The Life of Frank O. Lowden* (Chicago: University of Chicago Press, 1957), II, 690.

[6] Many of the points mentioned in this and the preceding paragraph are discussed at length in Henry O. Evjen, "The Republican Strategy in the Presidential Campaigns of 1936 and 1940" (Ph.D. dissertation, Western Reserve University, 1950).

[7] Landon to Frank Altschul, September 2, 1936; Malcolm Moos, *The Republicans: A History of Their Party* (New York: Random House, 1956), p. 399; Raymond Clapper diaries, n.d. (probably August 25, 1936), Raymond Clapper Papers, Manuscript Division, Library of Congress, Washington, D.C.; Henry Breckinridge to Landon, November 18, 1936; Grove Patterson, *I Like People: The Autobiography of Grove Patterson* (New York: Random House, 1954), p. 151.

trade barriers and yet afford additional tariff protection for farmers; how he could maintain and possibly expand existing services and yet balance the budget and perhaps reduce taxes; how he could effectively use state and local governments to conduct nationwide relief and social security programs. The governor was generally positive about programs but vague about how his programs could be implemented. Though many people were pleased with Landon and his programs, they concluded that Roosevelt would be as effective, and probably more so, in achieving the policy goals they favored. Another consideration is that the governor's campaign suffered from the unfounded charges and distortions of some of his opponents; much of the attack on Landon was effective because, being from a remote and small state, he was not well known before his nomination—either to the nation or within his party.[8] He was unable to correct this defect during the campaign.

Ironically, some of the governor's most appealing organizational efforts haunted him. By striving to reduce conservative control of the party and bring in new faces, Landon, an amateur in national politics, too often surrounded himself with other amateurs. Furthermore, coming from a state with few industries and no large cities, he was limited in his awareness of the subtleties of labor and urban problems.[9] Landon made no commitments on patronage or on policy beyond what he stated in his speeches, which deprived him of opportunities to control some of the activities of extreme elements in the party.[10] His tactic, instead, was to work the viewpoints of all the major elements supporting him into a campaign framework, along with his own ideas and the positions taken by the majority of Republicans in Congress. By attempting to harmonize the views of those supporting him, and by campaigning on this basis, Landon dampened the enthusiasm of some of his most influential backers. William Allen White, for example, could not understand that the nominee had to try to represent many people if he was to have a chance of creating a vigorous opposition party, or of educating that party to some of the political realities of the

[8] Memorandum from Roy W. Howard in Raymond Clapper diaries, August 27, 1936, Clapper Papers.

[9] Landon to W. M. Kiplinger, March 27, 1936; James L. Wright to Landon, August 3, 1936; Landon to Wright, August 10, 1936; Landon to William T. Mossman, August 3, 1936.

[10] Landon to James McMullin, May 11, 1936; Landon to Karl Lamb, April 4, 1957; William Hard to William E. Borah, October 20, 1936, William E. Borah Papers, Manuscript Division, Library of Congress, Washington, D.C.

1930s, or of winning election.[11] Many of his friends did not recognize that Landon—the fiscal conservative, the moderate on social welfare and on states' versus federal rights, the liberal on questions of civil liberties, agriculture, and conservation—was one of the few Republicans who could represent the diversity of views among President Roosevelt's opponents. As unfortunate as this lack of understanding among many of his supporters was Landon's belief that he had to state—as well as represent—all of these views. The result was that he covered more issues during the campaign than his supporters or the general public could understand.

Landon and the Republicans, of course, did not lose the election entirely because of their deficiencies. The long depression had made most of the voters unreceptive to Republican campaign efforts, which (except for Landon's) reflected considerable ignorance of most people's difficulties and aspirations. This unreceptiveness contrasted sharply with the impression the Roosevelt administration made—of giving the highest priority to helping people. But this was not all; the *political* effectiveness of the New Deal was at least as important as Republican defects in deciding the result. In Franklin D. Roosevelt the New Deal possessed not only a remarkably skillful commander but a personable candidate who could point to a well-known national record of accomplishment. His administration controlled more federal, state, and local patronage, and possessed more in-office leadership, than any previous political group. It had spent almost twice as much public money as any other peacetime American government, and had obligated—through relief activities—about one-sixth of the population. The Roosevelt forces were understandably not reluctant in using all this for political purposes.[12] The Republicans, even with a very large campaign fund, could scarcely hope to combat such a political force as had been constructed by the New Deal.[13]

[11] See Walter Johnson, *William Allen White's America* (New York: Holt, 1947), pp. 452 ff., for a sympathetic analysis of White's feelings.

[12] Bureau of the Census, U.S. Department of Commerce, *Historical Statistics of the United States, 1789–1945* (Washington, D.C.: Government Printing Office, 1949), pp. 299 ff.; Broadus Mitchell, *Depression Decade* (New York: Rinehart, 1947), p. 315; Milton Plesur, "The Republican Congressional Comeback of 1938," *Review of Politics* (October, 1962), p. 526.

[13] The Republicans and allied groups were reported to have spent $14,198,202.92 during the campaign and to have incurred a deficit of $960,771.73; the political groups supporting President Roosevelt spent $9,228,406.85 and had a deficit of $373,481.65. See *Senate Investigation of Campaign Expenditures in 1936*, Report 151, 75th Cong., 1st

It should be emphasized, however, that the Landon campaign did more than reveal Republican deficiencies. Under hostile circumstances, the campaign helped perpetuate certain ideas that have continued to receive attention in America—the concepts of an economy of plenty, the possibilities of new frontiers, unity of the people, efficiency, economy, state and local rights, exaltation of the Constitution, and a regulatory government rather than a managed state. Governor Landon also pointed out numerous New Deal defects and indicated paths of action that the New Deal itself followed; even during the campaign, government officials were prompted to take positive action to eliminate some of Landon's issues. Some examples of this were the President's extension of civil service regulations to postmasters, Harry Hopkins' interest in dealing with the political intimidation of WPA workers, the stepping up of the government's drought-relief program, and the establishment of a committee to devise crop-insurance proposals. After the campaign, the government worked harder to develop additional crop uses and to cultivate foreign agricultural markets.[14] Also, the Landon and Republican campaigns probably contributed to the downgrading of the planned-society elements in the government, the great battle in Congress to block Roosevelt's court reorganization proposals, the limitation of partisan activity by government employees, and increased executive and legislative interest in efficiency. Certainly the campaign publicized these issues before the government seriously wrestled with them.

One of the most interesting functions of the campaign was the way it marked out a road for the reconstruction of the Republican party. This the Landon forces accomplished partly by broadening the control of the party to include midwesterners, liberals, and young bloods, and partly by initiating the rebuilding of the party's political machinery.

sess. (Washington, D.C.: Government Printing Office, 1937), pp. 27, 29. Many commentators have evinced great concern over the greater campaign fund of the Landon forces, and many Democrats used it as an issue to enlist sympathy for their party. As Republicans saw it, though, their $5 million edge in campaign expenditures was insignificant compared with the " $5 billion" in spoils and patronage controlled by the New Deal.

14 James MacGregor Burns, *Roosevelt: The Lion and the Fox* (New York: Harcourt, Brace, 1956), p. 276; Robert G. Sherwood, *Roosevelt and Hopkins* (New York: Harper, 1948), pp. 81, 83; Harold L. Ickes, *The Secret Diary of Harold L. Ickes: The First Thousand Days* (New York: Simon & Schuster, 1953–54), p. 684; Chester C. Davis, "The Development of Agricultural Policy Since the End of the World War," in U.S. Department of Agriculture, *An Historical Survey of American Agriculture* (Washington, D.C.: Government Printing Office, 1941), pp. 317 ff.

There is great merit in historian Basil Rauch's suggestion that the liberal aspects of Landon's speeches kept many traditionally Republican farmers, workers, and middle-class elements in the party in 1936.[15] It should also be added that the governor, through his speeches and personal contacts, educated many Republicans to a recognition that such things as organized labor, government regulation of business, conservation, farm relief, and social security were realities in American life. In this, the Republican party—as well as the Democratic party—had traveled a substantial distance from its position in 1932.

Of course, Landon's campaigns—for nomination and especially for the Presidency—were only the beginning of the struggle for the intellectual and organizational reconstruction of the Republican party, a struggle that was to be carried on for many years afterwards. In viewing Landon's efforts, however, it is not fantastic to suggest he was significant not only in carrying out the role of an opposition candidate, under most difficult circumstances, but that he played an important part in shaping the development of his party into what, during the 1950's, would be known as Modern Republicanism.

Landon's supporters were of course disappointed with the election's outcome. Ogden Mills, whose confidence in Landon's election had gradually evaporated after the convention, was skeptical of a Landon victory by election day, but he was completely unprepared for the Roosevelt landslide. Robert R. McCormick, the volatile publisher of the *Chicago Tribune* (which daily during the campaign reminded its readers of the number of days remaining "in which to save your country"), was convinced that only a coalition ticket could have beaten Roosevelt. William Allen White, almost in desperation, wrote to a number of his friends to deny close connections with Landon's campaign—but he also wrote to others, as the shock of the overwhelming defeat wore off, to defend Landon. He said that Hoover could not have done better as the 1936 Republican candidate. Indeed, Hoover, as the nominee, would have stigmatized the party as opportunistic and expedient, whereas Landon gave it "any of half a dozen objectives."

Senator William E. Borah saw the defeat as a vindication of what he had been saying for years.

> The party can never again command the respect and confidence of the vast body of men and women who have heretofore been voting the Republican

[15] Basil Rauch, *The History of the New Deal, 1933–1938* (New York: Creative Age Press, 1944), p. 262.

ticket. The voters will never go back to that leadership. . . . The people do not believe in their philosophy of politics, or their philosophy of government. Landon was buried because it was believed by the masses that he would be the representative, if elected, of these political forces.

The discrediting of these men, Borah thought, put the Republican party in the position of having a stigma much like that carried by the Democrats after the Civil War.[16] Words of cheer and some doom came from Landon's Democratic supporters. Governor Joseph Ely was quoted as saying that the New Dealers did not really do very well for they had won the votes of only five or six million people who were not supported from government funds. Henry Breckinridge was dismayed at the failure of the Republican and Jeffersonian Democratic coalition to defeat Roosevelt, and he was at a loss to say how an effective opposition to the President could be established. The dissident Democrats, he reported, planned to meet again in late November or early December, but he was not sanguine about the results.

Landon did not consider his defeat a personal tragedy. Although he thought that George Norris and some of the other Republican dissidents were "meaner about little things than I would have expected," the Kansan was not bitter toward Roosevelt and did not sulk over the election results. He knew "it was a desperate fight from the start," but someone had to do battle.[17] Landon also knew that it had been better to take the nomination when he could get it, rather than wait until 1940 and hope that the chances for election would be better— because by then he might be in political oblivion.

Landon spent most of his time in November attending to state business—he was still governor of Kansas—and in acknowledging his post-election letters and thanking his supporters (whom he encouraged to think of future action). He wrote Henry Breckinridge that he was proud to have fought with him in pointing out "the dangers to the foundations of freedom." To Ben M. Anderson, Landon wrote that

[16] Ogden Mills to Gordon O'Neill, June 18, November 6, 1936, Ogden Mills Papers, Manuscript Division, Library of Congress, Washington, D.C.; Robert R. McCormick to Landon, December 3, 1936; W. A. White to George Norris, November 14, 1936; White to Thomas J. Norton, November 11, 1936; White to Erwin Canham, December 22, 1936, William Allen White Papers, Manuscript Division, Library of Congress, Washington, D.C.; William E. Borah to Thomas E. Whitten, December 5, 1936, Borah Papers.

[17] Henry Breckinridge to Landon, November 18, 1936; Clifford Hope to Robert J. Laubengayer, December 18, 1936, Clifford R. Hope Papers, Kansas State Historical Society, Topeka; Landon to W. A. White, December 17, 1936; Landon to Breckinridge, November 9, 1936.

Republicans should not consider that American freedom was lost as a result of the election because this conclusion would weaken Roosevelt's opponents for future battles.[18] He also wanted to go on record, for friends who had not supported him, about what had concerned him most during the campaign; and in a lengthy letter to Raymond Clapper he complained of Republican "stuffed-shirt leadership" and of the New Deal's methods, waste, expediencies, and carelessness.

> I have never been one of those who made a fetish of tradition, but democracies must be more careful of forms and traditions than monarchies. . . . We are struggling with the fundamental difficulty of maintaining a popular government, strong enough to adapt itself to our changing needs, strong enough to maintain effectively its own existence as a popular government. The following of the precedents established by this administration for many more years will, I am afraid, finish a popular government.
>
> You may say Congress cannot be trusted, but the answer is not to sink it still lower, but to build it up. Its present low state cannot be laid entirely at the door of this administration, although it has helped kick it still further into the gutter. Part of it is due to the constant lampooning of the newspapers over the years. Part of it is due to the machinations of big business. Part of it is due to its own incompetence. But the way to get anyone out of the gutter is not to keep on treating them with contempt. Both politicians in Congress and big business, governors and presidents, have been relying too much on supreme courts to stop legislation that ought to be threshed out on its own merits on the legislative floor.

Landon also blasted the corruption he saw in both parties. As for the Republican party,

> I think it has been criminally guilty in many states of corrupting the electors. I have been insurging against that type of leadership all my life. And, by the same token, I have contempt for the wholesale corruption of this administration which all their humanitarian manifestations cannot efface. . . . What does it avail a people to gain a shirt and lose its soul.

He closed his letter to Clapper with a postscript: "I can now tell you [that if elected] I was going to draft you to a position at my right elbow. I don't like yes-men around me." [19]

[18] Landon to Henry Breckinridge, November 9, 1936; Landon to Ben M. Anderson, December 17, 1936.

[19] Landon to Raymond Clapper, November 16, 1936. This is the only direct and written evidence that Landon had considered a particular individual for an appointive office. In an interview, however, he said that he would also have considered Charles P. Taft, J. Reuben Clark, and possibly Harold L. Ickes for appointments. Landon interview, January 9, 1962.

After taking care of his most pressing duties, Landon began to function as titular head of the Republican party. He wrote to key figures in the party, asserting "We must not let our organization backslide into the condition it was in after the 1932 election." He encouraged Ralph Robey and similar men to explore ideas for the development of a party of opposition, perhaps along British lines. Such a party should educate the public, have a moderating influence on government policy and public thought, and, through responsible investigation and audit, keep the government's power in check.[20] Landon also wanted to bolster national committee chairman John D. M. Hamilton, believing that he could be important in determining the strength of Landon's influence on party policy. On November 12 he wrote Hamilton, praising him for his "splendid efforts" and the "efficient work of your organization"—although some Republicans now called for Hamilton's resignation as national chairman. Congressman Hamilton Fish was critical of Hamilton's failure to develop a winning organization, and Richard Lloyd Jones asserted that he had used the chairmanship to gain the limelight. Landon agreed that there was something to what Jones said, but he pointed out that Hamilton "was up against an impossible situation." He told Jones: "I think John is the best we have now."[21] Landon kept in close touch with Hamilton, seeing him in Florida in early December, and later that month in Chicago and Washington.

In late November, with Lacy Haynes' help, Landon began working on a speech for the December meeting of Washington's Gridiron Club, the famous press punning and parody society, at which President Roosevelt also would speak. At Roosevelt's invitation, he also planned to visit the White House. Meanwhile, traveling with his old friend, oil tycoon L. E. Phillips, for a vacation in Florida, Landon looked forward to some uninterrupted fishing and reading (mystery stories and Sinclair Lewis' *It Can't Happen Here*); he planned to spend a couple of weeks on the Wacissa River near Tallahassee and to go fishing in the Gulf of Mexico. "I expect to have a better chance at catching fish than I did in the election," he said.[22] He returned to Topeka before

[20] Landon to William R. Castle, November 25, 1936; Ralph Robey to Landon, December 13, 1936.

[21] Landon to John D. M. Hamilton, November 12, 1936; Richard Lloyd Jones to Landon, December 10, 1936; Landon to Jones, December 16, 1936.

[22] Willard Mayberry to Marvin McIntyre, November 26, 1936, Franklin D. Roosevelt Library, Hyde Park, N.Y.; *Memphis Commercial Appeal*, December 1, 1936.

the middle of December, well rested and ready to plunge into public activities, and a few days later he left for Washington to deliver his Gridiron Club speech. On the way to Washington, he met with party leaders in Chicago to discuss the meeting of the Republican national committee, which was to convene there soon, and he went to Colonel Knox's for luncheon. Knox was civil, and observed all the amenties. (The former vice-presidential nominee, however, was unhappy with his campaign experiences and with Landon's leadership. He decided not to go to the Gridiron Club dinner, "especially since Landon is to speak. I have played second fiddle to that second-rater for the last time.")[23] Landon then proceeded to Washington, where he had a pleasant time and a good reception by the press. He was not, as Knox had predicted, at a disadvantage with Roosevelt; they got along famously at the White House, comparing their post-election fishing ventures and chatting about the Kansan's children and the President's grand-children.

At the Gridiron dinner, where the speeches of guests are off the record, Landon's remarks were as favorably received as those of the President, and the Kansan kidded himself and his conqueror. Using the intensity of the correspondents' roasting as his keynote, Landon said:

> Your skits and songs thus far have been brilliant and clever, but the burning doesn't compare to the last four months. . . . At first, I was a bit surprised that you picked Christmas week for a famed Gridiron dinner. Then, I realized that this is the season we devote to the honoring of Santa Claus. So, it occurred to me, that perhaps you were honoring Santa Claus in our good American personification of Santa Claus, our chief distinguished guest. Now, I am going to say before he does, even if he didn't wear the traditional Santa Claus whiskers in the campaign, the people recognized him on November third.

Landon closed his talk on a serious note; turning toward the President, he said:

> I want you to know that there is one thing on which I think we can agree. We know the American people want peace. And no matter how much we may differ on policies, I believe in the old American tradition that politics end at the water's edge. And to you, Sir, I pledge the utmost unity and co-operation in the difficult foreign situations confronting your administration. In all efforts to preserve peace in the world, there will be no party lines.

[23] Hill Blackett to Landon, December 16, 1936; Frank Knox to Annie Knox, December 10, 1936, Frank Knox Papers, Manuscript Division, Library of Congress, Washington, D.C.

Landon used his personality to captivate the Washington press corps and to show that he was a good loser.[24] He boarded the train back to Kansas with new prestige, which would help him in assuming a strange political role, titular leader of his party—a role that would be made even stranger by the events of the next three and a half years.

[24] Landon speech, Washington, December 22, 1936; *New York Times*, December 24, 1936; *Topeka Capital*, December 24, 1936; Harold L. Ickes, *The Secret Diary of Harold L. Ickes: The Inside Struggle* (New York: Simon & Schuster, 1954), pp. 21 f.

CHAPTER **15**

Titular Head

One night in June, 1937, while driving back from one of his oil properties in a heavy rain, Landon came to two wire-fence gates; he opened them, drove his car through, and then walked back to close them. Wet and muddy, and groping in the dark for the gates, he suddenly chortled, remembering that exactly a year before he had been nominated for President of the United States. Alf Landon had lost that election, but not his sense of humor.

Nor had Landon lost his sense of reality. During the depression, his governorship, and his campaign for the Presidency, he had slipped financially—and he had to make a living. He had held on to most of his properties and leases during the depression, but the income from them had been small: to remain prosperous, an oilman has to make strikes and have a good market. Although he was reputed to be a millionaire, he did not have the resources or income to match. Indeed he had to use some of his family's funds and his own emergency capital to buy 170 acres of undeveloped land west of Topeka after the 1936 election. It was here that he built a home, operated a small farm, and sold off his remaining acreage for building sites. The house (into which the family moved in December, 1937) was a large, Georgian structure, which caused one observer to quip that if Alf Landon could not get tenancy of the White House he would build a white house of his own.

Landon also had oil wells and gas properties in Kansas and Okla-homa, a farm in Miami County, and a ranch in Chautauqua County. His new oil operations were in Greenwood and Butler counties, where—the year after the election—he drilled seven wells and made five strikes, (none of the wells was greatly productive, but he said "all have been worth saving").[1] Landon resumed his oil operations early in 1937, and had drilled his first new well by March 19. Working at the well site—in high-top boots, leather jacket, and corduroy trousers—Landon was often surrounded by a crowd of curious farmers, oilmen, and friends. Many Kansans rejoiced with the *Emporia Gazette* that Alf Landon was again "a hard-working, two-fisted, square-shooting guy . . . about to become a shining example of how a man can recover who has once gone wrong." The *El Dorado Times* also joshed him: "There is more joy in heaven, y'know, over the one sinner saved than for the ninety and nine already in the fold."[2]

But Landon was not completely "saved." He was titular head of his party, which involved more than chatting with, writing to, and being viewed by the curious and the well-wishers, and Landon did not intend to neglect the responsibility of his opposition leadership. After his Gridiron Club speech, he pondered his new role in American politics: it had to be flexible, to match the times; it had to be constructive, because Republicans had been too negative to deserve the respect and confidence of the nation; it had to be moderate, to keep the almost 17 million Republican voters in the fold and to prevent the party's badly split leaders from going off on too many tangents. Besides, Landon was "not so much concerned about the Reds as I am about the Yellows—those who have no stomach for the fight"; so there had to be criticism, too—the type that would bring out the fight in Republi-cans. Landon decided to follow up his campaign criticism that the administration had evaded outlining its future policies: "Just what the election decided no one can be sure," he wrote. "Certainly [there is] no mandate from the people to change our basic political structure." This became a strong conviction with Landon, and in his correspon-dence he frequently charged Roosevelt with "artful dodging" on such issues as sit-down strikes, inflation, and tax reform. The nation, Landon thought, must demand moral leadership and character of its President.[3]

---

[1] *Portland Oregonian*, November 28, 1937; Landon to Alan Flory, January 6, 1937, Alfred M. Landon Papers, Kansas State Historical Society, Topeka.

[2] *Emporia Gazette*, March 19, 1937; *El Dorado Times*, March 20, 1937.

[3] Landon to William Hard, January 8, 1937; Landon to John D. M. Hamilton, February 5, 1937; Landon to A. H. Kirchhofer, March 27, 1937.

Landon soon realized that he had to develop his ideas further—as well as perfect his criticism of the New Deal—and his development was an expansion of his earlier ideas. He thought that many Americans had been blind to the problems involved in achieving an equitable distribution of wealth.

> I do not believe the Jeffersonian theory, that the best government is the one that governs least, can be applied today. I think that as civilization becomes more complex, government power must increase; but it is something to be approached slowly and with the caution, not of inertia, but of competence; whereas we have had too much of the slap-dash, jazz method.

He was not greatly concerned about specific economic systems, but he was greatly concerned with intellectual attributes; he contended that honesty, courage, inquisitiveness, and free expression were some of the necessary attributes for making whatever system might develop in the United States do its best. Of these, Landon exalted free expression; he worried that the people and the government were unwittingly taking steps that would ultimately lead to the loss of free expression,[4] and he was disturbed by the general unwillingness of President Roosevelt and his supporters to consider seriously the arguments of their opponents. He disliked those—including Republicans—who were rigidly committed to their own ideas and who closed their minds to what others said. This dislike was something Landon had carried with him since his Progressive party days, and it had been reinforced by his campaign experiences in 1936, when most Democrats and Republicans had interpreted everything he said according to their predilections. This attitude made Landon decide to use whatever prominence he had as titular head of the Republican party to support freedom of expression.[5]

The most important issues that Landon would be concerned with in 1937—and indeed generally during his titular leadership—were determined by forces beyond his control. On February 5, 1937, President Roosevelt delivered his congressional message on judicial reform, which included his plan to retire the older Supreme Court justices or to offset them with his own appointees, and the great issue of the year was born. The proposal led to intense struggles and bitter debates to determine the role of the judiciary in the nation's system of government.

[4] Landon to Raymond Clapper, June 14, December 6, 1937.
[5] *New York Times*, January 8, 10, 1937; Landon to Arthur Capper, January 19, 1937; Harold B. Johnson to Landon, February 3, 1937.

Most Republicans were eager to attack the President's plan, and the upcoming Lincoln Day functions presented a natural opportunity; however, Democratic opponents of Roosevelt's plan, led by Senator Burton K. Wheeler of Montana, asked the Republicans to be quiet on the issue. On February 6, William E. Borah, Charles L. McNary, and Arthur H. Vandenberg, the Republican leaders in the Senate, after conferring on their party's strategy, agreed with Wheeler's contention that vocal Republican opposition to the Court-packing plan would unite the Democrats and lead to its enactment. The Senate Republicans agreed to let the Democratic insurgents lead the attack on the plan, with Republicans serving as silent partners.[6] Republican senators and representatives, particularly Senator John Townsend of Delaware, persuaded Landon not to attack the Court plan publicly. Although he had planned to make the President's proposal the target of his address at the National Republican Club's Lincoln Day dinner in New York, Landon agreed to follow the advice of the congressional Republicans, for they were on the "firing line."[7] Thus began the strategy that would contribute to President Roosevelt's first major defeat in Congress.

Landon, after he arrived in New York, plunged into a round of conferences and urged Republicans to work quietly with the Democratic opponents of Roosevelt's Court plan. He also met with editors, including those of the *New York Times*, to urge opposition to what he saw as Roosevelt's third-term aspirations and the country's possible drift toward dictatorship (his remarks were off the record). Landon's address to the National Republican Club was brief and restrained; aside from the customary eulogy of Lincoln, he referred—without naming them—to great national issues recently raised and urged unhurried, nonpartisan deliberation by Congress. He again said that politics end "at the water's edge." The speech was well received by Republicans and provided no political ammunition for Democrats.[8]

[6] Karl A. Lamb, "The Opposition Party as Secret Agent: Republicans and the Court Fight, 1937," *Papers of the Michigan Academy of Science, Arts, and Letters*, vol. XLVI (1961), pp. 540 f.; Burton K. Wheeler with Paul F. Healy, *Yankee from the West* (Garden City, N.Y.: Doubleday, 1962), p. 326; William Hard to Landon, March 23, 1937.

[7] Landon to Walter E. Edge, February 23, 1937; Landon interview, January 23, 1962. See George Wolfskill, *The Revolt of the Conservatives* (Boston: Houghton Mifflin, 1962), p. 252, for a different story.

[8] Landon to Julius Ochs Adler, April 15, 1937; *Vital Speeches of the Day*, March 1, 1937, p. 320; *Wall Street Journal*, February 15, 1937; *Washington Post*, February 14, 1937.

The strategy soon began to work; the Republican-Democratic coalition against the Court plan solidified in Congress, supported by well-publicized displays of public indignation. Landon wrote John D. M. Hamilton on March 1: "We all have a right to feel a bit elated over the opposition that is developing to the President's proposal to pack the Supreme Court." Landon, who disclosed his views in his correspondence, thought the bill documented the fact that "a short cut is the longest way home": although two years had passed since the Supreme Court had nullified the NRA, the President had sought no other way to achieve his goals than to pack the Court. Landon, who agreed that the Court had been an obstacle to some good legislation, said "there is something about a life term that makes a member of a federal court increasingly arrogant. . . . I would favor a Constitutional amendment, limiting tenure to the age of seventy, or seventy-five," but such a proposal, he contended, did not go to the heart of the issue, which was to secure good legislation. Because the National Industrial Recovery Act and the Agricultural Adjustment Act, for example, had been poorly constructed pieces of legislation, the administration should have worked for their refinement after experience and judicial invalidation had revealed their basic weaknesses.[9]

Although Landon was pleased with the growing opposition to the Court plan, he, like most Republicans, began to feel restive under silence. In late March he considered giving a radio interview in which he would make a case that the President had not been honest with the people on the Court issue, but he changed his mind within a few days. The temptation to speak out was so strong for Republican leaders that they took to writing reminders to each other of their vow of silence. Arthur Capper and Landon exchanged such letters; and when, in May, Hamilton began opinionating along the edges of the court controversy, Landon rebuked him. Others also chided the national chairman, including House Republican leader Bertrand H. Snell, who told Hamilton not to mention the issue and to discourage others from doing so.[10]

Opposition to the Court plan continued to develop. In late May, Landon concluded that the President's proposal was in bad shape, but he warned that it was too early for its opponents to boast of

[9] Landon to John D. M. Hamilton, March 1, 1937; Landon to Raymond Clapper, March 6, 1937.

[10] Landon to Frank Altschul, March 28, April 2, 1937; Arthur Capper to Landon, May 1, 1937; Landon to Capper, May 4, 1937; Landon to John D. M. Hamilton, May 10, 1937; W. T. Mossman to Landon, May 7, 1937.

victory, and he continued to urge Republicans to concentrate on defeating the proposal. "Any issue," he said, "is dangerous to press immediately until we have won the Supreme Court fight." But some thought the fight was won. Don L. Berry, in the June 24 *Indianola (Iowa) Record*, asked "Who Won?"

> Perhaps this modest man from Kansas won the campaign even though he lost the election. In New York he challenged the New Deal candidate for the Presidency to say what he proposed to do with the Supreme Court. The challenge was unanswered by the candidate; but numbers of his supporters voiced assurance that he would never touch the Supreme Court. There was therefore no "mandate" issued by the people for changing the Court.

Landon could forgive his newspaper friend this boast, for this was Landon's viewpoint,[11] but the Court fight had another month to run.

The Republican-Democratic opposition stood fast, and finally the President's forces surrendered. On July 22 the judiciary bill was recommitted in the Senate, which signified that only innocuous congressional legislation would result from the Court fight. W. K. Hutchinson, the chief Hearst correspondent in Washington, congratulated Landon on his role in defeating the plan, and said that if the Kansan had endeavored to make political capital of the President's judiciary proposals, a dozen opposition Democrats would have switched to Roosevelt's support. Landon, by keeping quiet, had set an example that was followed by Republican leaders across the land, and the strategy had prevented the President from securing a majority on the bill.[12]

Now that the battle was won, Landon wrote that the President's Court plan was extremely dangerous, and especially at a time when world conditions encouraged the development of dictatorial states. The independent judiciary was an ingenious American idea for preventing power over the people's representatives from being concentrated in the hands of one man. All Americans should have benefited from the better understanding the Court fight afforded of the "background, the real meaning and intent of the safeguards and limitations of power in our Constitution." This debate, the first great debate on the Constitution since the Civil War, also gave insight, Landon contended, into the

[11] Landon to W. T. Mossman, May 22, 1937; Landon to Channing J. Bullock, June 24, 1937; *Indianola Record*, June 24, 1937; Landon to Earle Evans, March 26, 1937. See also Merlo J. Pusey, *The Supreme Court Crisis* (New York: Macmillan, 1937), p. 67.

[12] *Congressional Record*, 75th Cong., 1st sess., LXXXI, 7381; W. K. Hutchinson to Landon, July 23, 1937.

problems posed by such men as Huey Long, by the urban machines, and by nazi and fascist theories.[13]

After the 1936 election Landon became intrigued by the possibilities of a Republican-Democratic coalition against the New Deal. Democratic insurgency against the Court plan moved him—and later other leading Republicans, including Frank Knox and Arthur Vandenberg— to explore more vigorously the possibilities of such a realignment of political forces. He was partly convinced, and he frequently asserted, that the Democratic party could not hold together until 1940 because there were "too many contradictory elements in the following of President Roosevelt."[14] Toward the end of December, 1936, after praising John Hamilton's suggestion that a summer round-table conference of leading Republicans be held, Landon sounded the national chairman out about inviting several Jeffersonian Democrats to the meeting. One week later Landon proposed that a set of common political principles be formulated at a week-long round-table conference that would be composed of Republicans and Jeffersonian Democrats.[15]

Landon had been in constant correspondence with his 1936 Jeffersonian Democratic supporters, and during his Lincoln Day visit to New York had met with Al Smith, Lewis Douglas, Bainbridge Colby, Colonel Breckinridge, and other dissident Democrats. Douglas, at least, was receptive to the idea of a conference of Republicans and Democrats for exploring questions of formal cooperation on particular issues and even a possible coalition. Landon urged Douglas to take the lead in developing a coalition, but he said that whether Republicans or Democrats took the initiative there must be "co-captains" in the endeavor.[16] Landon visited the Kentucky Derby in May and had a long chat with Ogden Mills, who, with other New York Republicans— Frank Altschul, for one—was talking with Democrats about coalition. Lewis Douglas, Mills said, would try to persuade Dr. Abel Wolman and Newton D. Baker to join himself and three Republicans in preparing a statement of common political principles, and Mills asked

[13] Landon to Henry Buzick, August 3, 1937.

[14] Wolfskill, *Revolt of the Conservatives*, p. 190; Landon to George Van Slyke, January 10, 1937.

[15] Landon to John D. M. Hamilton, December 30, 1936; Landon to Edward D. Duffield, January 5, 1937.

[16] Sterling E. Edmunds to Landon, January 29, 1937; Landon to Edmunds, February 1, 1937; Landon to Lewis Douglas, March 12, April 1, 1937; Douglas to Landon, March 22, 1937.

Landon to recommend three Republicans for this venture. One man whom Landon suggested was William Hard, because of his close acquaintance with Senator Wheeler and with independent Republican Senators Borah and Hiram Johnson. Landon said he would arrange for a meeting in New York between Mills and Hard, and suggested that at least one other Democratic leader, Governor Herbert Lehman of New York (Altschul's brother-in-law), should be considered for inclusion in the group of six. Mills then suggested that the statement of principles could become a round-robin affair, but Landon said he thought that following up the statement with a round-table meeting would be more effective.[17]

The Kansan saw several issues—including the Court plan, inflation, and economy in government—that might be bases for a coalition. He wanted the coalition to include liberals—such as Borah, Johnson, Lehman, and La Guardia—as well as moderates and conservatives, because a coalition party could fail in its program and its appeal (as the 1936 campaign had failed) if it did not attract liberal support. The legislative opposition to the President's program during the spring heartened Landon about the possibility of a coalition; he saw Roosevelt's "right wing crumpled and smashed; his center disorganized and wavering; his left wing advanced so far it has lost touch with his center; his line of communications is under shellfire." Roosevelt might not be able to regroup his forces: "The longer he waits the worse becomes his position."[18] But William Hard, who had many contacts with anti-Roosevelt Democrats, wrote Landon that he was doubtful about substantial intellectual agreement between Republicans and Democrats.

Landon replied to Hard that he would not pay much attention to what individuals said, for "the merger of Democrat and Republican ideas will not come about by the efforts of any one individual, or any group of individuals, no matter how powerful. Events will force it and it will come, if it is to come, as natural as the birth of a baby." He continued to encourage a new political alignment in his correspondence and visits with Republicans and dissident Democrats. "Personal Government vs. Representative Government," he thought, was the great issue that would spur a realignment. And Roosevelt's vindictive-

[17] Landon to William Hard, May 10, 1937.

[18] Landon to Arthur Calvert Smith, May 14, 1937; Landon to Gomer T. Davies, May 14, 1937.

ness would help do this—Landon was convinced the President would try to purge Democratic dissenters, one by one, for fear they would band against him in 1940.[19]

Discouraging news in July—after the defeat of the judiciary bill— was Arthur Calvert Smith's report that his contact during the Court fight thought the dissident Democrats were so pleased at having won that they were no longer interested in a coalition. William Hard reported that Senators Burke and Wheeler felt efforts at coalition would have to be kept quiet. Democrats are Democrats, after all, Hard concluded. Landon believed, however, that the President was boxed in; he was convinced that Roosevelt, like all men who build on personal leadership, could not ignore disloyalty. If he did not punish the insurgents, the morale of his organization would be destroyed, with the result that he would have less control over Congress and over the 1940 Democratic convention. "If he does punish them, he is going to split his party." Prophetically, Landon added: "The President may take advantage of the foreign situation and try to ease out of his own predicament." [20]

His conviction that President Roosevelt was in a dilemma prompted Landon to pursue coalition with even greater vigor in September. By October, however, when the full effect of the 1937 recession was evident, Landon was less certain that Roosevelt was boxed in. He thought the President had created the illusion of being the "master politician," in the political pattern of "the Grecian and Roman demagogues" who would give people "something to hate and give them doles, and make them believe you have transferred the taxes from the many to the few." Roosevelt would fortify that illusion, Landon thought, in his efforts to handle the recession: "He claims the greatest powers any President has ever had, yet will probably try to lay the blame for this depression on the fact that he doesn't have still greater powers." The President's speech of October, 1937, calling for a world quarantine of aggressors, seemed to support Landon's fears, because it might lead to a greater concentration of power in the executive's hands. A dilemma: If the isolationist path was followed,

[19] William Hard to Landon, May 18, 1937; Landon to Hard, May 22, 1937; Landon to Lacy Haynes, September 23, 1937; Landon to Joseph B. Ely, May 20, 1937; Landon to Theodore Roosevelt, Jr., June 22, 1937.

[20] Arthur Calvert Smith to Landon, July 23, 1937; William Hard to Landon, July 24, 1937; Landon to Hard, September 13, 1937.

Roosevelt could concentrate on securing control of the nation's production; if collective security against aggressors was sought, this would mean economic sanctions and a blockade, "which means war."[21]

Although the Kansan now grew doubtful about forming an effective coalition, he continued—on and off until 1939—to pursue this goal with dissident Democrats. When all was said and done, however, most anti-Roosevelt Democrats in the election year of 1940 preferred to take their chances with the President rather than with the Republicans. Ironically, the only startling realignment in 1940 was the entry of Republicans Frank Knox and Henry L. Stimson into Roosevelt's cabinet.

The coalition movement, which also suffered from intense bickering within Republican ranks during 1937, was to consume more of Landon's time than any other issue. After the 1936 election, however, Republicans had to contend with the fact that the great majority of voters were deaf to their appeals and that their party was almost politically impotent, holding only nine governorships, eighty-nine seats in the House of Representatives, and sixteen seats in the Senate. Moreover, the logical leaders of party policy, Landon and Hoover, had to exert their influence from positions of weakness because of their crushing defeats at the polls, their inability to work together, and the widespread conception of them as political bogeymen. But many Republican leaders, eager to see the party again an effective force in American life, were encouraged, in 1937, by Roosevelt's reverses in Congress and by the government's problems with labor. Some of them also saw the recession of that year as an omen that the President would fall from public favor.

To Landon, unity was the basic requirement for an improvement in Republican fortunes. He felt strongly, at the beginning of 1937, that he was the moderator of the party, that he must not line up publicly with any one faction of the party, that he had to "be true" to the millions who had voted for him. The Kansan further believed that the party had to serve as the nation's watchdog, and must be "fearless, plain-spoken and intelligent" in its opposition. It must insist on an accurate accounting of public funds and help bring about a realistic understanding of the government's proposals. Because Republicans

[21] Landon to Frank Altschul, September 7, 1937; Landon to William Hard, October 9, 11, 1937.

also had to appeal to a larger number of voters, Landon strove to make his party more representative of American life: the old guard had to be subdued, the party organization liberalized, westerners given a bigger part in program development, and the Negro vote recaptured. Landon was particularly concerned about the long-term, old guard control of the party in the east, which he believed could be solved by changing legislators and party officials more often. He lent his weight, especially in New York state, to efforts in that direction—which soon bore fruit with the resignation of Charles D. Hilles as national committeeman and the retirement of minority leader Bertrand H. Snell from the House of Representatives.[22]

Landon, who looked to the Republican national committee to coordinate the party's efforts, had not been completely satisfied with John D. M. Hamilton's service, and had been particularly displeased by his reluctance to make use of liberals during the 1936 campaign. But Landon shuddered to think who might take over—and how his influence on the national committee's operations would be affected— if Hamilton lost the chairmanship. Landon tried to strengthen the national committee headquarters, and his personal influence, by maneuvering William Castle and William Hard into important staff positions. Landon's relationship with Hamilton did not improve, and one of their first post-election clashes occurred early in 1937 over finances and organizational efforts. Because the party (despite its large 1936 campaign fund) had incurred a campaign debt of more than $900,000, Landon urged Hamilton to assume sponsorship of the Republican Lincoln Day dinners as a fund-raising device, but Hamilton decided against this; the chairman thought the state organizations would want part of the proceeds and his advisers had said that large contributors might use their donations to the dinners as an excuse for refusing to give more substantial amounts to the party. By March, other efforts were finally undertaken to liquidate the debt, with Landon, the first contributor, giving $1,000. Landon, however, was disappointed that the national committee had not used the Lincoln Day dinners for raising money and for appealing directly to rank-and-file Republicans, and chided Hamilton because he had

[22] Landon to John D. M. Hamilton, January 16, March 25, 1937; Harold B. Johnson to Landon, January 13, 1937; Landon to William Hard, June 18, 1937; Landon to Joe E. Dunne, January 21, 1937; Landon to L. C. Dyer, August 25, 1937; Landon to Johnson, February 22, 1937; Landon to Frank Altschul, February 23, 1937.

thought the national chairman had also been convinced of the wisdom of a wide organizational appeal and would undertake it immediately.[23]

In June, 1937, there was considerable agitation to force Hamilton to resign; he had come under fire for an alleged lack of executive ability, for his marital difficulties, and for "abandoning" his post to take a trip (reportedly accompanied by a valet) to Great Britain to study the organization of the Conservative party. Although Landon thought Hamilton had shown poor judgment in several activities, he defended him against his critics, and upon Hamilton's return he suggested that they talk things over. Hamilton went to Topeka on July 29 to confer with Landon, but little came of this—only a statement on the "good future" that awaited the Republican party.[24] Landon continued to back Hamilton because (as wrote the national chairman) "it is imperative that we should preserve the appearance of harmony and unity within the party," but he made it clear he thought Hamilton was not keeping in close touch with the national committee members and that it was not the business of the national chairman "to be continually discussing national issues."[25]

Landon's disagreements with Hamilton, however, were not as serious as his disputes with Herbert Hoover. In April, Hoover suggested that a convention of Republican leaders be held in June to draw up policies for party members. The convention was to be made up of Republicans who had been national convention delegates, state chairmen, or congressional or gubernatorial nominees between 1932 and 1936. Hamilton asked Landon if he would sign a letter, along with other Republican leaders, calling for this convention, and Landon replied that he could not accept the idea because it would result in a convention of "ghosts from the boneyard." Hamilton advised him that if he did not endorse the convention idea its proponents would take the leadership of the party away from him. Landon said: "All right, tell them to go ahead, if they can." Although Landon favored a gathering, he wanted one that was representative of the party, off the record, and small enough to permit a candid discussion of party

[23] *Baltimore Sun*, March 9, 1937; Landon to John D. M. Hamilton, December 30, 1936; January 26, 21, April 16, 27, 1937.

[24] Landon to Lacy Haynes, June 16, 1937; Landon to William Hard, June 23, 30, July 10, 1937; Hard to Landon, June 21, 28, 1937; *Topeka Capital*, July 30, 1937.

[25] Landon to John D. M. Hamilton, October 28, 1937. For a view of Hamilton's national chairmanship that is more favorable than Landon's, see Karl A. Lamb, "John Hamilton and the Revitalization of the Republican Party, 1936–1940," *Papers of the Michigan Academy of Science, Arts, and Letters*, vol. XLV (1960).

policies—not a big, highly publicized convention open to domination by a clique. When Hoover was told of Landon's position, he replied that the matter might as well be dropped for the time being.[26] Landon, skeptical that "the time being" would be very long, discussed Hoover's mid-term convention idea with former Treasury Secretary Ogden Mills and was pleased to learn Mills had told Hoover that he opposed it.

Landon was certain the convention idea was part of a plan to enable Hoover—and the old guard—to regain control of the party, a conviction that was bolstered by the "revive Hoover" movement attempted by Hoover's former Secretary of Agriculture, Arthur M. Hyde of Missouri. During the spring Hyde had written letters to Republicans declaring that only Hoover could repair the party's defeatism and disruption—which was interpreted by some as an endeavor to remove Landon from the higher party councils and to advance Hoover for the Presidency in 1940. Although Landon and Hoover were not openly battling each other, their political associates were obviously maneuvering for positions of strength within the party. Concrete issues also were involved, for Hoover did not like the strategy of silence and had been the only major Republican leader to speak out on the Court issue. It was also said that he was flatly opposed to a coalition with anti-Roosevelt Democrats.[27]

Landon thought Hoover's activity was further evidence of the former President's "childish inclination to make himself the center of every incident, whether trivial or major." Toward the end of June, after Hyde had discussed the convention proposal publicly, Landon again tested the party sentiment, and in July he went to Chicago—at Hill Blackett's invitation—to confer with leaders from Illinois and other midwestern states on developing opposition to Hoover. He also asked Knox to confer with him privately, and Knox consented, though he wrote his wife: "I will do a heavy job of listening. I have no slightest intention of getting involved in any partnership with Landon."[28] But Knox, despite himself, was headed for another partnership with Landon.

[26] Landon to John D. M. Hamilton, April 27, November 3, 1937; Landon to George H. Mayer, November 17, 1960; Hamilton to Landon, May 6, 1937; Landon to Arthur H. Vandenberg, June 24, 1937.

[27] Landon to William Hard, May 10, 1937; Landon to Arthur Calvert Smith, May 14, 1937; *Des Moines Register*, June 10, 1937; *Buffalo Evening News*, June 10, 1937.

[28] Landon to Lacy Haynes, June 23, 1937; Landon to Arthur H. Vandenberg, June 24, 1937; Frank Knox to Annie Knox, July 19, 1937, Frank Knox Papers, Manuscript Division, Library of Congress, Washington, D.C.

Before and during the Chicago meeting, Landon was strongly urged by his friends to speak out publicly, in part to counter Hoover and in part to give the party direction. Consequently, Landon made preparations to take to the stump immediately after the adjournment of Congress. Draft after draft of a radio speech to the "seventeen million Republicans" was made, but until early in autumn Landon went no further than to make a short press statement that criticized President Roosevelt for his "tricky scheme in springing the Court proposal on the people without having discussed it in the campaign." [29] The Kansan still hoped that antagonism between Roosevelt and his Democratic opponents in Congress would result in an irreparable split in the Democratic party, and he feared that any outpouring of Republican oratory would prevent such a breach. "I have not yet seen," he wrote in September, "where we have lost anything by continuing to follow Fabian tactics." Meanwhile, on August 9, Hoover had repeated his assertion, this time publicly, that a special Republican convention should be held to revive the party and to prepare for the 1938 elections. Since April, he had traveled all over the country, urging the idea in meetings with Republican leaders. Landon condemned it in his correspondence, adding that Hoover's convention would exclude the party's most ardent supporters, the Young Republicans and the Women Republicans. Also, Landon compared Hoover's convention idea with the Springfield "grass roots convention" of 1935, which in its planning stages had sounded wonderful but which turned out to be dominated by the old guard. [30]

By September, Frank Knox also had become alarmed by the continued talk of a mid-term convention; he too feared that Hoover wanted to control the party, or get the Republican nomination in 1940. Within the party, however, there was a softening of resistance to the convention idea. Hamilton wrote Landon that national committeeman Harrison E. Spangler of Iowa appeared to be working successfully among his fellow committeemen for the proposed meeting. To William Hard, who was beginning to think some kind of a Republican gathering was inevitable, Landon wrote that he still could not see the value of a convention, and that the Republican congressional leaders opposed it.

[29] William Hard to Landon, July 7, 23, 1937; Arthur Calvert Smith to Landon, July 23, 1937; *New York Times*, September 25, 1937.

[30] Landon to W. T. Mossman, August 27, 1937; Landon to William Hard, September 13, 1937; *Pittsburgh Press*, August 9, 1937; Landon to Harold B. Johnson, August 14, 20, 1937.

A mass convention would not have any authority and would be dominated by those who have expense money to attend. . . . What we want is a quiet, efficient building up of our local organizations. We want to urge the state chairmen to see that the lists are purged of disloyal precinct committeemen who supported Roosevelt both in '32 and '36. . . . If you had a Republican convention, who would you have on the front row on the platform? Pat Hurley, Jim Watson, George Moses, Herbert Hoover. Read 'em and weep.[31]

Formal consideration of the mid-term convention proposal began on September 23, when an attempt was made to get the executive committee of the Republican national committee to recommend the convention proposal favorably to the entire national committee. Before the executive committee met, John Hamilton claimed authorship of the idea, apparently in an effort to allay opposition to it. Nevertheless, after four hours of debate the chairman of the Republican congressional campaign committee, Joseph W. Martin, Jr.—with the help of several others—persuaded the executive committee merely to refer the convention proposal to the national committee for consideration.[32]

Probably as a result of this standoff, Hoover decided to discuss the issue directly with Landon, and a copy of a telegram, secretive in tone, was sent to Landon from Sinnissippi Farm, Frank Lowden's country seat, indicating that Hoover would like to talk confidentially with Landon, with Lowden serving as the mediator. Landon was not opposed to meeting Hoover, and Lowden therefore made arrangements for Landon and Hoover to meet with him at Sinnissippi on October 3. The only thing the three men were able to agree upon was set forth in Lowden's carefully worded but meaningless statement: "The three of us canvassed the national crisis at great length, and we find ourselves in agreement on every essential problem, both of the country and the party."[33]

As for the proposed convention, however, the three men apparently came away with divergent understandings of what had been said. Landon has contended that he agreed to go along with the convention if he could name its temporary chairman and all of the members of the

[31] Frank Knox to Annie Knox, September 10, 1937, Knox Papers; Knox to Landon, October 9, 1937; John D. M. Hamilton to Landon, September 1, 1937; William Hard to Landon, September 10, 1937; Landon to Hard, September 13, 1937.

[32] *New York Times*, September 24, 1937; Henry P. Fletcher to Landon, October 20, 1937.

[33] Larry [probably Lawrence Richey, Hoover's aide] to Arch W. Shaw, September 24, 1937; Landon to William Hard, November 4, 1937; *New York Times*, October 13, 1937.

resolutions committee—to which, the Kansan thought, Hoover consented.[34] Lowden's impression was that Landon and Hoover agreed on a convention that would be dominated by the Republican members of Congress and composed not only of recent Republican congressional and gubernatorial nominees but also a number of public and party officials on the state and local levels. According to Lowden, they also reached substantial agreement on a policy committee made up of Landon, Hoover, Lowden, Knox, Vandenberg, and possibly Borah, and any others these men would choose.[35] That Hoover did not interpret the conversations in the same way as Landon or Lowden was indicated by subsequent events; Hoover, when he called Frank Knox to try to secure his support, said Landon had agreed to the convention without reservation.

When Landon heard of this, he reversed his agreement with the former President, reverting to the position that he and Representative Joseph Martin, the leader of Republican congressional opposition to the convention, had developed in late September: support of a study committee rather than the proposed convention. Landon, after telling the press that he had not agreed to the convention, sounded Frank Knox and Senator Vandenberg out on the study committee idea, which they approved. Vandenberg's lack of enthusiasm for the convention, which Hoover still pursued, was typical of most Republican senators and representatives. Vandenberg considered a mid-term convention inadvisable because a declaration of opposition to Roosevelt, and principles to match—issued two years before the next presidential election—would be premature. Moreover, it would not help in the congressional elections of 1938, which would center mostly on local issues.[36]

As the struggle developed, other Republican leaders also began to oppose Hoover. Former national chairman Henry P. Fletcher, Senator Styles Bridges of New Hampshire, Hoover's former Secretary of Labor James J. Davis (at the time a senator from Pennsylvania), Senator Arthur Capper, Senate minority leader Charles L. McNary, and

---

[34] Landon to George H. Mayer, November 17, 1960; Landon interview, January 23, 1962.

[35] William T. Hutchinson, *Lowden of Illinois: The Life of Frank O. Lowden* (Chicago: University of Chicago Press, 1957), II, 724 ff.

[36] Landon to George H. Mayer, November 17, 1960; Landon interview, January 23, 1960; *New York Times*, September 26, October 13, 1937; Landon to Joseph W. Martin, October 5, 1937; Arthur H. Vandenberg to Landon, October 9, 1937.

Senator Borah joined forces with Landon, Martin, Vandenberg, and Knox. Landon was pleased with the reception the study committee proposal was getting, despite reports that the majority of the national committeemen favored the mid-term convention.[37] Nevertheless, Landon was increasingly disturbed by the effects of Hoover's persistence on the convention issue: it was not only confusing and dividing Republicans, it was also causing people who might desert Roosevelt to support him because they preferred the New Deal, with all its faults, to a party that might be dominated by Hoover. Landon heard that Hoover had spent $80,000 for political purposes since the election and had visited sixteen states that summer. He feared that Hoover was out to control the party, or was pursuing the 1940 presidential nomination—at the expense of party unity and of any success in appealing to anti-Roosevelt Democrats. Certainly it was a harmful diversion for Republicans at a time when Roosevelt was under attack for his Court-packing plan, the recession, labor strife, his quarantine speech, and his Supreme Court appointment of Hugo Black, a former Ku Klux Klan member.[38]

Landon, meanwhile, decided to hold his own convention—a "convention of 17 million Republicans." On short notice, arrangements were made for him to broadcast a speech nationally on October 19, although the speech had been in preparation since early February, when the President's Court plan was announced (Landon's 1936 speech aides, Arthur Calvert Smith, Sherwin Badger, and Ralph Robey, had been working on it for several months). Landon dominated his "convention." He even failed to send copies of the radio speech to the national committee headquarters for distribution. When William Hard complained that the headquarters was embarrassed by the situation, Landon answered: "I quite appreciate it was embarrassing to you; but frankly, the National Headquarters so completely ignores us that we never thought of sending them anything."[39]

The October 19 radio performance—despite its preparations—did not mark a brilliant reentry on the national political stage. Landon's

[37] Henry P. Fletcher to Landon, October 20, 1937; Landon to Joseph W. Martin, November 1, 1937; James J. Davis to Landon, October 18, 1937; *New York Times*, November 23, 1937.

[38] Landon to Arthur Calvert Smith, October 12, 1937; Landon to Don Berry, October 14, 1937; Landon to William Hard, October 11, 1937.

[39] William Hard to Landon, October 19, 1937; Landon to Hard, October 22, 1937.

delivery was flat, and he occasionally hemmed and hawed; moreover, the speech was negative, and dealt with a bewildering variety of topics —except, of all things, the current economic recession. Landon recited at length the case against Roosevelt's Court plan, and urged adherence to the Constitution. He also explained that his long silence was required so as to eliminate partisan consideration of the Court plan. What the President needed was less power and more administrative ability— new advisers, drawn from both the Democratic and Republican parties. Social security was unworkable in its present form—so was the Wagner Act—so were the New Deal tax measures. Roosevelt had allowed the labor strike situations to get out of hand because he had not sought genuine collective bargaining. He should have presented Justice Black's entire background, including his alleged Ku Klux Klan membership, when he appointed him. The President had been rushing the nation into foreign entanglements that could lead to war. After proclaiming agreement with the basic goals of the administration —which, presumably, were recovery, relief, and reform—Landon arrived at his two main points: (1) The President had refused to try to achieve his objectives Constitutionally; and (2) "Mr. Roosevelt asks for more power, and still more power, to accomplish his purposes. As long as he uses lack of power as an alibi we will never make any real progress. Most of the mistakes he has made have been because he has been given too much power."[40]

The speech had been given, and Landon was on record and back in the headlines. He had also asserted his claim to party leadership. Although he had made no Democratic friends with the speech, he had reminded Republicans that they were Republicans and of what they were to fight against. He had abandoned the strategy of letting the Democrats fight among themselves because he had concluded that the prospects for a coalition party in the near future had faded. Moreover, Republicans could not be silent for four years.

In some quarters Landon's speech was viewed as a bid for re-nomination. After the 1936 election Landon had said that he would not run again, and again he assured his friends that he did not intend to run; he had "no illusions . . . as to any possibility of renomination." Indeed, the Kansan thought there was far too much talk of the 1940 presidential nomination.[41]

Landon expanded on this idea in a letter to—among others—the

[40] *St. Louis Post-Dispatch*, October 21, 1937; Landon speech, October 19, 1937.

[41] Landon to Harold B. Johnson, October 26, 1937; Landon to Lacy Haynes, October 25, 1937.

Washington correspondent of the *Buffalo Evening News*, James L. Wright. " I have no more idea of being nominated in 1940 than of seeing Hoover nominated. It will probably be either Vandenberg or a Democrat." Hoover, Landon believed, was becoming "the dominant figure in the Republican party," and the Kansan deplored this because of the unfavorable opinions most people held about the former President. "I think he undoubtedly will be able to dominate the activities of the Republican Party because he has both the time and the money to spend at it; while I have neither in the amount that he has." Landon suggested a reason for Hoover's recent activities: "Mr. Hoover was mad all through the last campaign because we did not defend his administration."

The Kansan was further irritated as Hoover apparently began to seek national publicity. A week after Landon's speech, Hoover followed with a radio address of his own, which borrowed one of Landon's lines in calling for "new blood and new faces." *Life* magazine, treating the former President kindly, saw him as offering principles and a program in addition to being against the administration. Hoover's speech was also seen as a rebuke of Landon.[42]

Landon, it was evident, would not let Hoover proceed with the mid-term convention idea without opposition. Landon made it clear to the members of the national committee (a week before its meeting on November 5) that he wanted a policy committee instead of a convention. Then, if a policy committee should be established, Landon wanted the House and Senate minority leaders to have the right of veto over the committee so that Republicans in Congress would not be embarrassed by the committee. He also wanted a representative intermediate committee that would select the policy committee members, especially since the latter would presumably be asked to report to the Republican national committee on the advisability of a national convention in 1938. Landon thought that if the national committee called a mid-term convention, that convention should concretely state the Republican position on measures pertaining to agriculture, labor, unemployment, tariffs, and silver and gold purchases. Conversely, it should avoid issues on which the party's stand was well-established: executive usurpation of legislative power, attempted control of the judiciary, and excessive regulation of the economy.[43]

[42] Landon to James L. Wright, October 25, 1937; *Life*, November 8, 1937, p. 73.
[43] Landon to R. B. Creager, October 29, 1937; John D. M. Hamilton to Landon, November 1, 1937.

Although it was obvious that Landon's demands were obstructionist in nature, national chairman Hamilton, on November 2, used them as the basis for a counterproposal. Hamilton's compromise contemplated the establishment of a policy committee composed of at least 100 members, who would be representative of all party elements, including the Young Republicans and the Women Republicans. Frank Lowden, after consultation with congressional leaders, would appoint most of the members, and the national committee could designate additional members. The policy committee, once appointed, would consider the major issues before the country and report its conclusions to the national chairman, who would forward the report to a national Republican conference (a euphemism for a mid-term convention).

Hamilton would also ask that a committee on arrangements for a national conference be established; Hamilton would be chairman of this committee, and would appoint its twenty-five members after consultation with Republican congressional leaders and the executive committee of the national committee. The arrangements committee, besides determining the time and place of the meeting, would determine the method for selecting the membership of the national conference. Hamilton asserted the need for a national conference so as to point up the significance of the policy committee's work—it was one thing to report to the national committee chairman and another thing to report to the chairman *and* a national party conference.[44] Landon, who refused to accept Hamilton's compromise, took the position that the national committee could do as it pleased.

Hamilton's proposal showed that the convention—or conference—advocates were uneasy; moreover, the strength of their adversaries had steadily increased, in reaction to Hoover's efforts. Frank Knox wrote that even Lowden felt the party was in danger of becoming "Hooverized." As the national committee members arrived in Chicago for their regular meeting on November 4, they were cannonaded by statements of opposition to a convention *or* a conference, by sources ranging from the conservative chairman of the Senate campaign committee, John Townsend, to the party's unpredictable radical, William E. Borah. The *Chicago Daily News* ran a two-column, front-page editorial by Colonel Knox that predicted disaster for the party if the convention were approved and held. That evening, led by Henry P.

44 John D. M. Hamilton to Landon, November 2, 1937.

Fletcher, the executive committee members who were in opposition to the convention idea forced a compromise—the recommendation that only a policy committee be established.[45] The airing of the issue, largely forced by Landon, had led to this compromise.

On November 5 the Republican national committee, substantially following the recommendation of its executive committee, created a "Committee on Program for the consideration of pertinent policies and issues of government." The new committee was to be composed of not less than 100 members, chosen by the national committee's executive committee after consultation with Republican members of Congress and other leading Republicans. The program committee was to "ascertain as fully as possible the various views held by the rank and file of the Republican party, its national and local leaders including auxiliaries of men, women and youth, upon such questions as may properly come before it for consideration." It was added, in an attempt to save face, that the committee was to report its recommendations to the national chairman, who would call a meeting of the national committee "to determine the most effective and practical manner, whether by a national general forum, conference or otherwise, of presenting such report for the consideration of the nation."

Hoover had been rebuffed and Hamilton embarrassed. Landon, however, did not emerge from the dispute with any feelings of victory; he viewed the decision of the national committee as a delaying action: "The convention idea was sidetracked for the time being. They had the skids all greased and I presume will try to put it over again later on next spring. But I believe the opposition is growing."[46]

Although it did not determine his basic position on the matter, Landon was irritated that Hoover had not originally consulted him on the mid-term convention proposal, and he was disappointed that John Hamilton had not fully confided his views. Landon wrote William Hard, Hamilton's assistant, that he realized his chief was under great pressure from Hoover (who, Landon thought, was not Hamilton's friend) and various big contributors, but he hoped Hamilton would

[45] Frank Knox to Annie Knox, November 5, 1937, Knox Papers; *Chicago Daily News*, November 4, 1937; *New York Times*, November 5, 1937.

[46] *New York Times*, November 6, 1937; "Resolution Adopted by the Republican National Committee, November 5, 1937" (mimeograph); Landon to Gomer T. Davies, November 16, 1937.

come to realize that his true friends were in Kansas. Declaring he held
no grudge against Hamilton, because the important thing was the
"present and the future," Landon said:

> I would be glad if I had no responsibility in party matters other than being
> a back-seat driver, because it costs me time and money that I can ill afford.
> . . . But I do want to do the job that so many expect of me. And I am
> terribly anxious to see John do the job that is expected of him. Neither of
> us can do this unless John appreciates the necessity of working in closer
> touch with me. . . . I really think it should mean more to him than it does
> to me, for after all, he has a more tangible responsibility than I do.

Hard conveyed Landon's comments to Hamilton, who soon wrote
Landon of his plans to make the program committee a truly representative operation, and he asked Landon to nominate people who shared
his views. Hamilton explained that the breakdown in communications
had been unintentional, caused by the press of work.[47]

The rapprochement between Landon and Hamilton was not to last
long; the two men did not see the issues confronting their party in the
same light. Hamilton, however, took pains to solicit Landon's nominations for the program committee and to inform him of the progress
being made in constituting the committee, but Landon suggested only
one man for the committee, Fiorello La Guardia, mayor of New York—
with whom he had little in common. This nomination represented
Landon's concern "that the views of every group in the party shall be
represented. There has been too much tendency on the part of some
to close the door against Republicans whose views they might not agree
with." Landon was urged by many of his friends to accept appointment
to the committee; Henry P. Fletcher, especially, pleaded with him to
do so, for it seemed that Hoover expected to be appointed—and to
have a great deal to do with writing the program. Fletcher was also
alarmed because Hoover was still talking about a mid-term convention.
Landon knew that by staying off the committee he would retain his
freedom of action, and he wanted to avoid being put in a position where
he might be forced to battle publicly with Hoover and Hamilton,
which would of course shatter the appearance of party unity that he
wanted to preserve. Therefore, when on December 16 Hamilton

---

[47] Landon to Frank Altschul, November 5, 1937; Landon to William R. Castle,
November 15, 1937; Landon to William Hard, November 4, 1937; John D. M.
Hamilton to Landon, November 15, 1937.

officially requested him to serve as a member and as honorary chairman, Landon declined.[48]

Although La Guardia was Landon's only nomination for membership on the program committee, he suggested—to Henry Fletcher and others —that several anti-Roosevelt Democrats be named to the committee. Landon also recommended Kenneth Simpson, Will Chadbourne, Harold B. Johnson, and Edwin F. Jaeckle, insurgents against the old guard in New York, and Amos and Gifford Pinchot, Frank E. Gannett, William Allen White, Henry J. Allen, Iowa insurgent Don Berry, Charles P. Taft, Nebraska state chairman Lyle E. Jackson, Wilbur Denious of Colorado, Richard Lloyd Jones of Oklahoma, Henry Haskell of the *Kansas City Star*, Robert P. Bass, ex-Governor Alvan T. Fuller of Massachusetts, and Hearst's general counsel, Francis Neylan, one of the few Hearst men noted for saying no to his employer. These men, and the groups they represented, Landon thought, would not otherwise be considered, because they were either opposed to the old guard or of independent minds. When the final decisions were made, however, the executive committee of the Republican national committee tried not only to secure representation of the various party elements on the program committee but to confer membership on Bass, Gannett, and Amos Pinchot. Moreover, Dr. Glenn Frank, former president of the University of Wisconsin, and William Hard—both of whom were considered to be members of the liberal wing of the party—were appointed committee chairman and secretary, respectively.[49]

The appointments to the program committee, however, were not an insurmountable obstacle to domination of the party by Hoover or by the old guard, nor had the door been closed to a mid-term convention or to Hoover's candidacy as the Republican presidential nominee in 1940. Before the committee's membership was announced, Landon had considered ways of thwarting Hoover's control of the party other than through the program committee or by open attack. He would attend the Washington Gridiron dinner, on December 11, then visit New York, and in both places—in private conferences—he would urge opposition to Hoover and the old guard. He would meet Thomas E. Dewey,

[48] Landon to John D. M. Hamilton, November 23, December 19, 1937; Henry P. Fletcher to Landon, November 23, 1937; Hamilton to Landon, December 16, 1937. Landon to Hamilton, December 19, 1937.

[49] Landon to Henry P. Fletcher, November 16, 1937; Landon to Robert P. Bass, December 6, 1937; *New York Times*, December 17, 1937, January 8, 1938.

already mentioned as a possibility for the 1940 presidential nomination, and lend his support to the young district attorney's attacks on New York's Republican old guard. In Washington, after paying a courtesy call on President Roosevelt, he would attend a dinner at William Castle's, where he would meet with Frank Knox and the Republican congressional leaders to discuss ways of preventing Hoover from using the program committee to seize party leadership. (Knox was also in favor of thwarting Hoover, if only to even the score for having been used as Hoover's ploy during the 1936 convention.) [50]

Landon had still another stratagem in mind, other than private encouragement of opposition to Hoover. Landon and Knox rode together on the train from Chicago, and Landon showed his former running mate his announcement that he would not be a candidate for the presidential nomination in 1940, and would decline the nomination if it were offered him. Knox approved the statement. On December 10, in a Washington press conference, responding to the question "What about 1940?" Landon said his actions were frequently thought to be motivated by ambition.

> For that reason, and because personalities frequently confuse the clear-cut consideration of problems, especially in politics, I am glad to answer that question without any equivocation: I will not be a candidate in 1940 and I will not accept the nomination in the remote contingency that the Republican national convention would offer it to me.
>
> I say this with full regard and appreciation of the honor in it, but I feel it incumbent on me to take this position in order to keep the faith with the millions who have trusted me with their confidence.
>
> A man who is in the position of being suspected of being either an active or a receptive candidate cannot render the service to his party or to his country that I conceive to be a patriotic duty in the critical situation that now confronts us.

Knox wrote to his wife: "It puts Hoover on a spot and there can be but one interpretation if he refuses to follow suit at once." Knox thereupon made an equally blunt statement disavowing his candidacy for the 1940 nomination.[51]

[50] Landon to Frank Altschul, December 6, 1937; W. T. Mossman to Landon, December 2, 1937; *New York Times*, December 11, 1937; Frank Knox to Annie Knox, December 10, 1937, Knox Papers.
[51] Landon press statement, Washington, D.C., December 10, 1937; Frank Knox to Annie Knox, December 10, 1937, Knox Papers; *New York Herald Tribune*, December 12, 1937.

The press reaction was favorable. The *New York Herald Tribune* welcomed the Landon and Knox statements, saying they cleared the air. The *Chicago Tribune* interpreted the move as an invitation that Hoover take himself out of the running. The Kansan's withdrawal, according to the *Des Moines Register*, allowed the Republican party to concentrate on important issues of policy. The Democratic *Louisville Courier-Journal*, and Arthur Krock in the *New York Times*, compared Landon's forthright statement to General Sherman's in 1880. The *Los Angeles Times*, though never a great admirer of Landon, said "Landon's withdrawal, to large numbers among his 17 million supporters of 1936, will be an occasion for regret." [52]

Landon's statement and covert opposition to Hoover undoubtedly blunted the effectiveness of the former President's political weapons and helped keep the way open, in the years ahead, for the new leadership in the Republican party that Landon wanted.

Foreign policy became an important factor in the maneuvers for position within the Republican party when, on December 13, 1937, Japanese airplanes sank the United States gunboat *Panay* and two other American vessels in China's Yangtze River. The United States government immediately demanded an apology and explanation for these unprovoked attacks, but national reaction to the incident was mixed. Representative Louis Ludlow of Indiana had recently proposed an amendment to the Constitution that would require (except for an invasion of the United States) a national referendum before the nation could declare war. Such an amendment, of course, would have crippled an administration in its conduct of foreign relations, but the Ludlow proposal, riding a high tide of pacifism, rapidly gained support from congressmen of all parties.

Landon was alarmed to discover that the entire Kansas delegation in the House of Representatives—five Republicans and two Democrats —had signed a petition (which was later successful) to discharge the Ludlow resolution from committee. Moreover, thousands of Topeka citizens were signing petitions urging the withdrawal of American forces from China. On December 19, after Senator Capper in a radio address urged adoption of the war referendum, Landon concluded it was risky to weaken the President's hand, especially at a time when his

[52] *New York Herald Tribune*, December 12, 1937; *Chicago Tribune*, December 11, 1937; *Des Moines Register*, December 12, 1937; *Louisville Courier-Journal*, December 11, 1937; *New York Times*, December 22, 1937, *Los Angeles Times*, December 13, 1937.

administration was trying to impress the Japanese government with the seriousness of sinking an American naval vessel. He decided to support Roosevelt in defeating the referendum proposal because there was no "surer way to war than to give the bullies of the world an idea we will not fight under any circumstances." [53] Landon drafted a telegram, consulted with Roy Roberts and a few other friends on its contents, and then sent it to the White House, on Monday afternoon, December 20. At 6 p.m. the telegram from Topeka was read by the President's press secretary, Stephen T. Early.

Referring to his statement at the Gridiron Club in 1936 that "politics end at the water's edge," Landon said:

> It means there must be no demagogic playing of politics at the expense of the country's unity in dangerous situations as now confront us.
>
> Therefore I want to renew my pledge, especially in view of the fact that so many members of Congress, of both parties, seem to have forgotten this basic principle of American politics and by their actions help create the impression on foreign nations that they do not trust your administration of foreign affairs. They would hamstring your conduct of extremely delicate foreign situations.
>
> These members are pursuing the same dangerous course followed by those members of the British Parliament who early in 1914 gave the impression that England either would not or could not fight under any circumstances.
>
> I congratulate you on your firm NO to the proposed legislation that would take away the power of Congress to declare war. You and I both know the American people want peace, but they want a peace that will enable us to maintain the respect of the other nations of the world. [54]

Roosevelt was surprised and gratified by the message, and he replied to Landon the next morning.

> The generous spirit of your telegram helps me to meet the problems which confront our country in the field of foreign relations during these troubled times.
>
> The pledge which you gave at the Gridiron dinner a year ago carried force because of the patriotic motive which prompted it. The renewal of that pledge not only strengthens the hand of government but gives all of our citizens a good example.

Soon after the President's telegram was sent, the White House telephoned to ask if Landon would object if the two telegrams were

[53] Landon to E. G. Bennett, January 12, 1938.
[54] Landon to Franklin D. Roosevelt, December 20, 1937, Franklin D. Roosevelt Library, Hyde Park, N.Y.

published, and Landon responded that it could do anything it wished. The telegrams were shown to Secretary of State Cordell Hull, who agreed that they should be given to the press at once.[55]

Newspaper reaction was generally favorable. The *Louisville Courier-Journal* called Landon "a broadminded patriot." The *Washington Post* wrote that Landon "serves timely warning on those foreign powers which are banking strongly on American isolationism." The *St. Louis Post-Dispatch*, re-enamored of its 1936 hero, declared that Landon's telegram would be a strong factor in defeating the Ludlow amendment, a defeat "devoutly to be wished." The *New York Herald Tribune* thought the telegram showed the nation would be as one with Roosevelt on the *Panay* crisis. The Hearstlings were confused: there was no editorial comment, but columnist Isaac Don Levine interpreted the exchange of telegrams as a blunder similar to those that had led to World War I, and George Rothwell Brown viewed Landon's action not only as patriotic but also of value in twitting Hoover.[56]

There were, of course, criticisms. The *Chicago Tribune* noted, with a suggestion of conspiracy, that Landon had visited the President on December 10. Representative Hamilton Fish advised Landon not to interfere with the foreign policy positions taken by Republican members of Congress. Hulbert Taft, of the *Cincinnati Times-Star*, told Landon that his telegram could be used to support an administration decision to send our military forces to fight in the Far East.

Landon was not the only Republican who supported Roosevelt— Frank Knox soon sent a letter to the President in support of his stand on the *Panay* incident, and former Secretary of State Henry Stimson wrote a widely publicized article that opposed the Ludlow amendment.[57] However, the practical results of the Landon-Roosevelt exchange were mixed. The surveys of the Gallup Poll before and after the exchange indicated that an overwhelming number of Americans favored the withdrawal of United States armed forces in China. Nevertheless, with the support of Landon, Knox, and Stimson, and exerting strenuous pressure, Roosevelt was able to secure the defeat of

[55] Franklin D. Roosevelt to Landon, December 21, 1937, FDRL; *Washington Daily News*, December 24, 1937.

[56] *Louisville Courier-Journal*, December 22, 1937; *Washington Post*, December 22, 1937; *St. Louis Post-Dispatch*, December 22, 1937; *New York Herald Tribune*, December 23, 1937; *San Francisco Examiner*, December 25, 24, 1937.

[57] *Chicago Tribune*, December 23, 1937; *New York Herald Tribune*, December 22, 1937; Hulbert Taft to Landon, December 22, 1937; *Louisville Courier-Journal*, December 23, 1937.

the Ludlow amendment in the House of Representatives by a vote of 209 to 188. Moreover, it appeared that the exchange had helped resolve the immediate crisis, for it was reported that Japan took the Landon-Roosevelt telegrams as a representation of national unity on the Far Eastern question. After the exchange, the Imperial headquarters admitted responsibility for the attack on the *Panay* and the Japanese government announced that steps would be taken to prevent the repetition of such an incident.[58]

Although Landon was in the vortex of controversy at the end of 1937, and was neither the country's nor his party's most popular statesman, he was showing some of the qualities that had made people flock to Topeka to see him before his nomination in 1936. As Arthur Krock of the *New York Times* put it: "In his every act and word Mr. Landon has revealed that he is a thoroughbred in the truest sense, an intelligent patriot and a common-sense leader of a political cause." Krock said Landon deserved the highest commendation for his 1936 Gridiron Club statement, his withdrawal from the race for the 1940 presidential nomination, and his telegram to Roosevelt on the *Panay* incident and the Ludlow amendment. "A man of Mr. Landon's unusual quality can put aside ambition, but in so doing he enters automatically upon a higher plane of leadership."[59]

[58] Hadley Cantril (ed.), *Public Opinion, 1935–1946* (Princeton: Princeton University Press, 1951), p. 1074; *New York Times*, December 23, 25, 1937; *Congressional Record*, 75th Cong., 3d sess., appendix, LXXXIII, 204.

[59] *New York Times*, December 22, 1937.

CHAPTER 16

A Practical Liberal ?

Landon's actions during the latter part of 1937 disturbed many Republicans. His support of Roosevelt on the *Panay* and Ludlow questions and his refusal actively to support the Republican program committee led many to conclude that his positions were divisive of the party's strength. Some Republicans even charged that he might desert the party for a place in Roosevelt's cabinet. Landon scoffed at the idea of a position in Roosevelt's cabinet, which he said he would not accept. As for the program committee, Landon still viewed it, despite its membership, as an attempted tour de force against the liberals and the younger leaders of the party.[1] Moreover, he used his aloofness to forestall the party from writing a mid-term platform, an action that would be "the height of stupidity" because it could help unite the Democrats behind the President.

As Landon saw it, the chief issue before the country was the fight for power between "the spirit of the Anglo-Saxon people" and those "whose racial heritage and background is not the village moot, but who only admire power, ruthless power, and the nerve to wield it." Although this was a jot of racism that occasionally cropped up in his letters in the mid-1930s, it was well-meant. Landon's wish was that

[1] Verne Marshall to Landon, January 8, 18, 1938; Willard Mayberry to Landon, January 6, 1938; Landon to George Sibley, January 11, 1938; Alfred M. Landon Papers, Kansas State Historical Society, Topeka.

those—presumably of non-Teutonic origin—who esteemed the exercise of raw power would come to value the traditions he connected with the Anglo-Saxon village moot. For the present, however, he thought that the issue between democracy and political power might split the Democratic party, with the result that a majority coalition would be formed of Republicans and Democrats—liberals, moderates, and conservatives—who feared the New Deal's fiscal policies and its loose construction of the Constitution. Because he thought such a Constitutionalist coalition would be dominated by liberals and moderates, he believed it could offer the voters real economic progress and still preserve the best of America's traditions.[2]

While Landon dreamed of a coalition that was never to be, he was still the titular head of the Republican party, and he received all kinds of requests for assistance and advice. Advice the Kansan gave freely, but assistance was limited by his inclinations. He encouraged party liberals and moderates to participate in organizational activities in their states, and he even volunteered to lend an Iowa faction the services of his secretary, Carl Rott. To those who, disappointed with John Hamilton, urged Landon to assume the national committee chairmanship, Landon replied that though he had willingly made sacrifices to work for the party, the national chairmanship would be too great a sacrifice. Five years' absence from business affairs—and his inability even in 1937 to give them the time they required—had weakened his financial position: "I could not afford to take the national chairmanship without a salary and I could not afford to take it with a salary."[3]

Although Landon became more active in Republican affairs during 1938, his relations with the national committee headquarters deteriorated. Between December, 1937, and March, 1938, Landon and Hamilton did not write to each other (Landon was not asked by the national chairman to speak on Lincoln Day, and as a result did not accept other invitations). When Hamilton wrote, on March 2, to solicit Landon's support in raising funds, he received the terse reply: "Not able to make any contribution at this time to the Republican National

[2] Landon to E. G. Bennett, January 12, 1938; Landon to J. Reuben Clark, December 21, 1937.

[3] Landon to Thomas E. Dewey, February 2, March 22, 1938, Thomas E. Dewey Papers, University of Rochester Libraries, Rochester, N.Y.; Landon to William A. Sheaffer, January 10, 1938; Sheaffer to Landon, December 30, 1937; Landon to Frank E. Gannett, January 12, 1938.

Committee."[4] Thereafter, the correspondence between Landon and Hamilton was infrequent and usually inconsequential.

Landon became most actively involved in Republican politics early in 1938 in Pennsylvania, where he privately encouraged Gifford Pinchot's effort to reclaim the Pennsylvania governorship—against the opposition of the Pew-Grundy group. This plunged Landon into the most serious intraparty difficulty he was to encounter during 1938. Although the controversial Pennsylvania progressive Republican said he was confident of success in the primary election, in April Mrs. Pinchot—and later Pinchot himself—asked Landon for a public statement of support; Landon refused Mrs. Pinchot, but he apparently promised Pinchot that he would make a statement in his favor. Before Landon could make his statement, however, the Pennsylvania primary contest took a bitter turn, first one faction and then the other disparaging the purity of the other's Republicanism. Although Landon wanted to proclaim himself on Pinchot's side, he was dissuaded from this by Lacy Haynes, who thought his interference would help neither himself nor Pinchot. On Haynes' advice, then, Landon tried to soothe the antagonists. Late in April, he wired the *Harrisburg Telegraph*:

> There is no doubt of the loyalty of either [faction] to the issues the Republican party stands for. The country needs united leadership of all Republicans and I am sure after the primary is over personal interests will be forgotten in the complete unity for a crusade to restore decent government.[5]

Landon wrote Pinchot, apologizing for the telegram: "It didn't contain the 'red meat' which I know you wanted and which I promised. But as I watched the developments of the Democratic row, I became increasingly convinced that the kind of a telegram which I sent would do you more good." Landon believed that Pinchot's real fight would be in November, and that his strongest support should be reserved for the general campaign in order to get full party backing for Pinchot at that time. He urged Pinchot, after his anticipated nomination, to "start healing the wounds of the party in a natural way," and Landon

[4] John D. M. Hamilton to Landon, March 2, 1938; Landon to Hamilton, March 4, 1938.

[5] Landon to Gifford Pinchot, March 2, April 19, 1938; Cornelia Pinchot to Richard Lloyd Jones, April 4, 1938, enclosed in Jones to Landon, April 6, 1938; Landon to Jones, April 9, 1938; Lacy Haynes to W. A. White, April 21, 1938, Lacy Haynes Papers, Kansas State Historical Society, Topeka; Landon to L. W. Sheridan, n.d. (probably late April, 1938).

volunteered to go to Pennsylvania to help the old Progressive do this. But the Kansan offered even more; in an effort to commit Pinchot to the idea of party unity, Landon offered him an opportunity to reach the political heavens:

> I don't think you can appreciate how much I desire your nomination and election. . . . I have already talked to Roy Roberts and William Allen White about the possibility of your nomination for President in 1940, providing you are elected Governor. So I think, both from the point of view of the November election and the point of view of the possibility of your future national leadership and the throat-cutting among the Democrats, you want to be more of a harmony candidate than you have ever been previously. I don't mean by that that you will be what is known in political circles as a harmony candidate. That is impossible as far as you are concerned, and would lessen your strength. But I do want to urge the wisdom of modifying somewhat a vicious intra-party attack.[6]

Landon had planned to visit the east in the latter part of May in order to make several speeches and to perk up the party in preparation for the fall elections. Because he was convinced that Pinchot would win the gubernatorial primary, Landon did not schedule a visit to Pennsylvania, but fresh trouble erupted there when Landon's original backer for the Presidency, Richard Lloyd Jones, made statements on behalf of Pinchot and accused the Pew brothers of losing Pennsylvania for Landon in 1936. James A. Veasy, a mutual friend of the Pews and Landon, asked the Kansan to make a public statement exonerating the Pews. Landon wrote Veasy that he had asked Joseph Pew to use Pinchot in Pennsylvania during the campaign, and that he understood Pew had tried to do so, though without success; but he refused to make a statement in defense of the Pews, probably because he agreed with Jones' charges.[7]

The Pennsylvania situation was aggravated when Pinchot was swamped by his opponent, Arthur H. James, in the primary election. Landon was in an unpleasant position; the victorious Pew faction thought Landon had conspired to remove Pew from the political scene, and Pinchot probably harbored the feeling that Landon, though meaning well, had let him down. Landon authorized Roger W. Straus to telephone Pew and Pinchot and urge them to pull the party together in order to fight the New Deal. Pew answered that Landon, in fighting Hoover, had tried to manipulate the Pennsylvania situation,

---

[6] Landon to Gifford Pinchot, May 7, 1938.

[7] Landon to James A. Veasy, May 12, 1938; Lacy Haynes to W. A. White, April 21, 1938, Haynes Papers.

and that if this continued the Republican party would be crippled in Pennsylvania—a result that would have national repercussions. Straus could only reiterate the argument for party harmony. Landon replied, however, that he had not been fighting Pew, and he added that there was no Landon–Hoover battle, except as Hoover made it appear so to feed his candidacy. (Such a struggle for the Republican party, Landon wrote Duke Shoop of the *Kansas City Star*, "would be like two undertakers fighting over the corpse.")[8] Landon was finally successful in calming Pew, and thereby helped the party in Pennsylvania compose itself enough to win the fall elections.

Landon's only clash with the national administration in early 1938 concerned its wheat policies, which he believed would hurt the farmers of the plains states. The administration had taken the position that there would be great overproduction of wheat in 1938, but the Kansan was persuaded by his contacts among farm experts, agricultural journalists, and grain dealers that this would not be so. In February, Landon wrote Representative Clifford Hope, a member of the House Agriculture Committee, that weather, crop, and world trade conditions pointed to an improved market for American wheat in the months ahead.

> The American farmer is in the saddle for dictating prices. . . . Yet every time the market has tried to advance in these past few months, the Secretary of Agriculture has come out with a statement lamenting our burdensome surpluses. Thus the whole world is being misinformed as to our true conditions. . . . This is not the way to obtain the prices for our wheat and corn to which our farmers are entitled.

Landon contended that Secretary Henry A. Wallace had based his conclusions on acreage reports rather than on crop conditions; although there was a surplus of wheat, it was not a surplus of good bread wheat. Landon wrote similarly to Senator Arthur Capper, in a public letter, adding that Capper should call the President's attention to this situation in order to bring pressure on Wallace to revise the official methods for estimating wheat crops—and to stop his complaints of a wheat surplus. Although Capper said he would pursue the matter with Wallace, he cautioned that the problem was complicated.[9]

[8] Roger W. Straus to Landon, May 31, 1938; Landon to Straus, June 2, 1938; Landon to Duke Shoop, n.d. (probably late May, 1938).

[9] A. W. Erickson to Landon, January 28, 1938; John H. Parker to Landon, February 24, 1938; Landon to Clifford R. Hope, February 7, 1938; *New York Times*, February 17, 1938; Landon to Arthur Capper, February 16, 1938; Capper to Landon, February 23, 1938.

Later in February, Landon received information that there had not been sufficient snow to bring spring wheat production up to the levels estimated by the Department of Agriculture. There was confirmation of this from English sources, including the Liverpool Corn Association and *Broomhall's Corn Trade News*, which contradicted the forecast of the International Wheat Advisory Committee and asserted that a world wheat surplus was unlikely in 1938. Meanwhile, Congressman Hope had replied, implying that Landon had joined the grain dealers' attack upon the government's statistical service. Landon answered that he was not opposed to the service, that he wanted it amplified, and that he objected to the interpretation of data for propaganda purposes —or, as he believed was the case, to aid enactment of the administration's proposals to control surpluses. Landon pointed out that the Bureau of Agricultural Economics had assumed, on January 26, that there was no reason for revising its wheat-production forecast of December 1, 1937—although insufficient rainfall between these two dates precluded a good wheat crop. Landon said, moreover, that he had consulted experts at the Kansas State Agricultural College, who thought his position was "an understatement rather than an overstatement." Landon, having also written to Representative Frank Carlson, had been advised that the issue had to be seen in the context of the battle between the Department of Agriculture and the big grain organizations on new farm legislation. Carlson said further that overt action by Kansans on the wheat surplus issue might jeopardize appropriations for higher parity payments on wheat, and he thought the moisture received in February should increase the wheat harvest.[10]

Landon had the backing of grain dealers, millers, and many farmers in Kansas and Missouri, but he could not move his congressional friends. He wrote Carlson: "Very frankly, I can't understand you chaps. You all seem to be under the spell of Wallace and the Department of Agriculture." Representative Hope, by early March, had abandoned any attempt at diplomacy; he told Landon that he thought the department's statistics were not inaccurate. By late April, Capper had conveyed Secretary Wallace's comments on the matter: although the 1938 crop would be a bit smaller than in 1937, it would exceed the average wheat production of 1932–36 by 160 million bushels; the stock for export and the surplus on hand on February 1 was 243

[10] A. W. Erickson to Landon, February 19, 1938; David G. Page to Landon, February 25, 1938; Clifford R. Hope to Landon, February 23, 1938; Landon to Hope, February 26, 1938; Frank Carlson to Landon, February 26, 1938.

million bushels—70 million bushels more than in the preceding year; and Canadian, Argentinian, and European wheat yields would probably be higher in 1938 than in 1937. Capper said the department must make these estimates, even though they might be inaccurate, so that the grain dealers would be prevented from taking advantage of farmers, and he added that he did not think Wallace had used his information services for political purposes.[11]

Landon and his allies had lost their fight to revise the method of estimating wheat production, having been repulsed by Wallace and by the Kansas congressmen; all that remained was to see who was right. Landon was dead wrong on wheat prices: the Kansas farmer was not "in the saddle" but flat on his back, receiving only 57 cents a bushel—a drop of 44 cents from the previous year and substantially less than at any time since 1932. Landon's only consolation was that the Department of Agriculture had overestimated the size of the 1938 wheat crop. The initial estimate for Kansas had been 220,000,000 bushels, but this had been scaled down (perhaps in response to criticisms) to 163,576,000 bushels, and the actual winter wheat yield was only 149,394,000. Moreover, the quality was low.

Landon, in disgust, wrote that crop reporters all over the state were resigning in protest at the way their figures had been handled; the estimates of one Kansas State College staff member, for example, had been hiked 25 per cent by the Department of Agriculture. Landon attributed these actions to the department's wish to use the fear of big surpluses as a weapon to force legislation of the Agricultural Adjustment Act of 1938. Although he was sincere in his belief that government juggling of crop estimates was an "outrageous shame,"[12] he rarely afterward mentioned that issue.

While still engaged in the wheat issue, Landon took up one of the most admirable fights of his political career—the defense of the right of freedom of speech for the Socialist leader, Norman Thomas. In February, 1938, Landon first spoke out vigorously about freedom of speech in responding to the request of the editor of the University of

[11] Landon to Frank Carlson, February 28, 1938; Clifford R. Hope to Landon, March 4, 1938; "Summary of the Present Wheat Situation, Prepared with Reference to the Landon Criticisms," enclosed in Arthur Capper to Landon, April 22, 1938.

[12] Kansas State Board of Agriculture, *Kansas Agriculture—Centennial Report* (Topeka: State Printer, 1961–62), p. 517; *Topeka Capital*, August 12, 1938; Landon to E. H. Taylor, August 5, 1938.

Kansas student newspaper, the *University Daily Kansan*, for his thoughts about a proposed legislative investigation of alleged Red activities at the university. Landon wrote that

> freedom of speech must permit a man to say what he thinks, although we may not agree with his views, and academic freedom is essential to free speech. The true test of our belief in freedom of speech comes when we listen to someone who expresses views which we abhor, and when we are willing to make the fight to permit the expression of such views.[13]

Some of the state legislators groaned; if the movement for a probe had had any chance of success, Landon's statement had seriously undercut it.

The test of Landon's conviction came in April, when, in Jersey City, New Jersey, Norman Thomas was roughed up, prevented from speaking, and thrown out of the city by the political corporals of Mayor Frank Hague. The Kansan protested immediately. In a public letter to Thomas, he wrote:

> I am shocked at your treatment in Jersey City, and at such a gross violation of our sacred right of free speech.
>
> I do not want this threat of our priceless heritage of freedom to pass without protest on my part. This is not a fancied threat at democracy. It is shocking evidence that even America is not isolated from a rising tide of hate and intolerance. It only illustrates that the oppression and injustice which is so much in evidence under the tyrants of Germany, Italy and Russia is contagious. It is time we recognize our danger. And this incident should draw together all those who have common ideals of freedom and tolerance in order that we may stand united in defense of the principles which lead to peace and security. Our American heritage does not yield complacently to ruthless power and the nerve to wield it.
>
> I am glad to note that you have just begun to fight. I want you to know that I stand shoulder to shoulder with you in this fight for the right of free speech.[14]

Immediately, Landon was flooded with protests, especially because he was the only nationally known Republican or Democratic political leader to speak out in defense of Thomas' right to free speech. In his replies to the critics, Landon reiterated his position, and in a letter to a member of the Kansas senate he warned that no one could be

[13] Landon to Marvin Goebel, February 24, 1938; *Topeka Capital*, February 25, 1938.
[14] Landon to Norman Thomas, May 1, 1938; *New York Times*, May 2, 1938.

trusted to decide who may or may not properly speak. "You can't arbitrarily stamp out social or political views by repression. If that had worked, the Bourbons of France and the Czarists of Russia would still be on the job." Landon also pointed out that he could sympathize with Thomas: "No one has been treated more unfairly than I have been by a lot of [the intellectuals], and by the New Republic and all that group who not only misrepresented my views but my record."[15]

Thomas asked Landon if he would cooperate with a nonpartisan committee in holding a meeting in Jersey City for free speech and assemblage, either on Flag Day or July 4. The Kansan said it was impossible for him to return to the east so soon after his two-week tour of the region (in May), but he was interested in such a meeting, and he asked Roger Straus to keep in touch with developments. Writing Straus "I want to help," he said he would be willing to speak to the meeting from Topeka over a national network if the right group of sponsors could be assembled. Network time could not be arranged,[16] but the issue kept Landon busy for many months. In his May swing around the east he often referred to it, and throughout the summer and into the fall he worked the question into many of his letters and speeches.

The May trip back east was Landon's first extended speaking tour since the 1936 campaign. His main concern was to stimulate interest among Republicans in the approaching mid-term elections, which he thought the national committee—being "broke and busted, higher than a kite"—was not able to do.[17] Landon left Topeka on May 16, and arrived in Chicago the next morning, to speak to the Inland Publishers' Association. He swung into the freedom-of-expression issue with the force of a crusader, relating the question to an attack on the New Deal. The ejection of Norman Thomas from Jersey City and the later denial there of speaking rights to two congressmen showed America was not immune to an international tide that was corroding freedom. Liberty was safe only when everyone—excepting proponents of violence—had the right of free expression. Speaking pointedly to Republicans and anti-Roosevelt Democrats, Landon said: "If we meant what we said in '36 and '37 in praise of the Constitution and of the Supreme Court, and the rights of the minority guaranteed

[15] Landon to Thale P. Skovgard, May 4, 1938.

[16] Norman Thomas to Landon, May 13, 1938; Roger W. Straus to Landon, May 31, 1938; Landon to Straus, June 2, 1938; Landon to Thomas, June 2, 1938.

[17] Landon to Robert H. La Follette, May 4, 1938.

under the Constitution and by the Supreme Court, we must be prepared to grant the right of free speech to those persons who have views we do not share." He warned the newspaper publishers of subtle attacks on freedom of the press, citing the Works Progress Administration's withholding of official information and the bill of Senator Sherman Minton of Indiana for censorship of material that was "proved" false by the government and yet knowingly published. Although he did not believe Congress would take the bill seriously, Landon declared: "Apparently it reflects the New Deal attitude toward the press of the country, and I'm afraid it may reflect the President's attitude. The President's views have, no doubt, encouraged Senator Minton and others."[18]

Immediately after his I.P.A. address, Landon left by automobile for Indiana, where he had hoped to encourage the state's Republicans and anti-New Deal Democrats to join in reelecting Democratic Senator Frederick Van Nuys as an independent candidate and in supporting the Republican nominee for governor. The Kansan saw this as a useful strategy for achieving a Constitutionalist coalition in states where anti-Roosevelt Democratic senators were marked for purging at the polls by the President, but the movement was unsuccessful because the Democrats whom the administration wanted removed decided to stand on their own in their party's primary elections. In Indiana, the chance of a coalition ticket was slim because Van Nuys appeared determined to run as a Democrat, and the state's Republicans —despite the urgings of Landon, Frank Gannett, and Roy Howard— seemed equally set on nominating their own candidate.[19] The situation appeared so hopeless, in fact, that Landon, even before he arrived in Indiana, deleted references to Van Nuys from his speech for the Indiana Governor's Day banquet at Lebanon. Then, before the banquet began, he had to throw away his entire talk—which was to have been a sarcastic commentary on the "Democratic recession" and the White House "boss-type" politics—because the Democratic governor of Indiana refused to attend otherwise. Landon talked extemporaneously, repeating the essence of his Chicago address to the publishers.[20]

Landon's first talk in the east was on May 19 at the Northeast

[18] Landon speech, Chicago, May 17, 1938.

[19] Landon to J. P. Goodrich, March 14, 1938; Landon to Henry P. Fletcher, June 10, 1938; Frank E. Gannett to Landon, May 10, 1938; Landon to Gannett, May 13, 1938.

[20] Landon speech, Lebanon, Ind., May 17, 1938.

Methodist Conference in Lynn, Massachusetts. (He had given an increasing amount of attention to church affairs since he had left public office, serving as a trustee of Baker University and of the Methodist-Episcopal Home for the Aged in Topeka. He had also spoken on a national radio hook-up and at church affairs in the midwest urging the union of the three branches of Methodism in the United States, cooperation with other Protestant sects, and better financial support for the clergy and for the church's educational and welfare programs.) At Lynn, he praised the work of the century-old Boston University Theological School. The church, he said, had a great responsibility in imbuing people with "lofty ideals and high vision." Intensely interested in strengthening the church as a bulwark of morals, Landon said: "If we fail in building character, democracy will fail. And if democracy fails, free religion and a free church, as we know them, are gone too." [21]

Landon also attended three political meetings in Massachusetts and met hundreds of Republican politicians and anti-Roosevelt Democrats. He then went to Vermont, where he fished and chatted with Governor George D. Aiken about strengthening Republican liberalism. Over the weekend the Kansan went to New York for a series of conferences with Republicans, and stayed the night of May 22 at the Waldorf Towers as a guest of Frank Knox. Unexpectedly, Landon and Knox encountered Herbert Hoover the next morning and a consequence of this brief but well-publicized meeting was that many Republicans were relieved, believing the three party leaders had had a harmony meeting. Landon spent several days in New York City; then, on his way upstate, he had "a fine visit" in Pawling with Thomas Dewey. [22]

Urging the need for new blood in the Republican party, Landon spent most of his time in New York State with the younger and insurgent elements, and he encouraged broadening the party to include anti-Roosevelt Democrats. In upstate New York, he visited insurgents Harold Johnson of the *Watertown Times*, Frank E. Gannett at Rochester, and Edwin F. Jaeckle, chairman of the Erie County Republican committee. This emphasis on youth and independence culminated in

[21] *New York Times*, February 6, 1938; Landon speeches, Chicago, February 5, 1938, and Lynn, Mass., May 19, 1938.

[22] Landon to Orie Phillips, June 22, 1938; Daniel L. Marsh to Landon, May 9, 1938; Landon to Sterry Waterman, June 10, 1938; *New York Times*, May 24, 1938; Herbert Hoover to Landon, May 23, 1938; Landon to Hoover, June 2, 1938; Landon to Duke Shoop, n.d. (probably late May, 1938); Landon to Arthur Calvert Smith, May 16, 1938; Landon to D. B. Flemming, June 28, 1938.

the only purely political talk of Landon's tour, in the speech he gave at Niagara Falls to the New York State Young Republican convention on May 28. He exalted youth and enjoined it to work toward putting the millions of jobless back to work, an objective that was central to the solution of the nation's other problems because "people who are hungry think more in terms of bread and butter than political liberty." He was greeted with a roar of approval when he added: "I don't want to be personal about this, but it is too bad we don't have somebody in Washington who can get this job done."

It was because of the unemployed's natural concern with bread and butter, Landon said, that the New Deal had grown strong, but it was deplorable that the administration had taken advantage of that concern to drive toward the dangerous policy of "complete government control of everything." This policy was markedly different from the ideas of Theodore Roosevelt and Woodrow Wilson, the difference being that government now told people what they must do instead of telling them what they could not do. To Landon, the difference marked the arrival of a great basic issue that could "form the foundation for distinct and strong party alignments," and he called for the creation of a Republican Jeffersonian party based on opposition to the concentration of power in the hands of government or private corporations, on respect for property rights and civil liberties, and on dedication to opening the channels of production and distribution in order to raise the living standards of all Americans. This new party could come about if the Republican party resolved "to free this country from all oppressive dictation, whether by bureaucratic official or financier, whether by industrialist or by labor leader, whether by public money or by private money, whether by the force of the militia or by the force of the mob." If the Republican party would take this broad a view of its mission, it could become an effective bulwark against oppression in America.[23]

Although the Young Republicans cheered, neither the Republican leaders nor the Jeffersonian Democrats were enthused, and Landon's idea of an idealistic and moderate party was "buried" in the country's newspapers.

Landon returned home perturbed by political developments within and outside his party. He had been subjected to sharp attacks from fellow Republicans—from conservatives because he had seen Governor Aiken, who was a consistent and outspoken critic of John Hamilton,

[23] *New York Times,* June 28, 30, 1938; Landon speech, Niagara Falls, N.Y., May 28, 1938.

and from liberals because he had seen Hoover. He thought these attacks were unreasonable, but—even worse—they did not augur the party unity that was necessary for the solution of national and world problems, problems that were increasingly alarming. People of all classes seemed reluctant even to try to replace federal aid with programs based on private initiative, and the east seemed to think a new world war was inevitable. The reaction to the freedom-of-speech issue had too often been indifferent, even hostile, and Landon was also alarmed by a swelling of anti-Semitism and "a rising tide of feeling between the haves and the have-nots." All this seemed to be tied in with the "hardening attitudes," the stubbornness that he encountered on his tour. "I find," he wrote, "an increasing tendency on the part of Republicans everywhere to be against the New Deal, horse, foot and baggage, and an increasing tendency on the part of the New Deal not to give an inch." He later wrote that "spiritual and moral leadership" was desperately needed to offset the "apathy and cynicism" of the times.[24]

Although he was convinced that his analysis of the situation was right, he found it necessary to redefine his role in coping with it. Some things were easy to do: he could use whatever influence he had to defend freedom of expression, to protest intolerance at home or abroad, to speak up in church circles on the need for a spiritual and moral leadership, and to deplore unnecessary reliance on government handouts. Yet he was caught in several dilemmas. How could he cooperate with the administration but maintain his position within the Republican party? How could he work effectively toward a more moderate Republican party without seriously impairing the unity of the party? How could he work in opposition to the government policies he deplored and still expect the administration to change them? How could he recruit new voters for his party and yet build confidence in administration circles that he was honestly seeking compromise and cooperation?

It seemed that he could resolve none of these dilemmas. He could only choose a particular course in a specific situation, hoping the advantages would outweigh the disadvantages, while keeping in mind that as titular head of the opposition party he must not destroy that party. He was convinced that the destruction of the Republican party

[24] Landon to Orie Phillips, June 22, 1938; Landon to Richard Lloyd Jones, June 20, 1938; Landon to Frank L. Perrin, June 7, 1938; Landon to Solon H. Wiley, June 17, 1938.

could lead to the loss of the two-party system, and possibly of democracy, and he determined to make every effort to maintain that democracy regardless of personal consequences. Secondly, "a sound middle-of-the-road program" had to be developed, for, as he wrote Gifford Pinchot, this was the only thing "practical liberals" could do when caught between Republican and Democratic obstinacy.[25]

By the spring of 1938, Kansas politics began to take more of Landon's time; although it was important for his national prestige that Kansas be recaptured for Republicanism, he had to be actively interested in the state's politics for another and more personal reason. Since early 1937 he had been under pressure to run for the Senate seat held by Democrat George McGill, and it had also been suggested that he again run for governor, but Landon had no intention of running for any office—he had had enough. He had tried to forestall a Landon-for-senator movement in 1937 by encouraging Fred Brinkerhoff to run for the post, but the Pittsburg publisher resisted the temptation. The pressure continued into early 1938, and Landon tried to counteract it by publicly stating his intention not to run for the Senate or the governorship; and again he tried to encourage a "good man" to run for the senatorship, either Clifford Hope or Homer Hoch— both of whom decided against running.[26]

Landon was disappointed when, by the spring of 1938, the choices for the Republican senatorial nominee narrowed to Clyde M. Reed, with whom he thought it impossible to work, and Gerald B. Winrod, the publisher of the anti-everything *Wichita Defender*, who was totally unacceptable. Landon decided—if it became necessary—to help Reed win the nomination; he would rather see Reed in Washington than himself. But the pressure upon Landon swelled even more during and after his tour of the east; he had excited many of his Kansas friends with his defense of free expression and his warning against concentrations of power. Moreover, the rise of Winrod's senatorial ambitions alarmed many people, who feared that Kansas would be represented by a fascist prototype. Landon's statements on tolerance were the opposite of Winrod's anti-Jewish, anti-Catholic preachments. Duke Shoop, the Washington correspondent of the *Kansas City Star*—one of

25 Landon to Gifford Pinchot, June 8, 1938.

26 Landon to John M. Henry, February 4, 1937; Landon to Jack Harris, July 2, 1937; *New York Times*, January 23, 1938; Landon to Lacy Haynes, January 12, 1938; Clifford R. Hope to Landon, January 19, 1938; Landon to Hope, January 21, 1938.

those who urged Landon to run, reported that even Harry Woodring would help him in a race against Winrod.[27]

Others urged Landon to run for senator so that he might use the position as a stepping stone to the Presidency, but his answer was that he would not exchange "the comparatively simple but intelligent life of Kansas . . . for a stuffy old political office." He was pleased that he was still carried in the Gallup Poll, but he had no political ambitions. In any event, he knew "that the forces that probably will control the next national Republican convention are finding out that their budget balancer has some other views which make them rather unhappy. . . . But more than that, I know a man can't take the licking that I took and come out of Kansas . . . and have any hopes of repeating." Landon's interest was "in doing a job for my country in this particularly trying hour," or, as he later wrote, to be an influence for sanity in a nation imperiled by "a world turning to barbarism" and rocked at home by an erratic President and stubborn old guard factions in both parties. The nation needed political figures who, because they were not running for office, could speak freely. Landon thought he fitted that description: "Now, I am a free Negro. The only limitation on my actions is not to get out on a limb where I would be a political eunuch."[28]

Because he believed that neither Kansas nor the party would benefit from the outcome of the senatorial contest, Landon during the spring gave most of his attention to the race for governor. He had thought of a number of acceptable candidates for the governorship, including Frank Carlson, Harry Darby, Homer Hoch, and a dynamic state senator of partly Jewish descent, Payne Ratner. Although Landon repeatedly said he would keep out of the primary contests for governor, he did not feel this pledge prevented him from trying to encourage good candidates for the nomination—nor did his closest political associates. The Landon group increasingly favored Ratner, thinking he had a good chance to beat Democratic Governor Walter Huxman because of the state's reaction to the general decline of business,[29] and Landon became more and more involved in the Ratner campaign.

In March, Landon advised Willard Mayberry on the conduct of

[27] Landon to Harold B. Johnson, June 7, 1938; Duke Shoop to Landon, n.d. (probably late May, 1938).

[28] Landon to Roger W. Straus, June 11, 1938; Landon to Roy Howard, June 13, 1938; Landon to Raymond Clapper, August 9, 1938.

[29] Landon to W. C. Gilmore, February 14, 1938; Willard Mayberry to Landon, March 24, 1938.

Ratner's campaign in western Kansas, and urged his former secretary to "take your shirt off and pitch in for him as hard as you can." Mayberry immediately went to work for Ratner, though he warned that Landon might be labeled a boss if he became involved in the campaign without being on the ticket. Landon said he intended to stay out of the primaries, as far as public action was concerned, but "I can't refuse to talk to fellows who drop in." He also answered telephone and mail inquiries, and, once asked his position and advice, left no questions unanswered. Landon favored Ratner for governor—in opposition to his fellow Montgomery Countian, former Congressman Harold McGugin, whose argumentativeness left him open to attack; and he favored Reed for senator—despite (in Landon's opinion) his factional disloyalty and because of Winrod's alliance with forces of intolerance.

As Mayberry had warned, Landon was soon accused of bossism. On April 9, McGugin charged Landon with attempting to dictate the state's Republican nominees, and took him to task for bolting the party in 1924 and 1930 when his choices for the gubernatorial nominees were not selected.[30] This, in fact, was the beginning of a standard Republican ploy that would be used in the state for the next ten years: "Boss" Landon was to be the perennial bogeyman—until the tactic succeeded, in 1948, in removing him as the prime political influence in Kansas.

During most of April and May, Landon was not active in Kansas politics because of his involvement in the national scene, but by June he was once again in close touch with the Ratner forces. He then came under harsh attack by A. L. "Dutch" Shultz, the old guard political columnist of the *Topeka State Journal*, who said that if McGugin won the gubernatorial nomination "Landon's organization hasn't the slightest notion of supporting him for the election." Shultz added that Landon, Mayberry, Justice William Smith, Lacy Haynes, and others were also greasing the skids for Clyde Reed in November. Landon retorted privately that Shultz was the "most unreliable newspaper man in Kansas" and was reflecting the bitterness engendered by McGugin's supporters. Yet the furor raised by Shultz and McGugin was such that Landon, on June 25, decided to make a press statement. He said that his announcement that he was not going to run for public office did not mean he had retired from politics. As for McGugin, Landon held

[30] Landon to Willard Mayberry, March 26, 1938; Mayberry to Landon, March 28, 1938; Landon to Jay Scovel, March 30, 1938; *Wichita Eagle*, April 10, 1938.

it was "always a mistake to nominate a candidate with weak spots who is on the defensive, because you can give the enemy a lot of free ammunition to use." He hoped that "none will deny me my right as a Republican and a citizen of Kansas to support whomever I think is for the best interests of the Republican party and the general best interest of Kansas."[31]

Landon kept quiet after this because he was convinced that a public statement for Ratner would win votes for McGugin, and any statement against Winrod would only help the Wichita fundamentalist's candidacy. Landon's task, despite the pleas of those who begged him to speak out, was accomplished behind the scenes; as he wrote Vic Sholis of the *Chicago Times*: "The Kansas people don't like to be told by anyone whom to vote for or not to vote for." Acting on this premise, Landon spent most of his free time in July and early August trying to engineer, through organization channels, Ratner's victory in the gubernatorial primary and Winrod's defeat in the senatorial contest.[32] Ratner's ensuing nomination, as well as Winrod's defeat, led to attacks on Landon and others for making "Kansas Jew-Conscious." One pamphlet attributed Clyde Reed's triumph to

> secret opposition on the part of former Presidential candidate Alfred M. Landon (Jews are rumored to have come to Kansas from the East and threatened to "paint his name mud" if he didn't "crucify Winrod"); opposition of William Allen White, who "fronted" for Winrod's enemies; opposition of Republican National Committee Chairman John D. Hamilton—all of whom were Jew-surrounded in the last Presidential election; and who apparently continue to feed at the same trough.[33]

Landon was congratulated by his friends and acquaintances on the primary's results, but a number of them asserted that his silence had probably hurt him nationally. Landon knew this, but he also realized that he would have been in disfavor—deservedly so—with the responsible political elements of the land if Winrod had been nominated. Referring to Herbert Hoover, Landon wrote: "The old boy on the Pacific coast certainly would have done a lot of cackling over the

[31] *Wichita Beacon*, June 19, 1938; Landon to Stella Pryor, June 23, 1938; memo to North American Newspaper Alliance, June 25, 1938.

[32] Landon to Vic Sholis, July 9, 26, 1938; Landon to Roger W. Straus, August 5, 1938; Henry Haskell to Raymond Clapper, August 15, 1938, Raymond Clapper Papers, Manuscript Division, Library of Congress, Washington, D.C.; Walter Johnson, *William Allen White's America* (New York: Holt, 1947), p. 469.

[33] *Kansas Jew-Conscious*, Leaflet, New York, September 2, 1938.

country." The important thing was not who got credit but that Winrod had been defeated: "I was following a policy that would insure his defeat."[34]

Although he was involved behind the scenes in the state primary, Landon had not been inactive on the national scene. When Bertrand Snell resigned as House minority leader, Landon supported Joseph W. Martin as Snell's successor, and he also concerned himself with the national committee's poor work in raising funds for the fall campaign. Again, he supported Martin, agreeing that the congressional campaign committees were the proper vehicles for fund-raising because they would carry the greatest burden of campaigning in 1938. Martin and Landon were alarmed by the national committee's apparent inability to support the congressional committees: by August 1, $320,000 in assistance had been promised but only $133,750 had been given.[35]

During this time Landon also kept his "good sportsman" image alive by writing a series of four articles that appeared in the *New York Times* in August. The articles set forth his impressions of the presidential campaign and the compensations of losing—the franchise to be himself rather than an overburdened executive.[36] Yet during the summer Landon had also renewed battle with his adversary of 1936, President Roosevelt.

Roosevelt, in late June—in a fireside chat—had finally made public his intention to purge the Democratic party of its conservative elements; then, almost as an afterthought, he deplored suppressions of free speech and assembly. This presented a fine opportunity for a direct clash between Landon and Roosevelt. Landon, who immediately issued a press statement, called the speech an admission of an effort "not only to centralize all federal or national government in the President's hands [but also] to turn the weight of government spending against those state political organizations that are not 'yes' organizations." While Landon welcomed Roosevelt's reference to the need for free speech and discussion, he asked, alluding to the treatment of Norman Thomas in Jersey City, "Why does he not apply it to one of

[34] Vic Sholis to Landon, n.d. (probably early September, 1938); Landon to Sholis, September 24, 1938; Landon to Roger W. Straus, August 5, 1938; Landon to Harry Newman, August 3, 1938.

[35] Landon to Joseph W. Martin, June 20, 23, 29, July 1, 5, 1938; Martin to Landon, August 1, 1938.

[36] *New York Times*, August 21–24, June 28, 1938.

his own sponsors [Frank Hague], the Vice Chairman of the Democrat National Committee . . . ?"[37]

The President, in a hypocritical manner, had touched on the issue to which Landon was most sensitive, for whatever bitterness Landon had as a result of the 1936 campaign and subsequent events was epitomized in the question of free speech. The "raspberry tirade" of 1936, the tactic of making rash and extreme statements about anyone who opposed Roosevelt's policies, had reached its height in the attempt to eliminate from office those Democrats who did not agree with the President, and it was all the more galling because the announcement of the purge policy was combined with a defense of free speech. This bitterness, and his adherence to copybook maxims on freedom of expression, explained Landon's defense of Norman Thomas and many of his later statements. He had become convinced that the administration, instead of handling criticism intelligently, was out to suppress it by derogation, innuendo, and pressure.

Concluding that his statement to the press was insufficient for dealing with this most recent example of Roosevelt's repressive attitude, Landon arranged to answer the President over the network of the Columbia Broadcasting System (from Council Bluffs, Iowa) on July 6. Landon first took up the bread-and-butter questions, saying the recent economic reversal was "purely a *political* depression—a depression brought on by the *methods* and *policies* of the present administration." Recession was not what the New Deal wanted but recession was what the administration got because it refused to listen to those who tried to show "some of the *unplanned* results that would come from the planning of his advisers." The issue before America was not, as President Roosevelt indicated, the protection of reforms begun under the New Deal. The issue was making them work—and leading the country to economic recovery. Nor was the question one of who was liberal and who was reactionary. It was a matter of developing a government strong enough to solve the nation's problems, but "within the framework of the American constitutional system." The truth was, the Kansan said, that the possibility of developing this kind of government was being endangered by a loose fiscal policy, by the practice of playing politics with social security taxes, relief work, the Wages and Hours Act, and by the nagging at business to cover up the administration's failures. The price, high though it may be, would be worth paying had the nation been

[37] *New York Times,* June 26, 1938; Landon press statement, June 25, 1938.

restored to a lasting prosperity, had the future been made more secure, and had living standards for all Americans been raised. The tragic fact, however, was that the price had been paid and these objectives had not been attained. Furthermore, infringements of free speech— as in Jersey City—had not been ensured by the administration.

Landon called for

> a fundamental change in our attitude toward life and government. . . . As long as we are resigned to crookedness and waste in government, we will have a wasteful government. As long as we depend upon intellectual trickery instead of truth, we will continue to have crowd psychology and propaganda. . . . Let Mr. Roosevelt only practice what he preaches, and we will not only cooperate with him—we will fight shoulder to shoulder with him to achieve the social progress and the economic recovery which we all desire and need.[38]

Aside from chiding the President, Landon's speech was designed to encourage responsible parties to address themselves to service in the public interest. The Kansan still believed that only a coalition of responsible conservatives, moderates, and liberals from both major parties could bring the nation back to sound government and economic recovery. Yet he knew that such a coalition was unlikely because of the inability of business elements to see what they had to concede and support in order to achieve just and effective government for themselves as well as for others. Because social security, collective bargaining, and many other social issues had been decided upon, it was now the duty of the responsible business elements to make them work. Landon wondered if they would do this—when their attitudes toward the nation's problems resembled those of the French aristocrats of the eighteenth century.[39]

In late July, Landon began preparing for the fall campaign. It would not be a coalition campaign against the New Deal, as he had inter- mittently hoped: not only had he failed in his efforts to encourage a coalition, he knew he had offended too many people—as a defender of a Socialist and as the wrecker of the mid-term convention. His chief consolation was that the Republican program committee had limited its scope to inquiry and recommendation; at most, it would

[38] Landon speech, Council Bluffs, Ia., July 6, 1937.
[39] Landon to Lewis H. Brown, July 22, 1938.

suggest, he wrote, "the Ten Commandments and the Lord's Prayer and the Bill of Rights . . . as principles of the Republican Party."[40]

As titular head of the Republican party during the 1938 campaign, Landon contributed time and encouragement. Although he wrote letters of support for Republican candidates all over the country, his greatest encouragement went to the party's New York liberals, where Thomas Dewey, who was seeking the Republican gubernatorial nomination, and Kenneth Simpson, the leader of the state's liberal Republican factions, had to battle not only the Democrats but also the Republican old guard. Simpson, the youthful New York national committeeman-designate, contrasted Landon's support to the brick-bats he had received from Wall Street and the National Republican Club for supposedly selling out to communism by cooperating with the American Labor party in backing several candidates for office. Landon had for some time been encouraging Dewey, and in early September he even alluded to the possibility of the young district attorney's nomination for President in 1940. He fully approved Simpson's and Dewey's appeals to liberals, a technique that had been successful in rallying "good-government elements" behind Mayor Fiorello La Guardia in his 1933 and 1937 campaigns in New York City. After the Republican state convention had nominated Dewey for governor, Landon urged Dewey and the upstate insurgents, Edwin Jaeckle and Harold Johnson, to rally New York's liberal Republicans into a force that could control Republican state politics while attracting votes from outside the party in order to win New York in the elections.[41]

Landon had another pet project, in the south. Like all Republicans, he was intrigued by the difficulties of finding southern support, and, after the 1936 campaign, Landon had met an impressive young Arkansas Republican, Osro Cobb. Cobb, the Republican state chairman for Arkansas, thought the party had a future in his state, and he persuaded Landon that southern Republicanism would be greatly helped if the Kansan began his 1938 campaign with a speech in Arkansas.[42]

[40] Landon to J. Reuben Clark, March 3, 1938; *New York Times*, August 4, 1938; Landon to Paul Block, August 1, 1938.

[41] Landon to George Sibley, October 18, 1938; Kenneth F. Simpson to Landon, August 10, 1938; Landon to Thomas E. Dewey, September 3, 1938; Landon to Hugh A. Butler, November 18, 1938; Landon to Harold B. Johnson, October 17, 1938.

[42] Landon to L. E. Phillips, August 23, 1938.

Landon therefore accepted an invitation to attend the Republican state convention in Little Rock on September 13 and to give a nationally broadcast speech in the city that night. The Kansan was royally received by the convention delegates and by the local press; according to the *Arkansas Gazette*, even the state's Democrats welcomed "this upstanding and liberal-minded American."[43]

Landon gave a fighting speech in Little Rock, addressed primarily to the Democrat who "does any thinking for himself." The times urged action, but six long years of lack of accomplishment had bred resentment and hate. Men had to be put back to work, but chaotic government, produced by the political considerations of the New Deal, could not do the job. The President wondered why business had not taken up the load, but the government's vacillation and the lack of real encouragement of business provided the answer: "First, a stimulant is mixed for the business patient. Then he is given a depressant. Then the President wonders why the patient doesn't get up and go to work, and attributes it to his being a slacker anyhow!" Although the President could claim credit for partial economic recovery, Landon said, he must also accept the blame for the fact that recovery had been only partial. An unsound fiscal policy, the attack on the Supreme Court, the ballyhoo about a wheat surplus, the condoning of sit-down strikes, and the President's fault-finding with everyone but himself was not the tonic for business or political health. The removal of chaos in government and the achievement of full recovery required "the healthful influence of intelligent opposition," an opposition that could come about if Americans, regardless of party, voted Republican.[44]

Landon contributed five other speeches, all in the middle west, to the Republican mid-term election campaign. For his major effort—an effort to emphasize the importance of reaching the grass roots—he chose Vienna, a town of 900 people in southern Illinois. The county Republican leaders, unsuccessful in securing nationally known Republican speakers, and thinking they might as well be turned down by the party's titular head as well as by almost everyone else, invited Landon. To their surprise, he accepted, thereby making dramatic what otherwise would have been a drab occasion. On October 19 Republicans flocked in from all of southern Illinois to hear Landon rip into the New Deal at an open-air, afternoon meeting.

The new "depression" the country then suffered from, Landon said,

[43] Landon to Osro Cobb, September 6, 1938; *Arkansas Gazette* (Little Rock), September 15, 1938.
[44] Landon speech, Little Rock, September 14, 1938.

was brought about by the same policies that the President had earlier boasted of by saying "We planned it that way." It was evident, then, that the administration had planned badly, which was particularly true of the New Deal's agricultural, employment, and relief programs. Landon condemned the contradictory policies of increasing the restrictions on planting quotas while permitting food imports to multiply and while mounting huge projects to reclaim unproductive land. The failure of the administration's employment program was evidenced in the great size of its relief program, and proof of the weakness of the relief program was its failure—despite its extravagant overhead—to meet the needs and yearnings of the citizens on its rolls. The inadequacies of these programs, he contended, not only reflected the failure of the New Deal to achieve recovery but had helped bring about new economic miseries.

Landon then turned to the administration's political practices.

> Every politician knows that Mr. Hopkins and the President are just having their little joke when they say relief is free from political manipulation. Every politician of both parties knows that the spending machine and the WPA pressure machine will deliver votes just like the city machine does.
>
> We see this method forging control by the greatest political boss we have ever seen. Using the tactics of Croker and Murphy of Tammany, and of Pendergast of Kansas City, the President is making pikers of all of them.

The President's proposals for judicial and executive reorganization and his attempt to purge legislators who disagreed with him were simply part of an effort to establish a national political boss. Basically, Landon said, all this was "foreign and repugnant to a freedom-loving people" because it rested on the idea that all political and economic power was "to be concentrated in the federal government at Washington . . . in the executive head. . . . It is time to call a halt! We must act now and elect Republicans to Congress and to governorships if we are to turn the tide of the depression and turn back the trend toward an all-powerful central authority at Washington." [45]

Two days after his visit to Illinois, Landon spoke at Valentine, Nebraska, where he repeated the essence of his Vienna talk. At the end of October he went to Bartlesville, Oklahoma, to give his last out-of-Kansas campaign speech, reminding his audience that

> if the opposition party is to fill its most constructive role, it must criticize. The questions and suggestions which lead to an improvement of the administration's policies come out of such criticism. . . . We have many great

[45] *St. Louis Globe-Democrat*, October 12, 1938; Landon speech, Vienna, Ill., October 19, 1938.

problems pressing for decision in the next two elections. We must decide whether we are going to be a democracy or a fascist state. That means we must decide whether we are going to merely transfer the economic power of too few individuals, to a few powerful government bureaus, or whether we are going to break it up.

He once again declared that the nation could not go forward until it had a balanced budget—in order to consolidate the humanitarian gains made under the New Deal and to encourage the business activity necessary for restoring jobs. This required the courage to cut spending and "to levy the taxes" needed to "meet the bills which must be paid." Republican nominees had that courage, he implied.[46]

Landon also did what he could to help the Republican ticket in Kansas, giving his full backing to Clyde Reed and Payne Ratner, and raising money because the old guard was "not inclined to dig up anything" to support Reed, whom they thought erratic, and Ratner, whom they considered too friendly with labor.[47] Landon also gave two speeches in support of the ticket. In the first, at Fort Scott on October 10, he asserted:

> If we are to have good government in the nation we must first have good local government and good state government. If we are to halt the trend toward the management of all our affairs from Washington we must do two things. We must elect United States Senators and Congressmen who are not "yes men" [and repudiate] a state government that plays in with the Washington tendencies toward running everything. I am not in favor of making Topeka a "Little Washington."

Landon then warmly endorsed Ratner, Reed, and the Republican congressional nominees. He concluded his campaigning November 4, at Mankato, where he predicted a landslide for Ratner and Reed. He also made a final jab at Roosevelt, portraying him as in the dilemma of deciding whether he had caused the 1938 depression or had been a miserable failure in doing something about the 1929 depression.[48]

During the course of the campaign there had been mounting evidence that Republican prospects were improving. This would, if true, be good for the nation because, Landon was convinced, Republi-

[46] Landon speeches, Valentine, Neb., October 21, 1938, and Bartlesville, Okla., October 31, 1938.
[47] Landon to Richard Lloyd Jones, September 20, 1938; Landon to Charles Welch, November 12, 1938.
[48] Landon speeches, Fort Scott, October 10, 1938, and Mankato, November 4, 1938.

can gains would stiffen the opposition in both major parties to Roosevelt's whimsical measures. He liked to think his 1936 message was at last being understood. What he had characterized as the defects of the New Deal now seemed abundantly clear; the only drawback was that some Republicans, because of their ingrained conservatism, might not be wise enough to benefit from the situation. Indeed, there were indications that Arthur James was conducting a "reactionary" campaign for governor in Pennsylvania, and Landon concluded that if James won, as was likely, it would be all the more difficult to enlighten Republicans in that state. And he was still unhappy with Hoover: the former President's speeches had been dreadful—"He just doesn't know what it is all about." Generally, however, Landon thought "it is becoming plainer every day that the next nominee of the Republican party will be able to take what's left of the Grand Old Party further to the left than I was able to take it in '36." [49]

The election results—for the first time in ten years—were good news to Republicans. The party had gained seven Senate seats and the number of Republican representatives had almost doubled, going from 89 to 164. The party had also netted an increase of fourteen governorships, and in doing so had swept the middle west. In New York, Thomas Dewey was defeated for governor, but he had run so strongly that he was considered a possibility for the 1940 Republican presidential nomination. Landon was delighted by his party's gains, and after it had been established that Reed and Ratner had won in Kansas, he wrote an old friend: "Yes, we are all happy about the results, not only in Kansas but elsewhere. It looks as if the American people are once more getting their balance." He agreed with Harold Johnson that although Dewey had lost he had "won" because he had displaced the old Republican leadership in New York and had given people someone to vote for. Landon thought Dewey could go far if he handled himself properly. [50]

Despite the generally happy results, Landon persuaded himself—after further reflection—that the party "could have won many more seats in Congress, and I think, some more governors, if we had had strong organizations and good candidates." He was still troubled by

[49] Landon to George Sibley, October 18, 1938; Landon to Raymond Z. Henle, October 24, 1938; Landon to Harold B. Johnson, October 5, November 3, 1938.

[50] Landon to Chester Stevens, November 12, 1938; Harold B. Johnson to Landon, November 9, 1938; Landon to Johnson, November 19, 1938; Landon to William R. Castle, November 15, 1938.

the fear that the Republican party was not yet ready to assume responsibility for national government. Too many Republicans believed in
ideas that might create an artificial prosperity for the nation. If the
conservatives should control the government, Landon wrote, "we are
liable to see the biggest boom and the greatest bust we have ever seen
and I don't think we can stand it."[51]

[51] Landon to Don Berry, November 16, 1938.

CHAPTER **17**

Days of World Crisis

Although domestic issues had determined the Republican election victories in 1938, the party's fortunes for the next eight years were to be conditioned by world affairs. Landon had not been fully aware of this change in 1938, although he had become increasingly concerned with the international consequences of German and Japanese aggrandizement, and he was worried by the administration's handling of foreign relations. Roosevelt's position, as Landon saw it, was neither that of an internationalist nor an isolationist; it was "hasty, impulsive." As the United States became more involved in world crises, the Kansan quickly developed a stand: he would back the administration on issues of national defense and would support a strong hand for the President in countering intimidation from abroad—as he had during the *Panay* incident and the debate on the Ludlow proposal. Landon believed that any other stance "would encourage the Japanese to the false belief that they could push us around as they please," and thus lead to war. The government's discretion in negotiating international disputes must not be limited: "In a matter of negotiation, there always comes a time when there is a psychological moment to withdraw or to strike and close the deal."[1]

The Kansan's heightened interest in foreign policy brought him in

[1] Landon to Hulbert Taft, January 12, 1938, and Landon to E. G. Bennett, January 12, 1938, Alfred M. Landon Papers, Kansas State Historical Society, Topeka.

407

touch with men who had long been concerned with it, such as Salmon
O. Levinson, Borah's chief adviser on international relations, and
George Fort Milton, special assistant to Secretary of State Hull.
Milton even visited Landon in Topeka, in January, 1938, in an
attempt to induce Landon to accept membership on Hull's Economic
Policy Committee for the support of reciprocal trade. Landon refused,
but he stayed in touch with the committee and with Milton, showing,
as Milton put it, a "kindly attitude" toward the reciprocal trade
program.[2]

As Landon became more aware of specific world problems, he
became less sure of the practical steps that could solve them. He had
thought world peace and international and national prosperity would
benefit if the "punitive peace treaty of Paris" were revised, but he
knew that affairs had gone too far for this approach to be practical.
He also knew that the developing crises had to be resolved if the
United States was not to become deeply involved in them. Landon
compared America to Rome, surrounded by barbarism abroad and
disturbed at home by "the Antony of the old guard"—of both parties—
and "the Augustus of Roosevelt." The nation needed force as well as
prestige for defending its interests abroad and achieving economic
development and stability at home.[3] Yet Americans were not the
masters of their destiny.

> Events in Berlin are going to be as significant for the American people as
> events in Washington. A general war of any duration at all would certainly
> feed the fires of Communism everywhere. On the other hand, if Hitler has
> his way, it may give impetus to Fascism, even of some modified sort, in not
> only the democracies of Europe but in South America.

Landon could only hope that the thrust of totalitarianism would be
blunted in the natural course of events.

Writing to a business acquaintance who thought that Germany
wanted only commercial supremacy in central Europe, Landon agreed
that such a development would *temporarily* promote peace, prosperity,
and stability. France, then, would sink to the level of "a more or less

[2] Salmon O. Levinson to Landon, April 26, 1938; Landon to Levinson, May 12,
1938; George Fort Milton to Landon, January 5, 8, June 1, 1938, and Landon to
Milton, January 8, 1938, George Fort Milton Papers, Manuscript Division, Library
of Congress, Washington, D.C.; memo of conversation with Felix Morley, December
20, 1937.

[3] Landon to Edmund E. Lincoln, March 30, 1938; Landon to Raymond Clapper,
September 9, 1938.

second-rate power—a mere satellite in the English orbit [and] England and Germany working together will open up the channels of trade for the time being." After the Munich agreement, in 1938, which permitted Germany to annex the Sudetenland, Landon announced his relief that the United States had not been committed "to help preserve the boundary lines fixed by the Treaty of Versailles." We would have had "to go to the aid of Czechoslovakia or break our solemn word as a nation. I believe the American people are happy that we were not bound by such a treaty." [4]

It was obvious that the Kansan recognized the danger of nazi imperialism to the United States as well as the danger inherent in American military involvement abroad. At the same time, he shared the bewilderment of the great majority of Americans, who wanted world peace *and* freedom. This dilemma led the nation farther down the path of noninvolvement—in the hope that things would work themselves out.

The nazi pogrom against the Jews in November led Landon to join Herbert Hoover, Harold Ickes, and Catholic and Protestant clergymen in a nationwide radio protest against these "inhuman actions." [5] That same month Landon became more immediately involved in world affairs as a result of the administration's decision to display national unity, where possible, in the conduct of foreign affairs; on November 11 the State Department asked him to serve as vice chairman of the United States delegation to the Conference of American States at Lima, Peru, in December. After consulting with some of the Republican leaders in Congress, Landon agreed to accept the appointment as "a patriotic duty." He also wanted to use this opportunity to broaden his experience and "to find out firsthand just how much Fascist and Communist penetration there is in [the Latin-American] countries." Moreover, he wrote, "There is a decided domestic advantage in pulling together once again. Anything that will help us forget our bitterness, divert our minds from our own trouble, and bring a sense of solidarity to America will be helpful." [6]

Landon had only two weeks for settling his affairs and preparing for

[4] Landon to Raymond Z. Henle, September 27, 1938; Landon to Herbert L. Bodman, September 30, 1938; Landon speech, Vienna, Ill., October 19, 1938.

[5] *New York Times*, November 15, 1938.

[6] Landon to G. Winne, November 19, 1938; Landon to William Hard, November 12, 1938; Landon to W. W. Waymack, November 19, 1938; Landon to Don Berry, November 16, 1938.

his assignment. He consulted chiefly with J. Reuben Clark, Coolidge's
Under Secretary of State and the author of the famous Clark Memorandum, which had effectively argued against the policy of United
States intervention in Latin America. Clark, correctly predicting that
the Roosevelt administration valued Landon's cooperation and would
give him its full cooperation in this venture, urged Landon not to
make a minority report at Lima because the Latin Americans would
ridicule the United States if its delegation did not stand united. He
also warned the Kansan to be prepared to hear the United States—
as Clark had heard—libeled and abused by Latin Americans. Landon
left the United States by ship in late November and arrived in Lima
on December 9, in company with several members of the United
States and Central American delegations. Most of his briefing was done
on shipboard, where Landon soon became a popular figure, using his
ability as a listener to acquire information and to ingratiate himself
with American Democrats and Latin-American delegates.[7]

The Roosevelt administration regarded the Lima conference as
crucial in United States foreign policy; and Roosevelt and Hull, with
great success, had used the foundations laid by Clark and President
Hoover to persuade Latin-American governments that the United
States was not aggressive. Now, as the Roosevelt administration strove
for hemispheric solidarity in a troubled world, it was essential to show
the Latin-American countries that the United States was united in its
effort to achieve inter-American cooperation. Secretary Hull, as
chairman of the United States delegation at Lima, asserted that our
object was to strengthen the hemisphere's resistance to foreign intervention, and the American states had to go beyond the pledge of
consultation (made at Buenos Aires in 1936) in order to be successful
in averting common dangers.[8] Hull's statement reflected the United
States' alarm over German propaganda and economic pressures, and
the rise of nazi political parties in the southern countries. Secretary
Hull's chief goal was to offset fascist pressure and intimidation in the
hemisphere, and Landon's presence at Lima supported this objective
because it gave "a valuable proof to the Latin Americans that both
major parties were united on the Good Neighbor policy."

[7] J. Reuben Clark to Landon, November 21, 1938; *New York Times*, November 26,
December 4, 1938.

[8] Donald M. Dozer, *Are We Good Neighbors? Three Decades of Inter-American Relations,
1930–1960* (Gainesville: University of Florida Press, 1959), p. 39.

As it developed, his view was well-founded. Hull, on his way to Lima, had received word that Foreign Minister José María ⌐antilo of Argentina would reject any collective security arrangement proposed by the United States on the grounds that the Latin-American nations could not rely on the northern republic for protection—that United States foreign policy would shift because of "the possibility of changes in [its] internal politics." Despite Hull's efforts, Cantilo's opposition caused the security-pact idea to be dropped, but the contentious Argentineans—and their sympathizers among other Latin-American delegations—were persuaded by the show of United States unity to give unanimous support to a compromise measure, the Declaration of Lima. The declaration affirmed hemispheric solidarity, the desirability of consultation in crises, and the use of "measures which in each case the circumstances may make advisable" to thwart threats to the peace, security, or territorial integrity of New World nations. Other resolutions condemned racial and religious bigotry, wherever found, and the political activity of aliens in the hemisphere. The actions taken at Lima, although they did not completely satisfy Hull, were a sharp criticism and a collective warning to fascist powers.[9] The conference therefore produced the basis for effective collective security in the Americas.

Landon had done more than serve as an example of his country's unity, or mix with the other delegates and gaining goodwill for the United States; he served on two committees—the Committee on the Organization of the Peace and the Committee on the Pan American Union and Conferences—and he made two addresses to the conference. In his first speech, in general debate, he stressed the bipartisan agreement in the United States on the necessity for opposing foreign intervention in the western hemisphere. In his major address, on December 18, Landon said the conference's resolutions reflected the agreement of the American nations on common principles and their warning against intruders. The policy of settling "all disputes by peaceful means and to cooperate in every way for our mutual advancement and security . . . will be sustained [by the United States] irrespective of what political party may in the future hold office." He urged the delegates not only to express but to live the spirit of

---

[9] Cordell Hull, *The Memoirs of Cordell Hull* (New York: Macmillan, 1948), I, 601 ff.; Dozer, *Are We Good Neighbors?* pp. 53 f.

inter-American solidarity in a world that was threatened by totalitarian brutality.[10]

The Kansan later broadcast a similar speech from Lima, which was
carried in the United States over the National Broadcasting Company,
warning of the aggressive efforts that communism, fascism, and
nazism were making "to gain positions of influence and control in our
sister republics south of the Rio Grande."

> Regardless of election results, the United States will not tolerate any
> foreign government gaining a foothold on this continent. And if I am any
> judge, there is. . . the same patriotic determination on the part of our fellow
> Americans down this way to maintain this independence.[11]

The reactions to Landon's efforts were favorable. The chairman of
the Senate Foreign Relations Committee, Key Pittman, usually sparing
of praise, called Landon's statements "very frank and able." The
Louisville Courier-Journal said the Republican's efforts fully supported
the work of Secretary Hull. David Lawrence, in his syndicated column,
said Landon had emphasized American unity and had reflected the
democratic approach. William Philip Simms, foreign editor of the
Scripps-Howard syndicate, wrote that Landon went to Lima to work
and not for the ride, and the result was that "Landon at Lima boosted
the prestige of U.S. democracy." Only Under Secretary of State
Sumner Welles carped about Landon's speech to the conference; he
feared that the failure to mention the Good Neighbor policy would be
taken in many Latin-American quarters as an indication that it was
only a Roosevelt policy. Welles, with the President's approval, tried to
remedy this by stating that the whole nation supported the principles
of the Good Neighbor policy.[12]

The conference crystalized Landon's ideas on world affairs. Before
the Lima Conference he had thought the United States required

[10] Hull, *Memoirs*, I, 611; Cordell Hull to the Acting Secretary of State, December 24,
1938, 710.H Continental Solidarity/106, National Archives, Washington, D.C.; *Octavo
Conferencia Internacional Americana, Diario de Sesiones* (Lima: Imprenta Torres Aguirre,
1938), pp. 217, 739, 1050 f.

[11] *Vital Speeches of the Day*, VI (January 1, 1939), 191 f.

[12] *Des Moines Register*, December 19, 1938; *Louisville Courier-Journal*, December 20,
1938; *Buffalo Evening News*, December 22, 1938; *New York World-Telegram*, December
29, 1938; Sumner Welles to Cordell Hull, December 19, 1938, 710.H/313, National
Archives. Hull reminded his second-in-command that Landon's speech represented
the Republican leader's personal views. The Secretary wrote that there were "no
unfavorable repercussions" in Lima to the speech. Cordell Hull to Sumner Welles,
December 23, 1938, 710.H/328, National Archives.

rearmament, though not as much as President Roosevelt wanted; after his return, however, he believed the President's defense estimate was too low to allow Roosevelt to stand behind his recent bold statements. It was with this in mind, and also to point up the lessons he had learned at Lima, that Landon decided to speak to the people. At the Kansas Press Association meeting in Topeka—on January 21, 1939—Landon pictured the results of the Lima Conference as a compensation for the loss of prestige democracy had suffered at Munich; but the agreements required application as well as expression if the propaganda and intrigue that European dictators had directed against democratic ideals in the Americas were to be combated. Furthermore, the antagonism between democratic and totalitarian powers had been declared as an economic war in the hemisphere, which was "just as dangerous to representative government as new war machines." Because he thought the greatest problem of the United States in meeting totalitarian threats was internal discord, Landon addressed himself to the national administration: "The use of class hatred as a political weapon must stop . . . if we are to pull together in meeting either difficult foreign situations or domestic problems." Finally, the United States must be fiscally prepared for the possibility of armed conflict between democracy and totalitarianism. "Any government, head over heels in debt, is in a bad position to defend itself. . . . The present state of world affairs, instead of being a justification for continued deficits, is a mandate for a balanced budget." [13]

As international tensions increased in 1938 and early 1939, acquaintances pressed divergent views on Landon. Some contended that Germany sought only economic stability and a revision of the Versailles Treaty; others were horrified by the brutality of Hitler's government; and there were those who thought that a firm United States stand against German aggressiveness would prevent war. There were those who felt that European nations, even France and Great Britain, were tending toward fascism, and that America's only course was noninvolvement; others did not trust Roosevelt to put up a stiff policy, or did not trust him to remain aloof enough, or did not trust him at all. Landon tried to develop a position that might accommodate all of these views: The United States should be firm in meeting foreign threats to the western hemisphere, and should avoid involvement in war beyond the hemisphere; Republicans should support the President

[13] Landon to W. W. Waymack, November 19, 1938; Landon to Sterling Morton, January 23, 1939; Landon speech, Topeka, January 21, 1939.

in these two policies but be critical of other policies in order to maintain the two-party system. This position, Landon thought, was essential for the preservation of the nation's traditional values. The United States, and democracy, could not stand another world war; and bold and vigorous action for hemispheric defense and world peace was the country's only chance of avoiding war. He was pessimistic that the United States would be given that chance: "Mr. Roosevelt is too timid for that sort of a game." [14]

Landon's reservations about the President were soon documented to his satisfaction. In January, 1939, the crash of an American bomber—with a French official aboard—indicated that the administration had been secretly encouraging the sale of United States military equipment to France. The covertness of this procedure was widely criticized, and members of the Senate Military Affairs Committee were invited by the President to discuss the situation confidentially. Afterward, Roosevelt was quoted as having said that America's first line of defense was the Rhine River, that the United States should do everything short of war to strengthen Germany's opponents, and that Great Britain and France knew of his position; but in a news conference, on February 3, Roosevelt called these reports deliberate lies. The source of the stories, however—allegedly a senator—refused to retract the statements. Landon's reaction was that the President had vacillated, and had aroused suspicion of his motives on all sides. [15]

Landon began to speak out, saying what he thought the President lacked the courage to say. In February, in an article for the National Editorial Association, Landon lashed out at Europe's "mass brutality." He condemned the "accents of force" in Europe, the vast military mobilizations, "the intense activity in the spread of doctrines inspired by hatred," and the "cruel persecution for political, racial and religious reasons."

> New World society can no more isolate itself from the moral and psychological effects of the horrors being lived by the Jews of Austria and Germany than it can isolate itself from international broadcasts. . . . The mind that views brutality and injustice with indifference . . . is not awake to the real danger. [16]

[14] Landon to Arthur Calvert Smith, January 26, 1939.

[15] William E. Leuchtenburg, *Roosevelt and the New Deal, 1932–1940* (New York: Harper and Row, 1963), p. 287; *New York Times*, February 8, 1939; Landon to Sterling Morton, February 13, 1939. See also John Morton Blum, *From the Morgenthau Diaries: Years of Urgency, 1938–1941* (Boston: Houghton Mifflin, 1965), pp. 64–78.

[16] *Topeka Capital*, February 18, 1939; see also revised version in *National Jewish Monthly*, LIII (March, 1939), 222.

As discouraging as the times were, Landon could not accept the view that world war and American involvement were inevitable. The question was how to prevent the former, and, failing that, preclude the latter; but action by any one country, he believed, was insufficient. Toward the end of February, 1939, he considered crusading for a world conference in which all international issues could be discussed. That it would become a marathon event did not discourage him because he thought time was on the side of those who wanted peace. Moreover, such a conference might extend a fair hearing to Germany's legitimate grievances, which might soften her aggressiveness. Landon asked several friends to consider the feasibility of such a conference, but their response was not enthusiastic; it was feared that the administration would consider the suggestion a partisan proposal for embarrassing the President, or that—if the idea were accepted—it would hamper the development of America's foreign policy. Others thought the President would take the credit if such a conference succeeded, and would blame the Republicans if it did not. Failing to get support from his friends on the proposal, Landon set aside the idea.[17] Then, during the spring, Roosevelt called for a world peace conference, which Landon happily supported.

Landon, in the spring of 1939, combined his concern with foreign affairs with his interest in his church, having since 1936 been active in Methodist-Episcopal work and as a trustee of several Methodist colleges and charitable organizations. He had also been an outspoken defender of religious toleration and a leading advocate of union among the various Methodist groups, and because of this work he was elected a delegate-at-large to the Uniting Conference of Methodism in Kansas City in April (within weeks after Germany declared its protectorate over Czechoslovakia and Italy seized Albania).[18] At the first session of the conference, Landon spoke in favor of the union of the Methodist-Episcopal, Methodist-Episcopal Southern, and Methodist-Protestant churches. The conference, he said, was seeking not only the welfare of Methodism but "of all churches and all peoples," and this by setting an example of humble cooperation, not self-aggrandizement.[19]

Although the conference made great progress in uniting the three sects, Landon was disturbed by its tendencies on international affairs: some of the leaders had prepared a resolution favoring prohibition of

[17] Landon to Raymond Gram Swing, February 22, 1939.
[18] Charles L. Mead to Landon, November 11, 1938.
[19] Landon speech, Kansas City, Mo., April 24, 1939.

the shipment of war materials to Japan, and the churchmen had already claimed a broad right of conscientious objection in case of war and conscription. Landon thought that adoption of these two ideas would put Methodism in an unrealistic position; he recognized the right of conscientious objection but thought that it could not be used to shelve "all responsibility." In his major speech to the conference, on May 3, he pleaded for a dispassionate approach to foreign affairs, and again he pledged his support of the President—"whether he deserves it or not"—on international matters.

To show that his pledge was not an idle one, Landon endorsed Roosevelt's message of April 14, which asked Hitler to give assurances that Germany would not violate the sovereignty of thirty-one specified Middle Eastern and European countries. Although the German chancellor's response had been insulting, Landon thought it left

> the door slightly open for further discussion of the common destiny of the common people of this world. . . . I urge we explore constructively the possibility for further discussion which Herr Hitler's speech offers. . . . Henceforth, we must not allow friendship or animosity or emotion to influence our foreign policy. We must learn that negotiations between nations are cold and ruthless, and we must play the game the same way.

The only immediate interest of Americans should be the United States; and Landon reprimanded American citizens who organized themselves in pro-Hitler bunds or stop-Hitler parades: "I like Americans who are for our country, first, last and all the time." Any taking of sides, he was sure, would lead to America's entry into war.

Landon then urged support of President Roosevelt's call for a world peace conference. "The United States is the one great power which has the chance to offer something other than the mere choosing-up of sides before going to battle." In any case, the nation should act vigorously and impartially for peace because war in Europe would probably mean war for America. Even if it did not,

> How long can popular government survive in a world armed to the teeth and constantly attacking or threatening to attack, with trade between nations at a low ebb, with monetary systems disorganized and a world going bankrupt by [a] gigantic armament race?. . . The only way to have peace is to talk peace.[20]

Landon, in this nationally broadcast address, had spoken for peace and democracy, but he had also asked the question that would con-

[20] Landon to J. Roscoe Drummond, May 21, 1939; *New York Times*, May 10, 4, 1939.

vulse American politics as war came to Europe: Could the United States have peace and still maintain its democracy? Landon's answer was "perhaps"; certainly, though, the alternatives to peace were war, the probable death of democracy, and economic ruin.

Landon's prestige in the Republican party increased after the disaster of November, 1936, partly because of his subsequent activities and partly because of the administration's many failures. The *Emporia Gazette*, writing of Landon and the 1936 campaign, said:

> A lot of moon-eyed, star-gazing, rainbow-chasing liberals were on our necks three years ago for not whooping it up for the old smiler in the White House. To which we wish to reply in hissing tones: "Well, what have you got now that you wouldn't have had with our man? and how about a little recovery? and boys, wouldn't it be swell to be sure that we weren't being backed into a European war?"

Some observers inquired why Landon was not being discussed as the Republican nominee for 1940. The *Boston Sunday Post* noted that Landon had "gained considerable public confidence as a humanitarian. He is not a relentless prosecutor nor an engineer. It would seem that many Republican leaders would estimate Landon's worth higher because of this quality."[21]

Although Landon was keenly interested in the Republican presidential nomination, he did not want it for himself, nor was he prepared to commit himself to any of the contenders for the nomination. Although he had encouraged Thomas E. Dewey, he refused to support the New Yorker's candidacy. As Landon wrote (not unkindly) to Roger Straus in April, 1939, it remained to be proved that Dewey was the best man, but he thought Dewey could be nominated if he handled himself well during the year. Dewey should not allow himself to be pictured as a Hoover man, which it seemed the New Deal was doing in order to stop him. The Kansan also told the Dewey men that they needed all the support they could get within New York State; the fight that had developed between Dewey and national committeeman Kenneth Simpson would not help Dewey's chances for the nomination, and Dewey needed Simpson more than Simpson needed Dewey. Although Dewey thought Landon's stand was motivated by dislike of Hoover, the Kansan was genuinely interested in seeing Dewey's

---

[21] *Emporia Gazette*, April 3, 1939; Boston *Sunday Post*, March 26, 1939.

campaign develop; he did not want it to seem that he—or anyone else—dominated the young New Yorker.[22]

Because his business affairs were precarious and he did not have the money for carrying on far-flung political activities, Landon did not participate extensively in party politics at this time. Early in 1939, in fact, at least two friends contributed money to help defray the expense of answering his voluminous political correspondence. Sterling Morton, the "When It Rains It Pours" salt heir, sent Landon $1,000 for this purpose, as did Hill Blackett, the recently elected Republican national committeeman from Illinois.[23] Landon eked out his income in order to take a political swing of the east in June, and spent most of the summer shoring up his business enterprises. His few civic ventures were essentially of a religious nature, to emphasize the need for Christian unity in a "world that is largely ruled by pagan ideals."

Then, late in the summer, the Kansan again involved himself in controversy with the Department of Agriculture. Secretary Henry A. Wallace, in a radio address on September 8, had stressed the problem of dealing with the great surpluses of wheat, corn, cotton, and hogs. Landon, in reply, said that once again Wallace, by talking about surpluses, was "knocking the first decent general price he has had in prospect for years. . . . He is not helping the farmer get the full benefit of a fair price for the produce still in his hands by this kind of talk."[24] This time the Kansan was right as the coming of World War II pushed commodity prices steadily up.

With the coming of war in Europe—in September, 1939—Landon was back in the headlines. There was considerable public sentiment for a special session of Congress, and President Roosevelt called a special session for late September; in preparation for the session, he also called a conference of political leaders at the White House for September 20. Originally, this was to have been a conference between the President and congressional leaders, but Landon and Frank Knox were later invited so that the meeting would not be composed only of

[22] Landon to Roger W. Straus, April 3, 1939; Thomas E. Dewey to Leonard C. Reid, April 14, 1939, W. A. White to David Hinshaw, May 22, 1939, and Lacy Haynes to Straus, April 13, 1939, Thomas E. Dewey Papers, University of Rochester Libraries, Rochester, N.Y.; Landon to Blackett, May 15, 1939.

[23] Sterling Morton to Landon, January 18, 1939; Hill Blackett to Landon, January 7, 1939.

[24] Landon, "Christian Unity in Purpose and Action," *The Christian-Evangelist* (September 14, 1939), pp. 965 f.; *Topeka Capital*, September 9, 1939; *Kansas City Star*, September 13, 1939.

congressional leaders nor seem overly weighted with Democrats. Landon accepted the invitation.

Immediately before the White House meeting, at a press conference with fifty reporters—at Washington's Willard Hotel—Landon urged that Congress meet continuously during the war—"There is more confidence in the united judgment of the representatives than in any one man's opinion." He also declared his support of President Roosevelt's wish to revoke the embargo provisions of the Neutrality Act and otherwise ease the law's restrictions so that the United States could conduct a cash-and-carry trade with European nations during the war. Such actions, Landon said, had commercial merit.[25]

At the White House conference, which lasted more than two hours, Landon sat between minority leader Joseph W. Martin and Frank Knox. It seemed to the Kansan that the Republican leaders had been invited primarily as window dressing, and Landon's participation was only minimal, though he again urged that Congress remain in session during the emergency. After the conference he told the press that nothing had occurred that had changed his views on the Neutrality Act. Because of Republican congressional reluctance to cooperate with Roosevelt, he weaseled, though, by stressing that United States foreign policy would require careful legislative consideration and debate.[26]

Landon then went to New York, where he expressed the concern he had felt since 1937 over the rumors that Roosevelt would seek a third term as President. This concern had been heightened by Roosevelt's request that Congress "adjourn partisan politics" in considering American policy during the European war.

> I heartily agree with the President that this should be done. But I submit that he himself should make the first move in that direction by removing the biggest stumbling block of all in the path of nonpartisan discussion, namely the third-term issue. . . .
>
> All the underbrush should be cleared away. Everything that could possibly obscure or distort the vision should be removed. Dispassionate reasoning is difficult at best in times like these, hence the President should facilitate the task of Congress by taking the step suggested. He owes it to himself, to his party and to the nation.

[25] Franklin D. Roosevelt to John Garner, September 13, 18, 1939, Franklin D. Roosevelt Library, Hyde Park, N.Y.; *St. Louis Post-Dispatch*, September 20, 1939.

[26] Landon to Eliot Janeway, May 29, 1947; Landon to James L. Wright, December 6, 1941; *New York Herald Tribune*, September 21, 1939; James F. Byrnes, *Speaking Frankly* (New York: Harper, 1947), p. 8. See *New York Times*, September 21, 1939, for a garbled account of Landon's position after the White House meeting.

Roosevelt smiled when he heard Landon's suggestion—but the President's mother was reported to have said: "I wish you would, son." The *Christian Science Monitor* wrote that Landon had "put his finger frankly on one crucial point in the present grave discussion," a question that deserved the most serious consideration. Most responses to Landon's statement, however, were more partisan. It was reported that Democratic congressional leaders thought the statement was sheer politics. The *New York Herald Tribune* said Landon's activities in Washington and New York revealed his "usual clear-headedness" and had rendered "great public service." The *Boston Post* termed the Kansan's statement about the third-term a "shrewd bit of Republican strategy," although "it will hardly succeed."[27]

While in Washington, Landon had given an interview to Ralph McGill of the *Atlanta Constitution* that stirred great controversy within Republican ranks. Landon, who had called upon the party's leaders to send delegations to the Republican national convention that represented the best Republican elements, had been particularly critical of the delegations from the south, which had been disproportionately Negro in composition. Moreover, these Negroes had not been representative of the best of their race.

> The real trouble with the Republican party in the South was not the Civil War. Nor was it the tragic period of reconstruction. The trouble was the fatal error of the Republican party in believing that it paid off its obligations to the Negroes of the North by appointing Negro delegations to the conventions from the Southern states.

The development of a two-party system in the south required, as a beginning, that delegations to the Republican national convention be composed of representative persons of both races. McGill, in his column, hailed Landon's statement; and pointed out that traditionally the Republican national committee had had no respect for the southern delegations because it had assumed, with few exceptions, that they were for sale. McGill added that the southern Republican state conventions had rarely shown great integrity. "Not until the present unofficial head of the party was bold enough to speak out was the problem brought before the public.[28]

[27] *New York World-Telegram*, September 23, 1939; *Christian Science Monitor*, September 27, 1939; *Washington Post*, September 24, 1939; *New York Herald Tribune*, September 24, 1939; *Boston Post*, September 25, 1939.

[28] *Atlanta Constitution*, September 23, 1939.

Landon was vehemently attacked for his statement. Bascom Slemp, who had been a Republican congressman from Virginia and President Coolidge's secretary, declared that Landon's ignorance of southern voting conditions had led him to condemn the southern Republican leaders unjustly, and that the fraudulent voting practices of the Democrats surpassed anything the southern Republican leaders were guilty of. Landon was also attacked by Negroes, who interpreted his position as being anti-Negro; in Kansas, Daniel A. Sawyer, the president of the Negro Young Republicans of Shawnee County, charged that there had been a trend toward reducing Negro influence within the party.[29] Indeed, most of the Negro press assumed that Landon's objective was to eliminate Negroes from leadership in the Republican party. C. A. Barnett, of the Associated Negro Press, wrote Landon that almost every headline he had seen on Landon's interview indicated that this was his intention.

Negroes who knew Landon well, and those who were convinced of the wisdom of his suggestions, went to his defense. The *Kansas City Call* praised Landon for criticizing the many Negro politicians who were "generals without an army"; and his formal denial of wanting a lily-white Republican party was widely circulated by the Associated Negro Press. Bishop J. Arthur Hamlet, of the African Methodist-Episcopal Church of Kansas City, also worked to show that Landon was not prejudiced against Negroes. Some newspapers, in defending Landon, criticized the *Atlanta Constitution* and other southern Democratic newspapers for trying to use the statement to encourage antagonisms among southern Republicans.[30]

Landon, who had been aware of the unfavorable political conclusions that would be drawn from his statement on the southern delegations, wrote Ralph McGill that this incident should at least prove that he was not thinking of being a presidential candidate. (McGill had written articles saying Landon had grown in strength and that his party might draft him for the nomination.) The fact, however, was that Landon's public-opinion poll strength as a possible nominee had diminished between December, 1936—when 32 per cent of the

[29] *Richmond Times-Dispatch*, September 26, 1939; Daniel A. Sawyer to Landon, September 28, 1939.

[30] *Baltimore Afro-American*, September 30, 1939; Claude A. Barnett to Landon, October 7, 1939; *Kansas City Call*, September 29, 1939; *Nashville Defender*, October 13, 1939; Landon to Barnett, October 5, 1939; Landon to C. A. Franklin, October 7, 1939; *Topeka Plain Dealer*, October 13, 1939.

Republicans had wanted him as their nominee—and 1939—when only 7 per cent favored him. Perhaps it was surprising that he was mentioned at all—in view of his many denials of wanting the nomination and his forthrightness on touchy issues. Most professional observers did not mention Landon in connection with the nomination, but many of the rank-and-file stood by him. In a poll taken in October by radio station KMA (Shenandoah, Iowa) of people in Iowa, Nebraska, and Missouri, the Kansan ranked surprisingly high. He had not been listed by the station among the possible Republican nominees, but of the 6,040 votes cast he received 806 write-in ballots.[31]

Meanwhile, Landon had declared his support of Senator Arthur Capper for the Republican presidential nomination, a choice that most Republicans in Kansas regarded as binding upon their 1940 convention delegation. The veteran editor of the *Topeka State Journal*, Arthur Carruth, then publicly raised the question that many Kansans were asking: "What about Alf Landon?" This question was repeated in a number of other Kansas newspapers, including Capper's *Topeka Capital*, and it was also asked outside the state. As late as April, 1940, Gifford Pinchot wrote Landon: "I wish to goodness that you might be a candidate again."[32]

Landon, however, was serious; he would not permit his name to be considered. His chief political aide, Lacy Haynes, wrote to reassure the Dewey forces of this—and that there would be no serious Capper-for-President movement. Capper would be presented, Haynes wrote, only to give him the honor of having been placed in nomination.[33] By nominally supporting Capper, Landon retained freedom of action: he did not intend to commit himself prematurely, inasmuch as a third term for Roosevelt and the issues of peace or war might have to be decided. It was only October, 1939, and much could happen before the convention in 1940.

[31] Landon to Ralph McGill, October 6, 1939; *Atlanta Constitution*, September 23, 24, 1939; *Des Moines Sunday Register*, October 22, 1939.

[32] *Topeka State Journal*, October 9, 1939; *Topeka Capital*, October 11, 1939; *Elkhart Tri-State News*, October 26, 1939; M. Nelson McGeary, *Gifford Pinchot, Forester, Politician* (Princeton: Princeton University Press, 1960), p. 422.

[33] Lacy Haynes to Roger W. Straus, October 20, 1939, Dewey Papers.

CHAPTER 18

Politics in Time of Peril—1940

Landon, although firm in his decision not to seek renomination, was displeased with the prospective crop of Republican presidential nominees. Dewey was not campaigning adroitly; even worse, the views of Borah, Vandenberg, and even those of Capper would take the Republican party back to a nineteenth-century isolationist position.[1] Moreover, although he agreed with Roosevelt's statements that Republicans and Democrats must, in the national interest, cooperate on foreign affairs and defense measures, Landon thought the President insincere in his calls for unity.

Particularly disturbing was the incident created by the President on the occasion of the capital's Jackson Day dinner on January 8, 1940. Roosevelt had announced that his address would be nonpartisan, and as a gesture of unity had invited three Republicans to attend; because it was a Democratic meeting, however, the Republicans declined. Roosevelt's scolding of the three Republicans seemed to Landon the action that "might be expected of a national chairman." He told the press:

> It wasn't necessary for the three Republican leaders to attend the Democratic meeting to portray national unity. The way to get national unity is for the President to invite them to the White House and talk things over. He

[1] Landon to W. A. Sheaffer, December 27, 1939, Alfred M. Landon Papers, Kansas State Historical Society, Topeka.

needn't do all the talking himself, either, and attempt to tell them what they should do. He should talk it over and then agree what to do.

Landon also commented on the incident in a letter to William Allen White. "I have gone further in support of his foreign policy than any other Republican, and I have been severely criticized for it. I have done this because I know that every move we make in America is being closely watched by all the foreign countries." The President had not reciprocated.

> Instead of leading this spirit of unity, he attempts to pull his usual slick political stunt. In the first place, his speech was not nonpartisan, as he announced it would be; in the second place, instead of magnifying for the foreign observer an appearance of disunity, where none existed, he should have been playing it down. He has played a rotten trick on the country.[2]

Despite his anger with Roosevelt, Landon continued his friendly relations with other Democrats. For example, he responded to a call for financial help from George Fort Milton—who was trying to establish a liberal Democratic newspaper in Chattanooga—by buying ten shares of stock in the newspaper, the *Chattanooga Evening Tribune*, and subscribing to it.[3]

As his interest in Dewey flagged, Landon began to promote Joseph W. Martin for the Republican presidential nomination. As early as May, 1939, the Kansan had mentioned the House minority leader as a possible nominee, and later that year he had been instrumental in securing Martin as the chief speaker at the 1940 Kansas Day celebration. Martin was also mentioned by the press in connection with the nomination. *Life* magazine, in reviewing the possible Republican nominees, featured Martin, Vandenberg, and Dewey. The magazine pictured the minority leader as a man adept at using persuasion and encouragement in developing a "vigorous, intelligent, effective opposition" to the President in the Congress, an opposition that had resulted in increased government economy and in the passage of the Hatch Act, which restricted partisan activities in the federal civil service.[4]

[2] *Kansas City Star*, January 9, 1940; Landon to W. A. White, January 9, 1940.

[3] George Fort Milton to Landon, January 5, 1940; Landon to Milton, January 8, 17, 1940.

[4] Henry J. Allen to David Hinshaw, December 8, 1939; Landon to Lacy Haynes, January 5, 1940; *Life*, January 1, 1940, pp. 48 ff.

By January, 1940, Landon had made the arrangements that would make Kansas Day a meeting of national importance. Although Martin was to give the main address, Dewey had not been overlooked; one of Dewey's assistant district attorneys, Francis E. Rivers, also would speak. The festival reflected Landon's flexibility on the selection of the party's next nominee. Leaders from most parts of the country were on hand: Martin; New York national committeeman Kenneth Simpson; William Hornbeck, chairman of the Young Republican National Federation; J. Russell Sprague, Dewey's campaign manager; national committeeman Hill Blackett of Illinois; and Jake Meckstroth of Ohio, who was a Robert Taft leader. Other party leaders came from Iowa, Nebraska, Utah, Oklahoma, Arkansas, Missouri, South Dakota, and North Dakota.

The Kansas Day event made it clear that most of the midwestern Republican leaders would go to the national convention unpledged. They were, as James A. Hagerty of the *New York Times* wrote, "prepared to vote for the nomination of a man, who in their judgment, would make the best President, if elected, and who would make the best candidate, when nominated." Hagerty said these leaders were not necessarily hostile to Dewey's candidacy, but they were displeased with reports that the New Yorker would probably be unable to command all of the delegates from his state at the national convention. There was considerable interest in Martin, but it was clear that he could be nominated only by a shift of delegates after a deadlock among the other candidates. This was as Landon wanted it; he was interested in a Martin movement chiefly as a device to make it impossible for any candidate to claim—before the convention—that he had clinched the nomination. Landon's encouragement of Martin also served to warn the presidential aspirants that they would have to work for the nomination, and that the party would therefore have to remain flexible on program and strategy until the convention.[5]

The warning was not sufficient, however. Landon had been told by Gifford Pinchot that the Pew brothers, encouraged by their success in Pennsylvania in 1938, were striving for complete control of their state's delegation. Other reports indicated they would also try to control the delegations from Oklahoma, Florida, Indiana, and Illinois. Lacy Haynes called Frank Knox to warn him of the plans of the conservative

[5] *New York Times*, January 29, 30, 31, 1940.

Pennsylvania leaders, and Knox, Landon, and Pinchot joined together in an attempt to block the Pews.[6]

In early April, Landon openly espoused flexibility in the Republican party. In a nationally broadcast speech he told the Kansas Republican convention in Wichita: "This is our year!" but the party "must show it is prepared . . . to solve . . . the problems of business, agriculture, and the workingman." To do this, the national "Republican convention must not be of the boss-ridden kind that the Democratic Convention will be. It must be one in which the voice of the people will prevail." In an obvious reference to Joseph Pew and the American Liberty League, Landon said: "We must not permit one man, or any group of money-raisers, to pick our nominee."[7]

Landon, of course, was concerned with expanding the representativeness of the Republican party in order to secure a liberal or moderate nominee and the adoption of liberal farm planks—the essential platform demand of the midwest—and his many allies in this struggle included Senate minority leader Charles L. McNary, Minnesota Governor Harold Stassen, Frank Knox (who had become reconciled to many of the reforms of the 1930's), Joseph Martin, Gifford Pinchot, and Senator Arthur Capper. Gaining the support that would assure an open convention required concessions on other vital issues, and, although Landon disagreed with the widespread Republican sentiment for the repeal of reciprocal trade legislation and for a declaration of absolute neutrality during the war in Europe, he decided to remain silent for the time being. By late March, however, the Kansan thought he had lined up 140 delegates who would help him block control of the convention by the party's extreme elements and nominate a man with a broad outlook and appeal.[8]

Because the task of formulating an acceptable platform would be as difficult as finding a suitable presidential nominee, Landon—and many others—proposed that the resolutions committee meet at least a week before the beginning of the convention. This proposal won wide

[6] Frank Knox to Landon, January 12, 17, 1940; Landon to Knox, January 16, 1940.

[7] Landon speech, Wichita, April 4, 1940. Surprisingly, at the national convention Landon found Pew to be open-minded. The people the Kansan found difficult to deal with were Governor Arthur H. James and former Senator Joseph R. Grundy, who really controlled the Pennsylvania delegation and spearheaded the most conservative forces at the convention. Landon interview, May 2, 1963.

[8] *New York Times*, April 7, 1940; Landon to Raymond Clapper, March 29, 1940.

support, which reflected the party's desire to avoid a convention battle on platform questions. In May, 1940, Landon disclosed his position on a number of platform issues. He planned to fight the protectionists on the tariff plank, which he tied in with the question of farm subsidies: if the party went on record—as many Republicans wanted—for reduced agricultural subsidies, it must also oppose the great subsidies that industry would get from the imposition of high tariffs. He also made it clear that he would fight any attempt to reject the best of the New Deal measures, such as social security, the regulation of utilities and stock markets, the wages-and-hours law, and the provisions for collective bargaining.[9] Repudiation of such legislation would ruin any chance of a Republican victory at the polls; more importantly, the Kansan believed, it would injure national stability.

Landon also hoped the party would support the development of strong defense forces so as to make it understood abroad that the United States intended to defend its interests; this, however, had to be coupled with a foreign policy that would keep the United States out of other nations' affairs. Landon had opposed the Declaration of Panama (adopted by the Conference of Inter-American States in October, 1939) and President Roosevelt's wish to implement the declaration by means of a 300-mile-wide neutrality belt around the western hemisphere and an American naval patrol. Such a patrol, Landon said, raised questions "full of peril to our neutral position," and because this policy could lead to incidents that might result in war, the Kansan believed that Republicans should not give advance support to the President's conduct of foreign relations.[10] But the necessity of resisting involvement in the war did not mean the United States could ignore what was happening in Europe. Landon wrote, in early April, that the nation should continue to exert pressure for world peace, even to the extent of helping arrange a peace settlement—and even if it had to lend its gold to restore peace and stability in Europe. He also thought that, when peace came, the United States should materially encourage democratic movements in central Europe. (As for the use of American gold, Landon did not care if it were lost in the process; because gold then seemed worthless to the United States, it might as well be applied where it could be of use.) [11]

[9] *Christian Science Monitor*, May 4, 1940.

[10] William L. Langer and S. Everett Gleason, *The Challenge to Isolation, 1937–1940* (New York: Harper, 1952), p. 214; Landon to Preston Wolfe, February 19, 1940.

[11] Landon to E. H. Taylor, April 8, 1940.

After the nazi conquests of Denmark, Norway, and the Low Countries, Landon's peace program became impracticable. He still believed, however, that the United States should assist the postwar reconstruction of Europe because of the mutuality of American and European stability; not only did he cling to this belief, he was bold enough to state it publicly—as early as May, 1940.[12] Discussion of this forerunner of the Marshall Plan was impossible at that time because other, more pressing problems had to be solved for America.

Republican discord bubbled to the surface in early spring as Vandenberg's candidacy gained momentum. Landon was unhappy with this development, and particularly with the announcements of Senators McNary and Capper in support of Vandenberg. Landon felt that Capper should have discussed the endorsement with him because the senator was the presidential candidate of the Kansas Republicans and because Capper's support of the conservative Vandenberg might split the forces working for a liberal platform.[13] In reading between the lines, it would seem that Landon feared Vandenberg's candidacy would be used by eastern industrialists to dominate the national convention. Despite the increasing interest among Republicans as to who the nominee should be, Landon, in partnership with Knox, continued to emphasize the need for a "good progressive declaration of principles" by the party in the convention. Both men talked with many Republican leaders about this; Knox, who traveled throughout the country, was the field man in this endeavor, and Landon worked on the telephone. Knox reported considerable support from a variety of sources for such a declaration, from such men as Senator McNary, Representative Martin, Senator Styles Bridges of New Hampshire, and the prominent Taft leader, Clarence Brown of Ohio; it even appeared that Senator Vandenberg would accept it. Although the Dewey forces would support such a declaration, Knox thought they could not spearhead it because Dewey's chances for the nomination appeared to be slipping. Other good news came when national chairman John D. M. Hamilton, in one of his infrequent letters to Landon, wrote that he would like to assemble the resolutions committee well in advance of the convention. Landon thought this was excellent; it was in line with

12 *Washington Star*, May 23, 1940.
13 Landon to E. H. Taylor, April 8, 1940.

his and Knox's suggestion for an unusually thorough consideration of the Republican platform.[14]

Events in Kansas, meanwhile, were giving Landon trouble. Senator Clyde Reed had exasperated Landon and the rest of the state organization, and Landon had decided that Reed, because of his cantankerousness, should not be a member of the Kansas delegation to the national convention. Although William Allen White tried to persuade Landon to endorse Reed as a delegate, Landon refused, thinking he "was entitled to have a *friendly* delegation." Reed decided to contest Landon's decision, and, against the advice of most of his friends, ran for election as a convention delegate. Landon, accepting this challenge to his leadership, declared that Reed would be defeated by a three-to-one margin, that there was harmony among the state's Republicans and that they were not going to permit the senator to disrupt it. Reed persisted in his struggle, and was crushed in the election, carrying only one of Kansas' 105 counties. As William Allen White said, "Landon won by something in between an avalanche and a house afire"; but the senator continued to fight Landon. Although he returned to Kansas with authority from the Senate to investigate the connection between the election and alleged relief frauds in Shawnee, Sedgwick, and Labette counties, he proved only that he had far fewer political friends who were willing to work for him than Landon had. In White's view, the "honorable Alfred Landon, is getting stubborner and stubborner, and . . . Senator Clyde Reed, is getting meaner and meaner."[15]

Throughout the spring Landon had avoided being pinned down on his choice for the nomination. He had grown increasingly fond of the flamboyant, energetic Knox, as well as of Joseph Martin, but preferred the latter because of his reliability and common sense. Landon wrote Knox, toward the end of April, that he had suggested the two as dark-horse candidates to Roy Howard, the head of the powerful Scripps-Howard newspaper syndicate. This interest in dark horses was a result of the Kansan's continued displeasure with the leading candidates: Dewey, Vandenberg, and Senator Robert A. Taft. Dewey, it seemed, did not know how to work with people, and apparently

[14] Frank Knox to Landon, April 19, 1940; John D. M. Hamilton to Landon, April 20, 1940; Landon to Hamilton, April 29, 1940.

[15] Landon to W. A. White, October 13, 1939; *Emporia Weekly Gazette*, June 6, 1940; Landon to Duke Shoop, March 7, 1940; Clyde M. Reed to G. W. Marble, April 15, 1940, enclosed in Lacy Haynes to Landon, April 18, 1940.

could not take advice; moreover—as far as Landon was concerned—he had not taken a stand on any of the chief issues before the party. The Kansan was also disturbed by the votes of Vandenberg and Taft against farm parity payments; he felt that this opposition—as well as widespread Republican hostility to fair labor legislation—was unwise. Farmers and workers were not going to vote against programs that had given them something in preference to programs that would not help them.

As Landon surveyed the crop of candidates, though, he could not avoid leaning toward Dewey, the most liberal of the contenders. Knox stood little chance because of his feuds with his fellow Chicago publisher, Robert R. McCormick of the *Tribune*, and his disagreements with many of the downstate Illinois Republicans. And Martin probably could not control enough delegates to carry him very far. By late April, Landon had again warmed up to the New Yorker. He felt that national committeeman Kenneth Simpson, who was bucking Dewey's leadership, was mistaken—another way of saying that Dewey, for all his faults, would be acceptable as the nominee.[16] Continuing to hope for a political miracle, however, he refused to go so far as to support Dewey for President.

By May, 1940, a new situation threatened to throw the Republican party off balance—Roosevelt's attempt to appoint Republicans to his cabinet. Rumors of this had begun as early as September, 1939, when Landon and Knox had been invited to participate in the White House conference on revision of the Neutrality Act. When Landon reached Washington, some of the reporters who met him said that he was being considered for a cabinet position, which Landon said was "Washington latrine gossip." But it was more than gossip. Roosevelt had toyed with the idea of bringing Landon and Knox into the cabinet as early as December, 1938, and had seriously considered it in September, 1939, but had decided against it after Landon had publicly demanded that he not run for a third term.[17]

16 Landon to Frank Knox, April 22, 1940; Landon to Harold B. Johnson, March 1, 25, 1940; Landon to R. W. Robbins, April 30, 1940.

17 Landon to Eliot Janeway, May 29, 1947 (most of this letter is reproduced in Eliot Janeway, *Struggle for Survival* (New Haven: Yale Univ. Press, 1950), pp. 128 ff.); Landon to Sterling Morton, January 13, 1949; Langer and Gleason, *Challenge to Isolation*, p. 509; Harold L. Ickes, *The Secret Diary of Harold L. Ickes: The Lowering Clouds* (New York: Simon & Schuster, 1954), pp. 8, 12, 21 ff.; Louis Brownlow, *A Passion for Anonymity: The Autobiography of Louis Brownlow* (Chicago: University of Chicago Press, 1958), pp. 433 ff.

In December, 1939, Roosevelt had offered Frank Knox the post of Secretary of the Navy, as a gesture of national unity. Knox told Landon he had turned it down, although reluctantly, because it might be thought he had betrayed his party if he were the only Republican to enter the cabinet. The publisher told Roosevelt that another Republican would also have to be appointed, because one Republican member would not make a coalition cabinet. Knox, later in December, wrote the President that he had heard rumors that Colonel William Donovan (one of the publisher's 1936 campaign aides) was being considered for Secretary of War, and Knox thought the appointment of himself and Donovan, on a patriotic basis, would be splendid. Roosevelt, in reply, said he understood Knox's position, but—even though Donovan would make a good cabinet member—he feared that the appointment of two Republicans "in charge of the armed forces might be misunderstood in both parties." Roosevelt indicated that he would let the matter lie for a while.[18]

During the months that followed, rumors persisted that Knox and Landon were being considered for the cabinet, and, for Landon, this passed beyond the rumor stage with a series of incidents in May, 1940. Frank Altschul, the brother-in-law of New York's Democratic governor, Herbert Lehman, telephoned Landon on May 13. Altschul, a Republican, asked Landon if he knew of Washington's discussions about the Kansan's appointment to a government post; and Landon said that he did. Altschul then asked if he would be willing to talk with the President about the matter, to which Landon replied: "I would be glad to talk to the President on any subject that he desired to talk to me about." Said Altschul: "Governor Lehman is going over to Washington tonight. Can he take that message?" Landon said he could.

On May 15, Roosevelt's military aide, General Edwin Watson, received a White House memorandum: "The President would like to have Governor Landon come to lunch on Wednesday or Thursday of next week"; and Watson called Landon, asking him for lunch on either May 22 or 23. Landon said he would be delighted to come, but he pointed out that he would broadcast a speech on foreign policies, from Warrensburg, Missouri, on May 17. Because he was going to take some "pokes" at the President, it would perhaps be best for the White House to wait until after the speech before making its invitation

---

[18] Landon to Eliot Janeway, May 29, 1947; Landon to Sterling Morton, January 13, 1949; Frank Knox to Franklin D. Roosevelt, December 15, 1939, and Roosevelt to Knox, December 29, 1939, Franklin D. Roosevelt Library, Hyde Park, N.Y.

public. Landon sent the President's office a copy of the speech, which General Watson showed to Frank Knox. Knox called Landon to say that he would ruin himself with the speech, that now—because the Low Countries had fallen—was no time to criticize the President. Landon asked if there was anything in the speech that hit below the belt. Knox agreed there was not, but he held that Landon's criticisms were poorly timed. Although Knox was upset by the speech, the White House apparently was not. On May 16 General Watson telegraphed Landon that Roosevelt would expect him May 22, and the Kansan accepted the luncheon date.[19]

Before leaving for Washington, Landon turned to other matters, the first of which was the delivery of his Warrensburg speech. Talking to the Johnson County Republicans—and a national radio audience—Landon declared that the United States was "going to keep out of this war" because the American people did not want their soldiers "to fight a foreign war on a foreign soil." Moreover, the country need not fear attack if it repaired the "deplorable" state of its national defense system. The Kansan praised the President for his new awareness of the immediate need for modernizing the nation's defenses, extending his support of efforts to prepare an impregnable defense and accomplish unity on foreign policy. But, Landon said, "the grave questions of foreign relations and national defense must be discussed, free of the usual invectives that characterize most of New Deal discussion, and as far as possible free from partisan bias."[20]

The next day, May 18, the White House released the news that Landon would lunch with President Roosevelt the following week. On May 19 the Kansan received telephone calls from Republican leaders all over the country saying that if he entered the cabinet, as was rumored, the 1940 election might as well be called off. Landon, who had not decided what he would do if Roosevelt offered him a cabinet post, and greatly affected by these telephone calls, met that night with Bernard Kilgore of the *Wall Street Journal*, Roscoe Drummond of the *Christian Science Monitor*, Alvin McCoy of the *Kansas City Star*, and Turner Catledge of the *New York Times* (all of whom had remained in Topeka after covering a speech by Senator Taft the day before). The

[19] Landon to Eliot Janeway, May 29, 1947; Landon to Sterling Morton, January 13, 1949; G. G. T. (presumably Grace Tully) to Edwin Watson, May 15, 1940, Watson to Landon, May 15, 1940, memorandum initialed by Watson, May 15, 1940, Watson to Landon, May 16, 1940, Landon to Watson, May 16, 1940, all FDRL.

[20] Landon speech, Warrensburg, Mo., May 17, 1940.

newsmen said the Republican party was facing the greatest crisis in its existence; with the impact of the world crisis, pressure was mounting that Republicans not contest the President's reelection. They pointed out that such influential observers as Dorothy Thompson and H. V. Kaltenborn were already urging this publicly.

Afterward, Landon and his visitors worked out a statement on the need for continuing regular election activities, and the statement was given to the *Kansas City Star* in Landon's name.

> In this critical period, when free government is under attack in the world, it becomes doubly urgent that we in America safeguard and maintain the essential functions of democracy. The very bases of these functions are free elections and party responsibility.
>
> I cannot observe without great concern proposals that we voluntarily place some limitations upon these functions as the result of the acceleration of the war in Europe. I regard as dangerous any attempts to decrease the vitality of the two-party system as it operates in this country or to obscure the meaning or purpose of the forthcoming party conventions and the national election. . . . We can, and will achieve any necessary degree of national unity without impairing the normal preparation of the conventions, the campaign and the election—the system by which the people themselves choose and support their leadership.
>
> Specifically, I am opposed to any suggestion that the Republican party postpone its National Convention or lend itself to any intangible coalition which would tend to decrease party responsibility. We Republicans can best serve the ends of national unity by maintaining ourselves as a patriotic and constructive party of the opposition until we are voted into power by the election next November. Thereafter, the country will need and expect the same service from our Democratic friends. Meanwhile all of us should avoid hysteria, keep our feet on the ground, and remain conscious of our opportunity to serve America and the world by strengthening the normal processes of democracy here at home.

After the statement had been sent, the newsmen said that Landon must know that this criticism of the idea of coalition meant he would not be offered a cabinet post. Landon replied:

> I know it, and that's the way I want it. I will only take it under one condition [that Roosevelt not run for a third term]. I don't think the President will meet that condition. Therefore, I want to save the President the embarrassment of offering me the cabinet position, and myself the embarrassment of refusing it.[21]

[21] Landon interview, April 16, 1963; Landon to Eliot Janeway, May 29, 1947; Landon press statement, May 19, 1940.

Landon left for Washington on May 20, so that he could visit with Frank Knox before his meeting in the capital, and, upon reaching Chicago, he refused to make a statement to the press about his appointment with the President. When he went to his hotel room he found that Frank Altschul was calling, and that General Watson had asked him to cancel the engagement with Roosevelt. Landon asked why the White House had canceled the engagement. Altschul replied that, because of Landon's Warrensburg speech and his press statement, the luncheon could serve no useful purpose. When Landon asked what Watson thought he should say about the matter, Altschul said the general had suggested that Landon say he had become suddenly ill and therefore had to postpone his visit to Washington. Landon replied: "I won't say any such damn thing." He hung up the telephone and turned to Arthur Evans, of the *Chicago Tribune*, who had been trying to get a statement from him, and said "I left for Washington at the invitation of my President. I am returning home at his invitation. I will go again whenever my President asks me to." Landon then arranged a press conference for the next morning—and had his telephone service shut off for the night.

The next morning Landon read a statement that repeated what he had told Evans the evening before, and, as he was finishing the statement, Hill Blackett told Landon the White House was waiting to talk to him on the telephone. "Hold everything," Landon said to the reporters, "I don't know what this means." When Landon answered the phone, President Roosevelt was put on:

> Alf, between Watson and Altschul, they got us all balled up. I didn't mean to cancel our luncheon. I wanted them to see if we could postpone it until Thursday. I have been wanting to see [Congressman James] Wadsworth and a committee, but I find I can see him this afternoon so you come on. We won't have any trouble understanding ourselves when we get our feet under the table.

Landon thanked Roosevelt and said he would be at the White House as expected. Withdrawing his statement to the newsmen, Landon told them simply that the President had called and asked him to come to Washington. (An explanation similar to the one told Landon was given to the newspapers by the White House, but newsmen who called Wadsworth's office found that the congressman was out of town.) [22]

That noon, as Knox and Landon lunched together, Knox said he was perturbed by the prospect of a nazi victory in Europe and by the

[22] Landon to Eliot Janeway, May 29, 1947; *Washington Star*, May 21, 1940.

threat this posed to the kind of civilization the two of them believed in—
as well as to the security of the United States. The publisher indicated
that, because of this, he was weakening on the matter of entering the
cabinet. Landon agreed that there were times when the country had
to be placed above a party, but he also thought "a third successive
term for any President is as great a threat to our institutions as anything
from the outside. If we go into the cabinet we might as well call off the
election." Landon said he had received this same expression from
persons all over the country after the announcement of his luncheon
appointment with Roosevelt. "While our country is in great danger,"
Landon added, "there has got to be *quid-pro-quo* for the 16 million that
honored and trusted us with their confidence in 1936, and that is that
the President will not be a candidate for the third term."

Knox declared that Roosevelt could not run again because of his
physical condition. Showing his trembling hands, the President had
once told Knox: "Look at me, Frank. How can I physically take
another term of this punishment?" "I know," said Landon, "but I
don't trust him." Knox then asked if the two of them might request the
President to write them a statement saying he would not be a candidate
for a third term. Landon believed such a request would put them in a
poor position, as Roosevelt had already said he was unable to run
again; it would appear, on the eve of possibly going into his cabinet,
that they were calling him a liar. Landon said they should agree to
enter the cabinet only if Roosevelt stated publicly that he would not
run for a third term.

Knox replied that he guessed Landon was right, and asked him to tell
Roosevelt that the Kansan spoke for both of the Republican leaders, but
Landon said he ought to tell the President that himself. He suggested
that Knox write the President of his agreement with Landon, and
the Kansan would take his note to Paul Leach, the *Chicago Daily News'*
Washington correspondent, who could deliver it to the White House
before Landon arrived for lunch with the President. Knox gave Landon
the note that afternoon:

> I have had a long and very thorough-going conference with Alf Landon
> and we have reached a mutual conclusion which he will convey to you
> when he sees you. In the light of events which almost hourly show graver
> implications for us and for the world our thinking was animated solely by
> the desire to promote national unity in the face of grave national peril.[23]

[23] Landon interview, April 16, 1963; Landon to Eliot Janeway, May 29, 1947;
Frank Knox to Franklin D. Roosevelt, May 21, 1940, FDRL.

Landon, at the train station, told Knox he doubted the President would
offer him a cabinet position the next day, and had therefore drafted a
statement, which he would read after leaving the White House, that
would again call upon Roosevelt to foster national unity by taking
himself out of the 1940 presidential race. Knox agreed to this and said
Landon should tell the press that he also spoke for Knox.

Landon's luncheon visit with the President on May 22 lasted for two
hours. The two men chatted pleasantly, although not seriously, about
domestic politics; then they turned to the foreign situation. Landon
was struck by the President's audacity when the latter commented that
he was going to tell Ambassador William Bullitt to suggest to Premier
Paul Reynaud of France that 450,000 soldiers guarding the Italian
border be withdrawn for a flank attack on Germany. The President
also said he would have to replace Charles Edison as Secretary of the
Navy because he was running for governor of New Jersey; and he added
that Secretary of War Harry Woodring and Secretary of Labor Frances
Perkins could no longer be permitted to remain in the cabinet. Roosevelt said he was considering some thirty or forty men to find replacements for these three officials. In response to a question by Landon, he
said he did not care whether the replacements were Republicans or
Democrats. "Alf, don't believe everything you read in the newspapers.
If you will just call me I will be glad to set you straight." As
Landon had expected, his appointment to the cabinet was never
mentioned.[24]

In a brief press conference, an hour after he left the White House,
Landon called upon Roosevelt—for the sake of national unity—not to
run for a third term. If the President ran for reelection, he said, any
Republican who entered the cabinet would be considered a party to
the third-term ambition. Before meeting the newsmen, Landon had
called Knox to tell him that he had not been offered a cabinet position,
and he had read Knox the final draft of his press statement. Knox said
"Bully!" and asked Landon to tell the press that he spoke for both of
the Republican leaders. Landon hesitated, and Knox—catching his
hesitation—asked: "Don't you think you should?" Landon replied
that he was "thinking of your own prestige and your own position of

[24] Landon to Eliot Janeway, May 29, 1947; Landon to Sterling Morton, January
13, 1949; Landon interview, April 16, 1963. The evidence from Landon and the
circumstances surrounding his luncheon at the White House contradict the assumption
by Langer and Gleason (in *Challenge to Isolation*, pp. 509 f.) that Landon had told
President Roosevelt he approved Knox's taking a post in the cabinet if another
Republican entered with him.

party leadership. It would be better for you to make your own statement."

Although Knox drafted a statement that said he would not enter the cabinet unless the President refused to run for reelection, he showed it to one of his senior editors, Paul Mowrer, who persuaded him that he was obligated to discuss the matter with the President. Knox wired Landon on May 24: "In considering matter discussed over phone became convinced that since proposal was made personally proprieties required that I respond personally before publicly discussing the matter." Knox said he was going to Washington that day on other business, and that he might be able to talk with Roosevelt.[25]

Although Roosevelt had once again changed his mind about inviting Landon to join the government, he still wanted Knox, and he was able to persuade the Chicago publisher to be receptive to a cabinet appointment. When Landon next saw Knox—toward the end of May, in Kansas City—it was apparent that the publisher's attitude had changed. Knox again appeared confident that the President would not run for a third term. Later, in a letter to Landon, Knox said he was depressed by the German advances in France and was convinced that speedy action had to be taken by the United States in preparing its defenses. Like the old soldier he was, Knox felt a duty to take part in the defense effort. (He was also distressed by the insularity of Republican politics in Illinois and in the country.) Landon, in trying to discourage Knox from entering the cabinet, said that he too was disturbed by foreign developments. "I find it difficult," he wrote, "to think about our own immediate political problems, in view of the terribly depressing news from Europe. The leaders of France and England have certainly made a terrible mess of their responsibility. I am commencing to wonder if the English are worth fighting for." Knox replied that he had no particular love for England, and that its leaders were responsible for much of their nation's trouble, but that he was concerned about the position of the United States. He believed that every day the allies could be kept resisting Germany would be a day's gain for the United States in preparing its own defense. That same day, June 11, Knox decided to join the government, as Secretary of the Navy, if another Republican were also appointed to the cabinet.[26]

[25] *Washington Star*, May 23, 1940; Landon interview, April 16, 1963; Frank Knox to Landon, May 24, 1940.

[26] Landon to Eliot Janeway, May 29, 1947; Frank Knox to Landon, June 8, 11, 1940; Landon to Knox, June 10, 1940; Frank Knox to Annie Knox, June 11, 1940, Frank Knox Papers, Manuscript Division, Library of Congress, Washington, D.C.

Meanwhile, toward the end of May, Grenville Clark and Felix Frankfurter had arranged with Roosevelt for the appointment of Republicans Henry Stimson and Robert Patterson as Secretary and Assistant Secretary of War, respectively. The entry of Knox, Stimson, and Patterson in the government not only eliminated several controversial persons from the President's official family—Secretary of the Navy Edison, Secretary of War Woodring, and Assistant Secretary of War Louis Johnson—but permitted Roosevelt to claim that he had formed a coalition, national-unity government. The Republicans were offered, and accepted, their posts on June 19, on the eve of the opening of the Republican national convention, a political advantage of which the President must have been keenly aware.[27]

Although by early June Landon had become convinced that Knox would enter the cabinet, he was sick at heart when the appointment was made. Having just sat down for one of his favorite meals—a New England boiled dinner—he was told of Knox's acceptance. He sent the dinner back to the kitchen, and had milk and crackers instead. Landon, however, did not criticize his former running mate for taking the position; as he later wrote: "I have never believed Knox wanted the job just for the sake of being in the cabinet."

The Kansan thought Knox's decision to accept the secretaryship was prompted by his desire to serve his country in a time of crisis, but other Republicans did not take the news so philosophically. The Stimson and Knox appointments, coming as they did just before the opening of the national convention, were widely interpreted as the rankest kind of political sabotage. The *New York World-Telegram* contended that the appointments did not make a coalition cabinet because Knox and Stimson were not representative of the Republican party. National chairman John Hamilton declared that Knox and Stimson were "no longer qualified to speak as Republicans or for the Republican organization," adding that their inclusion in the government made the Democratic party the "war party." Hamilton's comments contrasted with Landon's public statement that Knox and Stimson were good appointees.[28]

[27] Elting E. Morison, *Turmoil and Tradition, A Study of the Life and Times of Henry L. Stimson* (Boston: Houghton Mifflin, 1960), pp. 476 ff.

[28] Landon to Sterling Morton, January 13, 1949; *New York World-Telegram*, June 20, 21, 1940; *San Francisco Examiner*, June 21, 1940; *New York Herald Tribune*, June 21, 1940.

Despite his fencing with Roosevelt over the cabinet appointments, Landon, in May and June, had been chiefly interested in preparing for the Republican national convention. His main concern was the development of a satisfactory platform. By May, he had asked a variety of his political associates for their suggestions on the platform—such men as Knox, W. W. Waymack of the *Des Moines Register*, Henry Haskell of the *Kansas City Star*, Bruce Barton, William Allen White, Gifford Pinchot, and J. Reuben Clark. Landon wanted a platform that would "furnish all proper help to the democracies while avoiding commitments that would take us into war except in defense of vital American interests." The platform should also urge speedy and adequate preparation for national defense, encouragement of business expansion to absorb the millions of jobless, improvement of agricultural and social security programs, protection of the rights of labor, and planning for "a sound economic world order" after the war.[29] The Landon and Dewey forces cooperated on constructing the platform, partly because Dewey still sought the Kansan's help in gaining the presidential nomination. Landon, happy in turn to accept Dewey's support on platform matters, softened his attitude toward the New Yorker, though he remained committed to the idea of a convention in which the delegates, not the organization leaders, would select the nominees.[30]

It was partly because of Landon's commitment to an open convention that Thomas E. Dewey was not to have the support necessary to become the Republican presidential candidate in 1940 and that the nomination went to Wendell Willkie, who was virtually unknown to the party's leadership. Although Willkie, an attorney and former Democrat, had made headlines by defending the interests of southern electric corporations, and as a critic of the New Deal in 1938 and 1939, he was not a national figure until his nomination, in June, 1940. Nevertheless, he had attracted enough attention in eastern business circles to receive much support there for the nomination. Landon wrote in late April: "Somebody is spending a lot of money on Willkie, and

[29] Landon to Joseph W. Martin, May 8, 1940; "Mr. Haskell's version—The Republican Party Promises," n.d. (probably May, 1940).

[30] Landon to Thomas E. Dewey, May 6, 1940; Dewey to Landon, May 10, 15, 1940; Dewey to W. A. Sheaffer, May 31, 1940; Sheaffer to Dewey, June 6, 1940, Thomas E. Dewey Papers, University of Rochester Libraries, Rochester, N.Y. A letter from Landon to Henry P. Fletcher (May 20, 1940, in the Fletcher Papers, Manuscript Division, Library of Congress, Washington, D.C.) indicates that the Kansan was still encouraging Joseph W. Martin, whom Fletcher favored for the nomination.

it's silly, as far as nomination is concerned. He may get a lot of advertising that's worth something to him in his business." Despite the seeming impossibility of Willkie's nomination, his campaign went forward, and Landon was impressed. He wrote in late May that the Willkie campaign was amazing; and he thought it reflected Willkie's dynamic personality as well as widespread dissatisfaction with the other candidates. Although Landon had serious doubts about the advisability of nominating a public utilities spokesman, he thought this aspect of Willkie's background might be offset by the nation's preoccupation with foreign affairs.[31]

When Willkie visited Kansas, on Memorial Day, 1940, Landon had an opportunity to see him in action. He invited him to his house— along with thirty other politicans—for a buffet dinner, and he later heard him speak at an impromptu meeting at the railroad station, where 500 people were present. He wrote Senator Capper on June 5: "Willkie made a splendid impression in Topeka. And it's rather amazing, the letters I receive endorsing his candidacy. If he had ever held a public office, and was not a utility man, he would be a real contender because of his robust personality and ability to express himself." A week later, Landon wrote that Dewey had not slipped in the west, but Willkie was coming up remarkably.[32] To the Kansan, however, Willkie was then no more than a fascinating comet that would soon burn out.

Landon was making significant efforts on behalf of the Republican party. Early in 1940, the party's morale had been ebbing; although it had won great victories in 1938, no outstanding candidates for the 1940 presidential nomination had developed, and the German conquests in Europe seemed to favor President Roosevelt—in terms of a third term or the election of his hand-picked successor. Many Republicans, furthermore, were dismayed by the rumors that Roosevelt would appoint one or two Republicans to his cabinet. Landon, on every possible occasion, tried to rally the party's spirit by asserting its responsibility for continuing the two-party system and perpetuating American democracy. Repeatedly, he declared that Republicans would find a nominee who could win in 1940 if they formulated a platform

[31] Landon to R. W. Robbins, April 25, 1940; Landon to Harold B. Johnson, May 29, 1940.
[32] Landon to W. W. Waymack, May 31, 1940; Landon to Arthur Capper, June 5, 1940; Landon to Harold B. Johnson, June 12, 1940.

that would appeal to the American public. In effect, he served as a party whip, urging, cajoling, and threatening in order to reinvigorate the party and develop sentiment for an attractive platform and a freely chosen nominee. Landon was not unsuccessful in all this: the party regained some of its vitality, the 1940 platform represented another step away from conservatism, and the presidential nominee was freely chosen in a wide-open convention. Even if Landon later had regrets about that nominee, he was satisfied that the party had maintained its existence, its integrity, and its role of opposition.

Landon also suffered several reverses, notably the arrangements committee's decision not to invite him to address the convention. John Hamilton had recommended that Landon and Hoover both be asked to speak to the convention, and the motion to invite Hoover was carried in the committee. When it was moved that Landon be invited, Kenneth Simpson of New York, to everybody's surprise, objected, on the ground that Landon and Hoover were not in the same category: one had been President of the United States, the other had not. Rather than embarrass Landon with further discussion of the question, and possibly an adverse vote, the sponsors of his invitation withdrew their motion. Landon, who had not sought to address the convention, shrugged the matter off as a maneuver to help nominate Hoover.[33]

Landon arrived in Philadelphia on June 15 for the pre-convention meetings of the resolutions committee, of which he was a member. In a statement to the press immediately after his arrival, Landon said an Allied defeat would be a calamity. Although he took sharp exception to President Roosevelt's offer (at Charlottesville, Virginia, on June 10) of the nation's resources to "the opponents of force," the Kansan advocated selling the Allies "all the material supplies we can properly [furnish]. . . . All of us are agreed on preparedness; on going the limit on national defense. . . . But I am not ready to agree that we should go into the war and send our boys overseas." Because of his prestige and his middle-of-the-road position on foreign policy, Landon was elected chairman of the resolutions subcommittee on national defense and foreign policy. In this role he tried to devise a plank that would keep the United States out of the war but still permit some forms of aid to the Allies. He had to contend not only with diehard isolationists, and the stormy reaction to the Knox and Stimson cabinet appointments, but also with swift-moving developments abroad, for France was on the verge of surrendering.

[33] *Buffalo Evening News*, May 31, 1940; Landon to Frank Knox, June 10, 1940.

Landon held day-and-night meetings of the subcommittee, and even extended the number of days it deliberated, in order to achieve a moderate plank. Although the plank his subcommittee finally reported satisfied him, the reaction of the resolutions committee members was that it was pro-Allies. Extreme anti-interventionist members of the committee, headed by C. Wayland Brooks of Illinois and Senator Henry Cabot Lodge of Massachusetts, led the fight to turn the plank into an isolationist manifesto, so that the plank read:

> The Republican Party stands for Americanism, preparedness and peace. We accordingly fasten upon the New Deal full responsibility for our unpreparedness and for the consequent danger of involvement in war. . . . We shall support all necessary and proper defense measures proposed by the administration in its belated effort to make up for lost time.

Landon, supported by Walter Edge of New Jersey, was successful in adding the statement:

> We favor the extension to all peoples fighting for liberty, or whose liberty is threatened, of such aid as shall not be in violation of international law or inconsistent with the requirements of our own national defense.

Thanks to Landon, as the *New York Herald Tribune* put it, the platform committee was rescued "from its worst blunders."[34]

Although not enthusiastic about the plank, Landon found it acceptable; it represented the views of various interests in the party. It took into account pro-Allies sentiment yet satisfied Republicans who demanded that their party not condone actions that would lead to "American blood being spilled on foreign battlefields." It committed the party to a stepped-up American defense effort, yet allowed Republicans to claim that theirs was the peace party. Landon believed the platform was flexible enough to permit the party and the Republican nominees to adjust to the swift changes in world and national affairs in 1940. It was so ambiguous that the presidential nominee could interpret it as he wished—and that, Landon thought, was as it should be in a year of unprecedented crisis.[35]

The next battle was for the nomination. Landon had made it clear

---

[34] Landon press statement, June 15, 1940; *New York Herald Tribune*, June 27, 29, 1940; Donald B. Johnson, *The Republican Party and Wendell Willkie* (Urbana: University of Illinois Press, 1960), pp. 84 ff.; *Chicago Daily News*, June 20, 1940; *Proceedings of the Twenty-second Republican National Convention* (Washington: Judd & Detweiler, 1940), p. 142.

[35] Johnson, *Willkie*, pp. 84 ff.; *Chicago Daily News*, June 26, 27, 1940; Landon to Harold B. Johnson, July 12, 1940.

that the Kansas delegates could vote the way they wanted after Senator Capper released them, and the delegates had divided sentiments; some favored Dewey, some favored Taft, and a few favored Willkie. The Willkie sentiment was growing stronger, partly because of the impact of his personality and partly because of the work of the Associated Willkie Clubs of America, which represented the efforts of many young Republicans for a revamped party. Even before the convention, some observers believed Willkie was the man to beat, but Landon was not impressed with this; he and most of the others thought only Taft, Vandenberg, and Dewey—and perhaps Hoover—were serious contenders for the nomination. The effort in behalf of Willkie, however, was tremendous. Telegrams and letters by the bushel were received by leading Republicans; and Landon himself received thousands of messages urging Willkie's nomination. The Kansan acknowledged the wires and letters, with the assistance of Joseph Pew's Philadelphia National Bank, but it turned out that many of the messages were fabricated; eighteen mail sacks of his replies awaited him when he returned to Topeka, all stamped "ADDRESS UNKNOWN." The extent—and the questionable nature—of the campaign for Willkie was also seen in the packing of the convention's galleries with "We want Willkie" rooters, who had been admitted with counterfeit tickets.[36]

Friends and acquaintances also exerted pressure on Landon to support Willkie, and Willkie himself tried to see the Kansan, but was refused. Arthur Krock of the *New York Times* finally persuaded Landon to talk with Willkie to make sure there was nothing in the Hoosier's record that would "fly up and hit the party in the face" if he were nominated. When Willkie came to Landon's room—the night before the convention opened—Landon cross-examined him about his motivations, supporters, and tactics. The Kansan had been disturbed by the rumors that Willkie and Wall Street were buying delegates, as well as packing the galleries and financing a fraudulent campaign of telegrams. The Hoosier satisfied Landon that he was honest and that he was not responsible for the unscrupulous activities of some of his supporters. Willkie left with Landon's friendship, but nothing else.[37]

The convention seemed to be stalemated. None of the leading candidates and none of the favorite sons seemed to have a chance of attracting enough votes for the nomination. On the first ballot, which

[36] Johnson, *Willkie*, p. 75; Landon to Charles P. Blinn, Jr., July 8, 1940; *Topeka State Journal*, July 12, 1960; Landon Papers, Willkie file; Joseph Martin, *My First Fifty Years in Politics* (New York: McGraw-Hill, 1960), pp. 153 ff.

[37] Landon interview, May 2, 1963; Landon to Arthur Krock, July 12, 1940.

began Thursday afternoon, June 27, Dewey received 360 votes, Taft 189, Willkie 105, and Vandenberg 76. The rest of the votes were scattered among Styles Bridges, Harlan Bushfield, Frank Gannett, Arthur James, Charles McNary, Hanford MacNider, Herbert Hoover, Joseph Martin, and, of course, Arthur Capper. Dewey had not received the number of votes—at least 400 of the necessary majority of 501—his managers had anticipated, but Willkie had drawn support from twenty-five states. On the second ballot Willkie increased his votes to 171, and Taft to 203, while Dewey dropped to 338, and Vandenberg to 73. The rest of the votes were again scattered.

The convention then recessed for dinner, and Minnesota's young governor, Harold Stassen—who was Willkie's floor manager—immediately buttonholed Landon and tried to persuade him to switch the Kansas delegation to Willkie. Stassen and Landon were unable to understand each other in the din of the crowd, and ducked into a freight elevator to talk—but were apparently still unable to make themselves understood. Stassen has said it was in the elevator that the Kansan decided to swing his votes to Willkie; Landon's version was that he told Stassen the Kansas delegates, because of their divided sentiments, would not then switch to anyone as a group. Landon also said he neither opposed nor supported Willkie, and that it was not his prerogative to make decisions for the delegation.[38] The available evidence and subsequent events favor the Kansan's recollection of the elevator meeting.

Although Landon decided to support Dewey, he did not pressure his fellow Kansans to do likewise. The Kansan voted for the New Yorker on the third and fourth ballots, as the Kansas delegation, now released by Capper, split its votes among the leading contenders for the nomination. On the third ballot Dewey again lost votes, though with his 315 votes he still led the other candidates. Taft had gained 9, for a total of 212, but Willkie had added 88 and was in second place with 259 votes. (The proceedings became confused between the third and fourth ballots, amid the thunderous "We want Willkie" cries from the galleries.) On the fourth ballot Dewey, having lost 65 votes, dropped to third place; Willkie gained 47 votes to take first place, and Taft moved into second place with 42 new votes.[39]

---

[38] Landon interview, May 2, 1963; Johnson, *Willkie*, p. 96.

[39] Landon to Harold B. Johnson, July 12, 1940; Landon to Duke Shoop, July 12, 1940; Landon to Thomas E. Dewey, July 29, 1940, Dewey Papers; Johnson, *Willkie*, pp. 96 ff.

After the fourth ballot Landon came under increasing pressure from Willkie's supporters, particularly from Kansans Clifford Stratton, William Allen White, Jack Harris, and Oscar Stauffer. Willkie's managers wanted Landon badly, for he was the only national Republican leader they could hope to persuade to join their movement. They also wanted Kansas, hoping its surrender would crack the midwestern delegates and give Willkie the needed votes. Although not unfriendly to Willkie, Landon was still perturbed by the unorthodox pressure being applied to the delegates, and he discussed the situation with the convention chairman, Joseph Martin. He asked if the convention should not be recessed to prevent it from being stampeded, and Martin replied: "Alf, we agreed that this would be an open convention." Landon, chagrined, said "All right, let her go the way she's going."

Landon considered the dilemma he felt: Willkie's attractiveness on the one hand, and on the other his lack of political experience and his supporters' methods. But there were other factors as well. The Kansas delegation was under considerable stress; nerves were becoming frayed after four deadlocked ballots; continued stalemate within the delegation —and the convention—could jeopardize the unity the party needed to carry it through the general-election campaign. Moreover, Willkie's opponents might be strong enough and stubborn enough to prolong the contest for days. Landon could abandon Dewey with a clear conscience, for his appeal satisfied only those who "wanted to hear Roosevelt called names before breakfast, before lunch, before dinner, and for a bed-story at night." Finally, the Kansan could support Willkie because their current views on the issues largely coincided. It was on these grounds that Landon decided to vote for Willkie and recommend that the Kansas delegation do likewise.

On the fifth ballot Willkie continued to gain votes, and had already picked up 27 additional votes when the convention secretary called for the Kansas delegation's report. Alf Landon rose to give Willkie the state's 18 votes. Dewey's strength then disintegrated, as he lost 65 votes, many of which went to Willkie. The stalemate continued, however, for Taft also had gained on the fifth ballot: the Ohio senator had 377 votes and Willkie 429. Shortly after midnight, Governor John W. Bricker of Ohio, Taft's floor manager, tried to recess the convention in order to keep the Willkie tide from sweeping to the 501 votes necessary for nomination. Landon told Martin that he might get the nomination if he tried to form the holdouts into a stop-Willkie movement, but Martin resisted the temptation and immediately moved the convention

on to the sixth ballot. Vandenberg then released the Michigan delegates, most of whom voted for Willkie, and after that the Hoosier picked
up state after state and vote after vote, until, at the end of the ballot,
he had more than enough for the nomination.[40]

The *New York Herald Tribune* and the pro-Roosevelt New York
newspaper, *PM*, hailed Alf Landon as the man responsible for Willkie's
nomination. *PM*, for example, lauded Landon for switching Kansas to
Willkie—for taking a bold step "at exactly the right moment to rid the
Republican party of the old smugness, the old Hoover factionism, and
the newly developing threat of Pew-boss control." Neither *PM* nor
the *Herald Tribune* had the facts straight, however, forgetting that Taft
had been gaining strength until Vandenberg had released his delegates
on the sixth ballot. Nevertheless, Landon's shift to Willkie on the fifth
ballot had spurred others to do likewise, especially in the New York
delegation, where it became obvious—after Kansas voted for Willkie—
that Dewey had no chance of winning.

Landon sought no credit. Indeed he wondered what had been
accomplished by the Republican party's nomination of a politically
inexperienced man—and a former Democrat—for President of the
United States. When he retired to his hotel room after the nomination
his wife asked him why he looked "so white and scared." Landon
answered: "I wonder what I've done to my party and to my
country."[41]

The Republican platform had been written and the party's presidential nominee selected, and now the campaign had to be organized. One
of the first decisions was who would be the chairman of the national
committee. Willkie had promised to retain John D. M. Hamilton,
presumably as a reward for the assistance that Hamilton had given him
during the convention (despite Hamilton's pledge to treat all candidates
for the nomination equally). Willkie found, however, that there was
considerable distrust of Hamilton among Republican leaders, including
Landon. He therefore decided to ignore his promise to Hamilton and

[40] *Topeka State Journal*, July 12, 1960; Martin, *First Fifty Years*, p. 156; Landon to
Clifford Stratton, July 26, 1940; Landon to Duke Shoop, July 12, 1940; Landon to
Harold B. Johnson, July 12, August 23, 1940; *Twenty-second Republican National
Convention Proceedings*, pp. 302 ff.; Johnson, *Willkie*, pp. 98 ff.

[41] *New York Herald Tribune*, June 29, 1940; *PM*, June 28, 1940; Johnson, *Willkie*,
pp. 75, 95 ff.; *Topeka State Journal*, July 12, 1960. See also Mary Earhart Dillon,
Wendell Willkie, 1892–1944 (Philadelphia: Lippincott, 1952), pp. 161 ff., and Joseph
Barnes, *Willkie* (New York: Simon & Schuster, 1952), pp. 183 ff.

he asked Joseph Martin to accept chairmanship. The minority leader at first refused, but his friends in Congress, Willkie and his associates, Landon, and others persuaded him to change his mind—everyone thought the veteran Republican leader and the energetic but "greenhorn" nominee would make a good team. (An attempt was made to assuage Hamilton by having him remain with the national committee as its executive director.) Landon was enthusiastic about Martin's election as national chairman, and not entirely disconsolate about Hamilton's fall.[42]

After the convention, Landon went home to relax and to seek recreation in pitching hay and horseback riding, but soon he took an active part in the campaign. He would not return east, but he would do what he could for the ticket from Kansas. Although he still disapproved of the tactics used by the Willkie men in stampeding the convention, he was impressed with Willkie's charm and vigor, and he pitched in to help the nominee. He urged his friend, Franklyn Waltman, the national committee's publicity director, to check with state chairmen for their views on national publicity, especially on how it could fit into the state campaigns, and to sound out newspaper editors for information and advice. Martin, he suggested, should continue the process of ridding the party of the old Negro politicians and of replacing them with new, vigorous Negro leaders, and the new national chairman might consult Negro leaders from pivotal states—those who usually were outranked in party affairs by southern Negroes. Landon also encouraged Thomas E. Dewey—who he hoped would become the next mayor of New York City or governor of New York State—to take an active role in the campaign.[43]

Willkie appeared to be making a favorable impression on the people, but Landon was apprehensive that the campaign was off to a bad start. He was uncomfortable about Willkie's vacation at a fashionable Colorado hotel. He thought the Hoosier had said too much, and too acrimoniously, in the time between the convention and the formal opening of the campaign. He was also worried by occasional rifts between Willkie and Republican congressmen, though Landon hoped that he and Martin would be able to persuade the nominee and the

[42] Landon interview, June 2, 1963; *Topeka State Journal*, June 29, 1940; Martin, *First Fifty Years*, pp. 103 ff.; Johnson, *Willkie*, pp. 109 ff.; Landon to A. H. Kirchhofer, August 31, 1940; Landon to Harold B. Johnson, July 12, 1940.

[43] Landon to Harold B. Johnson, July 12, 1940; Landon to Franklyn Waltman, July 9, 1940; Landon to Joseph W. Martin, July 11, 1940; Landon to Thomas E. Dewey, July 13, 1940.

congressmen to compose their differences. Nor was the Kansan convinced of the effectiveness or the loyalty of the nominee's personal
campaign organization, the Willkie Clubs, as far as the party's general
interests were concerned; he feared the clubs' connections with big
business and their tendency to "gum up the campaign." He became
particularly angry with the Kansas Willkie Club: "While the regular
Republican organization went down the line for Willkie, this Willkie
organization . . . was trading off the Governor [Payne Ratner] and we
came darn near losing him."[44] Landon did not blame Willkie for that
situation, but he thought the Hoosier was not effectively supporting
Republican candidates for congressional, state, and local offices. Too
often these candidates did not feel welcome when they arrived on
Willkie's campaign train—nor were they used effectively in support
of Willkie.

The Landon was not expressing any personal pique, for he had been
cordially treated by Willkie; however, the nominee's treatment of other
Republican candidates reflected political naiveté, as did his frequent
references to "you Republicans," something that might prevent solid
identification between the party's rank-and-file and its presidential
candidate, who just a few years before had been a registered Democrat.
Landon did not keep these criticisms to himself; he told Willkie he
should make greater use of local and state candidates in his campaign
appearances and that he needed a "boss" as his spokesman in handling
unpleasant incidents and coordinating affairs on the campaign train.
He also suggested that Willkie visit the newsmen more frequently in
order to exchange ideas about the campaign. By October, Landon was
fearful that Willkie was trying to cover too many issues ("I made the
same mistake in '36," he said). Landon thought Willkie should confine
himself to the rising public debt, extravagant federal expenditures,
relief abuses, to hammering home the necessity of keeping the country
out of war and the theme that—under a Republican administration—
there would be greater wealth for a larger proportion of the American
people.[45]

The Kansan kept up a constant stream of correspondence with
Republican leaders across the land, encouraging them to give full
support to the ticket and advising them on tactics. His central theme

[44] Landon interview, May 2, 1963; Landon to Raymond Clapper, November 30,
1940; Landon to Harold Knutson, November 29, 1940.

[45] Landon to Wendell Willkie, September 17, 1940; Landon to Raymond Moley,
October 5, 1940.

was that victory could come only as a result of hard work in reaching the voters, and he made plans to deliver some political statements and addresses during the campaign. In September, he answered the Secretary of Agriculture's contention that Republicans were appeasers of fascism. "Mr. Roosevelt and his official family, immediately following Munich, proudly boasted of the part that Mr. Roosevelt had played in bringing about the Munich settlement." [46]

On October 1, at Hastings, Nebraska, Landon gave the first of his four major campaign speeches. He charged that the Democratic national convention of 1940, unlike the Republican convention, had not been free and open. "So it is perfectly evident that [the United States has] a one-man party, and, unless the Republicans win next November, we will practically be reduced to a country without a substantial political opposition." In this free-swinging speech Landon also asked a series of questions that were reminiscent of the 1936 campaign.

> Will the President have Congress actually declare war after the election? Or, will he so conduct our national affairs that declaring war is a mere formality? No one can be sure. . . . What new trick will be sprung on the American people by this administration if Mr. Roosevelt is elected for another four years? How far will this administration go in curtailing American rights? No one can be sure.

There was, said Landon, only one safe answer for Americans, and that was to elect Wendell Willkie. Landon then turned to the third-term issue, asserting the tradition set by President Washington

> has been recognized by the American people as a rule more sacred than a written law. Today the American voter must answer for the first time this challenge to our high tradition—a demand for a third term—a fourth term—a fifth term—yea, a life term. [47]

The Hastings speech was not just campaign oratory. Landon was in earnest about the issues he raised, and especially about the third-term issue. He wrote Raymond Clapper that the Republic could not survive the precedent of a third term. Landon admitted that Roosevelt had created a new civic consciousness and had brought the government "more into line with industrial life," but he believed that the short cuts taken by the administration were destructive to the fabric of the

---

[46] Landon press statement, September 17, 1940.
[47] Landon speech, Hastings, Neb., October 1, 1940.

Constitution and that the President's election to a third term could set the stage for the rise of lifetime, authoritarian presidents.[48]

Landon again trod the campaign trail in the middle of October; this time he was alarmed by foreign reactions to the controversies of the campaign. At Atlantic, Iowa, on October 15, he prefaced his speech by saying:

> I want to say to the dictators who are offering us alternate threats and bribes, that they are making a very grave error if they mistake the rivalry of a political campaign for disunity in the United States.
>
> We Americans do not conduct our political affairs with that attitude. As soon as this election is over, Democrats as well as Republicans will rally in the nation's interests to the support of the President of the United States. This vital and dominant attitude will not be changed by the bitterness of this campaign.
>
> Whoever is elected will be my President for the next four years.[49]

Four days later, in Quincy, Illinois, he delivered another speech, which was nationally broadcast. In this, one of his most bitter speeches, he emphasized the third-term issue—"the question of a life term for the President of the United States." He believed the election of Wendell Willkie

> is the only chance for the future life of the Republic. . . . A life term for Mr. Roosevelt means the possibility of a life term for *any* President who may follow him. If you are one of those people who trust Mr. Roosevelt not to abuse his powers, remember this: a man may follow who can not be trusted. A vote for a life term *now* is a vote for the principles for dictatorship.

Landon made it clear that he did not trust Roosevelt. He asserted the President, in effect, wanted to use his powers without subjecting his decisions to the checks and balances provided by the Constitution.

> Last June the President . . . wanted Congress to adjourn and go home. And think of all the legislation that has been passed since then because of the international crisis. But the President wanted neither public debate nor check of any kind by the Congress on his decisions.

The Kansan connected this with what he saw as the administration's efforts to undermine the people's confidence in Congress, the Supreme Court, and the press.

Landon then turned to the foreign question. To discredit the

[48] Landon to Raymond Clapper, October 12, 1940.
[49] Landon speech, Atlantic, Ia., October 15, 1940.

administration's claims of sincerity in its pledge to keep the nation out of war, he picked up Secretary of the Navy Frank Knox on his statement that there are enemies to the east and the west of America. Landon asked:

> What does this mean? An enemy is a country with which we are at war. Are we at war with Japan? Is Japan literally our enemy, and if she is our enemy, what kind of diplomacy or lack of preparedness have we had in the past seven years that has failed so signally to protect our interests in the Far East?
>
> Let us have done with the nonsense about there being no difference between the foreign policies of the White House and the Republican party. There is a difference, and that difference may be written in the blood of our youth and in the loss of our liberties, if the life-term candidate is elected in November.[50]

Landon's last major campaign speech was also nationally broadcast, from Sioux City, Iowa, on October 31, 1940. He compared the defense record of President Wilson between April and October, 1917, with President Roosevelt's between the same months in 1940. "The amazing and terrifying fact is that this country armed under Woodrow Wilson, in his six months' period, *twenty-eight times faster* than we are in 1940." He saw no hope in Roosevelt's record that confusion and uncertainty would be swept away in the effort to make the country impregnable. He urged that the nation not cling to an ineffectual leader: "Instead of being afraid to change horses in the middle of the stream, cold chills are running down the backs of all familiar with the dangers confronting us, unless we do make that change." Landon then contrasted the Republican nominee with Roosevelt.

> Under Wendell Willkie we are . . . taking no chances of sending an armed expeditionary force to Europe or Asia. Under the leadership of Wendell Willkie we will expand our productive capacity to its peak, because he possesses the temperament and executive ability to get the job done. He is no glamour showman. He does not substitute words and ever-changing theories for acts. He possesses the qualities we desperately need in the White House; a belief in private enterprise, and the ability to meet hard problems and stay with them until they are solved.[51]

Landon's 1940 campaign speeches tended toward immoderation, reflecting not only the partisan antagonisms that had survived the

[50] Landon speech, Quincy, Ill., October 19, 1940.
[51] Landon speech, Sioux City, Ia., October 31, 1940.

1930s but the lack of trust most Republicans had in Roosevelt—and their conviction that his reelection would jeopardize the nation's safety. The tragedy in 1940 was that neither Roosevelt nor the Republican leaders could set aside the bitterness that had accrued during the preceding decade, that the President could not abandon the deviousness with which he too often acted, and that his opposition could not set aside its too frequent immoderation. At a time that cried out for American equanimity in considering the issues, the President was not big enough to seek it and the opposition was not humble enough to offer it.

Landon had been so caught up in Willkie's campaign for the Presidency that, toward the end, he believed the Hoosier would be elected.[52] Landon was wrong again. Although Willkie ran the closest race for President since 1916, he trailed Roosevelt by 5 million votes out of the 50 million cast between the two men.

Landon, who had contributed to the bitterness of the campaign because of his belief the national interest demanded Roosevelt's defeat, was nevertheless convinced that American unity should not appear to have disintegrated. Therefore, the night after the election, Landon sent a statement to be read at the America United Rally in New York City. He repeated his Atlantic, Iowa, pledge that "whoever is elected will be my President in the next four years." He said he had meant it in Atlantic and "I mean it tonight."

> The safety of the Republic requires our full cooperation on our national defense program, and at the same time continued active political opposition. . . . We have taken an intelligent interest in this election. Let us continue an intelligent interest in our government, which is our greatest organized effort for human welfare.[53]

Landon, thoroughly disappointed with the election results, reviewed the causes for the Republican defeat. He felt that Willkie had not made the appropriate appeals for united Republican support, but this was not the main reason for his defeat. Nor was the conservatism of much of the party. "The plain truth of the matter is that the Republican party is not so reactionary in its thinking as it is stupid and dead on its feet." Landon cited the party's failure to fight for the labor vote, the continued identification of Republicans with prohibition, the fact that Republicans

52 Landon to L. M. Kyes, October 25, 1940.
53 Landon statement, America United Rally, New York City, November 6, 1940.

had traditionally staked the Democrats the southern electoral votes, and the widespread disbanding of Republican political machines and the New Deal's effective use of its machines. Of course, the depression "broke us all to pieces" and the New Deal had been able to exploit the depression and drench the Republicans in the acid of class hatreds. Further, Roosevelt's political position had been fortified by the pumping of defense-program money into the economy.[54]

Whatever the reasons, the Republicans had once again lost a presidential election. Whatever Landon's prescriptions for Republican recovery, the party would lose two more.

[54] Landon to Harold B. Johnson, November 12, 1940; Landon to Raymond Moley, November 14, 1940; Landon to William P. Simms, November 13, 1940; Landon to Chester Stevens, November 14, 1940.

CHAPTER **19**

The Road to War

Landon after the election of 1940, like all American politicians, was preoccupied with the question of war or peace. Remembering World War I and its aftermath, he feared war not only because of the deaths, blood shed, and economic disruption that would occur but because it might mean the end of American democracy. Democracy in the United States, as Landon saw it, had already suffered from the rise of authoritarianism abroad, from the domestic bitternesses of the 1930s, and from the concentration of power in Washington and in a leader who regarded himself as indispensable. If this was followed by a presidential dictatorship, which Wilson's administration had indicated war would bring, democracy might not recover.

These were the major reasons that led the Kansan to resist any move he thought might lead to war, but his anti-war convictions did not resolve all of the questions in his mind. He doubted that Germany could attack the United States, but he believed that Germany posed an economic threat, especially in terms of Latin-American markets. He wrote friends for advice on this and other questions. "How can a nation on a forty-hour [work] week ultimately beat a nation that is on an eighty-hour week?" If Great Britain fell, would Germany be able to attack the western hemisphere? What role would the British fleet play if Britain were defeated by Germany? Must the United States inevitably be drawn into war? If our merchant ships were allowed to enter war zones, would this not be tantamount to

454

involvement in the war? Landon thought the Pearl Harbor base protected the western hemisphere from Japanese attack, but an attack upon the Philippine Islands could involve the United States in a war of national honor. Could we not, however, "sacrifice a part in order to preserve the whole?"[1]

The Kansan had fairly well formed his mind on these and other questions by the end of November, 1940, when—in a speech before the Cooperative Club of Kansas City—he entered the debate on foreign affairs. The United States could avoid war

> if we choose wisely our course of action now and in the months to come. . . . It is not a question of determination by the chief executive to keep us out of war. It is a question of avoiding policies which will stir the American people to the point where they will be engulfed in a wave of hysteria, which has swept us before, and which can sweep us again.

Landon expressed his sympathy for the embattled British and his willingness that the United States extend credit and share the produce of its factories and farms, but he drew the line at allowing American ships to transport these goods into the war zones, which would be equivalent to declaring war against Germany. He then tried to calm fears that the United States would be attacked by Germany in the unlikely event that Britain were defeated.

> Herr Hitler is not going to be in any position . . . to come to America or even to any spot in the Western Hemisphere, with an armed expeditionary force. Regardless of the duration or the outcome of the war, his hands are going to be full for a long time.

On the other hand, if America plunged itself into the war,

> it will mean fighting Germany and her allies in Europe, with Japan in the Far East, and with the Red Bear watching from the sidelines and licking its chops. . . . [But] we may be able to save ourselves, and ultimately the rest of the world, if we will only unite in this country, forget class hatred, and pull together, with the fire of conviction in the glorious destiny of the Republic.[2]

[1] Landon to Felix Morley, November 10, 1940, and Landon to William Phillip Simms, November 19, 1940, Alfred M. Landon Papers, Kansas State Historical Society, Topeka.

[2] Landon speech, Kansas City, Mo., November 26, 1940. In December, Landon showed he was serious about helping the British when he publicly suggested that the United States might give them an outright grant of $5 billion. Such a grant would help Britain bolster its defenses without broadening the President's discretionary powers. *New York Times*, December 13, 1940; Landon to J. Roscoe Drummond, January 3, 1941.

A new tack in foreign affairs was taken by the administration after the President, in a "fireside chat" on December 29, 1940, expressed his fears for the nation and the dangers associated with German aggression, and proposed that he be authorized to lend or lease goods and equipment to the democracies fighting Germany. This proposal was outlined in detail in Roosevelt's message to Congress, January 6, 1941, and marked the beginning of the great foreign policy debates of 1941.

January 11, from Tulsa, Oklahoma, Landon made the first major Republican response to the lend-lease proposal. In a nationwide broadcast arranged by national committee chairman Martin, the Kansan said there had been serious confusion about the form of American aid to Britain because the United States had not decided whether its first interest was British success or staying out of the war. Aid to the British, he said, was following the pattern of America's involvement in World War I:

> First, materials; second, money; and third, men. I am willing to take the first two steps, but not the third. Baldly stated, this brings little disagreement —publicly, at least. But the way we do the first and the second is the answer to the third.

Landon declared that Roosevelt, in his message to Congress, had proposed that the United States underwrite British victory by stating that Hitler could not be allowed to dictate the peace terms—a far different interpretation of national foreign policy than the President had given during his reelection campaign.

> *Then* he advocated "all aid to Britain, short of war." *Now* he says that we do not intend to let the dictators win. Instead of "aid short of war" the President further committed himself to a war policy by urging "full support of all those resolute peoples, everywhere, who are resisting aggression."

If this new policy prevails, Landon asserted, the country would have to go to war "in order to make the President's words good."

Landon then discussed the legislative heart of the lend-lease proposal; and he chided the President on its vagueness and deplored his reasoning that such a program could be carried on without cost to the taxpayers. The proposal, if implemented, could also be "the seed of future friction between England and America. It is like endorsing a blank check for a friend. You never know how much it is going to cost." Landon suggested an outright subsidy to Great Britain so that the United States would know the exact cost of the program and could stop it at will.

> I don't favor helping England as a matter of charity. . . . I favor helping her because it is to America's interest to do so. And we should charge the cost as part of our national defense. . . . Let's stop kidding ourselves on . . . lending and leasing without cost to the American taxpayer. The lending of war material—the garden-hose scheme—might better be compared to lending a cake of ice in July in Kansas, with the same hope of recovery.

Whatever action was taken, Landon thought the American people would suffer. If England won the war, Americans would suffer great social and economic disturbances; if Hitler won, the disturbances would be greater still.

> If we get into this war with fighting forces, when the end comes, we will suffer the *greatest* economic, social, and political disturbances. Add a long war to the personal government the President admits with the suspension of the Bill of Rights and other Constitutional safeguards—more short cuts in the name of emergency—more blank checks by the Congress to the chief executive, and representative government in this country will be on thin ice. Then add also a fourth term, plus the terrible economic suffering and racial hatred of minorities which will be the aftermath of our participation in the war, and the Republic may well go through the rock crusher. In defeating totalitarianism abroad, we will strengthen its hold here at home.[3]

Landon's position, as he stated it at Tulsa, was the position of the Republican moderates: Give aid to Britain without directly involving America in the war and without giving the President additional discretionary powers. Wendell Willkie, however, the new titular head of the party, endorsed the lend-lease proposal, calling only for a time limit on the President's extraordinary power. Landon therefore declared that there was no real difference between Roosevelt and Willkie on the chief issue before the nation; their position seemed to be "We must get into the war, if necessary, to help England win." Landon contended that if the two men had acknowledged this position earlier, Willkie would have not been nominated and Roosevelt would have not been reelected.[4] Landon, however, had no illusions about the result of the battle over lend-lease. "I know," he wrote to a newspaper friend, "I am on the losing side." He was nevertheless determined to continue

[3] Landon speech, Tulsa, January 11, 1941.
[4] *Kansas City Times*, January 13, 1941.

the debate because "I believe America has more to lose by getting into this war than by staying out, and that is the whole thing with me." [5]

The Kansan fired his next broadside on February 1, over the Columbia Broadcasting System. "I am not neutral in this European war. Nazism and Communism stand for more than merely totalitarianism. They mean inhuman brutality on a scale not witnessed for ages." But the lend-lease concept was "phony," and revealed the end-justifies-the-means philosophy of "those who are emotionalizing us into a war fervor." He opposed the lend-lease bill "because it delegates to the President the Congressional power to declare war; because it repeals the provisions of the present laws prohibiting ships from entering the war zones; because its delegation of powers to the President is so vague and limitless that no one can accurately define its extent." Although "the people did not have the opportunity last November to vote on this question of how close we shall get to war," Landon thought something still could be done about it, and he urged the people to tell their views to members of Congress—"in this way casting our vote—the vote that was denied in November." [6]

The lend-lease bill was introduced in Congress on January 10 and hearings were scheduled shortly thereafter. Representative Hamilton Fish, the leader of the opposition in the House Foreign Affairs Committee, asked Landon to testify before the committee, but Landon replied that he would not: "I am against the whole damned bill, from start to finish. You can't amend basically wrong legislation." Landon recommended, however—because the bill would probably be passed—that the power to implement it should not be given solely to the President but, perhaps, to a commission composed of the President, the chairmen of the House and Senate Foreign Affairs Committees, and minority representatives. Landon again was asked to appear before the House and Senate committees (Republican Senator Robert A. Taft and Progressive Senator Robert M. La Follette, in particular, pleaded with the Kansan to appear), and finally, on February 6, Landon decided to go before the Senate Foreign Relations Committee in opposition to the bill. [7]

[5] Landon to Theodore Alvord, January 21, 1941; Landon to Duke Shoop, January 21, 1941.

[6] Landon speech, C.B.S., February 1, 1941.

[7] Hamilton Fish to Landon, January 12, 14, 1941; Landon to Fish, January 13, 1941; Robert M. La Follette, Jr., to Landon, February 4, 1941; Robert A. Taft to

The hearings before the Senate committee began on January 27 and continued through February 11, 1941. The testimony was sharply pro or con, and received enormous publicity. Many prominent Americans appeared to support, or oppose, the pending legislation. Secretary of State Cordell Hull, Secretary of the Treasury Henry Morgenthau Jr., Secretary of War Henry L. Stimson, Secretary of the Navy Frank Knox, Wendell Willkie, New York Mayor Fiorello La Guardia, president James B. Conant of Harvard University, theologian Reinhold Niebuhr, financier James W. Gerard, and representatives of the American Federation of Labor testified in favor of the bill. Opposing it were Landon, former Progressive Governor Philip F. La Follette of Wisconsin, Norman Thomas, historian Charles A. Beard, America First Committee chairman Robert E. Wood, president Allen Valentine of the University of Rochester, president James F. Kemper of the United States Chamber of Commerce, international law expert Herbert S. Wright, Gerald L. K. Smith, Robert R. McCormick, former Assistant Secretary of War Hanford MacNider, president Philip Murray of the Congress of Industrial Organizations, Charles C. Morrison of the *Christian Century*, and president Joseph Curren of the National Maritime Union. The list of opposing witnesses indicates the sharpness of the issue. Labor was split, religious groups were split, political parties were split. Men who but a few months before had been political enemies joined one another in support of or in opposition to the bill. The philosophies of the opposition were particularly disparate; dissenting Democrats, Socialists, Republicans, Progressives, fascist prototypes, businessmen, labor leaders, and intellectuals, all were alarmed by the provisions or implications of the lend-lease bill.[8]

Landon appeared before the committee Saturday morning, February 8, and his testimony was to be front-page news in almost every newspaper in the land. Although most Americans favored giving limited aid to Britain, Landon said, the lend-lease bill was a great departure from that concept. He opposed the bill, but he called for its fullest possible debate as an antidote to the notion that the United States was being tricked into war, which would be divisive of national unity in a time of great crisis. The Kansan deplored the "organized attempt to suppress

---

Landon, February 5, 1941; Landon to Taft, February 6, 1941; Landon to La Follette, February 6, 1941.

[8] *To Promote the Defense of the United States—Hearings before the Committee on Foreign Relations, United States Senate, 77th Congress, 1st Session* (Washington, D.C.: Government Printing Office), *passim.*

public speaking and public opinion in this country on the bill" and protested the attribution of "partisan or petty factional motives" to those who were against it. Landon then turned to the bill itself, which he characterized as a "guess-and-be-damned policy." He said: "I might be pardoned not attempting to discuss it in detail, when even members of the President's cabinet have been unable to answer the questions of the committees of the House and Senate as to a clear-cut definition of its powers."

Senator Alben Barkley had contended that the bill did not authorize the use of American vessels for the delivery of war materials to combat zones, but Landon cited section 3–a, subsection 2, which provided authority "to sell, transfer, exchange, lease, lend, or otherwise dispose of, to any such government any definite article," and he called the committee's attention to the word "transfer." "Transfer," according to *Webster's New International Dictionary*, meant "to convey from one place, person, or thing, to another; to transport, remove, or cause to pass, to another place, person, or thing." Landon thought the Attorney General, if asked by the President whether this language authorized him to transport "any definite article," would reply in the affirmative. In short, the word "transfer" could authorize the use of American ships for transporting defense articles into war zones.

Landon, again calling for an outright subsidy to Great Britain, said neither the nation's defense nor our interest in Britain's survival made it necessary for Congress to grant the President powers—as the Kansan interpreted the bill's wording—so extensive that they could be used at any time, in any place, and for any purpose—and could put American soldiers into battle. He warned of possibly disastrous implications in President Roosevelt's pledge not to let Hitler dictate the peace and in his January 6 message to Congress that called for freedom of expression and worship and freedom from want and fear "'everywhere in the world.'" Landon declared: "I have heard it stated that it is preposterous to suggest that the President would use these powers. Then I suggest that it is equally preposterous to suggest that the Congress grant these powers."[9]

After his Senate testimony, Landon continued his fight against the lend-lease bill. In a press statement six days later, February 14, he answered the charges by administration spokesmen that Republican opposition to the bill proved the Republican party was one "of

[9] *Ibid.*, pp. 661 ff.

negation." The confusing actions and policies of the administration, he retorted, had withered American values, and "out of this destruction of values will finally very likely come Fascism—although the administration is not planning it that way." It was not, he asserted, a policy of negation "for the Republican leaders to attempt to jolt the people out of a war hysteria"; it was not negation for Republicans to attempt to keep the United States a republic; and it was not negation for Republican leaders to oppose repression of "freedom of debate." Landon pictured Republican opposition not as obstructionist partisanship but as a "sturdy fight against great odds for principles which, while they may appear drab and colorless, are fundamental to the continued life of the Republic." [10]

Throughout the lend-lease battle Landon kept in touch with the bill's opponents across the country, all the while receiving great quantities of mail that either commended or deplored his activities. He answered those who wrote cogent letters of protest with stiff, sometimes lengthy rebuttals. To an acquaintance in Junction City, Kansas, he wrote:

> It's all right with me if you want to start fixing national frontiers all over the world, and start on another "Peter the Hermit" crusade to make the world safe for democracy. . . . That is O.K., if that's what you want and you are honest about it. But I never have kidded the American people, and I do not propose to do so now. The lease and lend bill is a war bill, and I am telling them that.[11]

On February 24 he delivered a fifteen-minute broadcast on the Blue Network of the National Broadcasting Company. Disagreeing with two supporters of the bill, Senators Barkley of Kentucky and Bailey of North Carolina, Landon said lend-lease was "not simply a bill to aid Great Britain 'short of war.' This is a war bill." It was also a "dictatorship bill" because it gave "one man, the President, the authority to conduct the foreign affairs of the nation entirely by himself, on his own, without the advice and consent of the Senate," and because it gave him "practically complete control over American industry, American resources, and American men." Landon again charged that the President's aims, as set forth in his December 29 radio address and his January 6 message to Congress, were to police the world and to restore, remake, or preserve national boundaries throughout the world.

[10] Landon press release to International News Service, February 14, 1941.
[11] Landon to F. W. O'Donnell, March 1, 1941.

He did not know exactly what the President planned to do if the bill were passed, but he knew that "social gains are going to be lost, that civil rights are going to be impaired, that the cost of living will increase, and the standard of living will be lowered." He called upon his listeners to tell their senators that "the American people do not want war. Tell them that the American people do not want to guarantee the boundary lines of nations everywhere and anywhere in the world."[12]

In the last days before the Senate acted upon the bill (the House had passed it by a vote of 260 to 165 a month earlier), Landon explained his position in letters to influential newspapermen. Having always believed "we cannot escape the responsibility of world leadership," he based his opposition to lend-lease on the "sight unseen" features of the bill. The eventual public reaction to the deceptive wording of the bill would, he thought, "destroy any constructive attempts toward a sound and workable cooperative peace. . . . Collective security, or even cooperative security, has been damned because of the 'whole hog or none' way in which it has been advocated."[13]

Landon had planned to give another radio address, over the Mutual Broadcasting System on March 10, but by then it was too late. The Senate, on March 8, passed the lend-lease bill—with only eleven minor modifications—by a vote of 60 to 31. A small consolation for the Kansan in the final version of the bill was that "transfer"—in subsection 2 of section 3–a—had been altered to "transfer *title*," as he had suggested.[14] He believed, however, that this change was of no final importance, that sooner or later President Roosevelt would find a way to use American ships to transport goods into the war zones, thereby jeopardizing America's neutrality.

A leading participant in the controversy over the lend-lease bill early in 1941, Landon had also been caught up in the controversies over party leadership that confronted Republicans. The question of Wendell Willkie's renomination for President, which arose soon after the 1940 election, would not be answered until 1944, but Joseph Martin's statement, on November 13, 1940, that he would resign the chairmanship of the national committee the following January caused problems of immediate concern. Martin's loss, Landon believed, would

[12] Landon speech, N.B.C. Blue Network, February 24, 1941.
[13] Landon to Roy Howard, March 7, 1941; Landon to James L. Wright, March 7, 1941.
[14] 55 *U.S. Stats.* 31.

split the party wide open because no other man was readily acceptable to all of the major Republican elements. The Taft forces were split between David S. Ingalls, the Ohio national committeeman, and former Representative John M. Hollister of Cincinnati. The older national committee members seemed to prefer West Virginia's Walter S. Hallanan, who was not committed to any of the potential candidates for the 1944 nomination. Some of the Willkie forces supported Bruce Barton, the party's unsuccessful New York senatorial nominee in 1940. Still others—especially in the middle west, and among Republican congressmen—wanted to retain Martin as national committee chairman. Landon also wanted Martin; he thought the minority leader could double as chairman if he were given an executive assistant to handle the details of running the national headquarters. In late December, 1940, when it was obvious that the party was badly split on the chairmanship, Willkie and others were able to persuade Martin to defer his resignation until March.[15]

Time, however, only complicated the matter: party opinion was divided on the lend-lease bill, and many Republicans believed Willkie was becoming a stooge for President Roosevelt. Landon, however, worked to keep Martin as House minority leader and as national committee chairman; he wrote that it was good for the opposition party to combine the two roles—especially because the party's present titular head was "not much inclined to work with the party leadership in Congress." As the list of nominees for the chairmanship grew longer, Landon found it ironic that members of the Hoover faction seemed to want the Kansan to take the position—which, in any case, he was unwilling to do.[16] Finally, in March, the matter was settled. After great pressure from Landon, Willkie, Dewey, Senator Taft, and other Republican leaders, Martin agreed to continue as national chairman, with executive assistance, until after the 1942 elections.[17]

After the lend-lease battle and Martin's decision to stay on, Landon thought he would have time to relax from the pressures of politics; moreover, his business still had not recovered satisfactorily from the

[15] Landon to Arthur Capper, December 5, 1940; Donald B. Johnson, *The Republican Party and Wendell Willkie* (Urbana: University of Illinois Press, 1960), pp. 167 ff.

[16] Johnson, *Willkie*, pp. 173 ff.; Landon to Thomas E. Dewey, January 21, 1941, Thomas E. Dewey Papers, University of Rochester Libraries, Rochester, N.Y.; Landon to Arthur Capper, January 4, 1941; Landon to Lacy Haynes, February 13, 1941.

[17] Johnson, *Willkie*, pp. 183 f.; Landon to Clifford Stratton, March 14, 1941.

depression. He also felt a need to escape the unhappy prospects of public affairs. "I am looking for a good fishing hole," he wrote Roy Howard, "one that doesn't have a good view of the pleasant road which we are traveling to hell." It was only a matter of time, he thought, before war would be upon the country.[18] But his respite from politics was brief; by April, he had become involved with the America First Committee, the country's best-known organization of anti-interventionists and isolationists. Landon's connections with the committee were so highly publicized that many people thought he was one of its leaders, but Landon never joined the committee and had little in common with its members. Although he opposed America's intervention in the war, especially through deception, he advocated an adequate national defense and preparedness for war. Unlike most of the America Firsters, Landon favored giving substantial aid to Britain and to any other democracy attacked by the Axis powers.

Landon's concern with what he saw as the administration's efforts to gag discussion of foreign policy (which he had indicated in his testimony before the Senate Foreign Relations Committee) was the key to his involvement with the America First Committee. In April, he had endorsed a magazine statement by Charles A. Lindbergh that emphasized the need for building strength and character at home rather than crusading abroad—which was fully in line with Landon's ideas.[19] Then, toward the end of the month, Lindbergh was refused permission to speak in Miami, and Lindbergh and Robert Wood (the America First chairman) were personally castigated by Roosevelt and Ickes. Landon thereupon donned his civil-liberties armor in defense of the America Firsters. On April 28 he accepted an invitation—which he had previously declined—to speak at an America First meeting in Kansas City. In accepting, he said:

> It is shocking to see the smear campaign that is being conducted against those who are simply exercising the prerogatives of every American citizen by speaking their honest convictions on the greatest issue that ever confronted people—that of peace or war. Obviously there is an attempt to smear everyone who dares stick up his head in opposition to war. But the time for free discussion has not yet passed.[20]

[18] Landon to W. K. Hutchinson, March 22, 1941; Landon to Roy Howard, March 17, 1941.

[19] R. Douglas Stuart, Jr., to Landon, April 16, 1941.

[20] Landon to Robert E. Wood, May 2, 1941; Landon to Ray F. Moseley, April 28, 1941. The standard work on the Committee is Wayne S. Cole, *America First, The Battle against Intervention, 1940–1941* (Madison: University of Wisconsin Press, 1953).

At the Kansas City meeting, on May 2—where he shared the platform with Democratic Senator Bennett Champ Clark of Missouri—Landon praised the "fight to help the American people maintain the determination they have expressed repeatedly to stay out of war." Although he was "willing and anxious to help England with materials," he was unwilling to help with manpower, a view that was also held by the people—as had been shown during the 1940 election. If the President wanted to reverse America's peace policy, Landon said, he must openly seek congressional action in an atmosphere of free discussion.

> There is now, and there always has been, a plain attempt by this administration to discourage discussion of its management of the country's affairs. Americans cannot even be as critical of the British management [of the war] as the British themselves, without being accused of being disloyal to our country. . . .
> This republic can survive only if we preserve the freedom to carry on enlightened discussion of the administration's management of our affairs. In time of peace and in time of war, this freedom is a part of our elementary heritage. Those who exercise that freedom should not be subjected to smears and sneers, as they have been from this administration since its inception. Let no foreign dictator mistake free discussion for disunity in the United States, and let no one seek to destroy that free discussion at home.[21]

The press almost completely ignored this plea for freedom of discussion of foreign policy and the warning that such discussion should not be mistaken for disunity. As a result, Landon's participation in the meeting generally served to link him with the nation's most extreme anti-war elements—a connection that was strengthened, in the public mind, by the Kansan's opposition to the administration in May and June. Convinced that war fever was rising, Landon thought the only hope for peace lay in exerting stronger pressure on Roosevelt to abide by his 1940 campaign promise to keep America out of war. This conviction, and his concern with civil liberties, explains most of Landon's activities during May and early June. Less than a week after the Kansas City meeting he issued a press release stating that the recent course of the administration justified the Republicans' 1940 campaign charge that Roosevelt would involve the country in another European war.

> Again we are hearing, from administration sources, the same fine humanitarian slogans that took us into the last war. Again we are hearing, from

[21] Landon speech, Kansas City, Mo., May 2, 1941.

administration sources, the same provocative speeches attempting to build up public sentiment in this country for war.[22]

Landon again cooperated with the America First Committee on May 10. In response to a request by Robert L. Bliss, the A.F.C. organizational director, Landon sent a telegram to be read at a huge meeting in Minneapolis, where Lindbergh was to speak. The Kansan, again stressing the need for freedom of speech, contended there was a contradiction between President Roosevelt's statements about peace and the recent demands of several cabinet members for sending American convoys to England, which "certainly requires discussion." He also warned the administration and the A.F.C. that the electorate had approved neither war nor isolation but "intensive national defense preparations and support of England with materials."[23] Landon then agreed to make a fifteen-minute radio speech, under the auspices of the America First Committee, on May 18. He again charged the administration with trying to suppress free speech by discrediting the government's opponents and he demanded that the President be frank with the country on foreign-policy matters. At the same time, the United States should arm itself sufficiently so "that we can lick any nation or combination of nations that are foolish enough to attack us."[24]

His May 18 speech was Landon's last activity in connection with the America First Committee; he had concluded that his ideas and the committee's, particularly on aid to Britain and national defense, were too dissimilar to permit further cooperation. This was not, however, the end of his personal crusade for peace and for open discussion of foreign-policy issues. His next public appearance was May 21, in a commencement address at the Burlington, Kansas, high school, in which he foretold an uncertain future—in a world of "blood-crazed despots, concerned only for power for power's sake." He exhorted the graduates to have faith in themselves, and cited the "rough, tough bunch of cookies with plenty of fire in their bellies" who had established the state of Kansas against great odds. The United States needed

[22] Landon to Preston Wolfe, May 8, 1941; Landon press release, May 7, 1941.

[23] Landon to Robert L. Bliss, May 10, 1941. An earlier draft of this telegram had been sharper in tone. It had included the assertion that if the United States went to war it would cost the country several hundred billion dollars and the lives of hundreds of thousands of soldiers. Landon also had asked: "Are we going to start out on a crusade to bring the Four Freedoms to every nation in the world, without first even having them in America?" Landon to Bliss, n.d., not sent.

[24] Landon speech, C.B.S., May 18, 1941.

a similar toughness for protecting its liberties during the present crisis, and should not condone the administration's short cuts or repressive tactics.[25]

Landon carried on his campaign in a nationally broadcast commencement speech at Simpson College, in Indianola, Iowa, on June 2. Again he asked for free discussion of the war issues, frankness by the President, and a firm and realistic foreign policy. He deplored talk about the United States getting into the war and "carrying the Four Freedoms to all the world." Before it plunged into war, the country should "understand all the facts." How well prepared, he asked, was America for war? What would be its war aims? What could be expected from possible allies in terms of wartime cooperation and reconstruction policies?

The Kansan then attacked the President's contention that the western hemisphere was in danger of nazi attack from Dakar.

> Now Dakar, Africa, is picked as the jumping-off place to Brazil for the Nazi invasion of the Western Hemisphere. Well, Dakar, Africa, is French territory at the present. But, waiving that, get down your maps and figure out how far Dakar, in Africa, is from the real base of operations, Germany. There isn't a military or naval expert in the United States that will challenge the statement that the real base of operations is in Germany. Consider the distance from Germany to Dakar, Africa. Consider the woefully inadequate transportation facilities, the enormous quantities of equipment, munitions, guns, food, and men that would have to be transported from Germany to Dakar—Dakar, Africa, before they were even started for Brazil. For even though the airplane has revolutionized warfare, it has not eliminated the doughboys. And all this material and all the ships and all these millions of men would have to be assembled in Dakar, Africa, *4,000 miles* from their base of operations in Germany. And still 1,600 sea miles further to go, to their objective in Brazil.

Furthermore, he asked, was it not conceivable that the United States, Brazil, and the other nations supposedly endangered would find a way to defend themselves if this hypothetical menace materialized?[26]

Landon, in all his efforts, was stating the position of many Republicans—and some Democrats. As Joseph Martin put it, President Roosevelt's requests for wartime powers, without an honest acknowledgment of the imminence of American involvement in war, offered little encouragement to the Republican leadership to temper its

[25] Landon speech, Burlington, Kan., May 21, 1941.
[26] Landon speech, Simpson College, Indianola, Ia., June 2, 1941.

opposition. Landon was therefore able to speak authoritatively for many of the leaders of his party; furthermore, he was frequently in touch with them, especially the congressional leaders, and many of them began to look not to Wendell Willkie but to Landon and Herbert Hoover for the party's prime leadership. As Representative Harold Knutson of Minnesota, for one, saw it, Wendell Willkie had vacated the leadership of the opposition, which had therefore been reassumed by Alf Landon, who had vigorously opposed interventionism. And Landon continued this opposition, in speeches and correspondence, until the Japanese attacked Pearl Harbor. He did this partly because of his conviction that the prime job of the opposition party was to oppose the administration wherever necessary, and partly to defend the unique aspects of American government, which he thought were slipping away. That he had no conviction of ultimate success was revealed in a letter he wrote his Democratic ally, Senator Bennett Champ Clark of Missouri: "I imagine the future student of this period will be amazed at how easy it was for a highly educated people to lose the Republic and their individual liberty." [27]

In June, 1941, Landon took an active interest in the government's emergency petroleum policies, particularly with the limitation of the distribution of petroleum products in the eastern states because of the use of American oil and tankers for supplying the British armed forces. Not only could this harm the area's industry, the threat of insufficient oil for winter heating would put many people to needless extra expense in finding substitutes. In a press release the Kansan presented his analysis of the situation and outlined the steps that could be taken to prevent a domestic oil shortage. "Get the oil to England necessary for her vital defensive service. Give her such tankers as are necessary for this purpose. But only after she has put all her own tankers into this use." Then, in the United States, the many idle railroad tank cars should be put into service to relieve the oil shortages. "Suspend the antitrust laws and other rules and regulations prohibiting the immediate cooperation which will increase the delivery of oil. Build short connecting links that increase the efficiency of the present network of pipelines. And I don't think there will be any need for gasless

[27] Joseph Martin, *My First Fifty Years in Politics* (New York: McGraw-Hill, 1961), p. 91; Harold Knutson to Arthur Schwab, May 21, 1941; Landon, "The Job of the Republican Party Now," *Liberty*, May 31, 1941; Landon to Bennett Champ Clark, June 5, 1941.

Sundays and shortages of fuel oil next winter in even the North Atlantic states." [28]

As for the government's interest in building a large-diameter pipeline from Texas to the east, Landon wrote Senator Capper that Federal Oil Administrator Harold Ickes was playing into the hands of four or five big oil companies that were more interested in profits than in national defense. Landon thought the proposed pipeline would cost too much and would require too much steel and construction time to serve defense interests well. He was therefore delighted when, in September, the Office of Production Management refused to approve construction of the Texas-Eastern pipeline; but there was still the problem of increasing the flow of oil to various parts of the nation. He wrote Frank Knox, who as Secretary of the Navy was greatly interested in the supply of petroleum, that short connecting links between existing pipelines could satisfactorily increase oil flow to the east, and in one-tenth the time it would take to build a large Texas-Eastern pipeline. Landon was also convinced that the smaller connecting loops would be far more economical in terms of cost and construction materials. If necessary, the Texas-Eastern pipeline could be constructed later, when the necessary steel was more readily available. Knox replied that Landon's idea was good and that he would follow it through with the Office of Production Management. [29] Eventually the government decided to build both the connecting loops and a through pipeline between the southwest and the east.

Landon and Knox had earlier been in touch with each other on questions of foreign policy, and Knox, in June, had attempted to change Landon's position:

> Things are growing very tense. . . . The situation is that we must get in or see England go down with Hitler dominating the world. . . . I know . . . that you are just as good an American as I am and just as willing to serve your country as I am. I want to tell you that in my judgment the time has come when all of us must subordinate everything else to national unity regardless of personalities or past events.

No one, Knox declared, could contribute more to this unity than Landon.

[28] Landon press statement, June 12, 1941.

[29] Landon to Arthur Capper, June 18, 1941; Landon to Frank Knox, September 10, 1941; Knox to Landon, September 17, 1941.

Landon answered:

> I agree with you as to the terrible need for national unity. And I will not
> deny that a combination of things has placed me in a position of terrific
> responsibility in that connection. But in the final analysis, Frank, there is
> only one man in this country who can bring about national unity—and he
> must prove himself by deeds, not words.

If that man, President Roosevelt, would really strive for national unity,
Landon said he would follow him.

> But I won't break the ice for him. For I still insist that before such a move
> is made the people and the Congress are entitled to an explanation for the
> change of front since the election.

Moreover, it was essential to national unity that the President make
clear what his labor, business, and price-control policies would be; and
additional efforts would have to be made to equip the army adequately
and to eliminate waste in the construction of army camps.

Landon also told Knox that the people needed definite information
about the operations of the American naval patrol in the Atlantic.

> I think you were terribly wrong in your [recent public] statement to the
> effect that it is none of their business. How can they be alarmed, when
> they are given the stand that the administration is still conducting "business
> as usual"? [Hence] the public confusion, and the apathy, and the indifferent
> understanding of the urgency of our own situation. The President must
> furnish us definite clear-cut leadership, to be the unifying force of the
> nation's life that his predecessors have been.

Part of the blame for the present confusion lay with the President,
Knox replied, but the overall situation was so complicated that
presidential action could not await unlimited debate in the Senate and
decisions that could not be reached by Congress in less than two or
three months.[30]

Neither partner of the 1936 campaign was to change his position;
each remained true to his duty as he saw it. Landon could not change
his position when what he feared most—an edging toward war under
the guise of preparing the nation's defense—seemed to be happening.
The Lend-Lease Act, the assumption of the defense of Greenland, the
seizure of German and Italian ships in American harbors, the establishment of a North Atlantic naval patrol, the occupation of Iceland, and

[30] Frank Knox to Landon, June 11, 1941; Landon to Knox, June 18, 1941; Knox
to Landon, June 27, 1941.

other acts by the United States all could be construed as steps toward war. When, in June, the United States merchantman *Robin Moor* was sunk by the Germans, Landon concluded that war would come in a few days. He was filled with gloom and pessimistic that after the war, if the Republic survived, the Communists and their anti-war fellow travelers would, and perhaps successfully, blame the whole thing on the capitalist system.

The sudden outbreak of war, in June, between the two dictatorships, Germany and Russia, although it did not alter Landon's convictions on the administration's "duplicity" or on the unwisdom of American entry in the war, caused him to ponder his position. After a while, he began making contacts to resume the attack upon the administration, and angrily protested the Copperhead epithet that was being applied to those who opposed the President's policy. Landon wrote newspaper tycoon Roy Howard, one of his most frequent correspondents:

> This Copperhead business is not only for the purpose of suppressing opposition at the present time, but is also with the idea of laying the foundation for a 1942 campaign along 1862 lines. That is, if you elect the opposition you will give aid and comfort to the enemy, and prolong the war.[31]

Publicly, Landon stated that the people were confused about their proper course of action because of the silence of the nation's officials on several major issues, their contradictory statements on others, and the fact that

> some of these administration officials get mad when they are asked by anyone to clarify this confusion. . . . It is a tragedy in this great emergency that we have this misunderstanding, and growing cynicism. The President's trail is as hard to follow and figure out as the trail of an old bull racoon in a swamp. This may be smart politics, but it is not the kind of leadership that promotes national morale in such times as these.[32]

At the end of June, Landon worked to gather support for a foreign-policy statement by a group of national leaders who opposed the President's policies, which he thought was especially needed now that the Soviet Union was in the war. The reaction was favorable, and for the next five weeks Landon was involved in drafting the statement—along with Herbert Hoover, president Felix Morley of Haverford College, and president Robert Hutchins of the University of Chicago. Landon had begun the project as a result of a conversation with

---

[31] Landon to Preston Wolfe, June 18, 1941; Landon to Roy Howard, July 17, 1941.
[32] Landon statement at Sabetha, Kan., July 19, 1941.

Raymond Moley, Roosevelt's disaffected Brain Truster; Moley had been enthusiastic about the idea and Landon had asked him to discuss it with Hoover. Moley soon called the Kansan to say that Hoover was very much interested, and Hoover later called Landon to say that he had asked Robert Hutchins to draft the statement. Hutchins sent the first draft to Hoover and Landon for revisions, after which copies were circulated among the three of them until agreement was reached. On July 19, Harry Woodring and Landon discussed the statement, and the former Democratic governor and Secretary of War showed interest in signing it because of indications that the President would run for a fourth term in 1944. Roosevelt's former ambassador to Great Britain, Joseph P. Kennedy, also indicated an interest, and Felix Morley, who had the task of getting the signatures, worked hard to enlist him. The release of the statement was delayed for more than a week in the hope that Kennedy and Woodring would sign; in the end, however, Kennedy decided not to sign, and Woodring did not want to be the only Democrat among the signatories.

The question then was who should issue the statement. Landon preferred that it be released by Hoover, but Hutchins recommended Frank O. Lowden, the former Illinois governor, which won Landon's and Hoover's approval.[33] Lowden issued the statement on August 5, and it had been endorsed by Lowden, Landon, Hoover, former Vice-President Charles G. Dawes, humorist Irvin S. Cobb, author Clarence Buddington Kelland, labor leader John L. Lewis, Robert Hutchins, opera singer Geraldine Ferrar, J. Reuben Clark, Henry P. Fletcher, Stanford president Raymond Lyman Wilbur, Felix Morley, Hanford MacNider, and Philadelphia businessman J. Henry Scattergood. It read in part:

> The American people should insistently demand that Congress put a stop to step-by-step projection of the United States into undeclared war. Congress has not only the sole power to declare war but also the power and responsibility to keep the country out of war unless or until both Houses have otherwise decided. Exceeding its expressed purpose, the lend-lease bill has been followed by naval action, by military occupation of bases outside the Western Hemisphere, by promise of unauthorized aid to Russia and by other belligerent moves. Such warlike steps, in no case sanctioned by Congress, undermine its Constitutional powers and the fundamental principles of democratic government.

[33] Landon to Clifford Stratton, July 1, 1941; Landon to his children, July 19, 1941; Landon to Felix Morley, July 14, 19, 1941; Landon to Herbert Hoover, July 29, 31, 1941; Landon to Robert M. Hutchins, August 4, 1941.

Referring to Russia's involvement in the war, the document noted that

> Recent events raise doubts that this war is a clear-cut issue of liberty and democracy. It is not purely a world conflict between tyranny and freedom. The Anglo-Russian alliance has dissipated that illusion. . . . Insofar as this is a war of power politics, the American people want no part in it. . . . The hope of civilization now rests primarily upon the preservation of freedom and democracy in the United States. That will be lost for a generation if we join in this war.

American lives and defense efforts should be expended only for the protection of American independence or to prevent invasion of the western hemisphere. The fifteen Republicans asserted that the Axis powers were not, nor would they be, in a position to threaten the hemisphere if the nation's defenses were properly prepared. "Energies of this country should be concentrated on the defense of our own liberties. Freedom in America does not depend on the outcome of struggles for material power between other nations."[34]

A new issue developed almost simultaneously with the Republican declaration: the extension of terms of service under the Selective Service Act of 1940. There was stiff Republican and Democratic opposition, with almost all of the Republican congressmen opposing the extension the moment it had been proposed by the administration (in July). Landon, however, differed with his fellow Republicans on this issue because defeat of the extension might be disastrous for national defense. In a July 20 coast-to-coast radio address, although he described the legislation as the "beginning of a sad revelation to the American people," he gave "reluctant support" to extending the terms of the draftees and national guardsmen.

> The President has the country out on the limb now, and we have got to strengthen the tree at the base. . . . [because] if there is no stopping of Mr. Roosevelt's war policies, he will throw the finest untrained and unequipped army in the world into a shooting war.[35]

The measure passed in the House of Representatives by the slimmest margin—203 to 202—and went into effect after the Senate approved it in August.[36] Landon's stand on the continuation of the draft brought

[34] *New York Times*, August 6, 1941.
[35] Landon to Lewis H. Brown, January 26, 1945; Landon speech, C.B.S., July 20, 1941.
[36] Martin, *First Fifty Years*, pp. 96 ff.

him little praise in his party. When Congressman Frank Carlson, his 1932 campaign manager, wrote Landon in protest, the Kansan replied with a statement of William Allen White: "If the Republicans in Congress vote to dissolve the army in the face of the enemy, and then we get into the war, it is going to be pretty tough in the campaign." Among the prominent Republicans, only Franklyn Waltman, the publicity director of the Republican national committee, wrote Landon to congratulate him for supporting the extension of the draft.[37] Landon perhaps did not persuade any Republicans in Congress to support the measure, but he gave strong support to the few who voted for it—and that may have been enough to ensure its passage.

Landon's position on the extension of the draft did not make him an outcast; his speeches and correspondence against the "repressive" tactics of the administration continued to win praise from Republicans and dissident Democrats. He repeatedly condemned the administration's defensive tactic of name-calling in this time of emergency, and he continually stressed the issue of war or peace. To suggestions that Roosevelt wanted to avoid war, Landon wrote: "If the President is determined to keep us out of war, but bolster up all the opposition to Hitler everywhere in the world, his policies then become understandable, and really masterful strategy. In that event, the opposition is his greatest asset." Although Landon doubted that this was Roosevelt's strategy, he conceded that "if we are going to get into this war, Hitler himself must force the issue."[38]

Doubt was cast on this conclusion, however, with the August 14 announcement of the Atlantic Charter conference between Roosevelt and Prime Minister Winston Churchill of Great Britain. Landon, in an interview with the press, said the conference was a

> well-staged effort to mislead the American people as to the purpose of this meeting. All the emphasis was placed on desirable peace aims. . . . It was not revealed until later in the day that the military and naval high commands were present also. Their presence instead of the Secretary of State gives weight to great misgivings that this long conference dealt with military and naval collaboration, rather than collaboration with Britain by peaceful means.

[37] Frank Carlson to Landon, July 21, 1941; Landon to Carlson, July 28, 1941; Franklyn Waltman to Landon, July 21, 1941.

[38] Landon to Theodore Alvord, August 11, 1941.

Landon praised the peace aims of the two leaders but wondered if the United States had been further committed to warlike means. Also, he found it "rather strange" that the Atlantic Charter had called for freedom of the seas, national self-determination, and other freedoms, but had not mentioned freedom of worship. "Could it be that this omission was caused by a desire not to offend atheistic Communist Russia?"[39]

In August and September Landon gave some special consideration to domestic politics. Roosevelt, he believed, must be defeated for a fourth term in 1944, and fundamental to accomplishing this was the mid-term election of Republican governors in some of the key states. New York was most important, and it was Dewey's job to capture that state. Landon had also become convinced that the party could no longer support Republicans (such as Fiorello La Guardia) who always sided with the administration. Political opposition, not cooperation, would sustain the party in an emergency and give meaning to the concept of a democratic, two-party system in America. The Kansan was distressed by Republicans who had joined the administration in trying to shout down the critics of its foreign policy with accusations of partisan politics. Willkie had done this, Landon believed, and therefore obviously did not think of himself as the leader of the opposition party, responsible for maintaining party cohesiveness and perpetuating the American party system. Opposition was essential in times like these, when the greatest stress was placed on popular government; after the war, moreover, only a responsible, cohesive opposition could facilitate a return to government by the ballot box. As he explained to Henry L. Mencken, "[this is] why I, who have never been such a staunch party man, am putting so much stress on the necessity for active and effective party organization."[40]

In September the question of the national chairmanship rose again. Senator Hugh Butler of Nebraska called Landon to say there was a mounting demand for a full-time national chairman, and considerable talk of Adam McMullen, the editor of the *Farm Journal*, for the position. Landon replied that the election of McMullen to the chairmanship would brand the national committee as belonging to Joseph Pew, who owned the *Farm Journal*. Furthermore, Landon said, Joseph Martin's problems were caused by the lack of money: the chairman did not have

[39] Landon press statements, August 15, 1941.

[40] Landon to Harold B. Johnson, August 15, 1941; Landon to Henry L. Mencken, September 11, 1941.

enough money to hire the executive assistant Willkie had promised him earlier in the year. Butler then said that industrialist Ernest Weir and his New York City contacts would guarantee sufficient money to engage a full-time national chairman. "To hell with them," Landon retorted; "they came over to Philadelphia and told us that before the convention. And look what happened." Landon said he would not allow Wall Street to dominate the national committee and name its chairman. Butler suggested that either Landon or Hoover could pick the man, but Landon was not interested. Later, in a letter to Landon, Butler denied that he wanted to remove Martin from the chairmanship. He professed his loyalty to Martin and his strong desire to cooperate with Landon, and said that Willkie was not the party leader as far as he was concerned.[41]

Nor was Willkie the party's leader as far as Landon was concerned—and the Kansan made this clear in a speech at Sparks, Kansas, on August 30. Landon lashed out at the new firm of Roosevelt and Willkie, charging that their "war party" favored "personal loyalty to the President."

> It means the attempt to eliminate from public life all who disagree with the President's policy. That is exactly the course Mussolini and Hitler and Stalin followed in building their power and maintaining it.

Landon declared that Willkie, in effect, approved the administration's attempt "to smother political debate in this country."

> This attempt to eliminate all opposition has reached the point that the row now is not over the question of whether the administration is doing wrong but that we who think the administration is making mistakes may not even debate it. . . . As far as I am concerned, I am going to continue to speak my mind; and I am going to insist on the freedom of others to speak their minds, whether on all points or no points I agree with them. While a declaration of war means that we will close ranks behind the flag, as we always do, it does not extinguish the rights of citizens to discuss the war and its prosecution. But the last one of us will fight for America, under any kind of leadership.[42]

Landon continued to combat the administration through fall of 1941. In Kansas, despite the efforts of the "war press" and the "war party," he found little sentiment for war. There was, instead, largely "a fatal-

[41] Landon to Lacy Haynes, September 24, 1941; Hugh Butler to Landon, October 2, 1941.
[42] Landon speech, Sparks, Kan., August 30, 1941.

istic acceptance of the fact that the President has at last worked us into war." This was a reference to the President's September 11 announcement that American warships had been instructed to fire at German or Italian naval vessels on sight, a policy that resulted from the attack a week earlier on the destroyer *Greer* while on its way to Iceland.[43]

October 9 saw a new turn in the foreign-policy debate, as Roosevelt asked Congress to repeal the sections of the Neutrality Act that prohibited the arming of American merchant vessels and their sailing directly to Allied ports. During the debate on this proposal—on the day that news came of a torpedo attack on the American destroyer *Kearney*—Landon again spoke out publicly. He told the second congressional district's Women's Republican Club in Kansas City, Kansas, that "while the President has repeatedly proclaimed a national policy of destroying Hitler, we are unprepared for the physical fact of war." There had been, he declared, an "alarming failure of our defense production," which he ascribed to "the tragedy of a President selfishly playing politics and denouncing all disagreement with him as 'playing politics' when there should be none. We have the tragedy of a President hiding behind the bushes, unwilling to call on the American people for the sacrifices they must make. To date, he is still feeding us sugar, when he ought to be feeding us iron."

In this speech Landon for the first time made public his belief that it was only a matter of time before the United States would be in the war. All the country could do was prepare for war as best it could. But it had to exert more pressure upon the administration to increase the preparation.[44]

By November, Landon was almost exhausted—intellectually, physically, and spiritually. He wrote to Harold Johnson: "Brother, I am slowing up. There isn't any question about it. The only victor out of the upheaval, anyhow, is going to be Communism or Fascism." He added that perhaps "a man thinking only of his own skin should join up with the 'commies.'" Landon also wrote Roy Howard, saying he would like to "sail away to some quiet island where there are no telephones and no telegraph stations, smash the radio, sink the boat, and content myself there for another twenty years at least." Yet he kept up the battle. On November 13 he suggested to Senator Bennett Champ Clark that he talk with Clarence Streit, the proponent of the union of

---

[43] Landon to Franklyn Waltman, September 27, 1941.
[44] Landon speech, Kansas City, Kan., October 17, 1941.

the English-speaking countries. "I am not plugging for Union Now. I am simply exploring every possible avenue, however crackpot it may seem, in the hope of finding the way out of the holocaust ahead of us." [45]

Writing to Roscoe Drummond of the *Christian Science Monitor*, which he read every day, Landon complimented the newsman for making "the best defense of Roosevelt's tactics that I have seen, when you say you are not going to be kept 'from supporting sound policies . . . by his unsound arguments.'" But Landon thought those unsound arguments might sabotage sound policies.

> How about the average man on the street, when he finds he has been tricked into war. God protect us from their bitterness in the inevitable days ahead, when we have the reaction to deficit spending and war. Their bitterness will not be confined to having been tricked into war. Until within recent months the President has been assuring them of "business as usual," and that they should keep all their social gains. You and I know that is impossible in the years ahead of us. But what about the psychology of the man who doesn't know it is impossible, when he finds out he has been lied to by the man that is almost God to him. . . .
>
> You have got to have ideals to fight for, and there is none in this situation. And there have been none in the eight years of the New Deal administration, except that of security—which is another softening effect, on account of the way so many people are getting it. . . . Fighting a war under a Churchill is one thing, but fighting a war under a boondoggler is another. [46]

Landon continued his fight against the administration to the eve of Pearl Harbor. On December 4 he went before the Young Republicans of Kansas to proclaim "There is more patriotism than politics building in the Republican party." He condemned the administration's "continual support of those who believe our capitalistic system is a failure and no longer can perform its historic function." Of an alleged campaign to discredit the newspapers, he said: "If [the administration] can make the people of the country lose confidence in the press, and eliminate any real worthwhile minority party, then anything is possible. We will have a one-party system, and the machinery to perpetuate it." On December 6 he wrote that although the United States was not yet a one-party country, "we are creating the same sort of collective system in the United States that we are fighting to destroy in Germany." He

[45] Landon to Harold B. Johnson, November 4, 1941; Landon to Roy Howard, November 14, 1941; Landon to Bennett Champ Clark, November 13, 1941.
[46] Landon to Roscoe Drummond, November 13, 1941.

hoped the war would cause a political revolt in the United States that would reverse the trend toward a one-party state.

He had not long to wait for the arrival of the conditions under which that idea would be tested. The next day Japanese sea and air forces attacked Pearl Harbor. America was in the war. Landon telegraphed the President:

> There is imperative need for courageous unified action by the American people. The Japanese attack leaves no choice. Nothing must be permitted to interrupt our victory over a foreign foe. Please command me in any way I can be of service." [47]

[47] Landon remarks, Topeka, December 4, 1941; Landon to James L. Wright, December 6, 1941; Landon to Franklin D. Roosevelt, December 7, 1941.

CHAPTER 20

Political Opponent in Time of War

During the war much was said about adjourning partisan politics. Indeed, the day after Pearl Harbor, December 8, 1941, this became the official theme of the Democratic national committee chairman, Edward J. Flynn, and was warmly approved by President Roosevelt.[1] Landon's reaction was that this would be as unpatriotic as sabotaging the war industry. Believing the administration's "forget politics" theme must be combated so that it would not lead to the Republican party's destruction, Landon was in the forefront of those who urged Republicans to continue playing the role of the opposition. On January 29, 1942, he told the diners at the Kansas Day banquet that the work of the minority party called for

> absolute devotion to the interests of our country, and loyal support for all policies that will tend to bring victory to our common cause. But it also requires honest and fearless discussion and impartial criticism of mistakes and inefficiency on the part of the administration. . . . By furnishing advanced leadership of public opinion, it has very definitely the duty of pulling and pushing and shoving the national administration along the road to victorious war production.[2]

[1] Edward J. Flynn to Franklin D. Roosevelt, December 9, 1941, and Roosevelt to Flynn, December 10, 1941, Franklin D. Roosevelt Library, Hyde Park, N.Y.

[2] Landon to Mark M. Jones, January 7, 1942; Landon to Raymond S. Springer, January 13, 1942; Landon remarks, Kansas Day dinner, Topeka, January 29, 1942; Alfred M. Landon Papers, Kansas State Historical Society, Topeka.

The Kansan was invited to be the chief speaker at the Lincoln Day dinner in Washington, D.C., on February 11—in an address that would be carried over a national network. National chairman Joseph W. Martin and the other sponsors of the meeting thought his speech should be patriotic rather than political, but Landon disagreed. He believed that he should "proclaim the necessity of politics; that we can't abandon our form of republican processes; that politics is as essential in war as it is in peace." Landon acted on this conviction in his address. Speaking before an audience studded with Republican senators and representatives, he said that the job before the country was "to win the war as speedily as possible." This, however, did not mean that discussion of the domestic war effort was out of order. He conceded that some waste would be caused in the exigencies of preparing to fight, and said that should be excused, "but the risk is too great and the stakes are too high for any patriotic American to sit silent in the face of incompetency and unsettled rules that interfere with the maximum efficient prosecution of the war."

Having called for politics almost as usual, Landon enumerated the points in his wartime policy. He asked President Roosevelt to sound a

> clear call to patriotic concentration, to united effort and sacrifice in our common cause.... The country is not interested in criminations and recriminations between isolationists and interventionists.... Any attempt to arouse group or racial dissension and bitterness can only be in the interests of the Axis nations. That is true whether it is anti-Semitism or Jim Crowism, or playing politics with economic group prejudices.... Now is no time to try to fit the American people into ideological patterns for the future.

He also called upon the government "to make at least a twenty-five per cent cut in expenditures for non-military purposes," to curb inflation, and to make better use of "little business" in the war effort. "The test of the ability of a free people to survive is their freedom to point out the weak spots of their leaders, and their ability at the same time to cooperate with them."[3]

Landon's declaration that partisan politics should not be adjourned was the foundation of Republican action during the war. It made an impact because it was stated in the capital, and nationally over the radio, on Republicanism's high feast day. It carried even more force because it followed Landon's well-publicized visit with President

[3] Raymond S. Springer to Landon, January 10, 1942; Landon to Springer, January 13, 1942; Landon speech, Washington, D.C., February 11, 1942.

Roosevelt earlier in the day, when the two men agreed that the immediate task was to hold fast until the United States was ready to strike back.[4] In any event, the party line was set and Republicans were to act on it throughout the war—though eventually they would have needed no urging from Landon to do so.

While the Republicans were deciding to strike for freedom of action, they had to combat turmoil in their own ranks, which centered on attempts by conservative industrialists and by monied, eastern Willkie supporters to capture control of the national committee headquarters from the moderates. In the struggle, the men of wealth tried to starve the moderates out by withholding financial support from headquarters activities, with the result that in 1941 and 1942 national chairman Martin and his two principal assistants, Frank E. Gannett and Clarence Buddington Kelland, served without pay. The group was also forced to give up its spacious quarters on Jackson Place for an old brownstone house on Connecticut Avenue.[5]

Even the moderates were at odds, among themselves. Martin wanted to quit the chairmanship, against the opposition of many moderates who feared that his resignation would end their control of the national headquarters. On the other hand, there were conservatives—such as Senator Robert A. Taft of Ohio—who wanted Martin to resign because they believed the burdens of national chairman and House minority leader were too much for one man. Senator Taft led a movement to have Landon succeed Martin because he felt the Kansan was the most active and prestigious Willkie opponent, and could therefore be elected chairman. Victor Murdock, the old Kansas Progressive leader; Ernest Weir, the Pennsylvania industrialist; and Herbert Hoover also suggested that Landon take the position. Landon refused, writing Taft that although he would do almost anything to help the party, he could not accept the chairmanship because of the time it would take from his business.[6] Lacking a candidate who was acceptable to most of the Republican factions, the national committee would not elect a new chairman until after the 1942 elections.

[4] *Washington Star*, February 11, 1942; *San Francisco Examiner*, February 12, 1942.

[5] Joseph W. Martin, *My First Fifty Years in Politics* (New York: McGraw-Hill, 1961), pp. 122 f.; Landon to Edward F. Colladay, February 27, 1942.

[6] Robert A. Taft to Landon, February 20, 1942; Victor Murdock to Landon, March 7, 1942; Landon to Richard Robbins, September 28, 1942; Landon to Harry Darby, April 8, 1942; Landon to Taft, February 21, 1942.

Meanwhile, Landon was concerned with the level of the country's morale; in February, he reported an unwelcome change of sentiment in Kansas. "People are very critical, almost bitter, at England." They were dismayed by the fall of Singapore, and by the movement of German ships through the English Channel under the guns of Britain. Moreover, the rumor that Churchill had boasted of getting the United States into the war touched off "criticism that is extending to the President himself." When on February 23, 1942, Roosevelt attempted to rally the nation, Landon felt better; he thought the speech was good and that it contained some inspired words, though he found virtually no one who agreed with him. Nevertheless, Landon was still dismayed by the President's partisanship. "It is a hell of a situation, to have to be fighting a war abroad, and when you want to support the administration 100 per cent to be confronted with the evident build-up for a fourth term and an increasing destruction of state functions." Some of the concentration of power in the hands of the national administration was unnecessary, even in wartime, and he saw it as a deliberate attempt by a few New Dealers to take advantage of public support for the President to push "their ideas of totalitarian collectivism." This, he thought, industry must fight, but he did not expect much from industry. "It always amuses me to hear some businessman accusing Congress of being a rubber stamp, while nine out of ten of them are afraid to stick their necks out."[7]

In March, Landon again took to the radio to express his views. He deplored time-wasting issues—the discussions of war aims and whether the interventionists or the isolationists were to blame for Pearl Harbor—when the task was to achieve the "swift defeat of those who have attacked American soil." Anti-Semitism and racial and economic prejudices were also condemned as interfering with "our concentration on winning the war." The Kansan was convinced that "those who are attempting to suppress all suggestions on the conduct of this war are unconsciously great aids to Hitler"—as were those who tried to push domestic social and economic changes. "We must immediately and forthwith accept willingly for the sake of victory, a Spartan existence.... All the frills and the nonessentials everywhere must go." The situation demanded "some tough guys in high office, who have

[7] Landon to Arthur Krock, February 19, 1942; Landon to Joseph W. Martin, February 24, 1942; Landon to H. A. Meyer, March 3, 1942; Landon to Otto D. Donnell, March 4, 1942.

only one thought, one ideal, one single purpose. That is, winning the war."[8]

Although at that time the press was filled with stories about the administration's errors and inefficiency, Landon's speech was not favorably received. One of the sharpest criticisms was a *Cleveland Plain Dealer* editorial:

> There is much to be criticized about Washington's conduct of the war, but Alf Landon, like the man who lives in a glass house, is in no position to throw stones. . . . A better role for him would be to don sackcloth and ashes in repentance for the part he played in trying to obstruct the President's defense program before the war started.

The Kansan was hurt by this because he had repeatedly emphasized— long before Pearl Harbor—the necessity for greater defense efforts; and he saw this criticism as another instance of fomented antagonism between former interventionists and isolationists. He was also displeased by signs that Wendell Willkie would make use of the isolationist-interventionist issue. All this was reprehensible because it created division in the party—even worse, in the country—at a time when the United States desperately needed unity. Administration spokesmen, and Willkie, had frequently referred to the pre–Pearl Harbor record, and Landon wrote that interesting questions could be asked about promises of peace, defense preparations, and America's involvement in the war. Although such a debate should be deferred until after the war, "as long as the Democrats insist on opening the pre–Pearl Harbor record, we will have to meet them."[9] Landon's reaction to being labeled an isolationist, and his later determination to prevent Willkie's renomination for President, were largely responsible for his growing political friendliness with former President Herbert Hoover and Senator Robert A. Taft.

During the summer Landon thought the main issue was still victory, but the time had come for discussion of what would happen after the war was over. In a Flag Day speech, at Marshalltown, Iowa, he called for clarification of Allied war aims "as a part of the preparedness for peace." This should be done to avoid dissension among the Allies during the war, and to alert the American people that they could not, at the war's end, go "back to normalcy."

[8] Landon speech, N.B.C. Blue Network, March 8, 1942.

[9] *Cleveland Plain Dealer*, March 10, 1942; Landon to William Hard, March 30, 1942; Landon to Harry Darby, April 8, 1942; Landon to Harold B. Johnson, July 15, 1942.

We have had the fatal weakness of assuming that everyone in the world wants to live as we do, and under the same kind of government that we do. ... We must approach the greatest problem of all times, a just and durable peace, with justice born of wisdom, and a sober appraisal of the realities. ... We must avoid the old-fashioned camp-meeting way of approach. That hallelujah foreign policy has been disastrous repeatedly throughout our history. It is based on the smug assumption that all the world likes American ice-cream sodas. Strange as it may seem to most Americans, they don't.[10]

On the basis of his recognition of pluralism in the world, Landon was to join with fellow Republicans in seeking a reasonable foreign-policy position, one that might remove the stigma of isolation from their party and yet steer clear of the incaution they saw in President Roosevelt's brand of internationalism.

Landon participated actively in the campaign of 1942. He spent much time urging a broader base of contributions to the party because he was fearful that a few big-money contributors would dominate the policies of the Republican national committee. In Kansas, he worked to round up support for the corporation commissioner, Andrew Schoeppel (a former all-American football player), as governor. Landon also strongly encouraged Thomas Dewey's campaign for the governorship of New York, and supported Kenneth Wherry in his campaign against Independent Senator George Norris in Nebraska. The Kansan wrote to Dewey: "Nothing is of greater importance in the Republican party than your election."[11]

To assist Wherry, Landon agreed to make his major speech of the 1942 campaign to a Republican mass meeting in Lincoln, Nebraska, on October 9. He attacked the "chaos, confusion, bickering and jealousy ... in Washington [that] is certain to cost many thousand American lives on the battlefield and even put in jeopardy the victory for which we are all sacrificing." He lauded the Democratic and Republican members of Congress who, through their investigations, had revealed the "delay, inefficiency, red tape, and personal feuding that are clogging our war efforts." These investigations, he charged, indicated that America was sending inferior planes to meet the enemy, and that bureaucracy was obstructing the efforts to produce the amount of synthetic rubber necessary for war needs. Landon also

[10] Landon speech, Marshalltown, Ia., June 14, 1942.

[11] Landon to Richard Robbins, September 28, 1942; Landon to Willard Mayberry, July 16, 1942; Landon to Thomas E. Dewey, July 30, 1942, Thomas E. Dewey Papers, University of Rochester Libraries, Rochester, N.Y.

contended there might be shortages of food and oil because of the administration's inability to allocate enough manpower for production of these commodities and increase the payment received by producers for their work. "The peaceful ways of a republic may result in errors at the beginning of a war. But this is the end of the tenth month." The administration was trying to "fight through a program of social reform, maintain our standard of living, and successfully fight a war at one and the same time"—which he thought could not be done. "Electing Republicans is the only way the people can crack the whip over this well-meaning but inefficient administration."[12] His Lincoln speech was so enthusiastically received that it became the model for Landon's campaign speeches in Kansas and the surrounding states.

"Ti-Ra-La-La-I-Ta! I gloat" wrote Landon in reacting to the Republican victories in 1942. The party gained forty-four seats in the House and nine in the Senate. Wherry defeated Norris in Nebraska, and a Republican, Edward H. Moore, was elected senator from normally Democratic Oklahoma. Dewey won in New York—one of several new governorships the Republicans acquired—and Schoeppel was elected by a large majority in Kansas. Landon attributed the Republican gains to Roosevelt's broken peace promises of 1940, political interference by Mrs. Eleanor Roosevelt, and—most of all— the lack of a major military victory. "The American people," Landon said in a press statement, "also resented the continual ding-donging from Washington that they were soft and weak when they felt that the administration was soft and weak."[13]

Landon also had a private life to lead during the war. His oldest daughter, Peggy, had married in October, 1941, and within a year Landon had a grandson. The Kansan's business improved because of the increased demands for oil and gas, and, although his profits (and those of other oil independents) were restricted by price regulations, he sold all of his production and made a substantial profit. The Landons, like most Americans of means, had trouble securing help to run the house and their adjoining farm. During 1943 the Landons were without a maid most of the time, and the statesman found that "my training at drying dishes which I acquired as a boy is

12 Landon speech, Lincoln, Neb., October 9, 1942.

13 Landon to Thomas E. Dewey, November 4, 1942, Dewey Papers; Donald B. Johnson, *The Republican Party and Wendell Willkie* (Urbana: University of Illinois Press, 1960), pp. 220 f.; Landon to Arthur Krock, November 4, 1942; Landon press statement, November 4, 1942.

doing me in good stead." In the fall of 1943, Landon's hired hand quit, and Landon and his nine-year-old son, Jack, fed the hogs and chickens and pailed the cow. As a result, Landon worked off about ten pounds in the spring of 1944. "There is," he said, "something to be said about this manpower shortage after all."[14]

The Kansan also gave inspirational speeches during the war. In 1942 and early 1943 he frequently reviewed America's naval heritage and lauded the fleet's current performance. Or he would tell an audience: "The time is here when we must all fight for America. Then pray God, 'Come, peace, not like a mourner bowed, but proud, to meet a people, proud with eyes that tell the triumphs tasted.'" He was also concerned with the problems of education during the war (he was a trustee of Southern Methodist University), and in several speeches he declared that "the crowning glory of America has been the liberal arts colleges scattered throughout our land." He urged support for these colleges: "It would be a great tragedy to America if the strong liberal arts college for any reason is weakened and permitted to languish. Come what may, in this world of ours, good literature will be just as necessary, good music just as beautiful, and good character just as inspiring."[15] Landon cooperated in the war bond program, and was frequently in touch with federal and state officials and fellow oilmen on ways to increase oil production and facilitate the flow of petroleum products to points where they were needed. He also worked to "clean up" conditions around military camps, particularly to restrict the availability of liquor near camps that soon would be training eighteen- and nineteen-year-old draftees.[16]

Republican leaders, who began preparing for the presidential campaign of 1944 immediately after the 1942 elections, first had to select a new national chairman; on November 12, Joseph Martin announced his resignation as chairman so that he might concentrate on his duties in the House of Representatives. At least fifteen different

[14] *Topeka State Journal*, October 4, 1941; *Topeka Capital*, July 6, 1942; Landon to W. K. Hutchinson, June 8, 1943; Landon to Harold B. Johnson, March 3, 1943; Landon to Alfred G. Hill, November 8, 1943; Landon to Edmund I. Kaufmann, June 16, 1944.

[15] Landon speeches: *e.g.*, Lyndon, Kan., October 27, 1942, and Carleton College, Northfield, Minn., May 12, 1943.

[16] Vincent F. Callahan to Landon, November 2, 1942; Landon speech, Topeka, January 26, 1944; Landon to Harold L. Ickes, March 13, 1942; Landon to Ralph O. Brewster, June 12, 1942; Landon to Edwin H. Hughes, October 21, 1942; Landon to Henry Stimson, October 29, 1942.

successors were seriously considered, including Werner W. Schroeder, the Illinois national committeeman (the conservatives' choice); Massachusetts national committeeman Sinclair Weeks; Governor Ralph Carr of Colorado; former Congressman John Hollister of Ohio; and national committeeman Harrison E. Spangler of Iowa. Martin favored Spangler, as a compromise between the various Republican factions, and was able to secure enough backing to have him elected at the December 6 national committee meeting.[17] Landon also had been mentioned as a compromise candidate; he had, in fact, been urged by Hoover, Robert Taft, Arthur Capper, William Allen White, and Ralph Robey to take the position. Although Landon thought he could have been elected unanimously, he refused to consider it, because it meant "a dog's life" for the incumbent. "A chairman's job is that of organization," the Kansan said. "He is circumscribed, when it comes to policies." Landon did not want to be silenced on the issues before the nation.[18]

Because of his continuing prominence, Landon was often asked what the Republicans would stand for in 1944, but he answered that so much could happen between 1942 and 1944 that no one could be certain. Although he did not know what his party's 1944 position would be, he was convinced that Republicans would have to prepare early for the campaign—and should begin by making common cause with anti-Roosevelt Democrats. He repeatedly urged this tactic upon other Republican leaders, pointing to the 1942 election of Republican Senator Moore in Oklahoma as an example of a successful fusion of Democrats and Republicans. Landon also encouraged Harry Woodring's efforts to form a third party—the proposed Commonwealth party—or, failing that, to join with Republicans in opposing Roosevelt. He told Gomer T. Davies, the editor of the *Concordia Kansan*, "Don't jump on Woodring. He represents a great [flock] of Democrats that are coming our way. Let's woo them."[19]

[17] Martin, *First Fifty Years*, pp. 132 ff.; Johnson, *Willkie*, pp. 222 ff.

[18] Arthur Capper to Landon, November 21, 1942; Ralph Robey to Landon, November 23, 1942; Landon to Charles M. Harger, December 4, 1942; Landon to W. D. Archie, December 21, 1942; W. A. White to Wendell Willkie, November 30, 1942, White to Herbert Hoover, November 30, 1942, and Hoover to White, December 2, 1942, William Allen White Papers, Manuscript Division, Library of Congress, Washington, D.C.

[19] Landon to Harrison E. Spangler, January 4, February 9, 1943; Landon to Eugene Meyer, February 9, 1943; Landon to Edward H. Moore, June 16, 1943; Landon to Gomer T. Davies, July 12, 27, 1943.

In October, 1943, Landon could write: "We might nominate a Democrat for Vice President." He pointed out to many of his correspondents that he believed the Republicans had attracted about a million and a half Democratic votes in 1936, and even more Democratic votes in 1940, "because the clay feet of the New Deal were further exposed." He looked forward to even greater Democratic support in 1944. Landon was in almost constant touch with Harrison Spangler in 1943, and was one of those who persuaded the Republican chairman to take a serious interest in the Kentucky elections of that year. Landon saw Kentucky as a test of whether Republicans and Democrats could join in support of Republican candidates, a fusion he directly encouraged. This interest from outside the state was probably effective, for the Republican ticket in Kentucky, headed by gubernatorial candidate Simeon S. Willis, won all except one of the state offices—which Landon took as an omen of Republican victory over Roosevelt in 1944.[20]

In February, 1943, Landon renewed his personal campaign against the New Deal, in Omaha, Nebraska. His Lincoln Day speech dealt more harshly with the Democratic administration than any of his previous speeches.

> We are being compelled to fight on two fronts—one a global war, the other a Nazi bureaucrat war. Instead of a leadership uniting us with "an eye single to the task" on the war front we have a bureaucratic leadership in Washington obviously thirsting for power and just as obviously determined to establish a permanent control of our lives thus creating a second front at home.

Landon urged Republicans to be critical of New Deal policies on the grounds that "what might seem a mere partisan blanket attack is really an effort to spur a win-the-war policy." He also appealed to "real Democrats" to work to this end within their party, and with Republicans to keep Vice President Henry Wallace and "his fellow travelers" from leading "us down the same disastrous primrose path which Hitler has led his people." As harsh as Landon was with the administration, he told his fellow partisans that "the mere election of Republicans will not 'save the country' unless we are equal to the

---

[20] Landon to W. D. Ferguson, October 8, 1943; Landon to Harrison E. Spangler, June 18, August 6, 1943; Spangler to Landon, August 9, November 4, 1943; Landon to D. O. Becker, August 10, 1943; Johnson, *Willkie*, p. 253.

problems of reconstruction not only in the United States, but in the postwar world-at-large." [21]

Landon became increasingly angry with the secrecy and apparent confusion of the New Deal on international issues. Early in April he scored the chairman of the Senate Foreign Relations Committee on his statement that hearings before that committee on "postwar peace proposals are to be secret." "The average citizen," Landon declared, "today feels that we need more news out of Washington instead of less. . . . Any plan which directly concerns the future welfare of the American citizen doesn't have to be hidden behind the veil of secrecy."

He reiterated this issue throughout 1943 and 1944. In a nationally broadcast speech on April 16, 1943, Landon said:

> It is obvious that there are certain difficulties in discussing at this time, all questions of the postwar future. It is also obvious to the observant citizen that there are currents and counter currents of opinion in the [fighting] United Nations. To discuss these "differences of opinion" with complete frankness subjects one to the charge of creating disunity in the war coalition and of threatening victory. But if we remain silent on the pitfalls and dangers —both domestic and foreign—which confront the American people, we threaten America. But in spite of these difficulties there are certain questions that must be faced today. They must be dragged out into the open.[22]

Dragging these questions into the open was the task the Kansan set for himself.

Landon's April 16 speech was made during a pulse-taking tour of the east, in which he conferred with Thomas Dewey, Governor John Bricker of Ohio, Herbert Hoover, chairman Spangler, and other Republican leaders—as well as with President Roosevelt and Secretary of State Cordell Hull. (Whenever Landon went to Washington— from 1939 until Hull's retirement in 1944—he visited the Secretary of State at his invitation. Hull used the Kansan as a sounding board for his ideas and his complaints. Some of Landon's public criticisms of the President were reinforced by Secretary Hull, and perhaps even derived from him.) Landon returned from the east alarmed by the impression he had received—from Hull and others—that Washington seemed at loose ends in approaching foreign problems and that politics played too great a role in policy-making. He was shocked when Roosevelt told him he was out to discredit the Free French leader, Charles de Gaulle.[23]

[21] Landon speech, Omaha, February 12, 1943.

[22] Landon press release, April 2, 1943; Landon speech, C.B.S., April 16, 1943.

[23] *Topeka Capital*, April 9, 1943; *Des Moines Register*, April 18, 1943; Landon to Richard Lloyd Jones, April 19, 1943; Landon interview, September 17, 1963.

"The tragedy," Landon believed, "is that no one in the State Department knows what [Roosevelt's] foreign policies are." He thought the administration was blocking congressional consideration of resolutions on peace and international organization because it was afraid such debate might shatter the New Deal's political coalition. Even matters of refugee resettlement and international distribution of food were seldom freely discussed.[24]

Landon was therefore encouraged to continue roiling the political waters to get support for his position of open discussion. On May 13, just before making a major address in Minneapolis, he said:

> The Republican party has a whole fist full of governors and senators—and at least one ex-candidate—from which to select its presidential nominee in 1944. . . . Roosevelt can be beaten in 1944—war or no war. And he will be defeated not only by Republican votes but by the votes of real Democrats who are not going to stand for a life term for any President.

Later, in an interview, he asked for less government control in the United States, warning that "the New Deal is following the economic pattern of Hitler's early-day national socialism." The pattern could be seen in the

> government-managed and -manipulated economy . . . government-planned management of production . . . government-planned management of labor . . . government-planned management of agriculture. (Remember the government's destruction of six million little pigs.) [And] government-planned management of the press and the radio. . . . That was the prewar New Deal and it is the plan for the postwar New Deal.[25]

[24] Landon to Harold B. Johnson, April 27, 1943. Criticism, by Landon and others, of the secrecy about non-military diplomacy exasperated Roosevelt. This is seen in a remarkable letter the President sent to Arthur Capper, who was not only a Republican senator but also a newspaper publisher. Writing of the World Food Conference in Hot Springs, Roosevelt justified restricting contacts between the conference delegates and the press on the ground that "certain newspaper owners like McCormick and the Pattersons [had] ordered their people to [create] trouble and controversy." Sputtering about the "very large percentage of rumors" in the newspapers, President Roosevelt said that much of the press was a "purveyor of false news." He even declared that the Pan-American conferences at Montevideo and Lima "were nearly torpedoed" because of the unhampered access newsmen had to the delegates, Franklin D. Roosevelt to Arthur Capper, June 16, 1943, Arthur Capper Papers, Kansas State Historical Society, Topeka. It is not surprising that Roosevelt's extreme sensitivity to criticism made his opposition all the more suspicious of him.

[25] *Minneapolis Star-Journal,* May 13, 1943; *Minneapolis Morning Tribune,* May 14, 1943.

In his Minneapolis address, which was broadcast over the N.B.C. Blue Network, the Kansan spoke of foreign relations. He sharply disputed the charge that the Republican party was the party of isolationism. He justified the rejection of the Versailles Treaty because it had been based upon "an imperfect and outworn balance of power" and had ignored Russia, accepted secret treaties, partly sanctioned Japanese aggression in the Far East, and necessitated economic policies that "planted the seeds of war." Landon then described the Republican governments of the 1920s as administrations that had worked ceaselessly for international peace and stability—in contrast with the comparative isolationism of the Democratic party in the 1920s and much of the 1930s. Yet the crux of his Minneapolis speech was not who had been isolationist or internationalist, but what policies the country should presently adopt. He called for open discussion of the non-military aspects of United States foreign policy and congressional minority representation in the formulation of that policy.

Landon also demanded that the administration face up to the fact that "tragic misunderstandings between ourselves and our allies as to the future are beginning to develop." Criticizing the tendency to ignore disagreeable facts—"the hallelujah approach"—he said:

> Russia has already let it be known that she has no intention of restoring Eastern European boundaries. . . . Mr. Churchill and others have also served notice that Great Britain is not going to liquidate her empire and that the French and the Dutch empires are to be restored. How does this fit in with Under Secretary of State Welles' statement that "the age of imperialism is ended"?

Having asked for a realistic consideration of world affairs, Landon reached the high point of his speech—his outline of postwar American objectives. He proposed that representatives of the fighting United Nations should, for several years after the war, sit as "an interim world council" to supervise punishment of war criminals, disarmament and political reconstruction in enemy countries, restoration of world-trade relations, and famine relief. Such a council should also set up commissions to consider plans for better international economic relations, for the government of undeveloped lands, for machinery to ensure a lasting peace, for world disarmament, and "for international recognition of the principle of religious liberty and for the autonomy of nations." He also urged that the United States soon recognize the desirability of some form of "permanent international organization"—

perhaps coordinated world and regional organizations—for achieving its prime objective, the prevention of conflicts between nations. This "new high and ethical system of justice," he said, could be approached only with dispassionate understanding and maturity.[26]

The Kansan took this position because, like most American leaders, he had been searching for an acceptable instrument that might prevent future international wars, and because—after the initial shock of the war had worn off—only an international organization could offer a feasible solution. Partly the result of his own thinking, he had also been persuaded to this conclusion by William Allen White, with whom he had discussed the idea since December, 1942, and by those (particularly Hoover and Secretary of State Hull) with whom he had talked on his tour of the east. In any event, Landon, in his Minneapolis speech, had joined Hoover and Willkie in urging the establishment of an international peace organization. It is probable that this widely publicized agreement of the three Republican leaders made easier the adoption of a similar resolution by the party's policy conference in September, and that it aided adoption by the House and Senate of resolutions in favor of American participation in a world peace organization.

Landon returned from his 1943 tours of the east and the upper midwest convinced that his party should soon begin preparing for the 1944 election campaign. Because the national committee was still in a weak financial condition, he had urged the necessity of supporting the organization, and he came back to Topeka hoping—as he wrote chairman Spangler—that "we have pretty well taken care of the ridiculous charge that the Republican party is isolationist. Therefore, we can hammer now on the home-front sins such as bureaucracy, blundering and needless government waste." Displeased that the Republican party was getting only spotty coverage from the newspapers and the radio networks, he urged the national committee headquarters to work for better coverage of Republican activities.[27]

Although he had served as a herald of Republican victory on his trips, Landon had found that Republicans were in a defeatist mood, believing Roosevelt could not be beat while the war was on. It was possible, however, that Republicans could be reinvigorated if they could

[26] Landon speech, Minneapolis, May 13, 1943 (from manuscript and phonograph record).

[27] Landon to Harrison E. Spangler, May 21, 1943; Landon to James P. Selvage, May 26, 1943.

be convinced that "the Democratic party is split in two"—but the Republicans, in turn, would be divided if there were an attempt to picture Wendell Willkie as a turncoat Republican. Although the Kansan thought Willkie, because of his inability to act in the party's best interests, should not be renominated, he decided not to attack him frontally—even taking what he thought was an unfair gibe without retorting. (Willkie, at Oberlin College to receive an honorary Doctor of Laws degree, had told reporters "Ham Fish is against me, Gerald L. K. Smith is against me and I understand Landon is against me. If this keeps up I may be nominated in spite of myself.") Landon kept to his strategy and would not allow himself to be provoked; the target, he said, was "the mess in Washington." The strategy, which the Kansan helped develop, was that favorite son candidates in key states would control their delegations, thereby depriving Willkie of popular support in the primary elections. Landon worked with some of the national committee staff members in devising the plan.[28]

Willkie was the strongest contender for the nomination, but Landon was encouraged by the fact that the Hoosier had broken with a number of his 1940 supporters: such as Harold Stassen, who had been Willkie's floor leader at Philadelphia; Bruce Barton, who had seconded his nomination; and Clarence Buddington Kelland, his chief southwestern supporter. Also, the thinking of most publishers and newsmen—many of whom had been enthusiastic for Willkie in 1940—was that either Dewey or General Douglas MacArthur would be drafted by the 1944 Republican convention. By mid-1943, the Republican picture was confused. Although Landon was convinced that MacArthur would remain on active military duty, Senator Leverett Saltonstall of Massachusetts and Governor Dwight Green of Illinois were showing signs that they might seek the nomination—and Governor Dewey was of course a strong contender. If these rivals contested Willkie's leadership of the party, the Hoosier could be stopped. And the indications were that he would be contested.

Landon, although he believed Willkie was disrupting the Republican party, soon demonstrated his own rebelliousness by publicly backing the claims of the United Mine Workers to higher wages—even suggesting they could not be criticized for threatening to strike during the national crisis. He wrote to John L. Lewis that he was disgusted with Republicans who bayed against Lewis, a man who had shown his

---

[28] Johnson, *Willkie*, p. 237; Clarence Buddington Kelland to Landon, June 11, 1943; Landon to Kelland, June 23, 1943.

"guts and courage" in swinging to the Republican party in 1940. "Besides that, I think first, the miners have some just merit to their claims, and second, the national administration encouraged the operators to refuse to negotiate with you." Landon also displayed his contentiousness by upbraiding the senators who were supporting a resolution to restrict the presidential tenure to two terms. Its adoption, he felt, would only help the incumbent—to whom it would not legally apply—in his campaign for another term.[29]

In July, Landon aimed a haymaker at Vice President Henry Wallace. Wallace, in a speech at Detroit, had labeled President Roosevelt's opponents "the American fascists." Landon rejoined in an angry address, "Who Are the American Fascists?" over the N.B.C. network. "Vice President Wallace declared civil war. He declared that war on ... every American who might ever hope to do his own independent thinking to solve his own problems." Therefore, the soil had been prepared "for a bitter political campaign." Landon declared that "schisms and hatred stalk the land" and that "fascist New Dealers" were responsible for it.

> The bitter controversies so deplorably characteristic of this administration are the results of life-term ambition. It is upon the meat of confusion that it feeds.
> The administration has abandoned the original New Deal. In other words, the postwar plans of the palace-guard bureaucrats are to relieve the businessman of all responsibility. And to relieve organized labor of all responsibility. And to relieve the farmer of all responsibility. And to relieve the elected representatives of the people in the Congress of all responsibility.
> That is the fascist's theory of a planned economy.

This bitter speech received a great deal of commentary. It was front-page news in the Hearst newspapers, which obviously approved it. Others thought that Landon, not Wallace, was "seeing spectres in the woodshed." The *Louisville Courier-Journal* asked, in an editorial, "What's the Matter with Kansas?" Even Landon's friend, G. B. Parker, the editor-in-chief of the Scripps-Howard syndicate, cautioned Landon against overuse of the fascist label. Landon answered, however, that Wallace had used this double-edge term in "a deliberate attempt to muddy the waters"; and he was pleased that the issue—as he saw it, man against the state—had been raised. It might unite Republicans

[29] Landon to Henry Baker Reiley, June 12, 1943; Landon to W. K. Hutchinson, June 24, 1943; Landon to John L. Lewis, May 28, 1943; Landon to Robert A. Taft, June 1, 1943.

and millions of Democrats into a coalition that could subdue statist forces.[30]

Landon's ferocity was loosed again in August. In a radio address James F. Byrnes, the Director of War Mobilization—like so many administration spokesmen before him—urged an adjournment of politics for the duration of the war. Landon responded in a press release: "That is exactly what we ought to do. But it takes two sides to adjourn politics." How could politics be adjourned, he asked, when "a lot of behind-the-scenes theorists in Washington" were using the war "to stand our social and economic system on its head." On August 31, Landon took to the air to reply to a statement by Herbert H. Lehman, the director general of the United Nations Relief and Rehabilitation Administration, that the United States must go on a cereal diet—after Wallace had earlier asserted that the United States should stand everyone in the world to a bottle of milk a day.

> The New Dealers are proposing to take our food—our money, away from our own [people] and hand it over to someone on the other side of the world. And they think we should say "thanky-sir" while they are doing it. . . . The New Dealers changed Thanksgiving, killed the little pigs, and now they want to put us on the rice and fish diet of the Orientals.

This, he said, was all part of the unrealistic idea that Americans could achieve their ideals by thinking of themselves last in a world where all other peoples thought first of themselves. "It is high time you and I speak first for America."[31]

The chief event of the Republican party, as autumn approached, was the Mackinac Island policy conference. Chairman Spangler had decided, in consultation with other party leaders, to form a Republican Post-War Advisory Council. On May 31 he announced the appointment of forty-nine Republicans—all national committee members or high officeholders—to the council, which would meet at Mackinac Island on September 6 and 7. (Neither Alf Landon, Herbert Hoover, nor Wendell Willkie were named to the council or invited to attend the conference. Landon was pleased that the former presidential nominees had not been invited because he thought their presence would result in

[30] Landon speech, N.B.C., July 31, 1943; *San Francisco Examiner*, August 1, 1943; *Louisville Courier-Journal*, August 2, 1943; G. B. Parker to Landon, August 4, 1943; Landon to Parker, August 9, 1943.

[31] Landon press release, August 18, 1943, Landon speech, N.B.C., August 31, 1943.

unnecessary arguments on foreign policy among Republican leaders.) The conference met as planned, and with surprisingly little disagreement adopted a statement pledging Republican support of "responsible participation by the United States in postwar cooperative organization among sovereign nations to prevent military aggression and to attain permanent peace with organized justice in a free world." This confirmed the general position that Landon, Hoover, and Willkie had already taken.

Although Governor Dewey originally had opposed the Mackinac conference, he used the meeting as a showcase for his opinions. He arrived at the island fashionably late, then snatched the headlines by proposing a postwar alliance between the United States and Great Britain, which he hoped China and Russia might also join. The independent tone of Dewey's remarks and his publicity-seeking irritated a number of Republican leaders. Landon, who had been favorably disposed toward Dewey's nomination in 1944, was distressed by news of the New Yorker's performance. He believed that Dewey had "a vein of sarcasm that crops out at the most inopportune moments" and that his statements at Mackinac would hurt him, with the isolationists as well as with those who wanted collective security. Landon also thought that Dewey would have to overcome his New York City provincialism, and hinted that he should be careful about talking too much.[32]

Landon, quite pleased with the Mackinac conference itself, wrote Roy Howard that the policy group had swung around to the position the two of them had been advocating—"a willingness to cooperate with the rest of the world in the way that our humanitarian instincts require and our interests and strength demand by reserving our blank-check commitments until we see what kind of a world we are called upon to guarantee." The Kansan also set out to make his position clear —in opposition to Dewey's—on an alliance between the United States and Great Britain; on October 1, 1943, he voiced his views to a national radio audience. "It is now time for plain talk," he began, and he argued that an alliance with Britain would restrict America's constructive influence in the world. Such an alliance would limit the United States in seeking a permanent settlement of the Jewish problem, in encouraging Indian self-government, and in upholding China's rights because of Britain's interests in Palestine, India, and China.

[32] Johnson, *Willkie*, pp. 243 ff.; Landon to L. E. Phillips, September 17, 1943; Landon to E. G. Bennett, September 22, 1943.

Nor could Americans "talk to Russia about the rights of small nations while we are talking about a partnership with imperialistic Britain," or "insist on 'open convenants openly arrived at' regarding the whole colonial question with Holland, [France,] and Great Britain." Landon demanded that the President make the nation's peace plans clear, fair, and realistic so that the American citizen would not put "his hands in his pockets and walk off from a lot of world chores that could and should be done." [33]

The speech was interesting if for no other reason than that the Kansan had called for settlement of the Jewish question. For some time, Zionists had been seeking his aid in forcing the establishment of a Jewish homeland, but—although in sympathy with the movement—Landon had done no more than offer approval and encouragement. He was convinced that the Moslem world, as well as the British administration in Palestine, would have to work with the Zionists in settling the matter if there was to be harmony and stability in the Near East. Landon was well enough thought of that he was offered the chairmanship of the American Resettlement Committee for Uprooted European Jewry—in August, 1943—but he refused the position because he thought that Jews had to be united on their goals and the other interested groups had to be brought to a point where they would negotiate. [34]

With the news of an impending Anglo-American declaration of an anti-Zionist policy, Zionists became all the more eager to enlist Landon's support—either as national chairman or as honorary president of the resettlement committee. As the administration's policy on the Palestine problem became murkier, Landon demanded—in a speech before the resettlement committee in New York City (in December, 1943)—that the United States "push the permanent settlement of the Jewish problem." He urged the United States to take up "the question of the resettlement of the millions of Jewish sufferers of the European holocaust." In April, 1944, he broke his long-standing rule against joining special-interest committees and accepted membership on the national committee of the American Committee against Nazi Persecution and Extermination of the Jews. [35]

[33] Landon to Roy Howard, September 8, 1943; Clarence Streit to Landon, August 27, 1943; Landon speech, C.B.S., October 1, 1943.

[34] Landon to Pierre Van Paassen, December 29, 1942; Landon to William Hard, July 30, 1943; Isaac Don Levine to Landon, August 2, 1943; Landon to Levine, August 5, 1943.

[35] Isaac Don Levine, George Sokolsky, and Eliahu Ben-Horin to Landon, August 12, 1943; Landon speech, New York, December 10, 1943; Landon to Norman Littell, April 25, 1944.

Landon also continued his battle against an American-British alliance. In a talk at the University of Kansas Debate Institute, October 22, 1943, he hit at this possible alliance and at the secrecy that surrounded its discussion.

> The only foreign policy the administration has approved, and that by indirection, is the old discredited theory of a balance of power alliance. Alliances tend to separate the nations of the world rather than to pull them together. Especially is that true of the proposed exclusive alliance.

Speaking for "world collaboration," Landon submitted that "the proposed British-American alliance is joint isolationism." [36]

His speech caused an immediate division of opinions. H. V. Kaltenborn, the National Broadcasting Company news analyst, agreed that there was a need for American cooperation with all nations and that an Anglo-American alliance might be "joint isolationism." On the other hand, Walter Lippmann made a surprisingly brusque attack on "Governor Landon's boner." Denying that an exclusive British-American alliance had been proposed, Lippmann said that Landon should have read the newspapers before making "his inflammable speech." Landon rejoined in a letter to Lippmann, copies of which were circulated widely among the Kansan's friends:

> Mr. Churchill while a guest in the White House in a carefully prepared speech envisioned a "common citizenship" between Britons and Americans. The whole spirit of his studied statement contemplated the most exclusive kind of an alliance. That has been the common acceptance of his speech as frankly discussed in the newspapers. . . . I am one of those old-fashioned Americans who believes that to be an American citizen is to have the greatest privilege in the world. I believe such a priceless possession is not divisible. "Common citizenship" means common sovereignty. Who is going to be the King's first minister: Roosevelt or Churchill?

Accusing Lippmann of serving as the President's spokesman, Landon asked: "Why don't you speak for yourself, Franklin?" [37]

In the late fall of 1943, Landon's reactions to world happenings involved him in a new controversy. On October 30, in Moscow, the United States, Britain, and the Soviet Union announced that they "recognized the necessity of establishing at the earliest practical date a general international organization based on the principles

[36] Landon speech, Lawrence, Kan., October 22, 1943.

[37] Excerpts from Kaltenborn broadcast of October 22, 1943, enclosed in Frank E. Millin to Landon, November 4, 1943; *Washington Post*, October 26, 1943; Landon to Walter Lippmann, October 30, 1943.

of sovereign equality of all peace-loving states, and open to membership by all such states, large and small, for the maintenance of international peace and security." The three powers had also declared that "after the termination of hostilities they will not employ their military forces within the territories of other states, except for [occupation of present enemy powers] and after joint consultation." The Moscow declaration was greeted in the United States as a victory for peace, and Landon also accepted it as such—until Constantine Oumansky, the former Soviet ambassador to the United States, then stationed in Mexico, stated that Russia planned to retain the Polish territory it had seized in 1939. "It was like a dose of cold water," Landon said. He took Oumansky's statement as a threat of Russia's "likely supremacy on the entire European continent." Landon's concern about the direction of American foreign policy was greatly intensified; he was angry with the United States, not with Russia. "I don't assume that Russia is misleading us," he wrote William Phillip Simms; "I think we are building false illusions and hopes. I think Russia has been perfectly frank and open." [38]

Landon also objected to the suggestion of Secretaries Knox, Stimson, and Hull that the Republican and Democratic parties adopt identical foreign-policy planks in 1944. On December 4, in Washington, the Kansan spoke to the freshmen Republican senators and representatives about the identical platform planks idea and the Moscow agreements. He opposed the foreign-policy proposal because identical planks would deprive the country of the debate that was necessary for bringing the facts and issues of foreign policy into the open. Moreover, Landon asked, "what foreign policy does the President stand for? . . . He doesn't stand still long enough" for Americans to know. In opposition to Willkie, the Kansan then advised against Republican endorsement of the Moscow declaration because there was "no evidence that the Russians have yielded one inch in regard to their well-known territorial aspirations or political ambitions in Europe." Landon also urged stepped-up "antitrust proceedings under existing legislation, higher inheritance tax to redistribute inherited capital and power, regulations administered to protect the little fellow, and the fostering of cooperatives." [39]

[38] Ruhl J. Bartlett, *The Record of American Diplomacy* (New York: Knopf, 1954), p. 658; *New York Times*, November 14, 1943; Landon to Simms, November 19, 23, 1943.

[39] *Kansas City Times*, December 1, 1943; Landon speech, Washington, D.C., December 4, 1943; Johnson, *Willkie*, pp. 256 f. In speaking for the "little fellow,"

Landon did not neglect his political chores during this trip to the east. In Washington, and later in New York, he frequently said that Dewey was the favorite for the Republican nomination, predicting that the New Yorker would be nominated not later than the second ballot—and that, before June, Willkie would be almost entirely out of the running. Asked if he was angry with Willkie, he answered, smiling, "I am not mad at anybody." [40] Nevertheless, Landon's comments on the Moscow declaration and the identical party planks—not his politics—received the greatest amount of attention. Willkie saw Landon's statement as a retreat to isolationism which, if accepted by the party, would make renomination unattractive to the Hoosier. Hoover, feeling he had to explain the Kansan's comments, stated that Landon wanted lasting peace but "has rightly objected to advance pledges of Republicans to commitments on peace settlements until these proposals are made known." The *Philadelphia Evening Bulletin* thought the American people considered the Moscow agreement great statesmanship, and that "sniping at the conference or at any of its participants isn't the way to bring about party harmony. Nor to win next year's election." The *Wilkes-Barre Record*, however, agreed with Landon, saying "many will want to know in black and white what is proposed. . . . Our foreign relations are too vital for identical planks in the party platforms unless advance interpretations of them are identical." The *Pittsburgh Post-Gazette* called upon Landon "to clarify his own nebulous and negative views on foreign affairs." [41]

Landon himself thought his comments needed clarification. On December 13, in a nationally broadcast speech, he declared: "The Moscow agreement, so far as we can ascertain, is an expression of the principles of peace, and world cooperation based on justice and decency. The American people are for those principles." But they would ask: "Just what, in practice, does this mean? . . . They have a right to be answered—answered honestly and in detail." On the question of identical foreign-policy planks, Landon said he had told

---

Landon revealed his belief that big business, in order to make money, was allowing the government's price policies to squeeze small businessmen out of competition. In this, the Kansan saw a parallel with the relationships between Hitler and big business in Germany in the early 1930s. Landon to Richard Lloyd Jones, November 15, 1943; Landon to Theodore Alvord, November 16, 1943.

[40] *Des Moines Register*, December 5, 1943; Johnson, *Willkie*, pp. 256 f.; *New York World-Telegram*, December 7, 1943.

[41] Johnson, *Willkie*, p. 257; *Philadelphia Evening Bulletin*, December 10, 1943; *Wilkes-Barre Record*, December 11, 1943; *Pittsburgh Post-Gazette*, December 11, 1943.

Secretary of State Hull that three practical problems had to be resolved. First, the Republicans would have to have a complete and detailed report—"the kind that the Secretary of State is expected to make to the President following any important foreign conversation and negotiation." Second, the two parties would have to agree upon the exact wording and meaning of the text. Third, "there would have to be a firm commitment . . . that the Democratic party in its convention would adopt the exact same plank." Although Landon knew that such conditions would be difficult to achieve, anything less "would not be fair to the American public. If the President in any administration is told he has blank-check powers, that he can just go ahead and shoot the works without having to face open public discussion, what becomes of democracy?" Landon again faced a barrage of hostile criticism; gossip columnist Elsa Maxwell, for example, called the speech the "reactionary regurgitation" of the "braying old burro, . . . a deliberate attempt to destroy the very foundations of permanent peace."[42]

Landon knew he was sticking his neck out, that "brickbats and dead cats and rotten eggs" would be thrown at him "by the lunatic fringe of our so-called internationalists."

> The Moscow conference came as a great relief to the American people and they wanted to believe everything good that was said about it. The emphasis and slant that was given to my speech, which went even further than I did, was a shock to them, but I don't believe events have ever so rapidly justified a man's position as they have mine.

He saw the effects of Russian aggrandizement—in December and January—in Roosevelt's and Churchill's recognition of the Communist Tito as leader of the Yugoslav resistance, in the Soviet-Czechoslovak pact of cooperation, in Russia's proposal to swap German territory for Polish, and in the warning of the South African elder statesman, Jan Smuts, that a barrier must be erected in Europe against Russia. Landon's prognosis was further confirmed by statements of Oumansky and the Russian newspaper, *Izvestia*, that contradicted Secretary Hull's interpretation of the Moscow agreement. Landon, however, was not gratified that his views had been vindicated; it meant that the concept of collective security had been discarded.

[42] Landon speech, N.B.C., December 13, 1943; *New York Post*, December 16, 1943.

"We are facing a Communist Europe [but] I hope from the bottom of my heart that I am wrong." [43]

In the meantime, events had developed that were to make Landon a leader in the movement to frustrate Wendell Willkie's drive for the presidential nomination in 1944. In October, 1943, Landon heard that Willkie, in an off-the-record speech to the freshman Republican representatives, had threatened to bolt the Republican party if it did not endorse his positions at the national convention. Landon's informant, Kansas Congressman Frank Carlson, added that minority leader Martin had suggested that Landon journey east and work to coordinate the groups that opposed Willkie. Landon replied directly to Martin, saying that he was willing to undertake the job "providing I will have your help." He would do some of the work during his December visits to Washington and New York. [44]

Willkie, however, had already played into his opponents' hands. On October 15 he had gone to St. Louis, to attend a partisan rally, and at a luncheon presided over by industrialist Edgar Monsanto Queeny had been introduced as "America's leading ingrate." Queeny said: "In 1940, I raised $200,000 in his behalf and never got a thank you"; and Willkie answered: "I don't know whether you're going to support me or not and I don't give a damn. You're a bunch of political liabilities anyway." Landon thought this statement, as well as other comments Willkie had made in St. Louis, advanced the view that "the minority, not the party in power, is to blame for everything that has gone wrong in the country." [45]

The anti-Willkie movement was encouraged by the results of the elections of November, 1943. The Republican candidate was elected lieutenant governor of New York in a special election; Republican governors were elected in Kentucky and New Jersey; and many local elections were won by Republicans in Pennsylvania, Connecticut, and California. Landon was jubilant:

[43] Landon to Clifford Stratton, December 22, 1943; Landon to Hulbert Taft, January 11, 1944; Landon to Richard Robbins, December 31, 1943; Landon to Theodore Alvord, December 23, 1943.

[44] Frank Carlson to Landon, October 21, 1943; Landon to Joseph W. Martin, October 26, 1943.

[45] Johnson, *Willkie*, pp. 250 f.; Landon to George Rothwell Brown, October 22, 1943.

The election results Tuesday showed the trend started in 1938—interrupted by the German blitz in 1940, resumed in 1942—is still on the upswing. By all past experience, it spelled defeat for Roosevelt in 1944. It has fired the Republicans with confidence. It encourages the real Democrats to cut his throat. . . . It will encourage the independence of Congress.

Equally important, Willkie had not been encouraged: the Republican victory in New York put Dewey "in the forefront."[46]

Landon's anti-Willkie strategy was simple. He would encourage a "fist full" of candidates for the nomination, detaching support from Willkie, and he would plug Governor Dewey as the leading candidate. Landon had help in this from his former secretary, Willard Mayberry, who was then on a speaking tour of the east and the south. Mayberry outlined the plan to scuttle Willkie when he wrote Landon that "your 'native-son finesse' at this point is the maneuver for they then become traders, something Willkie doesn't even understand." For example, Saltonstall of Massachusetts, tempted by his own ambitions, was already withdrawing from the Willkie camp, and Mayberry thought that southern Republicans could be bargained with to help Dewey. Yet, some observers even thought of renominating Landon. George Rothwell Brown, in his column in the Hearst newspapers, said Landon's "speeches and public addresses during the past year or two have been among the ablest that have been heard in the opposition." And Senator Capper wrote Landon: "Speaking for myself, I would like to see you run for President again. I think you are just the type of man we need in the White House in this emergency."[47] But Landon had neither ambitions nor illusions; he had had his chance and he knew that he would not get another. His goals were to keep Roosevelt from winning a fourth term and to deny Willkie renomination.

Still seeking to win Democratic support for the Republican party, Landon, in identical Lincoln Day addresses in Knoxville and Nashville, Tennessee, declared that he was speaking not as a partisan but as an American. Then, in a rip-snorting speech, he asserted that the New Dealers were trying "to undermine the Democratic party" by working with independents and political bosses, which he saw as an integral part of the National Socialist tendencies of the administration.

But, you say, the New Deal does not display the same brutality and inhumanity as the Nazis. That's correct. It does not. But it is playing with the

[46] Johnson, *Willkie*, p. 253; Landon to Merryle S. Rukeyser, November 8, 1943.

[47] Landon to Richard Robbins, November 23, 1943; Willard Mayberry to Landon, November 19, 21, 1943; *Chicago Herald-American*, December 2, 1943; Arthur Capper to Landon, December 7, 1943.

same fires of intolerance and hate. Furthermore . . . we have learned by bitter experience that centralization of political power creates of itself more centralization. We know intolerance breeds more intolerance; arbitrary bureaucracy always breeds more master bureaucrats. After you have taken away a man's rights, his hope of a decent livelihood of his own choosing, his right to manage his business or his farm, or work as he pleases, what difference does it then make if you forego lashing his body, and, instead, put him to work on the paltry pay of the WPA so he can barely manage to keep himself and his family in food and is forced to go to the relief office for his clothing and his medicine? Let us not wait until the fateful handwriting appears on our walls. Let us read what has been written on the walls of other nations which drank in the opiate of indispensability and trusted one man too long—and too far!

The Kansan was not precise about the Republican alternative or the things his party stood for: "Intelligent use of income, inheritance taxes and price reductions to effect . . . distribution . . . in the public interest, . . . [taxation] planned from the point of view of encouraging individual enterprise and activity as well as sharing the wealth." To favor Democrats—and Tennesseans particularly—he added that Secretary of State Cordell Hull should be "the second man at the peace table under a Republican President."[48]

Landon was pleased with the reception of his Tennessee speeches. The *Knoxville Journal* had commented that there would be an open partnership of Republicans and Democrats in some areas against "the life term." Moreover, the Nashville meeting was said to have been "the largest and most enthusiastic Republican gathering in the history of Tennessee," and at least a fifth of his Knoxville and Nashville audiences were thought to have been Democrats.[49]

In February, 1944, Landon began preparing in earnest for the Republican platform and campaign, helped chiefly by economist Ralph Robey, who was then on the staff of *Newsweek*. Landon's Tennessee talks had already indicated some of the things he wanted incorporated in the 1944 Republican platform, and with Robey's encouragement he continued to test new ideas in his pre-convention talks in order to give the resolutions committee "something to chew on long before the National Convention." In speeches and correspondence Landon emphasized the need for a balance between imports and

[48] Landon speeches: Knoxville, February 11, 1944, and Nashville, February 12, 1944; *Knoxville Journal*, February 11, 1944.

[49] *Knoxville Journal*, February 12, 1944; Landon to James L. Wright, February 15, 1944.

exports, pointing out that if a nation's trade balance remained either favorable or unfavorable over a long period of time, that country would be in economic distress. The solution lay in competitiveness in international commerce, which could be achieved by lowering tariffs and by persuading nations to abandon trade quotas, artificial controls on currency and exchange, and preferential treatment within empires. Stabilization of foreign currencies was an important part of this program because it would stop other countries from devaluing their currencies and competing for business "on a bargain basis." The United States could help stabilize foreign currencies by giving its gold. Landon also urged that Americans increase their purchases of foreign goods, because nations become politically intertwined "with those countries upon which they are economically dependent. If we are not willing to purchase the products of other nations after this war, Russia will and can." [50]

The Kansan's trade policy depended, of course, on the maintenance of peace, and he doubted that enduring peace could be accomplished through "the closely guarded secret conferences of three men." A world council was needed that could meet "the fundamental need for building step by step the vital cooperative attitude among the United Nations." Peace would also have to be based on a realistic view of things as they were—not on idealism, or myths, or trick statements such as the Atlantic Charter. World organization must recognize all national interests. "We might," he said, "divide the world between Russia, Britain and America and have peace for a while—but only for a while." It was inherent in Landon's thinking on world trade and peace, as the *New York Herald Tribune* pointed out, "that peace is not simply the absence of war. It is a condition that is so attractive to the nations that they will not risk breaking away from it." [51]

Also concerned with the domestic economy, Landon believed the United States had to plan for a return to peace. The nation needed "a blueprint for free industry and not a socialistic state so that businessmen are assured of a fair profit, labor will be assured full employment, good pay and higher standards of living and farmers are assured of a

[50] Landon to Ralph Robey, February 16, 1944; Robey to Landon, February 29, 1944; Landon speeches: Kirksville, Mo., February 17, 1944, Topeka, March 31, 1944, and Chicago, May 16, 1944.

[51] Landon to Richard E. Berlin, May 1, 1944; Landon speeches: Chicago, May 16, 1944, and Topeka, April 16, 1944; *New York Herald Tribune*, April 18, 1944.

better price for their crops." Simplification of economic regulations and of the tax structure was needed so that idle capital would be encouraged to open new industries and businesses and create new jobs. In order to stimulate business and stave off monopoly, however, these changes would have to favor the man starting out instead of the man whose fortune was already made and the producer instead of the wealthy investor.[52]

Landon was active in other platform areas. Working with Negro businessman Lloyd Kerfoot (of Atchison) and his associates, Landon assumed a prime role in fighting for liberal civil rights planks that would put the Democrats "in the hole." These planks, incorporated by the 1944 national convention almost without change, demanded immediate congressional action for ending racial segregation and discrimination in the armed forces, a permanent fair-employment practices commission, a Constitutional amendment to abolish poll taxes, and federal legislation against lynching. This was the first time in the twentieth century that a major political party had dealt in such detail with civil rights. (With less success, Landon worked with John L. Lewis' representatives in behalf of a plank favorable to organized labor.)[53]

The Kansan meanwhile was pleased by Wendell Willkie's withdrawal as a candidate for the nomination—after running fourth in the April 4 Wisconsin primary—and Landon thought the Hoosier's withdrawal would help the Republican party maintain a reasonable degree of unity on candidates and policies. Landon was therefore inclined to believe that things were developing well for the party and for Dewey, who he was convinced would be nominated. Furthermore, the Republicans should have a good platform, the issue of the President's declining health would work against the Democrats, and the voters would be at least suspicious of the administration's world-first America-last orientation. Landon took Willkie's Wisconsin defeat as the warrant for much of this thinking. He also felt the President would

---

[52] Landon speech, Topeka, March 31, 1944; Landon to Ralph Robey, March 9, 1944.

[53] Landon to Carroll Reece, July 6, 1944; Memorandum initialed by Landon, July 7, 1944; *Kansas City Call*, April 16, 1948; Landon to B. K. Litowich, July 6, 1944; Landon to John L. Lewis, July 14, 1944; *Official Report of the Proceedings of the Twenty-third Republican National Convention* (Washington: Judd & Detweiler, 1944), p. 146.

be hurt by the government's seizure of the Montgomery Ward company and by its inability to prevent unrest among coal miners and railway workers.[54]

There were, however, some drawbacks. The Kansan had concluded that Spangler had been an unfortunate choice as the national chairman because he lacked the necessary drive. And by late May, Landon and Hoover agreed that Republican enthusiasm was low. The former President contended that this was the result of attacks on Dewey by the political action committee of the C.I.O., New Dealers, and Communists, and he complained that he and Landon were widely pictured as political lepers. Landon thought the loss of enthusiasm had been caused by the primary-election victories of liberal Democratic Senators Claude Pepper of Florida and Lister Hill of Alabama, and by special-election victories of Democrats elsewhere.[55]

As the convention date drew closer, Landon's prominence in it was ensured by his election as chairman of the Kansas delegation and as chairman of the foreign-trade subcommittee of the resolutions committee. But when Landon reached Chicago, he was not in a happy mood. He expected to be set upon by high-tariff men, he was alarmed by recent indications that Britain and the dominions would maintain imperial-trade preference—and he was suffering, as he would throughout the convention, from an ulcerated tooth.[56] Despite everything, he became one of the hardest-working delegates in Chicago. He argued day and night and worked on hundreds of pages of plank drafts, fighting for a liberal foreign-trade policy.

The struggle went on for five days, with Landon and former Senator Joseph R. Grundy of Pennsylvania, the high priest of the high tariff, the chief antagonists. Landon had secured the assistance of the chairman of the resolutions committee, Robert A. Taft, by telling him: "Bob, you know my position on the tariff. If the committee will not accept a plank which is acceptable to me, I give you warning that I'll make a minority report and fight for it." In the committee meetings Grundy charged Landon with "undoing everything that has made America

[54] Landon to Thomas E. Dewey, April 21, 1944; Landon to A. H. Kirchhofer, April 26, 1944; Landon to James L. Wright, May 2, 1944; Landon to Roy Howard, May 3, 1944.

[55] Landon to A. H. Kirchhofer, April 24, 1944; Herbert Hoover to Landon, May 27, 1944; Landon to Hoover, May 29, 1944.

[56] Landon to B. I. Litowich, July 6, 1944; Landon to Robert A. Taft, August 7, 1944; *Chicago Tribune*, June 26, 1944.

great and powerful and prosperous. You are undermining all the factors and forces which gave us the prosperity of the 1920–30 era." Landon rejoined: "And what, Mr. Grundy, came after all those prosperous years of 1920 to 1930?" Grundy faltered, searching for an answer, and finally grumbled: "The American people simply went nuts in that period. The depression was their own fault, you can't blame it on us." This was greeted by a roar of laughter.[57]

The Grundy forces, knowing they were losing ground, tried to specify that existing tariffs could be altered only by treaties, but Landon was able to broaden this so that the party could go on record favoring tariff changes through reciprocal agreements. The Kansan at first had to battle for tariff flexibility by himself, with only incidental support from Senator Taft. Finally the Dewey men, who agreed with Landon's position but who had maintained neutrality on platform issues, swung forcefully in support of Landon. (Landon thought his threat of making a minority report if he lost in committee brought them around in order to maintain the appearance of party unity.) The result, nevertheless, was a compromise. The plank, as it was incorporated in the platform, proposed that the United States "establish and maintain a fair protective tariff on competitive products so that the standards of living of our people shall not be impaired through the importation of commodities produced abroad by labor or producers functioning upon lower standards than our own." But it also declared the necessity of a great expansion of trade for postwar world reconstruction and for lasting peace. The party pledged to "join with others in leadership in every cooperative effort to remove unnecessary and destructive barriers to international trade" and to support modification of American tariffs by reciprocal bilateral agreements approved by Congress. The *Des Moines Register* gave "three cheers and a tiger for Alf's influence at Chicago in at least getting the door left open for a party policy on international trade that doesn't date back to the 1880s."[58]

Landon had fought a good fight. He had not played statesman, like Hoover, who except for a speech stayed in his hotel room (Willkie stayed in New York). As one newspaperman put it:

[57] Letter from Ralph Robey in *New York Times*, October 21, 1944; *Oskaloosa* (Kan.) *Independent*, July 6, 1944.

[58] Landon to Henry J. Haskell, July 3, 1944; *Chicago Tribune*, June 28, 1944; *Des Moines Register*, July 13, 1944; *Twenty-third Republican National Convention Proceedings*, p. 144.

The 1936 candidate was down on the floor with the foot soldiers, a Kansas placard over his shoulder, marching and stomping and yelling, his shirt wringing wet, his face grimy and slick, his eyes tired and droopy from loss of sleep in the committee room. But, by George, there he was in the infantry, working for the ticket.

The Kansan was pleased with the convention results. Dewey had been nominated on the first ballot, and Landon thought the nomination of Ohio Governor John Bricker for Vice President would strengthen the ticket's appeal, especially in the middle west. Landon also believed he had committed the party to a flexible foreign-trade policy, and he was particularly happy that Dewey had liberally interpreted the foreign-trade plank as a "promise to work with other nations for greater trade." Landon was also delighted with the adoption of the civil rights planks and the recognition by the new national committee chairman, Herbert Brownell, Jr., that the national headquarters would have to give more attention to the problems of Negroes.[59]

The Republican ticket had been chosen and the platform adopted. Although Landon's assistance—somewhat to his irritation—was not solicited by Dewey's headquarters, the Kansan did his best to contribute to the campaign. As early as August he made a speech urging Dewey's election, and again he fidgeted about the conduct of the campaign. He wrote Lacy Haynes that too little publicity was being issued by the Republican headquarters, and that Dewey should let John L. Lewis know if he wanted his help. Landon repeatedly urged the New Yorker to espouse a realistic—that is, a Landon—foreign policy, and to speak out boldly on racial problems. He wrote national chairman Brownell that Dewey must make more public appearances:

> [Dewey] has a warm and charming personality that is being buried under propaganda of cold efficiency. . . . As Willkie needed to spend more time with the party leaders, I think Governor Dewey should spend more time with the general public.[60]

Landon was not pessimistic about the outcome; as he wrote Felix Morley, on September 19, it was a unity not a class campaign. By

[59] *Kansas City Star*, July 2, June 30, 1944; Landon to Kelly Kash, August 3, 1944; Landon to Robert Patchin, August 25, 1944; Landon to Herbert Brownell, Jr., July 7, 1944.

[60] Landon speech, Topeka, August 8, 1944; Landon to Lacy Haynes, August 25, 1944; Landon to Thomas E. Dewey, July 14, August 22, 28, September 29, 1944; Landon to Herbert Brownell, Jr., September 19, 1944.

early October he was highly optimistic about Dewey's chances, and his optimism continued until election evening. He made several speeches during October and early November. In Chicago, on October 6, he told the Executives Club: "Our incomparable war production was made possible only by that willing cooperation of the traditional American economic system, which the Roosevelt administration for the first nine years had done its utmost to injure." This cooperation, with a change in government, could be built upon in peacetime to "provide the jobs the New Deal couldn't." Speaking like a Manchester liberal, he also lashed out at international cartels, monopolies, high tariffs, subsidies, unnecessary public works, managed currencies, and trade quotas. In Sabetha, Kansas, on October 24, he condemned the Allies' demand for unconditional surrender and the Morgenthau plan, which would strip Germany of its industrial power. Both policies, because they had fortified the Germans "with the desperate courage of despair, [would cost] the lives of untold numbers of American soldiers."

A week later, in Harrisburg, Illinois, Landon again lashed out at the Morgenthau plan. "Morgenthau's inhuman threats—from the White House steps—discredited all the reasonable statements we have been distributing in leaflets over Germany." He urged that Morgenthau be removed as Secretary of the Treasury to show America's repudiation of the plan.[61] In November, in Manhattan, Kansas, and Oakland, Nebraska, Landon called Roosevelt "the great promiser" and the "artful dodger." The President, he declared sarcastically, had recently promised shorter hours, higher wages, 60 million postwar jobs, continued high prices and more prosperity for the farmers, and a tax reduction program, thereby proving himself "a friend of everyone." The Kansan then charged Roosevelt with twenty-four major contradictions in promises and performance while in office. His 1940 "promise of a new President" by 1945, Landon proclaimed, "is one promise the people are keeping for him by electing Governor Dewey."[62]

Victory again eluded the Republican party as the American people went to the polls on Tuesday, November 7. Dewey and Bricker

---

[61] Landon to Felix Morley, September 19, 1944; Landon to Edward F. Colladay, October 6, 1944; Landon to Herbert Hoover, October 18, 1944; Landon to W. K. Hutchinson, November 3, 1944; Landon speeches: Chicago, October 6, 1944, and Sabetha, Kan., October 24, 1944; *Chicago Tribune*, November 1, 1944.

[62] Landon speeches: Manhattan, Kan., November 3, 1944, and Oakland, Neb., November 4, 1944.

lost to Roosevelt and Truman by 3.5 million votes, out of 48 million cast. The Republicans lost eighteen seats in the House of Representatives, though gaining a seat in the Senate. Roosevelt was elected to a fourth term—as it turned out, a life term. Landon, in his musings on the election, thought a coalition ticket might have made the difference. He also felt that Dewey had not clarified the differences of principle between the New Deal and the Republican party, and had not used the Morgenthau issue early enough. Nor had Dewey overcome the handicap of appearing to be a cold, efficient machine. Whatever the reason, though, Roosevelt was still the President.[63]

[63] Landon to Sterling Morton, December 6, 1944; Landon to A. H. Kirchhofer, December 18, 1944.

CHAPTER 21

The Postwar World

As victory over the Axis became a certainty, Landon turned his attention completely to the problems that peace would bring. America's increasing belief, as he saw it, that the ends justify the means—and the fuzziness about the ends—did not bode well for the future. For one thing, the Kansan worried about influence-peddling in Washington, through which fortunes had been made during the war: with the result that the "money-changers haven't been driven from the temple—a new crowd has simply been brought in." He thought that favoritism and corruption would become even worse after the war, and that the only way to stop it was to diffuse "responsibility among labor, capital, and government. Concentration of power as with concentration of wealth must be prevented."[1]

Landon was also concerned with the disorder and suffering that afflicted Europe, and with Russia's efforts to set up puppet states in eastern Europe. Because the United States was giving "the hush-hush, everything is hunky-dory treatment" to world affairs, he feared the nation would be unprepared for its postwar problems. He could hope that America would act to become the world's economic mooring post, and the nations meeting in San Francisco to establish a new world

[1] Landon to Raymond Moley, December 8, 1944, and Landon to Thomas E. Dewey, February 6, 1945, Alfred M. Landon Papers, Kansas State Historical Society, Topeka.

513

organization might succeed in providing political stability. These were weak hopes for Landon, however, because of his pessimism that a nation led by Roosevelt and a peace organization based only on the good intentions of a few nations could oppose Russian expansion or effect reconstruction.[2]

Then, on April 12, 1945, the situation changed drastically with Roosevelt's death. A new President took office; and a new executive meant fresh viewpoints and different lines of attack. Harry S. Truman's succession to the White House was almost agreeable. Although Landon had personally liked Roosevelt and regretted his death, he had trusted neither his judgment nor his integrity. Truman, the man from Independence, Missouri, was a President the man from Independence, Kansas, could like and trust—even though they often disagreed. Both men spoke the same political language.

The Kansan continued to speak out publicly during the spring and summer of 1945, but not in a partisan vein: world events were moving at a frightening pace; the President would require several months for adjusting to his burdens; and Landon had pledged cooperation. As for the United Nations meeting in San Francisco on April 22, Landon said: "We can hardly overstate, overemphasize, or exaggerate what the outcome of that conference means to the future of the world." He hoped the United States could move from a three-man win-the-war autocracy to a cooperative effort by the nations of the world to fashion an effective world organization. And he hoped the Lord would give President Truman "strength and courage and fidelity to bear what he must bear."[3]

While the United Nations conference was in session, Landon again addressed himself to its problems, in a speech at Manhattan, Kansas, in June. The chief problem facing the meeting, he said, was the world confusion that had been caused by the destructiveness of war and the lack of planning for reconstruction. "Russia seems to be setting up by ruthless force puppet states in this vacuum that was once Europe. . . . And we are still listening to the birdies sing as we have done from Moscow to San Francisco—under the assumption that there is accord on postwar policies among the Allies." The United States could not ignore the situation any longer; its statesmen must "build a bridge of cooperation for peace between a ruthless totalitarian dictatorship and

[2] Landon speech, Cleveland, January 18, 1945; Landon to David Lawrence, March 27, 1945; Landon to Roy Howard, April 11, 1945.
[3] Landon speech, Topeka, April 22, 1945.

other nations whom the Russians consider equally ruthless." Although America had been working for world harmony against Russian opposition, Landon warned against those "who are not making it easier by their loose talk that we must eventually fight Russia." He also warned against those who insisted that all of Russia's policies were justified and that criticisms of them were Fascist-inspired lies. "If we in the United States make plain that we are not and will not be a party by action or inaction to any scheme or intrigue to gang up on Russia, or Great Britain, or China, or any other nation, then we have laid the cornerstone for lasting peace." This, he believed, was President Truman's policy, and it deserved the people's support.[4]

The Manhattan speech won widespread praise for Landon—for the first time in years. The *New York Herald Tribune* headlined his support of President Truman; and Ralph McGill, in the *Atlanta Constitution*, said "Alf Landon talks good sense."[5] The Soviet Union's policies had jarred the war-generated idealism of the American people, and Landon now could call for a realistic foreign policy and be hailed as a far-sighted statesman. Moreover, his words were all the more acceptable because they were couched in gentleness toward President Truman, and Landon was sincere. Working with Truman, he believed, "Congress will once more occupy its Constitutional and traditional position in shaping policies that express the needs and aspirations of the American people. That's all to the good. Truman is nobody's fool and he has a good political eye." Landon, however, also felt the new President posed no threat to Republican victory in 1948, because he would be unable to hold the Roosevelt coalition together. Specifically, the Kansan thought the Democratic party would be split by the rise of a New Dealish "third party headed by Wallace," whose aim would be to teach the Democrats that they could not win without it. But Landon was genuinely pleased with Truman's moderate tack during his first months in office; he wrote Roy Howard: "It's a great thing once more to be 'Dimmecrats' and Republicans instead of New Dealers and reactionaries."[6]

Landon's goodwill gestures toward Truman were reciprocated. On May 24 Truman asked Landon to call at the White House when he came to Washington because "there are certain problems facing the

[4] Landon speech, Manhattan, Kan., June 7, 1945.

[5] *New York Herald Tribune*, June 8, 1945; *Atlanta Constitution*, June 10, 1945.

[6] Landon to Raymond Moley, April 26, 1945; Landon to Roy Howard, June 13, 1945.

country which I should be pleased to discuss with you." The Kansan answered that he would be happy to meet with the President, and Truman suggested that they meet in Kansas City within the month. Truman's gesture went beyond Landon, for he also asked Herbert Hoover and Thomas E. Dewey to meet with him;[7] nevertheless, Truman and Landon met at the Hotel Muehlebach in Kansas City for forty-five minutes on June 30. Among other things, Landon urged a method for facilitating freight car delivery of farm produce to the market, which was especially necessary at the time when starvation was common in many parts of the world. Taking up a suggestion by Norman Thomas, he also asked Truman's serious consideration of Japanese surrender offers in order to avoid further slaughter and to work out terms for a lasting peace in Asia on democratic and anti-communist bases. After the meeting, Landon told the press that Truman had offered the country a basis for closing ranks on foreign policy. When asked what the country thought of Truman, Landon replied, "Judgment suspended," though he observed that the nation was relaxed under Truman.[8] This was the beginning of a pleasant acquaintanceship between the two men that would endure over the years.

Although Landon hoped for Truman's success in dealing with national security and equitable world reconstruction, success was elusive; and on October 25 the Kansan publicly expressed his apprehensions about foreign policy before the Kiwanis Club of Lawrence, Kansas. He asserted that America's "foreign policies involve not only our future peace and prosperity but such everyday affairs as—how long your boy is going to stay in the Army or Navy—whether your boy is to be conscripted under a permanent peacetime compulsory military draft—how much of your earnings we are going to give to Great Britain—and other foreign countries—as subsidies—and the atomic bomb in the hands of other countries." He was not opposed to giving other countries economic assistance, but he was convinced that the world would not recover as long as Germany, the economic heart of Europe, remained unproductive. He saw other obstacles to world reconstruction in "the mass shifting of peoples around like cattle" and the use of United States forces to restore British, French, and Dutch colonialism.

[7] Harry S. Truman to Landon, May 24, June 2, 1945; Landon to Truman, May 28, 1945; *Topeka State Journal*, May 28, 1945.

[8] Norman Thomas to Landon, March 19, May 24, 1945; Landon to Thomas, May 3, July 20, 1945; *Kansas City Times*, June 30, 1945; *Baltimore Sun*, June 30, 1945.

All this was complicated by the inability of the United Nations and of the foreign ministers of the major powers, mainly because of Russia, to reach agreement on world problems. Drastic measures by the United States were therefore necessary, instead of merely sitting on the lid of the world's explosive forces. Landon made six recommendations.

1. The United States should become "a sound financial mooring post for the rest of the world to tie to" by reversing its fiscal policies of unlimited borrowing and spending.
2. The policy of keeping Germany to a pastoral economy should be scrapped.
3. Extraterritorial privileges should be surrendered and all colonies should be prepared for self-government.
4. The United States should demand honest and intelligent "application of the principles of the Atlantic Charter."
5. The internationalization of the atomic bomb should be considered by a joint committee made up of the legislative bodies of America, Britain, and Canada, the nations that developed the weapon.
6. The internationalization of strategic locations should also be considered.

This six-point program, along with on-going efforts to seek peace and to give friendship, should show the sincerity of the peace-loving nations. It should be, Landon declared, the test of whether Russia was merely suspicious of other nations or whether she was bent on aggression; and if "Russia refuses the proffered hand of the peace-seeking nations, we must not shrink from the tragic fact that a new aggressor is on the prowl." [9]

The Lawrence speech also was widely praised. The *Cincinnati Times-Star* suggested that the United Nations "would do well to listen to this man from the plains of Kansas"; and Clarence Streit's *Freedom Union World* lauded Landon's idea of a joint legislative committee of the United States, Canada, and England to consider world control of the atomic bomb. Streit, in fact, publicized the idea as widely as he could, contacting—among others—White House press secretary Charles Ross and Senate leaders. Landon cautioned Streit, however, that he could not expect a Democratic administration to be enthused about "the Landon joint atomic committee"; he advised keeping the concept in the foreground and the Republican in the background.[10]

Landon's anxiety over world developments increased toward the end

[9] Landon speech, Lawrence, Kan., October 25, 1945.

[10] *Cincinnati Times-Star*, October 26, 1945; *Federal Union World*, November, 1945; Clarence Streit to Charles Ross, October 30, 1945; Streit to Landon, October 31, 1945; Landon to Streit, November 6, 1945.

of 1945. In November he wrote that the United States was moving toward an Anglo-American coalition that would eventually put the nation squarely in opposition to Russia. Instead of being an "honest broker" for peace, the country was being "pushed into bloc leadership," and America had to make an all-out effort to make the United Nations succeed before its work could be obstructed by power politics. He was consoled by the thought that Truman also felt this way; but the situation got no better. Truman, despite his fine intentions, Landon believed, had "worked himself into a bad hole and the . . . country along with him." By the beginning of 1946 an Anglo-American bloc seemed to be developing rapidly. The Kansan saw this in America's participation in the Palestine Commission, in Lord Halifax's statement that the European policy in Java was Anglo-American, and in America's proposed loan to Great Britain. An Anglo-American coalition, though better than yielding to Moscow on all important issues, was still an unsatisfactory answer to the world's problems.[11]

After the 1944 election Landon had diversified his activities. Although he continued to assist Red Cross work and war bond drives in Kansas, he became associated with a variety of national committees and movements. The latter included membership on the board of trustees of the Committee on Inter-American Cooperation, the use of his name for the support of liberalized immigration procedures for Indian nationals, and membership on a committee to commemorate the nazi destruction of Lidice, Czechoslovakia. He also signed an appeal to save the life of the non-Communist Yugoslav leader, General Mihailovich, and a memorial that called for Polish freedom from Soviet domination; and he endorsed Senator Elbert D. Thomas' proposal to turn war forces into peace forces, and Ewing Cockrell's program for world disarmament and the abolition of war.[12] Landon was active in religious work as well. In 1946 he spoke on "The Bible Comes to Life," over the Columbia Broadcasting System, in a program sponsored by the American Bible Society; he also served on the National Christian Committee in support of the American Jewish Appeal; but his main religious efforts were on

[11] Landon to Felix Morley, November 15, 1945, January 4, 1946; Landon to Fred Mahan, December 10, 1945.

[12] Landon to Joseph C. Ravensky, November 13, 1944, November 8, 1945; Landon to J. J. Singh, February 20, 1945; Landon to Christopher Emmet, July 10, 1945, May 3, 1946; Landon to Elbert D. Thomas, July 10, 1946; Landon to Ewing Cockrell, July 10, 1946.

behalf of the National Conference of Christians and Jews. During and after the war he served on the N.C.C.J. national board of directors, and late in 1946 he became a member of the executive committee. His affiliation with the conference was not nominal; Landon actively participated in organizing Brotherhood Week activities, serving as Kansas state chairman in 1946–47 and as southwestern United States regional chairman in 1948. He was also, in 1947, the chief speaker at the Wichita Brotherhood Week dinner, where he declared that "on the battlefield all men are brothers and comrades. What a travesty on Christian civilization if this conception of a beautiful world is the attribute of war, but not of peace." [13]

Landon's economic worth had risen during the war because of the increased demand for crude oil and natural gas; consequently, he was able to regain a solid financial footing and considerable venture capital. Convinced, however, that the future of independent oil enterprisers would be difficult, he set out to diversify his interests. An economical and astute operator, he derived a sizable return from his oil and gas leases, but he wanted to find more stable sources of income. One of his searches, in the 1930s, had led him to invest in farm and ranch lands, but without notable success. In 1944 he leased a large area of land for development as a rock quarry, but after losing $10,000 he withdrew from the business.[14]

Finally, in 1947, Landon found his new economic mainstay, radio, and he used his wartime profits from oil and gas to acquire broadcasting properties. He had originally considered setting up stations (with local partners) in El Dorado, Abilene, Liberal and Leavenworth, Kansas, and in Denver and Englewood, Colorado, but problems of financial feasibility and an FCC permit led him to drop his plans for Abilene, El Dorado, and Englewood. He at last received permission to go on the air in Liberal and Leavenworth, and in Denver, Colorado:[15] KCLO in Leavenworth, KSCB in Liberal, and KTLN in Denver opened during 1948. Landon also filed an application for what would have been Denver's first television station, believing "the day is not far

[13] Landon to Francis C. Stifler, December 3, 1946; Landon to Everett Clinchy, March 28, October 28, 1946; Clinchy to Landon, March 25, 1946; *Wichita Beacon*, February 21, 1947.

[14] Landon interview, October 6, 1959.

[15] Charles M. Harger to Landon, January 20, 1947; Landon to Rolla Clymer, February 3, 1947; Charles R. Depuy to Joseph W. Martin, February 26, 1947; Martin to Landon, May 29, June 6, August 7, December 4, 1947; Landon to Martin, March 7, May 26, July 17, 1947.

off when television will do more to mould the political destiny of this country than any other single medium. In a few years candidates will have to be 'telegenic' to be nominated. And they'll have to possess what Hollywood calls 'it' to be elected." Landon, however, did not go into television because, as he later put it, "the margin of profit in radio is 15 percent and in television 5 percent."[16]

Although the Kansan had forsaken oil as his chief economic interest, he occasionally engaged in selective drilling for the development of profitable wells, and he retained his oil and gas properties that were still producing. Nevertheless, Landon felt he had been pushed out of the oil industry by the competitive efficiency of the major companies and the prohibitive costs of digging deep wells and making extensive geophysical surveys. An independent producer could keep up only by being "Johnny at the rathole when a new field is opened. While the big companies' representatives are phoning Wichita, and Wichita phones Tulsa, he can close a deal."[17] Playing "Johnny at the rathole" did not appeal to Landon.

Partisan politics, however, was still his main interest, and Landon was convinced that the best hope for maintaining American democracy was the election of a Republican President in 1948. He saw many potential Republican nominees—Governors Dewey of New York, Warren of California, Bricker of Ohio, Green of Illinois, and former Governor Stassen of Minnesota; Representative Martin; Senators Taft, Vandenberg, Saltonstall, and Lodge; and Generals Eisenhower and MacArthur. As for issues, foreign relations was the most important, but America's ability to carry out an effective policy for world peace and security depended not only on events abroad but also on those at home. Two domestic issues were therefore crucial: economic stability and a "balanced-budget administration" (rather than "national tinhorn financing").

Landon did not contend that the Republican party was without fault, or thoroughly competent. Republicans, for example, had to learn to understand and cooperate with management and labor, to be fair to both, and to recognize and deal harshly with injustices in both

16 *Leavenworth Times*, March 17, 1948; *Rocky Mountain News* (Denver), March 29, 1948; *Denver Post*, May 3, 14, 1948; *Southwest Daily Times* (Liberal, Kan.), July 24, 1948; Landon interview, October 6, 1959.

17 Landon to Harold B. Johnson, September 25, 1947.

groups.[18] To emphasize the importance of cooperation with labor, Landon continued his contacts with union leaders, and especially with John L. Lewis and other United Mine Workers officials. Landon and Lewis had corresponded since their meeting at the Republican national convention of 1940, and their friendship reached its rhetorical peak in 1946 when Landon wrote Lewis that he was "the smartest, squarest and ablest labor leader in America today." Landon also preached the gospel of national unity to labor. Speaking before the Kansas State Federation of Labor, on May 2, he urged that labor, industry, and agriculture cooperate and recognize each other's rights in order to achieve peace and progress. "There can be no permanent peace among nations if the greatest nation of all is torn by internal strife." [19]

His beliefs were tested later that month when he was asked to comment on President Truman's proposal to draft workers during a nationwide strike of railroad employees. The Kansan, reluctantly accepting the President's policy, said that labor "has its responsibilities" to the public, but he rapped Truman by saying that "a wise leadership, exercised in time, . . . should have prevented us getting into a situation where the President's proposal seemed to be the only thing left to do." He warned that the draft proposal was a "step in the direction of the Communist and Fascist technique of settling economic disputes." He could not restrain himself from saying that President Roosevelt, in 1936, had declared that he was the master of business—and labor had cheered. "In 1946 as President Truman proposed to make the Presidency the master of labor, business cheered. Thus does liberty languish." [20]

Landon's sympathy for labor reflected his concern for achieving balance between the nation's interests, which he thought essential to the maintenance of the Republic and of Constitutional guarantees. He also thought that a variety of viewpoints among Republicans would

[18] *Nashville Tennessean*, January 20, 1946.

[19] Landon to John L. Lewis, January 2, 1946; Landon speech, Topeka, May 2, 1946.

[20] *Wichita Beacon*, May 27, 1946; *Topeka State Journal*, May 28, 1946. In a private letter, probably as an afterthought, Landon flatly opposed the drafting of workers because "it places too much power in the hands of our presidents—who after all are only human. I don't believe that we should take the slightest step in the direction of settling our economic disputes by the firing squad and the concentration camp. When you propose to draft men in the army in the settlement of labor disputes, that is exactly what you are doing." Landon to Theodore Alford, May 29, 1946.

ensure the party's health. This belief had been behind his efforts to improve the quality of Negro Republican leadership and to make John L. Lewis feel comfortable in the party; and Landon carried it further by enthusiastically welcoming Progressive Senator Robert M. La Follette, Jr., back into the party. After La Follette announced in March, 1946, that he was returning to Republicanism, Landon wrote: "You will be a very healthy and constructive influence in shaping our policies." To show that he was earnest, the Kansan agreed to boost the Wisconsin senator in his contest for nomination, against Joseph R. McCarthy. Speaking before the Nebraska Young Republican convention (on May 11), Landon praised La Follette and other Wisconsin Progressives for "their healthy influence and vigorous championship of a practical progressive program," and said their return to Republicanism would help the party offer the nation better government than was being given by the Democrats.[21] This and other out-of-state help, however, was insufficient to bring La Follette victory; his distinguished career was ended and McCarthy's senatorship had begun, with ramifications that no one could then foresee.

The Kansan also interested himself in the reorganization of the Republican national committee. Herbert Brownell, Jr., in the spring of 1946, resigned the chairmanship and Landon supported conservative Representative Carroll Reece of Tennessee, who he thought could moderate the conflict among the various factions. Landon worked through Representative Frank Carlson and national committeemen Harry Darby of Kansas and Edward Colladay of the District of Columbia. Reece, who secured the support of most Republican moderates and liberals, was elected to the chairmanship.[22]

Landon's participation in the 1946 campaign was limited. In his one major speech, July 10, at the Kansas Young Republican convention at Newton, he said: "It is obvious that the Republican party will win the election this November [and] the swing is so marked that we can hardly be maladroit enough to lose in 1948." Because of the probability that Republicans would regain national power, Landon said the party had to deal with three great changes that had been brought about during the New Deal years.

[21] Landon to Robert M. La Follette, Jr., March 22, 29, 1946; La Follette to Landon, March 27, 1946; Landon speech, Grand Island, Neb., May 11, 1946.

[22] Carroll Reece to Landon, April 5, 1946; Landon to Frank Carlson, March 11, 1946.

1. Increase of monopolistic power, which we must break up ruthlessly.
2. Increase of labor unions power with which we must deal understandingly and sympathetically, but firmly, in the best interest of labor and the public.
3. Increase of government power which has been administered so erratically and badly as to demoralize the economic life of the nation.

As for the other problems confronting the nation, Landon said inflation was the worst. Rejecting price control as a remedy, he maintained the cure was to be found in more free enterprise, governmental economy, higher federal taxes, and a balanced federal budget. Although he conceded that the Republican party did not have all the answers for the country's problems, the path to good government lay in a return to Republican principles: "competent and efficient administration" and a refusal to "cater to any minority pressure group."[23] These same points were repeated in Landon's two other campaign speeches, which also were given to Young Republican groups.[24]

Convinced that the Republicans would win the congressional elections, Landon remained in Kansas during the 1946 campaign. He was correct. Using the slogan "Had enough?" Republicans swept the country and gained enough seats to control both houses of Congress—for the first time since 1930. The Democratic tide seemed to be receding.

The days that followed the 1946 election were busy and eventful as Republicans prepared to assume leadership in Congress, but—although there was much positive thinking—their ingrained spirit of opposition remained strong. The first controversy after the election was caused by the proposal of many Republicans that President Truman appoint a Republican as Secretary of State and then resign, so that the Republican Secretary could succeed him as President. This was justified on the ground that, by electing a Republican Congress, the nation had voted its lack of confidence in Truman. The group also contended that responsibility would be better fixed if the Republicans controlled Congress and the executive branch. Landon disagreed, stating "The Republican landslide gives Mr. Truman an opportunity to pursue whatever policies he may believe in—he is free to be himself" because he did not have to cater to a Democratic majority and would not cater to a Republican Congress. The Kansan added that the suggestion that

[23] Landon speech, Newton, Kan., July 10, 1946.
[24] Landon speeches: Sabetha, Kan., September 17, and Topeka, October 4, 1946.

Truman resign was a New Deal–type of "attempt to sidetrack the established processes of our government."[25]

Landon gave much thought to what the goals of the Republican Congress should be and the legislation his party should concentrate on during the next two years. He concluded that an equitable, non-punitive labor practices act was needed, that all Republican enactments should be undergirded by the principle that "you cannot continue to take out of the till more than you put in," and that the budget should be balanced before Congress acceded to the mounting pressure to reduce taxes. One of the biggest tax-reduction opportunities was world disarmament, he pointed out, and greater "efficiency of government by a thorough housecleaning of a lot of overgrown federal bureaus" would also lead to reduced expenditures.[26] In December, Landon journeyed to Washington to try to bolster sentiment for a balanced budget and a reduction of the national debt. He also expressed his hope—in an effort to ward off punitive labor legislation—that Americans would enter an era of cooperation between industry, labor, and government in 1947.

On his way home from the capital, during a stop in Buffalo, he said there were signs that the administration was turning to "a middle-of-the-road policy in handling business cycles," which he saw as indicative of cooperation between Congress and the executive branch in "rescuing from the garbage pail some of our own fundamental American principles." Landon again warned against a punitive labor policy, and called for stepped up antitrust action and increased salaries for American diplomats. On the eve of the convening of the new Congress, in a press statement, he renewed his suggestion that "Congress should invite the British and Canadian parliaments to send bipartisan delegations to meet with its own delegation in a consultative committee on their tripartite affairs." He also favored giving the atomic bomb to the United Nations under the government-sponsored Baruch plan.[27]

As the Eightieth Congress got under way, Landon was in frequent touch with its leaders, Senator Robert A. Taft and House speaker Joseph W. Martin, and with Republican national committee chairman

[25] *Topeka Capital*, November 8, 1946.

[26] Landon to Harold B. Johnson, November 12, 1946; *Pittsburgh Sun Telegraph*, November 22, 1946.

[27] *Washington Times-Herald*, December 19, 1946; *Buffalo Evening News*, December 19, 1946; Landon press release, January 2, 1947; Landon to Wiley S. Smith, December 30, 1946.

Carroll Reece and Governor Dewey. Although Landon was concerned with domestic issues, he emphasized foreign affairs in his speeches and letters, and on January 14 he gave his first speech of 1947 before the Junior Chamber of Commerce in Minneapolis. He tried to inspire confidence that the United States could handle the nasty problems of the postwar period, evidence of which he saw in America's war record.

> Where Russia fought on a two thousand–mile front and a mere pond called the Baltic Sea—where Britain guarded a coast of eight hundred miles and a lifeline through the Mediterranean and the Indian Ocean ten thousand miles long—the United States waged war on seven oceans, every sea, and on scores of fronts that totaled not two but tens of thousands of miles. Our invasions of Jap-islands alone were military feats heretofore never dreamed of. The invasion of Europe by British and American forces combined was a titanic operation which even the military mind still has difficulty grasping. The world has never seen the equal of the military achievements and military resources of our great and glorious Republic.

Those achievements, he said, derived not from a "totalitarian system, but from a mighty, free, competitive system, a republicanism which we have chosen to call democracy." He urged that the United States not turn its back on the world, because with this "greatest dynamic force in the world today" the nation could keep the peace and strive for greater world equity. Trouble was upon the world, but Americans could not ignore it.

> With oceans reduced to mere rivers, and with weeks reduced to mere minutes by the advent of jet propulsion and the harnessing of atomic energy, no minor disturbance of the peace . . . is beyond our concern. No longer can America close its eyes to the fact that, as a street fight may turn into a riot, so may a minor border dispute flare into the next world war.[28]

Although Landon urged confidence in America's ability to deal with world problems, he was personally disquieted. Communism, by its intransigence and aggrandizement, was creating international chaos and instability, and this was forcing the United States to forsake the the goal of world cooperation for a balance-of-power policy. Even this shift, he thought, was "ineffectual" because of the administration's unwillingness to disavow the Morgenthau plan, which was eating up manpower and time and accomplishing nothing. But even a reversal of the policy of restricting Germany would not be enough to meet Russian aggrandizement; other non-communist areas also had to be

[28] Landon speech, Minneapolis, January 14, 1947.

built up, as the administration had recognized in proposing a loan to Great Britain and assistance to Greece and Turkey. The question was:

> Are we strong enough to carry on our shoulders alone the burden of financing England, France, Belgium, Germany, Italy, Greece, China, and other countries, in order to prevent a vacuum into which Russia plans to move? . . . If we are to become a modern Atlas, then we must certainly pull in our belts here at home and sit down for a long siege, which no one can tell when, where or what the end will be. [29]

Despite his discouragement he supported the Truman Doctrine, which proposed giving assistance to Greece and Turkey to enable them to resist communist pressures. Speaking on March 19, 1947, in Wichita, he praised President Truman for throwing down "the gauntlet to the imperialist and aggressive policies of Russia," and he pointed out that the doctrine meant "We are in European power politics up to our necks, and in it to stay." Whether we liked it or not, the United States would have to reverse its German and Italian policies, return to the Good Neighbor policy in the western hemisphere, and keep its armed forces at the highest level of efficiency. Despite the cost, these measures were necessary for maintaining freedom and security, and because they were necessary, Landon said, the President should be given (even if it unbalanced the budget) "everything that he asks." [30] The Scripps-Howard newspapers thought Landon reflected "the thinking and sturdy confidence of the solid Americanism at the nation's grass roots, and on the Main streets of thousands of cities, towns, and villages." [31]

Landon was not happy with the new foreign policy, but he thought there was no alternative. "Backing Truman seems to me to be the only way out of a bad mess which the [New Deal's] tragic bungling of our foreign affairs has gotten us into." Nor was Landon sanguine about the success of the policy—there were too many complicating factors. One uncertainty, of course, was whether the President would follow through; another was whether Republicans would go as far as they should in supporting the President; and then there were the attacks of the "peace" advocates, like Henry Wallace, which Landon thought were "disgraceful." In an effort to compensate for these factors, Landon

[29] Landon to Felix Morley, March 4, 1947.
[30] Landon speech, Wichita, March 19, 1947.
[31] *Wichita Beacon*, March 22, 1947; *Washington News*, March 20, 1947.

during the spring of 1947 supported the President's hard line against Russian expansion.[32]

His support of the Truman Doctrine did not mean Landon had lost hope in the United Nations or in the possibility of disarmament. He urged that there be a provision in the United Nations charter for an effective, universal disarmament program, believing that if the United States took the leadership in a disarmament movement, and were the least bit successful, the Soviet Union would not dare stay out of it— though if she did "we should then mobilize the world against her."[33] In June, in a speech in Philadelphia, Landon linked the disarmament question and Secretary of State George Marshall's proposal for a large scale United States assistance program in Europe. He said he wanted to support Marshall's recommendations, but that more details were necessary. Moreover, the program would be expensive, which pointed to the need for America to find a better—and less expensive—way out of world disorder, which would have to be world disarmament. Disarmament was the only way to lighten the people's financial burdens, to avoid "living in an armed camp," and to stop "a rising militarism" from "eventually engulfing our Republic"; it was the only road to world peace and harmony. As additional steps, Landon again recommended the internationalization of strategic areas—including the Panama and Suez canals, Gibraltar, and the Dardanelles—and "a consultative committee of the legislative bodies" of (at least) France, Britain, Canada, and the United States to assist the work of world reconstruction.[34]

The Kansan also commented on domestic issues. On April 11, 1947, speaking to the western states conference of Young Republicans at Salt Lake City, he lauded the manner and technique of the Eightieth Congress. "No longer are bills rushed through in shameful hysteria without thorough consideration and debate." He interpreted the mandate to the Republican party as the development of a reasonable diffusion of power, responsibility in government, a solvent and fully productive

[32] Landon to F. E. Spicer, March 26, 1947; Landon to William Hard, April 4, 29, 1947; Landon to Willard Mayberry, April 16, 1947; *Denver Post*, April 9, 1947; *Rocky Mountain News* (Denver), April 11, 1947; *New York Herald Tribune*, April 25, 1947; Landon speeches: Topeka, May 9, 1947, and Philadelphia, June 26, 1947.

[33] Landon to John C. McCall, May 13, 1947; Landon to Herbert Bodman, June 6, 1947.

[34] Landon speech, Philadelphia, June 26, 1947.

nation, and protection against the dangers of inflation. He also spoke vigorously in favor of legislation that would give every person, regardless of race or financial status, his full rights as an American citizen.[35]

Later in the month, addressing the Republican national committee in Kansas City, Missouri, Landon decried criticism of Congress as a do-nothing body. He said that the Eightieth Congress' critics "do not realize how much New Deal underbrush must be cleared away or how much bureaucratic rubble must be removed before actual work can begin on the construction of sound laws to replace the jerry-built flimsies of the New Dealers." He called for national unity and cooperation in tackling the problems of the day, and particularly demanded the help of business. "I think it is time for business leadership as a whole to get over the idea that we have to have a boom-and-bust business trend in this country." He said that, with wise management and by discarding the concept of "large profits now," business could seek plans for long-term prosperity. "It could do wonders in the way of adding a substantial stability. It would mean that a business could establish prices today which would yield it a profit margin which over the long pull is adequate to attract capital to the industry." He also urged management to "get rid of its 'follow the leader' psychosis" in setting wages and prices—which led only to the inflationary spiraling of wages and prices. He asked labor to "gamble on the future," contending that if it would "hold fast and let us get our economy back on to a sound, productive, competitive basis, not only labor but everyone else will benefit." Nor was economic self-interest the only reason why Americans should cooperate in working for economic stability; they had a duty to do so. "Russia is waiting hopefully for another 'bust' when she confidently expects us to succumb to totalitarian economic planning and control of everything—including labor."[36] The Kansan spoke sincerely about unity and economic cooperation, but few members of a society of competing interests would heed his words.

Support of the Truman Doctrine and world disarmament was the gist of Landon's comment on the issues before the nation between April and October, 1947. Then, when he resumed his speechmaking, he smugly minimized the possibility of war between America and Russia. "Modern warfare is technological and nuclear physics. The Russians are babes in the woods at that kind of business."[37] As the details of the

[35] *Salt Lake Tribune*, April 12, 1947.
[36] Landon speech, Kansas City, Mo., April 22, 1947.
[37] *Boston Sunday Globe*, October 19, 1947.

Marshall Plan were developed, Landon spoke in support of it, demanding that America give long-term aid as a matter of humanitarianism and economic good sense. He suggested, however, that the

> government in advancing money should impose conditions of performance which really are tough from the point of view of production. I can see no conceivable reason why we should continue to provide funds for the perpetuation of governments which, by their policies, make it impossible to reestablish sound economic conditions within their countries.

This reflected Landon's concern, as he wrote Herbert Hoover, that the terms of the Marshall Plan were so vague that the formulation of a program was determined largely by the aided countries.[38]

As relations between the United States and the Soviet Union grew worse during the late fall of 1947 and the following winter, Landon became less confident of America's military superiority. In December he warned that the disagreements between the two countries were likely to continue for a long time, and that the United States must prepare for trouble. He called for a "constantly improving air force," "the biggest navy in the world," a greatly expanded regular army, larger national guard and organized reserve forces, and "proper and efficient intelligence facilities"; even more important, the nation must keep its lead in nuclear physics. (He rejected any form of conscription in favor of "seeing more youths enter the fields of science and research.") In February, 1948, he amplified his stand. While emphasizing that he did not believe war was inevitable, he recommended three general policies for the United States. "1. We must proceed at once to make ourselves as nearly invulnerable as possible in this atomic age. . . . 2. Go right ahead with a sound and coherent foreign-aid program. . . . 3. Make it perfectly plain that we stand ready to come to an understanding with Russia." Landon said the nation was stressing foreign aid more than the other two policies, when equal attention should be given to all three.[39]

The Kansan spoke with greater urgency as communism spread. After the 1948 coup d'état in Czechoslavakia, he recommended that American military experts be given a greater role in preparing for war, and even suggested that prices and profits be frozen. Early in April,

[38] Landon speeches: Garnett, Kan., October 29, 1947, and Kansas City, Mo., November 18, 1947; Landon to Herbert Hoover, November 24, 1947.

[39] *Topeka State Journal*, December 10, 1947; *Somerset* (Pa.) *Daily American*, December 10, 1947; Landon speech, Ottawa, Kan., February 4, 1948.

at a meeting of Washington's Gridiron Club—Landon lauded the Eightieth Congress' tax reduction bill and increased appropriations for the air force as "two great steps toward peace." As he saw it, the tax reduction would stimulate the country's material development through private enterprise.[40]

The next month, as the Trade Agreements Act came under consideration for renewal by Congress, Landon lashed out at the Republican Congress, deploring its failure to understand the international importance of this reciprocal tariff legislation. On May 22, 1948, while in Washington to confer with House speaker Joseph Martin, Landon said the Republican plan to extend the act for only one year threatened the entire European recovery program; he favored extension of tariff reciprocity for the usual three years, and without the limiting amendments that had been proposed (he also supported, though reluctantly, a temporary revival of conscription in order to build up the army).[41] Although he fought in vain for a liberal tariff policy, the foundations of Landon's foreign policy views were set. National rearmament, trade and aid to strengthen non-communist countries, and the seeking of peace with freedom—these were the things with which to combat Russian aggression.

The year 1948 was a year of great expectations for the Republican party. With the right nominee, the party could capture the Presidency, and Landon intended to test the leading candidates to see who would be most attractive to the voters. In January, 1947, the most likely candidates for the nomination seemed to be Governor Dewey, Harold Stassen, and Senator Robert A. Taft; but Landon looked beyond the field to General Dwight D. Eisenhower, who could upset the nominating routine. He believed the delegates from the plains and the Rocky Mountain areas would support the World War II hero if he declared for the Presidency, and Kansas, the general's home state, would "feel very friendly toward Eisenhower, and would be very sympathetic with any statement he might make at any time as to his political principles and policies." Although Landon was attracted to Eisenhower, he retained his freedom of action; he was not convinced of the ability of the contenders and he thought the convention would be "sewed up tighter than a tick" for several ballots. Landon refused to respond to pleas to support Dewey, asserting that the New Yorker—and Taft as

[40] *Wichita Eagle*, March 24, 1948; *Watertown* (N.Y.) *Times*, April 9, 1948.
[41] *Denver Post*, May 14, 1948; *Washington Post*, May 23, 1948.

well—was weak in popular and political appeal. The Kansan was still bothered by the fact that neither Dewey nor his organization had contacted him during the 1944 campaign. This, Landon thought, revealed a great weakness because "when a man gets down in the dust of the arena it takes not only endless work, but back-breaking attention to human relationships." [42]

Landon remained uncommitted in the summer of 1947. The convention's choice of its nominee should depend, he thought, on whether Henry Wallace's third party materialized and on the course of Russo-American relations. The latter situation, if it worsened, might lead to a soldier or an educator being chosen. (The *New York Times* observed that Eisenhower, who had recently been selected president of Columbia University, fitted both categories.) Landon's activities in 1947 also led to speculation that he might again run for the nomination; it was noted that he frequently made public appearances and that he saw political leaders wherever he traveled. John M. Cummings commented in the *Philadelphia Inquirer*: "A nice guy to meet, Alf Landon. It may be that, like Governor Dewey, he is not a believer in the theory that lightning never strikes twice in the same place." Gladstone Williams, in the *Atlanta Constitution* in July, asked: "Landon a G.O.P. Candidate Next Year?" Williams contended that Landon was thinking of the Presidency and that this posed a threat to Governor Dewey, who needed the midwestern delegates upon whom Landon would draw in a battle for the nomination. Indeed, one of Dewey's leaders in the west, E. G. Bennett of Utah, reported to Dewey there were rumors that Landon would be a dark-horse candidate; but later, when Bennett asked the Kansan point-blank if he might be a dark horse, Landon jumped two feet from his chair and replied, "Hell, no." [43]

Landon had no thought of running for President, and his correspondence revealed none of the preparations that a candidate would have to make. To friends who would have been needed for launching a Landon boom, he wrote that the Republican party "needs at least one leader who is not worrying about having an office"—and that leader was Landon. It seemed clear by July, however, that he was not a

[42] Landon to Richard E. Berlin, January 24, 1947; Landon to Kenneth Hogate, February 4, 1947; Landon to A. H. Kirchhofer, February 27, 1947.

[43] *New York Times*, June 29, 1947; *New York News*, July 1, 1947; *Philadelphia Inquirer*, June 28, 1947; *Atlanta Constitution*, July 10, 1947; E. G. Bennett to Thomas E. Dewey, July 8, 1947, Thomas E. Dewey Papers, University of Rochester Libraries, Rochester, N.Y.; Landon interview, September 17, 1963.

Dewey man. When Dewey, on a supposedly nonpolitical tour of the country, lunched in Kansas City with Kansas and Missouri Republican leaders, Landon did not attend. "It was nothing personal," he said; he was staying home for business reasons; but his absence was widely interpreted as a snub.[44]

Landon was involved in the Eisenhower-for-President movement, something Dewey's supporters had feared. They had observed— according to Doris Fleeson, a Scripps-Howard political columnist— that New York, where the general lived, "has been artfully linked to the Eisenhower boom by Alfred Landon." This, of course, imperiled Dewey's base of strength. Landon, during this period, knew nothing of the general's intentions but he thought he could be a winner, and he frequently wrote the general's brother, president Milton Eisenhower of Kansas State College, and enclosed clippings about "Ike" and the presidential nomination. He went so far as to write Milton Eisenhower, on July 22, that "the tempo is picking up." Landon also wrote to his friends about Dwight Eisenhower's attractiveness: he told Harold Johnson that "Eisenhower's move to Columbia has tremendously stimulated an interest in him," and Frank E. Gannett that Eisenhower would have the political appeal of a combination Ulysses Grant and Woodrow Wilson.[45]

Although not committed to Eisenhower or anyone else in the summer of 1947, Landon was convinced that the party could find a better nominee than Dewey had been in 1944. The Kansan was searching for that nominee, and he encouraged the leading contenders for the nomination, even Dewey and Taft, to show what they could do.[46] But Eisenhower was Landon's main hope. In August, 1947, a wave of Eisenhower publicity began to spread, for which Landon, Senator Capper, and Roy Roberts of the *Kansas City Star* were widely credited. *Life* called the Eisenhower boom "the hottest shoptalk" of politics because the general seemed to be popular with everyone; it reported that Dewey and Taft—and Truman—were perturbed. The Eisenhower boom continued into the fall; and the Gallup Poll in late September

[44] Landon to Harold B. Johnson, September 25, 1947; Landon interview, September 17, 1963; *Topeka Capital*, July 11, 1947.

[45] *Kansas City Times*, July 16, 1947; Landon to Milton Eisenhower, July 22, 1947; Landon to Harold B. Johnson, July 16, 1947; Landon to Frank E. Gannett, July 22, 1947.

[46] Landon to Harold B. Johnson, July 16, 1947; Landon to Frank E. Gannett, July 22, 1947; Landon to Felix Morley, August 13, 1947; Landon to Thomas E. Dewey, August 6, 1947.

showed that the general had the support of 48 per cent of the voters compared to 39 per cent for Truman. It was also in September that Landon came out publicly for Eisenhower: "We believe in Ike like we believe in Kansas."[47]

Eisenhower, however, said he wanted to stay out of politics, but Landon continued to boom him for President in his letters and visits with newspapermen and Republican leaders—and was occasionally chided by his friends. Herbert L. Bodman said he remembered when Landon told him that as the army could not make generals out of corporals so politicians could not nominate political greenhorns for President. Unhappily for Landon, the Eisenhower movement collapsed in January, 1948, when the general declared he "could not accept nomination to high political office." Landon rejoined: "unanswered is whether the American people will accept his statement as their final decision." Regardless of what the people thought, Eisenhower had made his decision for 1948 and Landon found himself without a leading contender for President.[48]

In addition to his trouble on the national scene, Landon was also encountering difficulties in Kansas. Since 1932 he had been the prime leader of the Kansas Republicans, but events in 1947 and 1948 broke his hold on the state party. Landon had had disagreements with Governor Andrew Schoeppel in 1945 and 1946, and had broken with Schoeppel because of his ineffectual enforcement of the state's prohibition law, his questionable financial activities, and his alleged interference in the work of the state Corporation Commission. In 1946, Landon supported the successful gubernatorial candidacy of his former state chairman, Representative Frank Carlson, hoping Carlson's election would raise the level of state administration. Meanwhile, however, Landon had been pictured as the bogeyman of Kansas politics; Democrat Harry Woodring, in his unsuccessful attempt to regain the governorship, inveighed against the "Landon machine," as did some of the defeated candidates in the 1946 Republican primaries. The situation was further complicated by the rise of sentiment to

[47] *Washington Post*, August 20, 1947; *New York News*, September 16, 1947; *Life*, August 25, 1947, pp. 33 ff.; *Saturday Evening Post*, November 15, 1947, pp. 15 ff.; *Newsweek*, September 15, 1947, p. 22.

[48] Jack Wells to Thomas E. Stephens, October 6, 1947, Dewey Papers; Landon to Harold B. Johnson, September 25, 1947; Herbert Bodman to Landon, October 13, 1947; *Topeka Capital*, January 24, 1948.

rid the state of prohibition, but Landon came under the fire of the prohibitionists because the law had not been fully enforced and because he was not fighting against a referendum on prohibition that would come up in 1948. Landon's position was that he was not "an all-powerful influence," though he believed that Carlson, as governor, would enforce the liquor laws; if he did not, Landon promised he would protest. As for the referendum, Landon held, as he always had, that the voters should decide the issue: "I don't believe in maintaining any law that the people are not for." [49]

The chief threats to Landon's leadership came in 1947, when Schoeppel decided to run for senator against the aging Arthur Capper, and there was strong sentiment that Landon would not choose the winner in the race for the Republican nomination—or, if he did, that his nominee would lose the 1948 general election. In June, 1947, Landon counterattacked in a speech "for the good of the party," criticizing Schoeppel's senatorial ambitions because of his lax enforcement of liquor and gambling laws. A month later, new stories broke about Schoeppel. An informant told the Kansas Corporation Commission that the Republic Natural Gas, Panhandle Eastern, and Northern Natural Gas companies had been favored at the expense of small producers in the Hugoton gas field during Schoeppel's administration. The commission, apparently in response to this information, ordered ninety-two gas wells shut down, including sixty-three of Republic's, because of "excessive and illegal withdrawals." Landon added to this in his attempts to stymie Schoeppel's political advancement. He pointed out that Schoeppel, upon leaving the governorship, had joined the law firm that represented Republic, and that the head of that firm was a large Republic stockholder and a director. Landon also used the issue to try to prevent the *Kansas City Star* from supporting Schoeppel. Landon wrote Willard Mayberry that he should tell Roy Roberts he had always trusted the *Star*, but "it breaks your heart to see the *Star* being taken over by the big utility gas, oil, etc., corporations, which is the plain truth of what is occurring if they, in any way, countenance the campaign of Schoeppel for United States senator." Landon also suggested that Mayberry point out that Schoeppel had

[49] Landon interview, September 17, 1963; Landon to Harold B. Johnson, November 12, 1946; *Salina Journal*, September 9–14, 16–17, 1946; Frank Carlson to Lacy Haynes, August 12, 1946, Lacy Haynes Papers, Kansas State Historical Society, Topeka; Landon to Milton Amrine, November 8, 1946.

undoubtedly been under obligation for the $25,000 in campaign funds he received from a Republic Natural Gas official in 1942.[50]

The "scandal and disgrace" of Schoeppel's relations with the gas corporations strengthened Landon's determination to frustrate his ambitions. A problem, however, was that no one of any standing could be persuaded to enter a primary in which he would face not only the aggressive Schoeppel but possibly the beloved Senator Arthur Capper as well. Landon therefore felt he had to support the eighty-three-year-old Capper if he ran for renomination. Capper decided to run, and announced his decision in November, 1947; a few days later Schoeppel announced his candidacy, which was seen as the beginning of a struggle to tip the balance of power away from Landon.[51] Landon immediately began working for Capper. He wrote that although the senator was old, his voting record was good. "Schoeppel has neither the grasp of the problems confronting us, nor the sympathy for the common man that Capper has" and he charged that Schoeppel's sympathies lay with big business. Landon knew it would be a tough fight, because even most of Capper's backers thought he was too old to continue in the Senate. Moreover, as Clifford Stratton, Capper's assistant, pointed out, most of the newspaper opposition to the senator came from his former supporters, the *Kansas City Star* and the Jack Harris newspapers.[52]

The first attack on Landon came from William L. White, the son of William Allen and his successor as publisher of the *Emporia Gazette*. Comparing Landon to a heroic statue, White viewed Landon's opposition to Schoeppel

as conduct unworthy of a statue. It is as unseemly as if, in a circus parade, the gilded lady who rides high on her golden throne as a living statue, would suddenly hop down off the wagon, grab a convenient bedslat, and take out after one of the clowns.

We cannot in this hard world always have what we want, but in a free country there is no harm in asking for it. And this is why, in all humility, we beg Alf Landon to withdraw from these undignified, back-alley brawls and to climb back upon his pedestal. And if he needs any help, we are not

[50] *Wichita Eagle*, June 26, 1947; *Wichita Beacon*, August 1, 1947; Landon to George E. Burket, August 4, 1947; Landon to Willard Mayberry, August 8, 1947.

[51] Landon to A. E. Kramer, October 15, 1947; Landon to J. N. Tincher, December 5, 1947; *Topeka Capital*, November 2, 1947; *Wichita Eagle*, November 5, 1947.

[52] Landon to L. F. Metzler, November 6, 1947; Landon to Clifford Stratton, November 10, 1947; Stratton to Landon, November 14, 1947.

only willing but eager to steady the stepladder. For there he has sat in the past and there he should sit today, high above the rest of us, ignoring our petty jealousies, his noble profile thrust up against Heaven's blue vault, with cumulus clouds drifting lazily past his ears, thunderheads tickling him under the chin and the cold winds of immortality blowing up his pants legs. That's how we like him best.

This did not deter Landon from opposing Schoeppel. He was telling all comers the same thing he had written to his New York friend, Harold B. Johnson.

> I never was more disappointed in my life than I was in the record Schoeppel made as governor. I am opposing him because in the Senate he will simply be the errand boy for the utilities, big pipeline companies and oil companies. I think the Republican party is the only agency that can save America. And, we are not going to do that job if we are dominated by big business as we were in the '20s.[53]

The Republican party in Kansas appeared to be breaking up as the fight soon extended to the selection of delegates to the national convention. Friendships and alliances dissolved to an extent that the party had not experienced since Clyde M. Reed's defeat for governor in 1930. Landon's old friend, Lacy Haynes, made it clear that he would not support Capper because of his age. Haynes, also, had joined the Dewey forces, which was another point of conflict with Landon. All the possibilities of a bitter struggle developed because Schoeppel would not cease and Capper would not desist. The bitterness was seen again when the Republican state central committee, in January, 1948, changed the rules for the representation of congressional districts in the national convention: the district including Topeka, which usually contributed four or five of the state's seven at-large delegates, could send no more than two. This change, which equalized the representation of the state's congressional districts, struck at control of the party by Landon and Capper, who had greatly benefited from the old arrangement.[54]

Landon's friends and supporters deserted him rapidly. The resolution that changed the composition of the delegation had been offered by Claude Bradney and supported by Fred Brinkerhoff. And the struggle

[53] *Kansas City Star*, November 17, 1947; Landon to Harold B. Johnson, November 21, 1947.

[54] Lacy Haynes to J. H. Jenson, December 3, 1947; Haynes to Herbert Brownell, Jr., December 3, 1947; Harry Darby to Hugh A. Hope, May 19, 1948, Haynes Papers; *Kansas City Star*, January 29, 1948.

for power went on in a fight for delegates after the state central committee adjourned. In the contest for delegate from the fifth congressional district, Willard Mayberry was opposed by Jess C. Denious and Richard W. Robbins, both of whom had been close to Landon politically. Even though Mayberry was victorious in the fifth district delegate race, the war—as the *Kansas City Star* commented—was already won. The Landon forces had bid for only six of the eighteen district delegates, which meant that the Landon men could not win the majority of the state's delegates. Yet the Landon-Capper forces continued the fight; using their press allies, and especially Capper's *Topeka Capital*, they tried to stir up the state against Schoeppel. The *Capital* raised the issue of "out-of-state domination," making much of the comment in John Gunther's popular book, *Inside U.S.A.*, that Kansas was a colony of Missouri's *Kansas City Star*. *Time*'s dubbing of Roy Roberts as "Kansas' top GOPower" and of his headquarters at the Kansas City Club as the "unofficial capital of Kansas" was also used in the attack on Schoeppel.[55]

After the district delegate fights had been settled, Landon's forces found themselves with only six delegates; and twelve delegates supported Landon's opponents. The *Star* crowed: "The balance has been tipped." The tipping of the balance also meant that Harry Darby, who supported Dewey for President and Schoeppel for senator, would be reelected national committeeman and would become chairman of the state's convention delegation, thereby strengthening the anti-Landon forces. The only concession to Landon was that the delegates were not formally committed to any of the candidates for the presidential nomination.[56]

The struggle nevertheless went on, concentrating on the senatorial nomination, and once again William L. White entered the fray. Capper, he wrote, was universally loved, and had done great service for his state, but he was "a very old man" who had continued to do his job only at great personal sacrifice. White charged that Landon had pushed Capper into an unwanted contest in the belief that "the heavens will totter and the Republic will crumble" if Schoeppel was elected to the Senate. He urged that Landon run for the Senate himself if he wanted Schoeppel opposed. Fay Seaton's *Manhattan Mercury-Chronicle*

[55] *Kansas City Star*, January 29, March 21, 1948; *Wichita Eagle*, March 12, 1948; *Topeka Capital*, March 13, 16, 1948.
[56] *Kansas City Star*, March 24, 1948; *Topeka State Journal*, April 8, 1948; *Kansas City Times*, March 30, 1948; *Wichita Eagle*, March 30, 1948.

replied: "Let's let Arthur decide." The newspaper said that Landon had not put Capper in the race, nor could he withdraw him. "Since before Alf Landon put on long pants, Arthur Capper has been making his own decisions." Capper also answered, saying he had not decided to run at the urging of any one person, and that his concern was that the Senate Agricultural Committee chairmanship—which he held—remain with a midwesterner (the next Republican in line was a New Englander, Senator George D. Aiken). The *Kansas City Star*, not impressed with the statement of the "frail 83-year-old Capper," continued to view the campaign as one between Landon and Schoeppel rather than Capper against Schoeppel. Capper's deafness, age, and uncertain health were pointed up as reasons why he should not be renominated. Finally Capper gave in. On June 7, 1948, it was announced that he would not file for renomination because he was beginning to tire of work after more than thirty years in office. Capper's withdrawal was lovely news to Landon's opponents; the senator's decision, as the *Garden City Telegram* wrote, signified his refusal "to play rubber-stamp for Alf Landon and his tightly knit group of mobsters."[57]

Landon was politically destitute in 1948—without a leading candidate for the presidential nomination, without control of the Kansas delegation, and without a candidate for United States senator. His opponents had gambled and had won all the chips.

Even if Landon's luck had run out, he could rejoice in one thing: it also appeared that the Democrats' luck had turned. Truman seemed unable to prevent the Wallace group from pulling away on the left and the southern states' righters from pulling away on the right; it seemed the city bosses would no longer be able to produce the votes they had delivered for Roosevelt; and in state after state, especially in the midwest, Democratic organizations no longer were worthy of the name. Although Landon believed Truman would lose, he still admired the President for his forthrightness and his refusal to engage in duplicity.[58]

Although Landon had been sidelined, and most of his team had found a new captain, he still searched the sandlots of the Republican party for a presidential candidate. His initial choice was House speaker

[57] *Emporia Gazette*, April 29, 1948; *Manhattan* (Kan.) *Mercury-Chronicle*, May 3, 1948; *Kansas City Star*, May 10, 1948; *Topeka Capital*, June 7, 1948; *Garden City* (Kan.) *Telegram*, June 7, 1948.

[58] Landon to George Rothwell Brown, January 7, 1948; Landon to Lewis H. Brown, February 16, 1948; Landon to Raymond Henle, March 2, 1948.

Joseph Martin, the Republican leader with whom he had worked closest over the years. But the two disagreed on strategy, Landon urging a wide-open campaign and Martin deciding to gamble on a deadlock and his selection as a compromise candidate. In May, Landon tried to force the matter by telling Washington newsmen that the convention need look no further than Martin for the best possible candidate. Martin, however, said, that he was not a candidate, though the *Washington Star* observed he left the door open for a draft.[59]

Meanwhile, the Stassen and Taft forces strenuously solicited the Kansan's support, and Landon, who respected Taft's ability, persuaded himself that the Ohio senator might be a winner. With the senator's knowledge, Landon worked on a Taft-Stassen coalition, and when Stassen visited him late in May, Landon told him that only the coalition could prevent Dewey from winning the nomination. Stassen indicated his willingness to consider merging his forces with Taft's, and Landon thereupon visited the Ohioan to suggest Stassen for Vice President. Taft was cold to the idea, but receptive to Landon's alternative suggestion that the former Minnesota governor be named Secretary of Defense or Attorney General. Taft, however, delayed so long in contacting Stassen that the Minnesotan was offended, and refused to discuss the matter when it was finally broached. Other attempts to bring Taft and Stassen together came too late to be effective in defeating Dewey for the nomination.

Disappointed by Taft's lack of political astuteness, Landon swung back to Martin as his candidate, and although he was constantly importuned by Dewey supporters at the national convention, he stuck to Martin to the end. Dewey, of course, was nominated; Martin never had a chance. All of Landon's efforts had been frustrated.[60]

Although the Kansan thought it looked as though "we are on the way to a winning ticket," his enthusiasm for the fight had waned. He yearned, he told A. H. Kirchhofer, for

> some of our old-time crusading friends in the Republican party, like Borah, Johnson, and Bob La Follette, to keep us from zigging too far to the right. Too many of us old-time Progressives have either passed on or been taken

[59] Landon to Joseph W. Martin, April 22, 1948; Landon to A. H. Kirchhofer, July 8, 1948; *Washington Star*, May 23, 1948.

[60] Landon interviews, October 16, 1959, September 17, 1963; Clarence Brown to Landon, May 5, 1948; *Topeka State Journal*, May 31, 1948; William S. White, *The Taft Story* (New York: Harper, 1954), p. 124; Landon to A. H. Kirchhofer, July 8, 1948.

over by the New Deal or have been crushed by the propaganda that all liberals were to be labeled and defined by their stand in favor of a free-giving and free-wheeling foreign policy.

Although he still thought Dewey could win in 1948, he asked:

> Can the G.O.P. have a responsibility and not a license? The coming victory imposes on the party, from its leader in the White House to its lowest member in Congress, great public responsibility. There are many great problems facing the country in both the domestic and foreign fields and these problems cannot be solved by giving heed to self-interested and selfish vested interests.
>
> Keeping these swarms of looters in check is going to be one of the real problems of the new administration. These cookies are going to feel that the honey pot is just waiting for them to grab and run and they will be all over Washington.[61]

After the convention, Landon tried to bridge the gap between Dewey and himself; he wrote the New Yorker encouraging letters during the campaign, and supported him in his other correspondence. Landon saw his new role as that of "the conscience of the Republican party," and in playing this role he made known his fear that "irritations over domestic politics . . . will give both foreign foes and foreign friends, the idea of disunity in this country." He argued that the people were not interested in Republican "bickering" about President Truman's call for a special session of Congress, and even urged House speaker Martin to try to cooperate with President Truman in minimizing partisan divisions during the special session in order to allay impressions of American disunity. The Republican party's control of Congress, Landon repeated again and again, was "a responsibility and not a license." [62]

Virtually inactive as a speaker during the campaign, Landon's only major address was in August, before the World Affairs Institute, at Estes Park, Colorado. He accused the Truman administration of having bungled foreign affairs; and urged that steps be taken to halt inflation by increasing interest rates on consumer credit and by restraining government spending at home and abroad. Landon became increasingly optimistic as the campaign went on. In September he said "there is no doubt about the election of Dewey," but he thought the Repub-

[61] Landon to A. H. Kirchhofer, July 8, 1948.

[62] Landon to Robert S. Allen, July 30, 1948; Landon to William H. Burnham, July 20, 1948; Landon to Robert Humphreys, July 19, 1948.

licans might lose control of the Senate. On October 7 he wrote Robert Humphreys that Dewey would make a good President, adding wryly that "The boys out here are certainly rubbing my nose into the dirt. I have to laugh at the way they are determined to keep me out of any local publicity." Partly because of resentment and partly because he thought Dewey would not have a "tough fight," Landon did not attend Dewey's October rally in Kansas City.[63]

Toward the end of October the Kansan wrote that "the election of a Republican President [is] inevitable"—but after the election returns came in he was writing "What an upset. When I said that Dewey's honeymoon would be over before it starts, I did not think it would be this soon." He ascribed Dewey's defeat to his inability to work with other Republican leaders. As for Truman, Landon said that as a result of his almost single handed triumph "President Truman occupied a place unique among modern American presidents, in that he owed neither his nomination nor election to a single man, and that the responsibility for what happened in the next four years was uniquely that of the President." The Kansan attributed Truman's victory to the "deep-seated distrust of the Republican party by farmers ever since President Calvin Coolidge vetoed the McNary-Haugen bills in the '20s" and to the fact that "the people didn't trust the Republicans to handle the inflation situation."[64]

Once again Landon had been wrong about the result of a presidential election, but this time he did not seem too unhappy.

[63] *Commercial and Financial Chronicle* (New York), August 12, 1948; Landon to William H. Burnham, September 14, 1948; Landon to Robert Humphreys, October 7, 1948; Landon to Thomas E. Dewey, October 14, 1948, Dewey Papers.

[64] Landon to John A. Danaher, October 28, 1948; Landon to Robert S. Allen, November 3, 1948; *New York Times*, December 8, 1948; *Topeka Capital*, December 12, 1948; *Washington Times-Herald*, December 12, 1948.

CHAPTER 22

Ten Years Down on the Farm

Landon had been rusticated. After the events of 1948, he found himself out of power in Kansas and out of grace with the national Republican leadership; and consequently came to do what he wanted to do. He no longer felt he must consider the impact of his positions on his party, or that he must travel about the country as a salesman for Republicanism. He could play a private role as the party's conscience, and enjoy himself.

After 1948 the Kansan turned increasingly to his private concerns. He lived a gracious life in his Georgian house, which now, with shrubbery and trees well grown, was splendidly adapted to its site. He spent more time with his charming wife, and gave increased attention to his two teenage children, Nancy and Jack. He rode his horse for an hour or two a day in good weather, and went duck hunting in season. His correspondence was heavy, but most of it was with veterans of the 1936 campaign and old friends, such as Sterling Morton of the Morton Salt Company, publisher Roy W. Howard, newsman Arthur Krock of the *New York Times*, politician Fred Seaton (who was to become Secretary of the Interior under Eisenhower), and John L. Lewis. He wrote of his opinions on public affairs to his friends—and lifted sentences and paragraphs from their letters for inclusion in his speeches—but his letters increasingly contained comments that were prefaced by "Back in 1936 . . ."

Landon gave more of his time to civic affairs. He was an area fund-raiser for the National Boys' Clubs of America from 1950 to 1952. He also served with CARE in 1951, and his association with the National Conference of Christians and Jews continued into this period. Although not a great philanthropist, Landon gave some Standard Oil stock to the Menninger Foundation and contributed regularly to the athletic scholarship fund of the University of Kansas; he also served on the advisory board of the university's museum of natural history. In 1957 the newly elected Democratic governor, George E. Docking, appointed Landon a member of the Kansas Commission on Constitution Revision, which recommended that the only state elective officers be governor, lieutenant governor, and attorney general, and that they be elected for four-year rather than two-year terms. As chairman of the commission's finance and taxation committee, Landon brought out a report that called for uniform rates of assessment and taxation of property.[1]

Landon's varied business affairs during the 1950s brought him increasing prosperity. He sold KTLN, Denver, in 1949, and in 1952 his interest in KCLO at Leavenworth, but he retained his interest in the 1,000-watt station in Liberal, KSCB, and he acquired control of WREN in Topeka and KEDD in Dodge City. Landon continued to profit from his oil and gas properties, and every year he acquired a few new leases. He further diversified his activities, becoming interested in anything that might turn a profit: land, industry, and stocks and bonds.

Retired as a national leader by the events of 1948 but retaining his interest in the issues before the country, Landon continued to make speeches—to luncheon clubs and school and church groups, which regarded him primarily as history on the hoof. His ideas seldom made the headlines, even in Kansas, but this did not deter him from speaking out on public affairs. His statements and correspondence constituted a chronicle of a tough-minded man's reactions to national and international events, which exasperated his fellow Republicans almost as often as they did Democrats.

The Kansan displayed this quality in December, 1948, during a visit to Washington and New York, by criticizing the Truman administration for "colossal blunders in China" and by assailing Republicans for

[1] Kansas Commission on Constitution Revision, *Progress Report, January 30, 1959* (Topeka: State Printer, 1959), pp. 6 f.

"placidly accepting a corruption of bipartisan foreign policy which has turned it into a booby trap for both the Republican party and the country." These actions, he contended, would forfeit China to communism. He called upon Republicans to initiate a vigorous debate on foreign policies so that the issues would be placed before the country, which many were quick to do. Landon also reproved the President for insisting that congressional investigation of leaks of information to Russian agents was only a red herring. Then, during a visit to the White House, the Kansan told the President that the tideland oil reserves should be owned by the federal government. This idea was contrary to the 1948 Republican platform plank, but Landon believed the reserves belonged to the entire American people, not just to the states that bordered the offshore oil pools.[2]

Landon's chief public concern during the decade after 1948 was foreign affairs, and he repeatedly warned that the conflict between the communist and western countries would last a long time. "It would be as bad a mistake to believe that the end of the cold war is in sight" as it would be to believe "that a third world war was inevitable." As Landon saw it, the struggle necessitated the recruitment and training of scientists and technical personnel, which meant the United States had to provide money for educational programs—and use it efficiently.[3]

As international tensions steadily mounted after 1948, Landon approved the enlargement of America's armed forces. The build-up, however, would have to be conducted carefully, avoiding authoritarianism and national bankruptcy—particularly if Congress approved many of the President's requests for increased domestic expenditures. Although Landon conceded the desirability of "a comprehensive education program—decent racial relations—high health standards," he contended that a ceiling on federal expenditures was of paramount importance because the Marxists were "waiting for us to knock ourselves out through our own excesses." These excesses, he declared in 1949, could be in the form of greater federal expenditures, the increased power of the state, and inflationary pressures. "It is ruinous to assume that it is within our means adequately to prepare our

[2] *New York World-Telegram*, December 8, 1948; *Topeka Capital*, December 10, 12, 1948; *Washington Times-Herald*, December 12, 1948.

[3] E.g., Landon speeches: Manhattan and Topeka, March 31, 1955, and Salina, Kan., November 19, 1957, Alfred M. Landon Papers, in the possession of Alfred M. Landon. (All typescripts and manuscripts, unless otherwise identified, are in the Landon Papers, which, to 1949, can be found in the Kansas State Historical Society, Topeka. Those dated 1949 and later are in the possession of Alfred M. Landon.)

national defense and at the same time continue profligate spending for new and greater government services at home." [4]

Convinced, however, that mere rearmament was insufficient as a foreign policy, Landon proposed that the country express its willingness "to place all our vast atomic development under an international control." Further, the policy of "containing" communism was also of limited use; it, too, was a negative policy. But negativism could not be charged exclusively to the administration: "Our foreign relations are also disturbed by the purely negative talk of some Republican leaders." Landon strenuously disagreed that the United States should withdraw from the United Nations, believing this action—advocated by Senator Schoeppel and others—would be "playing into the Soviet's hands." Nor would ultimatums and threats—from Democrats or Republicans— maintain world peace. Rather than badger Russia, Landon suggested that the United States develop its own strength and that of its allies; even West Germany should be given permission to rearm. But even more important, the United States "should take a leaf from the Communists and talk peace—and not war." [5]

In June, 1950, the United States entered the Korean War, and Landon fully supported the "police action" and the President— unlike most Republicans, he praised Truman's decision. He thought the President should have consulted the Republicans beforehand, but "The President has reared back and said in effect—'Look—we have tried everything to get along with you people—now you are looking for trouble and we are going to act.' I applaud the raw courage of the President." [6]

Landon's wholehearted support of intervention in Korea probably was one of the bases for the rumors, circulated late in 1950, that Truman was considering inviting some Republicans, including Landon, into his cabinet. In response to an inquiry from Robert S. Allen, Landon wrote that the President should name a Republican, preferably one not closely identified with bipartisanship, either as Secretary of State or Secretary of Defense. Contrasting the situation with that of 1940, Landon wrote that he "would feel entirely different about going into Mr. Truman's cabinet . . . , if that remote possibility

---

[4] Landon to A. H. Kirchhofer, February 25, 1949; Landon speech, Topeka, April 30, 1949; *Los Angeles Examiner*, December 9, 1948; *Manhattan* (Kan.) *Mercury-Chronicle*, October 20, 1949.

[5] Landon speeches: Wichita, April 12, 1950, and Salina, February 25, 1952.

[6] Landon speech, Hamilton, N.Y., July 11, 1950.

should ever present itself," because the nation was at war; and he added that he trusted "Mr. Truman more than I did Mr. Roosevelt." An appointment, of course, was never offered, for President Truman fought the war without resorting to a coalition cabinet.[7]

As the war continued, Landon deplored the lack of support given the United States in Korea by other members of the United Nations. Although the United States could "do the job alone," he believed this would force the American people into militaristic isolationism. He opposed those who urged drastic military measures, particularly the use of the atomic bomb, saying this would be "like using a sledge hammer to drive home a tack."[8] Chinese armies swarmed into the fight, in late November, 1950, and pushed the United Nations forces back, but as resistance to the Chinese stiffened, Landon became convinced that the Communists could not conquer Korea because of their inability to supply their troops adequately. The key to their inadequacy was oil, which the Chinese lacked, and which was in short supply in Russia.

> Instead of America being pinned down in Korea, Russia is pinned down there. She can't abandon the Communists. As a matter of logistics, it is easier for us to supply our armies if we can hold the tip of the Korean peninsula with our superior firepower than it is for the Russians to supply the Chinese with trucks and gasoline in a quantity to feed an army of the size that they have in Korea.

This thinking caused Landon to fly in the face of strong Republican sentiment that the United States withdraw from Korea.

On January 29, 1951, at the Kansas Day meeting, Senator Joseph R. McCarthy called for America's withdrawal. Speaking two days later, Landon rebutted the harum-scarum Republican senator and backed the President's policy. The Kansan also backed the administration's proposal that the United Nations brand China an aggressor; he demanded, moreover, that the United Nations apply economic sanctions to China and that "the fetters" be taken off Chiang Kai-shek's forces on Formosa.[9]

Landon's disagreement with McCarthy pointed up his ambivalence about the extreme right wing in American politics, which had been

[7] Landon to Robert S. Allen, December 4, 1950.

[8] Landon interview with International News Service, July 25, 1950; Landon to Merryle S. Rukeyser, December 20, 1950.

[9] Landon to Deane W. Malott, January 4, 1951; *Topeka Capital*, February 1, 1951; Landon speech, Topeka, January 31, 1951.

symbolized by his absence at the Kansas Day dinner. But Landon also criticized the administration—particularly Secretary of State Dean Acheson—for permitting allies to profit from trade with communist nations while the United States was fighting a war against communism. He also criticized the President for relieving General Douglas MacArthur of command in Korea: the general had been "thrown on the junk pile for [his] convictions."[10]

His criticism of the administration and his eagerness to get information from a variety of sources led Landon into an extended correspondence with Alfred Kohlberg, one of the leaders of the radical right and the head of the so-called China Lobby, during the early 1950s. Landon's exaggerated phraseology and frequent criticism led many to believe that the Kansan was a radical, but when extremists approached him for public support, they were disappointed. When Kohlberg, for example, suggested that Soviet agents were influencing United States foreign policies, Landon asked "What's your proof?" and told Kohlberg and his associates that they must deal in facts. Although Landon sympathized with the radical right's demands to develop the strongest possible deterrents to war, to weed out communist conspirators in the United States, and to extend military and economic aid only to cooperating allies, he did not agree that the United States should withdraw its recognition of communist nations. He wrote Kohlberg in 1955: "I can see no advantage in that policy while there are many advantages for us to maintain diplomatic connections."[11] As Landon saw it, fighting the cold war demanded flexibility in both strategy and tactics.

Fairness, as well as flexibility, demanded ambivalence of Landon. Appearing before a bar association, Landon lauded the work of the House Un-American Activities Committee in exposing subversive threats to the Republic and urged citizens to cooperate with the committee, which he thought had "proved its value"—although he thought investigating committees should "set up some standards and principles of procedure." Of the most prominent right-winger, Senator McCarthy of Wisconsin, Landon wrote: "He owes much to his enemies. They have done more to build him in the minds of thousands of people than anything he has done himself." McCarthy's tactics, he thought, were "nothing but New Dealism. That is the end justifies the means." He found it ironic that "many of those now talking about

10 *Wichita Eagle*, April 24, 1951; Landon speech, Kansas City, Mo., April 24, 1951.
11 Landon to Alfred Kohlberg, May 7, 1951, January 21, 1955.

McCarthyism applauded as delightful such epithets as princes of privilege, economic royalists, tories, reactionaries, and applied them liberally to everyone who disagreed with the New Deal." [12] Although the Kansan thought McCarthy had uncovered some vital information, he felt that the senator's temperament and his bull-dozing tactics had "greatly weakened his usefulness." When in 1954 the permanent Senate Subcommittee on Investigations refereed the struggle between McCarthy and the army over alleged communist infiltration of the service, Landon urged the discontinuance of the hearings, not only because they were hurting the party but because the trend of opinion seemed to be in favor of McCarthy. [13]

Landon made several attempts to regain political strength after 1948, but all were unsuccessful. In 1949 there was talk of joining his forces with those of Senator Clyde M. Reed and of backing Reed for reelection and Willard Mayberry for governor; but the proposal collapsed with Reed's death in November, 1949. Landon's opponents in state politics were further strengthened by the appointment of national committeeman Harry Darby as Reed's successor in the Senate, and the understanding that Governor Carlson would run for the post in the 1950 election. Despite the failure to form a coalition, Landon in 1950 contested the dominant Republican element in Kansas by supporting Mayberry in the gubernatorial primary, against Attorney General Edward Arn, and former national American Legion commander Harry Colmery, against Carlson. Although Mayberry and Colmery were defeated in the primary, Landon said he would vote for the Republican ticket because of his belief that "the preservation of our Republic depends upon the election of Republicans to office." He made it clear, however, that he disapproved the party's promise of additional and expanded government services with no indications of how they would be financed. [14]

Although he was the hobgoblin of Kansas Republicanism, Landon tried to maintain friendly relations with Thomas E. Dewey, the

[12] Landon speech, Topeka, January 11, 1949, Landon to J. P. Kassebaum, April 20, 1953.

[13] Landon to Whittley Austin, June 18, 1954; *Newsweek*, August 10, 1953, p. 42; Landon to Karl E. Mundt, April 28, May 8, 1954.

[14] *Kansas City Star*, November 9, December 9, 1949; *Topeka State Journal*, December 8, 14, 1949, March 16, 1950; Landon to Burton Bigelow, December 16, 1949; Landon speech, Topeka, September 28, 1950.

national party's titular head. In January, 1949, he predicted Dewey's renomination and reelection as governor of New York, because the people would "be begging Dewey to run." After Dewey won the renomination in 1950, Landon wrote that if he won the election—as the Kansan thought he would—Dewey would be a potent factor in deciding the 1952 presidential nomination, and might even be the nominee.[15]

Landon, however, was not sanguine about the Republican party's chances in 1952. The party had "lost its position. And there has been far too much ratification of the New Deal"; only Senator Robert A. Taft had given the party "a sense of direction." Landon therefore returned to the belief that a coalition of Republicans and Democrats might bring about a change in government, and he was encouraged by the development of Republican and conservative Democratic opposition to Truman's spending programs. "No one expected the Eighty-first Congress to slow up President Truman's fascist proposals as it has heretofore done. But we must send the coalition that has done such a good job some reinforcements in the 1950 elections if they are to continue to hold the line." An apparent revival of Republican en-thusiasm and the results of the 1950 elections further heartened him. He was gladdened by the primary-election defeats of liberal Demo-cratic Senators Claude Pepper of Florida, Frank Graham of North Carolina and Glen Taylor of Idaho, and by the fact that "many of the Democrat candidates in the fall elections openly repudiated the main points of the President's legislative program." The Kansan was also pleased that Robert Taft, in running for reelection to the Senate, had "carried all the industrial counties in Ohio except two. . . . The labor bosses have not been able to convince the rank-and-file of the soundness of the Truman policies and his administration."[16]

As 1952 approached, talk of Dwight D. Eisenhower for President increased. The draft-Eisenhower idea, which Landon could not put over in 1947, became popular in 1951 and 1952; but Landon would have no part of it. Indeed, in 1951 he had serious reservations about Eisenhower—probably because his political enemies in Kansas were

[15] Landon to A. H. Kirchhofer, January 14, 1949; Landon to Thomas E. Dewey, September 6, 1950, Thomas E. Dewey Papers, University of Rochester Libraries, Rochester, N.Y.

[16] Landon to Burton Bigelow, December 16, 1949; Landon to Walter Aldridge, January 4, 1950; Landon to Robert Humphreys, July 7, 1950; Landon to Raymond Moley, November 28, 1949, November 9, 1950.

enthusiastic about the general. If Eisenhower was successful as the commander of SHAPE (Supreme Headquarters, Allied Powers, Europe), Landon asked in July, 1951, "how can the Republicans make any campaign in criticism of Truman's foreign policy? The more we brag about Eisenhower's achievements in Europe, the more the ultimate credit reflects on Truman." By October, Landon was reciting his objections at length. Eisenhower was an integral part of the Roosevelt and Truman administrations. "High taxes and spending are going to be a big issue [and] if there was ever a military man who gave any consideration to economy and efficiency or to the waste of manpower in terms of dollars, I never knew him or heard him." There had been a deterioration of America's defenses while Eisenhower had been the army Chief of Staff after World War II. If the general left his post at SHAPE to seek the nomination, it gave Truman the opportunity of saying Eisenhower was abandoning his post during a national crisis or that he had not performed his duties adequately. Eisenhower's views on the issues—even his political affiliation—were unknown. And, if he were elected, the general might rely too heavily on the military for assistance.

Landon thought he would probably support Taft, but again he had reservations: "I don't know that Taft will spark [the necessary] enthusiasm. . . . He seems to have the unhappy facility of either not adequately stating his position or being misquoted in occasional press conferences."[17] By the spring of 1952, Landon thought Eisenhower "missed the boat" by his withdrawal from the presidential primaries of seven states, in which the votes of more than 300 delegates would be decided. When it was announced, in May, that Eisenhower would return from Europe to fight for the nomination, Landon thought the general would "attempt to duck on a lot of embarrassing questions. If he does, I am going to be greatly disappointed in him. . . . I cannot take a pig in the poke." Landon made his decision within a few days: he would support Taft.

With Eisenhower's return to the United States, Landon's resolve was strengthened; confusion seemed to underlie the general's press conferences and speeches, and the fellow Kansan did not seem to be of presidential timber. Landon wrote Mrs. Helen Reid, in response to her request that he support Eisenhower:

> I am still confused on the General's position on some highly important issues. For illustration, he said last week in New York that he was not for

[17] Landon to A. H. Kirchhofer, July 28, October 26, 1951.

farm subsidies. The A.P. report today from Denver says he does not know for sure, but he thinks he favors farm price-support without controls of production. If that is not subsidy, I do not know what it is. I do not know any more devastating policy as far as the United States Treasury is concerned. Yet, he is going to reduce appropriations [$]40 billion.

As the date of the Republican national convention drew nearer, many of Landon's friends pleaded with him to support Eisenhower, and criticized him for supporting Taft because of the reactionary elements that surrounded the Senator. Landon's response was that Eisenhower had not been impressive in his appeals to the country, and that Taft should not be condemned because of his followers: "After all, he cannot kick them in the teeth and tell them to go away." [18]

Landon was again on the losing side. He was unable to win the Kansas delegation for Taft because the appeal of another Kansan being nominated for President was too strong. In the national convention the general's forces overwhelmed Taft's. Although Landon thought Eisenhower's victory would turn out to be a "Pyrrhic victory" for the party, he wrote "There is only one thing for us to do, and that is we must all put our shoulders to the wheel and work for Eisenhower's election."

But Landon took no part in the campaign; he neither asked nor was invited to participate. Eisenhower's campaign organization probably viewed him as a vengeful, diehard conservative, and Landon thought the general was the big-business candidate. Nor was he impressed by Eisenhower's campaigning; Landon referred to the nominee's speeches and rallies as "amateur nights." He found it difficult, after five successive Republican defeats, to believe that Eisenhower would be elected President. He would only venture—in October—to say that it looked like Eisenhower would be elected, but he added that anything could happen. [19] The general, of course, was elected by a substantial majority, and Landon was more left out than ever. Unlike Truman, Eisenhower did not speak the same political language as Landon.

[18] Landon to Merryle S. Rukeyser, March 28, 1952; Landon to Sterling Morton, April 4, 1952; Landon to Carl A. Rott, May 15, 1952; Landon to Robert A. Taft, May 19, 1952; Landon to Roy Howard, June 10, 1952; Landon to Helen Reid, June 17, 1952; Landon to Don L. Berry, June 25, 1952.
[19] *Topeka State Journal*, April 11, May 23, 1952; Landon to Sterling Morton, July 17, August 28, 1952; Landon to A. H. Kirchhofer, July 18, 1952; Landon to William Hard, October 10, 1952.

With the general's election, Kansas' Republican leaders rubbed their hands in anticipation of patronage. One of the first major appointments was that of C. Wesley Roberts, the former state chairman, as the chairman of the Republican national committee—an ill-advised move for an administration that said it would be "as clean as a hound's tooth." Roberts, in 1951, had been instrumental in getting the state of Kansas to purchase the Ancient Order of United Workmen hospital for $110,000, a building that under an earlier agreement would soon have become state property without cost. For this service to the A.O.U.W., Roberts received a commission of $11,000 (Roberts said that he served only in a "public relations" capacity).[20] Early in February, 1953, Alvin S. McCoy—in the *Kansas City Star*—and state senator William D. Weigand and Lieutenant Governor Fred Hall—both Republicans—charged that the national chairman's hands were not clean.

Landon immediately joined the battle, declaring Roberts was the Kansas equivalent of the "five per center" peddlers of political favors whom Republicans had inveighed against during the campaign. Landon, who became the most active of those who worked for Roberts' removal as national committee chairman, sent material on Roberts to leading newspapermen—and especially to Colonel Robert S. Allen, who circulated the material on Capitol Hill and shared it with his former partner, Drew Pearson, the controversial news commentator. Landon also publicly contested a White House statement of confidence in Roberts.

> President Eisenhower's satisfaction with the ridiculous explanation of National Republican Chairman C. Wesley Roberts for his prostituting of his political influence in a raid on the public treasury of Kansas, which stinks to high heaven, does not satisfy the people of Kansas by a long shot. Furthermore, it is unpleasantly reminiscent of the loose standards of public honesty and morality which the people of America voted to change in the last election.

Landon became increasingly angry as the affair went on. Because the out-of-state news media—and, surprisingly, the Democrats—largely ignored the charges, Landon thought there was a conspiracy to smother all derogatory information about the national chairman. He was further irritated because Roberts would not resign.

The campaign against Roberts dragged on through February and into March. Kansas press opinion became increasingly hostile, and a

[20] *Washington Post*, January 18, February 14, 23, 1953.

committee of the legislature was assigned to investigate the affair, despite the opposition of Governor Arn. The national committee and the Republicans in Congress were said to be uneasy, thinking the party might be defending a man who had done the same type of thing for which it had belabored Democrats during the Truman administration. In the middle of March the state legislative committee unanimously condemned Roberts' lobbying procedures—"spiritual rape" of the law one newspaper called it. Roberts was pressed to resign by national committee members, Republican congressmen, and newspapers. As the *Washington Post* said, "His usefulness to the Republican party is at an end"; and Roberts quit the chairmanship on March 27.[21]

One result of this affair was that Kansas received little patronage from the Eisenhower administration, and the state organization took a dimmer view of Landon than ever before. Moreover, a punitive campaign was directed against the politicians and journalists who had been involved in revealing Roberts' background, especially against Lieutenant Governor Fred Hall, attorney general Harold Fatzer, state committee chairman C. I. Moyer, and Alvin McCoy—who the following year received a Pulitzer prize for his reporting of the scandal.[22] At the same time, public reaction to the Roberts affair gave Landon and the Republican mavericks a political opportunity. Fred Hall, a liberal Republican who had opposed Darby and Arn in winning the lieutenant governorship in 1952, challenged the organization for the governorship, and Landon and former Governor Payne Ratner joined the Young Turks in the legislature to support Hall. Their campaign, begun late in 1953, carried through to victory in the gubernatorial primary in August, 1954, and in the general election in November.[23]

Hall, however, was an unpopular governor—as Landon put it, "He talks to people, not with people"—and his independence, which had made him a perfect candidate for combating the organization, contributed to his unpopularity. Landon defended Hall, saying he was

[21] Landon to A. H. Kirchhofer, February 14, 1953; *Washington Post*, February 28, March 14, 19, 20, 22, 28, 1953; *Topeka Capital*, March 28, 1953; Landon to James C. Hagerty, February 17, 1953; Landon to Sterling Morton, February 21, 1953; Landon to Robert S. Allen, February 13, 17, 27, March 12, 14, 19, 1953; Allen to Landon, February 23, 1953.

[22] *Wichita Eagle*, October 21, 1953.

[23] Landon to William Weigand, John C. Woelk, Philip J. Doyle, John Anderson, and Dillard C. Croxton, February 2, 1954; Landon to William Weigand, October 12, 1954.

"doing a good job for the state," but he realized that the young governor's lack of cooperation with the legislature *and* the organization would cost him renomination. Landon again supported Hall in 1956, although he believed the governor would be defeated in the primary by an alliance of the Darby-Arn forces and his former supporters, who had been disillusioned by his temperament. Hall was defeated in the primary, but the victorious Republican nominee, Warren Shaw, was defeated in the general election by George E. Docking, who became Kansas' first Democratic governor in twenty years.[24]

In national politics, Landon maintained formal loyalty to the Eisenhower administration but did not esteem the President, largely because he believed that party loyalty and discipline—the essentials of effective administration—did not mean much to Eisenhower. After Eisenhower's heart attack, in 1955, it appeared that the Republicans would have to seek a new presidential nominee the following year. Landon, who thought Eisenhower should not run again—that the burdens of the Presidency were too great for one whose health had been even slightly impaired—considered Chief Justice Earl Warren the best candidate, though Vice President Richard Nixon and Harold Stassen were also acceptable.[25]

Landon also had reservations about his party's health: "The Republican party is going the way of the Whig party which failed to develop a basic philosophy in keeping with the problems of government." He also believed that if Eisenhower ran for reelection he might be defeated because of the political liabilities of his administration, especially Secretary of Agriculture Ezra Taft Benson and Secretary of State John Foster Dulles. Nevertheless, after Eisenhower's decision to run, Landon publicly predicted that the President and Nixon would be reelected, because "this time we're 'in' and have the prosperity issue." He also cited "the critical foreign situation, confidence in Mr. Eisenhower, [and] peace issues."[26]

After the 1956 elections Landon was still regarded with disfavor by the national administration, and he had no significant influence in

[24] Landon to Whittley Austin, March 27, 1956; Landon to Leila Elliott, July 31, 1956.

[25] Landon to Joseph W. Martin, September 24, 1953; Landon to George Rothwell Brown, May 26, 1955; Landon to Louis Marx, January 10, 1956; Landon to Doris Fleeson, October 26, 1955; Landon to Leonard E. Thomas, October 21, 1955.

[26] Landon to Sterling Morton, January 31, 1956; Landon to Barry Faris, December 29, 1955; *Denver Post*, August 12, 1956.

Kansas because a Democrat held the governorship. Among the state's Republicans, however, he enjoyed increasing favor. His role in the Roberts affair and his sponsorship of Hall in 1954 had created new respect for him among his opponents, and moderate and maverick Kansas Republicans came to look upon him as their elder statesman. Moreover, having lost the governorship, Republican leaders felt compelled to restrain their quarreling in order to regain control of the state. There was even talk of Landon for governor, which Landon privately and publicly discouraged. In 1958 he supported publisher Clyde M. Reed, Jr., the late senator's son, for governor. Reed won the Republican nomination easily, but was buried in a Docking landslide in the general election. Landon, however regretfully, had predicted this result, as Governor Docking was able to rally Democratic voters and attract Republican conservatives with his policy of "fiscal sanity."[27] Landon would not find a winning candidate for governor until 1960.

After Eisenhower's 1952 election Landon tried to summarize the voters' expectations of the new administration. The President-elect should seek national unity: "There has been too much deliberate nursing of hate between different groups of Americans, either for short-term political benefits or for long-term Communist aims seeking the ultimate destruction of our great and beloved Republic." A high level of honesty was expected of the administration, which would set "the tone for morality in public office . . . throughout the nation." And the Western democratic countries should be instilled with a new spirit of "working together instead of huddling together."

After Eisenhower had been in office ninety days, Landon evaluated his Presidency as "slowly but vigorously and surely making definite progress in fulfilling the major platform pledges of the Republican party of adequate military force—a sound dollar—lower taxes—elimination of socialistic expansion of government—and a peaceful, even though it be uneasy, world." His only criticism of the administration in April (he tactfully ignored the Roberts affair) was its handling of party matters; Landon thought the administration had been inept in collaborating on policy decisions with Senator Taft, speaker Martin, and other Republican leaders in Congress.[28]

[27] *Wichita Eagle*, June 30, 1957; Landon to Lee Larrabee, October 14, 1957; Landon to G. H. Wilson, April 21, 1958; Landon to Ray Johnson, October 27, 1958.
[28] Landon speeches, Topeka, January 7 and April 10, 1953.

Despite his acknowledgments, Landon was distressed by Secretary of State John Foster Dulles; and the new government had scarcely taken office before Landon wrote that he did not like Dulles' policy of delivering ultimatums. The problem, as Landon saw it, was that Dulles "did not leave himself any apparent ground for maneuvering. This has contributed materially to further division among the free states." By the summer of 1954, Landon was so irritated by Dulles' tactics that he publicly charged the administration's "startling, ominous, and belligerent statements" had "alienated world opinion and support." America's need to meet force with force did not justify rushing to the brink of war in every crisis, with the possibility of skittering over the edge. Instead of this policy, the Kansan urged, the United States should make better use of the United Nations in dealing with international disputes and Americans should reveal "the real America" to the world.[29]

During the summer of 1954, Landon differed with his party's attitude on another issue: right-to-work legislation. These measures, which were to come before a number of states for adoption, provided that workers could not be compelled to join trade unions; in effect, they outlawed the union shop. "It is plain," Landon said, "that the right-to-work legislation interferes with the rights of both labor and management and is another example of the pernicious paternalistic theory that government can tell both business and labor what [they have] to do to be wise and competent in the management of their own affairs." Although Landon condemned the proposals, he believed in the "right of the public to be protected from harassment and violence and loss of essential services through labor strife." The answer to the problem, he said, could be found in an adaptation—with the right of appeal—of Kansas' Industrial Relations Court, which had had the power to decide industrial disputes.[30] The right-to-work issue increasingly became a compelling issue for Landon as many states adopted the legislation. Landon's concern over heightened government interference in labor-management affairs finally led him to repudiate his suggestion of an industrial court.

Foreign affairs, however, were still the Kansan's main interest. Although during the Korean War he had called for a blockade "by all the free governments of the world of all the slave states," after the war

[29] Landon to Sam M. Jones, January 21, 1953; Landon to Lester F. Kimmel, March 31, 1954; Landon speech, Kansas City, Mo., June 15, 1954.

[30] Landon speech, Topeka, July 7, 1954.

he contended that channels between East and West must be kept open. In 1953 he called for consideration of communist China's admission to the United Nations as a way of possibly detaching it from the influence of the Kremlin; and he thought the United States should be willing to enter negotiations with the communist nations. Consistent with this view, Landon refused to sign the petition of the One Million Against Admission of Communist China to the United Nations. As a result, the former Secretary of the Navy, Charles Edison, the organization's treasurer, called upon Kansas to repudiate Landon. Landon retorted by saying the group's ideas were based on "emotionalism." [31]

In October, 1954, Landon—motivated in part by the partisanship of the congressional elections—viewed Eisenhower's foreign policy favorably. He thought the administration, at the international conferences in London and Paris (which led to German rearmament), had produced "unity out of discord—decision in place of indecision—strength in place of weakness—victory out of defeat." The new accord among Western nations might be "the beginning of the effective building towards America's goal for the free world—security and peace by an administration that knows how [to do it]." Landon, by this time, had also changed his mind about Chiang Kai-shek's belligerency. In response to an appeal from the Chicago Committee on the Far Eastern Crisis for help in developing pressure for a cease-fire between the two Chinas, and for the admission of Red China to the United Nations, Landon sent the text of his speeches and a press interview for the committee's use; he also volunteered additional help. [32]

Although his general support of the government's foreign policy on the eve of the 1954 congressional elections may have seemed like campaign talk, Landon was genuinely pleased with the pattern of world events during and after the fall of 1954. When Soviet Premier Georgi Malenkov resigned, in February, 1955, Landon told the press: "It is a world-shaking event. It is evidence of the breaking up of the ruling tyranny of the slave states." He was most impressed that a tyranny had permitted a top leader to live after a major political upheaval, which he thought reflected considerable dissension in the Soviet bloc that would encourage even wider divisions of opinion. The Geneva Conference of heads of state, in July, and President Eisenhower's proposal

[31] Landon speech, Oskaloosa, Kan., December 27, 1951; Landon to Raymond Moley, November 24, 1953; *Topeka State Journal*, February 23, 1954.

[32] Landon to F. A. Miller, October 25, 1954; Harry Barnard to Landon, January 31, 1955; Landon to Barnard, January 31, 1955.

for "Open Skies" and the exchange of aerial information, "broke through the maze of propaganda and diplomatic maneuvers to the common peoples. They were thrilled with its potentialities." He was also pleased with Soviet Premier Nikolai Bulganin's counterproposal of ground inspection of armaments. In October, despite the lingering atmosphere of mistrust among the nations, Landon urged continued exploration of disarmament. He also recommended three principles that might further contribute to world peace: " 1. A stable government, responsible to its obligations. 2. Freedom of [exchange of] information and [of] travel. 3. The freest possible exchange of goods and services." [33]

Landon thought there was a steady improvement of world conditions in 1955 and 1956: the Austrian Peace Treaty, the rearming of West Germany, the admission of Spain to the anti-communist alliance, the relaxation of the China situation, increasing travel of Westerners behind the Iron Curtain, freer exchanges of ideas, the establishment of the South East Asia Treaty Organization, the increasing strength of Western countries, and the overthrow of a communist government in Guatemala. All this seemed to prove Landon's conviction that, although the United States had to be vigilant and armed, the nation must realize that communist truculence was not always insuperable. Distrust of Russia must not become "a conditioned reflex" that would force the United States to neglect opportunities that might end the cold war. [34]

The Kansan discerned favorable omens even in Russia's brutal repression of the Hungarian revolution of 1956: it "shook Communist circles the world over," and was related to the reaction that forced the Russian government to disavow the worst aspects of Stalinism. "Public opinion is more of a factor today than heretofore in Russia and its colonies." He was also pleased by the frustration of the Anglo-French invasion of Egypt in October, 1956: "For the first time in the life of mankind, collective security stopped two major powers' invasion of a smaller and weaker country." These were signs, Landon told a college group in May, 1957, that the message of Norman Angell's 1913 book, *The Great Illusion*, was being received at last. As the Kansan put it, "Wars are the product of the stupidity, cupidity, the arrogance,

---

[33] Landon to Felix Morley, February 10, 1955; Landon speech, Wichita, October 21, 1955.

[34] Landon to Robert S. Allen, March 27, 1956; Landon to Dorothy Thompson, June 29, 1956.

or the fanaticism of the Napoleons, the Kaisers, the Hitlers of the world."[35]

Landon believed that the United States could not relax its guard: peace could be found only if security was maintained. And fortunately for world peace, the enemy weakened as the West grew stronger. Everything seemed to indicate that Russia was in a poor position for pursuing belligerent policies; internal pressures and the West's strength forced the Soviet Union to loosen state controls at home and to seek peaceful coexistence with the rest of the world.[36] This meant permanent peace was possible if the United States was wise enough to recognize that the Russians knew they could not "afford" a war with the West. The solution was to avoid placing ourselves or the Soviets in a position where war was the only out. This solution demanded that the United States—though maintaining its defenses—do everything possible to encourage a relaxation of tensions between the East and the West.

[35] Landon speech, Topeka, May 31, 1957.
[36] Landon to Eliahu Ben-Horin, July 8, 1957.

CHAPTER 23

Elder Statesman

The decade of rustication ended in 1958, when Landon, because of the intensity of his feelings on the issues, took vigorous measures for making his views known. Another factor was that he regained some stature as a political leader when the moderate and liberal Republicans in Kansas took over the party machinery, in 1958, and the governorship, in 1960. And his growth as an elder statesman was enhanced by the fascination of political observers that, as the *Wichita Eagle* put it, "Landon has been known as a conservative, but the label has refused to stay pinned on him." [1]

Landon's new vigor was seen in his foreign-policy pronouncements. Although he approved President Eisenhower's peace statements, he deplored what he considered was the administration's inconsistent foreign policy. In 1958 he suggested: "Somebody ought to write a song 'What's Our Wandering Foreign Policy Tonight'." Landon thought American foreign policy should be explicit, that "we must not make the mistake of either purely negative thinking or letting our guard down." To those who were pessimistic because of the long duration of the cold war, he said: "When you stop talking, you start fighting. Peaceful relations between neighborhoods and countries are never established by threats of force or the use of force." The United States, in Landon's view, should make it clear that although the

[1] *Wichita Eagle*, May 7, 1963.

country was prepared to fight aggression it was also eager to lay the foundations for permanent peace.[2]

In January, 1958, Landon created his first great stir since the crusade against national chairman Roberts: before a meeting at Minneola, Kansas, of some 300 school teachers, he called for the replacement of John Foster Dulles as Secretary of State. Landon blasted Dulles—for his

> negative attitude on discussions with the Soviet—[for his] massive retaliation—ultimatums—[and] brinkmanship policies. While Secretary Dulles is boasting about them at the front door—the Soviet is making important and significant gains at the back door.... Secretary of State Dulles' adamant stand against a meeting at the summit with the Soviet because he doubts their sincerity—is taking the world down a dangerous road that threatens disaster for all mankind. Therefore, the first requirement of a positive constructive instead of a negative foreign policy—a policy that does not leave the initiative always in the Soviet's hands—is a new Secretary of State.[3]

The United States should maintain an effective military defense and yet be willing to negotiate with the Soviets; this was the basis of Landon's foreign-policy views. He also believed that the country could not allow other nations to determine its foreign policy. When President Eisenhower announced support of nationalist China in its defense of the islands of Quemoy and Matsu, Landon wrote it was "horrible for us to get into a position where the Nationalist Chinese can declare war for us"; the only winner in such a situation, he thought, would be communist China. He reacted calmly to communist activities. He knew that the repeated threats to the status of West Berlin could lead to war, but he was convinced such crises had value for the free world. Russia's 1959 ultimatum to the Western powers "to get out of Berlin or else," the Red Chinese takeover of Tibet, and the Soviet pressures on Iraq dramatized—for neutrals as well as anti-communists—the menace of communist aggression, which could only bolster resistance to Red aggrandizement.[4]

[2] Landon to Arthur Peine, October 3, 1958; Press statement, September 28, 1959; Landon speech, Topeka, February 15, 1958, Alfred M. Landon Papers, in the possession of Alfred M. Landon.

[3] *Christian Science Monitor*, January 15, 1958; Landon speech, Minneola, Kan., January 13, 1958.

[4] Landon to Leonard E. Thomas, September 15, 1958; Landon speech, Topeka, April 9, 1959.

The United States, however, needed to do more than maintain anti-communist defenses in order to maintain world peace. As the Kansan saw it, international control of armaments, particularly of nuclear weapons, was essential. He was given an opportunity to discuss these views when the Committee for a Sane Nuclear Policy, headed by Norman Cousins of *The Saturday Review*, arranged for him to speak—along with Mrs. Eleanor Roosevelt, Walter Reuther, Norman Thomas, and Governor G. Mennen Williams of Michigan—at a mass meeting in Madison Square Garden on May 19, 1960. World tension was especially strong: it had just been revealed that an American U–2 reconnaissance plane had been shot down over Russia, and in Paris, after the United States had originally attempted to disclaim responsibility for the flight, Soviet Premier Nikita Khrushchev canceled a summit conference with President Eisenhower. Landon saw his role at the New York rally as that of speaking common sense at a moment of crisis—in his first speech in the east since 1950.

He went before the audience of 17,000 as a politically conservative representative of those who wanted to overcome the threat of nuclear war, and pointed out the risks of the atomic age: a war there was "no adequate way of surviving," which could be set off in an instant by democratic or by communist nations—a war that was increasingly likely as more nations acquired atomic weapons, or the ghastly alternative of generations of children deformed by fall-out from the "preparation to fight a war that might never occur." These perils must be avoided, but "unilateral action by the United States would be the height of folly"—and at this point he was booed by a bloc of "better Red than dead" believers. "Multilateral action with questionable controls would be absurd. Equally ridiculous is the thinking that if the free world alone lays down its atomic weapons—others will automatically do likewise."

The solution, Landon declared, was

> to seek and agree upon a realistic nuclear-policy relationship between nations by definite treaties controlling atomic tests and the employment of nuclear energy as a blessing instead of a curse to mankind.

The crisis caused by the failure of the Paris summit meeting, he said, could lead to war, but it should not be overlooked that Khrushchev

> has political pressures to contend with, both abroad and at home. Furthermore, he is proud of the new factories, dams, schools built in the U.S.S.R. in the past ten years at great human cost. He would not happily see them

destroyed overnight. I am also sure that even Khrushchev, or at least Mrs. Khrushchev, would recoil at the thought of deformed or sterile great-grandchildren.

Landon called for another meeting, as soon as possible, of the heads of state of the atomic powers to pursue a settlement of the nuclear crisis.[5]

Agreement by the atomic powers on nuclear weapons, Landon knew, was not enough: world government was necessary for peace and for justice. When in April, 1959, Vice President Nixon had urged a re-examination of America's self-imposed bar against membership in the International Court of Justice, Landon agreed; but he disagreed with Nixon that the United States could establish the rule of law in the world if it reserved "the right to determine what are domestic matters." The court, to be effective, would have to decide "what are or are not domestic matters," and would have to include all nations—even Red China—in its jurisdiction. Such a broadening of the court's jurisdiction would be a "slow and evolutionary process," but the United States should begin by "trying to orient the world to the idea that it had better get used to abiding by accepted laws—or else there won't be any world left."[6]

His conviction of the need for urgency in pursuing world peace led Landon to argue expansion of the powers of the United Nations, and he told a luncheon of the Daughters of the American Revolution—in Topeka, on June 11, 1960—"There is no room for juvenile senti-mentality at the present time, just hard facts." Although the United States was bound to resist communist aggression with force, defensive action by one nation was insufficient to preclude catastrophe—for that nation or for the world. The General Assembly of the United Nations "holds the key if we participate in a clearly defined policy to make it the central and key body in the United Nations." Stipulating that membership in the United Nations must be open to all nations, Landon said the General Assembly should be made responsible for the economic development of underdeveloped countries, for immediate and effective international disarmament, for the internationalization of major trouble spots and strategic positions, and for examining govern-ments' "statements and charges" and censuring "any member nation for verbal acts of war." The General Assembly should be empowered

[5] *Topeka Capital*, May 9, 20, 1960; Landon to W. David Ferguson, May 25, 1960; Landon speech, New York, May 19, 1960.
[6] Landon speech, Manhattan, Kan., May 28, 1959.

to "expose the truth to the world and act to maintain a climate conducive to peace."[7]

The Kansan knew his proposals were idealistic, but he was convinced that idealism was essential: if people did not talk peace they were unlikely to act for peace. Although Landon believed world government or the peaceful adjudication of all international disputes would not be developed in his lifetime, he thought such a body or process would never be developed if the United States did not add a positive program for world cooperation to its defensive policies.

Right-to-work legislation, which he opposed, was one of the domestic issues behind Landon's emergence as an elder statesman. He was not, as some charged, "tender on the subject of labor"; he believed many labor leaders were "making the same mistake that business had made too frequently, of pursuing a 'public be damned' policy." Landon, however, did not think that additional public regulation would solve the problem. He was not opposed to regulation in theory, but he thought the labor-regulation being sought was of a repressive or punitive nature. Until there were signs that regulative legislation would be fair to all parties, the development of a sense of public responsibility among labor leaders was the only approach to the problem.[8]

In 1958, when the Kansas legislature submitted a right-to-work proposal to the voters as a constitutional amendment, Landon opposed the move; he also sought an alternative. In June, in a letter to Charles P. Taft—one of the few nationally prominent Republicans who was also opposed to right-to-work legislation—Landon suggested that a national study committee be formed of "fair-minded" representatives from the National Association of Manufacturers, the United States Chamber of Commerce, and organized labor. At the same time, he issued a statement that the AFL–CIO could use in the states where right-to-work legislation was an issue:

> There is no greater domestic problem today than working out sound relations involving the public, employees, managements, in our complex industrial economy. But these so-called right-to-work laws are not the answer. [America] needs strong unions, not weak. Strong unions mean leadership with a sense of public responsibility. Weak unions mean rabble-rousing leadership.

[7] Landon speech, Topeka, June 11, 1960.
[8] Landon to Thomas McNally, November 18, 1957.

And weak unions—and more labor unrest—would be the result of right-to-work laws.

There was also political reasoning behind the Kansan's position. He differed with Senate minority leader William F. Knowland of California, who encouraged right-to-work legislation, and urged him to develop a sympathetic approach to labor's problems. The political aspect of the issue hurt the Republican party, he said, and he gave Kansas as an illustration: "Two years ago we drove thousands of votes into the Democrat party by blanket abuse of all labor leaders as 'goons' and 'racketeers.'"[9]

In the fall of 1958, when the chief issue before the Kansas voters was the proposed right-to-work amendment, Landon decided upon a one-man campaign against the amendment. At his own expense, he made a speaking tour to six of the smaller cities of the state. September 24 was a hot day, but the 71-year-old former governor campaigned for fifteen hours; he traveled almost 300 miles and spoke to about 500 people. The legislature, he said, should have decided the state's labor policy, and not foisted the decision upon the voters. Moreover, the amendment "puts our government in a strait-jacket. It puts Kansas in a position of attempting to settle for all time what the world has not been able to settle up to now." (At five of his six stops, Landon was heckled by an employer-association manager from Toledo, Ohio, but Landon told his listeners: "He doesn't bother me—I've been heckled by experts.") This tour helped put Landon back in the public eye—there was public interest about the conservative bogeyman's campaigning in support of organized labor—but it was not enough to defeat the amendment.[10]

Landon's interest in labor matters continued after the 1958 elections. Speaking to the state AFL–CIO convention in July, 1959, he argued the need for mass unionism as a "needed check and balance on economic power in our nation's life"; and he praised labor leaders for supporting civic improvements and for effectively opposing communism. He said, however, that organized labor should reconsider its support of increased governmental expenditures, which would lead

[9] Landon to Charles P. Taft, June 2, 1958; Press statement, June, 1958; Landon to William F. Knowland, June 27, 1958.

[10] Landon speeches: Junction City, Clay Center, Washington, Marysville, Frankfort, and Manhattan, Kan., September 24, 1958; *Topeka Capital*, September 25, 1958; *Lawrence* (Kan.) *Journal-World*, September 25, 1958; Landon to Peter Jacoby, October 30, 1958.

only to inflation. Inflation, he warned, robbed labor, which had no hedge in the form of land, stock, or merchandise. Later, before the Junction City Chamber of Commerce, he said that if labor and business did not settle their differences the government would have to act to protect the people. The result would be a "totalitarian state," which no one wanted. But he did not blame the government for this possibility so much as business, which had "time after time forced upon the government the necessity of taking more and more power" to deal with the problems that business refused to meet.[11]

Although Landon had become increasingly independent on issues, he was still vitally interested in his party, and he was particularly concerned that its behavior should not ensure its defeat in future elections. After 1958, when Republicans for the third consecutive election lost congressional seats, Landon categorized the party's liabilities: "The Republican party is now tagged with one group as an anti-labor group; with a second group as an anti-farmer party; [with] the third group as being no different from the Democratic party on basic issues." It could not, he thought, oppose everything or favor everything; it must stand for basic principles—such as sound money, *fair* regulation of the worst labor abuses, strengthened collective bargaining, and the end of subsidization of agriculture. He regarded the January, 1959, election of Barry Goldwater as chairman of the Republican Senate campaign committee and of Charles Halleck as House minority leader as indications of a lack of realism in the party leadership.[12]

By the spring of 1959, Landon became interested in the selection of the party's presidential nominee for the 1960 election. Support was already developing for Governor Nelson Rockefeller, and Landon tended to agree with the New Yorker's contention that the front-runner, Vice President Nixon, could not be elected President. The Kansan liked Rockefeller because of his courage in demanding that expenditures be covered by taxes—and he probably thought Rockefeller would be more flexible on foreign policy than Nixon. But the Rockefeller-for-President campaign did not progress rapidly enough, as Landon saw it, and in October he concluded that Nixon had the

[11] Landon speeches: Topeka, July 16, 1959, and Junction City, Kan., November 19, 1959.

[12] Landon to Meyer Miles, December 24, 1958; Landon to Warren Zimmerman, December 26, 1958; Landon to James A. McCain, January 27, 1959; Landon to John M. Henry, January 20, 1959.

nomination sewn up. Landon foresaw the possibility of a Nixon-Rockefeller ticket: if the ticket won, Rockefeller could exert a salutary influence on government; if it lost, his nomination for the Vice Presidency would give the New Yorker an edge for the presidential nomination of 1964. By spring, however, when it was obvious that Rockefeller was not interested in accepting second place on the ticket, Landon backed Fred Seaton (one of his aides in 1936) for the vice-presidential nomination. He described Seaton, who was then Secretary of the Interior, as "amply qualified not only for Vice President but, in the event of tragedy, to be President"; in addition, Seaton's midwestern background would "help the Republican ticket where it needs strengthening."[13]

Landon had been fascinated by the astuteness of Senator John F. Kennedy's pursuit and capture of the Democratic presidential nomination, but the Kansan's interest in the senator from Massachusetts was not an endorsement. Kennedy's election to the Presidency, Landon said in an interview in Colorado on August 28, would be a case of "sending a boy to do a man's job." He thought this had been proved by the senator's inability to fulfill his promise to use the 1960 special session of Congress, with its huge Democratic majority, to begin implementing the Democratic party's platform. Landon supported Nixon, who, he asserted, had emerged as "a statesman, a man who exercises mature restraint, leadership and understanding for other nations' problems."[14]

After the candidates had been nominated and the campaigns had got under way, Landon became less impressed with Kennedy and skeptical of Nixon. He thought both nominees were running a "somewhat stumbling kind of campaign." Kennedy was trying to "both connect and disconnect Nixon with having anything to say about international as well as administration domestic policies. Nixon is trying to establish the important part he had in shaping administration policies and yet trying not to get too completely identified with them. Therein, both candidates seem to be trying to have their cake and eat it too." It was incredible, Landon believed, that such issues as foreign policy, automation, and "soft" money had not been discussed with any profundity.

[13] Landon to John M. Henry, May 27, 1959; Landon to R. L. Thompson, June 18, 1959; Landon to Eliot Janeway, October 22, 1959; Landon to Edward F. Colladay, November 17, 1959; *Topeka Capital*, May 6, 1960.
[14] Landon to Rudo S. Globus, June 27, 1960; Landon to Arthur M. Schlesinger, Jr., May 16, 1960; *Topeka Capital*, August 29, 1960.

"Instead, we have had the discussion of where Mrs. Kennedy buys her dresses and which [nominee] is the more mature or experienced in government. And, tragically, religion has engulfed the basic issues." He snorted at the televised debates between the nominees: their performances had discredited them as men of stature. Their "jack-in-the-box program where each candidate pops to his feet every two-and-one-half minutes has the aspect of a Punch and Judy show." Landon was also dismayed by the Hughes Tool Company's loan to Nixon's brother and by the possibility that it had involved the Vice President, and by the "unsavory reputation of the Kennedy money spent for the nomination." All this, Landon thought, left "the American voter with little choice on the matter of decency, honesty and ethics between the two candidates."[15] Except for the gallows optimism, Landon's opinion was expressed by one of the 1960 bumper stickers: "Cheer up! You can't elect both of them."

As for Kansas—although he liked George Docking as a man—Landon felt the Democratic governor had carried his "fiscal sanity" too far, that he was not facing the state's need for tax revision, economic development, or the expansion of educational facilities. Landon emphasized development of the state's schools: even with efficient handling, education "costs more money every year. . . . We have children who must be educated and that number is going to increase. If we want good teaching we must be willing to pay for that." When Docking said that the staff of the University of Kansas was "overpaid and underworked," Landon accused him of attacking the university in "an attempt to direct public attention away from the whole state college problem."

Landon continued to urge better educational facilities in Kansas—for the state's development and for "our modern military requirements for national security"—and he countered the governor by calling for an increase in "the ridiculously low salaries of our state civil service employees." Docking's policy of holding the line on the budget was absurd, he declared, when the chief issue before Kansas was the distribution of surplus state funds.[16] Landon and Docking clashed again, in the spring of 1960, and made the front-page headlines. When Landon criticized the governor for "capriciously" commuting the sentence of a convicted killer from death to life imprisonment,

15 Landon to Rudo S. Globus, October 12, 1960; Landon to Donald G. Brownlow, October 21, 1960; Landon to Don L. Berry, October 31, 1960.

16 Landon speech, Topeka, November 21, 1958; *University Daily Kansan* (Lawrence), February 24, 1959; Landon speech, Topeka, January 5, 1960.

Docking rejoined: "Since he likes capital punishment so well, we'll just offer him the job of executioner at $100 a throw." Landon called the comment "psychopathic"; if the governor didn't believe in capital punishment, Landon asked, "why hasn't he recommended repeal of the law?"[17]

When, in 1960, Docking decided to run for a third term—which the old Republican thought would set a bad precedent—Landon redoubled his efforts to get the short-tempered, tight-fisted governor out of office. With other Republican liberals and moderates, Landon pressured the popular Republican attorney general, John Anderson, Jr., into running for governor. Docking, partly because he handled himself ineptly during the campaign, lost to Anderson by a substantial margin in the November election. Landon and the moderate and liberal Republicans were once again in charge, not only of their own party but also of the state government.

Landon had not been impressed by John F. Kennedy's campaign, but he was pleased with the President-elect's cabinet appointments. Moreover, Kennedy's preparations for assuming office led Landon to believe the new President would be in closer touch with public and party matters than Eisenhower had been. He was particularly pleased that Kennedy, who had "proven himself to be a top politician," was using the flexible techniques of a politician rather than Eisenhower's "chief-of-staff military methods." "History," he thought, "might well begin and end with John Fitzgerald Kennedy." The great decisions that might finally lead to a peaceful and honorable accommodation between East and West might be made—and have to be made—during the Kennedy administration.[18]

Landon went east in January, 1961, to speak before the American Whig–Cliosophic Society of Princeton University. The United States, in seeking its economic stability, he said, must make "grave new choices" because of the growing competitiveness of the world economy. America's deficit spending and its unfavorable balance in international trade had to be reversed to maintain the country's prosperity and the confidence of its allies. Moreover, the nation would have to return to highly competitive trade practices, in terms of quality and price.

Landon then developed the standard arguments against foreign aid into an argument for a strengthened United Nations, contending that

[17] *Lawrence Journal-World*, April 15, 1960.
[18] *Kansas City Times*, December 29, 1960; *Topeka Capital*, January 11, 1961; Landon to Lester F. Kimmel, January 23, 1961.

the United States could no longer afford to underwrite the expenses of world economic development and defense against aggression. If these tasks were given to the United Nations, not only could America reduce its expenditures but it could realize its frequently stated policy of developing the United Nations into "the critical international force, responsible for the maintenance of peace and the protection of the rights and sovereignty of all member states and their peoples." Even as a generous contributor to United Nations efforts to assist under-developed lands, the nation could still save money—money that was needed for bolstering its own economy. Wasteful spending and un-productive use of resources could be ended if the United Nations would provide the defense needs of the smaller member states and if the major powers were prohibited from supplying military aid to the weaker nations. The development of the United Nations into an agency for world economic reconstruction and a "chamber of security," Landon thought, offered many advantages: more dollars could be used to develop healthier trade competition among the nations; the arms race might be halted; and the possibility of American economic isolation through foreign trade alliances might be lessened.[19]

Landon was optimistic about such achievements because of the historical precedents for the accommodation of contending power blocs: "One hundred years ago," he told a University of Kansas audience, "the Catholics and Protestants were at mortal war with each other. They learned to get along. I'm not pessimistic. In time, com-munism and capitalism can live together without mortal danger to each other."[20]

Almost as Kennedy took office and his administration was formed, crisis upon crisis developed: the struggle in the Congo, the threat of communist absorption of Laos, and increasing difficulties with Fidel Castro's revolutionary government in Cuba presented tremendous challenges. The Kansan had hoped the United Nations would meet those challenges, but it seemed it would not be given the opportunity, or would prove inadequate because its member nations would not support a firm policy. Landon consequently feared that "a great calamity may be in the making, with the United Nations fading away as did the League of Nations."[21]

He was also dismayed by affairs in the United States. The new administration's talk of big budgets and more economic controls, he

[19] Landon speech, Princeton, N.J., January 6, 1961.

[20] *University Daily Kansan*, January 18, 1961.

[21] Landon speech, Topeka, April 9, 1961.

thought, was impairing business development at home. Nor could Landon look to his own party for remedies; he was still convinced that the Republican party, with its small minorities in the House and Senate, might be going the way of the Whig party. Certainly, it was being harmed by the activities of the radical right, especially by the John Birch Society, which he believed was "incipient Nazism. Instead of book-burning, they're burning the professors." [22]

By the spring of 1961, the international situation seemed to be worse. Several governments were shirking their obligations, not only to the United Nations but also to the North Atlantic and the South East Asia treaty organizations. President Charles de Gaulle of France and Foreign Minister Paul Henri Spaak of Belgium had indicated their unwillingness to support the United Nations fully, and Prime Minister Harold Macmillan of Great Britain, Chancellor Konrad Adenauer of Germany, and President Kennedy had given signs of strengthening NATO at the expense of adequate support for the United Nations. Landon wrote, on April 20, that Kennedy—contrary to his stated aims —had allowed the emphasis to be shifted from the United Nations "to building up a stronger military bloc." Landon, hoping this shift of emphasis could be prevented, urged Ralph McGill of the *Atlanta Constitution* to consider organizing a "strong expression of public sentiment by a big United Nations rally in Madison Square Garden." Then, in a public statement, Landon declared: "The United Nations needs now strong manifestation of popular support from peoples of the free world. On the extent of favorable public opinion depends the success of the United Nations." [23]

The failure of the American-supported invasion of Cuba in late April added to world tension and led to widespread criticism of the United States, either for trying to overthrow or for failing to overthrow the Castro regime. In May, the Kansan concluded that the Kennedy administration was "floundering in the handling of our international relations." Not only were the chances for world government diminishing, America's defensive alliances seemed to be weakening and its unilateral actions failing. [24]

Because of his forceful statements in support of the United Nations,

[22] Landon to Bernard Kilgore, March 6, 1961; Landon to Rudo S. Globus, March 6, 1961; Landon to Robert S. Allen, April 6, 1961; Landon to Arthur M. Schlesinger, Jr., November 18, 1960.

[23] Landon to Ralph McGill, April 20, 1961; Landon to Whittley Austin, April 12, 1961; Landon speech, Topeka, April 25, 1961.

[24] Landon to Robert S. Allen, May 19, 1961.

Landon had become the darling of Kansas' UN advocates, by the spring of 1961—ironically, just at the time he had become pessimistic about its survival. The discouraging events of early 1961 were topped, during the summer, by a new crisis over the status of West Berlin and the rights of the Western powers in the city. No solution seemed to be in sight, as the power blocs stiffened their opposition to each other; it seemed ridiculous even to suggest that the Berlin question be settled by the United Nations. "The United Nations has lost so much prestige at home and abroad," Landon wrote a friend, "that I think perhaps a referral of the dispute to that organization is somewhat futile." Then, on September 23, Landon pessimistically stated:

> The ideals and principles of liberal democracy are fading under pressure of tyrannical dictators of the right and left. . . . Isn't it time for us to face the facts—that discussion of disarmament, world court and rule of law—world citizenship is nonsensical and a waste of time—and that the United Nations is collapsing.[25]

A few days later, however, the administration showed that it had not abandoned the United Nations as President Kennedy went before the General Assembly to tell the nations, and particularly the small states, that the future of the world depended upon the preservation of the United Nations.

Landon applauded Kennedy's statement, but he thought something more positive than a speech was needed "to preserve our ideals of equity, justice and freedom" and to find the way to peace; and Landon had been searching for a positive measure. At the same time, support had been developing (largely as the result of a non-partisan report by Truman's former Under Secretary of State, Will Clayton, and Eisenhower's former Secretary of State, Christian Herter) for greatly liberalizing presidential discretion in fixing tariffs. This proposal demanded that the United States act to preclude being economically cut off from the European Common Market area of France, Germany, Italy, and the Benelux countries. The Common Market nations had been moving steadily toward creating a rich, free-trade area for its almost 300 million people—and toward increased tariffs against non-member states. The results of high European tariffs could be disastrous, not only for American trade but also—as the Kansan saw it—for maintaining Western unity against communism.

[25] Landon to Rudo S. Globus, September 11, 1961; *Kansas City Star*, September 24, 1961.

By late October, 1961, Landon's course was clear. The President was said to be uncommitted on the trade question and Landon decided to try, as others were doing, to force his hand—or, if the President requested additional powers for negotiating trade agreements, to help create sentiment for the liberalization of reciprocal trade legislation. If the legislation were liberalized, the President could negotiate substantial trade-barrier reductions between the United States and the Common Market. Landon was to address the National Press Club in Washington on December 8, and he decided to use this forum for airing his proposal. He started working on his speech late in October, made more than a dozen drafts, and analyzed each draft with his friends. The White House and the State Department had meanwhile been alerted that they could expect help from the Kansan if the President should decide to ask for liberalization of foreign-trade legislation. The speech would be doubly important because it would come from a Republican whose roots were deep in the midwest, a region usually thought of as a desert of liberal thinking on international economics.

Kennedy had responded favorably to the pressures for the liberalization of reciprocal trade legislation, and the day before Landon's speech, in an address to the National Association of Manufacturers in New York City, had said he would ask for increased authority to negotiate favorable trade agreements with foreign countries, especially with the Common Market. Landon, who arrived in Washington on the evening of December 7, was pleased with the President's New York speech and happy that he could support him on this issue—believing, because of the timing of Kennedy's speech, that he had helped force the President to declare himself. Landon, on his arrival, made a good impression on the capital. A Washington reporter saw the Kansan as "a round, ruddy, chipper 74, [a man who had] emerged out of the obscurity which has enveloped him since 1936, as a tiger for free trade." Landon surprised the newsmen by calling President Kennedy a "strong leader" and by describing himself as a "great admirer" of Harry Truman.[26]

The next day, in his formal address to the press club, Landon said: "It is time to wake up. Our dreams for a civilized approach to world problems through the United Nations have been shattered by fast-moving recent events." The beachheads "Imperial Communism" had secured in North Vietnam and Laos, Cuba, and East Germany must

[26] *Washington Star*, December 9, 1961; *Kansas City Star*, December 9, 1961.

be offset, he said, by the consolidation of the strength and resources of the free peoples of the world. Militarily, the United States should

> coordinate and strengthen our multilateral engagements, global and regional. We should revamp our regional defense systems—NATO, SEATO, CENTO—to merge and pool their military forces in a really co-operative association with unified command to maintain peace in the world and defend equity and justice.

Economically, America should

> support the expansion of the concept of the Common Market of Europe to include all nations everywhere that are willing to join a cooperative enterprise to create higher standards of living in all countries by freer exchange of goods and services.

Substantial liberalization of the President's powers in negotiating trade agreements should be the first step in seeking this goal, a goal in which eventual free trade was implicit.

Because economic interests reinforced, in fact required, common political interests, Landon placed "as much emphasis on using the European Common Market as a national survival policy as I do a trade policy." [The intertwining of economic and political interests would mean a sound dollar would have to be sought in order to persuade the hard-money Common Market nations that the United States would be a valuable addition.] A free-world common market had several advantages: Prosperous countries would be strengthened and under-developed nations would be assisted toward economic security, with the result that the economy of the free-world bloc would be so strong that the "Communist bloc would have to trade with it. The Communist bloc would be isolated unless and until it changed its ways."

> A correlative result of the neutralization of Communist terror by the power of free peoples would be the salvation of the United Nations. The powers of the free peoples to checkmate forces of aggression and subversion would give greater force to the decisions of the United Nations. Rather than show contempt for the U.N., the Soviet Union would need the United Nations as a forum for the honest discussion of problems affecting both the Communist and the free nations. It would attach more—much more—importance to the United Nations' decisions than it does now.

Landon concluded:

Free nations' determination to subordinate short-sighted nationalism to a broader goal is the decisive factor. Herein is the real test of Western strength —of the determination to live and die as free people—not slaves in a police state. Our United States of America must pass that test of leadership. We delude ourselves and we flatter our enemies if we think that the only choice before us is peace at any price—or war at any cost.[27]

The address won wide acclaim. The *Washington Post* said in an editorial: "His forthright support of free trade stands in happy contrast to the nervous-nelly protectionism of Sen. Barry Goldwater." The *Wichita Eagle and Beacon* praised the speech, calling it "common sense from the prairies." Mary McGrory commented in her syndicated column: "To the astonishment of a National Press Club luncheon, he made a high-level, 40-minute defense of the Common Market which would have done credit to George Bundy or Paul Henri Spaak." And the *Council Bluffs Nonpareil* said: "We need more men like Alf Landon in public life. Kansas has two excellent U.S. senators, but if there should be a vacancy in the next few years, Alf Landon would make a good Senator."[28]

Landon was in earnest about the trade issue, and about the liberalization of the President's tariff powers. On December 13, substituting for former Governor LeRoy Collins of Florida in a speech before the annual dinner of the Kansas City, Missouri, Chamber of Commerce, Landon repeated the essence of his National Press Club address. On December 17 on "Washington Conversation," a televised interview program of the Columbia Broadcasting System, when asked if he would break with the Republican party, Landon answered that if trade liberalization "got to be an issue between the two parties, a clear-cut issue, I'd be very much tempted." He thought, however, that the Republicans would support the President on the matter. Conversing on another topic, the Kansan derided the "silly antics" of right-wing extremists.[29]

[27] Landon speech, Washington, D.C., December 8, 1961.

[28] *Washington Post*, December 9, 1961; *Wichita Eagle and Beacon*, December 8, 1961; *Atlanta Constitution*, December 15, 1961; *Council Bluffs Nonpareil*, December 18, 1961. The *Nonpareil*'s view was echoed in Kansas after the death of Kansas' senior senator, Andrew Schoeppel, on January 21, 1962. The sentiment for Landon's appointment to the Senate was so widespread that newsmen asked him about the possibility. He replied: "If I had any desire to serve in the U.S. Senate, I would have been a candidate many years ago." *Topeka Capital*, January 26, 1962.

[29] *Kansas City Times*, December 13, 1961; "Washington Conversation" transcript, December 17, 1961.

In January, 1962, Landon repeated his call for the revision of the nation's foreign-trade policy—this time in Kansas at the Great Bend Chamber of Commerce annual dinner. The speech evoked favorable responses from many Kansas newspapers. (The *Great Bend Tribune* commented of the audience, which was drawn from one of the state's most conservative sections: "They needed it.") In February, Landon spoke in Des Moines before the National Farm Institute in support of broadening the President's power to negotiate trade agreements, which was then embodied in the trade-expansion bill before Congress. The action taken on the pending legislation, he said, "will be a historic turning point in not only trade, but political relations that can—and probably will—mean the difference between peace and a nuclear war." He appeared in March on "Face the Community," a television interview program in Kansas City, where he again spoke out on the need for the United States to take steps to join the Common Market. He also wrote an article in support of the trade-expansion bill, which appeared in a new wide-circulation magazine, *This Month*. In April, Landon gathered representatives of leading economic groups—including the state presidents of the Farm Bureau, the League of Women Voters, the Grange, the Chamber of Commerce, the Farmers' Union, and the vice president of the Kansas AFL–CIO—to speak at a Topeka rally "in support of the President's tariff legislation request."[30]

Landon returned to Washington in May to speak to the District of Columbia Bar Association of the need to give the President "wider-reaching powers in concluding foreign-trade agreements."

> It's a question of whether we are going to survive in ever-sharper world-trade competition, or whether we are going to fold up, gradually weakening our economic, political and military strength by inbreeding.... The situation is this simple. If we do not at least keep pace in selling our goods abroad, we will not be able to sustain prosperity at home, or maintain our influence abroad. If we do not sustain prosperity at home—we will find it exceedingly difficult to support adequate military defenses against aggression. If we do not maintain our influence abroad, we will not be able to keep up a high spirit of united free-world resistance to imperial Communism. In addition to these—loss of prosperity at home also obviously means serious recessions and maybe depression—serious strains on our already burdened finances—and a political disunity that could rent the political fabric of the free world.

[30] *Great Bend Tribune*, January 11, 1962; *Lawrence Journal-World*, February 17, 1962; Landon, "We Must Enter the Common Market," *This Month* (April, 1962), pp. 48 ff.; *A Call to Kansas: Our Stake in World Trade* (April, 1962), n.d.

Passage of the trade-expansion bill, however, was not enough. Nor were revisions in the tax laws for the encouragement of business. Nor were attempts to maintain a sound dollar.

> We must seek more than just government action. We must be ready to compete like Yankee traders. We must be prepared to engage once again in price competition. We must compete in quality—in service. And, with increasing automation of industry, we can't say that we cannot afford to do it.[31]

The Kansan was feted like a visiting prime minister during his stay in Washington. He breakfasted with twenty Republican congressmen from seven states, chatted with the President for an hour, and was the guest at a luncheon given by presidential assistant Arthur Schlesinger, Jr.—which was attended by the British ambassador and Secretary of the Treasury Douglas Dillon. He told the congressmen: "The Republican party's great mistake was that it took its cue from the [National Association of Manufacturers] instead of the free-enterprise system." He added that it was also "great foolishness" for the party to tie itself to right-to-work legislation.[32]

Landon had intended the Washington visit as his last effort in support of the trade-expansion bill, but when the measure came up for a vote in the Senate—in September, 1962—there were reports that attempts would be made to cripple it by amendments. Again the Kansan spoke out. Addressing a high school debate institute in Topeka, on September 15, he called for a liberal enactment. A few days later—to show he meant business—he told the press that there should be no limitations on petroleum imports: oil, too, must accept the idea of freer trade. Coming from an oilman who had always favored import restrictions, Landon's declaration left no doubt of his sincerity.[33] The Trade Expansion Act, passed by Congress and signed in October, was not all that President Kennedy had asked for or that Landon had hoped for, but it gave the President greater discretion in negotiating trade agreements for the reduction, and in some cases the elimination, of duties. It was a big step forward, and Landon was proud of his work in making it possible.

Although Landon was not the only Republican who had fought for the trade-expansion bill, his contribution was unique because he was

[31] Landon speech, Washington, D.C., May 8, 1962.
[32] Landon to D. R. McCoy, May 23, 1962; *Hutchinson News*, May 31, 1962.
[33] *Wichita Sunday Eagle*, September 16, 1962; *Great Bend Tribune*, September 19, 1962.

its most vigorous midwestern advocate. His role, moreover, was recognized by President Kennedy's appreciation of Landon's "great contribution" in making its passage possible: "You were among the first to perceive the importance and implications of the successful enactment of the trade bill and to speak out in support of it with force and conviction." The President asked Landon to continue to act in behalf of what "you believe to be the highest national interest" on matters of international trade. Landon, acknowledging he had "gone the last mile" in supporting the legislation, replied that he would continue to seek freer world trade.[34]

Although he had supported President Kennedy on trade expansion and had cordial relations with the administration, Landon was not in the President's pocket; he opposed various domestic policies of the administration. When, for example, Kennedy asked for authority to adjust income taxes, subject to congressional review, and to initiate public works programs, the Kansan condemned such grants of power not only as unnecessary but as tipping the balance of power between the White House and Congress.[35] In Kansas, Landon actively supported the Republican ticket in the election campaign of 1962—especially Governor John Anderson's reelection and the election as Senator of James B. Pearson, who had been serving in the Senate since Andrew Schoeppel's death in January.

Landon poured criticism on the Democrats. After the election he analyzed the Republican sweep of state and congressional offices in Kansas as the "people's healthy reaction to one of the lowest-level political campaigns, from the President on down, I've ever seen in an off-year election." He charged there had been "what might be classed as wholesale bribery in the form of handouts from the executive branch of government for state and congressional districts that vote right." Nevertheless, Landon was pleased with Kennedy's "skillful handling" of the Cuban crisis in October and November, during the time of the Soviet installation of missile bases in Cuba. He supported the President's blockade of the island, forcing the dismantling of the bases and evacuation of Russian troops and technicians.[36]

The Kansan, not surprisingly, remained unhappy with the ad-

[34] John F. Kennedy to Landon, October 30, 1962; Landon to Kennedy, November 7, 1962.

[35] *Topeka Capital-Journal*, January 14, 1962.

[36] *Topeka Capital*, November 7, 1962; Landon to John F. Kennedy, November 21, 1962.

ministration's domestic policies. When in January, 1963, President Kennedy requested that federal taxes be substantially cut and appropriations greatly increased in order to boost the economy, Landon deplored this "startling departure in fiscal policy." He was not sure that this would increase spending, keep prices down, provide jobs for the several million who were unemployed, ease the citizens' tax load, (or merely permit hard pressed state and local governments to raise their taxes), improve relations with the hard-money Common Market countries, or reverse the nation's unfavorable balance of trade. Some of these results might come, Landon thought, but the touchy international situation was a compelling argument against such a drastic experiment, which affected so many aspects of American economics and politics. He later said of the President's proposal: "He got too much hay down." [37]

Although skeptical of the merits of Kennedy's domestic program, Landon continued to support the administration's foreign policy. Of the Cuban question, which dominated the front pages until the spring of 1963, Landon said the policy of quarantining the Castro regime was realistic "if it isolates the threat of Communism in the Western Hemisphere." In a speech to a Young Republican group in May, Landon said the Cuban problem was "not going to be resolved . . . either by blockade or invasion. I cannot conceive of a greater mistake than getting bogged down in the jungles and mountains of Cuba as we were in Korea, with as great a force of men as were involved in that war." Moreover, world peace was at stake, because intervention in Cuba would be an attack not only upon Castro but—indirectly—upon Khrushchev. If the relatively moderate Soviet premier chose to fight over Cuba, it might mean a world war; if he backed off, it could mean his downfall—and the rise of more aggressive Communists, especially China's Mao Tse-tung. The Kansan called for support of President Kennedy's Cuban policy.

> As Republicans, our first duty is to our unique Republic. . . . We must not become so concerned with partisan advantage that we would rush the nation into disaster—and criticism for criticism's sake can mean disaster. There is plenty of room for legitimate differences between our national administration and its bipartisan opposition. Unless we stick to these legitimate differences and keep our eyes on our great and beloved Republic's true interests, our [party's] future is sure—it is defeat.[38]

[37] Landon speeches: Topeka, February 6, 1963, and Kansas City, Mo., May 2, 1963.
[38] Landon speeches: Bartlesville, Okla., February 28, 1963, and Kansas City, Mo., May 2, 1963.

Flexibility and moderation, at home and abroad, were the themes of Landon's speeches from that point on—after President Kennedy's tragic death and even during the political campaign of 1964.

Alf Landon in his later years was a curiosity in the American political scene. He had come back into public view without holding, or seeking, office; he had come back by asserting his particular brand of independence at a time when independence seemed rare in American politics. He became something of an elder statesman.

Once again, he was mentioned by columnists and newspapermen. Leonard Lyons carried the item that Landon, upon meeting Norman Thomas, introduced the socialist leader to Mrs. Landon with the quip: "Dear, this is the man I've been telling you about—the one I licked in '36." Landon was also the subject of feature articles in newspapers. Occasionally there were such headlines as "NEW LANDON BEGINS TO EMERGE," in the *Christian Science Monitor*; "WISE WORDS BY LANDON," by Ralph McGill; "THE 'KANSAS COOLIDGE' SPEAKS OUT ON TRADE," in the *Washington Post*; and—in celebration of his seventy-fifth birthday— "ELDER STATESMAN AFTER A BAD DEFEAT," from the Associated Press.

The *New York Post*, never noted for its sympathy with hard-money advocates, called Landon's support of the trade-expansion bill "good news for the country."[39] John K. Jessup, writing in *Life*, said "The politicians who most deserve support during these next ten years will be those who act on the maxim which Senator Paul Douglas once echoed from Alf Landon: 'To be a liberal, one does not have to be a wastrel.'" The Kansan was particularly pleased by the estimates of his contribution to the passage of the Trade Expansion Act. Roscoe Drummond, in his syndicated column, observed that passage of the act required Republican support, and "Few worked for it harder and to better effect than Alf Landon, the unforgotten man of the 1936 Presidential election."[40]

There were other signs of Landon's position as an elder statesman. The Kansas AFL–CIO, with great fanfare, established a Hall of Fame for Kansas that was based on an opinion survey for the ten most illustrious men in Kansas history. Landon, of course, was named

[39] *Lawrence Journal-World*, February 9, 1963; *Christian Science Monitor*, February 11, 1961; *Kansas City Times*, April 19, 1961; *Washington Post*, January 28, 1962; *Kansas City Star*, September 9, 1962; *New York Post*, March 20, 1962.

[40] "Choices Ahead for New Prosperity," *Life*, August 24, 1962, p. 72; *Washington Post*, July 2, 1962.

among the ten, and the *Topeka Capital* commented that he not only ranked well in history but was one "whose statesmanship is undiminished." Alf Landon was also pleased when the Topeka board of education named a new junior high school after him—though in deference to Mrs. Landon's wishes it was named the *Alfred* M. Landon Junior High School.[41]

The silver-haired gentleman received his share of the intangible rewards of civic service; more important and valuable, however, was his pride in having fulfilled his duties as an independent throughout most of his life. He had brought a new deal to government in Kansas, and, despite his occasional crankiness, had been one of the champions of a broad-gauged Republican party. Landon had pursued national and world stability because of his belief that this was a necessary condition for personal and group accomplishment. Stability demanded a balance among contending interests, and reasonable solutions to problems. Negotiation was the means to achieve balance and satisfaction, but majority rule, freedom, and a government of laws could not be bargained away.

The sources of Landon's values were varied. His family background and schooling had exalted stability, integrity, democracy, law, and liberty of conscience. Hard work and free-enterprise ventures had resulted in real achievement and had taught him the value of negotiation. His political experiences had taught him to distrust extremists, and he had had the strength to fight them. For more than fifty years he had been a politician, and he had played the role honorably, forthrightly. A republic could not demand more of a citizen.

[41] *Topeka Capital*, October 30, 1961, February 19, 1962.

Bibliographical Note

Because there are very few books that deal at any length with Alfred M. Landon, it would serve no significant purpose to burden this volume with the usual bibliography of all the sources consulted. This list is confined, therefore, to the political biographies of Landon and to a few other works that are invaluable for background materials.

BINGAY, MALCOLM. *Two Candidates: Landon and Roosevelt*. Detroit: Malcolm Bingay, 1936.

BRIGHT, JOHN D. (ed.). *Kansas, The First Century*. 2 vols; New York: Lewis, 1956.

BURNS, JAMES MACGREGOR. *Roosevelt: The Lion and the Fox*. New York: Harcourt, Brace, 1956.

COMER, BURT. *The Tale of a Fox*. Wichita: Burt Comer, 1936.

FOWLER, RICHARD B. *Deeds Not Deficits, The Story of Alfred M. Landon*. Kansas City: Richard B. Fowler, 1936.

HINSHAW, DAVID (ed.). *Landon, What He Stands For*. New York: Mail and Express, 1936.

HUTCHINSON, WILLIAM T. *Lowden of Illinois: The Life of Frank O. Lowden*. 2 vols; Chicago: University of Chicago Press, 1957.

ICKES, HAROLD L. *The Secret Diary of Harold L. Ickes*. 3 vols; New York: Simon and Schuster, 1953–54.

JOHNSON, DONALD B. *The Republican Party and Wendell Willkie*. Urbana: University of Illinois Press, 1960.

JOHNSON, WALTER. *William Allen White's America*. New York: Holt, 1947.

MARTIN, JOSEPH. *My First Fifty Years in Politics*. New York: McGraw-Hill, 1961.

MAYER, GEORGE H. *The Republican Party, 1854–1964*. New York: Oxford University Press, 1964.

PALMER, FREDERICK. *This Man Landon*. New York: Dodd, Mead, 1936.

SCHLESINGER, ARTHUR M., JR. *The Politics of Upheaval*. Boston: Houghton Mifflin, 1960.

SCHRUBEN, FRANCIS W. (comp). *Harry H. Woodring Speaks: Kansas Politics During the Early Depression* (Los Angeles: Francis W. Schruben, 1963).

THORNTON, WILLIS. *The Life of Alfred M. Landon.* New York: Grosset and Dunlap, 1936.

TINNEY, CAL. *Is It True What They Say About Landon? A Non-Partisan Portrait.* New York: Wise-Parslow, 1936.

WELLS, JOHN W. *Meet Mr. Landon.* Topeka: John W. Wells, 1936.

WHITE, WILLIAM ALLEN. *The Autobiography of William Allen White.* New York: Macmillan, 1946.

———. *What It's All About.* New York: Macmillan, 1936.

WOLFSKILL, GEORGE. *The Revolt of the Conservatives.* Boston: Houghton Mifflin, 1962.

ZORNOW, WILLIAM F. *Kansas.* Norman: University of Oklahoma Press, 1957.

Most information on Landon must be dug out of manuscripts, archives, and newspapers, as the footnotes attest. The most important of these sources are Alfred M. Landon's files of letters, speeches, press releases, and newspaper clippings; those up to 1949 are in the archives of the Kansas State Historical Society, Topeka, and those of subsequent date are still in Landon's possession. Other useful materials at the Historical Society include the papers of Arthur Capper, Rolla Clymer, Lacy Haynes, Clifford R. Hope, and George McGill, and the Kansas State Archives' gubernatorial records of Clyde Reed and Alfred M. Landon. The manuscripts in the Franklin D. Roosevelt Library at Hyde Park, New York, are invaluable to any student of the New Deal years. The papers of Thomas E. Dewey, which are in the University of Rochester Libraries, shed much light on Landon's post-1936 political activities. Records at the University of Kansas are illuminating in respect to his student years. Some records on aspects of Landon's life and some background material can be found in the National Archives, Washington, D.C. The papers of Frank Knox and William Allen White, which are in the Manuscript Division of the Library of Congress, are invaluable sources of information. Other papers consulted in the Manuscript Division included those of Newton D. Baker, William E. Borah, Henry Breckinridge, Raymond Clapper, Edward T. Clark, Bainbridge Colby, James J. Davis, Henry P. Fletcher, James Rudolph Garfield, Harold L. Ickes, William M. Jardine, Charles L. McNary, Ogden Mills, George Fort Milton, George W. Norris, Gifford Pinchot, Theodore Roosevelt, Jr., James W. Wadsworth, and Wallace H. White.

Many newspapers were consulted during the course of research, but this task was made simpler by virtue of the many clippings in the Landon Papers. Among the newspapers examined in the Kansas State Historical Society, the most valuable were the *Topeka Capital, Topeka State Journal, Kansas City Star, Kansas City Times, Wichita Beacon, Wichita Eagle,* and *Emporia Gazette.* At the Library of Congress, a quantity of relevant material was discovered in various Scripps-Howard and Hearst papers, sources that are not used frequently enough by historians. Other newspapers of importance to this study were the *Atlanta Constitution, Chicago Tribune, Christian Science Monitor, Denver Post, Des Moines Register, Los Angeles Times, Louisville Courier-Journal, New York Herald Tribune, New York Times, St. Louis Post-Dispatch, Washington Post,* and *Washington Star.*

Except for manuscripts and archives, this note attempts to mention only the chief sources used. The footnotes include references to other helpful books, published documents, magazines, and newspapers.

Acknowledgments

The facts and ideas that go into a book come from innumerable sources, and behind the sources stand people: the men and women who have been interviewed or who have chatted with the author, who have written letters and supplied printed and documentary materials, and who have commented on portions of the manuscript. In the present instance the most important and generous contributor was the book's subject, Alfred Mossman Landon, who did all of these things unstintingly. It has been my good fortune to know Alf Landon personally, and I doubt that any biographer could have had a more cooperative subject. I am deeply indebted to him, not only for granting me full access to his papers but for a hundred hours of interviews during which he discussed himself with the utmost candor and straightforwardness.

I am also indebted to many others. I am grateful for the help of manuscript curators, archivists, and librarians, such as Nyle Miller, Edgar Langsdorf, and Robert Richmond at the Kansas State Historical Society; George Caldwell and Laura Neiswanger at the University of Kansas; Herman Kahn, Robert Jacoby, and George Roach at the Franklin D. Roosevelt Library; David Mearns and Joseph Vance at the Library of Congress; Jane Smith at the National Archives; and John Russell and Margaret Butterfield at the University of Rochester. For information and insights about Landon, Kansas, Republicanism, and the New Deal, I am thankful to scores of people, particularly George Anderson, John D. M. Hamilton, Karl Lamb, James Malin, Roy Roberts, Ralph Robey, Richard Ruetten, and Arthur M. Schlesinger, Jr. I benefited greatly from readings of drafts of the manuscript by George Lobdell of Ohio University, George Mayer of Purdue University, and Elmo Richardson of Washington State University. LANDON OF KANSAS probably would have been a better book had I heeded more of their suggestions, but errors of fact and judgment are my responsibility alone.

Finally, I wish to acknowledge the generous support of the University of Kansas General Research Fund, which was of material assistance in carrying out this project.

Donald R. McCoy

Index

Acheson, Dean, 547
Adams, John Truslow, 229
Adenauer, Konrad, 571
Afro-American, 311–12
Agriculture, Department of, 386–87
Agricultural Adjustment Act, 145, 216, 222, 248, 335, 357, 387
Agricultural Adjustment Administration, 146, 148–49, 199, 201, 241, 297
Aiken, George D., 391–92, 538
Aikman, Duncan, 229, 328
Albaugh, Morton, 22
Alford, Theodore, 212
Allegheny College, 4
Allen, H. R., 100
Allen, Henry J., 34–35, 59, 213, 274; as Progressive leader, 15, 17–18; campaigns for governor, 18, 21–23, 29; as governor, 25–30; and 1920 presidential nomination, 27–28; at 1920 Republican national convention, 29; opposes Ku Klux Klan, 31; supports Clyde Reed for governor, 36–38, 40, 48; and U.S. Senate, 52–54, 57, 60–61, 63–66, 92; and oil industry stabilization, 83; and 1932 Republican campaign, 106, 110; supports Landon for President, 246, 251, 253–54; and Republican program committee, 375
Allen, Robert S., 547, 552
Allen, Wilbur, 28
Allied Independent Banks of Kansas, 163

Allis, Barney L., 240
Altschul, Frank, 291, 359–60, 431, 434
America First Committee, 464–66
American Committee Against Nazi Persecution and Extermination of the Jews, 498
American Federation of Labor–Congress of Industrial Organizations, 564
American Hotel Association, 240
American Labor party, 401
American Legion, 25, 33, 58–59, 61, 91, 94, 97, 285, 290
American Liberty League, 225, 236, 264, 269, 271, 293–94, 296, 301, 327, 342, 426
American Medical Association, 91
American Petroleum Institute, 68, 71, 138, 203, 205
American Resettlement Committee, 498
Amrine, Milton, 53
Anderson, Ben M., 229, 267, 348
Anderson, John, Jr., 569, 578
Angell, Norman, 558
Arkansas City Traveler, 157
Arkansas Gazette, 402
Arn, Edward, 548, 553–54
Associated Negro Press, 240
Association of Young Republican Clubs, New York, 243
Atchison Globe, 162
Atlanta Constitution, 421
Atlantic Charter, 474–75, 506, 517
Ayres, Leonard P., 267

Bachman, Carl, 250, 258
Bacon, Gaspar, 257
Badger, Sherwin, 267, 369
Bagby, Wesley M., 29 n.
Bailey, Joseph W., 270
Bailey, Josiah, 461
Bailey, Roy, 115
Bailey, Willis J., 22
Baker, Newton D., and 1936 Republican politics, 258, 310, 316, 328; and political realignment, 359
Baker University, 391
Baltimore Sun, 301, 315, 320
Banking, 1933 problems of, 125–27, 161–67
Barkley, Alben, 460–61
Barnett, C. A., 421
Barnsdall Oil Co., 71–72
Bartley, E. Ross, 267
Barton, Bruce, 439, 463, 494
Baruch Plan, 524
Bass, Robert P., 267, 281, 375
Bates, Sanford, 171
Beard, Charles, 459
Beck, Clarence, 157
Beck, Will T., 183, 213, 250
Becker, Carl L., 8
Bell, William B., 267–68
Bennett, E. G., 531
Benson, Ezra T., 554
Berlin, 561, 572
Berlin, Richard E., 230
Berry, Don L., 358, 375
Berry, George L., 273–74, 318
Bever, Ellis D., 150
Bigelow, W. F., 278
Bingay, Malcolm, 242
Bingham, Hiram, 254
Black, A. H., 11, 94
Black, Hugo, 369–70
Blackett, Hill, 365, 425, 434; and 1936 campaign, 310; assists Landon financially, 418
Blakely, George, 193
Bleakley, William F., 333
Bliss, Robert L., 466
Block, Paul, 232, 258, 333 n.
Blount, William M., 190

Bodman, Herbert L., 533
Borah, William E., 360, 539; and 1936 presidential nomination, 218, 220, 224, 226, 230, 235–36, 242, 244–47, 250–56, 258; and 1936 campaign, 310, 343, 347–48; and Roosevelt court plan, 356; and struggle for Republican leadership, 368–69, 372; and 1940 presidential nomination, 423
Boston Post, 341, 417, 420
Boston Transcript, 219
Boston University Theological School, 391
Boyd, Tom, and Finney scandal, 153–54, 156, 158, 160
Boynton, Roland, and oil industry stabilization, 74; and 1932 campaign, 111; and Finney scandal, 154–55, 157, 159–61
Bradney, Claude C., 124, 536
Bradshaw, William M., 45, 56, 98
Brady, Joseph H., 102
Brann, Louis J., 299
Brazil, 467
Breckinridge, Henry, 269–71, 348, 359
Brewster, Sardius M., 153, 183, 186
Breyfogle, John W., 62
Bricker, John W., 317, 520; and 1940 Republican national convention, 445; meets Landon, 490; and 1944 campaign, 510–11
Bridges, Styles, 259–60, 368, 428, 444
Brinkerhoff, Fred, 223, 394, 536
Brinkley, John R., 293; medical activities of, 91–92; campaigns for governor, 92, 101–104, 106–13, 111 n., 182–83; supports Democrat for governor, 186
Brisbane, Arthur, 231
Bristow, Joseph L., 14–15
Brooks, C. Wayland, 442
Broomhall's Corn Trade News, 386
Brotherhood of Railway Trainmen, 53
Browder, Earl, 3
Brown, Clarence, 428
Brown, G. A., 103
Brown, George Rothwell, 379, 504
Brown, Walter, 261
Browne, Charles H., 193–94

Brownell, Herbert, Jr., 510, 522
Bryan, William Jennings, 6
Buck, C. Douglass, 245
Bulganin, Nikolai, 558
Bullitt, William, 436
Bullock, Channing J., 249
Bundy, McGeorge, 575
Burch, John, 41
Burdick, Usher, 310
Burke, Edmund, 116
Burke, Edward R., 361
Burr, Harry, 193
Burton, Ella J., 103
Bushfield, Harlan, 444
Butler, Hugh, 475–76
Buzick, Henry, 124
Byrd, Harry, 232, 258
Byrnes, James F., 496

Caldwell, Leland, 155–56, 161
Campbell, Philip P., 15
Canada, 295, 517, 524, 527
Canham, Erwin, 298
Cannon, Joseph, 15
Cantilo, José María, 411
Capper, Arthur, 34, 38, 57, 212, 233, 309, 469, 532; and campaigns for governor, 17–18; runs for Senate, 21; and oil industry stabilization, 73, 75, 77, 79–80, 82–84, 136, 138, 206; and 1932 Republican campaign, 106, 110; and farm relief, 144, 176, 197–98, 289; and banking legislation, 161; and utility rates, 166; supports Landon for President, 226, 235, 251, 504; on Landon's nomination, 264; and Roosevelt's court plan, 357; and the struggle for Republican leadership, 368; and Ludlow resolution, 377; and crop statistics, 385–87; and 1940 presidential nomination, 422–23, 426, 428, 440, 443–44; for Landon as national chairman, 488; and press criticism of Roosevelt, 491 n.; retires, 535–38
Carlson, Frank, 522; as Landon's 1932 campaign manager, 98, 102; as state chairman, 104–105, 109, 111; supports Landon for President, 219; on 1936

Republican national convention, 264; and crop statistics, 386; and 1938 elections, 395; and Selective Service extension, 474; and Wendell Willkie, 503; runs for governor, 533–34; nominated for Senate, 548
Carr, Ralph, 488
Carruth, Arthur, 422
Carter Oil Co., 72
Casement, Dan, 229
Castle, William, 326, 363
Castro, Fidel, 570–71, 579
Catledge, Turner, 432
Chadbourne, Will, 375
Chase, D. A. N., runs for gubernatorial nomination, 39, 41, 43; appointed budget director, 128, 151; and Finney scandal, 155
Chattanooga Evening Tribune, 424
Chautauqua Lake Assembly, 4, 7, 20
Chiang Kai-shek, 546, 557
Chicago Daily News, 372
Chicago Defender, 312
Chicago Tribune, 220, 377, 379
China, 497, 515, 543–44, 546–47, 557, 561, 563
Christenson, W. E., 223
Christgau, Victor, 201
Christian Science Monitor, 420, 580
Church, Robert R., 311–12
Churchill, Winston S., 474, 478, 483, 492, 499, 502
Cincinnati Times-Star, 341, 517
Cities Service Co., 166, 169–70
Civil Service Commission, 330–31
Civil Service League, 248
Civil Works Administration, 147, 166, 172–73
Civilian Conservation Corps, 142, 172, 320
Clapper, Raymond, 300 n., 349, 449; and Landon campaign for President, 230, 328, 337 n.
Clark, Bennett Champ, 465, 468, 477
Clark, Grenville, 438
Clark, J. Reuben, 349 n., 439; and Landon's campaign for President, 249, 251, 267, 326; and Latin American

Clark, J. Reuben—*Continued*
  policy, 249, 410; and Republican
  anti-war statement, 472
Clayton, Will, 572
Cleveland, Richard, 271
Cleveland Plain Dealer, 484
Clugston, W. G., 29 n., 57
Cobb, Irwin S., 260, 472
Cobb, Osro, 401
Cockrell, Ewing, 518
Coffman, Clyde W., 63
Cogswell, Carl C., 185, 216
Colby, Bainbridge, 337; supports Landon
  for President, 269–71, 342; criticizes
  New Deal, 328; meets with Landon, 359
Cole, William P., Jr., 203–204, 206–207
Colladay, Edward, 218, 522
Collins, LeRoy, 575
Colmery, Harry, 251, 548
Comer, Burt, 103, 292–93
Committee for a Sane Nuclear Policy, 562
Communist party, 262–63, 279, 508
Conant, James B., 459
Congress of Industrial Organizations, 508
Connally Act, 204, 206–207
Consumers' Council, 179
Cook, Clarence, 185
Coolidge, Calvin, 29, 52, 218–19, 237,
  316, 421, 541
Coughlin, Charles, 294, 332
Council Bluffs Nonpareil, 575
Cousins, Norman, 562
Couzens, James, 209 n., 310, 343
Cox, Dale, 228
Cox, James, 341
Crawford, Schuyler, 173–74
Cuba, 570–71, 578–79
Cummings, John M., 531
Curren, Joseph, 459
Curtis, Charles, 57; runs for Senate, 18;
  and H. J. Allen, 25–26; nominated for
  Vice President, 40, 44, 51; supports
  J. D. M. Hamilton for governor, 34,
  39, 41–42; resigns from Senate, 52–54;
  and 1932 campaign, 99, 101, 103,
  105–106, 111; supports Landon for
  President, 226
Czechoslovakia, 409, 415, 529

Dakar, 467
Dale, Kirke, 183
Darby, Harry, 522, 553–54; as director
  of Highway Department, 150; and
  1938 campaign, 395; and 1948
  campaign, 537; appointed to Senate,
  548
Darling, Jay N., 267
Davies, Gomer T., 488
Davis, Chester, 176, 201
Davis, James, J., 284, 368
Davis, John W., 230, 271
Davis, Jonathan M., 30–32, 103
Dawes, Charles G., 472
De Gaulle, Charles, 490, 571
De Mille, Cecil B., 271
Democratic party, 1928 state platform of,
  49; representation of in state legisla-
  ture, 51, 188; 1932 state platform of,
  104; 1932 campaign expenditures of,
  111 n.; 1934 state platform of, 184;
  state of in 1936, 262–63; and attack on
  Landon, 293–94; funds of in 1936,
  345–46 n.; state of in 1948, 538
Democrats, Jeffersonian, 258, 269–71,
  279, 301, 332, 348, 359, 392
Denious, Jess C., 537
Denious, Wilbur, 375
Denman, Arthur, 70
Dern, George H., 286
Des Moines Register, 306, 377, 509
Dewey, Thomas E., 475, 490, 516, 525;
  meets with Landon, 375–76, 391; and
  1938 campaign, 401, 405; and 1940
  presidential nomination, 417, 423–25,
  428–30, 439–40, 443–46; and 1940
  campaign, 447; and Joseph Martin,
  463; and 1942 campaign, 485–86; and
  1944 presidential nomination, 494, 497
  501, 504, 507–509; and 1944 campaign
  510–12; and 1948 presidential nomination, 520, 530–32, 537, 539; and
  1948 campaign, 539–41; and 1950
  campaign, 548–49
Dewhurst, Frederic, 249, 267
Dickinson, Lester, and 1936 presidential
  nomination, 218, 244, 252–53, 256–57;
  and 1936 campaign, 276

Dillon, Douglas, 577
Disney, Wesley, 202–203
Dixie Oil Co., 72
Docking, George E., elected governor, 554; as governor, 543, 568–69; re-elected, 555; defeated, 569
Doherty, Henry, 109–10
Donovan, William, 431
Douglas, Lewis, 258–59, 267, 359
Douglas, Paul, 580
Drought conference of 1936, 286–89
Drummond, Roscoe, 432, 478, 580
Dulles, John Foster, 554, 556, 561
Dutch Shell Pipeline Co., 72, 85

Eagle Home News, 312
Early, Stephen T., 320, 378
Eaton, Melvin C., 230, 251
Edge, Walter, 254, 260, 331–32, 442
Edison, Charles, 436, 438, 557
Edmonds, Leslie, 45, 48, 97
Edmunds, Sterling, 270
Egypt, 558
Eisenhower, Dwight D., 3; and 1948 presidential nomination, 520, 530–33; and 1952 presidential nomination and campaign, 549–51; and C. Wesley Roberts, 552–53; and health, 554; administration of, 554–58, 560–62; compared with John F. Kennedy, 569
Eisenhower, Milton, 532
El Dorado Times, 354
Elliott, John B., 134–35, 236
Ely, Joseph, 258, 269–71, 348
Empire Oil Co., 72
Emporia Gazette, 61, 96, 354, 417
Enfield, Frederick, 266, 268
Ericsson, Arthur, 105
Eskridge Independent, 96
European Common Market, 572–74
Evans, Arthur, 434

Farley, James A., on Springfield "grass roots" conference, 217; on Republican national convention, 247; and 1936 campaign, 292, 295–96, 340
Farm Credit Administration, 147, 149
Farm strike, 147–48

Farrell, J. F., 179
Fatzer, Harold, 553
Federal Board of Vocational Education, 144
Federal Emergency Relief Administration, 143–45, 172–73, 175–78, 198, 200
Federal Farm Board, 61, 64, 100, 316
Federal Home Loan Bank, 121–22
Federal Oil Conservation Board, 74, 85, 134
Federal Radio Commission, 91–92
Fees, Walter, 251
Ferguson, Miriam, 136, 172
Ferrar, Geraldine, 472
Filene Foundation, 308
Finney, Ronald, 153–61, 183
Finney, Warren W., 153–56, 158–61, 183
Fish, Hamilton, 494; visits Kansas, 230; and 1936 Republican national convention, 253; wants J. D. M. Hamilton to resign, 350; chides Landon on foreign policy, 379; and lend-lease bill, 458
Fitzgerald, Frank, 276, 318
Fitzpatrick, W. S., and 1920 delegate fight, 28; supports Landon for national committee secretary, 60; and 1930 campaign, 65; and oil industry problems, 73–75, 79; and 1932 campaign, 106
Fleeson, Doris, 532
Fleming, William, 20
Fletcher, Henry P., as Republican national chairman, 213, 215, 225, 250, 255, 261, 269; and struggle for Republican leadership, 368, 372; and Republican program committee, 373–74; and 1940 presidential nomination, 439; and Republican anti-war statement, 472
Flynn, Edward J., 480
Foraker, Joseph, 6
Ford, Henry, 318–19
Fort, Franklin W., 247
Fowler, Richard B., 11, 239
France, 389, 408, 413–14, 436–37, 492, 498, 516, 527, 558
Frank, Glenn, 375

Frankfurter, Felix, 328, 438

Franklin, Ben, 110, 151, 190–91

Franklin, Wirt, and the oil industry, 68, 77, 86, 89; and 1932 campaign, 108; and 1933 oil conference, 131

Frelinghuysen, Joseph, 331–32

Fremming, Harvey H., 226

French, Will J., 62, 154–61

Fuller, Alvan T., 375

Galena Times, 42

Gannett, Frank E., 532; supports Borah for presidential nomination, 253; and Republican program committee, 375; and political realignment, 390; meets with Landon, 391; and 1940 national convention, 444; as national committee aide, 482

Garber, Milton C., 77, 83

Garden City Telegram, 99, 538

Garfield, James Rudolph, 337, 340

Garner, John Nance, 88

Garner, Robert L., 270

Geddes-Carpenter bill, 80–81

Geneva conference, 557–58

Gerard, James W., 459

Germany, 226–27, 233, 388, 407–409, 413–15, 436–37, 454–56, 467, 478, 511, 516–17, 525, 545, 557

Gilchrist, Fred, 282

Glass-Steagall Act, 161–63

Goldwater, Barry, 566, 575

Gompers, Samuel, 318

Good, James W., 54

Good Neighbor League, 263, 293, 311

Goodell, Lester, 153–54, 156, 159

Goodrich, James R., 254

Gore, Thomas, 77

Graham, Frank, 549

Grange, 53, 115

Great Bend Tribune, 576

Great Britain, 248, 409, 413, 437, 454–57, 465–66, 469, 483, 492, 497–99, 506, 515–18, 524–27, 558

Greece, 526

Green, Dwight, 494, 520

Green, James, 7–8, 11

Greenleaf, Jesse, and Clyde Reed, 38–39,

42; and Public Service Commission, 41, 114, 128; and 1932 campaign, 110

Gridiron Club, 350–51

Griffith, Evan, 195, 288 n.

Grundy, Joseph R., 218, 383, 426 n., 508–509

Guck, Homer, 230

Gulf Pipeline Co., 72, 79, 85

Gunther, John, 537

Gypsy Oil Co., 72

Hagerty, James A., 425

Hague, Frank, 388, 399

Hale, Frederick, 300

Hall, Fred, 552–55

Hallanan, Walter S., 463

Halleck, Charles, 566

Hamilton, John D. M., 52, 62, 97, 392; runs for governor, 39–43; opposes Clyde Reed's renomination, 58; as state chairman, 66, 99; and 1932 campaign, 106, 112; as Republican national committeeman, 114, 213, 215–17; supports Landon for President, 211, 218, 221, 224, 230, 237–38, 250–52, 254, 256–60; elected national committee chairman, 261; and 1936 campaign, 265–67, 269, 280–82, 286, 296, 300, 307, 320, 326–27, 333, 338, 342; and post-election work, 350, 359; and Roosevelt court plan, 357; and struggle for Republican leadership, 363–64, 366–67, 372–73; and party program committee, 374; relations with Landon deteriorate, 382; and 1938 campaign, 397; and preparations for 1940 national convention, 428, 441; on Knox and Stimson cabinet appointments, 438; and Wendell Willkie, 446–47

Hamlet, J. Arthur, 421

Hanna, Mark, 6

Hard, William, 239, 249, 267, 277, 296; doubts political realignment, 360–61; on national committee staff, 363, 366, 369, 373; and Republican program committee, 375

Harris, Fred, 156, 159, 186

Harris, Jack, 445, 535
Harris, William A., 6
Harrisburg Telegraph, 383
Haskell, Henry, 375, 439
Hatch Act, 424
Haucke, Frank, 102; runs for governor, 58–59, 61–66, 91–92; and 1932 nomination race, 96; and 1932 campaign, 106, 110; and 1936 Republican national convention, 251
Hawkes, Kirby, 266
Hawley, William C., 83
Hawley-Smoot Tariff Act, 77
Hayes, Ralph, 328
Haynes, Lacy, 510; supports Landon for governor, 94–95, 98, 105; supports Landon for President, 221, 223, 229, 267, 278; and Landon's Gridiron Club talk, 350; and Gifford Pinchot, 383; and 1938 campaign, 396; and 1940 presidential nomination, 422, 425; and 1948 election, 536
Hearst, William Randolph, supports Landon for President, 230–33, 236, 246–47, 279–80, 285, 294, 296, 320, 342
Helvering, Guy, criticized by Landon, 98, 107; as Democratic state chairman, 102; criticized by Republicans, 105, 109
Henderson, David, 56
Herring, Clyde L., 148, 288–89
Herter, Christian, 572
Hiawatha World, 95
Hibbs, Ben, 208
High, Stanley, 218, 293
Hill, Lister, 508
Hill, Thurman, 157, 173
Hilles, Charles D., 230, 251–52, 363
Hitler, Adolf, 408, 413, 416, 455–57, 460, 469, 477, 489, 491, 501 n.
Hobbs, Charles, 127
Hoch, Homer, 52, 59; and oil industry stabilization, 77–78, 82, 84; suggested as House speaker, 88; appointed to Public Service Commission, 114, 128; and utility regulation, 169–70; and 1938 campaign, 394–95
Hodges, Frank, 292

Hodges, George, 229
Hoffman, Harold G., 245, 247, 278
Hollister, John M., 267, 463, 488
Holloway, W. J., 74
Holt, Rush, 263
Hoover, Herbert, 34, 44, 57, 99, 101, 213, 216, 232, 301, 347, 391, 397, 409, 417, 468, 476, 484, 490, 496, 509, 516, 529; nominated for President, 40, 51; and Charles Curtis, 52–54; and oil industry stabilization, 70, 73, 75, 79, 83, 85; and 1932 campaign, 99, 101, 103, 110–11, 340; and 1936 presidential nomination, 208, 218, 220, 222, 224–26, 231, 235–36, 244–46, 250, 255; and 1936 campaign, 279–81, 309, 311, 316, 320, 327, 342; and struggle for Republican leadership, 363–77, 384–85, 405; and Latin American policy, 410; and 1940 national convention, 441, 443–44, 446; and Republican anti-war statement, 471–72; for Landon as national chairman, 482, 488; and world organization, 493, 497; on Republican enthusiasm, 508
Hope, Clifford, 224; and farm relief, 145; supports Landon for President, 237, 254; on 1936 Republican national convention, 264; and 1936 campaign, 267; and crop statistics, 385–86; declines Senate race, 394
Hopkins, Harry, 182, 403; as relief administrator, 143–44, 146, 174, 176, 197–98, 200, 288 n.; criticizes Landon, 229, 235, 240; and 1936 campaign, 292, 346
Hopkins, Richard J., 31, 56–57
Hormel, George A., 327
Hornbeck, William, 425
Howard, Roy, 429, 464, 471, 477, 497, 515, 542; and political realignment, 390
Howe, Ed, 289
Howe, Louis, 292
Hughes Tool Co., 568
Hull, Cordell, 305, 379, 408, 505; and Lima conference, 410–12; and lend-lease, 459; and Landon's visits, 490;

Hull, Cordell—*Continued*
and world organization, 493; and bipartisan foreign policy planks, 500, 502
Humphreys, Robert, 541
Hungary, 558
Hurley, Patrick, 211, 367
Hutchins, Robert, 471–72
Hutchinson, W. K., 358
Hutchinson News, 157
Huxman, Walter, 395
Hyde, Arthur M., 64, 211, 365

Ickes, Harold L., 263, 293, 349 n., 409; and 1933 oil conference, 131–35; and Petroleum Code, 139–40, 202; as public works administrator, 146–47; and oil regulation, 204, 206–207; and 1936 campaign, 252, 274, 278, 322; castigates America Firsters, 464; and oil for defense, 469
Independence Daily Reporter, 14, 93
Independence Evening Star, 14, 17
Independent Petroleum Association, 25, 68, 76–77, 89–90, 131, 134, 136, 203, 205, 207
Independent Petroleum Association Opposed to Monopoly, 135
India, 497
Indian Territory Illuminating Oil Co., 11, 13
Ingalls, David S., 463
Insurance regulation, 58, 63, 127
International Union of Mine and Smelter Workers, 193
Interstate Commerce Act, 78
Interstate Commerce Commission, 38, 62–63, 75
Interstate Oil Compact, 86, 203–207
Ise, John, 285
Italy, 388, 415
Izvestia, 502

Jackson, Lyle E., 375
Jaeckle, Edwin F., 251, 375, 391, 401
James, Arthur H., 384, 405, 426 n., 444
Japan, 377, 380, 407, 415, 455, 479, 492, 516, 525

Jardine, William M., 159, 211, 240
Jessup, John K., 580
Jews, and the 1936 campaign, 267, 278, 292, 311, 332–33; and 1938 Kansas campaign, 394–95, 397; and nazi persecution, 409, 414; and Palestine, 497–98
John Birch Society, 571
Johnson, Harold B., 391, 477, 532, 536; and Republican program committee, 375; and New York politics, 401
Johnson, Hiram, 310, 343, 360, 539
Johnson, Hugh, 162, 182
Johnson, Louis, 438
Johnson, Thomas C., 70
Johnston, William A., 52, 118
Jones, A. R., 155–56, 243
Jones, Richard Lloyd, supports Landon for President, 211, 221, 236, 242, 252; suggests Herbert Lehman for Vice President, 258; and 1936 campaign, 281; criticizes J. D. M. Hamilton, 350; and Republican program committee, 375; and Gifford Pinchot, 384

Kaltenborn, H. V., 241, 433, 499
Kansas, Board of Administration, 151, 171, 191; Commission on Constitutional Revision, 543; Corporation Commission, 128–29, 136–37, 166–67, 169–70, 190, 533–34; Court of Industrial Relations, 26–27, 33, 49, 556; Debt Conciliation Committee, 149, 176; Emergency Relief Committee, 146, 172–73, 178, 195–96; 4-H Fair, 167; Highway Department, 98, 105, 107, 120, 122–23, 125, 150–52, 166, 169, 172, 192; Highway Patrol, 153; Income Tax Division, 150; Inspections and Registration Department, 125, 129, 150–51; Legislative Council, 123, 129, 164–65, 190; Medical Registration and Examination Board, 92; National Guard, 153, 173–74, 193–94; Oil Advisory Committee, 137; Planning Board, 188, 190; Public Service Commission, 55, 58, 80–81, 88, 110, 114, 123, 128, 166; Public Utilities

Commission, 29–30, 38, 41, 49; School for the Deaf, 167; School Fund Board, 153, 156; State Agricultural College, 386–87; State Commission on Labor and Industry, 56; State Penitentiary, 151–52, 171–72, 191–92; State Tax Commission, 56, 58, 63; University of, 7–11, 25, 285, 387–88, 543, 568
Kansas Banking Association, 163
Kansas City Call, 421
Kansas City Journal-Post, 57
Kansas City Star, 32, 35, 55, 61, 92, 96–98, 109, 433, 534–35, 537–38
Kansas City Times, 128
Kansas Daily Newspaper Association, 239
Kansas Farmers' Union, 35
Kansas Medical Society, 92
Kansas Natural Gas Co., 7, 10
Kansas Press Association, 220
Kansas Progressive party, 17–18, 20
Kansas State Federation of Labor, 185, 195, 580
Kansas State Teachers' Association, 123
KCLO, 519, 543
KEDD, 543
Kelland, Clarence Buddington, 472, 482, 494
Kemmerer, Edwin W., 233
Kemper, James F., 459
Kennedy, John F., 283; and 1960 campaign, 567–68; compared with Dwight Eisenhower, 569; administration of, 570–80; and trade expansion law, 572–78
Kennedy, Joseph P., 472
Kennedy, Michael J., 314
Kerfoot, Lloyd, 507
Ketchum, Omar, 184–87
Keynes, John Maynard, 314–15
KFKB, 91–92
Khrushchev, Nikita, 562–63, 579
Kilgore, Bernard, 432
Kinsley, Earl, 261
Kiplinger, W. M., 214–15
Kirchhofer, A. H., 539
Kirkpatrick, E. L., 146
Kiro Dam proposal, 142–43

KMA, 422
Knapp, Dallas, 119
Knapp, George S., 143
Knock, D. Clyde, 44
Knowland, William F., 565
Knox, Frank, 391, 500; and 1934 election, 208; at 1935 Kansas Day, 211; and 1936 presidential nomination, 214, 218, 220, 226, 235, 245–46, 250–53, 255–58; nominated for Vice President, 258–60; and 1936 campaign, 265–67, 281, 286, 295–97, 301, 303, 317, 319–21, 327, 342; on Landon, 212, 304, 351; and election results, 341 n.; and political realignment, 359; and struggle for Republican leadership, 365–66, 368–69, 372, 376–77; and *Panay* incident, 379; attends White House conference, 418–19, 430; and preparations for 1940 Republican national convention, 425–26, 428–30, 439; and cabinet appointment, 362, 430–38, 441; and 1940 campaign, 451; and lend-lease, 459; on national unity, 469–70
Knoxville Journal, 505
Knutson, Harold, 468
Koeneke, H. W., 125–26, 154, 161
Kohlberg, Alfred, 547
Korea, 545–47, 556, 579
Krock, Arthur, 380, 443, 542
KSCB, 519, 543
KTLN, 519, 543
Ku Klux Klan, 31–32, 39–42, 312, 369–70

Labor's Non-Partisan League, 318
La Follette, Philip F., 343, 459
La Follette, Robert M., 14, 32 n., 42, 539
La Follette, Robert M., Jr., 293, 343, 458, 522
La Guardia, Fiorello, 263, 293, 360, 374–75, 401, 459, 475
Lambert, John T., 219, 231
Lambertson, William, 226
Lamont, Robert P., 75, 78–80
Landon, Alfred Mossman, family background of, 3–4, 13–14; boyhood of, 4–7; and religious matters, 5, 6, 13, 391,

Landon, Alfred Mossman—*Continued*
415–16; as University of Kansas student, 7–11; and early political interests, 8, 17–18; and business activities, 11–13, 21–22, 24, 67–69, 354, 382, 418, 486, 519–20, 543; marries Margaret Fleming, 20; and 1918 campaign, 21–23; and death of Margaret Fleming Landon, 23; army service of, 23; as a joiner, 24–25; as aide of Governor Allen, 25–29; and 1924 campaign, 30–32; on Gifford Pinchot, 33; and 1928 primary campaign, 34–43; as Republican state chairman, 43–45, 47–66; political thought of, 45–46, 210–11, 349, 355, 388–89, 581; endorsed for Senate, 53; marries Theo Cobb, 58; suggested for national committee secretary, 60; and oil industry stabilization, 67–90, 129–40, 170–71, 201–207; runs for governor, 92–113; as governor-elect, 113–17; and 1933 legislative program, 118–29; and national oil conference, 131–34; and unemployment relief, 140–44, 164–66, 172–74, 189, 195–96; and conservation, 24, 140–41, 174–76, 199–200, 288, 300, 302; and farm relief, 144–49, 176–80, 197–201, 275–76, 286–88; and Finney scandal, 153–61; and special session, 1933, 161–67; and special session, 1934, 167–68; and budget administration, 168–69, 190–92; and utility regulation, 166–67, 169–70, 190, 322; and prison problems, 152, 171–72, 191–92; runs for re-election, 181–87; and 1935 legislature, 187–90; and miners' strike, 192–95, 274–75; and early speculation about presidential nomination, 208–20; and campaign for presidential nomination, 220–61; and early part of 1936 campaign, 263–90; and special session, 1936, 268; and first campaign tour, 282–86; and 1936 drought conference, 286–89; and campaign issues and problems, 291–97, 307–12, 341–49; and second campaign tour, 297–301; and third tour, 302–

306; and fourth tour, 313–20; and final tour, 321–38; on election day, 338–39; and election results, 339–41; immediate post-election activities of, 347–55; and Roosevelt's court plan, 355–59, 366, 370; and political realignment, 359–62, 382, 390, 392, 400, 488–89, 504–505; and struggle for Republican leadership, 362–77, 384–85; denies interest in renomination, 370–71, 376–77; opposes Ludlow resolution, 377–80; talked about as cabinet member, 381, 430–37, 545–46; and Republican affairs in 1938, 382–85, 391–94, 417–18; clashes with Henry Wallace, 385–87, 418, 449, 489, 495; defends free speech, 387–90, 398–400; civic service of, 13, 24–25, 391, 487, 518–19, 543; and Kansas politics, 1938, 394–98; on recession, 399–400; and 1938 campaign, 400–406; increases concern for foreign relations, 407–409, 413–15; and Lima conference 409–13; attends White House conference, 418–19, 430; on third term for Roosevelt, 419–20, 422, 449–51; and Negro Republican leadership, 420–21, 447, 510, 522; prepares for 1940 national convention, 421–30, 439–41; early interest in postwar reconstruction 427–28; and Knox's entry into cabinet, 430–38; and 1940 national convention, 442–46; and 1940 campaign, 447–53; and views on war, 454–55; and aid to Britain, 455 n., 457; and lend-lease, 456–62; supports Joseph Martin as national chairman, 446–47, 462–63, 475–76; and America First Committee, 464–66; on oil for defense, 468–69; and coming of war, 464–67, 470–79; and Selective Service extension, 473–74; on Atlantic Charter, 474–75; as opponent of New Deal during war, 480–512; suggested as national chairman, 382, 482, 488; and 1942 campaign, 485–86; favors world organization, 492–93, 497, 506; opposes Wendell Willkie's renomination, 494,

503; and Jewish homeland question, 497–98; opposes Anglo-American alliance, 497–99, 518; prepares for 1944 national convention, 505–508; at the 1944 convention, 508–10; and 1944 campaign, 510–12; on problems of victory, 513–18; and postwar building of Republican party, 520–23; on railroad strike, 1946, 521; and 80th Congress, 523–30; and disarmament, 527–28, 558, 562–63, 570; and Marshall Plan, 428, 527, 529; and 1948 Eisenhower for President movement, 530–33; defeated as Kansas Republican leader, 533–38; and 1948 elections, 538–41; as an independent Republican, 542–81; on Korean War, 545–47, 556; on Joseph McCarthy, 546–48; and 1950 elections, 548; and 1952 political affairs, 549–51; and the Eisenhower administration, 552–58, 560–62; on East-West tensions, 557–64, 569–70; opposes right-to-work laws, 556, 564–65; and 1960 campaign, 566–69; and trade expansion law, 572–78; and 1962 campaign, 578; on Kennedy administration, 578–80; viewed by others, 580–81

Landon, Anne Mossman, 4, 13–14
Landon, Helen, 4
Landon, Jack, 238–39, 487, 542
Landon, John M., marries, 3–4; and business, 4, 7, 10, 20; and politics, 6, 15–17, 47; family life of, 13–14, 23; on Alfred Landon, 234
Landon, Manuel, 4
Landon, Margaret Anne, birth of, 21; childhood of, 23–24; and plot to kidnap, 158; and 1936 campaign, 238–39, 336; marries, 486
Landon, Margaret Fleming, 20, 23
Landon, Nancy Jo, 102, 238–39, 542
Landon, Theo Cobb, 542, 580–81; marries, 58; and investment in Hill Packing Co., 158, 183; and 1936 campaign, 238–39, 336, 338–39; at Republican national convention, 446
Landon, Thomas, 4

Landon, Thomas, Jr., 4
Landon-for-President clubs, 223, 237, 239–40, 246
Langer, William, 147
Langworthy, Herman, 253
Lawrence, David, 412
Lawson, E. B., 73
Leach, Paul, 435
League of Nations, 253–54, 570
Lee, Marvin, 83
Legge, Alexander, 64
Lehman, Herbert, 258, 360, 431, 496
Lemke, William, and 1936 campaign for President, 268, 294, 310, 313, 341
Lend-lease, 456–62, 470, 472
Levand, Louis, 236
Levine, Isaac Don, 379
Levinson, Salmon O., 408
Lewis, John L., 507, 510, 522, 542; and 1936 campaign, 318; and Republican anti-war statement, 472; praised by Landon, 494–95, 521
Lewis, Sinclair, 350
Life, 371, 424, 532
Lima Inter-American Conference, 409–13, 491
Lindbergh, Charles A., 464
Lippmann, Walter, 326, 399
Little, Arthur W., 260, 312
Little, Chauncey B., 47, 49–50
Liverpool Corn Association, 386
Lodge, Henry Cabot, 442, 520
London Economic Conference, 325
Long, Chester I., 36
Long, Huey, 359
Longworth, Alice Roosevelt, 333
Longworth, Nicholas, 83–84
Los Angeles Daily News, 293
Los Angeles Times, 377
Louisville Courier-Journal, 377, 379, 412, 495
Lowden, Frank O., and Springfield "grass roots" conference, 216; and 1936 presidential nomination, 220, 252; and 1936 campaign, 306; and Landon and Hoover, 367–68; and Republican mid-term convention, 372;

Lowden, Frank O.—*Continued*
and Republican anti-war statement, 472
Lucas, Robert H., 220
Ludlow, Louis, 377
Ludlow resolution, 377, 379–81, 407
Lyons, Leonard, 580

MacArthur, Douglas, 494, 520, 547
McCarthy, Joseph R., 522, 546–48
McCloud, C. A., 245–46
McCormick, Robert R., 347, 430, 459, 491 n.
McCoy, Alvin S., 432, 552–53
McFarland, Russell M., 327
McGill, George, 92, 112, 143, 394
McGill, Ralph, 420–21, 515, 571, 580
McGrory, Mary, 575
McGugin, Harold, 396–97
Mackinac Island conference, 496–97
McKinley, William, 317
McLean, M. R., 174
Macmillan, Harold, 571
McMullen, Adam, 475
McNary, Charles L., 209 n.; and 1936 campaign, 310; and Roosevelt court plan, 356; and struggle for Republican leadership, 368; and preparations for 1940 national convention, 426, 428; and 1940 national convention, 444
McNary-Haugen legislation, 541
MacNider, Hanford, 58–59, 444, 459, 472
Malenkov, Georgi, 557
Mallon, Paul, 222, 231
Malloy, Pat, 81
Manhattan Tribune, 154
Marietta Academy, 6–8
Markham, W. T., 155
Marland, E. W., 136, 138, 195, 203–207
Marshall, George, 527
Marshall Plan, 428, 527, 529
Martin, Joseph W., 524, 530, 540; and 1936 Republican national convention, 255; and 1936 campaign, 278, 282; and struggle for Republican leadership, 367–69; as House Republican leader, 398; attends White House

conference, 419; and 1940 presidential nomination, 424–26, 428–30, 439 n., 444–45, as national chairman, 446–47, 456, 462–63, 475–76, 481–82; criticizes Roosevelt, 467; resigns as national chairman, 487–88; opposes Willkie's renomination, 503; and 1948 presidential nomination, 520, 539; and Eisenhower administration, 555
Maxwell, Elsa, 502
Mayberry, Willard, on 1932 campaign, 112; as Landon's secretary, 151, 181, 267; and 1938 campaign, 395–96; opposes Willkie's renomination, 504; and 1948 election, 534–35, 537; runs for governor, 548
Meckstroth, Jake, 425
Mencken, Henry L., 475
Mercer, Joseph, H., and 1928 gubernatorial nomination, 35–36; as state livestock commissioner, 148; and farm relief, 177, 179; and 1934 campaign, 185; and 1936 Republican national convention, 251
Merriam, Carroll B., 144
Merriam, Frank F., 244, 322
Methodist affairs, 391, 415–16
Methodist-Episcopal Home, 391
Meyer, Agnes, 267, 278, 326
Meyer, Eugene, 226, 229, 267
Michelson, Charles, 229
Mid-Continent Oil and Gas Association, 25, 76
Mihailovich, Draja, 518
Miller, Clyde, 244
Miller, Nathan, 326
Mills, Ogden, 268; and 1936 presidential nomination politics, 225, 253, 264, 267; and 1936 campaign, 297, 347; and political realignment, 359–60; and struggle for Republican leadership, 365
Milton, George Fort, 408, 424
Minton, Sherman, 390
Moley, Raymond, 472
Monroe Doctrine, 249
Montgomery Ward, 508
Moore, Edward H., 486, 488
Morgan, William Y., 30, 41, 62, 97

Morgenthau, Henry, Jr., 147–48, 287 n., 459, 511–12
Morgenthau Plan, 511–12
Morley, Felix, 471–72, 510
Morrison, Charles C., 459
Mortgage redemption legislation, 121, 124, 129, 148, 167–68, 190
Morton, Sterling, 418, 542
Moscow Foreign Ministers Conference, 499–502
Moses, George H., 252–54, 367
Mossman, Robert, 4
Mossman, William H., 4
Mossman, William H., II, 4–6
Mossman, William T., 6; supports Landon for President, 209, 212, 217–18, 221–22, 224–26, 231, 233; on Republican vice presidential nomination, 258; and 1936 campaign, 278
Motter, Harvey H., 22–23, 35
Mowrer, Paul, 437
Moyer, C. I., 553
Mulvane, David, 34, 57, 62; as Republican national committeeman, 44; considered for national chairman, 60; and 1932 primary election, 96, 99; dies, 114
Munich agreement, 409, 449
Murdock, Victor, as a Kansas Progressive leader, 15, 17–18; runs for Senate, 18; and 1930 primary election, 59; advice of to Landon, 98; for Landon as national chairman, 402
Murray, Cicero, 85
Murray, Philip, 459
Murray, William H., and oil industry stabilization, 74, 84–85, 136–38, 171, 204; and 1936 campaign, 324
Myers, William I., 149

National Association of Manufacturers, 264, 564, 577
National Boys' Clubs, 543
National Conference of Christians and Jews, 519, 543
National Economy League, 239, 342
National Industrial Recovery Act, 138–39, 152, 170, 183, 201–204, 207, 357

National Recovery Administration, 144, 162, 273, 299, 329, 334, 336, 357
National Republican Club, 401
National Resources Board, 175
National Youth Administration, 172
Neeley, Earl, 194
Negroes, 522; in 1928 campaign, 45; and Reed administration, 56; and 1932 campaign, 98, 103–105; and 1936 campaign, 240, 277, 297, 311–12, 332–33; in Southern politics, 420–21; and 1940 campaign, 447; and 1944 campaign, 507, 510
Netherlands, 492, 498, 516
Neutrality Act, 325, 419, 477
New Republic, 389
New York Herald Tribune, 377, 379, 420, 442, 446, 506, 515
New York Post, 580
New York Times, 308, 356, 377, 398, 531
New York World-Telegram, 438
Neylan, Francis, 280, 375
Nice, Harry, 257, 259–60
Niebuhr, Reinhold, 459
Nixon, Richard M., 554, 563, 566–68
Norbeck, Peter, 310
Norris, George W., and 1936 campaign, 263, 293, 310, 348; and 1942 election, 485–86
Northern Natural Gas Co., 534
Nye, Gerald P., 77, 84, 263, 310

Ohio Oil Co., 20
Ohio State Journal, 219, 228
Oil States Advisory Committee, 85–86
Oklahoma Pipeline Co., 72
Oumansky, Constantine, 500
Owens, Jesse, 297

Palestine, 497–98
Palmer, Frederick, 239
Pan-American Petroleum and Transportation Co., 83
Panama, Declaration of, 427
Panhandle Eastern Gas Co., 534
Park, Guy B., 195
Parker, G. B., 495
Parker, John J., 61

Patterson, Eleanor, 232, 491 n.

Patterson, Robert, 438

Paulen, Ben, 34, 52; runs for governor, 30–32; as governor, 32–33; favors Landon for governor, 97; runs for Senate, 105–107

Peake, A. W., 74

Pearson, Drew, 552

Pearson, James B., 578

Peek, George, 303

Pepper, Claude, 508, 549

Perkins, Frances, 229, 436

Petroleum, efforts to stabilize industry of, 67–90, 129–40, 170–71, 201–207; Kansas legislation on, 80–82, 129; excise on imports of, 89–90, 130; national conference on, 131–35; and National Industrial Recovery Act, 138–39, 170, 201–204, 207; interstate compact on, 203–207; and national defense, 468–69, 487; and offshore ownership, 544

Pew, J. Howard, 383–84, 425–26

Pew, Joseph, and 1938 election, 383–85; and 1940 Republican national convention, 426, 443, 446; and Adam McMullen, 475

Phi Gamma Delta, 8–9, 25, 316

Philadelphia Evening Bulletin, 501

Phillips, L. E., 350

Pihlblad, Ernest, 159

Pinchot, Amos, 267, 326, 375

Pinchot, Cornelia, 249, 267, 326, 383

Pinchot, Gifford, 394; in Kansas, 17; Landon on, 33; and 1936 campaign, 249, 264, 267, 281, 284; and Republican program committee, 375; and 1938 campaign for governor, 383–84; and preparations for 1940 national convention, 422, 425–26, 439

Pittman, Key, 412

Pittsburg Advertiser, 157

Pittsburg Sun, 162

Pittsburgh Post-Gazette, 501

Pleasanton Herald, 124

PM, 446

Poling, Daniel A., 185

Porter, P. G., 312

Powell, Hugh, 28

Prairie Oil and Gas Co., 15, 28, 65, 68–75, 79

Progressive National Committee, 263, 293

Prohibition, 18, 34, 44, 49–51, 61, 63, 101, 106–107, 109, 162–65, 190, 240, 534

Public Works Administration, 147, 166, 168, 172–73

Queeny, Edgar M., 503

Railroad regulation, in Kansas, 30, 34, 37–39, 41–42, 44, 55–56, 58, 61–63

Railway Employees' Journal, 42

Rathbone, Albert, 270

Ratner, Payne, 395–97, 404–405, 448, 553

Rauch, Basil, 347

Reconstruction Finance Corporation, 131, 141, 144, 179

Red Cross, 144–45

Reece, Carroll, 522, 525

Reed, Clyde M., 91–92, 114, 536; early political career, 25–29; campaigns for governor, 30–31, 34–45, 48–51; as governor-elect, 51–52; as governor, 53–63; runs for renomination, 58–66; and oil industry stabilization, 69, 71, 74; and 1932 campaign, 96–97, 106; and 1936 campaign, 310; runs for Senate, 394, 396–97, 404–405; runs for convention delegate, 429; dies, 548

Reed, Clyde, Jr., 555

Reed, David, 252, 254, 261

Reed, James, 51, 269, 271, 337

Reeser, Edward B., 71–72, 171

Reforestation Act, 140–42

Reid, Helen, 550

Republic Natural Gas Co., 534–35

Republican Assembly, California, 244, 246

Republican party, 1912 national convention, 16; 1920 national convention, 28–29; 1928 national convention, 40; 1928 state platform, 44; 1932 state platform, 105; 1932 campaign expenditures in Kansas, 111 n.; representation in legislature, 119, 188; 1934 state platform, 183–84; Springfield "grass roots" conference, 213–17, 366; 1936 national convention, 251–61; 1936 national platform, 253–54, 256–57; state of in 1936, 260–63; national committee headquarters, 277, 369, 382, 482; Landon on, 341–42, 349–50, 392–93, 452–53, 539–40; 1936 campaign funds of, 345–46 n.; effect of 1936 campaign on, 340–42, 346–47; and mid-term convention issue, 364–73; program committee, 373–75, 381, 400–401; financial troubles of, 398, 482; 1940 national platform, 442; 1940 national convention, 442–46; and Mackinac Island conference, 496–97; 1944 national platform, 507–10; wins control of Congress, 523

Requa, Mark, 261
Reuther, Walter, 562
Reynaud, Paul, 436
Richey, Lawrence, 218, 367 n.
Right-to-work legislation, 556, 564–65
Ritchie, Albert, 269
Rivers, Francis E., 425
Robbins, Richard W., 537
Roberts, C. Wesley, 552–53, 555, 561
Roberts, Roy, 218, 384; supports Landon for President, 221, 223, 226, 235, 255, 259, 267, 326; and Ludlow resolution, 378; and 1948 election, 532, 534, 537
Robey, Ralph, and 1936 campaign, 266, 268; and post-election political work, 350, 369; for Landon as Republican national chairman, 488; assists Landon 505
Robin Moor, 471
Robins, Raymond, 17
Rochester, E. S., 131–32
Rockefeller, John D., Jr., 70
Rockefeller, John D., Sr., 70
Rockefeller, Nelson, 566–67
Rodeheaver, Homer, 185
Rogers, George E., 173
Rogers, Will, 242
Romig, C. C., 53
Roos, Charles F., 267

Roosevelt, Eleanor, 486, 562
Roosevelt, Franklin D., 129–30, 218, 376, 440, 463, 480–81, 483, 485, 490–91; and 1920 campaign, 341 n.; runs for President, 102, 110, 112; and 1933 oil conference, 131, 133, 135; and oil regulation, 137–38, 170, 205; and National Industrial Recovery Act, 138–39; and conservation, 140–42, 175, 288; and salutes for governors, 143; and relief, 148, 172–74, 197–98, 200, 276, 286–88; and 1934 Kansas campaign, 184, 186–87; 1935 reaction of to Supreme Court, 216; policies of assessed by Landon, 217, 222–24, 265–66, 354, 370, 398–400, 402–403, 407; and preliminaries to 1936 campaign, 230–32, 243; as Democratic party leader, 262–63; and 1936 reelection campaign, 264–338, 343–46; and 1936 drought conference, 286–89; and election results, 339–41; and judicial reorganization, 346, 355–58; invites Landon to White House, 350–51; political position of viewed by Landon, 360–61, 366; and 1937 political problems, 369; and Ludlow resolution, 378–80; and "purge" of Democratic opponents, 390, 398; Latin American policy of, 410; and secret sale of aircraft, 414; seeks world peace, 415–16; invites Landon to embargo conference, 418–19; and third term ambition, 419–20, 422, 449–51; and preliminaries to 1940 campaign, 423; and talk of Landon and Knox in cabinet, 430–38; appoints Knox and Stimson to cabinet, 438; and national preparedness, 441, 451; and 1940 campaign, 449–53; and lend-lease, 456–58, 460–62; castigates America Firsters, 464; and the coming of war, 465–67, 470–79; discusses war with Landon, 481–82; complains about press, 491 n.; and Anglo-American alliance, 499; and 1944 campaign, 511; dies, 514
Roosevelt, James, 217
Roosevelt, Nicholas, 214, 217, 221

Roosevelt, Theodore, 6, 14–17, 45, 78, 130, 241, 316, 330, 332, 337, 392
Roosevelt, Theodore, Jr., 333
Roraback, J. Henry, 250
Ross, Charles, 517
Rott, Carl, 267, 382
Rowell, Chester, 236
Runyon, Damon, 219, 230
Russia, 148, 388–89, 455, 472–73, 475, 492, 497, 499–500, 502, 506, 513–15, 517–18, 525–30, 545, 557–59, 561, 574, 578
Rust, H. B., 225
Ryan, Frank J., 39, 41, 43

St. John, John P., 3
St. Johns, Adela Rogers, 230
St. Lawrence Seaway Project, 313
St. Louis Post-Dispatch, 301, 379
Salina Journal, 116
Saltonstall, Leverett, 494, 504, 520
San Francisco Chronicle, 307
San Francisco Examiner, 239
Sawyer, Daniel A., 421
Scattergood, J. Henry, 472
Schlesinger, Arthur, Jr., 577
Schoeppel, Andrew, reduces Ronald Finney's sentence, 160; runs for governor, 485–86; as governor, 533–34; runs for Senate, 534–38; and United Nations, 545; dies, 575 n., 578
Schroeder, Werner W., 488
Scott, Charles, 35–36, 39–40, 43
Seaton, Fay, 537
Seaton, Fred, 542; and 1934 campaign, 181; supports Landon for President, 227, 243; and 1936 campaign, 267; mentioned for vice presidential nomination, 567
Selective Service Act, extension of, 473–74
Seubert, E. G., 74, 79
SHAPE, 550
Sharp, Harry, 62
Shaw, Warren, 554
Shawver, Ernest B., 204
Sholis, Vic, 397
Shoop, Duke, 212, 385, 394–95

Shouse, Jouett, 91
Shultz, A. L., 44; and 1928 election, 41–42, 49; and 1932 campaign, 97, 104; and 1938 campaign, 396
Simmons, Roscoe, 312
Simms, William Philip, 412, 500
Simpson, Kenneth, and Republican program committee, 375; and New York politics, 401, 417; and preparations for 1940 national convention, 425, 430, 441
Simpson, Lacey, runs for gubernatorial nomination, 96–97, 99, 101–102; and 1932 Republican state council, 105; and 1932 campaign, 106, 110; as prison warden, 171
Sinclair, Harry F., 13
Sinclair Oil Co., 69, 81, 87
Slemp, Bascom, 218, 421
Sloan, E. R., 50
Smith, Alfred E., 300; and 1928 campaign, 47, 49–50; and 1936 campaign, 269, 271, 308–309, 320, 332–33, 342; and political realignment, 359
Smith, Arthur Calvert, 266, 361, 369
Smith, Frank, 261
Smith, Gerald L. K., 294, 459, 494
Smith, William, 98, 105, 396
Smuts, Jan C., 502
Snell, Bertrand H., and oil tariff, 77, 84; and Republican 1936 national convention, 256; at Landon's notification ceremony, 272; and Roosevelt court plan, 357; retires as House minority leader, 363, 398
Synder, Ralph, 59
Social Security Act, 249, 295–96, 305–306, 308, 334, 336, 370, 427
Socialist party, 262–63
Soil Erosion Service, 198
Southern Methodist University, 487
Spaak, Paul Henri, 571, 575
Spangler, Harrison E., and Springfield "grass roots" convention, 215; and mid-term convention proposal, 366; as Republican national chairman, 488–90, 493, 496
Sprague, J. Russell, 425

Sproul, W. H., 59, 83
Stalinism, 558
Standard Oil of Indiana, 65, 68–69, 72–75, 79, 83, 85, 171, 236, 244
Standard Oil of Kansas, 79
Standard Oil of New Jersey, 79, 85
Standolind Pipeline Co., 72, 75, 81
Stassen, Harold, 426; and Wendell Willkie, 444, 494; and 1948 presidential nomination, 520, 530, 539; and 1956 presidential nomination, 554
Stauffer, Oscar, 223, 267, 281 n., 445
Steiger, Charles W., 45, 48, 57
Steiwer, Frederick, 255, 268, 276
Sterling, Ross S., 84
Stetson, Eugene W., 270
Stewart, R. G., 83
Stimson, Henry L., and Ludlow resolution, 379; appointed to cabinet, 362, 438, 441; and lend-lease, 459; and bipartisan foreign policy planks, 500
Stone, J. F., 175–76
Stratton, Clifford, on 1929 Senate vacancy, 53–54; on Landon as possible governor, 93; on 1932 election, 107; on Finney scandal, 155, 183; on Landon's political ambitions, 212, 222; and Landon's presidential campaign, 229, 231; and 1940 Republican national convention, 445; and 1948 election, 535
Straus, Mrs. Oscar D., 311
Straus, Roger W., 267, 384–85, 417
Streit, Clarence, 477, 517
Strong, James G., 52
Stubblefield, E. M., 171
Stubbs, Walter R., 14–16, 30, 62
Stutz, John G., as state relief director, 146, 150, 173–74, 182, 189
Sudetenland, 409
Sullivan, Mark, 212, 214, 224, 233
Swing, Raymond Gram, 249, 278

Taber, Louis, 276
Taft, Charles P., 349 n.; supports Landon for President, 249, 253–54, 266, 268–69, 296, 316, 342; and Republican program committee, 375; opposes right-to-work laws, 564
Taft, Hulbert, 379
Taft, Robert A., 432, 484, 524; and 1936 presidential nomination, 244, 250, 257; and 1940 presidential nomination, 428–30, 443–46; and lend-lease bill, 458, and Joseph Martin, 463, 482; for Landon as national chairman, 488; and 1944 Republican national convention, 508–509; and 1948 presidential nomination, 520, 530, 532, 539; and 1952 presidential nomination, 549–51; and Eisenhower administration, 555
Taft, William Howard, 14–16
Tariff questions, 249, 304–305, 321, 408, 506, 508–11, 530, 572–78
Tax reform, in Kansas, 37, 44, 51, 55–60, 92, 95, 106–107, 120, 122, 127–29, 187, 189–90
Taylor, Earl H., 266, 268
Taylor, Glen, 549
Tennessee Valley Authority, 175
Texas Co., 72, 79
Theta Nu Epsilon, 9
This Month, 576
Thomas, Elbert D., 518
Thomas, Elmer, 84, 202–203, 205–206
Thomas, Norman, 580; in Topeka, 210; and 1936 campaign, 274–75, 327; and free speech, 387–89, 398–99; and lend-lease, 459; and Japanese surrender, 516; and nuclear policy, 562
Thompson, Dorothy, 433
Tilson, John Q., 84
Time, 234–35
Tito, 502
Toledo Blade, 307
Topeka Daily Capital, 38, 53, 107, 116, 171, 230, 537, 581
Topeka State Journal, 220
Townsend, Francis, 229, 276, 313
Townsend, John, 276, 356, 372
Trade Expansion Act, 576–78, 580
Tri-State Zinc and Lead Ore Producers' Association, 193

Truman, Harry S., 550–51, 572–73; early days as President, 514–18; visits to from Landon, 516, 544; and railroad strike, 521; resignation of suggested, 523; and aid to Greece and Turkey, 526; and 1948 election, 532–33; 538, 540–41; and Korean War, 545; and 81st Congress, 549
Truman Doctrine, 526–28
Tucker, Howard, 154
Tugwell, Rexford, 199
Tulsa Tribune, 242
Turkey, 526
Twentieth Century Fund, 308

Umberger, Harry, 177–79, 199
Union Now, 478
Union Oil Co., 4
Union party, 262–63, 268
United Mine Workers, 494, 521
United Nations, 514, 517–18, 527, 545–46, 556–57, 563, 570–74
United States Chamber of Commerce, 264, 564
University Daily Kansan, 388
U.S.S. Greer, 477
U.S.S. Kearney, 477
U.S.S. Panay, 377, 379–81, 407
Utility regulation, in Kansas, 30, 38–39, 41, 44, 55, 58, 61, 63, 121, 165–67, 190, 322

Valentine, Allen, 459
Vandenberg, Arthur H., and 1936 presidential nomination, 218, 220, 235, 245–46, 250, 253, 255–57; and vice presidential nomination, 258–59, 260 n.; and 1936 campaign, 318; and Roosevelt court plan, 356; and struggle for Republican leadership, 368–69; and 1940 presidential nomination, 371, 423–24, 428–30, 443–44, 446, and 1948 presidential nomination, 520
Van Nuys, Frederick, 390
Veasey, James, 170, 384
Vernon, William H., 119
Versailles, Treaty of, 408–409, 492

Villard, Oswald Garrison, 292
Voiland, Fred, 39, 41–42

Wadsworth, James, 251, 259, 434
Wages and Hours Act, 399, 427
Waggener, Will, 50–51
Wagner Act, 370
Wagstaff, Thomas, 44, 251
Walker, Ida, 45
Wallace, Dan, 304
Wallace, Henry A., 148, 263, 293, 489, 515, 526; and farm relief, 145, 149, 176–77, 179, 197–98; and 1936 campaign, 303; clashes with Landon, 385–87, 418, 449, 495; and third party, 531, 538
Wallace, J. P., 303
Waltman, Franklyn, 447, 474
Warburg, James P., 264, 267, 310
Warren, Earl, 244, 323, 520, 554
Washington Post, 228, 260, 341, 379, 553, 575, 580
Washington Star, 539
Water conservation, 140–41, 174–76
Watson, Edwin, 431–32, 434
Watson, James, 218, 220, 367
Waymack, W. W., 439
Wedell, Hugo T., 159
Weeks, Sinclair, 488
Weidlein, Edward, 225
Weigand, William D., 552
Weiner, Carl, 70
Weir, Ernest T., 225, 476, 482
Welford, Walter, 276
Welles, Sumner, 412
Wells, Bert, 173
Wells, John, 50, 292
Wells, Seth G., 44, 53; supports Clyde Reed for governor, 37, 43, 48; supports William Sproul for Senate, 59; as director of Inspections Department, 150
West, William G., supports Clyde Reed for governor, 48; as Reed's secretary, 61; supports Landon for governor, 98, 105; as Landon's secretary, 114, 119; resigns, 151; runs for governor, 340
Westbrook, Lawrence, 197

Wheeler, Burton K., 294, 356, 360–61
Wheeler, Frank, 5
Wherry, Kenneth, 485–86
White, Wallace, 297
White, William Allen, 9, 34, 43, 57, 59, 94, 213, 384, 424, 439, 535; as a Progressive leader, 15–18; opposes Kansas' labor laws, 27, 29; campaigns against Ku Klux Klan, 31–32, 312; and anti-Bill White law, 33; and 1928 Republican politics, 35–36, 40; and Herbert Hoover, 53–54; and 1930 campaign, 60; and 1932 campaign, 96–98, 112; patronage requests of, 113; and Finney scandal, 155, 160; chides J. D. M. Hamilton, 215; avoids Springfield "grass roots" conference, 216; supports Landon for President, 217, 221, 226, 229, 231, 235, 237, 239, 246, 249–55, 267, 269–70, 276, 291–92, 310, 327, 344; on vice presidential nomination, 258–59; on 1936 campaign, 347; and Republican program committee, 375; and Reed-Landon fight, 429; and 1940 national convention, 445; on Selective Service extension, 474; for Landon as national chairman, 488; and world organization, 493
White, William L., 535–37
Wichita Beacon, 40, 128, 220, 271, 575
Wichita Eagle, 560, 575
Wilbur, Ray Lyman, 71, 73, 75–76, 472
Wilkes-Barre Record, 501
Williams, Al F., 62
Williams, G. Mennen, 562
Williams, Gladstone, 531
Williams, James T., 235
Willis, Simeon S., 489
Willkie, Wendell, 482, 496, 509–10; and 1940 presidential nomination, 439–40, 443–46; and J. D. M. Hamilton, 446–47; and 1940 campaign, 340, 447–53; and lend-lease, 457, 459; and problem of Republican national chairmanship, 446–47, 462–63; as party leader, 463, 468, 475–76, 484; and world organization, 493, 497; as contender for renomination, 494, 501, 503–504; withdraws as contender, 507
Willkie Clubs of America, 443, 448
Wilson, John, 170
Wilson, M. L., 198–99
Wilson, Woodrow, 392, 451, 454
Wingfield, George, 261
Winrod, Gerald, 394–98
Wisconsin Progressive party, 522
Wolman, Abel, 359
Women's Christian Temperance Union, 164
Wood, Robert E., 459, 464
Woodring, Harry, 93, 101, 142, 150; runs for governor, 66, 91–92; and oil industry stabilization, 71, 74, 79–81, 84; runs for re-election, 102–104, 106–13; and the Kiro Dam proposal, 142–43; and Finney scandal, 155, 157, 186–87; and utility rates, 166; and 1938 election, 395; leaves cabinet, 436, 438; and anti-war statement, 472; and opposition to Roosevelt, 488; and 1946 campaign, 533
Work, Hubert, 48
Works Progress Administration, 195, 287–88 n., 313, 330, 346, 390, 505
World Court, 253–54, 563
WREN, 543
Wright, Herbert S., 459
Wright, James L., 337, 371

XER, 103